Law and Justice

An Introduction

to the American Legal System

Fifth Edition

HOWARD ABADINSKY

Upper Saddle River, New Jersey 07458

Library of Congress Cataloging-in-Publication Data

Abadinsky, Howard, 1941-
    Law and justice : an introduction to the American legal system / Howard Abadinsky.--
5th ed.
        p. cm.
    Includes bibliographical references and index.
    ISBN 0-13-098180-X
        1. Justice, Administration of--United States. 2. Law--United States. I. Title

KF384.A75142002
349.73--dc21   2002024601

Publisher: Jeff Johnston
Executive Editor: Kim Davies
Production Editor: Naomi Sysak
Production Liaison: Barbara Marttine Cappuccio
Director of Production and Manufacturing: Bruce Johnson
Managing Editor: Mary Carnis
Manufacturing Buyer: Cathleen Petersen
Creative Director: Cheryl Asherman
Cover Design Coordinator: Miguel Ortiz
Marketing Manager: Jessica Pfaff
Editorial Assistant: Korrine Dorsey
Cover Designer: Amy Rosen
Cover Photo: Michael Nelson, FPG International
Composition: Naomi Sysak
Printer/Binder: Courier Westford

Pearson Education LTD, *London*
Pearson Education Ausstralia PTY, Limited, *Sydney*
Pearson Education Singapore, Pte. Ltd.
Pearson Education North Asia Ltd., *Hong Kong*
Pearson Education Canada, Ltd., *Toronto*
Pearson Educación de Mexico, S.A. de C.V.
Pearson Education–Japan, *Tokyo*
Pearson Education Malaysia, Pte. Ltd

10 9 8 7
ISBN: 0-13-098180-X

CONTENTS

CHAPTER 5   THE LEGAL PROFESSION AND THE PRACTICE OF LAW   110

CHAPTER 6   THE STRUCTURE AND ADMINISTRATION OF STATE AND FEDERAL COURTS   136

CHAPTER 7   THE APPELLATE PROCESS AND JUDICIAL REVIEW   166

CHAPTER 8   JUDICIAL INTERPRETATION AND POLICY-MAKING   183

CHAPTER 11   NEGOTIATED JUSTICE: PLEA BARGAINING   285

CHAPTER 12   CIVIL JUSTICE   310

CHAPTER 13   JUVENILE JUSTICE   335

CHAPTER 14   ALTERNATIVE DISPUTE RESOLUTION AND THERAPEUTIC JUSTICE   356

PREFACE

This book offers a thorough examination of the system of justice used in the United States: civil and criminal, juvenile and therapeutic. It is designed for courses on the law and judicial process that transcend the disciplines of political science, sociology, and criminal justice. The writer has attempted to take advantage of his background in these disciplines to provide a comprehensive book that can be used alone or along with more particular treatments of the topics contained in this fifth edition.

The book opens with a chronology so students can more easily trace the evolution of law and justice and the important historical events related to them. It concludes with a glossary of key terms used in the text. There are related Internet sites and review questions at the end of each chapter that provide sources for further research and term assignments. The fifth edition has been updated and expanded into 14 chapters.

Chapter 1 prepares the reader for subsequent chapters by examining the problem of defining law, the unique philosophical role of natural law, and a modern society's need for rational law.

Chapter 2 examines and contrasts common law and equity with civil (code) systems of law. The chapter discusses statutory law, legal reasoning, case law, administrative law, and the application of law through a comparison of the inquisitional system used in continental Europe and the adversarial system used in England and the United States.

Chapter 3 is a history of the development of American law and justice from colonial times into the twenty-first century, providing a grounding for topics in later chapters.

Chapter 4 examines legal education, the law school curriculum, differences between law schools, and criticism of legal education. The chapter ends with a discussion of legal realism, critical legal studies, the law and economics perspective, and the emerging therapeutic jurisprudence.

Chapter 5 reviews the development of bar associations, the practice of law, and the stratification of the legal profession. The chapter ends with a discussion of federal legal services and attorneys practicing public interest law.

Chapter 6 reviews the history and development of court systems, the variety of ways in which they are organized, court administration, and reform.

Chapter 7 explores the appellate court process and judicial review, the issue of legitimacy, and the implementation of appellate decisions.

Chapter 8 examines the processes involved in interpreting statutes and the Constitution, issues such as plain meaning, originalism, textualism, and legislative intent. The chapter discusses the controversies surrounding the policy-making role of the judicial branch and the related issues of judicial restraint versus judicial activism

Chapter 9 looks at judges, prosecutors, and criminal defense attorneys. The role of the trial judge is discussed and methods for selecting judges are compared and contrasted. The office of prosecutor is examined, including the ways in which it can be organized and their implications. The discussion of the criminal defense attorney—private counsel, public defender, court-appointed counsel—focuses on the very difficult problems encountered in the practice of criminal law.

Chapter 10 begins with a review of the evidence needed to convict in a criminal case, the due process guarantees to which every criminal defendant is entitled, and the relevant Supreme Court decisions that have affected defendant rights. The trial process is examined from pretrial activity, to the *voir dire* hearing, to the judge's charge to the jury. The differences between the indeterminate and various types of determinate sentencing are reviewed as a prelude to the presentence report and the sentencing hearing. The chapter ends with a discussion of probation, parole, and executive clemency.

Chapter 11 provides an in-depth examination of the method most frequently used to decide criminal cases, and the controversy surrounding plea bargaining.

Chapter 12 contrasts the civil trial process with the criminal trial and examines issues surrounding the contingency fee and class action lawsuits.

Chapter 13 examines the system of juvenile justice, the important Supreme Court decisions that have affected the juvenile court, the movement away from *parens patriae* and toward a justice model of responding to juvenile crime.

Chapter 14 examines alternative methods of dispute resolution in both civil and criminal matters, mediation and arbitration, and the emerging field of therapeutic justice.

The writer is grateful for the confidence shown in his work by Kim Davies, Prentice Hall Executive Editor. He would like to thank development editor Susan Beauchamp for her outstanding work on this edition. And a special thanks to production editor Naomi Sysak, and copyeditor Natalia Morgan, for their attention to detail and special care in editing this edition. A special thanks and recognition to Alex delCarmen, University of Texas–Arlington; Frank Afflitto, Arizona State University; Greg Plumb, Park University; and Kathleen Simon, Appalachian State University, for their careful review and suggestions for this edition.

The author encourages comments about his work. He can be reached at Saint Xavier University, 3700 W. 103rd Street, Chicago, IL 60655; abadinsky@att.net.

ABOUT THE AUTHOR

Howard Abadinsky is professor of criminal justice/law and society at Saint Xavier University/Chicago. He was an inspector for the Cook County Sheriff's Office for eight years and a New York State parole officer and senior parole officer for fifteen years. The author holds a B.A. from Queens College of the City University of New York, an M.S.W. from Fordham University, and a Ph.D. from New York University. He is the author of several books, including *Organized Crime*, 7th edition, *Probation and Parole*, 8th edition, and *Drug Abuse*, 4th edition.

Dr. Abadinsky encourages communication about his work, and can be reached at: abadinsky@att.net.

LAW AND JUSTICE CHRONOLOGY

1950–1792 B.C.E.	Hammurabi
1200–1080	Moses
621	Draco's law
638–558	Solon's law
450	Twelve Tables of Rome, a written code
384–322	Aristotle
300	Greek Stoics
106–43	Roman statesman Marcus Tulius Cicero
533 C.E.	Code of Justinian
1086	Origins of English common law
1225–1274	Thomas Aquinas
1492	Columbus reaches the Americas
1607	Jamestown, the first English settlement in America, is established
1620	Mayflower lands at Plymouth
1765	Blackstone's Commentaries on the Laws of England
1776	Declaration of Independence
1781	Articles of Confederation ratified
1783	Revolutionary War ends
1787	Philadelphia Convention
1788	*Federalist Papers*; Constitution ratified
1789	Judiciary Act sets the Supreme Court's membership at six and creates three circuit courts; French Revolution begins
1791	Bill of Rights ratified

1793	*Chisholm* v. *Georgia* (states can be sued in federal court by citizens of other states)
1798	Eleventh Amendment ratified (in a reaction to *Chisholm*, affords states sovereign immunity)
1803	*Marbury* v. *Madison* (power of judicial review)
1804	Napoleonic code
1816	*Martin* v. *Hunter's Lessee* (upheld the appellate jurisdiction of the Supreme Court as the "final word" over all federal *and* state courts)
1819	*McCulloch* v. *Maryland* (extends the power of the federal government by discovering the Constitution's "implied powers")
1820	Missouri Compromise (Maine is admitted as a free state and Missouri as a slave state, and slavery is banned in much of the Louisiana Purchase)
1824	*Gibbons* v. *Ogden* (asserts the federal government's supreme authority over the regulation of interstate commerce)
1829–1837	Jacksonian era
1833	*Barron* v. *Baltimore* (Bill of Rights does not apply to states)
1848	"Field Code" of civil procedure enacted in New York
1857	*Scott* v. *Sanford* (while a state can confer citizenship on a Negro, this does not affect his status in another state nor does it give rise to a claim of constitutional protection even within the granting state)
1861–1865	Civil War
1868	Fourteenth Amendment ratified (applies Bill of Rights to states)
1870	Christopher Columbus Langdell at Harvard
1873	*Slaughterhouse* Cases (recognition of "states' rights" against federal authority)
1875	Judiciary Act (provides federal courts with extensive jurisdiction)
1876	Reconstruction Era ends
1879	West Publishing Company establishes the *National Reporting System*
1890	Sherman Antitrust Act (criminalizes restraint of trade/monopoly)
1895	*United States* v. *E.C. Knight & Co.* (limits the application of the Sherman Antitrust Act)
1896	*Plessy* v. *Ferguson* ("equal but separate" accommodations for the whites and blacks is reasonable)
1905	*Lochner* v. *New York* (New York statute providing maximum hours for bakers is unconstitutional)
1908	*Adair* v. *United States* (Congress has no power with respect to union activities)
1914	War begins in Europe; *Weeks* v. *United States* (establishes exclusionary rule in federal cases)
1917	Russian Revolution; United States enters First World War

1918   First World War ends

1919   *Schenck* v. *United States* (limits free speech when there is "a clear and present danger")

1920–1933   Prohibition

1920   Nineteenth Amendment grants women the right to vote

1928   Mussolini dictatorship

1929   Great Depression begins

1932   Franklin D. Roosevelt elected president; Norris–La Guardia Act (strips federal courts of their power to issue injunctions in labor disputes); *Powell* v. *Alabama* (if a defendant in a capital case lacks an attorney and a fairly chosen jury, he or she cannot be convicted)

1933   Hitler named chancellor

1935   Wagner (National Labor Relations) Act (gives explicit protection to the rights of workers to organize)

1937   Court packing plan

1939   War begins in Europe

1940   *Minersville School District* v. *Gobitis* (requiring pledge of allegiance in school is constitutional)

1941–1945   Second World War

1943   *West Virginia Board of Education* v. *Burnette* (overturns the 1940 *Gobitis* decision)

1944   *Korematsu* v. *United States* (upholds a relocation order for Americans of Japanese ancestry)

1950–1953   Korean War

1952   *Youngstown Sheet and Tube Co., et al.* v. *Sawyer* (rules that President Truman had acted beyond his constitutional authority in seizing steel mills during the Korean War)

1953   Earl Warren appointed to Supreme Court

1954   *Brown* v. *Board of Education* (school segregation is unconstitutional)

1957   Federal troops sent to Little Rock, Arkansas, to enforce *Brown*

1961   *Mapp* v. *Ohio* (applies the exclusionary rule to the states)

1961–1973   Vietnam War

1962   *Baker* v. *Carr* (Gerrymandering unconstitutional—"one person, one vote"); *Engle* v. *Vitale* (prescribed religious ceremonies in public schools are unconstitutional)

1963   *Gideon* v. *Wainwright* (states must provide counsel for all indigents in felony cases)

1965   *Griswold* v. *Connecticut* ("right to privacy" voids statute prohibiting birth control devices)

1966   *Miranda* v. *Arizona* (prior to questioning, the police must warn a suspect of the right to remain silent)

1967	*In re Gault* (extends due process protections to juvenile court)
1969	Warren Burger appointed Chief Justice
1973	*Roe* v. *Wade* (strikes down laws prohibiting abortion)
1974	*United States* v. *Nixon*; President Nixon resigns
1986	William Rehnquist appointed Chief Justice
1989	Dismantling of the Berlin Wall presages the collapse of European communism
1991	Soviet Union dissolved
1992–2000	Decisions favoring states' rights; *Miranda* reaffirmed
2001	*Bush* v. *Gore* ends the presidential recount in Florida

1

An Introduction to Law and Justice

This chapter introduces themes and concepts discussed throughout the book. We will examine the law, its attributes and definitions. We will move from the concept of natural law to capitalism's need for rational law. This will prepare the reader for more detailed examinations of law and justice in later chapters. But first, what is meant by "law?"

LAW: THE PROBLEM OF DEFINITION

The concept of law is ancient—references to written law date back to about 2400 before the Common Era (B.C.E.) (Draper 1989). Most modern books on law, however, do not define the phenomenon—as if the obvious need not be defined— yet the definition of law can be as complex as its application. The word *law* is believed to be derived from one of two Old Norse terms, *log* or *lag*. The former means to lay down or determine; the latter refers to a team, the concept of binding people together (Aubert 1983). Although central to the functioning of society, law has defied authoritative definition. Even lawyers and judges have no generally agreed-upon definition of law: "For them it is simply what they practice and what courts do" (Loh 1984: 23). The noted jurist Jerome Frank (1970: xiii) admits that he "seriously blundered" in offering a definition of the word law because "that word drips with ambiguity," and he concluded that efforts of defining are futile. The German philosopher Immanuel Kant (1724–1804) faulted lawyers for being unable to agree on a definition of the subject matter of their profession. He proceeded to construct his own definition, which found no more universal acceptance than the others that have been offered (Berman and Greiner 1980).[1] John Zane (1998: 2) noted that "no jurist has yet achieved a definition of law that does not require the use of the idea of law, either implied or expressed, as part of the definition."

"The existence of laws presupposes human beings living in a social complex" (Zane 1998: 2) and society is possible only on the basis of order. Therefore "law can be conceived of as simply a body of rules governing a social order" (Hoebel 1974: 12). The earliest societies, however, knew no law, but instead relied on the force of custom, magic, religion, and social pressure (Draper 1989). Social scientists disagree over the point at which law can be said to exist in a society: How is law to be distinguished from social rules and customs, the norms of a society? (Sigler 1986). A *norm* indicates societal expectations of what is right, or "normal;" in short, of what ought to be. In his well-known elaboration, William Graham Sumner (1840–1910) ordered norms in a hierarchical manner:

- *Folkways* are unplanned social rules enforced by informal controls such as ridicule and ostracism. There is a sense of obligation, but it is relatively weak—for example, holding open a door or allowing women or children to enter first.

- *Mores* are similar, but there is an imperative to comply, and violations are met with a strong sense of moral indignation—for example, removing one's hat (or, in some cultures, one's shoes) when entering a residence or perhaps a restaurant.

- *Customary law* involves rules enforced by specific sanctions imposed by the community as a whole, although certain persons may be delegated to carry out the task—for example, prohibitions against sexual relationships between blood relatives.

- *Enacted law* is similar to customary law but, as the term implies, the rules are deliberately set out by official representatives of the community—they are explicit and carry the weight of the community—the criminal statutes of a state, for example.

Laws not based on societal norms are unlikely to gain general compliance: prohibition in the United States (1920–1933) is a good example.

According to Max Weber, laws are "norms which are directly guaranteed by legal coercion" (1967: 14). Conduct that violates a social norm may be impolite or perhaps eccentric, and it can cause the violator to be shunned by those who are aware of the norm-violative behavior. Behavior that violates the law, however, draws punishment. Punishment, if it is to be "lawful," must be imposed by persons specifically authorized by society; thus, law represents the rules of conduct backed by the organized force of the community (Abraham 1998).

Laws and formal mechanisms of enforcement emerge when societal complexity renders custom ineffective in controlling behavior and the need for explicit controls becomes increasingly greater. Homogeneity gives way to heterogeneity. Common interests shrink

---

[1]For a discussion of the elements included in "law," see Hart (1961).

*S*OCIETAL *N*ORMS AND *P*ROHIBITION

Herbert Packer (1968: 263) reminds us that people do not necessarily respond to new criminal laws by acquiescence, particularly when they do not conform to the norms of a large part of the population. He points out that resistance can be fatal to the new law, and moreover, when this happens "the effect is not confined to the immediate proscription but makes itself felt in the attitude that people take toward legal prescriptions in general." Thus, primary resistance or opposition to a new law such as Prohibition can result, secondarily, in disregard for laws in general: negative contagion. During Prohibition a "general tolerance of the bootlegger and a disrespect for federal law were translated into a widespread contempt for the process and duties of democracy" (Sinclair 1962: 292).

in relation to special interests. Face-to-face relations exist not between all of the members of the society, but only among a progressively smaller proportion of them. Genealogical kinship links not all the members as it did before, but only a progressively smaller proportion of them. Access to material goods becomes more and more indirect, with greater possibilities for uneven allocation, and the struggle among the members of a given society for access to the available goods becomes intensified. Everything moves to increase the potential for conflict within the society. (Hoebel 1974: 293)

"It is the formality of legal processes which makes legal relations a special and unique type of social relations, distinct from informal (that is, undefined, spontaneous, intimate) relations" (Berman and Greiner 1980: 28).

"Law is distinguished from mere custom in that it endows certain selected individuals with the privilege-right of applying the sanction of physical coercion" (Hoebel 1974: 276).[2] Benjamin Cardozo (1924: 52) adds the necessity of regular enforcement by courts of law. Law, he says, "is a principle or rule of conduct so established as to justify a prediction with reasonable certainty that it will be enforced by the courts if its authority is challenged."[3] That norms require a formal mechanism for enforcement presupposes that there may be those who do not, or will not, support them in all instances, although Weber (1967) points out that custom may be far more determinative of conduct than the existence of legal enforcement machinery.

In sum, law appears to have four components:

1. Norms
2. Regularly enforced by coercion
3. By persons authorized by society
4. As applied by courts of law

---

[2]Edwin Schur (1968: 75) finds this problematic because it fails to distinguish between law and government: "Not only does this seeming indistinguishability make their separation for analytical purposes impossible, but also it renders the notion of a government *subject* to law meaningless."

[3]The term "court" is derived from a time when the king in his court served as a judge. Medieval English judges acted as agents of the king, conducting their business in court (Rabkin 1989).

PRIVATE RULES TO PUBLIC LAW

There is an "increasing tendency for the norms of private legal systems to be judicially recognized, as, for example, in a medical malpractice suit in which the code of ethics of the American Medical Association is invoked; in a suit involving the internal relations of a trade union in which the union's constitutional provisions are accorded legal status by the court; or in a suit by a student against a college or university in which the institution's disciplinary rules are judicially recognized" (Evan 1962: 176). The once private nominating practices of political parties are now rigidly governed by (public) law.

"Some laws compel conduct while others serve to facilitate voluntary actions by providing guidelines for them.[4] It is useful to think of law as comprising a set of authoritative and prescriptive rules for conduct. Some rules instruct persons in what they must or must not do (for example, 'pay your taxes'; 'do not segregate public school pupils on the basis of race'); others tell people how to do what they wish to do so that their actions are legally enforceable, that is, backed by the power of the state (for example, 'this is how to make a valid contract'; 'follow these steps in setting up a partnership')" (Loh 1984: 24). There are also laws that create benefits, such as Social Security, while others deal with the functions of bureaucratic entities such as a department of transportation responsible for building and maintaining public roads.

As we have defined it, law is amoral—witness the laws of Nazi Germany or the Fugitive Slave Act of the United States. The idea of morality in law is associated with the concept of natural law. Before there was law in the form of rules deliberately set forth by a human society—*positive law*—there was the "law of nature," or natural law.[5]

A DEFINITION OF LAW

Law consists of norms[6] regularly enforced by coercion, by persons authorized by society, as applied by courts of law.

---

[4]The assertion that some laws simply facilitate private action poses a problem because there are instances when law may actually hamper such efforts: "A rule that demands high levels of formality cannot simply be said to *facilitate* private ordering, but may instead facilitate ordering only for certain legally sophisticated parties with particular expectations about their dealings with others" (Kelman 1987: 233).

[5]See Heinrich A. Rommen (1897–1967), an opponent of the Hitler regime (for which he was imprisoned), for a critique of German legal positivism and his espousal of natural law: *The Natural Law: A Study in Legal and Social History and Philosophy* (1998).

[6]Admittedly, this definition is not without problems. Positive law may reflect the norms—the power—of economic elites and not necessarily societal norms.

*T*HE *F*UGITIVE *S*LAVE *A*CT 1850

"[W]hen a person held to service or labor in any State or Territory of the United States, has heretofore or shall hereafter escape into another State or Territory of the United States, the person or persons to whom such service or labor may be due . . . may pursue and reclaim such fugitive person. . . ."

NATURAL LAW

In the body of law revealed to Moses on Mount Sinai—for example, thou shalt not steal, thou shalt not murder—we can find universal elements that more contemporary observers refer to as natural law. "The term 'natural law' designates a theory which holds that law necessarily has a moral basis and its criteria are grounded in something more than ordinary experience—'in nature.' Natural law accepts as viable the quest for an absolute ideal of justice" (Levy 1988: 3). At its core, natural law posits a belief that humans have an inborn notion of right and wrong and, therefore, the very essence of law does not rest upon the arbitrary will of the ruler or upon the decree of the multitude (Rommen 1998). Natural law, while not requiring a belief in a deity,[7] refers to a higher law, primordial or law of nature[8]—in other words, rules for living that are binding on all human societies.

Natural law was expounded by Aristotle[9] (384–322 B.C.E.) and the Greek Stoics[10] (circa 300 B.C.E.), helping to form the basis of the legal philosophy of the Roman statesman Marcus Tulius Cicero (106–43 B.C.E.) as explicated in his *De legibus* ("On the Laws") and other works (Kelly 1993; Rommen 1998). In fourth century B.C.E. Greece, "men came to realize that societies which could not easily be dismissed as primitive cherished different and even conflicting customs. This shattering discovery

*D*ECLARATION OF *I*NDEPENDENCE, *J*ULY 4, 1776

"We hold these Truths to be self-evident, that all Men are created equal, that they are endowed by their Creator with certain inalienable Rights, that among these are Life, Liberty and the Pursuit of Happiness. . . "

---

[7]R.C. Van Caenegem divides natural law into that having religious origins, the other rational, for which " 'law of reason' is therefore more accurate than 'natural law'" (1994: 118).
[8]Richard Posner (1990) states that the term natural law is an anachronism—nature is amoral.
[9]That natural law could be invoked to defend both freedom and slavery has an early example in the apologetics of Aristotle.
[10]Stoicism, a philosophical movement that lasted about 500 years, emphasized the laws of nature and reason over emotion. Founded in Greece, it flowered in Rome, where it was popularized by Cicero (106–43 BCE).

provoked a search for universal principles of conduct based upon human nature, that might underlie the variety of customs and serve as criteria for their assessment. The philosophic doctrines fashioned in the course of this quest for these overarching norms were used by Roman lawyers" (Unger 1976: 76–77).

As derived from Aristotle and ancient philosophy, natural law doctrines were united into a Christian framework by Thomas Aquinas (1225–1274). In his *Summa Theologica*, Aquinas asserts that if positive law (law derived out of the political process) violates natural law, it is not law but a corruption of law. According to many references in Church doctrine, natural law is rooted in human nature, divine law written on the human heart (Fuchs 1965), the principles of which are known or at least knowable by anyone (Joseph Boyle 1992). In the language of the Declaration of Independence, truths which are self evident—a moral consensus.

During the Middle Ages (from the fall of the Roman Empire to the Renaissance), the concept of natural law served the interests of the Church in its dealings with secular powers, and in the hands of the Papacy it was an impediment to the growth of nation states (Aubert 1983). According to Church doctrine, the source of all natural law is divine and, thus, "the Church in her own Code emphatically refuses to recognize any legislation that contradicts the natural law" (Fuchs 1965: 8). The concept of natural law was later used by an emerging middle class in efforts to counter the power of feudal nobility and later the divine right of the monarch in order "to preserve an area of individual freedom and initiative secure from interference by the state" (MacDonald 1961: 4). Natural law necessarily places limits on political power, and in England it was embodied in the common law (discussed in Chapter 2).

Natural law stresses the importance of the promptings of conscience. Recurring themes appearing in natural-law tradition are an appeal to nature and human nature as sources of objective standards for ethics, politics, and law (Sigmund 1971): a "higher or natural law distinct from, and superior to, the customs of particular social groups and the commands of earthly sovereigns" (Unger 1976: 79). Out of the concept of natural law evolved the idea of natural rights, "certain qualities inherent in man and demonstrated by reason, which natural law exists to secure and to which positive [that is, manmade] law ought to give effect" (Pound 1975: 15–16). Natural rights are prepolitical and "the theory of natural law is always grounded in

Natural Law

"Congress shall make no law . . . prohibiting the freedom of speech." (*U.S. Constitution*, Amendment I)

Positive Law

The judge determined that Karlrobert Kreiten had indeed violated paragraph 91b of the Criminal Code; he sentenced the defendant to death. Kreiten was subsequently executed for making derogatory remarks to his friends about Hitler's regime (Müller 1991).

NATURAL LAW IN COLONIAL VIRGINIA

Now all acts of the legislature apparently contrary to natural right and justice, are, in our laws, and must be in the nature of things, considered void. The laws of nature are the laws of God, whose authority can be superseded by no power on earth. A legislature must not obstruct our obedience to him from whose punishments they cannot protect us. All human constitutions which contradict his laws, we are in conscience bound to disobey.

Source: George Mason's argument for plaintiffs in *Robin* v. *Hardaway*, found in Thomas Jefferson's *Virginia Reports* 109, 114 (1772). Mason, a wealthy Virginia landowner and delegate to the Constitutional Convention, opposed slavery and inspired the Bill of Rights.

the assertion that through reason we can know the nature of man and that this knowledge should be the basis for the social and legal ordering of human existence" (Schur 1968: 52).

Often seen as a liberalizing force, natural law stresses moral and rational elements in legal processes. "Even today," notes Russell Hittinger (1998: xvii), " 'natural law' often means any species of moral theory used by appellate judges when they interpret and apply law." Natural law exists whether or not there is a specific enactment by the authority of government. Thus, natural law transcends all formal human constructs and any law contrary to the natural law is based on the coercive force of the state, not the voluntary compliance of the governed. According to the *Commentaries* of William Blackstone (1723–1780), any human law contrary to natural law has no validity. Positive law, even that approved by a majority of voters, cannot transform evil into justice (Rommen 1998). However, stalwarts of natural law often had no qualms averring that its protections did not apply to certain "nonpersons": Native Americans, blacks, women, and children. Until the Civil War, property law, not natural law, defined the fate of slaves in the United States (*Scott* v. *Sandford* 1857). Natural law "has been used to defend slavery and freedom; hierarchy and equality; revolution and reaction" (Sigmund 1971: 206). Thus, natural law was invoked by patriots in the fight against Britain, while in postrevolutionary America natural law was invoked both for and against slavery. Natural law was used as a basis for denying women all political and many legal rights. Clearly, morality is relative; or, using Nietzsche, morality is a reflection of the needs and circumstances of the dominant group (Posner 1990).[11]

Natural law is expressed in the classical European Enlightenment concept of a *social contract:* a mythical state of affairs wherein each person agrees to a pact—a social contract—the basic stipulation of which is that, all men being created equal, conditions of law are the same for all. "The social contract establishes among the citizens an equality of such character that each binds himself on the same terms as

---

[11]"English settlers had to enact statutes designed to legalize and legitimate a system of bondage alien to English law and custom, a body of law and custom that by the early modern period had come to see the common law as a strong mirror of natural law and as a guardian of individual liberty" (Cottrol 1996: 729).

WOMEN ACCORDING TO "NATURAL LAW"

"Civil law, as well as nature herself, has always recognized a wide difference in the respective spheres and destinies of man and woman. The paramount destiny and mission of woman are to fulfill the noble and benign offices of wife and mother. This is the law of the Creator." *Bradwell* v. *Illinois* (1873), by which the Supreme Court upheld the right of Illinois to deny Myra Bradwell admission to legal practice because of her gender.

all the others, and is thus entitled to enjoy the same rights as all the others" (Rousseau [1762] 1954: 45). According to classical thought, man is free by nature and endowed with natural rights, a philosophical basis for the first ten amendments (Bill of Rights) to the Constitution. The natural law concepts of John Locke (1632–1704), according to which all men are by nature free, equal, and independent, and no one can be subjected to the political power of another without his own consent, were incorporated in the U.S. Declaration of Independence: "all men are created equal" whose "governments are instituted among men, deriving their just powers from the consent of the governed." The protection of property was a primary concern of Locke and it obviously influenced the Constitutional Convention (see Beard 1913).

For Englishmen, argues Edmund Morgan (1956: 16), including the American colonists, property was intertwined with liberty: "Where property was concentrated in the hands of the king and aristocracy, only the king and aristocracy would be free, while the rest of the population would be little better than slaves, victims of the external efforts of rulers to exploit subjects. Without property men could be starved into submission. Hence, liberty rested on property, and whatever threatened the security of property threatened liberty."

While Locke referred to the natural law right of "life, liberty, property," Thomas Jefferson enumerated the inalienable right to "life, liberty, and the pursuit of happiness." According to this view, the purpose of government was "largely to protect the natural rights retained by the people." And if "the government invaded these natural rights, the people could not only disobey, but resist and establish a new government as well" (Pohlman 1993: 10). "By the middle of the eighteenth century, the legal commentators of the Enlightenment had moved from thinking of natural law as a collection of moral abstractions to which conduct should conform, to the more particular assertion that natural law could be expressed in a body of legal precepts against which all positive law could then be measured" (Ferguson 1984: 62). Accordingly, natural law in the United States was expressed not in terms of the nature of man but, instead, in the nature of government, a government restrained by "the principles of natural constitutional law" (Pound 1975: 20).

Natural law was so deeply embedded in the American psyche that even before the adoption of the Constitution, state judges engaged in judicial review, invalidating legislation and overturning convictions not only on the basis of a conflict with a state constitution, but also on the basis of natural law. As the nation matured, the new federal courts joined state courts in using natural law to invalidate statutes, justifying and explaining their actions in the language of natural rights. "Court

NATURAL LAW → NATURAL RIGHTS → CONSTITUTION/JUDICIAL REVIEW

In the United States, the concept of natural law was transformed into something more practical: *natural rights*. The Constitution and judicial review are the instruments by which these rights would be guaranteed.

opinions spoke of such limits on legislation as 'natural rights,' 'inalienable rights,' 'inherent rights,' 'fundamental principles of civilized society,' and the 'immutable principles of justice.'" They also broadened the definition of natural rights, protecting not only property rights and the right to jury trial, but also the right of representation and rights against retroactive laws or laws granting special privileges (Sherry 1998: 16). "Many of the provisions of the Bill of Rights were clearly rooted in natural law thinking" (Atiyah and Summers 1987: 231).

In the United States, natural law was transferred into a secular document for ordering society, and the principles of natural law would be implemented through judicial review: "The judiciary would serve as an overseer to guard against unwarranted governmental usurpation" (Slotnick 1992a: 7). "After all, if the Constitution was thought to mirror natural law and natural rights, a politically insulated judge exercising judicial review was not merely enforcing the people's will (i.e., the Constitution) against the popularly elected branch of government, but was also defending the natural order created by God" (Pohlman 1993: 11).

There is an inherent conflict between natural law, which restrains and limits human enactments, and positive law: human enactments resulting from the popular consent of individuals who form themselves into a sovereign people. According to Locke (1952), the people may delegate lawmaking to a governmental agency (legislature) that is limited to those ends authorized by the people. Natural law, however, limits the ends that the people may authorize. "If legislatures should act beyond or against such ends, even with popular consent, their acts would not be valid. Thus, the laws that must be established by positive human authorities are in turn limited by natural law" (Smith 1985: 68). Natural law stands as a bulwark against totalitarianism, even that brought about by democratic means or the popular will (e.g., Fascist Italy

LEGAL POSITIVISM AND TOTALITARIANISM

The nationalist form of totalitarianism arose and flourished in the two countries—Germany and Italy—where moral and legal positivism had obtained a dominant position in the universities and the legal profession. Legal positivism conditioned an outlook of unqualified acceptance of the mythical *will of the state*—the state can do anything—as the controlling philosophy of law (Rommen 1998).

and Nazi Germany). The natural law doctrines limiting the power of government prepared the way for the institution of judicial review (Smith 1985; Sigmund 1971), which will be discussed in Chapters 3 and 8. Natural-law reasoning may be found in any number of contemporary Supreme Court opinions, whose authors hold that the Constitution "should be broadly interpreted in light of the fundamental rights of the human person that the Constitution was constructed to defend" (Conley 1991: 14). The prosecution of Nazi officials by the victorious allies, if it is to be justified beyond a simple expression of power or vengeance, is dependent upon a concept of natural law.

While it may be constrained by natural law, if a society is to advance into a more complex structure, that society must be governed by *rational law*.

RATIONAL LAW

In contrast to a rational legal order—*the application of general norms to specific cases*—Weber describes irrational legal systems in which decisions are "influenced by concrete factors of the particular case as evaluated upon an ethical, emotional, or political basis rather than by general norms" ([1925] 1967: 63). Irrational legal systems may exist when laws have theological origins and are enforced by agents of the prevailing religious order. Weber uses Islamic *kadi* justice as an example of highly particularized law. According to Weber, decisions are rendered by the religious judge, *kadi* or *qadi*, without recourse to generalized principles of law but, rather, according to what is deemed morally correct in each case. Each decision is made on a case-by-case basis, and its legitimacy is dependent upon the charisma of the individual judge.[12]

Under elementary social conditions this may suffice. "A close-knit, relatively homogeneous community can get along (perhaps) with a system where village elders reach decisions on the basis of their personal sense of fairness and their informed concern for the parties and the community." However, "that pastoral model cannot serve an ethnically and ideologically diverse nation where litigants are strangers to the judge and often to each other. The liberties and fortunes of citizens cannot be left at the mercy of each judge's personal sense of what procedures are fair, what outcome is just, who needs protection, and who deserves compassion" (Glendon 1994: 164). In such a system, since every dispute involves unique facts and parties, it would be difficult to predict the outcome of a given case. Thus, persons and businesses would be unable to adjust their behavior in order to avoid becoming embroiled in legal disputes (Beckerman-Rodau 1999).

Under an irrational legal system a modern capitalist economy cannot develop, "for modern rational capitalism has need, not only of the technical means of production, but of a calculable legal system and of administration in terms of formal rules" (Weber [1905] 1958: 25). Modern rational capitalism requires a legal order that is both prompt and predictable, one that is calculable in accordance with rational rules and guaranteed by the strongest coercive power. Weber

---

[12]For a different rendition of *kadi* justice, see Shapiro (1981), Chapter 5; Glenn (2000), Chapter 6; also Calder (1993).

notes that the development of capitalism occurs under rational legal orders wherein contractual obligations will be enforced between not only the primary parties, but also their agents: "Every rational business organization needs the possibility, for particular cases as well as for general purposes, of acquiring contractual rights and of assuming obligations through agents. Advanced trade, moreover, needs not only the possibility of transferring legal claims but also, and quite particularly, a method by which transfers can be made legally secure and which eliminates the need of constantly testing the title of the transfer" (Weber 1967: 122).

Without such guarantees, an economy must remain on the primitive level of barter or under control of the state.[13] Thus, for example, a merchant of the medieval period who placed his trust in a contract was in a quandary. There were several kinds of law, and the merchant would be uncertain as to which court had enough power to make the opposite party pay up or deliver the goods (Tigar and Levy 1977). Countries of Eastern Europe and the former Soviet Union are struggling with commercial law that has long been a staple of business relations in the West (Uchitelle 1992).

As opposed to laws and legal systems having divine or "natural" origins, the rational-law systems governing Western nations proceed from five postulates (Weber [1925] 1967):

1. Every legal decision involves the application of an abstract legal proposition to a concrete factual set of circumstances.

2. Every concrete case can be decided on the basis of abstract legal propositions derived by means of legal logic.

3. The law constitutes a gapless system of legal propositions, one that can deal with any and all possible concrete cases. In other words, there are no gaps in the legal system that render certain disputes outside the pale of law.

4. Every social action of human beings is construed either as an application or a carrying out of legal propositions or as an infringement thereof.

5. Whatever cannot be decided legally in rational terms is legally irrelevant.

In sum, *a system of modern or rational law involves the application of general principles to specific facts (cases).*

The legal philosopher John Rawls asks what makes a particular case "rational"? The answer, he offers "is that a judgment in a particular case is evidenced to be rational by showing that, given the facts and the conflicting interests of the case, the judgment is capable of being explicated by justifiable principle (or set of principles)" (1999: 10). What are these principles? They are encompassed in the two basic systems used in Western society for implementing a system of rational law, *common/case law* and *civil law*, topics for Chapter 2.

---

[13]John Noonan, Jr. (1976) states that a modern legal system in America also made bearable the institution of slavery. The legal process depersonalized participants to such an extraordinary degree that it was possible to deal with slaves using legal principles and processes that applied to the sale, transfer, and inheritance of property. For a similar rendition of the legal system in Nazi Germany, see Müller (1991).

INTERNET CONNECTION

Legal sites on the Web: *ih2000.net/ira/legal.htm*
Emory Electronic Reference Desk: *law.emory.edu/LAW/refdesk/toc.html*
Legal journals on the Web: *usc.edu/dept/law-lib/legal/journals.html*
Legal links: *gidc.com/links.htm*
Justice directory: *copnet.org/justice.html*
Meta-index for legal research: *gsulaw.gsu.edu/metaindex*
Global legal site: *hg.org*

REVIEW QUESTIONS

1. What has been the result of attempts to define "law"?
2. How is law distinguished from the norms of a society?
3. What are the societal conditions that lead to the emergence of laws and formal mechanisms of enforcement?
4. What are the four components that make up "law"?
5. How can laws serve to facilitate voluntary actions?
6. What are the basic concepts of natural law?
7. What are the characteristics of a system of irrational law?
8. How can natural law conflict with positive law?
9. What are the essential elements of a rational system of law?
10. Why is capitalism dependent on a rational legal system?

2

SYSTEMS OF LAW AND JUSTICE

Since legal tradition in the United States has borrowed from two rational systems of law—common/case law and civil law—we will examine and compare them. In this chapter, we will also distinguish between inquisitional and adversarial systems, and between statutory and administrative law.

COMMON/CASE LAW

England's rational system of law is based on judicial-lawfinding. Prior to the Norman conquest in 1066,[1] principles applied in local Anglo-Saxon courts (fifth to eleventh centuries) broadly reflected the customs of local communities as declared by their freemen or judges. In 1086, William I ("The Conqueror") sent commissioners throughout the realm to make a record (in *dooms* or *domesday books*—"doom" refers to law/judgment) of the names of towns, and the number of persons, cattle, and houses, as well as the customs and norms of the population. The Norman kings gradually wielded these local customs into a single body of general principles—*common law* referring to its application throughout the realm.

---

[1]The original Normans were Vikings—Norsemen—who had settled in France, from which Normandy derives its name. By the time of the Norman conquest, they had integrated with the native Gaulish population, had become Christians, and lost most of their Nordic character. They were well versed in Roman law, a source of the Latin words in common law (Zane 1998).

A legislative body—parliament—would not emerge for several centuries, and royal edicts did not extend to many legal issues confronting judges. Thus, in applying these principles, judges placed great reliance on previous judgments given in similar cases, a procedure that gave rise to the doctrine of judicial precedent (Tarr 1999). Toward the end of the thirteenth century, arguments of the barristers (trial lawyers) and the rulings of the judges were written down and circulated. These documents became the forerunners of the published Law Reports that are the basis for common law,[2] which was revolutionized with the advent of the printing press.[3]

"The common law of England evolved from spontaneously observed rules and practices, shaped and formalised by decisions made by judges pronouncing the law in relation to the particular facts before them" (Central Office of Information 1976: 4). The controlling element is *precedent*: "When a group of facts come before an English Court of adjudication," observes Henry Maine, "it is taken absolutely for granted that there is somewhere a rule of known law which will cover the facts of the dispute now litigated, and that, if such a rule be not discovered, it is only because the necessary patience, knowledge or acumen is not forthcoming to detect it" (1861: 24). If the circumstances of a particular case are unique, the common law resorts to reasoning by analogy from previous cases. The foundation of English common law is judicial decisions handed down from the earliest time to the present, each successive decision being founded on some preceding adjudication or a new application of a judicial principle already established. "The genius of the common law is that it proceeds empirically and gradually, testing the ground at every step, and refusing, or at any rate evincing an extreme reluctance, to embrace broad theoretical principles" (Aldisert 1989: 8). Because common law does not resort to written codes, it is sometimes referred to as "unwritten law" (Abraham 1998).

Basic to understanding common law is the notion that a judicial decision serves a dual function: "First, it settles the controversy, that is, under the doctrine of *res judicata* [final conclusive judgment] the parties may not relitigate the issues that have been decided. Second, in the common law system, under the doctrine of *stare decisis*, the judicial decision also has precedential value. The doctrine, from *stare decisis et non quieta movere*, 'stand by the decision and do not disturb what is settled,' is rooted in the common law policy that a principle of law deduced from a judicial decision will be considered and applied in the determination of future similar cases. [This doctrine] refers to the likelihood that a similar or like case arising in the future will be decided in the same way" (Re 1975a: 2). "The principle of *stare decisis* therefore creates a chain of cases, in which each decision is an interpretation of immediately prior decisions" (Post 1995: 32).

---

[2]"If the modern layman is bewildered by the language of the legal profession, he can blame William the Conqueror for his confusion, for the Norman Conquest made French the language of the royal household and the language of the royal courts. Anglo-French, or 'law French,' was used in pleading in the English courts, and the lawyer was forced to learn it as a second language. He had to learn Latin as well, for Latin was the language employed in the Middle Ages for formal written records. Anglo-French was a dialect from which the English legal profession first developed a precise vocabulary for the expression of legal concepts" (Hogue 1966: 7). Words such as *plaintiff, defendant, voir dire, en banc,* and *demurrer* are of French origin; *certiorari, subpoena, mens rea, actus reus, mandamus,* and *pro se* are Latin (Schubert 2000).

[3]There is also an Islamic influence in English law via the Crusades and the conquest of Jerusalem in 1099 (Glenn 2000).

However, the common law was not a "gapless system" capable of resolving all concrete cases. Common law remedies were confined almost entirely to money damages, and the procedures became increasingly complex and inflexible. Common law is made by judges as a byproduct of deciding cases (Posner 1990), and "common law judges are averse to deduction of particular rules from basic principles; the process is rather the inductive one of letting the general rule emerge from a succession of individual cases. Yet the courts do not respond with notable flexibility to social change because of the firmly held principle of binding judicial precedent" (McLaughlin 1984: 104). By about 1300, the common law had become so encumbered with artificial restrictions it was incapable of doing justice in a large number of legal issues, many of them of ordinary occurrence (Zane 1998). As a result, an alternative system of law—*equity*—developed alongside common law courts (For a detailed history of the common law, see Plunknett 1956; Cantor 1999).

EQUITY

The concept of equity expresses a concern for fairness that can be found in the Bible: "And thou shalt do that which is right and good in the sight of the Lord" (*Deuteronomy* VI: 18). Thus, it is not enough "to do that which is *right*," to act in accord with the letter of the law. One must also act fairly—do that which is "*good* in the sight of the Lord." The Hebrew concept of *yosher* is based upon this biblical imperative, according to which an individual must act beyond the mere rule of law (*din*) whenever the latter involves harshness or causes hardship (see Kirschenbaum [1991] for a discussion of this issue). As a system for correcting imperfections of positive law, equity is traced to Aristotle, who viewed equity as the application of natural law (Rommen 1998).

In more contemporary times the issue still remains: Should a rule be applied mechanically, no matter how outlandish or unfair the outcome, an approach advocated by Kant (1949)—positive law devoid of natural law restraints, or should there be room for ensuring a fair and reasonable outcome? While common law has been associated with rules, the nondiscretionary application of particular precepts (formalism), equity has been associated with the more flexible *reasonable standard* (situationism) component of law that has its own problems inherent in the exercise

RULES AND PRINCIPLES

A rule has one of two possible relationships to a set of facts: The facts either fall within the rule, in which case the consequences of the rule must be followed, or the facts are not relevant to the rule. Principles, however, are stated in general terms—they serve as guides—so that both their meaning and consequences are less clear; that is, open to more interpretation (Ducat 2000). "While a rule can emerge from a single case, a principle "emerges from a line of decisions as a broad statement of reasons for these decisions" (Aldisert 1989: 12).

of discretion. "Standards have the disadvantage of making it harder to predict the outcome of a legal dispute—there are more variables, which makes litigation more likely and also makes it harder for people to plan and to conduct their affairs" (Posner 1990: 45). "Most commonly, an equitable standard exists to counterbalance an overly harsh rule"[4] (Kelman 1987: 48).

"Equity," from the Latin *aequitas*, meaning equality or justice, is an Aristotelian idea (*Nichomachean Ethics*) found in the Roman concept of natural law as set forth by Cicero (and discussed in Chapter 1). It referred to fairness or equality of treatment between Roman citizens and foreigners in matters before the praetor, a powerful legal official in pre-Justinian Rome (Maine 1861). The Roman concept appears to have influenced English custom, particularly the practice of asking the king to intercede in the name of justice—for equitable relief—on behalf of a petitioner. "English judges have throughout history shown anxiety lest the effect of legal prohibitions should be weakened by equitable modifications designed to show mercy or compassion (or even justice) to those who committed prohibited acts in exceptional situations of stress or ignorance or lack of cognitive understanding" (Atiyah and Summers 1987: 38)—the dilemma exemplified in Melville's *Billy Budd* (1961).

In the early days of English common law, litigants were refused a hearing if their suits could not be settled by a narrowly drawn writ or order. Petitioners who argued that they could not find justice in courts of common law often begged the king to follow his conscience, rather than cause the petitioner to suffer because of the technicalities of common law procedures. Medieval kings were warrior princes with little time or patience for such matters; they typically referred petitions to the chancellor, a combination executive secretary and chief of staff (Hoffer 1990). In time, petitioners went directly to the chancellor, the "keeper of the king's conscience," for relief. From this practice came the chancery courts, or courts of equity. To John Zane (1998: 235) this approach is absurd: "One system enforced in many legal relations rules which the other system pronounced unjust and unrighteous, and boldly set at naught."

The chancellor, usually an educated clergyman with a staff of scribes, was in a unique position to provide relief for petitioners who could not gain swift justice in common law courts, which could proclaim duties and rights but could not compel any kind of action other than the payment of money. Equity, on the other hand, had a plethora of remedies. For example, the injunction could be used to command a person to do some specific act or to refrain from something he or she might be doing or planning to do. Injunctions were enforced by the chancellor's power to declare something in "contempt" for which he could order summary imprisonment. Henry Abraham notes that equity "begins where law ends; it supplies justice in circumstances not covered by law" (foreword to McDowell 1982: xii). While the common law provides for money damages, it cannot easily deal with nonmonetary issues such as divorce, administration of estates (trusts), civil rights, and labor disputes. Equity, however, has power over persons, *in personam* jurisdiction (but not over things, *in rem* jurisdiction). The injunction is an order addressed personally to the defendant. For example, equity could not force a transfer of land, although it could jail for contempt the party that refused to make such a transfer (Friedman 1973). Under equity, a judge can require specific performance; for example, where damages

---

[4]Known in law as estoppel doctrines.

would be inappropriate or inadequate, a judge can compel the fulfillment of terms of a contract. This court is characterized by flexibility and humane realism: "The chancellor peers behind the formalities to seek the real extent of harm" and retains jurisdiction over the case until satisfied with its resolution (Hoffer 1990: 8).[5]

Because the chancellor was empowered to settle controversies on the basis of general notions of fairness—equity—his decisions were often contrary to one of the principles of a rational system of law, the application of abstract legal propositions to concrete cases. The outcome of any dispute became difficult to calculate and predict with any certainty. Toward the end of the sixteenth century, however, the chancellor's decisions were published, and he began to follow the common-law practice of precedent—in equity, called *maxims*—when rendering decisions. As the role of the chancellor became more judicial, it evolved into a separate court of chancery and, by the eighteenth century, "was as much fixed by decisions and as much formed into technical legal rules as the rules of the Common Law" (Zweigert and Kötz 1987: 195). While equity began as an extraordinary intervention against the rigors of the common law, successive chancellors decided "disputes referred to them by consulting the records in order to see how such a question had been dealt with on previous occasions" (Archer 1956: 39). By the 1800s, the High Court of Chancery had become as complex and inflexible as common law courts and in 1875 it was dismantled by Parliament (Quillen and Hanrahan 1993).

Equity in America

The American colonists had a philosophical prejudice against royal prerogatives with which chancery courts were associated. While many colonies had courts of equity, after the Revolution, most states abandoned chancery courts and consolidated court jurisdiction so that the same judges would sit in law and equity. An important exception is Delaware which, although it did not have a chancery court before the Revolution, established one in 1792 (Quillen and Hanrahan 1993). As will be discussed later, this proved fortuitous to corporate America.

When rendering decisions, even in equity, judges are aware of the need for continuity and stability; the law must remain certain and predictable. "This demand for certainty, of course, runs counter to a demand for some flexibility, that the law be accommodated to changed conditions. Thus, when applied to new situations, the law should produce fair results yet still serve its original social purpose. Judges, being sensitive to these apparently contradictory demands and owing fidelity to the institutions of a well ordered legal system, do not likely disregard precedents, even though in theory they are free to do so" (Yiannopoulos 1974: 75).

The Constitution (Article III, Section 2) provides that a federal judiciary has power over cases arising in law and equity, and in most states, judges were similarly empowered to hear cases both of law and equity. The *Federal Rules of Civil Procedure*, adopted in 1938, empowers judges to provide a plaintiff in a single

---

[5]Many of the modern rules of "discovery" are taken directly from the procedures of equity—rules that promote fairness. Common law courts would not compel (subpoena) a defendant in a civil action to produce evidence such as record books (Hoffer 1990).

EQUITY COURTS IN TENNESSEE

The Tennessee Secretary of State describes the state's chancery court as based on the English system in which the chancellor acted as the king's conscience: "This is still fundamentally the court's role in modern time. Equity is the power to apply moral standards of justice in a given case by allowing the Chancellor the discretion to modify or soften the application of strict rules and thereby adapt or gear the relief in light of the circumstances of the particular case" (cited in Smith 1993a).

action with monetary damages (*in rem*) and order the defendant to comply with the law (*in personam*). This merger of law and equity provides lawyers with a basis for many civil rights actions (Labaton 1988a; see Hoffer 1990 for a history of the use of equity in the United States.)

The Constitution "guarantees the right to a jury trial in all cases that would have been tried in law courts at the time of the Revolution, but not in cases that would have been tried in equity courts at that time" (Neely 1985: 38). Since England did not provide for jury trials in cases of equity, there is no constitutional right to a jury trial in equity cases in the United States, although some states (e.g., Texas and Georgia) provide for such juries, and in some equity cases a judge can order a jury trial limited to specific factual issues. Modern interpretations of constitutional provisions have broadened the right to a jury trial, except when the remedy sought is an injunction (Hazard and Taruffo 1993).[6]

COMMON LAW OR EQUITY?

In 1988, a group of teamsters brought suit against their union, alleging a breach of fiduciary duty (obligation to act for the benefit of others). The Supreme Court had to decide if the case were one of equity or common law; if it were a case of equity, the plaintiffs would not be entitled to a jury trial. Cases involving fiduciary duty are equity determinations. However, the litigants were asking for monetary damages, and money remedies are relegated to common law. The Court has interpreted the language of the Seventh Amendment, which guarantees a jury trial in cases of common law, as requiring a historical analysis to "see whether it is the type of case that would have gone before an English jury at the time the Seventh Amendment was adopted" (Greenhouse 1990: 13). However, collective bargaining was unlawful in eighteenth century England, and the justices were unable to agree on a majority opinion, although by a vote of 6–3 they ruled that the litigants were entitled to a jury trial (*Chauffeurs, Teamsters, and Helpers* v. *Terry* 1990).

---

[6]Other types of litigation not using juries include admiralty (cases arising out of maritime activities), bankruptcy, and family (custody and divorce) matters.

In most states and in the federal system, the judge makes the equity determination "in good conscience," often granting a restraining order or injunction to prevent further or future harm to the plaintiff. The court may grant a temporary injunction where injury is imminent or continuing, the merits of the case to be determined subsequently at trial. Equity is uniquely suited to deal with matters of corporate law since the outcome is in the hands of experienced judges, rather than jurors who may have difficulty understanding the complex issues typically being litigated. Formalism is an effort to constrain judgments in advance by reference to a rule of law which advances predictability. As discretion, flexibility and the rule of man (represented by equity) increase, equal treatment and the rule of law (represented by formalism) decrease—a zero sum outcome (Sunstein 1996).

Some states (e.g., Illinois and Tennessee) have a separate chancery court/division; in Delaware, there is a Court of Chancery that has historically provided a speedy and clear resolution for corporate litigation, thus attracting major corporations. Almost half of the *Fortune* 500 corporations are incorporated in Delaware, and for jurisdictional purposes a corporation and its stockholders are considered a "citizen" of the state in which it is incorporated, giving the Court of Chancery an importance beyond the borders of the nation's second smallest state (Henriques 1995). Indeed, Delaware's size permits equity to be efficiently managed in a single centralized court.

Corporate takeovers and disputes involving management and stockholders are routinely adjudicated by the Delaware Court of Chancery, whose five members (a chancellor and four vice chancellors) are appointed by the governor for 12-year terms (Grunson 1986). In addition to the injunction, equity is often used in the cases of the stockholders' derivative suit: "A stockholder brings a derivative suit on behalf of the corporation, not to redress a wrong done him individually, but to obtain recovery or relief in favor of the corporation for all similar stockholders and to compensate the corporation as a collective entity for some wrong done to it by management" (Neely 1985: 39–40). Typically, in such actions, a group of stockholders seeks to enjoin the corporate directors from certain actions such as selling off assets. Corporate directors have a fiduciary responsibility to the corporation, and as trustees—persons obligated to act for the benefit of others—they can be held accountable in equity.[7] "The court is so

FORMALISM	EQUITY
rules	standards
legal imperative	good faith
ministerial	discretionary
predictable	uncertain
determinate	indeterminate
inflexible	arbitrary

[7] In corporate matters, in the absence of any federal statute or policy to the contrary, the federal courts typically defer to state law (L. Greenhouse 1991a).

highly specialized and its decisions so scholarly that corporations' legal counsels refer to Delaware rulings to order their companies' actions to avoid litigation"[8] (Milford 2001: 38).

Toward the end of the nineteenth century, the injunction was frequently used to enjoin strikes, a practice that continued until federal legislation favorable to labor unions was enacted during the New Deal era of the 1930s. Since the 1960s, the courts have used their equity powers to impose themselves in broad policy areas (e.g., they have reorganized the management of mental institutions and welfare agencies, and for several years courts presided over the operation of the Alabama prison system and Boston public schools in order to remedy violations of constitutional rights). Equity was used by the Supreme Court in *Brown* v. *Board of Education* (1954), marking the beginning of the end of *de jure* segregation in the United States. The expanding use of equity by judges is the source of controversy that will be discussed in Chapter 8.

CIVIL LAW SYSTEMS

Civil law systems use a detailed enumeration of rules and regulations, typically (but not necessarily) a code that provides the basis for settling all possible disputes. While common law and equity is a product of English history and tradition, other European nations (such as France and Germany) use civil law and have comprehensive codes that supersede earlier law—precedent is absent as a legal concept. The use of civil law (as distinguished from ecclesiastical or canon law) can be traced to Hammurabi, king of Babylonia, 1792—1750 B.C.E. In a quest for legal uniformity throughout his vast realm, Hammurabi authored a code inscribed on a block of diorite nearly eight feet high and about five feet in circumference. It had 8,000 Semitic words, equivalent to about 20,000 English words, comprising 282 clauses dealing with all aspects of Babylonian life, including rents, slavery, marriage and divorce, trade and commerce, adoption, wages, and criminal law (Harper 1904). Punishments were typically harsh and the law of damages was based on "an eye for an eye." It was not, however, a systematic attempt to cover all possible situations (Draper 1989; Sinha 1990). Many Babylonian laws, especially those dealing with commerce, passed to Palestine and Syria and to Asia Minor and its Greek cities, then to Greece itself where it formed the basis for the commercial code of Athens (Zane 1998).

Draco (circa 621 B.C.E.) authored Athen's first written code of law, whose punishments were so severe that the word "draconian" means an unreasonably harsh law. This code was refined by Solon (638–558 B.C.E.) and the courts became more accessible to the citizens of Athens. According to an ancient tradition, a commission from Rome traveled to Athens to study the laws of Solon from which they drafted the Twelve Tables (circa 450 B.C.E.), a code written on wood and bronze tablets that for several hundred years was the basic law of Rome (Kelly 1993). While comprehensive, like any code, the Twelve Tables could not fit every situation. In fact, "anything in the nature of a formal code, rigidly interpreted, cannot fully meet the needs of

---

[8]There are more than 160,000 corporations registered in Delaware that pay the state more than $150 million in fees and taxes.

present justice, and without elasticity of application, it cannot afford adequate guidance for the future" (Edmunds 1959: 147–48). This was recognized by the Romans, whose college of pontifices (priests) provided the expert interpretive process enabling the law to meet the changing needs of Roman society (Kunkle 1972).

The most important legacy of Roman law were the compilations of Justinian (Van Caenegem 1994). After the Roman Empire became permanently divided, the Emperor Justinian I, reigning in Constantinople from 527 to 562 C.E., appointed a team of scholars to systematize Roman law, which had grown heavy with commentaries and treatises written by legal scholars (jurisconsults): "He sought both to abolish the authority of all but the greatest of the jurisconsults of the classical period and to make it unnecessary for any more commentaries or treatises to be written" (Merryman 1985: 7). The published commentaries of the jurisconsults were a collection of answers, decisions, or rules derived from particular cases (Zane 1998). When the resulting Digest, *corpus juris civilis* or the Code of Justinian, was published in 533, the emperor forbade any further reference to the works of the jurisconsults as well as any commentaries on the *corpus juris civilis* itself, which to all appearances was honored mainly in the breach. Law always needs explaining, and legal scholars of the sixth century in fact produced abundant commentaries on the code even during Justinian's lifetime (McNamee 1998). With the fall of the Eastern Empire in 1453, the Code of Justinian was relegated to relative obscurity, although much of it was adopted by the Roman Catholic Church and the Holy Roman Empire, roughly Germany and Austria in the years 962–1806 (Van Caenegem 1994).[9]

Both Roman and canon law were ill suited to deal with issues of commerce,[10] "so from the twelfth to the fifteenth centuries, a customary and cosmopolitan commercial law was developed in practice. It was dictated essentially by the needs of practice and commercial efficacy in commodity and money markets, in trade fairs, corporations, banking operations and means of insurance and credit" (Van Caenegem 1994: 83). The commercial law that developed out of the activities of guilds and maritime cities became international in character, extending throughout the commercial world, even into areas such as England where the Roman civil law system had met with resistance. This common commercial law of Europe was later adopted by the nation-states and eventually incorporated into the commercial codes established throughout the civil law world in the eighteenth and nineteenth centuries (Merryman 1985).

Renewed interest in the study of Roman law emerged during the twelfth and thirteenth centuries at universities, most notably in Italy and France, but until the French Revolution, Roman law was largely in the form of a body of academic text and commentary rather than a set of statutory enactments. Nevertheless, "Roman law increasingly affected legal life and practice in Europe in general," providing authorities "solid compelling arguments for reinforcing state power against feudal fragmentation" (Van Caenegem 1994: 67, 73; Zane 1998). In Spain, *Las Siete Partidas*, a legal code that was apparently influenced by the Code of Justinian, was extended to Spanish colonies. It became part of the law in colonial Louisiana, remained in force in Texas until 1840, and operated for a decade later in California (Edmunds 1959).

---

[9]Modern civil code systems can be divided into the French and the German, both influenced by Roman law (Glenn 2000).
[10]Indeed, based on *Exodus* 22: 24 and *Leviticus* 25: 36–37, canon law prohibits the charging of interest.

The idea of a code reemerged during the Enlightenment period of the eighteenth century. With philosophical attachment to the law of nature, universal or natural law, Enlightenment scholars argued that the disorderly and patchy historical growth of law could be reworked into a comprehensible form through deliberate and planned legislation based on a rational system. To implement such an idea, however, required the powerful political impetus of the French Revolution and the authority and decisiveness of Napoleon. Beginning in 1804,[11] the emperor devoted himself to that task, constantly focusing legislators' attention "on the realities of life rather than the technicalities of law; he immediately saw the practical relevance of abstract rules; he put an abrupt end to any hairsplitting discussions, and by clear and simple questions kept bringing the discussion back to the practical and concrete; above all, he insisted on a style of drafting which was transparently clear and comprehensible to a non-lawyer like himself" (Zweigert and Kötz 1987: 195).

Napoleon's ideas are similar to the idea of those who today propose a "plain English" legal system for the United States.[12] In his egalitarian zeal, Napoleon wanted laws so clear that they could be understood even by the peasant with limited education. And there would be no need for lawyers. Civil law judges were to apply the provisions of the code literally to the cases that came before them. "At the beginning of his Civil Code, Napoleon put in a provision forbidding judges from laying down any general rule of law" (Edmunds 1959: 181). Prerevolutionary (ancien régime) judges were creatures of the crown, and revolutionary France sought to divide sharply legislative and judicial functions (Baudouin 1974), while putting in place a system that did not promote judicial independence: "Given the ancient régime, nobody wants a 'gouvernement des juges,' so the primacy of codes, and legislation in general, is reinforced by ongoing skepticism towards, and even surveillance of (through control of the career structure [discussed later]) the civilian judiciary" (Glenn 2000: 134).

But the Napoleonic Code was never a complete and exclusive body of statutory law, and during the nearly 200 years of its existence, the courts and legislators have adjusted the rules of the code in line with changing economic and social conditions. "The task of the court in this had been made easier because . . . the principles of Code Civil are often unclear and deliberately designed to require completion, the concepts used are frequently indefinite and ambiguous, many individual rules are incomplete, and the systematic interplay of different provisions is often faulty" (Zweigert and Kötz 1987: 96–97). In fact, the Napoleonic Code expresses only broad general principles laid down in simple terms. When a judge finds no positive rule in the code on an issue of law before the court, the judge uses the principles of equity in reaching a decision (Rommen 1998).

The legislature's failure to keep the codes up to date encouraged judges to rely on their own authority to extend provisions in new situations, while lawyers learned to search for relevant precedents and use them in their arguments (Provine 1996).

---

[11]The *Code Civil des Frances* was proclaimed on March 21, 1804. In 1807, the title was changed to *Code Napoléon*, but the original title was restored in 1816 with the fall of the Napoleonic regime. Napoleon III (1852–1870) restored the reference to Napoleon (Weber 1967).

[12]In 1999, Latin legalisms were barred from English civil courts: *in camera* is now "in private," a *subpoena* is a "witness summons," and an *interrogatory* is a "request for information."

Nevertheless, the utility of the code has been proven by its continued existence as basic law in France. (For an examination of current French law, see Kahn-Freund, Levy, and Rudden 1991; Provine 1996.)

In civil law systems "legislation is considered the one and only authoritative source of law to which all others, including case law, are subordinated" (Baudouin 1974: 7). Civil law is the product of legal scholarship. It is the legal scholar who "molds the civil law tradition and the formal materials of the law into a model of the legal system. He teaches this model to law students and writes about it in books and articles. Legislators and judges accept his idea of what the law is, and, when they make or apply law, they use concepts he has developed. Thus, although legal scholarship is not a formal source of law, the doctrine carries immense authority" (Merryman 1985: 60). Indeed, French judges "often cite academic authority to explain their decisions" (Provine 1996: 201).

The function of the judge is to discover the applicable provisions of the code and apply them to cases under consideration *without discretion* (Murphy and Pritchett 1986; Damâska 1986). Martin Shapiro notes that in practice, however, no civil system is so complete as to make unnecessary judicial discretion: "A code law judge would be almost completely bound by preexisting rules if his code were complete, consistent, specific, produced by a single authoritative legislator, and capable of rapid amendment by that legislator to meet changing circumstances. No code can fully meet these conditions" (1981: 26). A "purely deductive method in which decisions are explained merely by citing some code provision may seem to be simple, but it disguises the real choices that are inevitably involved" (Dawson 1961: 26). "Although the legislature tries to provide a clear, systematic legislative response for every problem that may arise, legislative practice falls far short of that objective. As a result, judges have a lot of interpreting to do. They frequently find themselves confronted by problems in which the only applicable legislation is so general as to be useless, is unclear or contradictory in application, or is obviously the product of a legislature that did not foresee the problem now facing the judge" (Merryman 1985: 82-83). In this respect, civil law systems are similar to those of the United States.

Differences between common law and civil law, Martin Shapiro argues, are often overdrawn. He observes that while the Continental judge "purports to be drawing a series of definitions, doctrines, and conclusions from the code by logical exegesis, in reality he is acknowledging the body of legal doctrines built up around the bare words of the code by previous cases" (1981: 135). Thus, while the civil law judge may avoid citing previous cases, other judges and lawyers are able to discern which prior cases are being followed, and some decisions will contain references to prior cases. While the importance of *stare decisis* is not given official recognition in civil law countries, there are hundreds of volumes of published decisions, and Continental lawyers frequently cite them when presenting their arguments in court.

However, civil courts do not defer to the authority of precedent established by a single case. If precedent is to command a particular outcome, it must be consistent with contemporary standards, not contradict legislation, and entail a continuous line of decisions that create a form of judicial custom or customary law (Baudouin 1974). Decisions of high courts are "not treated as exemplars of how a life situation had been resolved in the past so that the case *sub judice* [before the court] could be matched with these exemplars of earlier decision making" (Damâska 1986: 33). Unlike the common law judge who has been trained to find law in cases, the civil

DANGER OF LEGISLATIVE SUPREMACY

After the Second World War, Nazi judges claimed that they "were merely following the laws [of Hitler's Germany] and that, after all, this was how they had been trained by their democratic professors during the Weimar Republic" (Müller 1991: 220). They enforced laws which created a definition of who was a Jew so they could be deprived of their property and eventually their lives. French lawyers under German occupation performed similar roles; they even wrote briefs to determine if particular individuals could under Nazi legislation be defined as a Jew—and thus imprisoned (Weisberg 1997).

law judge is trained to look first at legislation in order to find answers to issues before the court. "Only if he cannot find a clear-cut answer in the code itself will he then try to deduce one from the broad general principles underlying the basic code rules. Cases will be used only to reinforce his arguments or as illustrations of what other judges have done in analogous situations. In other words, precedent [better expressed as legal custom] may enter only at the end of the second phase of his intellectual process" (Baudouin 1974: 15).

Many civil law countries, however, have adopted constitutions that limit the power of the legislative branch to amend laws by ordinary legislative action and, accordingly, impose some form of judicial review by which a court can declare a statute void because it conflicts with a constitutional provision (Merryman 1985; Volcansek 1996). France has a Constitutional Council—part of the legislative branch—"which reviews legislation before promulgation for adherence to legal and constitutional requirements" (Provine 1996: 179). Judicial review in Continental Europe, notes Mary Volcansek (1996), is a reaction to the Fascist/Nazi experience that gave unbridled power to the legislative branch. England, devoid of a constitution, has parliamentary supremacy—courts lack the power to undo legislative enactments (Coffin 1994; Volcansek 1996), although the House of Lords can exercise some restraint over parliamentary actions.

A great deal of the difference between common law and civil law systems can be explained by the manner in which courts are organized and judges selected.

COURTS AND JUDGES IN THE UNITED STATES AND CIVIL LAW COUNTRIES

In the United States, judges are typically attorneys who have been active in politics.[13] In civil law countries, there is a long history dating back to the seventeenth century of judicial officers being career bureaucrats (Damâska 1986). In France, the judiciary is, in effect, a part of the civil service, whose members enjoy life tenure (Abraham 1998). Continental judges opt for a judicial career early in life, receive specialized education and training for the position, and are appointed by the state after passing the necessary examinations (Zweigert and Kötz 1987). "Students decide to become

---

[13]For a comparison between lawyers in common law and civil law systems, see Abel and Lewis (1988).

ENGLISH JUDGES

In England, judges are appointed and promoted by the Lord Chancellor, an appointee of the prime minister, from the ranks of barristers (attorneys who handle cases in the higher courts) who have been designated "Queen's Counsel." This is an elite group representing about 10 percent of the United Kingdom's fewer than 6,000 barristers, and sometimes solicitors (lawyers who handle "paperwork," such as wills and contracts, as well as cases in the lower courts), in a process that is rather secretive (Darnton 1993). Since 1701, in the aftermath of the English Revolution (1688–1689), judges have enjoyed life tenure (Coffin 1994).

judges at the end of their professional training, and, if their grades are high enough, immediately enter into a largely anonymous civil service in which promotion is dependent upon a mixture of seniority and professional skill in interpreting the relevant codes" (Murphy and Pritchett 1986: 11). In France, for example, upon the completion of law school, aspiring judges are required to take a competitive examination to qualify to attend a special school, *Ecolé Nationale de la Magistrature*, for at least 28 months, during which they receive a government salary (Abraham 1998). While judges in the United States are typically drawn from the ranks of practicing attorneys, in a civil law country the judge is a specialist who has not previously practiced law. The opinions they render are unsigned and there is typically an absence of dissent even in appellate cases. In fact, most continental systems do not permit the publication of dissenting opinions (Damâska 1986). Civil law judges are usually independent and cannot be removed for any reason other than "cause" (personal impropriety).

In the United States, judges sit in either trial courts or appellate courts. The trial court is a fact-finding body that has jurisdiction in criminal and noncriminal matters. The fact-finding responsibilities of a trial court may be carried out by a jury or by a single judge in what is known as a bench trial. The trial court has primary responsibility for the enforcement of norms; its decisions respond to the single case at issue. Most cases that are brought to trial courts in the United States do not result in a trial. In civil—that is, noncriminal—cases they are usually resolved by a negotiated settlement (discussed in Chapter 12), and in criminal cases the outcome is often the result of plea bargaining (discussed in Chapter 11). Appellate courts do not use juries (they render decisions on issues of law, not fact), and, except in certain specific cases, they hear cases on appeal only after they have been decided by a trial court.[14]

An appellate court does not consider new evidence. The court's decisions are based on the formal record of the trial court (and any lower appellate court that considered the case) that has been officially transmitted by the court clerk, and the pleadings of attorneys. The decisions of an appellate court are typically elaborate documents that outline the issues presented by the litigants and the rationale underlying the court's decision, the *ratio decedendi*. These published decisions are available to other judges and lawyers and can be used to buttress cases litigated in other courts. As Alan Tarr

---

[14]One exception is the *interlocutory appeal*, raised prior to the completion of a trial, alleging errors by the judge that must be corrected if the trial is to proceed in a just and proper manner.

(1999: 6) notes, however, while they have generally adhered to precedent, "American judges have never viewed precedent as binding to the same extent as did their English counterparts. They have shown greater willingness to overrule earlier decisions and to alter the common law in response to changing circumstances."

In the United States, appellate courts render policy decisions, something very rare in trial courts. There are trial courts and appellate courts on the state and federal levels, the U.S. Supreme Court being the preeminent appellate court. (State and federal courts are the subject of Chapter 6.)

Continental courts do not use juries in civil cases. They are also rare in England, where less than 1 percent of noncriminal trials use juries (Kritzer 1996; Lloyd-Bostock and Thomas 1999). But juries have become widely used in criminal proceedings, a custom borrowed from England where criminals retain the right to opt for a jury trial in a superior–Crown–court (Damâska 1986; Lloyd-Bostock and Thomas 1999). In France, as in England, jury trials are reserved for serious crimes and the jury of nine citizens sits with one or more judges; verdicts are determined by majority vote (Abraham 1998). In general, plea bargaining is absent—a trial cannot be averted by a defendant's admitting guilt.[15] And the concept of equity is absent from civil law systems. While civil law judges may be empowered by statute to render equitable decisions in certain narrowly defined situations, they do not enjoy the power of injunctive relief (Merryman 1985).

In continental Europe, there is no clear distinction between trial courts and appellate courts, and policy issues are typically outside the purview of both. A single judge using simplified procedures has jurisdiction over minor cases, while a second level of courts hears serious cases and appeals from the lower courts. Judges in these courts sit in panels of three, and in some countries their decisions may be appealed to courts at a third level, whose judges sit in panels of three to seven. These higher courts may also conduct trials in special circumstances, or when the matter is particularly serious. At the highest level is a single supreme court, whose judges sit in panels of seven or more. The European appellate process allows for consideration of questions of fact and law; new evidence can be introduced, and often the appellate tribunal will hold a new trial (*trial de novo*) (Shapiro 1981). France and Italy also have a unique judicial tribunal, the *Cour de cassation*.

Established by Revolutionary legislation, the mission of the *Tribunal de cassation* is to ensure that courts do not deviate from the text of laws and thereby encroach on the legislative branch (a major political issue in the United States); it does not have the power of judicial review (discussed in Chapter 8). Napoleon renamed it the *Cour de cassation* and, with 6 specialized chambers, each with 15 justices, it continues to have the power to *casser* (quash) a judicial decision and remit the matter for rehearing to another court of the same level (Zweigert and Kötz 1987). While the *Cour de cassation* constitutes the French supreme court and frequently provides reasons for its decisions, they are persuasive at best and not binding on the lower court (Merryman 1985). The court has no original jurisdiction and does not try cases. As noted earlier, however, a number of civil law countries have adopted rigid constitutions and some form of judicial review with special courts authorized to deal with the constitutionality of statutes (Coffin 1994; Abraham 1998).

---

[15]This has been changing in Italy and Germany, where plea bargaining has also appeared (Goldstein 1996).

Civil law and common/case law systems differ in their approach to trials: civil law utilizes an inquisitorial system, common/case law an adversarial one.

INQUISITORIAL AND ADVERSARIAL SYSTEMS

The term inquisitorial (or inquisitional) carries negative connotations about the papal ecclesiastical courts, established in 1233, in which the judge was also the prosecutor, and the notorious courts of the Spanish Inquisition, established in 1478, which resorted to torture in their investigation of Jews whose conversion was not considered sincere and, later, extended to Muslims and any Spaniard suspected of heresy. However, the inquisitorial system today is a judicial procedure in which judges are at the center of the fact-gathering process. Thus, supporters of this system prefer the term *investigative* (and pejoratively refer to the adversarial system as *accusatorial* (Glenn 2000).

This system is used in civil law countries on the European continent and throughout Latin America. The parties must provide all relevant evidence to the court, and the judges, not the attorneys for the plaintiff and defendant, call and actively examine witnesses, although the attorneys may suggest questions to the judges. An attorney who wishes to ask a question directly must submit a brief in the form of "articles of proof," describing the matter(s) to be subject to questioning; the articles go to the court and opposing counsel. The court acts as an investigative body, somewhat akin to a legislative investigating committee in the United States. In countries using this system, there is a great deal of faith in the fairness and competence of the judges, who (as noted earlier) are not political appointees.

Continental legal systems are staffed by professional bureaucrats who typically employ lower ranking judges (such as investigating magistrates) to gather and prepare evidence in written form and present it to judges of higher rank. Written additions to the file continue as the case proceeds. "The parties have many opportunities to enter new evidence and argument and to respond to written pleadings filed by the other side" (Shapiro 1981: 149). Finally, the entire process ends with what appears to be a "trial"; actually, it is simply the time when the court finally decides the case that has been developed by the opposing attorneys and lower judges during a series of preliminary proceedings. "In the civil law system, no distinction is made between pretrial and trial" (Hazard and Taruffo 1993: 125). "There is a brief preliminary stage, in which the pleadings are submitted and a hearing judge (usually called the instructing judge) appointed; an evidence-taking stage in which the hearing judge takes evidence and prepares a written summary; and a decision-making stage, in which the judges who will decide the case consider the record transmitted to them by the hearing judge, receive counsel's briefs, hear their arguments, and render decisions" (Merryman 1985: 111–112).

"The Continental trial is, then, actually not the doctrinally proclaimed event of paramount importance that generates all material for disposition of the criminal case quite independently from prior (piecemeal) proceedings" (Damâska 1986: 53). Instead, information derived at preliminary hearings is checked independently by judges from material assembled over time and preserved in the written record. Information presented by attorneys is suspect, and thus continental lawyers rarely engage in independent investigative activities and expert witnesses are seldom called

CRIMINAL CASES IN FRANCE

"In Anglo-American systems, the crucial event is a trial, and the appropriate metaphor is combat, with the defense taking primary responsibility for articulating the interests of the accused. The civil-law alternative that France represents envisions a more cooperative relationship between participants, with careful investigation at the heart of the criminal process. Plea-bargaining is not part of the process because of the expectation that trial will occur whether or not the defendant confesses" (Provine 1996: 213). In France, a criminal trial is presided over by a three-judge panel whose members also form part of the jury panel: nine laypersons and the three judges. Verdicts require a majority of eight and ballots are secret.

by private parties; to be credible they must be called by the court and are treated as judicial assistants. In many civil law countries even plaintiffs and defendants are barred from testifying "on the premise that their interest in the outcome will bias their testimony" (Hazard and Taruffo 1993: 83). Thus, judges in inquisitorial systems perform many of the functions that would be performed by attorneys in adversarial systems. In France, for example, after a preliminary investigation by an investigating magistrate, judges "actively, often vehemently and acidly, participate in the courtroom questioning of witnesses as well as of the accused—who incidentally cannot invoke the Anglo-Saxon privilege of refusing to take the stand on grounds of possible self-incrimination" (Abraham 1998: 107).[16] In France, within the *Police Nationale* is a criminal investigation division (*police judicaire*) whose officers work under the supervision of the court system (Provine 1996). In Italy, prosecutors and judges are magistrates, a profession for which they qualify through a national competition. In the course of their career they may easily pass from the role of prosecutor to that of judge, and vice versa (Orlando 2000).

In contrast to inquisitorial systems, there is the laissez-faire role of the judge in adversarial systems;[17] each side is expected to pursue self-interest to the fullest, a legal correlate to free enterprise economics. In the adversarial system used in Anglo-Saxon countries,[18] each side is represented by an attorney, its advocate; the judge should be neutral, authorized to play the role of a referee who enforces the rules of "combat." In trial courts, the attorneys, not the judges, control the flow of information to the court, and a jury of citizenry determines issues of fact: guilty or not guilty, or blame in noncriminal cases. In appellate courts, however, justices typically

---

[16]While the civil law judge has authority to independently investigate facts, "in most countries this authority is conservatively exercised" (Hazard and Taruffo 1993: 86).

[17]There are differences between the roles of judges in the United States and England. While both are presumed neutral, in England the judge provides a " 'summing up' which can include, in addition to a summary of the evidence and legal instructions, comments on the relevance of pieces of evidence and on the credibility of witnesses" (Kritzer 1996: 106).

[18]The United States, however, is unique with respect to the degree to which the adversarial method is encouraged: "The American legal profession long has stressed the ethic of zealous advocacy, in contrast to the legal professions of England and Western European nations" (Kagan 1994: 37).

question attorneys directly in a process that resembles an inquisitorial system. In the adversarial system, inequalities in ability between parties often loom larger than in systems that rely primarily on judges: a party assisted by skillful counsel, or capable of expending the costs of pretrial discovery (discussed in Chapter 12) has a significant advantage over a weaker opponent (Damâska 1986). Contingency fees and small claims courts (both discussed in Chapter 12) are a partial response to this problem. In continental systems, however, there is a clear distinction made between judicial interrogation in criminal cases and that exercised in civil cases; probing in criminal matters can be vigorous, while judicial interrogation in civil cases can be anemic, and therefore, in practice, dependent on the adversarial skills of competing attorneys. In civil law countries, noncriminal cases are decided without the use of juries.

The absence of a jury in noncriminal cases accounts for much of the difference between civil and common law procedure. Since a jury cannot be kept together indefinitely, the American trial is more concentrated—and dramatic—than in civil law systems where a case is handled by judges over a series of hearings. Furthermore, since a legally unsophisticated jury can deal with factual issues only if they are presented in a focused manner, there is extensive pretrial activity (pleadings and discovery, discussed in Chapter 12) to sharpen contested issues, something far less pressing in civil law systems. And the distinction between issues of fact, for which the jury is responsible, and issues of law, for which the judge is responsible, is less relevant when only judges hear the case.

While common law has been dominant in the United States, civil law has left its imprint. As Patrick Glenn (2000: 232) notes, the particular genius of American law "has been its constructive combination of both civil and common law." This is clearly seen in the adoption of codes of procedure (Coffin 1994).

CODES OF PROCEDURE[19]

The British approach to common law was unyielding—"the law is the law"—and generally devoid of concern for American notions of "justice." The American colonists, and the United States after the Revolution, inherited this English system but found the procedural requirements far too rigid for their purposes. There was also an absence of uniform rules for the commencement of a particular action in law or equity. The language of the pleadings (formal written statements constituting the plaintiff's cause of action and the defendant's grounds for defense, or statements of the litigants' positions outlining the dispute) was antiquated and verbose. An action could be lost for failure to adhere to numerous technical details despite the merits of the case. As one lawyer wrote in 1844: "Its principal characteristics are a great many forms of an antique phraseology, according to which every controversy in the ordinary courts must be carried on; forms, the reasons for which perished long ago, and which are now become inadequate, uncouth, and distasteful" (Field 1965: 34). Procedural law was needed, that is, codes of civil and criminal procedure that could

---

[19]"Procedure implies structures and rules that endure beyond the controversies of the moment, that permit men and women to make reliable plans, that keep arbitrary discretion at bay" (Glendon 1994: 247).

simplify and standardize the commencement and resolution of legal actions (much as the development of *Robert's Rules of Order* helped bring procedural order to private organizations). A code of procedure could explain how to apply the substantive law to particular cases. While the substantive law defines certain behavior as criminal and provides for the recovery of damages in the event of a breach of contract or reckless behavior, questions remain concerning how a complaint is to be filed, what information can be received by the judge or jury, how is that information to be presented, and what are the standards of proof ("beyond a reasonable doubt," "preponderance of the evidence"?). The establishment of such procedural law is largely the result of the efforts of David Field.

David Dudley Field (1805–1894) was the son of a noted Massachusetts family; his brother Cyrus J. Field was responsible for the laying of the first transatlantic cable; brother Stephen J. Field became an influential justice of the United States Supreme Court, serving for more than 30 years; and another brother served as president of the Massachusetts senate. "Field entered the practice of law in New York City in 1828 and soon became known for his expertise in 'pleadings,' the stage of a lawsuit when the procedural complications were at their worst" (Gordon 1991: 18). Despite the handsome living he made as a result of common law complexity, Field soon became its opponent.

Field advocated codification. He believed law was a science whose elements could be categorized and classified according to central principles which could then be taught more systematically to law students and be more readily available in convenient form to legal practitioners (Hyman and Wiecek 1982). He campaigned vigorously for a uniform code of procedure for both civil and criminal matters and, later in his life, for a code of international law (Miller 1962). Field advocated legislative enactments that would simplify both the substance and the language of pleadings while abolishing distinctions between law and equity. His efforts, however, were opposed by those attached to the common law by education and training, and who favored the slow organic growth of common law as opposed to the swift legislative remedy that codes represented. Field's conservative opponents argued that substantive changes in legal development should come from the judicial branch of government and not from the legislature, which was prone to follow the whims of an electorate that might be bent on radical social and economic reformulations (Feldstein and Presser 1984). Thus, according to Rufus Choate, a vigorous opponent of codification, writing in 1845, "It is one of the distemperatures to which an unreasoning liberty may grow, no doubt, to regard law as no more nor less than just the will—the actual present will—of the actual majority of the nation" (1962: 264). There were also attorneys who saw codification as a simplification that would be harmful to their economic interests, and they proved a formidable lobby (Herget 1990).

In 1846, Field was able to have a requirement for codification made part of the new state constitution, and his code of civil procedure was subsequently enacted in New York in 1848. The "Field Code" served as a prototype for other states in codifying their rules of civil, and later criminal, practice. Among other changes, the Field Code removed distinctions between actions at law and suits in equity. Even Great Britain used his code to provide a basis for reforming the common law (Gordon 1991). The codification movement died down about the time of the Civil War (Gilmore 1977). During the 1890s, however, the American Bar

Association set up an affiliate, the National Conference of Commissioners on Uniform State Laws, that worked to codify various aspects of commercial law. These efforts resulted in the Negotiable Instruments Law (NIL) which was promulgated in 1896 and eventually enacted in all American jurisdictions. The NIL and other commercial codes drafted by the conference were eventually replaced by the Uniform Commercial Code, which is now in force in all jurisdictions except Louisiana, which has adopted part of it. (The Louisiana Civil Code, enacted in 1808, is based on the Napoleonic Code.) Its major architect was the legal scholar Karl Llewellyn (1893–1962). Morton Horowitz points out that codification resulted in the merger of law and equity: "It marks the final and complete emasculation of Equity as an independent source of legal standards" (1977: 265). And it was the ultimate rationalization of civil and criminal procedure, a move away from "natural justice" to formalism.

The National Conference is now a permanent organization whose membership consists of lawyers, law professors, and judges from the 50 states, with each state's delegation being selected by the governor. The conference meets annually in conjunction with the annual meeting of the American Bar Association, while day-to-day activities are conducted by a variety of standing and ad hoc committees. It should be noted that states usually adopt uniform law packages in modified form, changing or deleting some parts and, in many cases, adding new sections. "In short, by the time uniform laws have been adopted by the various states, they are no longer, strictly speaking, 'uniform'" (Elias 1989: 100).

In 1934, Congress authorized the Supreme Court to write general rules for the federal courts, and pursuant to this legislation, in 1938, the Court promulgated the *Federal Rules of Civil Procedure*, which were heralded for their uniformity and simplicity. However, these rules are general and permissive, failing to cover many topics on which federal courts must have a rule. Because of these shortcomings, the *Federal Rules* have been supplemented or expanded by about 5,000 local rules, undermining their uniformity and *raison d'être* (Coquillette, Squiers, and Subrin 1989). Nevertheless, most states' procedural rules are modeled on the federal code (Hazard and Taruffo 1993).

While the United States legal tradition includes codes, they have a meaning different from those of civil law countries: They make no pretense of completeness and a code provision will be interpreted in such as way as to avoid conflict with a common law precedent. In the United States, codes of procedure are the rules for enforcing substantive law. They prescribe the means of enforcing rights or providing redress of wrongs, the manner of pleading and practice, evidence, appeal, execution of judgments, representation of counsel, costs, transfer of property (conveyance), court costs, and related matters.

In sum, our system of justice has two basic types of law, substantive and procedural, and each is divided into criminal and civil:

Substantive criminal law defines the elements that constitute a crime, e.g., robbery, the unlawful taking of the property of another through the use or threat of force, and the penalties that attach for its commission.

Procedural criminal law controls the manner in which the substantive criminal law is invoked (e.g., rules of evidence and due process); thus, in order for a criminal conviction to be lawful, it must follow the rules set out in the procedural law.

Substantive civil law consists of the principles that determine "the rights we are said to have and the duties we are told we must accept" (Rembar 1980: 77), such as exercising care when we operate a motor vehicle. In a typical civil action, the law of torts determines who is liable for damages.

Procedural civil law is "the set of instructions prescribing how we redress a violated right, how our neglected duties are imposed" (Rembar 1980: 77), such as how to initiate a tort (suit for damages) action.

STATUTORY LAW

Statutory law is the province of legislative bodies that enact statutes—the Congress of the United States, state legislatures, county boards, and municipal councils. As in civil law countries, except when constitutional questions are at issue, statutes are superior to judicial decisions, but statutes must also be interpreted by judges at the point of application.

In general, one or more legislators introduce (sponsor) a bill into the house of which they are members. Serious bills (as opposed to those introduced solely to score points with certain constituents and that have no hope of passage) are usually introduced into both houses by a legislator in each body and referred to the appropriate committee (or committees) for consideration. Bills reported out by committee are referred to the entire house for consideration. Legislation that passes both houses (in bicameral legislative bodies) is sent to the chief executive—president, governor, county board chairman, or mayor—for his or her signature or veto. The signing of

*F*EDERAL *L*EGISLATION

When a member of Congress, senator or representative, introduces a bill, with few exceptions it is referred to the appropriate standing House or Senate committees. The bill may be referred to a subcommittee or considered by the committee as a whole. The failure to act on a bill effectively kills the legislation. If after hearings the committee fails to act, the legislation is dead. If the committee approves of the bill, it is sent to the House or Senate with a written report describing the intent and scope of the legislation, its impact on existing law and programs, the position of the executive branch, and the views of dissenting members of the committee. It is then placed on the calendar for floor action.

The legislation is debated on the House or Senate floor and if approved, with or without amendments, is sent to the other chamber, where it usually follows the same route as a newly introduced bill. If only minor changes are made, the bill is then sent to the president. If there have been significant changes, a House–Senate conference committee is formed to reconcile the differences. A failure to agree on changes kills the bill; otherwise, it is sent back to both houses for a vote, and then sent to the president. If the president signs the bill, or fails to take action within 10 days while the Congress is in session, it becomes law. The president may also veto a bill or, if the Congress is not in session, take no action ("pocket veto") and the legislation dies. A veto can be overridden by a two-thirds vote of the members of the Senate and House who are present in sufficient numbers for a quorum.

a legislative enactment, or the overriding of a veto (usually requiring a two-thirds vote), makes the bill a law. Legislative enactments are assembled and ordered in a systematic manner by a state code commission. They are then published.

All federal and state statutes and regulations (rules promulgated by administrative agencies pursuant to statutory authority) and all county and municipal ordinances are published in full. Federal statutes, the enactments of Congress, appear in several forms, the most convenient being the compilation authorized by Congress in 1925 and referred to as the *United States Code* (U.S.C.). There is also the *United States Code Annotated* (U.S.C.A.), which includes commentary on judicial decisions (case law) relating to the statutes contained in the code. State statutes are first published in volumes called session laws because they are prepared at the end of each legislative session. They are later printed in volumes arranged by subject matter and have different names in different states: statutes/laws/codes at large, compiled, consolidated, revised.

Statutory law is divided between criminal and civil/noncriminal enactments. The criminal or penal law (or code) defines those behaviors that are criminal and prescribes punishment, while civil law is concerned with the resolution of noncriminal disputes and the carrying out of government functions (e.g., the budget). The government has an important and direct interest in dealing with crime, so all criminal proceedings have the government (*United States* v. *Smith* or the *State of California* v. *Jones*) as the plaintiff, while litigation in civil disputes is typically brought by individuals or corporations (*Smith* v. *Jones*; "private law"), although the government may be a defendant or a plaintiff in a civil action ("public law"). Thus, while the government has a direct interest in whether or not you burglarize your neighbor's home, "it has only an indirect interest in whether you keep a promised contractual agreement with that neighbor. Private law, therefore, encompasses the major categories of substantive legal rules, such as contracts, real property, and torts" (Hall 1989: 7).

ƒORFEITURE

The Comprehensive Criminal Forfeiture Act "creates a rebuttable presumption that any property of a person convicted of a drug felony is subject to forfeiture if the government establishes by a preponderance of the evidence that the defendant acquired the property during the period of violation, or within a reasonably short period thereafter, *and* there was no likely source for the property other than the violation" (President's Commission on Organized Crime 1986: 274). To obtain a seizure order, the government must provide sworn testimony in an affidavit spelling out the property to be seized and why there is reason to believe that it is being used to commit crimes or was acquired with money from criminal activity. The filing of criminal charges against the owner is not required and the owner of the property is not informed of the action until his or her property is seized by U.S. marshals pursuant to the court order. The owner of the property has a right to contest the seizure only after it has occurred; he or she must prove that the money or property was earned through legal enterprise (Abadinsky 2000).

*F*EDERAL *F*ELONIES AND *M*ISDEMEANORS

Class A felony	Death or life imprisonment
Class B felony	25 years or more
Class C felony	Less than 25 years but more than 10 years
Class D felony	Less than 10 years but more than 5 years
Class E felony	Less than 5 years but more than 1 year
Class A misdemeanor	1 year or less but more than 1 month
Class B misdemeanor	6 months or less but more than 30 days
Class C misdemeanor	30 days or less but more than 5 days

In some instances, a criminal violation can result in damages and a civil action,[20] while the government can bring a civil forfeiture action against certain defendants in order to seize property that has been secured through the proceeds of or used in furtherance of criminal behavior. And the civil law is frequently used against criminal justice agencies and personnel who (allegedly) act beyond their authority or maintain jails and prisons in a manner that violates constitutional provisions, such as the Eighth Amendment's prohibition of cruel and unusual punishment.

The criminal law grades crimes in descending order according to their seriousness. For example, the *Illinois Criminal Law and Procedure* classifies all crimes in eight categories in order of seriousness: felonies as class X, 1, 2, 3, 4, and misdemeanors as class A, B, C. The *New York Penal Law* classifies crimes into seven categories according to seriousness: felonies as class A, B, C, D, E, and misdemeanors as class A and B. Both states also have numerous lesser offenses: violations or infractions, such as local (municipal or county) ordinances prohibiting jay walking or littering, and there are traffic-related violations.

JUDICIAL INTERPRETATION OF STATUTES[21]

While legislative bodies enact statutes, the system is dependent upon the judicial branch to interpret these laws in action. Interestingly, the Constitution does not have much to say about statutory interpretation, and what it does say is minimal and abstract. The Constitution does not provide explicit instructions to judges about the method(s) to use when interpreting statutes (Vermeule 2000). Therein lies a problem: "Words have no inherent significance; they are supplied with meaning by those who use them, and the problem before the judge is to determine meaning when it is not clear what the legislator meant when he used the words" (Merryman 1985: 44). In 2001, for example, the Supreme Court (*Toyota Motor Manufacturing*

---

[20]A civil action for behavior that violates the criminal law is permissible even in the absence of a conviction, such as in the case of O.J. Simpson.

[21]For a detailed discussion of the issues surrounding statutory interpretation, see Eskridge, Frickey, and Garrett (2000).

v. *Williams*) agreed to determine the meaning of "disability" in an effort to provide guidance for interpreting an 11-year-old statute. The Americans with Disabilities Act uses phrases such as "substantially limits" and "major life activities" that courts have struggled to understand and apply (Greenhouse 2001d). Legislation sometimes fails to define key terms. For example, there is no statutory definition of "restraint of trade" or "monopolization," although both are prohibited by federal statute. These terms have been given meaning through judicial interpretation—case law (Berman and Greiner 1980). "At the time of its enactment, a statute usually resolves the most pressing legal questions that gave rise to it, and resolves them in ways that are just as clear to the addresses as the authors of the statute. For such issues there is no need for 'interpretation'; the statute is clear. Interpretation is required for those issues that were either not anticipated or politically sidestepped" (Eskridge 1994: 9). "It is the function of the legislative organ to make laws," states Roscoe Pound, "but from the nature of the case it cannot make laws so complete and all embracing that the judicial organ will not be obliged to exercise a certain lawmaking function also" (1975: 51). In other words, the concept of a separation of powers is in reality tenuous.

Legislative enactments are the result of political compromise, and controversial laws may be deliberately ambiguous to protect legislators voting for them (Levi 1955). Legislators tend to avoid controversial issues since they generate negative publicity and may antagonize the media and turn off campaign contributions (Neely 1981). Legislators "are the world's only entrepreneurs devoted to shunning risk" (Alter 1989: 28). Lobbyists exert an influence that is usually hidden from constituents, and legislators often vote for bills about which they know little or nothing following the party leadership, so bills are often the result of political compromise, not rational lawmaking (Rembar 1980). Complex statutes are the result of an "intricate game of give-and-take in which legislators, nudged constantly at the elbow by constituents, play power poker with each other" (Friedman 1984: 106). At the federal level, a single issue may require compromise among dozens of committees that have authority over some part of any legislation; controlled substances (drugs), for example, fall under the aegis of no fewer than 80 congressional panels (Alter 1989).

Much, if not most, of a legislator's energy is expended on getting elected and reelected. As a result of these realities, legislation is often ambiguous, confused, contradictory, or unconstitutional. Legislators, with an eye toward satisfying constituents and winning reelection, typically disregard issues of constitutionality (Parsons 1997). Congress has devised its own language to obscure and confound, rather than anger, constituents; for example, budget-talk: "baseline," "outyears," "off-budget," "outlays," and "budget authority" (Alter 1989). "Some statutes are little else but back-room deals which distribute public benefits to groups that legislators want to help. This

Business as Usual

Late in the evening and early morning in 2002, the New York State legislature passed a health care bill—61 densely-worded pages still hot from the copying machine—that few legislators had any opportunity to read (Pérez-Peña 2002).

suggests that identifying the actual or even conventional purpose of a statute is just as difficult as identifying the actual or conventional intent of the legislature, perhaps even more so, since legislators may have incentives to obscure the real purposes of the statute" (Eskridge 1994: 27). And legislators engage in a great amount of symbolic politics: "At one extreme, symbolic politics consists of speechmaking and public position-taking in the absence of any real action or intention of taking action; casting the right vote is more important than achieving the right outcome. At the other extreme, symbolic politics consists of whole government programs that are ostensibly designed to achieve one set of objectives but are actually designed to achieve other objectives (in some cases simply the re-election of the politicians who can claim credit for them)" (King 1997: 48). Lobbying, the "pork barrel," and "logrolling," while synonymous with the legislative endeavor, are anathema to the judiciary. The courts are often left with the responsibility of cleaning up the legislative act. When interpreting legislation, the courts promulgate case law.

Case Law and Legal Reasoning

In place of English common law, judicial law-finding in the United States developed into case law guided by precedent. Case law is embodied in judicial decisions, generally those of appellate courts where the justices usually provide a written explanation of how the decision was reached. The principle upon which justices decide a case—the *ratio decedendi*—is based on a rigorous analysis of the facts of the case, rules that are applicable, and cases (precedents) cited by attorneys in an adversarial manner. (The cited cases must be from the United States—the renderings of foreign legal systems, no matter how germane to the issue at hand, are typically excluded from consideration [Posner 1990].)

The appellate decision embodies a principle that will govern this set of facts and others similar enough (Rembar 1980). Thus a court is bound by its own previous decisions and by the previous decisions of all higher courts. The role of the judge is to apply existing rules of law to the facts of each case in a deductive method known as *stare decisis*. Thus, *stare decisis* operates in two dimensions (Carter 1984): vertical and horizontal. The *vertical* dimension requires judges to honor the rulings of the highest court in any jurisdiction and, of course, those of the U.S. Supreme Court. The *horizontal* dimension refers to prior decisions of the same court. (Some decisions that provide neither vertical nor horizontal *stare decisis* can, nevertheless, exercise persuasive authority in courts considering similar cases—such as a state court decision influencing a federal appeals court.)

In order to apply the rule of precedent, the judge must analyze a case and distinguish between holding and *dicta*—sometimes far more easily said than done (Abraham 1998). The holding of a prior case refers to the rule or principle that was absolutely necessary for the resolution of the factual and legal issues actually litigated and decided. Any other remarks or observations in the decision are *obiter dicta*; dicta, at best, may have persuasive authority, particularly if the judge who authored the dictum has a reputation for legal scholarship (Re 1975a). For example, in *Gitlow* v. *New York* (1925), the dictum of Supreme Court Justice Edward T. Sanford (1923–1930) made judicial history by announcing the first application of two aspects of the Bill of Rights, speech and press, to the states; the first 10 amendments to the Constitution were (until *Gitlow*) applicable only to the federal government

(Abraham 1972). But "the distinction between holding and dictum is not hard and fast," as "shown by the inability of courts to agree on an operational definition of these terms" (Posner 1990: 96).

The use of precedent is justified by four elements:

1. *Predictability*. The doctrine of precedent allows for consistency of application and, thus, a degree of certainty—order and uniformity—vital to a rational legal system.
2. *Reliability*. People rely on the fact that courts will follow precedents.
3. *Equality*. Treating similar cases in a similar fashion.
4. *Efficiency*. If justice is not to be interminable, judges must have a source for the timely resolution of cases (Wasserstrom 1961).

Use of precedent also "helps secure legal compliance on the part of the losing parties, for they are more likely to see that decisions are not made against them personally, but apply to a class falling under a rule" (Atiyah and Summers 1987: 116).

The law must harmonize and reconcile two ideals: stability and change. "Stability requires a continuity with the past, and is necessary to permit members of a society to conduct their daily affairs with a reasonable degree of certainty as to the legal consequences of their acts. Change implies a variation or alteration of what is fixed and stable. Without change, however, there is no progress" (Re 1975a: 1). The "doctrine of *stare decisis* assumes that court decisions have been reasonable, that what was reasonable in one century may be reasonable in another—even though in the meantime the most revolutionary social and political changes may have occurred" (Hogue 1966: 9). The important word here is "reasonable."

The system is flexible. If the case at hand is to be governed by a particular precedent, it must be similar enough to the facts of the case that established the principle. "The determination of similarity or difference is the function of each judge" (Levi 1955: 2). The degree of similarity is a matter of judicial interpretation that provides flexibility in the system of case law. Thus, if the case is not essentially similar to an earlier case (usually cited by one of the litigants), or the reasons for that earlier decision are not good reasons, the court is not bound by the precedent. "In their legal arguments, lawyers are expected to advocate that each relevant authoritative precedent be followed, distinguished, or, less commonly, overruled" (Burton 1985: 30).

Ronald Dworkin distinguishes between two legal doctrines of precedent:

1. The *strict doctrine* "obliges judges to follow the earlier decisions of certain other courts (generally those courts above them but sometimes at the same level in the hierarchy of courts in their jurisdiction), even if they believe those decisions to have been wrong."
2. The *relaxed doctrine* "demands only that a judge give some weight to past decisions on the same issue, that he must follow these unless he thinks them sufficiently wrong to outweigh the initial presumption in their favor." (1986: 24–25)

Dworkin points out that "differences of opinion about the character of the strict doctrine and the force of the relaxed doctrine explain why some lawsuits are controversial. Different judges in the same case disagree about whether they are obliged to follow some past decision on exactly the question of law they now face" (1986: 26).

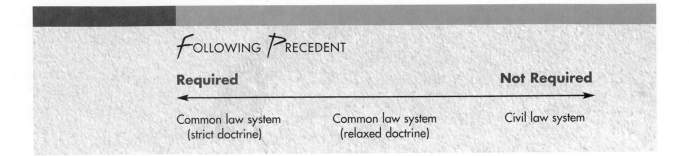

$\mathcal{F}$OLLOWING $\mathcal{P}$RECEDENT

Required ←————————————————————————→ **Not Required**

Common law system (strict doctrine)   Common law system (relaxed doctrine)   Civil law system

The basic pattern of legal reasoning in the system of case law is reasoning from case to case, that is, *reasoning by analogy*. It is a three-step process in which a proposition descriptive of the first case is made into a rule of law and then applied to a next similar situation (Levi 1955: 1):

1. Similarity is seen between cases.

2. The rule of law (precedent) inherent in the first case is announced.

3. The rule of law is made applicable to the second case (as per *stare decisis*).

"A precedent serves not as a rule but as an analogy to the extent that it is at least plausibly distinguishable from the case at hand, but suggestive of a more general principle or policy that seems relevant to that case" (Sunstein 1996: 71). For example, in 1913 the Supreme Court ruled in *Hoke and Economides* v. *United States* that the Mann Act, which prohibits the interstate transportation of women "for the purpose of prostitution, or debauchery or for any other immoral purpose," was constitutionally valid since the Court had already upheld the right of Congress to prohibit lottery tickets, diseased cattle, and obscene materials from interstate commerce (Levi 1955; see also Burton 1985):

■ The Mann Act case is similar to the (*ratio decedendi* in the) lottery ticket, diseased cattle, and obscene materials cases.

■ The precedent established in these cases is that Congress has the power to prohibit lottery tickets, diseased cattle, and obscene materials from interstate commerce.

■ Therefore, the Mann Act is constitutional: Congress also has the power to prevent interstate commerce in women for immoral purposes.

Reasoning by analogy can *uncover* agreement where it already existed (Sunstein 1996). But reasoning by analogy can also be more complicated. For example: Can the plaintiff recover expenses incurred saving the defendant's property when there was no contractual agreement or understanding between them? The court had previously ruled "yes" to that question when life, instead of property, was at stake. Suppose earlier cases had been based on an assumed willingness of the defendant to reimburse the plaintiff if he were asked before the emergency that endangered his life arose. Would this now apply to the question of property (Posner 1990)?

"Case law is neither in itself a fully worked out systematic whole, nor does it form a part of some logically coherent system. Instead, a variety of strands, only partly consistent with one another, exist side by side. We look now to the one, now

Sources of Law in the United States

After the Revolution, the Constitution became the supreme law of the land, and neither statutes nor judicial rulings can conflict with its provisions as construed by the Supreme Court. The rules of English common law were altered by legislation and many states purged the common law of its feudal elements, particularly during the Jacksonian era (1829–1837). While common law continues to provide certain avenues of civil redress, particularly in state courts,[22] the major sources of law governing the United States are the Constitution (constitutional law), legislative enactments (statutory law), and appellate court decisions (case law).

1. U.S. Constitution
2. Federal statutes
3. Federal administrative rules and regulations
4. Treaties
5. Federal court decisions
6. State constitutions
7. State statutes
8. State administrative rules and regulations
9. State court decisions
10. Municipal charters
11. County and municipal ordinances
12. County and municipal administrative rules and regulations
13. Municipal court decisions

to the other, as the particular case may require" (Llewellyn 1989: 45). We look to the published opinions of state and federal appellate courts. State decisions are found in the *National Reporter System*, which is divided into seven regional volumes, such as Atlantic and South Western, and additional volumes for New York and California. Federal appellate decisions are found in a series commissioned by the U.S. Supreme Court, *United States Reports*. The most important case law decisions, those of the U.S. Supreme Court, can be found in the official reporting system, *U.S. Supreme Court Reports* (abbreviated U.S.), or three private systems, *Supreme Court Reporter* (abbreviated S.Ct.), *Supreme Court Reports, Lawyer's Edition* (abbreviated L.Ed.), and more recently, *United States Law Week* (abbreviated LW). The use of computerized information systems has greatly facilitated the use of case law. CD ROM computer libraries which have put decades of legal decisions on a small number of compact disks and on line data bases, such as LEXIS and WESTLAW, increase access to a vast range of legal material, including some previously unpublished (Galanter and Palay 1991).[23]

---

[22]For example, claims of public services being applied in conflict with the common law duty to serve in an equal and adequate manner; see Haar 1986; Haar and Fessler 1986).

[23]See Brenner (1992) for a discussion of the result which she refers to as precedent inflation. Federal appeals judge Richard Posner (1990) notes that judges often use case citations to make an opinion look more solid than it really is.

The involvement of judges in determining what the law is in particular cases is (sometimes pejoratively) referred to as judge-made law. But Dworkin comments that judges "generally offer these 'new' statements of law as improved reports of what the law, properly understood, already is" (1986: 6). At issue is whether judges "invent" or simply "discover" law, and this could easily be settled, he argues, "if everyone agreed about what the law is, if there were no theoretical disagreement about the grounds of law." But lawyers and judges disagree, and "the debate about whether judges make or find law is part of that disagreement." (We will return to this issue in Chapter 8 in a discussion of policy-making by the judicial branch.)

ADMINISTRATIVE AND REGULATORY LAW

During the Progressive era of the late nineteenth century, complaints of economic exploitation by railroads and other monopolies led to the passage of state regulatory legislation. These efforts were declared unconstitutional by the Supreme Court—a violation of the exclusive federal jurisdiction to regulate interstate commerce. In response, in 1887 Congress created independent regulatory agencies such as the Interstate Commerce Commission. The number of such agencies multiplied during the era of the New Deal. Another expansion occurred during the years 1960 to 1980 with the creation of the Environmental Protection Agency (EPA), Occupational Health and Safety Administration (OSHA), and the Consumer Product Safety Commission (Pierce, Shapiro, and Verkuil 1999).

Statutory law is rarely self-implementing, and federal or state legislators may create an administrative agency to carry out a particular statutory function, for example, at the federal level to administer Social Security (Social Security Administration), to regulate labor management relations (National Labor Relations Board), to prohibit unfair methods of competition (Federal Trade Commission), or at the state level to regulate such professions as medicine and architecture and trades such as barbering and plumbing. There are liquor boards and zoning boards, and boards of examiners for security personnel and real estate brokers. Some agencies are part of the executive branch, for example, the Internal Revenue Service, and there are also numerous independent administrative agencies—commissions, examiners, and boards—such as the Federal Reserve Board. "Often the statutes that create them, even while placing them in political departments, contain special measures safeguarding against political influence; decisions of the Internal Revenue Service respecting the selection of individual taxpayers for investigation are shielded from political direction, for example" (Strauss 1989: 89). The independent agencies are typically bipartisan, with members who serve staggered terms that overlap (e.g., six years) that of the appointing authority, a governor or the president. Administrative agencies make regulatory law, and the bureaucrats enforcing these laws are governed by administrative law. For example, Federal Communication Commission (FCC) rules limit the number of commercial broadcasting stations a company may own, and IRS rules determine which groups need and need not pay taxes. "The IRS creates tax law, and the FCC makes communications law" (Carter 1983: 37).

While the executive branch contains a wide array of departments and administrative personnel capable of regulatory functions, Congress was concerned that "partisan presidential politics and the tremendous presidential powers to exploit the

On Administrative Due Process

"The vast expansion of this field of administrative regulation in response to the pressure of social needs is made possible under our system of adherence to the basic principles that the legislature shall appropriately determine the standards of administrative action and that in administrative proceedings of a quasi-judicial character the liberty and property of the citizen shall be protected by the rudimentary requirements of fair play." Chief Justice Charles Evans Hughes, *Morgan v. United States* (1938).

office could seep into regulation of sensitive areas like transportation and communications. "Besides," note Lief Carter and Christine Harrington (2000: 11), "presidents come and go quite frequently, and with them their cabinet appointees. Coping with technologically complex problems needs continuing expertise and leadership."

But how can legislative authority be delegated to an administrative agency when the Constitution (Article I, Section I) provides that all legislative power is vested in Congress? Indeed, courts have invalidated laws granting too much legislative power to an administrative agency. Nevertheless, the delegation of legislative authority to administrative agencies was gradually accepted by the U.S. Supreme Court as long as the scope of agency discretion was clearly delineated (Pierce, Shapiro, and Verkuil 1999).

Governments in colonial America (discussed in Chapter 3) often combined the executive, legislative, and judicial functions, a practice that came to an end when our Constitution created a delineation of authority. This has become a basic doctrine in American government: "The one who makes or implements a rule ought not be the same as the one who judges its fair application to particular circumstances" (Strauss 1989: 14). Nevertheless, many administrative agencies still enjoy a combination of these powers. For example, the EPA 1 ; 1 "exercises legislative powers when it issues rules and regulations to minimize industrial pollution of the air. These rules and regulations have the force of laws passed by Congress. The EPA exercises executive powers when it monitors and publicizes pollution levels throughout the nation and subsidizes the construction of municipal waste treatment plants. It exercises judicial powers when it determines whether a business firm has violated certain of its antipollution rules and regulations and then imposes penalties for the violation" (Auerbach 1983: 74–75).

Despite the problems inherent in combining legislative, executive, and judicial powers in a single agency, it has often been seen as the only logical and workable arrangement for the efficient regulation of huge, complex, rapidly changing, and often highly technical enterprises (Lorch 1980). Public agencies organized around specialized technocratic concerns, such as the EPA or the Nuclear Regulatory Commission, typically establish policy based on ad hoc, discretionary powers in response to scientific variables. Causal or scientific reasoning, rather than legal reasoning and the search for precedent and *stare decisis*, predominates (Stryker 1989), thereby reducing predictability. Many administrative agencies provide a mechanism for adjudicating disputes arising out of regulatory law, usually in the form of administrative hearings—the equivalent of a trial court. Some agencies, like OSHA, provide courtlike hearings before issuing rules. OSHA conducts such hearings before an administrative judge with provisions for cross-examination (Wilson 1989).

Instead of a trial judge, in the federal system there are about 30 agencies with over 1,100 administrative law judges (called hearing officers until 1978) empowered to take testimony and either render a decision or make a recommendation to the agency's governing board; more than 700 work for the Social Security Administration. Administrative law judges are required to have at least seven years' trial experience and pass an examination on general legal knowledge. They are then placed on a merit selection list from which various agencies select judges; appointments are for life. They adjudicate cases according to procedures set out in the Administrative Procedure Act, which was promulgated by the American Bar Association and adopted by Congress in 1946.

In the federal system:

> Administrative law judges are paid at the level of the senior executive service but—although formally located within the particular agencies they serve—are virtually beyond agency control. Appointments must be made on a competitive basis, from the top few names on a list supplied by civil service authorities. Once made, appointments are permanent (without [a] probationary period). Within the agency structure, administrative law judges must be free of supervision or direction from agency employees responsible for the cases that may come before them; neither salary, nor assignments, nor any disciplinary measure can be controlled from within the agency, but (if adverse) must be the subject of formal proceedings before the Merit System Protection Board. Any conversations administrative law judges may have with agency employees concerning the outcomes of formal proceedings they are hearing must be on the record—that is, there may be no private consultations (Strauss 1989: 95).

The decision of an administrative agency may sometimes be appealed to a specialized tribunal, for example, in tax disputes, to the Tax Court or the Courts of Appeals (discussed in Chapter 6). "Congress gave Courts of Appeals special responsibility to review the actions of federal regulatory agencies and to reconcile their conduct with law" (Howard 1981: 6). Courts of Appeals may hear petitions to review or enforce the orders of such agencies as the National Labor Relations Board or the Securities and Exchange Commission.

Statutes require that federal agency administrative regulations be published in the *Federal Register*, along with notices of agency meetings or hearings in order to provide interested parties with an opportunity to object. They are then published in

Administrative Law Judges

Administrative law judges for the New York State Public Service Commission, an independent regulatory agency, preside at formal evidentiary hearings on utility rates, the choosing of sites for electric generation or transmission facilities, and general commission policy. They analyze the hearing record and prepare recommendations for action by the commission.

the *Code of Federal Regulations* which is organized into 50 separate titles, such as agriculture and energy. State regulations are usually compiled by the agency involved and maintained in loose-leaf form. Copies may be filed with the secretary of state and are also found in law school or central public libraries.

Persons dissatisfied with the decisions of an administrative agency have to exhaust all other remedies, that is, follow agency review procedures, before turning to the courts. "Most statutes setting up administrative agencies provide for or imply the right of courts to review such agency decisions. The Administrative Procedure Act itself provides for review unless Congress firmly and explicitly says otherwise" (Friedman 1984: 118).

Now that we have looked at systems for implementing rational law, in the next chapter we will review the history of law and justice in America.

INTERNET CONNECTIONS

Lord Chancellor's Web site: *courtservice.gov.uk*
Legal sites on the Web: *ih2000.net/ira/legal.htm*
United Kingdom legal Web site: *infolaw.co.uk*
Global legal site: *lcweb2.loc.gov///law/GLINv1/GLIN.html*
'Lectric Law Library: *lectlaw.com/ref.html*

REVIEW QUESTIONS

1. What distinguishes a system of common law from a civil (code) law system?
2. With respect to rules and standards, how does equity differ from common law?
3. How do judges in civil law systems differ from those in the United States?
4. How does the inquisitorial system of adjudication differ from the adversarial system?
5. What distinguishes procedural law from substantive law?
6. Why is it essential that the judicial branch interpret statutory law?
7. What are the problems encountered in the judicial interpretation of statutory law?
8. How does the system of case law utilize the concepts of *stare decisis* and *res judicata*?
9. How does the use of precedent advance predictability, reliability, equality, and efficiency?
10. How does the use of precedent help to secure legal compliance on the part of losing parties?
11. What are the three basic steps in common/case law legal reasoning?
12. Why did some lawyers oppose the use of civil law codes in the United States?

13. In what way do administrative agencies combine the three functions of government (executive, legislative, judicial)?

14. What is an administrative law judge?

15. How does administrative or regulatory law differ from statutory law?

3

A History of Law and Justice In America

Law and legal structures reflect the complexity of a society at any given time in its developmental history. As a society grows larger and the economy expands, a greater division of labor ensues, relationships become more distant, and law and justice become more formal. This relationship between societal complexity and legal formalism has an ancient history that can be found in the Bible (Exodus Ch. 28). When Jethro, the father-in-law of Moses, visited the camp of the Hebrews, he saw "that Moses sat to judge the people; and the people stood about Moses from the morning unto the evening." After their departure from slavery in Egypt, life grew more complex for the Hebrews; the informal system used by Moses to deal with matters of law was no longer adequate. Jethro advised Moses to establish a formal system of courts and judges, to choose able men "to be rulers of thousands, rulers of hundreds, rulers of fifties, and rulers of tens. And let them judge the people at all seasons; and it shall be, that every great matter they shall bring unto thee, but every small matter they shall judge themselves."

As societies become more complex, they tend to substitute law and public officials—judges who can impose a settlement—in place of consensual third-party dispute resolution, mediation, and arbitration (Shapiro 1981). Legal systems of complex societies are characterized by a hierarchy of courts that implement laws guaranteeing reliability and predictability, yet remaining flexible enough to allow for successful application in particular cases, while adjusting to societal change. We will review these concepts.

THE LAW AND COURTS IN COLONIAL AMERICA

The primitive life of early American colonists was dominated by issues of survival. As time passed and life became more secure, the economy expanded and agriculture and commerce thrived. Important issues were not simply those of survival, but of more complex social and economic relationships. As the population increased, so did the complexity of relationships and the possibility of conflict. The shoemaker no longer dealt directly with the farmer, exchanging shoes for milk, meat, and vegetables. Now the farmer sold these items to a merchant, who in turn sold them to a variety of people, including the shoemaker. But what if there were defects or spoiled goods? Who was liable: the original producer? The merchant? Or was the ultimate buyer without recourse? The Puritans of New England could simply consult the Bible for guidance in matters of law and justice. But as Boston became a great seaport and commercial center, the greater complexity of society demanded a rationality greater than that offered by the Puritan Bible.

British colonization in America began in 1607 (during the reign of James I), a time when common law was quite formal and strict—equity and the Court of Chancery were still in a developmental stage. The common law of that period was heavily laced with Latin and French legal jargon developed in the Middle Ages, and unfit for a wilderness society that stressed individualism (Pound 1953). Some of the original colonies were corporations chartered by the Crown (e.g., Massachusetts Bay), and their legislative powers were limited to making bylaws and ordinances. Colonial charters required legislation to conform to the common law, and those deemed contrary could be reversed by an appeal to the Privy Council in England. Royal governors often interfered with the decisions of colonial courts, much as the Crown had done in England when judges ruled against its wishes or interests. Other colonies were royal colonies (e.g., Virginia) in theory controlled directly by the Crown, while still others were proprietary colonies (e.g., Maryland) in which a single owner exercised control (Hall 1989). "There could be little legal development under such a system" (Pound 1953: 134).

While colonial law was subordinate to English law, it was not clear which acts of Parliament and which court decisions were binding on the colonists. While each group of settlers brought with them an English legal heritage, each colony was founded at a different time (Massachusetts was founded 100 years before Georgia), and they differed in geography, immigration, religion, and economic and political development. Within each colony was a commercial center, a seacoast, and a hinterland. "The rugged independence which was born of the frontier brought about the scrapping of important common-law practices incompatible with life in the new agrarian communities" (Morris 1964: 20). Colonists were free of English supervision and tended to disregard the authority of the common law.

While the Crown never intended for distinctive legal cultures to develop in the colonies, dramatically different conditions in England and the colonies resulted in differing needs and thus differing laws (Hoffer 1992). For example, land was scarce in England, where it was a symbol of power and social status; it was bound up in centuries of land law handed down from feudal times. In colonial America, however, there was a shortage of people, not land. Land was important, but there were numerous landowners (Friedman 1973). Bradley Chapin notes that the labor supply influenced the law: "As a matter of policy it must have seemed that no great harm was done if the hangman thinned the horde of vagrant Englishmen.[1] In the colonies, the need for labor urged the use of penalties that might bring redemption" (1983: 9). Consequently, the use of capital punishment was severely restricted in the colonies. "Although the colonial law of crimes against persons remained basically English law," the colonial law of crimes against property was largely indigenous, and it virtually abolished the death penalty for property crimes, replacing it with branding, whipping, terms in the house of correction, and restitution (Chapin 1983). There were, however, several notable and historical exceptions: the banning and hanging of Quakers by Puritans in the Massachusetts Bay Colony and the subsequent witchcraft trials and executions. The Quakers of Pennsylvania eliminated capital punishment for all crimes except murder; however, blacks convicted of burglary, buggery (sodomy), or rape could still be executed (Walker 1980). In New Amsterdam the system of law resembled that of Holland—a civil code; while the Puritans of New England and the Quakers of Pennsylvania sought to establish a society based on the Bible. And there was also a French influence.

"The Dutch and French influence in different colonies gradually disappeared, and other variations between colonies also diminished. By the time of the American Revolution, religious influence had declined noticeably" even in Massachusetts and Pennsylvania (Walker 1980: 12). As colonial conditions stabilized, commerce flourished and economic growth required an increasingly commercial America to turn toward economically advanced countries for guidance in law. The only country that could provide a supply of law without the need for translation was England. "A distinctly American approach to law and justice emerged, based mainly on Anglo-Saxon legal heritage as modified by the colonial experience" (Walker 1980: 12).

Colonial courts assumed a wide range of responsibilities; they served as the legislative, executive, and judicial branches of county government—a reflection of the highly unspecialized nature of government during this time period (Walker 1980). For example, judges of the Superior Court of Massachusetts decided the validity of tax assessments and entertained damage suits against sheriffs, jailers, and customs officials (White 1976); the governor of colonial Maryland and his council sat as a chancery court (Katz 1971); and until the outbreak of the Revolution, the judges of Virginia's General Court were the governor and his council (Hoffer 1992). With significant economic and population growth, court structures moved from the simple to the more complex, from the undifferentiated to the hierarchical. Executive, legislative, and judicial powers that had not heretofore been clearly differentiated (e.g., legislatures heard appeals) became more distinct. English legal models, terms, and customs became more important and more frequently used (Friedman 1973). At the same time, the courts were increasingly seen as tools of the Crown and mistrusted by the common people, while legislatures generally supported popular

---

[1]In practice, however, mitigation was accomplished by the extensive use of pardons and the dismissal of indictments for technical reasons (Kelman 1987). Pardons typically required intercession by a powerful benefactor, gaining for local gentry the obligation and loyalty of the felon and his or her family (Turkel 1996). In England corruption, perjury, and jury-tampering were widespread, mocking "the common law's reputation for fairness" (Bordenhamer 1992: 14).

sentiment against the king (Chroust 1965). Chancery courts were controversial because governors, in their capacity as chancellors, sought political ends rather than justice (Hall 1989).

British equity, which had grown almost as complex as that of the common law, was not easily applied to colonial America. Some colonies established separate courts of equity; some merged equity with courts of common law; and in other colonies, equity powers were the province of the legislature or the governor. Colonial equity procedures were simplified, relief more accessible and swifter, but less predictable than in the English Court of Chancery (Hoffer 1992). "With the eighteenth century, however, we reach the era of more sophisticated adoption of the common law and the emergence of a distinctive colonial equity law" (Katz 1971: 262).

While common law in England was typically used by persons of power—nobility, commercial classes, and wealthy clergy—colonial law was substantially codified law, a response to frontier conditions. A newly settled colony cannot wait until a body of common law evolves before disputes are settled (Friedman 1973). Codes, on the other hand, can be reduced to knowable text in a single book or a short series of volumes. Common law is complex and unwieldy, while codes can be moved from one colony to another and adopted. Until the eighteenth century, some codes were borrowed in toto. The Inns of Court—English legal institutions—had their well established method of study. The introduction of a new book like Blackstone was not considered necessary, "but in the Colonies, where there were no schools of law, the Commentaries were hailed as absolutely essential to any legal education and as the only book in which extended legal knowledge could be easily acquired" (Zane 1998: 335).

The works of Sir William Blackstone (1723–1780) were widely cited in pre-Revolutionary American courts. While law books were quite scarce, Blackstone's four-volume work, based on his lectures at Oxford, *Commentaries on the Laws of England* (1765–1769), was generally available. This most influential writer on the common law undertook to demonstrate that England's legal system was not simply a confusion of rules justified only by their age. Blackstone organized the English common law into four areas: (1) the rights of persons, (2) the rights of property, (3) private wrongs (torts), and (4) public wrongs (criminal law). He provided the rules governing each legal topic and the logic behind them in an effort to gain support for the common law. Blackstone "tried to show that Englishmen had rationally, by trial and error through the centuries, worked out a system of social regulation which produced the greatest satisfaction for themselves, [and] the justest rule for their common existence" (Sutherland 1967: 23). He viewed the principles of common law as being derived from natural law or divine in origin. Blackstone's work was favored by the conservative Tory party in England and gained the support of colonial lawyers, for whom it provided "an up-to-date shortcut to basic English law" (Friedman 1973: 88). Since there was a paucity of readily available alternatives, the influence of Blackstone was pervasive.

THE REVOLUTION

On the eve of independence, the American colonies had a fully developed hierarchical court system, served by a professional bar operating under sophisticated procedural systems, although no two colonies had the same court structure. Colonial appellate courts were not necessarily comprised of judges; most consisted of the governor and council (Wiecek 1988). A fully developed separation of powers had to await the Constitution as influenced by the writings of Charles Louis de Secondat Montesqieu (1689–1755). In *The Spirit of Laws* (1748), Montesqieu advocated three branches of government, each confined to its proper sphere: "There is no liberty, if the judiciary power be not separated from the legislative and the executive" (1949:152).[2]

The Revolutionary War resulted in two bodies of law. The Crown authorized the British Army to seize goods for the war effort, to regulate prices, and to punish traitors, while the Continental Congress, driven out of Philadelphia in 1777, drafted its own legislation (Friedman 1973). The defeat of the British Army brought dramatic changes to the law and judicial process in America, though neither common law nor lawyers were any more popular in postrevolutionary America than they had been in the colonial era. However, the courts, now with patriotic judges, continued to conduct business using the only law they knew—English law—and much of it was based on common law.

While British statutes were put aside, the importance of common law remained. It was regarded as a source of protection for private rights and immunity from government oppression. "It would have been a political contradiction for the new states to jettison a legal system that they claimed [in the Declaration of Independence] as their birthright" (Hazard and Taruffo 1993: 6). Blackstone was frequently cited in American courts of this era, and popular British manuals of procedure were readily available and used in the United States.

There was a brief flirtation with France after the Revolution, and some even proposed basing the American legal system on that of the French codes. However, most Americans were unable or unwilling to read law books written in foreign tongues. The British common law prevailed, but not without vigorous opposition from those who favored codification. In general, the common law was favored by Federalists and, later, Whigs, who were aligned with commercial and business interests. They distrusted legislation that they feared might be used to promote the redistribution of wealth for egalitarian goals. They placed their faith in a judicial branch and common law. Codification or civil law was supported by Jacksonian Democrats. "The victory of common law in America was confirmed when [Judge James] Kent and [Justice Joseph] Story wrote their authoritative guides for judges and practitioners in the years between 1826 and 1845. After their texts were published, the cult of civil law virtually disappeared. They had restated the common law in American form. It was now so clearly presented that the energies of judges could be turned to applying common law principles to concrete cases" (Schwartz 1974: 29).

Except in Louisiana, the French and Spanish civil law of the West was eventually overwhelmed by the American settler invasion, although some of these traditions were incorporated into the common law tradition. A civil code enacted in 1825 in Louisiana was drawn primarily from the Napoleonic Code, and the law of Louisiana is a blend of French, Spanish, and common law traditions (Friedman 1973). However, most states added the part of the common law to their statutes that they found useful. This meant that each state had a different form of common law. Without recourse to a standard body of common law, judges and attorneys found

[2]England never adopted the concept of separation of powers: the Prime Minister is a member of Parliament, and the Lord Chancellor, a member of the cabinet, is speaker of the House of Lords while also head of the judiciary (Abraham 1998).

themselves without authoritative sources for their arguments and decisions, and "there can hardly be a legal system until the decisions of the courts are regularly published and are available to bench and bar" (Gilmore 1977: 9).

Prior to the Civil War, "most lawyers and judges relied on treatise writers, who ascertained the state of the law and provided voluminous citations to state, federal, and English cases" (Hall, Wiecek, and Finkelman 1991: 114). At the turn of the nineteenth century, states began introducing the *reporter system*, which published the decisions of the state courts. By 1821, there were more than 150 volumes of such reports available (Chroust 1965). Decisions of federal courts were also being published, "as well as American republications (with added local annotations) of English books and case collections" (Gilmore 1977: 23). In 1879, the West Publishing Company established the *National Reporting System*, and an overwhelming number of decisions became readily available to every lawyer; *stare decisis* became a quantitative as well as a qualitative challenge.

COURTS AFTER THE REVOLUTION

In postrevolutionary America, the concept of separation of powers developed slowly. Under the Articles of Confederation and Perpetual Union (1781), most functions of government were vested in a single-chamber legislature: Congress. Executive and legislative powers were not separated, and there was no national judiciary. State governments also reflected the absence of a clear separation of powers. Legislators and chief executives, often laypersons without legal training, served as justices of the states' highest courts (Friedman 1973). State legislatures began drafting detailed statutes setting out the structure and jurisdiction of the judiciary and the executive branches of government (Hurst 1950). But these were the years of legislative supremacy, and the legislatures frequently intervened in judicial activity, reversing decisions and passing special laws to the advantage of certain plaintiffs or defendants (Chroust 1965). State constitutions were viewed as inferior to legislative enactments, and the legislature had supremacy over the courts even when its enactments were contrary to the state constitution.

State court systems were characterized by decentralization, a Balkanization sometimes based on geographic jurisdiction, sometimes on the nature of the case, and sometimes both. This was caused by the need to bring the courts closer to litigants in an expanding nation where transportation was primitive. Each court played an important political and social role in the life of its community. When court convened in the county seat, often only once a month, it was a major event. Large numbers of people came to town, conducted business, discussed politics, and socialized with one another (Walker 1980). These were the days before radio, motion pictures, and television, and people flocked to the courtrooms to hear the oratory of noted attorneys. Courtroom oratory and successful advocacy gained an attorney a following and clients (Friedman 1973; Ferguson 1984).

Of particular importance in rural America was the justice of the peace (JP), who in colonial times was appointed by the royal governor and served at the county level. Requirements were minimal; legal training was not one of them, but political connections were. The JP was the basis of the states' systems for handling everyday disputes (Hurst 1950). The JP was empowered to try minor cases; the more serious ones were reserved for the higher courts that met infrequently. As a result, justice suffered. The justice-of-the-peace court was an effort to bring the administration of justice close to a scattered population at a minimum of public expense, so the office was usually operated on a fee-for-service basis.

Following the Revolutionary War, there was a trend throughout the states toward establishment of a separate appellate branch. Over the decades, the appellate process improved as specialized courts developed that could review cases without recourse to a *trial de novo*, a retrial in a higher court (Hurst 1950). The trial courts, however, were neglected and became unwieldy, inefficient, and in many areas tied to corrupt political machines, a link that would remain a problem in many urban areas well into the twentieth century.

From the Revolution until 1832, most states provided for both elected and appointed (by the legislature or governor) judges. In that year, Mississippi initiated the popular election of all judges; in 1846, New York did the same. Within 10 years, 15 of the 29 states that then made up the Union had followed suit, and every state that entered the Union after 1846 stipulated the popular election of all or most of their judges (Hurst 1950). A number of the other states experimented with both electoral and appointment systems, sometimes, as Texas did, going back and forth (Friedman 1973).

LAW AND JUSTICE ON THE FRONTIER

With the westward expansion, judges in the newly settled territories borrowed from a variety of state sources, but primarily from those states with which they were most familiar. In many areas there was little law. Justice was decided in a rather crude fashion by persons having rather limited knowledge of law and legal processes and often acting on their own instincts. Lawyers and judges carried weapons, and duels often settled legal questions. There was a paucity of law books, and lawyers were often not law school graduates. Many had simply been law clerks, and others gained their knowledge of the law through experience—and often resorted to tricks or to the few technicalities with which they were familiar (Friedman 1973). Court sessions were usually held in makeshift courtrooms by judges who were ignorant of the law; some were even illiterate. Judges were chosen on the basis of personal qualities— Indian fighters (who often engaged in America's version of "ethnic cleansing") were popular—rather than legal knowledge. Justice was dispensed without resort to precedent or decorum, so administration varied widely from court to court. Courts were filled with rowdy, tobacco-chewing participants. "The backwoodsman was intolerant of men who split hairs, drew fine distinctions, or scrupled over methods of reaching the right solution" (Chroust 1965: 96). But frontier justice also had some outstanding lawyers who presided over quality justice (Stevens 1971).

Out of these frontier sentiments, writes Richard Maxwell Brown, vigilantism and lynch law "arose as a response to a typical American problem: the absence of effective law and order in a frontier region. It was a problem that occurred again and again beyond the Appalachian Mountains. It stimulated the formation of hundreds of frontier vigilante movements" (1969: 156). The extralegal violence that emerged in late nineteenth and early twentieth century America—southern lynch mobs, western vigilantes, and northern and eastern "white caps"—had the support of many leading members of the legal profession, whose "conception of law and order in regard to the problem of criminal and disorderly behavior did not stress the method of *due process* of law but the *aim* of crime repression. In the vast majority of their actions these attorneys, jurists, and legal writers were law abiding in deed and thought. However, when the disorder of late nineteenth century America confronted their devotion to the strict letter of the law, the latter gave way to their primary desire for order" (Brown 1971: 96).

Lynch law was an extreme manifestation of popular local democracy—government by the people or popular sovereignty—responding to community sentiments and needs. Lynchings cut through the complexities of procedural law that thwarted "popular justice" and avoided the costs of jail and trial (Brown 1971). Lynch law prevented the obviously guilty defendant from escaping justice; it also imposed the ultimate penalty on the innocent, often in collusion with local officials sworn to uphold law and order. And in some regions, particularly in the South, lynchings served as an expression of racial hatred and intimidation.

THE SUPREME COURT

Shortly after the Articles of Confederation were adopted by the 13 sovereign states (1781), it became obvious that they were not a viable basis for governing the United States—federal authority was concentrated in a unicameral legislative body; there was no separate executive branch. The people were divided geographically—the journey from Boston to New York took a week, while Boston to Savannah was a trip of several months—and "by differences of religion, environment, and custom that bred fierce jealousy and local pride." Thus, "a man thought of himself as a Georgian, a Virginian, or a New Yorker but hardly ever as an American" (Cox 1987: 32).

Shay's rebellion (1787), in which destitute farmers in western Massachusetts, led by a Revolutionary War veteran, rebelled against onerous taxes, had revealed the inadequacies of executive power; the national currency was practically worthless, and there was real fear that European nations would take advantage of governmental anarchy as states squabbled over interstate trade. This commercial warfare led to the Philadelphia Convention: "The taxes levied upon goods moving through the Ports of New York and Philadelphia were bleeding portless New Jersey white. Virginia and South Carolina were bleeding North Carolina. Baltimore was fattening on the people of the interior valleys. When Virginia passed a law declaring that vessels failing to pay duty in her ports were subject to seizure, she was aiming at cargoes

*A*RTICLES OF *C*ONFEDERATION, *A*RTICLE 2

"Each state retains its sovereignty, freedom, and independence, and every power, jurisdiction, and right, which is not by this confederation expressly delegated to the United States, in Congress assembled."

from Massachusetts, New York, and Pennsylvania. In 1786 delegates from the States bordering on Chesapeake Bay met at Annapolis in an effort to stop the commercial warfare on the bay. The Annapolis Convention led to the broader summons to Philadelphia" (Cox 1987: 34). As criticism grew, Congress reluctantly called for a convention to meet in Philadelphia in 1787 to revise the Articles of Confederation.

Even though the delegates were not authorized to create an entirely new instrument of government, they did so. James Madison wrote (*Federalist* No. 40) that the convention had not exceeded its authority; but even if it had, he argued, it was justified by the need to protect the welfare of the nation. Out of this Constitutional Convention emerged the cornerstone of American government, separation of powers, which sought to answer one of the oldest problems of democratic government: how to provide for efficiency without tyranny.

A bicameral legislature (Article I) and a chief executive (Article II) were agreed upon after long and often acrimonious debate. The idea of a national judiciary was widely accepted, but delegates could not agree on the details. While there was general agreement on the need for a supreme court, the advocates of states' rights opposed creation of a system of inferior federal courts. They argued that state courts were sufficient, and a single federal appellate court was adequate to protect national rights and promote uniformity of judgments. In a compromise, delegates approved of Article III, which says in part, "The judicial power of the United States, shall be vested in one Supreme Court, and in such inferior Courts as the Congress may from time to time ordain and establish." They left it up to Congress to establish inferior courts and to set the size of the membership of the Supreme Court (Schwartz 1993).

The new Constitution needed to be ratified by nine of the original thirteen states, and the outcome was in doubt. A war of words broke out, and the press of the day was deluged with contributions from anonymous citizens writing under various *noms de plume* (Earle 1937). "Publius"—the pen name chosen for the joint writings of Federalists Alexander Hamilton, John Jay, and James Madison—wrote a series of 85 essays between October 1787 and May 1788 in support of the Constitution. These essays have become known as *The Federalist Papers*. Designed primarily to support ratification of the Constitution in New York, *The Federalist Papers* were known throughout the states. Although it is doubtful whether they had much influence in determining ratification, they provide an illuminating discussion of intent and a basis for interpreting the Constitution (Earle 1937).

The role of the judiciary was clear: "The courts were designed to be an intermediate body between the people and the legislature, in order, among other things, to keep the latter within the limits assigned to their authority. The interpretation of the law is the proper and peculiar province of the courts. A constitution is, in fact, and must be regarded by the judges, as a fundamental law. It therefore belongs to them to ascertain its meaning, as well as the meaning of any particular act proceeding from the legislative body" (*Federalist* No. 78: 506). Publius argued that "limitations of this kind can be preserved in practice no other way than through the medium of courts of justice, whose duty it must be to declare all acts contrary to the manifest tenor of the Constitution void. Without this, all the reservations of particular rights or privileges would amount to nothing" (*Federalist* No. 78: 505). In his assessment of *Democracy in America*, Alexis de Tocqueville, a French aristocrat studying the American prison system and writing in the 1830s, stated that "the power vested in the American courts of justice, of pronouncing a statute to be unconstitutional, forms one of the most powerful barriers which has ever been devised against tyranny of political assemblies" (1956: 76), and it is a methodological expression of the supremacy of *natural law*.

The *Federalist Papers* noted the relative weakness of the judicial branch and its dependency on the executive branch to carry out its decisions: "The Executive not only dispenses the honors, but holds the sword of the community. The legislature not only commands the purse, but prescribes the rules by which the duties and rights of every citizen are to be regulated. The judiciary, on the contrary, has no influence over either sword or purse; no direction either of the strength or of the wealth of the society; and can take no active resolution whatever. It may truly be said to have neither *force* nor *will*, but merely judgment; and must ultimately depend upon the aid of the executive arm even for the efficacy of its judgments" (*Federalist* No. 78: 504).

They also stressed the need for judicial independence, a principle that has become a cornerstone of the federal courts: "That inflexible and uniform adherence to the rights of the Constitution, and of individuals, which we perceive to be indispensable in the courts of justice, can certainly not be expected from judges who hold their offices by a temporary commission. Periodical appointments, however regulated, or by whomsoever made, would, in some way or other, be fatal to their necessary independence" (*Federalist* No. 78: 510). This warning was heeded—all federal judges are appointed to lifetime terms.

The Constitution was ratified by the ninth state, New Hampshire, on June 21, 1788, but the size of the Supreme Court was not determined until the Judiciary Act of 1789, which set membership at six: a chief justice and five associate justices. The act also created three circuit courts, each made up of two justices of the Supreme Court and a district court judge, and thirteen district courts, each presided over by a district judge (Carp and Stidham 1985).

The Supreme Court began operations in the Wall Street area of New York City on February 1, 1790 and the most immediate controversy concerned attire—the English wig was rejected, but robes were accepted (Schwartz 1993). A federal bar began to develop and, when the federal capital moved, a number of more prominent attorneys settled in Washington to argue cases before the Court (Chroust 1965). The justices appointed by President Washington were all loyal Federalists, three from the South and three from the North. (Washington established the traditions of appointing the party faithful and of geographic balance.) The chief justice was John Jay of New York. But when he was elected governor of New York, Jay resigned from the Court, because the judiciary was still the least important branch of government.[3] Several individuals declined appointments to the Court, and one, Robert H. Harrison, refused the appointment even after the Senate confirmed him; he chose, instead, to become chancellor of Maryland (Cox 1987). Particularly onerous was the requirement that members of the Court personally sit on circuit courts that had been set up by the 1789 Judiciary Act. This required a great deal of travel at a time when transportation was quite primitive (Schwartz 1993).

---

[3]Jay's view of the Court is highlighted by the appointment he accepted in 1794 as Special Ambassador to England where he negotiated the treaty that bears his name—without resigning as chief justice (Schwartz 1993).

The first Supreme Court was weak and ineffective and relegated to a room in the basement beneath the Senate chamber. Only two justices and John Jay were present on opening day. "Required by law to sit twice a year, it began its first term with a crowded courtroom and an empty docket. Appeals from lower tribunals came slowly; for its first three years the Court had almost no business at all" (Harrell and Anderson 1982: 15). For this reason Congress was reluctant to relieve the justices of their circuit riding responsibilities (Schwartz 1993).

When war raged between England and France, President Washington, hoping to keep America neutral, asked the Court for advice on 29 questions on international law and treaties. In a precedent-setting response, Chief Justice John Jay politely declined to provide advisory decisions, pointing out that each branch is responsible for acting as a check on the other and that such responsibility could not be fulfilled if the Court served as a presidential advisor. "However, as did many subsequent members of the Court, Jay acted extensively as a presidential advisor in an informal, behind-the-scenes capacity" (Wiecek 1988: 25).

During the Constitutional Convention, debates arose over the exercise of judicial review—the power to determine the constitutionality of an action by the legislative or executive branch—and they were inconclusive. "The convention delegates agreed to the establishment of a Supreme Court only after they had rejected proposals for a Council of Revision to scrutinize congressional legislation and another to allow Congress to veto state legislation. That the delegates debated these methods of constitutional oversight in the context of the judicial power indicates that they assumed the Supreme Court would oversee the constitutionality of acts of Congress and state legislatures" (Hall 1989: 73). While it seems clear that the delegates intended some type of judicial review, its content and scope were not defined and the Constitution remained silent about the issue. Leonard Levy concludes that "the evidence seems to indicate that the Framers did not mean for the Supreme Court to have authority to void acts of Congress" (1988: 100). While in state systems the practice of judicial review was beginning to emerge (Wiecek 1988), the Supreme Court did not assert this authority until its most important historical decision, *Marbury* v. *Madison* (1803), for which only three of the Court's six justices showed up to hear arguments. (For an examination of the origins of judicial review, see Sosin 1989; Stoner 1992.)

THE MARSHALL COURT

The Court moved to a site on the Potomac in 1800. In that year the Federalists were defeated. Chief Justice Oliver Ellsworth became ill and resigned, and Jay refused to serve again. In 1801, in an effort to "save" the Constitution from the "radical" Democratic Republicans led by Thomas Jefferson, lame-duck President John Adams appointed his secretary of state, the Virginia Federalist and Jefferson's cousin, John Marshall, as the Court's fourth chief justice. As a young man on Washington's staff, Marshall had experienced the horrors of Valley Forge, caused largely by selfishness and rivalry between states. He appreciated the need for national unity and had taken an active role in winning Virginia's ratification of the Constitution (Cox 1987).

Marbury v. Madison

In his last act before leaving office, President Adams appointed 42 justices of the peace for the District of Columbia, which the lame-duck Senate quickly confirmed. Although he had affixed the great seal of the United States, in the haste surrounding the appointments, Secretary of State John Marshall failed to send out the commission for William Marbury. When he took office, President Jefferson ordered that the commission not be delivered. In December of 1801, Marbury applied to the Supreme Court for a *writ of mandamus* (an extraordinary court order compelling a public official to perform his or her duty) ordering James Madison, the secretary of state, to give him his commission as justice of the peace. Although the Supreme Court agreed to hear the controversial case, Congress enacted a law that stopped the Court from convening for 14 months. In 1803, the Court finally heard the case of *Marbury* v. *Madison*.

Marry Ann Harrell and Burnett Anderson describe the quandary of the Court headed by Marshall:

> If the Court ordered Madison to produce that commission, he could simply ignore the order; President Jefferson would defend him. If the Court denied Marbury's right to his commission, Jefferson could claim a party victory. [Either decision would mean a significant loss of prestige for the Court.] Marshall found an escape from this dilemma. Point by point he analyzed the case. Did Marbury have a legal right to his commission? *Yes.* Would a writ of mandamus enforce his right? *Yes.* Could the Court issue the writ? *No.* Congress had said it could, in the Judiciary Act of 1789. It had given the Court original jurisdiction in such cases—power to try them for the first time. But, said Marshall, the Constitution defined the Court's original jurisdiction and Congress could not change it by law. Therefore that section of the law was void. (1982: 25–26; edited)

The Court could do nothing to help Marbury.

While Marbury never did get his commission, he was saved from historical obscurity "by the fact that he was the plaintiff in the most famous case ever decided by the United States Supreme Court" (Rehnquist 1987: 114). With this decision, John Marshall asserted the principle of *judicial review*, the power of the Supreme Court to determine the constitutionality of acts of Congress and actions of the president. While such power is inherent in the very idea of a written constitution (Tushnet 2000), "had Marshall not confirmed review power at the outset in his

MARBURY v. MADISON (1803)

"Certainly, all those who have framed written constitutions contemplate them as forming the fundamental and paramount law of the nation, and consequently the theory of every such government must be, that an act of the legislature, repugnant to the Constitution, is void."

Judicial Review

"Judicial review is the practice by which the Supreme Court scrutinizes state and federal legislation and the acts of state and federal executive officers and courts in order to determine whether they are in conflict with the Constitution" (Hall 1989: 1). However, "neither the words of the Constitution nor the provable intent of those who framed and ratified it justified in 1790 any certitude about the scope or finality of the Court's power to superintend either the states or Congress" (McClosky 1994: 5).

original magisterial manner, it is entirely possible it would never have been insisted upon, for it was not until 1857 that the authority to invalidate a federal statute was next exercised by the Supreme Court" (Schwartz 1974: 32–33).[4]

Marbury left unresolved the question of the scope of the power of judicial review (George 2000), but once the decision was made, the Court also claimed the right of judicial review over state legislation (*Fletcher* v. *Peck* 1810), and the Marshall court (1801–1835) overturned more than a dozen state laws on constitutional grounds (Carp and Stidham 1985). "Once Chief Justice Marshall had established the prerogative of the Supreme Court to declare statutes unconstitutional, the Court employed natural law thinking to protect vested property rights against legislative incursions" (Levy 1988: 13).

Marshall initiated a major change in the way decisions were presented by encouraging collective opinions in place of the usual *seriatim* (separate) opinions authored by each justice. He was responsible for the Supreme Court being the only one of our three branches of government that provides a written statement of its reasons when it renders a decision (Tribe 1985). "He created the judicial tradition," notes William Wiecek, "out of the scant and unpromising prospects he found when he took office in 1801" (1988: 55). G. Edward White sums up Marshall's contribution: "Appointed to a court that could easily have become and nearly did become a resting place for minor political officials, Marshall gave to succeeding judges a national judiciary able to stand equal alongside the other two branches of government" (1976: 35).

McCulloch v. Maryland

In 1819, the Court extended the power of the federal government when it found that among those powers specifically enumerated in Article I, Section 8, of the Constitution, were "implied powers" necessary for the proper implementation of the constitutional mandate. Accordingly, in *McCulloch* v. *Maryland* (1819), the Court upheld the power of the federal government to establish the Bank of the

---

[4]David Currie (1985) notes that the Court ruled acts of Congress unconstitutional prior to *Marbury*, but the Court had failed to justify the decisions by invoking the power of judicial review.

McCULLOCH v. MARYLAND (1819)

"A constitution, to contain an accurate detail of all the subdivisions of which its great powers will admit, and of all the means by which they may be carried into execution, would partake of the prolixity [tediousness] of a legal code, and could scarcely be embraced by the human mind. It would probably never be understood by the public. Its nature, therefore, requires that only its great outlines should be marked, its important objects designated, and the minor ingredients which compose those objects be deduced from the nature of the objects themselves. That this idea was entertained by the framers of the American constitution, is not only to be inferred from the nature of the instrument, but from the language."

United States and ruled that a state could not tax that bank. While President Andrew Jackson thwarted *McCulloch* in 1832 by vetoing legislation to extend the charter of the bank, the impact of Marshall's finding of implied powers "was the basis for the expansion of federal power and the rise of the welfare state that began during the depression of the 1930s" (Spaeth 1979: 200).

Supremacy Clause

The Court also transformed Article VI, the Supremacy Clause, into an operating reality, and this was not a simple task. At times, sectionalism was rife in New England, the West, and finally the South, threatening to tear the union apart (Wiecek 1988). While state court decisions had to conform to the Constitution, that document left enough room for diverse interpretations. Various states' courts might interpret the Constitution differently, while others might claim state sovereignty in certain cases. This issue came to the fore in a case that involved land in northern Virginia that had been part of the same tract as the John Marshall homestead; accordingly, in *Martin* v. *Hunter's Lessee* (1816) Marshall recused (disqualified himself). In his place, Justice Joseph Story upheld the appellate jurisdiction of the Supreme Court as the "final word" over all federal and state courts. The issue emerged again in 1821 in a case involving the sale of lottery tickets authorized by Congress but outlawed by Virginia (*Cohens* v. *Virginia*). Marshall wrote the opinion again upholding both the power of the Supreme Court and federal supremacy. The

ARTICLE VI $($$S$UPREMACY CLAUSE$)$

"This Constitution, and the Laws of the United States which shall be made in Pursuance thereof; and all Treaties made, or which shall be made, under the authority of the United States, shall be the supreme Law of the Land; and all the Judges in every State shall be bound thereby, any Thing in the Constitution or Laws of any State to the Contrary notwithstanding."

Supremacy Clause specifically obligates state courts to recognize the superiority of federal law and to apply the latter when state law has been superseded (Schwartz 1993).

Gibbons v. Ogden

In 1824, the Supreme Court handed down a decision that proved crucial for economic development in the United States. It was also one of the more popular decisions handed down by the Marshall Court. In 1803, Robert Fulton demonstrated his steam-powered ship on the Seine in Paris. Subsequently, the New York State legislature granted Fulton and his partner exclusive rights to issue licenses to run steamships on the Hudson River. In 1811, the territorial legislature in New Orleans granted them a similar monopoly; they controlled the two most lucrative ports in the country. Other states enacted similar legislation.

One of the licensees of the New York monopoly, ex-New Jersey Governor Aaron Ogden, sued his former partner, Thomas Gibbons, for navigating in New York waters without a state license. The New York courts found for Ogden and forbade Gibbons to operate in New York ports or to interfere with Ogden's monopoly. Gibbons appealed to the Supreme Court, arguing that his (federal) license under the Federal Coasting Act entitled him to trade between the ports of different states. The overriding legal issue concerned state and federal powers under the commerce clause, Article I, Section 8, Clause 3: regulation of intra- and interstate commerce. In his decision, Marshall asserted the federal government's supreme authority over the regulation of interstate commerce, while leaving the regulation of intrastate commerce to the states. The decision did not attend to the area of overlap between state and federal regulation, although subsequent cases for more than 150 years have clarified the issue.

Gibbons had an immediate and important economic impact—the destruction of state trade monopolies that stimulated business in their states, while other states retaliated against these protectionist measures. The decision facilitated the creation of the unified market essential for economic development in the United States and, later in the century, encouraged Congress to appropriate funds for improving interstate trade routes. "The modern free flow of commerce in the American economy's enormous national market is the legacy of *Gibbons* v. *Ogden*" (Richert 1987: 15).

THE ELEVENTH AMENDMENT AND SOVEREIGN IMMUNITY

While the Supreme Court dominated constitutional issues, it was the state courts' decisions that affected the day-to-day activities of most citizens. From the time of the ratification of the Constitution until the Civil War, the primacy of the state courts was not seriously questioned. The Judiciary Act of 1789 affirmed the primary role of the state courts and narrowly confined the jurisdiction of the federal trial courts. In 1793, however, the pre-Marshall Supreme Court, in its first constitutional decision, ruled in *Chisholm* v. *Georgia* that a state is not a sovereign entity and therefore a citizen in one state could sue the government of another state in federal court, in this case to recover a debt. States "feared ruinous suits on Revolutionary War debts that they had not paid on Tory property that they had confiscated" (Tribe 1985: 55). Congress responded with the Eleventh Amendment, ratified in 1795 (although the presidential proclamation was delayed until 1798) barring suits in federal court similar to the one sustained in *Chisholm:* "The Court's first constitutional decision conflicted with statements of Framers in 1788 and provoked an amendment to the Constitution to make it conform to a general understanding throughout the nation" (Levy 1988: 59).

In order to protect the independence of state courts—a practice known as *judicial comity*—the Eleventh Amendment provides that "the Judicial Power of the United States shall not be construed to extend to any suit in law or equity, commenced or prosecuted against one of the United States by Citizens of another State, or by Citizens or Subjects of any Foreign State." The Marshall Supreme Court, however, limited the impact of the Eleventh Amendment by holding that a suit against a *state officer* is not a suit against a *state*, if the officer was acting pursuant to an unconstitutional state law (*United States* v. *Peters* 1809; *Osborn* v. *The Bank of the United States* 1824). This interpretation would hold until the Reconstruction era, when the Supreme Court extended the protections afforded states—*sovereign immunity*—by the Eleventh Amendment, thus protecting state officers from lawsuits by nonresidents (Orth 1987). In 1890, the Court further extended sovereign immunity, prohibiting suits by citizens against their own states (*Hans* v. *Louisiana*), although a state may waive this immunity. People can still sue states on "equal protection" grounds, alleging a violation of the Fourteenth Amendment.

In 1946, Congress enacted the Federal Tort Claims Act, which provides the legal mechanism for compensating persons injured by the negligent or wrongful acts of federal employees committed within the scope of their employment. The injured party must first file an administrative claim with the appropriate federal agency. Only if the claim is denied or not acted upon within six months can the claimant file a suit in federal district court. Under the act, these lawsuits can only be tried by a bench (no jury) trial. States soon followed the federal lead and enacted legislation allowing citizens to seek redress against state actions in state court.

A person cannot sue a *state* government by invoking *federal* law, unless Congress specifically provided for an exception to sovereign immunity. State officials, however, can be held liable under federal law, 42 U.S.C. Sec. 1983: "Every person who, under color of any statute, ordinance, regulation, custom, or usage, of any State or Territory, subjects or causes to be subjected, any citizen of the United States or other persons within the jurisdiction thereof to the deprivation of any rights, privileges, or immunities secured by the Constitution and laws, shall be liable to the party injured in any action at law, suit in equity, or other proper proceeding for redress." Public officials may also be subject to an action in equity seeking an injunction to prevent them from acting *ultra vires* (beyond their power); or a tort action may ask for damages as a result of injury for behavior that was *ultra vires*.

The application of the Eleventh Amendment is still unclear. In 1989, for example, the Court held that while municipal (and county) governments are not protected by the Eleventh Amendment, states are immune from lawsuits growing out of constitutional violations committed by state agencies or their officials even when those lawsuits were brought in *state* courts (*Will* v. *Michigan*). During the same session, however, the Court ruled that Congress had the authority to authorize persons to sue their states in federal court to recover damages for cleaning up toxic waste for which the state was allegedly responsible (*Pennsylvania* v. *Union Gas*). In 1999, in three cases, all decided 5–4, the Court expanded the reach of the Eleventh Amendment when it ruled that states are immune from suits by state employees for violations of federal labor law (*Alden* v. *Maine*); by patent owners for infringement of their patents by state government (*Florida* v. *College Saving Bank*); and by people bringing unfair competition suits over states' activities in the marketplace (Greenhouse 1999).[5]

SLAVERY

The Constitution makes no direct mention of slavery, but as the result of a compromise to gain support of southern states, the document clearly recognizes that there could be *property in people*: Article I, Section 2, refers to "free persons" and "three fifths of all other persons," and Article IV, Section 2, refers to the escape of a "person held to service or labour," a clause essential for gaining southern support for the ratification of the Constitution. In the years preceding the Civil War, issues of states' rights and slavery were paramount. In 1857, for the first time since *Marbury* v. *Madison*, the Court exercised the power of judicial review over a federal statute: the case of *Scott* v. *Sandford*.

The case involved the status of a black man, Dred Scott, who had filed a suit for his freedom in a Missouri court in 1846. As a slave, Scott had been taken to a frontier U.S. Army post where slavery was forbidden (Illinois) and later to territory in which the Missouri Compromise banned slavery (Minnesota). He was subsequently taken back to Missouri, a slave state, where his master died. Scott, claiming that his sojourn on free soil released him from slavery, brought suit, and in 1850 a state trial court declared him free. The widow of Scott's master appealed, and the state's highest court ruled that, free on free soil or not, when Scott returned to Missouri he became a slave again. In an effort to make this a test case, Scott's lawyers arranged to have the widow pass title to her brother, John F. Sanford (misspelled in the records) of New York. This provided for the diversity of citizenship—Missouri and New York—necessary for bringing a federal appeal. Claiming Missouri citizenship, Scott sued for his freedom in St. Louis.

In 1854, the Circuit Court of Appeals ruled that Scott could not be a citizen because he was a Negro. The case was certified to the Supreme Court that same year. Abolitionist feelings were running quite high; that year Congress passed the Kansas–Nebraska Act (which repealed the Missouri Compromise),[6] opening up areas of the West to slavery, and fighting broke out in what became known as "Bloody Kansas." In 1856, the Supreme Court heard the case of *Scott* v. *Sandford*, and early the following year a majority of the justices, each of whom rendered a separate opinion, determined that Scott would remain a slave. While a state could confer citizenship on a Negro, this would not affect his status in another state, nor would it give rise to a claim of constitutional protections even within the granting state.

---

[5] It should be noted that while the Eleventh Amendment bars suits for damages, it does not bar equity lawsuits: for example, an injunction against a state official to enjoin the official from taking an action(s) that would violate the plaintiff's rights under the Constitution or federal law (Emanuel 2000a).

[6] The Missouri Compromise involved statutes passed by Congress in 1820 and 1821 to deal with the issue of extending slavery. Under the compromise, Maine was admitted as a free state and Missouri as a slave state, and slavery was banned in much of the Louisiana Purchase. By the time of the *Scott* case, Congress had already repealed the compromise (Hall 1989).

∫COTT v. ∫ANDFORD (1856)

[A] Negro of the African race was regarded by them [English colonists] as an article of property, and held, and bought and sold as such, in every one of the thirteen Colonies which united in the Declaration of Independence, and afterward formed the Constitution of the United States. . . . [T]herefore, it is the judgment of this court, that it appears by the record before us that the plaintiff in error is not a citizen of Missouri, in the sense used in the Constitution. . . ."

While the case before the Court did not require consideration of the wider issue of slavery, Chief Justice Roger Taney, a Marylander appointed by President Andrew Jackson, argued that according to the original intent of the framer's Constitution, members of the black race were "altogether unfit to associate with the white race either in social or political relations; and so far inferior, that they had no rights which the white man was bound to respect."[7] "The right of slavery," he declared, "is distinctly and expressly affirmed in the Constitution." Justice Peter Vivian Daniel, a Virginian, added that slaves were "*property*, in the strictest sense of the term." The Court would not invoke *natural law:* when natural rights—liberty—conflicted with property rights—slaves—property rights were supreme. Furthermore, the Court ruled, the Missouri Compromise was unconstitutional; Congress had no right to limit the expansion of slavery. Rather than minimizing the role of judges and limiting its decision only to those issues necessary for resolving the case—a concept known as *judicial restraint*, the Court decided *every* issue raised by the case (Sunstein 2000a). The scene was set for the most devastating war in American history.

RECONSTRUCTION AND THE EXPANSION OF FEDERAL AUTHORITY

Prior to the Civil War, the Supreme Court "had been perennially haunted by the danger that centrifugal forces would tear the nation apart, and their jurisprudence had been shaped by that terrible threat always in mind" (McClosky 1994: 67). Union victory changed the atmosphere in which the Court operated.

In the postwar era, African-Americans found themselves caught between two differing interpretations of emancipation: "Northerners assumed that once slavery was abolished the ex-slaves immediately and automatically ascended to all the rights and privileges and responsibilities of full citizenship, impeded by some racially based disabilities, to be sure, but nevertheless in possession of all civil rights whites enjoyed" (Wiecek 1988: 93). But southerners knew better—to them emancipation simply freed blacks from the authority of a master. Following the Civil War, southern states enacted *Black Codes*, denying to blacks many basic

---

[7]Chief Justice Roger Taney (1836–1864) tolerated dissenting and concurring separate opinions that, in slavery cases, gave rise to extreme positions, "which encouraged others on the Court to write their own extreme concurrences or dissents and, in turn, contributed to a widening spiral of polarization" (Wiecek 1988: 73).

rights secured to whites: freedom to move, to contract, to own property, to sue in courts, to assemble, to bear arms, and to be witnesses against whites (Curtis 1986; Wolfe 1986).

Blacks received no sympathy from President Andrew Johnson of Tennessee, a supporter of states' rights, but the Republican-controlled Congress reacted with passage of the Civil Rights Act of 1866 and the Fourteenth Amendment, ratified in 1868. It reads in part: "No State shall make or enforce any law which shall abridge the privileges or immunities of citizens of the United States; nor shall any State deprive any person of life, liberty, or property, without due process of law; nor deny to any person within its jurisdiction the equal protection of the laws." But Republicans had a particularly partisan concern. Instead of being counted as "three-fifths" for purposes of representation, black males in the South now constituted full persons who could strengthen the Democratic party in Congress and the Electoral College, while that same party was denying blacks the right to vote (Berger 1977). Instead of granting suffrage as part of the privileges of citizenship, the Fourteenth Amendment reduced representation in proportion to the number of males over 21 whose right to vote was in any way abridged. This also affected Northern states that denied blacks suffrage, but there were not enough blacks in those states to matter. "As a matter of law and as a matter of political objectives, most contemporaries distinguished between civil rights and voting rights" (Kaczorowski 1987: 49). In 1870, the Fifteenth Amendment was passed to prohibit the denial of suffrage based on race, and the Civil Rights Law of 1871 provided federal courts with jurisdiction in equity to remedy state encroachments on individual civil rights.

While Congress sought to protect and expand some of the rights of African-Americans in the South, southern officials were aided by the Supreme Court in efforts to deprive them of these same rights. The Court aided southern Democrats by supporting an antebellum view of federalism based on *states' rights* and *dual federalism*—"that state and nation were rival sovereignties that operated beyond the complete grasp of each other," with the "no-man's land" between them patrolled by an impartial Supreme Court (Hall 1989: 18). Thus, states continued to enjoy those aspects of sovereignty that had not been explicitly conveyed to the federal government by the Constitution; and states were the equal of the national government in the federal system, each with an independent structure and power to exercise sovereignty. According to this view, there are two sets of rights and privileges, state and federal, and only the latter could be secured by federal action (*Slaughter-House Cases* 1873). The Supreme Court thereby left the protection of the rights of

CIVIL RIGHTS ACT OF 1866

"All persons born in the United States . . . are hereby declared to be citizens of the United States; and such citizens, of every race and color . . . shall have the same right . . . to full and equal benefit of all laws and proceedings for the security of person and property, as is enjoyed by white citizens, and shall be subject to like punishment, pains, and penalties, and to none other."

African-Americans to legislatures and courts that were quickly becoming filled with ex-Confederates, ex-successionists, and racists. "In the late nineteenth century, the Court devised several doctrines and attitudes that resulted in a further erosion of the constitutional status of black people. This erosion occurred especially in three areas: voting, jury service, and public accommodations" (Wiecek 1988: 101). To provide African-Americans with equal access to public accommodations, Congress passed the Civil Rights Act of 1875, which ruled unconstitutional in the *Civil Rights Cases* of 1883. Despite its infamous past, the *Civil Rights Cases* would be cited by the Supreme Court majority in 2000 as a precedent for overturning the federal Violence Against Women Act (*United States* v. *Morrison*).

The Reconstruction era ended with the presidential election of 1876, when the last of the radical Republican regimes in the Old Confederacy were ousted, along with the hopes of black Americans in the South (Orth 1987). By 1900, the Fourteenth Amendment "had virtually ceased to shield blacks against discriminatory action" (Gerber 1981: 144).

BUSINESS, UNIONS, AND CIVIL LIBERTIES

It is of historical importance to note that the Bill of Rights (the first 10 amendments to the Constitution) was intended to apply only to the federal government (although many states had similar clauses in their constitutions, none were as extensive as those of the Constitution).

From the decision in *Barron* v. *Baltimore* (1833) until the ratification of the Fourteenth Amendment (1868), the Supreme Court held that none of the rights in the Bill of Rights limited the states, and there is continuing controversy over whether or not the Fourteenth Amendment was meant to apply the Bill of Rights to the states (see, for example, Berger 1977; Abraham and Perry 1994). "From 1868 to 1925 [the Court] found very few of these liberties protected from state action. Those the states were free to flout (so far as federal limitations were concerned) seemed to include free speech, press, religion, the right to jury trial, freedom from self-incrimination, from infliction of cruel and unusual punishment, and more. State constitutions, with their own bills of rights, were available to protect the individual, but too often proved to be paper barriers" (Curtis 1986: 1). This was exemplified by the *Slaughter-House Cases*.

Like many phrases in the Constitution, the wording of the Fourteenth Amendment allows for a variety of interpretations, and what is meant by "privileges or immunities of citizens of the United States" has been subject to vigorous debate. In a case alleging the unconstitutional nature of the granting of a slaughter-house

BARRON v. *BALTIMORE* (1833)

"These Amendments [Bill of Rights] contain no expression indicating an intention to apply them to the state governments. This court cannot so apply them."

monopoly by the Reconstructionist government of Louisiana, in 1873 the Supreme Court ruled: "[B]eyond the very few express limitations which the Federal Constitution imposed upon the states—such, for instance, as the prohibition against ex post facto laws, bills of attainder, and laws impairing the obligation of contracts . . . and a few other restrictions, the entire domain of the privileges and immunities of citizens of the states . . . lay within the constitutional and legislative power of the states."

Slowly, and over a long period of time, the Court began to apply these rights to the states. Ironically, they served to protect conservative business interests against legislative enactments designed to improve the conditions of workers. In an era swimming with legislative reforms, the judiciary remained a bastion of conservatives from the prosperous stratum of society. And it was to them that the owners of property turned for aid and protection. For these wealthy businessmen, the Fourteenth Amendment would prove to be a form of deliverance: "nor shall any State deprive any person of life, liberty, or property without due process of law." "Due process of law after the Civil War had two meanings—one procedural, the other substantive. The second stirred controversy. The phrase *substantive due process* meant that there existed an irreducible sum of rights that vested in the individual and could not be unreasonably or arbitrarily interfered with; this meant there were substantive limits on what legislatures could do" (Hall 1989: 26).

The Court decided it had the power to address the reasonableness of legislative interference with these rights, to determine if the rather vague doctrine of *substantive due process* had been improperly abridged—a judgment call with important policy implications.

> The Fourteenth Amendment had been adopted after the Civil War to assure the rights of the liberated slaves. But in a series of decisions from the Seventies on, the courts spelled out the doctrine that *any person* might also mean any corporate body, company, or association; and *property* might mean business or the profits of business. The courts, by interpreting the Fourteenth Amendment this way, opened the door to a long line of attacks on state laws that governed wages, hours, safety provisions, and the like— because such laws increased the cost of doing business and thus ate into the employer's "property." (Todd 1968: 9)

"Substantive due process became the Court's single most important doctrinal base for exercising the power of judicial review" (Hall 1989: 27). The Court's narrow construction of the Fourteenth Amendment when the case involved the civil rights of African-Americans must be contrasted with the Court's extension of the Fourteenth Amendment to protect corporate America (Schwartz 1993). A "constitutional amendment designed to protect the rights of liberated Negro slaves, became an instrument for the exploitation of industrial wage slaves" (Todd 1968: 9). Congress enacted legislation expanding the power of the federal judiciary with respect to federal laws in general, and civil rights in particular. However, despite Court rulings under Marshall, during Reconstruction the federal courts refused to sustain an action against a state official administering an unconstitutional law, on the grounds that the Eleventh Amendment prohibited such suits. "In a break with tradition, the Court held that it was without jurisdiction over a wide variety of suits against states" (Orth 1987: 58). Between 1875 and 1885, state governments, particularly in the South, used this shield and passed unconstitutional legislation to nullify debt obligations, "which profoundly disturbed the conservative elements of the community" (Warren 1966: 942). The Supreme Court, conservatives argued, should be able to compel a state to pay its debts.

This wide interpretation of the Eleventh Amendment would prove disastrous to the credit ratings of Southern states, many of which repudiated debts during the Reconstruction era. Bondholders were unable to sue in state courts, and their claims were barred in federal court. "It is one of the neglected ironies of history that federal judges firmly committed to the protection of property countenanced the repudiation of millions of dollars' worth of Southern bonds. Still more ironic, Southern courtroom victories were won by arguing the cause of state sovereignty within a generation of the military defeat of that principle in the Civil War" (Orth 1987: 8–9). While the rest of the country was undergoing industrialization and urbanization, the South was unable to finance industry by borrowing and reverted to an antebellum cash-crop economy.

As state governments fell under the sway of Populists and (later) Progressives who favored farmers and workers over banking and business interests, the Supreme Court reacted. In 1885, in *Poindexter* v. *Greenhow*, the Court "made a clear distinction between a suit against a State or a State official to compel it or him to perform an obligation of the State, and a suit against a State official to recover damages for an act performed in carrying out an unconstitutional State law." The Court, as it had under Marshall, ruled that "no official could claim an exemption from personal responsibility for acts committed under such an invalid law" (Warren 1966: 943). In an extension of *Poindexter*, the Court ruled in 1909 (*Ex parte Young*) that the Eleventh Amendment does not bar a suit against a state official where a violation of constitutional rights is alleged and that the sovereign immunity enjoyed by state officials is nullified when, under "color of law," they violate civil rights. When a state officer acts in violation of the Constitution, the official thereby loses "official capacity," making him or her, and not the state, liable for the official's actions. Since the state is not a defendant, the claim can be heard in federal court. These precedents have provided the basis for contemporary federal equity suits against public officials.

The increase in commerce and industry following the Civil War, and fears of state-court parochialism ("hometown decisions"), lent support to increasing the role of the federal judiciary at the expense of state courts. During the immediate postwar years there were important cases concerning currency laws and disputes between the states and the railroads. In what became a trend, the Court ruled in favor of business and against organized labor.

English common law, the "Tudor Industrial Code," considered any combination of workers to improve wages or conditions of employment as a criminal conspiracy, and this usage entered American law as a prohibition against any restraint of trade by workers acting in concert (Woodiwiss 1990). During the nineteenth century, until the time of the Civil War, the criminal conspiracy doctrine was used against labor organizations. This approach was subsequently replaced by the use of equity in the form of an injunction restraining the civil, rather than the criminal, aspects of organized labor (Blumrosen 1962). Injunctions deprived workers of their First, Sixth, and Eighth Amendment protections. Wiecek explains how the process worked: "A United States attorney hostile to unions and seeking to break a strike would find a sympathetic federal judge and persuade him to issue an injunction, often in an ex parte [only the plaintiff present] hearing. The injunction would restrain not only violence and concerted refusal to work, but also rights of speech, press, and assembly" (1988: 122). A failure to abide by the injunction would result in the union members being summarily imprisoned for contempt. This equity procedure permitted the plaintiff to avoid a trial by jury whose members might prove sympathetic to the strikers.

"Nineteenth and early-twentieth-century lawyers," Archibald Cox points out, "lived almost entirely in the world of business, finance, and property. It is unlikely that many of them could as judges wholly slough off the premises of their earlier years of private practice, whatever their effort to achieve detachment" (1987: 135). "The professional lives of the bar elite increasingly isolated them from other classes to the extent that they were able to create unreal images of the dangerous tendencies lurking outside their select social circle" (Hobson 1986: 68). In 1909, for example, the Populist government of Kansas enacted a law prohibiting "yellow dog" contracts, which required a prospective employee to agree to not join a labor union. The Supreme Court found the legislation unconstitutional because the worker was not coerced—he could forgo employment (*Coppage* v. *Kansas* 1914).

In the decades following the Civil War, when the powerless attempted to make the Constitution and the law work for them, "they found the constitutional high ground already occupied by powerful business interests, which were supported by the middle class and both political parties and backed by the military authority of the state. Buttressing the conservative legal structure was the Supreme Court under Chief Justices Morrison Waite [1874–1888] and Melville Fuller [1888–1910], which moved boldly to make the Fourteenth Amendment serve business but refused to make it work for the black Americans for whom it was intended. Business consolidated with the blessings of the law; labor's attempt to organize and bargain was opposed by an impressive array of legal stratagems" (Newmyer 1987: 814).

The Supreme Court transformed judicial review into a defense not so much of the Constitution but of a particular version of natural law: that is, natural rights, particularly property rights. With support from the legal profession, the Court "adopted a particular understanding of the property rights guaranteed by natural law, that of 'laissez-faire' capitalism. On the basis of that political philosophy, it struck down many attempts to regulate economic affairs in the period from 1890 to 1937" (Wolfe 1986: 4). The Supreme Court used the Fourteenth Amendment to create a national citizenship, "fitted it out with 'privileges and immunities,'

TAKING SIDES

"A Court committed by its tradition to the cause of property rights, composed of judges who were inevitably drawn largely from the ranks of the 'haves' and who were of course by definition lawyers and thus imbued with the conservative bias that has always characterized the American legal fraternity—such a Court was almost certain to throw its weight against the regulatory movement and on the side of the business community." (McClosky 1994: 69).

and placed this heritage from times of old beyond the power of the state government." According to the Court, "these privileges and immunities are nothing other than the natural rights of man"(Hamilton 1999: 7). From 1898 to 1937, the Court handed down 401 rulings invalidating state legislation; more than half relied on the Fourteenth Amendment. As Charles Hoffer points out: "The Supreme Court's decisions in labor, taxation, hours and safety regulation, and a host of other cases demonstrated antipathy to the claims of workers, reformers, and the local governments they had captured. Powerful minds on the bench made very creative use of law to defend corporate accumulation of wealth and power" (1990: 159). "It furnished the legal tools to further the period's galloping industrialism and ensure that public power would give free play to the unrestrained capitalism of the era" (Schwartz 1993: 174).

Organized labor sought relief from Congress, but the Supreme Court (*Adair* v. *United States* 1908) declared that Congress had no power with respect to union activities. It was not until 1932 and the Great Depression that Congress stripped the federal courts of their power to issue injunctions in labor disputes (Norris–La Guardia Act). In 1935, the Wagner (National Labor Relations) Act provided explicit protection to the rights of workers to organize and created an affirmative duty on the part of employers to engage in collective bargaining. The statute was declared constitutional by the Supreme Court in 1937 (*National Labor Relations Board [NLRB]* v. *Jones and Laughlin Steel Corporation*), which offered a more expansive view of the commerce clause than heretofore.

Congress voted to impose a federal income tax, but the Court ruled it unconstitutional (*Pollock* v. *Farmer's Loan and Trust Co.* 1895); this brought about the Sixteenth Amendment, which became part of the Constitution in 1913. In 1883, the Court again upheld the sanctity of property rights when it ruled that Congress did not have the power to outlaw racial discrimination in private accommodations. An 1875 statute that granted blacks equal access with whites to inns, theaters, and public transportation was declared unconstitutional (*Civil Rights Cases* 1883). As a result, eight states enacted legislation requiring railroads to maintain separate facilities for whites and blacks. In 1896, a seven-judge majority (*Plessy* v. *Ferguson*) ensured that the Fourteenth Amendment would be of little value to African-Americans when it ruled that a Louisiana law that mandated "equal but separate accommodations for the white and colored races" on all railroad cars was reasonable. One justice did not vote, and John Marshall Harlan, ironically a former Kentucky slave-owner, offered a powerful dissent: "Our Constitution is color blind,

NLRB v. JONES AND LAUGHLIN STEEL CORPORATION, 1937

"Although activities may be intrastate in character when separately considered, if they have such a close and substantial relation to interstate commerce that their control is essential or appropriate to protect that commerce from burdens and obstructions, Congress cannot be denied the power to exercise that control."

Sherman Antitrust Act (1890)

"Every person who shall monopolize, or attempt to monopolize, or combine or conspire with any person or persons to monopolize any part of the trade or commerce among the several States, or with foreign nations, shall be deemed guilty of a misdemeanor." The act does not define key terms such as "attempt to monopolize," leaving interpretation to the courts.

and neither knows nor tolerates classes among citizens."[8] Nevertheless, the doctrine of "separate but equal" received the blessing of the Supreme Court and remained the controlling decision in race relations until 1954. (For a full discussion of this case and its implications, see Lofgren 1987.)

During this period, state and federal judges routinely involved themselves in the formulation of public policy, substituting their policy choices for those of legislators. And these efforts were supported by bar association leaders allied with corporate America: "In the 1890s lawyers looked to the courts to act for the party of reason, order, and property and to restrain the parties of passion, ignorance, democracy, and socialism" (Hobson 1986: 34). In 1895 the Supreme Court refused to let stand a criminal prosecution of the American Refining Company for Sherman Act antitrust law violations, despite the fact that this Sugar Trust controlled almost all of the sugar refining in the country (*United States* v. *E.C. Knight & Co.*). During that same term, the Court unanimously upheld the issuance of an injunction against the American Railway Union under the Sherman Act (*In Re Debs*); this, despite assurances by the statute's sponsor, Senator John Sherman (R–OH), that it would have no effect on workers (Eskridge 1994). However, "while the courts trimmed many regulatory efforts, they left in place major pieces of federal legislation and retained for the state legislatures important, if somewhat hollow, authority to deal with economic matters" (Hall 1989: 238). (For an examination of nineteenth century state and local government regulation in the economy, public safety, and public health, see Novak 1996.)

A POLICY-MAKING JUDICIARY

After the turn of the century, Supreme Court rulings began to support the efforts of government in dealing with the giant trusts, such as Rockefeller's Standard Oil (*Standard Oil of New Jersey* v. *United States* 1911), whose restraint of trade was undermining capitalism, "and in this era the Court also handed down numerous decisions supporting state and federal efforts to protect workers" (Wiecek 1988: 126). The basic probusiness thrust of the Court continued, however, and in 1905

---

[8]For a biography of this "judicial enigma," see Yarbrough (1995).

five of the nine justices of the Supreme Court, contrary to the Court's decision in the *Slaughter-House Cases*, held that an 1897 New York statute providing maximum hours for bakers was unconstitutional. The law violated the Fourteenth Amendment and interfered with the baker's right to "liberty of contract" because the baker might want to work more than 60 hours a week (*Lochner* v. *New York* 1905).[9] In his famous dissent, Justice Oliver Wendell Holmes, Jr., argued that "liberty of contract" is not found in the Constitution, but was a concept created by judges. He accused his colleagues of embracing the social Darwinist philosophy of Herbert Spencer. The Constitution, he wrote, "is not intended to embody a particular economic theory, whether of paternalism and the organic relation of the citizen to the State or of laissez-faire." While Holmes himself was a supporter of free market economics and expressed support for the social Darwinist view (Novick 1989; Alschuler 2000; *Buck* v. *Bell*, 1927), he favored a system that allowed labor and capital to compete without judicial intervention that typically favored business (Wall 1981; Cosgrove 1987). Southern conservatives criticized *Lochner* on the basis of "states' rights" (Wall 1981).

In 1918 and again in 1922, the Court ruled that federal laws prohibiting child labor were unconstitutional–the right of young boys to work in coal mines and young girls in textile mills was upheld (*Hammer* v. *Dagenhart*; *Bailey* v. *Drexel Furniture Co.*). "If a ten-year-old child wants to work twelve hours a day in a textile mill, by what warrant is the legislature empowered to deprive the child's parents of their right to enter into such a contract on his behalf?" (Gilmore 1977: 63). In 1924, a frustrated Congress countered by attempting to amend the Constitution, a failed effort that was ratified by 28 states (Hall, Wiecek, and Finkelman 1991). It was not until 1941 that the Court reversed these child labor decisions (*United States* v. *Darby Lumber Co.*).

The Court's willingness to support laissez-faire economic rights, states Rogers Smith, stemmed from a variety of political, legal, and intellectual influences of the late nineteenth century. "Common law traditions, the legacy of Adam Smith's [1723–1790] economic liberalism, and the social Darwinism of Herbert Spencer [1820–1903] and William Graham Sumner [1840–1910] were combined into a legal ideology that justified opposition to the extensive reform legislation of the Populist and Progressive eras on higher law grounds." This involved "significant revisions in the natural law theories of the early liberals, but they appealed to those theories to justify their reading of the Constitution as intended to protect economic liberties" (1985: 75–76). Social Darwinism also played a role in legal decisions that supported segregation (Lofgren 1987), and the Court was criticized for using the Fourteenth Amendment to invalidate a state law protecting workers while restricting that same amendment so as to uphold a Kentucky statute requiring segregation even in private colleges (Wall 1981).

Kermit Hall argues that although the courts during these years are often portrayed as reactionary supporters of laissez-faire, their behavior was more complex than the stereotype suggests: "Appellate judges did invoke laissez-faire principles in a few celebrated cases, but in most instances state and federal courts 'moved

---

[9]In 1917, *Lochner* was overturned and the constitutionality of the ten-hour law upheld in *Bunting* v. *Oregon*. For a discussion of *Lochner*, see Kens (1990).

*S*OCIAL *D*ARWINISM

"Darwin's theory of natural selection supplied the conceptual ammunition for an ideology (later labeled as social Darwinism) which allayed the qualms of the rich about not helping the poor by telling them that the latter's sufferings were an inevitable price which could occur only through the struggle for existence ending in the survival of the fittest and the elimination of the unfit" (Andreski 1971: 26).

While Charles Darwin's (1809–1882) first book (*Origin of Species* 1859) was concerned exclusively with nonhuman organisms, his second (*Descent of Man* 1871) included humanity as being shaped by the forces of *natural selection*. According to Yale professor William Graham Sumner (1840–1910) "the truth is that the social order is fixed by laws of nature precisely analogous to those of the physical order" (1992: 172). Along with the English philosopher Herbert Spencer (1820–1903), Sumner applied Darwin to social evolution, a progressive phenomenon based on the "survival of the fittest" (Spencer 1961). This mitigates against activities on behalf of those who are "inferior," thereby providing a doctrine for persons who opposed governmental intervention on behalf of the downtrodden. "Whatever you do for any of the petted [poverty] classes wastes capital" (Sumner 1992: 222), while "the quality of a society is lowered morally and intellectually, by the artificial preservation of those who are least able to take care of themselves" (Spencer 1961: 313). For a discussion of social Darwinism, see Degler (1991).

consistently toward approval of a wide range of reform legislation' which although occasionally delayed in the courts, [was] not blocked there" (1989: 226; see also Wolfe 1986). And Joseph Wall (1981) denies that the *Lochner* Court was acting out of a philosophy of social Darwinism, as opposed to older concepts of laissez-faire and property rights (see also Schwartz 1993).

POLITICAL DISSENT

While the Court continued to provide protection for economic liberties, it had no difficulty denying other forms of liberty. "Beginning in 1895 the Court set itself as a bulwark against disorder from any source," particularly unions and political radicals (Gerber 1981: 181). In a unanimous decision the Court upheld the conviction of Eugene V. Debs and members of the Socialist party who, during World War I, campaigned against the draft, and it supported convictions in similar anti-free speech cases tried under the Sedition Act of 1918. In a decision written for one of these cases (*Schenck* v. *United States* 1919), Justice Holmes elaborated on the limitations of free speech: "The most stringent protection of free speech would not protect a man falsely shouting fire in a theater and causing a panic." Thus, "the question in every [First Amendment] case is whether the words used are in such circumstances as to create a clear and present danger that they will bring about the substantive evils that Congress has a right to prevent." In this case, "when a nation is at war many things that might be said in time of peace are such a hindrance to its effort that their utterance will not be endured." As a result "little constitutional protection was left for wartime critics of government policies" (Cox 1987: 219). Later that year, Holmes began to alter his opinion on free speech in favor of more liberal interpretations (*Abrams* v. *United States* 1919; also *Gitlow* v. *New York* 1925, which applied First Amendment protection to the states via the Fourteenth Amendment).[10]

During the 1920s, the attack on political dissidents shifted from Socialists to Communists, and the Supreme Court upheld the convictions of members of the Communist Labor party because their platform advocated syndicalism–a worker takeover and control of the means of production (Cox 1987). While the Court reined in on the rights of political "offenders," it began to expand the due process protections of criminal defendants. In cases that involved black sharecroppers who, in 1919, believing they had been cheated, rioted in Arkansas, the Court ruled for the defendants, declaring an obligation to ensure that criminal defendants received a fair trial in state courts. And in 1932, the Court decided the famous case of the "Scottsboro Boys." In 1931, nine black youths were arrested in Scottsboro, Alabama, and charged with raping two white girls on a freight train. They were found guilty in three trials that received international attention, and their convictions were twice reversed by the Supreme Court, which ruled that if a defendant in a capital case lacks an attorney and a fairly chosen jury, he or she cannot be convicted under law (*Powell* v. *Alabama* 1932; see Goodman 1994 for a historical examination of this case).

THE DEPRESSION

In 1929, the stock market collapsed and the Great Depression quickly ensued. Millions of Americans were unemployed, farmers were forced off their lands, and the economy was in ruins. In 1932, Franklin D. Roosevelt was elected president and enjoyed an overwhelmingly Democratic Congress. With New Deal inspiration, Congress enacted a series of laws designed to provide emergency relief for farmers, coal miners, and the unemployed. In a series of decisions denounced as "judicial activism" (an issue discussed in Chapter 8), the Supreme Court, seven of whose members had been appointed by Republican presidents, ruled these statutes unconstitutional.

The Depression was not limited to the United States—on its heels Hitler came to power in Germany. Radicals such as the "Radio Priest" Charles E. Coughlin[11] of Royal Oak, Michigan and Senator Huey P. Long[12] of Louisiana were gaining considerable followings in the United States, and "nine old men," appealing to the principles of natural law, were supporting the status quo. Between January 1935 and May 1936, twelve major pieces of New Deal legislation were ruled unconstitutional (Murphy 1986).[13] While Roosevelt was reelected by a landslide in 1936—Republican Alfred

---

[10]For a discussion of the "clear and present danger" issue, see Kessler (1993).

[11]See Warren (1996) for an examination of the Father Coughlin phenomenon.

[12]See Williams (1969) for a biography of the "Kingfish."

[13]New Deal lawyers were aware that much of their legislation was probably unconstitutional. They went ahead anyway, "based on a tacit understanding that in order to enhance recovery one had to operate, at least to some extent, outside the established boundaries of constitutional discourse" (Shamir 1995: 16; see also White 2000).

Landon won only Maine and Vermont—and Democrats took more than 75 percent of the seats in Congress, the Supreme Court remained a bulwark against legislative efforts to respond to the Depression.

The Court was attacked by judicial/legal realists[14] "who dismissed notions of natural law limits on governmental policies and methods as 'transcendental nonsense'" (Smith 1985: 78). Generally, the realists argued for a more utilitarian version of judicial lawmaking, although there was some disagreement over limitations that could be placed on government activity by the judiciary. It took a dramatic confrontation between the President and the Court to produce agreement that the rights of property and contract were not absolute.

Court-Packing Plan

Since 1789, Congress had changed the number of justices several times: from nine to seven in 1807, nine in 1837, ten in 1864, and back to nine in 1867. On February 5, 1937, the President asked Congress for the power to appoint an additional justice whenever a sitting member of the Court reached the age of 70 and did not resign, with the upper limit being 15 members. In 1937, six justices were over 70. Roosevelt at first based his legislation on the need to help senior justices carry out their responsibilities. In a radio speech ("Fireside Chat") on March 9, 1937, the president took a different approach, criticizing the Court for obstructionism: "I want—as all Americans want—an independent judiciary as proposed by the framers of the Constitution. That means a Supreme Court that will enforce the Constitution as written—that will refuse to amend the Constitution by the arbitrary exercise of judicial power—amendment by judicial say-so. It does not mean a judiciary so independent that it can deny the existence of facts universally recognized." Roosevelt argued that the Court had usurped the legislative function by "reading into the Constitution words and implications which are not there, and which were never intended to be there." The President promised to appoint justices "who will act as justices and not as legislators." (Similar sentiments against alleged "judicial activism" have been voiced by contemporary critics on the right, discussed in Chapter 8.)

The reaction to Roosevelt's "Court-packing" plan was overwhelmingly negative. Even congressional opponents of the Court did not want to tinker with tradition. On April 12, the Court reversed a previous position and ruled an important piece of New Deal legislation (the Wagner Labor Relations Act) as constitutional, and it backed away from a previous position on the constitutionality of minimum-wage legislation.[15] Shortly thereafter, a New Deal opponent announced that he was resigning from the Court, apparently in an attempt to influence the congressional vote (Rehnquist 1987). Later that same day, the Senate Judiciary Committee voted against the Court-packing legislation, and with Senate support waning, the bill was withdrawn by the administration. "In March 1937, with startling speed, the Court virtually adopted a whole new set of constitutional precedents" (Murphy 1986: 14).

[14]Judicial and legal realism are discussed in Chapter 4.
[15]In *West Coast Hotel* v. *Parrish* (1937) the Court upheld a Washington state minimum wage law for women and, "in doing so, announced their intention to disengage from further scrutiny of economic regulatory legislation on substantive due process grounds" (Hall 1989: 29).

Without a change in the total number of justices, the President soon enjoyed a Supreme Court majority that upheld the constitutionality of his legislation. Within four years, he was able to name six new justices. "By the end of the 1930s, federal authority had reached a new height. New grounds for executive power had been sanctioned. Previously limiting concepts like liberty of contract, economic due process, and strict commerce and taxing limitations had been rejected. The Court endorsed government regulation of the economy and approved changes in federal–state relations that increased government power and extended it into a variety of new areas" (Murphy 1986: 15).

In 1939, Roosevelt's Senate opponents saw an opportunity to strike back: Felix Frankfurter, the President's choice to succeed retiring justice Louis Brandeis, was required to appear in person at his confirmation hearings—the first time this was ever done. Frankfurter, a professor at Harvard Law School and presidential advisor, established what has now become routine for Court nominees: He refused to discuss how he might decide specific matters that might come before the Court (Zobel 1991). Frankfurter served until his retirement in 1962 and, despite his pre-appointment political liberalism, came to support judicial restraint: In his view, when exercising the power of judicial review, Supreme Court justices act as legislators and, as unelected officials, should therefore act with restraint (Wolfe 1986). This view enabled New Deal legislation to remain largely intact.

In the years leading up to America's entry into the Second World War, Democratic leaders were unwilling to advance the cause of black Americans for fear of alienating the southern wing of the party. The Supreme Court, however, handed down a series of rulings in favor of African-Americans, particularly in the area of education (Murphy 1986).

AMERICA AT WAR

As war raged in Europe and American involvement loomed large, the Supreme Court ruled 8–1 that public school students (Jehovah's Witnesses) who refused to salute the flag or participate in the pledge of allegiance (which they considered a violation of the Second Commandment) could be expelled (*Minersville School District* v. *Gobitis* 1940). In the wake of this decision, Witnesses were subjected to brutal mob attacks and police harassment. In the midst of the Second World War, the Court repudiated the *Gobitis* decision (*West Virginia Board of Education* v. *Barnette* 1943) with a telling comment: "If there is any fixed star in our constitutional constellation, it is that no official, high or petty, can prescribe what shall be orthodox in politics, nationalism, or religion, or other matters of opinion or force citizens to confess by word or act their faith therein." (In 1989, in a 5–4 decision [*Texas* v. *Johnson*] that cut across the Court's usual ideological lines, Justice William J. Brennen, Jr. cited *Barnette* in ruling that burning the American flag as part of a protest demonstration was protected by the First Amendment.)

In 1944, in a 6–3 decision, the Court upheld a relocation order for Americans of Japanese ancestry (*Korematsu* v. *United States* 1944), although no similar action had been taken against German-Americans or Italian-Americans. In his biting dissent, Justice Robert Jackson noted that being in a locality "was made a crime only if his parents were of Japanese birth. Had Korematsu been one of four—the others being, say, a German alien enemy, and Italian alien enemy, and a citizen of American-born ancestors, convicted of treason but out on parole—only Korematsu's presence would have violated the order."[16]

In 1951, the United Steel Workers Union demanded a raise, which the steel companies were unwilling to grant because they had been prohibited from raising prices by the Office of Price Stabilization; it was the era of the Korean War and there was fear of inflation. A strike that would impact on the war effort was set for April 9, 1952, and President Harry S. Truman reacted. By executive order, on April 8 he had the Secretary of Commerce seize the steel mills. In response to a legal action by the steel owners, a federal district court ruled against the government. The rules of the Supreme Court permit a losing litigant to petition the Supreme Court for an immediate hearing that is granted "only upon a showing that the case is of such imperative public importance as to justify deviation from normal appellate processes and to require immediate settlement in this Court" (Rehnquist 1987: 55). This extraordinary case received such a grant—*certiorari before judgment*.[17] In a 6–3 decision (*Youngstown Sheet and Tube Co., et al.* v. *Sawyer* 1952), the Court ruled that the President had acted beyond his constitutional authority, and Truman immediately ordered the Secretary of Commerce to return control of the mills to their owners. (For a detailed look at this case, see Westin 1990.)

In his very personal history of the Supreme Court, William H. Rehnquist argues that justices cannot isolate themselves from public opinion: "We read newspapers and magazines, we watch news on television, we talk to our friends about current events. No judge worthy of his salt would ever cast his vote in a particular case because he thought the majority of the public wanted him to vote that way, but that is quite a different thing from saying that no judge is ever influenced by the great tides of public opinion that run in a country such as ours. Judges are influenced by them, and I think that such influence played an appreciable part in causing the Steel Seizure Case to be decided the way it was" (1987: 98).

YOUNGSTOWN SHEET AND TUBE CO., ET AL. v. *SAWYER* (1952)

"The President's power, if any, to issue the order must stem either from an act of Congress or from the Constitution itself. There is no statute that expressly authorizes the President to take possession of property as he did here. . . . In the framework of our Constitution, the President's power to see that the laws are faithfully executed refutes the idea that he is to be a lawmaker. The Constitution limits his functions in the lawmaking process to the recommending of laws he thinks wise and the vetoing of laws he thinks bad. And the Constitution is neither silent nor equivocal about who shall make laws which the President is to execute."

---

[16]For an analysis (and defense) of *Korematsu* by the Chief Justice of the United States, see Rehnquist (1999).

[17]During a period of less than one year, some 300 federal district court judges had to address a major constitutional issue with respect to the federal Sentencing Reform Act. In response, the Supreme Court granted *certiorari before judgment* in the case of *Mistretta* v. *United States* (1989).

POLITICAL DISSENT, CIVIL RIGHTS, AND THE DUE PROCESS REVOLUTION

In the post-World War II/Korean War era there was a renewed attack on political dissidents by the House Un-American Activities Committee (whose first chairman, Martin Dies, sought to rid the government of communists, radicals, fascists, crackpots, and internationalists) and by Senator Joseph McCarthy of Wisconsin. "Loyalty oaths" and being "soft on communism" were the buzz words. At first the Court came down on the side of the anticommunist orthodoxy, but by the late 1950s and early 1960s there was a shift toward protecting the rights of dissidents (Cox 1987), which became intertwined with the civil rights movement.

The Civil Rights Movement

Linda Carol Brown, eight years old, had to cross a railroad yard in Topeka, Kansas, to reach a bus that would take her to a school 21 blocks away. There was another school five blocks away from her home, but it admitted only white children. Her father appealed to the federal courts which, in accord with *stare decisis*, ruled against him; the doctrine of separate but equal had been upheld by the Supreme Court in *Plessy* v. *Ferguson*. When the case (and three others from Delaware, South Carolina, and Virginia) reached the Supreme Court, a unanimous decision resulted (*Brown* v. *Board of Education of Topeka, Kansas* 1954). The Court found that equity required the abrogation of school segregation: "*Brown* was and remains the greatest 'equity' suit in our country's history" (Hoffer 1990: 4).

In equity cases, Hoffer points out, "the petitioner seeks fair play. The court probes deeply into the reality of social harms and tries to make the world whole. Defendants are given time and assistance to act in good faith, for the object is not to punish or deprive wrongdoers but to promote mutual justice" (1990: 180). Without rejecting the precedent of "separate but equal" established in *Plessy*, the Court, using controversial sociological and psychological evidence, held that "separate educational facilities are inherently unequal."[18] (See Patterson 2001). Instead of ordering immediate desegregation of all public schools, the Court used the phrase "with all deliberate speed," which served to encourage the South to respond with resistance and delay. In the years that followed, however, the Court summarily invalidated a host of other laws requiring segregation in public facilities and interstate commerce.

The Supreme Court, as the least democratic of our branches of government, is able to render unpopular decisions to support the interests of white people against the "natural rights" of persons of color, or the rights of employers against the interests of children, or in support of business against the overwhelming wishes of Congress and the President. It can also insist that, no matter how strong the opposition, black persons have *all* of the rights of white persons. But the Court has no powers of enforcement. As Alexander Hamilton wrote (*Federalist* No. 78), the Supreme Court is *the least dangerous branch*, having neither the "power of the purse nor

---

[18]It was obvious that segregation was designed to keep blacks in a subservient position, but the Court chose not to focus on this "political" reality (Posner 1995). Indeed, the average per student investment in Atlanta, which was typical across the South, was $570 for white children and $228 for black children (Menand 2001).

JEFFERSON IN OPPOSITION

"[T]he opinion which gives to the judges the right to decide what laws are constitutional and what not, not only for themselves in their own sphere of action but for the Legislature and Executive also in their spheres, would make the Judiciary a despotic branch."

—*Thomas Jefferson to Abigail Adams, 1804.* (University of Virginia Online Resources)

the sword." The judicial branch is totally dependent on the other branches, particularly the executive, to carry out its mandates. The President even appoints the U.S. marshals who are responsible for enforcing orders of federal courts. This has been a problem on a number of occasions.

President Andrew Jackson refused to enforce an order of the Court designed to protect the federal treaty rights of the Cherokee Nation against their violation by the state of Georgia. Jackson's attitude toward the Court had been expressed in 1832, when he granted the Court "only such influence as the force of their reasoning may deserve" (Veto of the Bank Bill, July 10). In a Maryland case (*Ex parte Merryman* 1861), on the eve of the Civil War, a writ of habeas corpus issued by (proslavery) Chief Justice Taney was defied by military authorities acting under an executive order from President Lincoln. "The lack of any formal connection to the electorate and its rather demonstrable vulnerability before the president and Congress mean that the United States Supreme Court must depend to an extraordinary extent on the confidence, or at least the acquiescence, of the public" (Caldeira 1986: 1209).

In 1957, Governor Orval Faubus of Arkansas defied a federal district court order based on *Brown* and called out the National Guard to prevent nine black students from entering Little Rock High School. An angry mob of whites surrounded the school. After several weeks of indecision, the National Guard was put under federal command and President Eisenhower ordered the U.S. Army's 101st ("Screaming Eagles") Airborne Division into Little Rock—however reluctantly, the decisions of the Supreme Court would be upheld. (Many of the briefs and case records for *Brown* can be found in Whitman 1993.)

BROWN v. BOARD OF EDUCATION (1954)

"Does segregation of children in public schools solely on the basis of race, even though the physical facilities and other 'tangible' factors may be equal, deprive the children of the minority group of equal education opportunities? We believe that it does. . . . To separate from others of similar age and qualifications solely because of their race generates a feeling of inferiority as to their status in the community that may affect their hearts and minds in a way unlikely ever to be undone."

Due Process Revolution

During the 1960s, the Court handed down a series of landmark (and highly controversial) due process decisions. In 1914, the Court (in *Weeks* v. *United States*) had ruled that evidence obtained in violation of the Fourth Amendment's prohibition against illegal search and seizure was not admissible in federal criminal cases. This decision established the *exclusionary rule*, and in 1961 (*Mapp* v. *Ohio*), the Court, citing the Fourteenth Amendment, extended the rule to state criminal cases. The Court recognized that the exclusionary rule (discussed in Chapter 10) would sometimes have the effect, as Supreme Court Justice Benjamin Cardozo had noted generations earlier, of permitting the criminal to go free because the constable had blundered. However, the Court also recognized the potential for a greater evil: unbridled police powers. In the *Mapp* decision the justices said, "we can no longer permit it [the due process clause] to be revocable at the whim of any police officer who, in the name of law enforcement chooses to suspend its enjoyment." In 1963, the Court ruled in *Gideon* v. *Wainwright* that the states must provide counsel for all indigents in felony cases, and in 1966 the Court determined (*Miranda* v. *Arizona*) that prior to questioning, the police must warn a suspect of the right to remain silent. (Due process is discussed at length in Chapter 10.)

Other Warren Court Decisions

Even as the populations of many states shifted from rural to urban, state legislatures remained dominated by rural voters because of a practice known as *gerrymandering*:[19] legislative districts were drawn in such a fashion that less populated rural areas had more legislators than heavily populated urban areas. In 1962, 1963, and 1964, the Court initiated a legislative revolution in the United States when it determined that legislative and congressional districts had to have populations that are roughly equal: "one person, one vote" (*Baker* v. *Carr*; *Gray* v. *Sanders*; *Wesberry* v. *Sanders*; *Reynolds* v. *Sims*). Rural domination ceased and Democrats took control of many legislatures in populous states that had heretofore been Republican.

In 1962 and 1963, the Court found prescribed religious ceremonies in public schools unconstitutional (*Engle* v. *Vitale*; *Abington School District* v. *Schempp*). In 1964, the Court ruled that in order for public officials to collect damages for libel, they need to prove actual malice. This decision (*New York Times* v. *Sullivan*) provides important protection for reporters and others writing on public affairs. In 1965, a Connecticut statute prohibiting birth control devices or the providing of information on contraception was ruled unconstitutional. The Court admitted that the statute did not violate any specific guarantee contained in the Bill of Rights. It was, however, contrary to the *right of privacy*, which the Court ruled is implied in the Constitution,

---

[19]Elbridge Gerry (1744–1814) was a signer of the Declaration of Independence, a member of the Constitutional Convention, and Vice President of the United States under James Madison. During his term as governor of Massachusetts, a law was enacted that redrew Senate boundaries in such a way as to ensure domination by Democratic Republicans. One district resembled a salamander, which gave rise to the term "gerrymander."

THE RIGHT TO PRIVACY AND ABORTION

Supporters of *Roe* v. *Wade* claim that the "right to privacy" is implicit in our constitutional tradition and, therefore, the logical implications of that principle regarding free choice are sufficiently clear to justify judicial support of abortion. Critics argue that the abortion issue is not properly subject to judicial authority because the Constitution does not explicitly endorse a "right to privacy" or "freedom of choice" or any other generalized principle that unambiguously provides support for abortion (Burt 1995).

insofar as it involved an intolerable intrusion into the bedroom of married persons (*Griswold* v. *Connecticut*). This case provided the precedent for *Roe* v. *Wade*, the case which struck down laws prohibiting abortion.[20]

The chief justice stepped down, and the era of the Warren Court was over. President Richard M. Nixon chose Warren Burger as chief justice. Nixon was overwhelmingly re-elected in 1972, and one year later there was a confrontation between the executive and judicial branches. The President claimed executive privilege in response to a *subpoena duces tecem*, an order to produce physical evidence, in this case the famous "White House Tapes." In 1974, the Supreme Court, three of whose members and the chief justice had been appointed by Nixon, upheld the rulings of the lower courts requiring the President to submit to sub-poenas issued by Watergate special prosecutors (*United States* v. *Nixon* 1974). Later that year Nixon resigned.

While judicial restraint—that judges should generally defer to legislators who are democratically accountable—was to be the cornerstone of the Burger Court, Stephen Wasby comments that the Court's overall record of invalidating federal and state legislative acts provides evidence of an activist Court, albeit in a more conservative direction (1993). In 1972, the Burger Court found that the then-current capital punishment laws violated the Eighth Amendment's guarantee against "cruel and unusual punishment"—"evolving standards of decency" can render once constitutional behavior unconstitutional (Tushnet 2000). The decision in *Furman* v. *Georgia* stopped executions until 1976, when the Court ruled that statutes imposing capital punishment, if drafted in a certain manner, were constitutional (*Gregg* v. *Georgia*). In 1973, the Court decided (*Roe* v. *Wade*) that state laws prohibiting abortion unconstitutionally restricted personal liberty and the right to privacy guaranteed by the Fourteenth Amendment. (In 1986, however, the Court refused to extend the right of privacy to adults engaging in consensual homosexual acts when it ruled that laws banning such activities were fully within the police powers of the state, *Bowers* v. *Hardwick*). In 1978, by a vote of 5–4, with six separate opinions,

---

[20]In 1989, a bitterly divided Court ruled 5–4 to limit the application of *Roe*. In *Webster* v. *Reproductive Health Services*, the Court upheld a Missouri law that prohibited the use of public funds, facilities, or state medical personnel to perform abortions except to save the life of the mother. The decision also upheld a requirement that doctors determine if a 20-week fetus is viable or capable of living outside of the womb: Missouri law prohibits abortions of a viable fetus.

the Court ruled that the quota system used by the University of California at Davis medical school, which reserved sixteen positions for black, Chicano, and Asian applicants, had unlawfully denied admission to an otherwise qualified applicant, Allan Bakke (*University of California Regents* v. *Bakke*).

The Court also began trimming some of the decisions of the Warren Court that provided extensive due process rights to criminal suspects and prison inmates (see Chapter 10). Associate Justice William J. Brennan, Jr. (1986), recalled that in 1963 the Warren Court sustained 86 percent of the cases involving constitutional issues, while in 1983, the Burger Court sustained only 19 percent of the cases. This led Christopher Wolfe (1986: 297) to conclude: "Fidelity to the original intention of the Constitution and even the coherence of constitutional doctrine (whether or not closely tied to the Constitution) do not seem to be the guiding lights of the Burger Court." In 1986, the Chief Justice stepped down, and President Reagan appointed Associate Justice William Rehnquist, a legal scholar—first in his class at Stanford—guided by issues of strict constructionism, original intent, and judicial restraint (discussed in Chapter 8), to be the Court's 16th chief justice.

As a result of the appointment of Rehnquist and associate justices by presidents Reagan and Bush, the Court took a clear turn toward the right, but without upsetting any significant precedents established by previous Courts. (From 1991 to 1994, there was only one justice who had been appointed by a Democratic president.) For example, in 2000, the Court affirmed the *Miranda* decision by a vote of 7–2 (*Dickerson* v. *United States*).[21] The business community, which supported Republican efforts to move the Court in a more conservative direction, was disappointed: instead of *pro-business*, the conservatism of the Rehnquist Court has been *pro-government* (Savage 1991). This was exemplified by a unanimous decision (*Whitman* v. *American Trucking Associations*, 2001) written by Justice Antonin Scalia in which the Court rejected arguments from industry lawyers attacking enforcement of the Clean Air Act by the Environmental Protection Agency.

With the election of Bill Clinton, appointments to the Supreme Court became decidedly more liberal, and for the first time in history, two women were serving as justices. Nevertheless, a conservative five-member majority has impacted on such areas as affirmative action. In *Adarand Construction* v. *Peña* (1995), the Court raised the legal standard required to invoke race-based criteria: "[W]e hold today that all racial classifications imposed by whatever Federal, state, or local actor, must be analyzed by a reviewing court under strict scrutiny. In other words, such classifications are constitutional only if they are narrowly tailored measures that further compelling government interests." In support of the chief justice's views of (dual?) federalism, the Court has modified the influence of federal courts and the power of Congress to expand federal authority. This was highlighted by several cases.

While conservative jurisprudence stresses deference to the legislative branch, in 1995 the Supreme Court ruled (*United States* v. *Lopez*) that Congress exceeded its authority when it enacted a law—the Gun-Free School Zones Act—making it a *federal* crime to possess a firearm in proximity to a school. In his 1999 annual message on the judiciary, Chief Justice Rehnquist appealed to Congress to refrain

---

[21]The Court held that *Miranda* was a *constitutional* ruling and, therefore, Congress could not supercede *Miranda* by legislative enactment—only a constitutional amendment can undo a constitutional ruling.

from creating federal laws that are redundant with existing state laws. He reprimanded the lawmakers for transforming highly publicized crimes into federal law, reminding Congress that crime and law enforcement fall within the jurisdiction of the state governments. Two decisions in 2000 continued the same theme: Congress exceeded its authority when it passed a law making federal statutes against age discrimination binding on state governments, an Eleventh Amendment issue (*Kimel* v. *Florida*), and in *United States* v. *Morrison* the Court ruled that Congress had overstepped its bounds by enacting a statute (Violence Against Women Act) permitting rape victims to sue their attackers in *federal* court. The trend continued in 2001, when the Court ruled 5–4 (*Board of Trustees of the University of Alabama* v. *Garrett*) that state employees cannot sue for damages for violations of the Americans with Disabilities Act: Congress does not have authority to permit such suits. In a historically familiar reframe, liberal critics accuse the Court of disregarding judicial restraint in favor of (a conservative-oriented) political activism (Greenhouse 2001a).

The Court's most controversial opinion concerned the presidential contest of 2000 which the five-member majority effectively ended by overruling the Florida Supreme Court and refusing to permit any further counting of disputed ballots, many, if not most, of which were from primarily African-American election districts (*Bush* v. *Gore Florida Recount*). The Court based its decision on the "equal protection" clause of the Fourteenth Amendment, which as noted earlier, was enacted to aid blacks in the post-Civil War South. Ironically, the use of the Fourteenth Amendment by the Warren Court in the 1960s had been criticized by political conservatives as an all-purpose tool for judicial activism (Dershowitz, 2001; Posner 2001).

In the next chapter we will turn to the history of law schools and examine legal education in contemporary America.

INTERNET CONNECTIONS

Legal Information Institute (Cornell University): *Law.cornell.edu*

Supreme Court project: *oyez.at.nwu.edu*

Legal history: *jurist.law.pitt.edu/sg_hist.htm*

University of Virginia digital resources:
lib.virginia.edu/speccol/eresources.html

Avalon project: *yale.edu/lawweb/avalon/avalon.htm*

Constitution project: *constitutionproject.org*

REVIEW QUESTIONS

1. What is the relationship between a more complex division of labor and formal legal structures?

2. What elements limited the use of common law in colonial America?

3. Why did most colonists favor the legislative branch over the judicial branch?

4. How did the courts in the postrevolutionary period differ from those of modern America?

5. Why were the works of William Blackstone used so extensively in early America?

6. Why did Federalists and Whigs who were supported by business interests favor common law over codes favored by Jacksonian Democrats?

7. Why were lawyers considered "a necessary evil" in colonial and postrevolutionary America?

8. Why was the bar in disarray following the Revolutionary War?

9. What led to the decentralization/Balkanization of state court systems?

10. What was the frontier problem to which vigilantism arose in response?

11. What was the relationship between the Industrial Revolution, the judicial branch, and the legislative branch?

12. Why did business interests favor the judicial branch over the legislative branch during most of the nineteenth and the first three decades of the twentieth century?

13. Why was it necessary to revise the Articles of Confederation?

14. What does the Constitution say about the judicial branch of government?

15. How did Supreme Court Justice John Jay respond to President George Washington's request for advisory opinions?

16. What was the importance of the case of *Marbury* v. *Madison*?

17. How did the decision in *Gibbons* v. *Ogden* (1824) prove crucial for economic development in the United States?

18. What was the purpose of the Eleventh Amendment?

19. Against what does sovereign immunity protect state governments?

20. How did the original Constitution recognize slavery?

21. What did the Supreme Court decide in the case of Dred Scott (*Scott* v. *Sandford*).

22. How did Congress attempt to protect blacks in the South during the period of Reconstruction?

23. Why did these efforts fail?

24. How did the Eleventh Amendment affect economic development in the post-Civil War South?

25. What was the relationship between Supreme Court decisions, business, and labor during the post-Civil War nineteenth century and the early twentieth century?

26. What was the importance of the 1896 *Plessy* v. *Ferguson* decision?

27. Why did the *Lochner* decision become a symbol of the attitude of the Supreme Court toward workers?

28. What was the attitude of the Supreme Court toward political dissidents during the early decades of the twentieth century?

29. What led to the confrontation between President Franklin Roosevelt and the Supreme Court during the Great Depression?

30. What was the outcome of the confrontation?

31. How did the Supreme Court rule against segregation in *Brown* v. *Board of Education of Topeka, Kansas*, without upsetting the precedent established in *Plessy* v. *Ferguson*?

32. Why is the judiciary described as the "least dangerous branch"?

33. How did the Supreme Court create a legislative revolution in its "one man, one vote" decisions?

34. What were the important due process rulings of the Supreme Court during the 1960s?

35. Why has the business community been disappointed with the type of conservatism manifested by the Rehnquist Court?

36. How can the Supreme Court during the Clinton administration be characterized?

37. What was so controversial about the Court's decision in *Bush* v. *Gore*?

4

LAW SCHOOLS AND LEGAL EDUCATION

Legal education is closely intertwined with the social, economic, and political changes in American history. In this chapter we will review that history from colonial times to the present state of legal education in the United States. We will examine the stratification and criticisms of legal education, and the positions offered by the legal realists, critical legal studies, and the law and economics movement.

EARLY LEGAL EDUCATION IN AMERICA

No law schools existed in the colonies, and only a small number of attorneys in the American colonies were trained in England. Some aspiring American lawyers traveled to England to attend the Inns of Court, companies of barristers in charge of legal training and admission to the upper branch of the English legal profession (solicitors make up the lower branch). The Inns represented a highly centralized and privileged source of legal education and controlled entry into the English legal community (McKenna 1986), a system that was not transferred to the American colonies.

The era of American colonialization was a time when education at the Inns of Court was in decay (Pound 1953; McKenna 1986), and many colonial lawyers learned through apprenticeship. Numerous lawyers combined their practice with being inn-keepers, soldiers, merchants, or clergymen (Friedman 1973). Only in urban areas could the apprenticeship be described as compulsory, and the quality of the apprenticeship was as diverse as those who acted as lawyer-mentors (Stevens 1971; McKenna 1986).

America's greatest chief justice, John Marshall, had little formal education in law or any other discipline—in fact, he attended law lectures for fewer than three months while on leave from military service (Schwartz 1993). Most American attorneys, however, including such notables as Thomas Jefferson and Alexander Hamilton, gained a legal education through the system of clerkship, serving as an apprentice to an established attorney. The law clerk studied common law as set down by Sir Edward Coke (1551–1634)[1] and, most importantly, by William Blackstone (1723–1780). He read statutes, copied legal documents, and watched his tutor practice law.

The first law schools evolved out of this system, as some attorneys found the teaching of law more rewarding than the practice of law. The earliest law office-school was established in a modest one-story building in Litchfield, Connecticut, about 1784, by a county judge, Tapping Reeve. At Litchfield, legal education-training was comprehensive and systematized. Students were exposed to lectures based on Blackstone's work and were concerned primarily with commercial law. They had to write up their notes, do collateral reading, and take a weekly examination. In later years moot courts and debating societies were part of the curriculum; the full course at Litchfield took 14 months. The largest class (1813) had 55 members. Its success gained Litchfield a national reputation, and by the time it closed in 1833, the result of heavy competition, more than 1,000 students had graduated, 28 of whom became U.S. senators, 101 Congressmen, 34 state supreme court justices, 14 governors, three justices of the U.S. Supreme Court, and three U.S. vice-presidents. Judge Reeve, however, never considered Litchfield a "law school" and no diplomas were issued, although for students that required it, he gave letters verifying attendance (McKenna 1986).

The first American professorship in law was established by Governor Thomas Jefferson at Virginia's College of William and Mary in 1779, to which he appointed George Wythe, a signer of the Declaration of Independence.[2] Wythe's students included James Monroe and John Marshall (Schwartz 1974). This led to the establishment of other positions in law at major institutions of higher learning: Yale, Columbia, University of Pennsylvania, University of Maryland, and the University of Virginia all established law professorships by the early part of the nineteenth century. "Overall, the efforts by the colleges to develop law as a scholarly study were not a success. Professorships frequently lapsed or remained sinecures. The common law content of courses was normally small, and serious professional training took place at the private law schools" (Stevens 1971: 415). It was not until 1817 that the first university law school was established at Harvard.

---

[1]Sir Edward Coke was the early 17th century English chief justice whose views greatly influenced the American colonists, particularly his assertion that even the king must submit to law as interpreted by the court—a government of laws, not of men.

[2]Wythe was poisoned in 1806 by his grandnephew who, apparently in debt, was eager to gain his inheritance (Schwartz 1974). Another version reports that a dispute over Wythe's will led to his murder (Noonan 1976). In any event, the only witnesses were two former slaves freed by Wythe. Under Virginia law, blacks were not permitted to testify against whites, and the murderer went free.

HARVARD LAW SCHOOL

Isaac Royall, a Loyalist, fled to England during the Revolution and died there in 1781. His will bequeathed an endowed chair to Harvard University for a "Professor of Physick and Anatomy" or a professor of law. The school chose the latter. Harvard had a great deal of difficulty securing the lands Royall left to the university, since there was hostility even toward dead Loyalists who had fled during the war. In addition, the idea of law as a course of study at an institution of higher learning was not universally accepted. While legal education as a legitimate object of university study was never questioned in Continental Europe (Herget 1990), this was not the case in England or the United States. Here, critics argued that if legal education were to be practical, it would not be academically respectable; on the other hand, if it were to be respectably academic, it would be professionally unprofitable (Sutherland 1967). It was not until 1815 that the Harvard Corporation chose the chief justice of Massachusetts, Isaac Parker, as its first professor of law.

Legal education at Harvard was hardly disciplined scholarship; no readings were assigned and there were no examinations. The school offered the degree of Bachelor of Laws (LL.B) to students who completed the prescribed 18 months of academic requirements. The degree could be earned by those who had already completed an apprenticeship in the law office of an attorney—a college degree was not necessary to attend law school. Blackstone's *Commentaries* and moot courts were the cornerstone of legal education at Harvard. Professors spent their time preparing cases for argument and classroom questions for their students (Sutherland 1967). Legal education floundered, and by 1828 only one student remained (Newmyer 1987).

In the early 1820s, colleges began to incorporate private law schools that were interested in the prestige of such an affiliation, because in most states only universities were empowered to issue degrees. Yale absorbed a local law school in 1824, and in 1829, Harvard reorganized its law offerings, bringing in a professor from the Northampton Law School (Stevens 1971). That same year, Joseph Story (1779–1845), a Harvard graduate and justice of the Supreme Court who rode the New England circuit, accepted an endowed (Nathan Dane) chair. As a result of his efforts the Harvard law library quickly became the largest in the country. By the 1830s Harvard was making a comeback, and there was an increasing study of judicial decisions—case law as analyzed and shaped by the energetic Story in his capacity as justice, professor, and author of legal texts. He helped transfer New England law into a national jurisprudence that would dominate the post-Civil War era and help foster an economic revolution (Newmyer 1987).[3] Harvard began to attract students from throughout the country. "By 1844, the school had 163 students—a remarkable number for the period" (Stevens 1971: 418). Declining standards for admission to

---

[3]Story, originally a Jeffersonian, joined with the Federalists in a strong defense of property and capitalism. In his Harvard inaugural address, he argued: "The sacred rights of property are to be guarded at every point. I call them sacred, because, if they are unprotected, all other rights become worthless or visionary. What is personal liberty, if it does not draw after it the right to enjoy the fruits of our own industry? What is political liberty, if it imparts only perpetual poverty to us and all our posterity. . . . One of the glorious, and not infrequently perilous duties of the Bar is the protection of property" (1962: 180–181).

the bar, however, led to a lowering of standards for admission to the Harvard Law School, and students not qualified for admission to Harvard College were allowed into the law school (Stevens 1971).

Other university law schools were established, and by 1840 there were nine university-affiliated law schools. By 1850, there were 15 law schools in 12 states (but none in the remaining 19). In the years just before the Civil War, there was a dramatic growth in formal legal education, "a revival of law teaching in the East (including Columbia, New York University, and the University of Pennsylvania) with the result that, by 1860, there were twenty-one law schools in existence" (Stevens 1971: 425). Despite their university affiliation, like their private law school counterparts, they were primarily trade schools (Stevens 1983), "little more than efficiently organized apprenticeship systems" (Herget 1990: 33). By 1870 there were 31 law schools (Friedman 1973), and in that year Christopher Columbus Langdell became dean of the Harvard Law School.

LANGDELL AT HARVARD

The nature of learning and science changed dramatically after the Civil War, and the methods of Charles Darwin became a key element in this change: "The late nineteenth-century scientific method was organic, inductive, and classificatory in its emphasis. Its adherents posited the inevitability of growth and change ('evolution') and argued that continuity and even permanency were linked to change. By examining the growth of an area of knowledge over time one could extract the core principles that had been retained and refined" (White 1980: 23–24). According to its proponents, science " 'taught' that knowledge, although infinite, was capable of being reduced to discernible units; science also taught the proper methods of discernment, the proper goals of these methods, and ultimately the proper persons to be using them" (White 1980: 25). This approach was applied to the study of law at Harvard by Christopher Columbus Langdell.

Born in New Hampshire in 1826, Langdell attended Exeter and Harvard, but left before finishing his degree requirements. He clerked in a law office for one and a half years, and then returned to Harvard, where he supported himself as the school librarian. In three years, without completing his undergraduate degree, Langdell finally earned his LL.B. in 1853. For the next 16 years he practiced law in New York. A poor trial lawyer, Langdell specialized in research for other attorneys (Sutherland 1967; Cosgrove 1987). Eventually he was appointed as a professor of law at Harvard, and in 1870 was elected dean of the three-member law faculty, a position he held until his resignation in 1895 (Feldstein and Presser 1984).

Legal education at Harvard "had no relation to Harvard College. Students in general chose either law school or college, not both." Most came directly from high school (Stevens 1983: 36). Under Langdell, however, admission standards were raised; only those who already showed intellect and possessed a Bachelor of Arts degree or passed a strenuous entrance examination could enter the Harvard Law School. (By 1909, the examination alternative was discontinued.) Langdell required proficiency in French or Latin, although in some cases another language could be substituted. In 1871, the course of study for the LL.B. was lengthened from 18 months to two years. In 1872, there were prescribed examinations required at the end of the first year as a condition of admission to the second year of study. And by 1899, the curriculum was extended to three years of residence, and examinations had to be passed at the end of each year (Sutherland 1967).

As important as these changes were, it was the method of instruction at Harvard that revolutionized the study of law in the United States. Grant Gilmore refers to Langdell as "an essentially stupid man" who early in his life hit on one great idea—the case method—"to which, thereafter, he clung with all the tenacity of genius" (1977: 42). Richard Cosgrove presents a more flattering view: "Langdell united academic ambition with experience of the world, and both elements colored his theories of law and legal education" (1987: 27).

Langdell introduced the case method as the basic pedagogical tool for educating lawyers at Harvard. Textbooks were abandoned in favor of casebooks containing appellate court decisions. By reading and analyzing the opinions of appellate judges, the law student learns how to spot similar issues in factually different situations and gains an understanding of judicial thinking. "The new system trained students to understand the sources as a practicing lawyer must understand them" (LaPiana 1994: 26).

Contrary to the older English view of law as a form of custom, Langdell taught that law was a *science* and legal education a search for the underlying principles of selected cases:

> Law, considered as a science, consists of certain principles or doctrines. To have such a mastery of these as to be able to apply them with constant facility and certainty to the ever-tangled skein of human affairs, is what constitutes a true lawyer; and hence to acquire that mastery should be the business of every earnest student of law. Each of these doctrines has arrived at its present state by slow degrees; in other words, it is a growth extending in many cases through centuries. The growth is to be traced in the main through a series of cases; and much the shortest and best, if not the only, way of mastering the doctrine effectually is by studying the cases in which it is embodied. But the cases which are useful and necessary for this purpose at the present day bear an exceedingly small proportion to all that have been reported. The vast majority are useless and worse than useless for any purpose of systematic study. (Langdell 1871: vi–vii)

Langdell "argued that the law was a science that could be reduced to a finite number of principles embedded in court decisions. Speculation into jurisprudence [the system of justice] and other, loftier disciplines [sociology, political science, psychology, economics] were banished from Dean Langdell's world. Cases, he maintained, were the lawyers' specimens, and law libraries were for them what laboratories . . . are to the chemists and physicists, the museum of natural history to the zoologists, the botanical gardens to the botanists" (Margolick 1983: 22).

While he attempted to wrap the study of law in the mantle of science, Langdell had little or no scientific education or training. Thus, his view of science, particularly biology, from which he drew many parallels, was limited and lacked sophistication even by the standards of his day (Stevens 1983; Cosgrove 1987). Indeed, as Richard Posner points out, adherence to precedent, a cornerstone of the case method, is in one sense a "refusal to correct errors—a posture that would be thought bizarre in scientific inquiry" (1990: 82). The study of law, Judge Posner argues, has more in common with theological exegesis than science.

THE CASE METHOD

The case method teaches students the skill of legal reasoning through cases that are carefully selected since, according to Langdell, the vast majority are useless and worse than useless for any purpose of systematic study. In his pioneering casebook on contracts, Langdell relied almost entirely on sequences of English cases, arranged chronologically, abridged, and organized in a systematic manner. In Langdell's view, the English common law "comprised an internally consistent body of precedents whose systemization proceeded from the application of induction and logic. Once identified, however, legal principles then became subject to a deductive process in which the judiciary used these rules to decide cases" (Cosgrove 1987: 28). Typically, a casebook does not explicitly state the basis for the selection and organization of the cases. Instead, guided by questions in the casebook or from the instructor, the student learns how to dissect an appellate decision and analyze its constituent parts. The student "learns to relate one case to another, to harmonize the outcomes of seemingly inconsistent cases so that they are made to stand together. By taking and putting together different cases, the student acquires a way of thinking and working with cases that constitutes the fundamentals of legal reasoning, as well as knowledge of doctrinal rules presented by these cases" (Loh 1984: 15).

The burden is on the student to make sense of the decisions. "There is no single correct way of analyzing or synthesizing opinions. In the case method of study, it is the process, not the outcome, that counts" (Loh 1984: 16). Each case has to be read several times to make sure nothing of importance has been missed, and students must come to each class prepared to discuss and analyze a group of actual appellate decisions. The role of the law professor is to goad and stimulate, asking questions in a Socratic method to explore the facts of the case, to determine the legal principles applied in reaching the result, and to analyze the method of reasoning used. The professor will often play the Devil's advocate, challenging students to defend their reasoning (*Prelaw Handbook 1982–1983*), and "students are given no advance notice of the positions they will be required to defend before their classmates under Socratic interrogation" (Kronman 1993: 111). "The idea is that students can simultaneously learn substantive doctrines, habits of analytical thought, and practical skills of public speaking" ("The Classroom Experience. . . " n.d.).

The Socratic method "familiarizes the student with legal materials, most of them written in the profession's standard style, which exaggerates the uniqueness and the power of the analytical methods that lawyers and judges use. And it imbues the student with that style, at the same time training him to exploit, by means of logic wielded as a critical tool, the indeterminacies in legal materials" (Posner 1990: 99). The student learns "to analyze the implications of each case for possible future disputes, and to integrate the lessons from groups of cases into a general understanding of each subject under study. The process of analyzing and synthesizing cases seeks to develop in the student a capacity to predict what the courts will do and persuade the courts to rule one way or the other in possible future cases" (Burton 1985: 15).

For every class session, appellate cases are assigned and the teacher generally begins by asking a student to summarize the facts of a case, the arguments of the parties, the application of the law to fact, the judge's rationale, and the rule of law as contained in the judge's decision. The teacher then asks the student a series of questions about the assigned material. Few of the questions have definite answers, nor are they designed to stimulate discussion. "Their nature is to probe issues systematically in the classroom, using the question and its answer to structure the information that the student receives, processes, and takes away from the class" (Gac 1988: 3). In the Socratic method there is "focused dialogue." The teacher then asks a series of hypotheticals—questions based on the case as altered slightly and the student is asked to decide if the results would be the same. Hypotheticals teach the student to explore the limits of law and the boundaries of case law. In law school, using hypotheticals is seen as "the most effective method for teaching critical thought and analysis" (Gac 1988: 3). Students also learn to think on their feet. Unprepared students can be the brunt of ruthless scrutiny.

As a first-year student at Harvard Law School, Scott Turow states: "I keep waiting for things to relent somehow. I'm blown out. I've never experienced mental exhaustion like what I felt by the end of each day this week. The ceaseless concentration on books and professors . . . left me absolutely blithering when I got home each evening" (1977: 61). But Robert Granfield and Thomas Koenig (1992) discount the "paper chase" myth as just that—myth. Students at Harvard are quite nonchalant about their grades and, particularly after the first year, feel little or no pressure to answer in, or even attend, class. (Chris Goodrich's [1991] portrayal of his first year at Yale Law falls somewhere between Turow and Granfield and Koenig.)

Absent from Langdell's curriculum was discussion of statutes, and his case-books were devoid of explanatory notes or comments—there was nothing to aid the student. Classroom lectures bewildered students as every possible legal principle was extracted from each case. By the end of Langdell's first year as dean, class attendance had dropped considerably, as had student enrollments. In 1872, nearby Boston University opened a law school for students who were not happy with the innovations at Harvard.

Contrary to the expectations of Langdell's critics, by 1874 enrollments at Harvard Law School were increasing, as Langdell's case method gained adherents. "Gradually the advantage of Langdell's technique became appreciated. By teaching students law from court decisions, an original source, Langdell taught legal reasoning more effectively than did the textbook professors" (Seligman 1978: 41). Harvard had "become a national law school freed from the parochial concerns of a particular state jurisdiction" (Cosgrove 1987: 28). By 1895, the year he stepped down as dean (he continued to teach until his death in 1905), it was clear that Langdell's reforms had brought a large and able student body to Harvard. Enrollments soared, and standards were raised. In 1896, law at Harvard became a graduate education requiring three years of study with vigorous examinations at the end of each year. There was also curriculum innovation: study of law was divided into patterns of specialization linked to professional training, for example, contracts, torts, and property. By 1895, Harvard Law School had 10 professors and over 400 students; by 1907, there were 14 professors and more than 700 students (Stevens 1971).

Harvard became the model for other university law schools, and the use of the case method spread rapidly. Many hired Harvard professors and law graduates to help them convert to the new system of teaching law. By 1908, there were more than 30 law schools using the case method (Seligman 1978). What started as innovation at Harvard led to a revolution that eventually became the norm for legal education in the United States. The other schools even copied the Harvard approach of required courses (adhering to the case method) during the first year of study, with electives for the next two years. In 50 years, "one school had, intellectually, socially, and numerically overwhelmed all others" (Stevens 1971: 434–435).

The case method also had economics in its favor, allowing for one professor to educate classes of as many as 150 students: Langdell "proved to the presidents of universities all over America that they, too, could make money by opening a law school and hiring just a few people to teach" (Turow 1977: 122). The case method resulted in a new profession: law professor. Prior to 1870 it was the practicing lawyer who became the teacher, often on a part-time basis. The case method, however, made stringent demands on time and intellect. Part-timers could not devote the time necessary for preparation, and those practitioners with leisure time "lacked the intellectual flexibility to cope with the analytical, inductive process that comprised the core of the case method" (Auerbach 1971: 552). Case-method law professors were frequently recruited right out of school without any practical experience in law. The teachers of law at the major schools came to comprise an influential elite that would affect the legal and political life of the United States. The influence of the new profession was enhanced by "law review," a student-run journal first established at Harvard in 1887, and subsequently copied by all law schools aspiring for national status. "Legal briefs and judicial decisions increasingly came to use ideas expressed by the professors in law review articles" (Hobson 1986: 408). There are more than 350 law reviews; several schools have more than one. Harvard, which established the first law review in 1887, for example, has about eight.

HARVARD PREVAILS

The model of education at Harvard was uncritical—it was law devoid of any political or social context. The lawyer *qua* scientist was to be rigorously educated to serve the interests of clients without regard to political beliefs or issues—the case method "makes every position respectable" (Kronman 1993: 114). But who could afford the price of such talented "scientists," persons with an undergraduate degree and three years of intensive graduate education? It was apparent that the Harvards of America were preparing lawyers to serve corporate America:

> At about the turn of the century, a number of the new corporate partnerships became convinced that Harvard Law School provided the most effective preparation for their type of practice. As a result, Harvard Law graduates initially received higher salaries than graduates of other law schools. In an unashamedly acquisitive age, such a reputation was no small matter. Harvard Law School could brag that it attracted students from every state of the Union. Law schools desirous of preparing their graduates to serve in the best-paying firms were inclined to follow Harvard's lead. (Seligman 1978: 44)

Entry into law schools, however, did not become truly competitive until the 1960s; as late as 1960, for example, Harvard Law School admitted 50 percent of all applicants (Abel 1989).

The jurisprudence that evolved out of the Harvard model, and which would grow to dominate legal education, is summarized by James Herget (1990: 37):

Law Schools and Law Students

1870	1880	1890	1900	1910	1920
31	51	61	102	124	143
1,653	3,134 (approx.)	4,518	12,516	19,567	27,000

Source: Hobson (1986)

- Law consists of principles, something apart from the cases themselves.
- These principles are the proper subject for intellectual study.
- Law changes over time in unplanned ways, such change being aided by judges.
- Rigorous legal analysis is the only rational way to understand the law and to make it applicable to new situations.

CONTEMPORARY LEGAL EDUCATION

"The shift from apprenticeship to academic education, which began about 1880 and was complete by 1920, had the unanticipated consequence of greatly accelerating the growth of the profession and facilitating entry by immigrants and their sons. The American Bar Association responded by promulgating standards that only some law schools could meet and seeking to persuade states to restrict entry to graduates of approved schools," a campaign that was largely successful (Abel 1989: 71–72).

Robert Stevens summarizes the relationship between legal education and the American Bar Association's (ABA) campaign to restrict the practice of law (discussed in Chapter 5): "It had begun in the 1870's as a requirement for some period of law study followed by a bar exam. The second stage was recognition of law school as an alternative to apprenticeship. The third stage was the requirement of law school without the alternative of office study; and the fourth was recognition only of ABA-approved law schools" (1971: 505). Thus, the organization which benefits from restricting the practice of law is in a position to restrict the number of law schools (Shepherd 2000).

As a result of ABA accreditation and the influence of the American Association of Law Schools (AALS), legal education in the United States has become standardized. In fact, the first year education of law students is fairly uniform across schools, with each student required to take most or all of the following courses (Law School Admission Council 1996: 3–4):

Civil Procedure. The process of adjudication in the United States: jurisdiction and standing to sue, motions and pleadings, pretrial procedure, the structure of a lawsuit, and appellate review of trial results.

Constitutional Law. The legislative powers of the federal and state governments, and questions of civil liberties and constitutional history, including detailed study of the Bill of Rights and constitutional freedoms.

Contracts. The nature of enforceable promises and rules for determining appropriate remedies in case of nonperformance.

Criminal Law and Procedure. The bases of criminal responsibility, the rules and policies for enforcing sanctions against individuals accused of committing offenses against the public order and well-being, and the rights guaranteed to those charged with criminal violations.

Property Law. Concepts, uses, and historical development in the treatment of land, buildings, natural resources, and personal objects.

Torts. Private wrongs, such as acts of negligence, assault, and defamation, that violate obligations of the law.

Legal Research and Writing. Students research and write memoranda dealing with various legal problems.

Legal Method. Introduction to the organization of the American legal system and its processes.

Uniformity of legal education ensures that attorneys will share an understanding of the law and its application. This is necessary to meet the needs of a rational legal system in which a lawyer is generally able to predict what a court will do, and judges, if they are to earn the respect of the legal community, will treat cases according to these shared understandings. In other words, "the conventions of the legal community can lead the lawyer with a problem case to see the important facts in the case as other lawyers and judges within the same legal system would see them" (Burton 1985: 97).

Harvard University J.D. Program

Most first-year courses are taught by full professors. Although most first-year classes are large (about 140 students), this format permits all students to experience the teaching of the most eminent legal scholars in their field, to other students, and to be exposed to a wide variety of perspectives and ideas. We try to give each first-year student a smaller class experience, and every first-year student takes one elective course.

Torts, Contracts, Property, Criminal Law and Civil Procedure are five of the six courses required in the first year. Legal Reasoning and Argument (LRA) is also a required course, complementing the other required work by explaining legal techniques, handling of precedent, judicial analysis, uses of litigation, etc. An important adjunct to LRA is the Ames Competition (moot court), in which pairs of students research, brief, and orally argue a hypothetical case.

In the second and third years, class size varies from seminars of 15–18 to classes of 25–200. In recent years, approximately half of upper-level courses or seminars have enrolled fewer than 30 students; two-thirds of the courses or seminars enroll fewer than 50 students. Courses in both the second and third year are all elective, but we strongly recommend four courses that are prerequisites to much advanced work: Corporations, Taxation, Constitutional Law, and Accounting. During the second and third years, students may cross-register for a limited number of credits within other departments of the University. The written work requirement may be fulfilled in either the second or third year. Wide latitude in choice of format and subject matter is allowed, and many options are available which satisfy the requirements for the paper.

The first-year curriculum is quite demanding, focusing on the analysis of appellate court opinions. At first:

> . . . the number of pages of assigned reading is not great, but the beginning student finds it extremely difficult. Not only is one confronted with a baffling array of unfamiliar concepts, but he or she must also master new intellectual skills. The student must learn to make sense out of the sometimes incoherent syntax of lawyers and judges, to think with analytical precision, and to distinguish legally relevant passages from the marginally relevant or irrelevant. He or she must acquire a new vocabulary, including numerous Latin and French words and phrases, the meaning of which varies according to the context in which they are used.
>
> All of this is made more difficult by the fact that the mastery of each of these skills depends in part upon ability in the others. For example, it is difficult to distinguish the legally relevant from the irrelevant until one understands the simple meaning of the sentences one is reading. But it is often difficult to pierce the nearly impenetrable veil of judicial syntax without some sense of legally relevant categories and some knowledge of legal vocabulary, neither of which is independently taught but instead is supposed to emerge from the cases. (Stover 1989: 46–47)

Soon, the amount of reading increases substantially, and the student is required to pursue deeper meanings as he or she is drilled in the Socratic method. "The traditional 'Socratic method' of legal instruction continues to be used in first-year law classes as an extremely effective technique for developing analytical skills, but is less dominant today in the upperclass years. It is supplemented by a diversity of teaching methods that, like the 'Socratic method,' are designed to foster fundamental skills and require students to make use of legal materials in performing lawyer-like functions" (American Bar Association Task Force on Lawyer Competency and the Role of Law Schools 1979: 13). Second- and third-year courses, however, are often taught in seminar-style rather than the confrontational (between instructor and student) manner of the Socratic method. Seminar courses may only be one-third as large as typical first-year case-method courses.

Besides an ABA-mandated course in professional responsibility and participation in a moot court and/or clinical experience, there are no additional course requirements common to all schools. Pressure by bar associations to reduce the cost of "on the job training" has led to the rise of clinical and legal skills training in the law school curriculum: "Legal educators have been forced to capitulate on their traditional exclusion of such matters from the curriculum and accept a dilution of the Langdell model geared solely to 'scientific' search for eternal truths found in judicial opinions" (Van Alstyne, Julin, and Barnett 1990: 72). "Langell's method was built upon two essential premises, each valid at the time: first, that there was a

CASE METHOD

"The case method reflects the general belief that the primary purpose of law school is not to teach substantive law, but to teach you to think like a lawyer" (Law School Admission Council 1996: 3).

Advanced Curriculum, University of California at Los Angeles

In the second and third years the student has an opportunity to engage in a number of different sorts of law and law-related study: Typically, these years fulfill several objectives. Some of the student's time will be occupied in further fundamental courses, including: constitutional law, which examines the framework of the national government and the guarantees of individual rights; courses that describe the legal framework within which much of the society's economic life takes place (corporations, labor law); and courses that examine the means by which various levels of government raise money—and the secondary effects of these efforts. Beyond these extensions of the student's knowledge of the fundamental legal bases for social organization are at least two other sorts of opportunities. First is the chance to explore the perspectives that history, philosophy, and the social sciences bring to the legal system; second is the possibility of acquiring a detailed working knowledge of particular areas of current legal concern which might range from the law governing the distribution of medical services to that regulating the conditions of monopoly and concentration of American industry.

manageable corpus juris which could and should be mastered by every 'educated' lawyer; second, that this corpus juris was essentially unchanging and thus, once mastered, was mastered forever." While neither premise is valid today, legal education has remained essentially unchanged and the casebook method remains the dominant model in legal education ("The Classroom Experience. . . " n.d.).

The increasing complexity of law, however, has brought changes in legal education. Scholars recognize that the social and behavioral sciences can inform the techniques, content, and conceptual vocabulary of the law. At the same time, initially inspired by the education of physicians, clinical education has found a niche in legal education. While early efforts in these directions suffered growth pains—borrowings from other disciplines were often superficial, producing work that neither clarified the law nor spoke seriously of the companion discipline—the more creative law schools are now on the brink of a second-generation approach to interdisciplinary studies and clinical education ("The Classroom Experience. . . " n.d.).

Many schools have broadened their required course offerings: The University of Virginia requires Agency and Partnership, Family Law, Introduction to International Law,[4] and Law and Economics. Cornell requires Legal Process, and two courses in Practice Training. Harvard requires Problems in Legal Practice and Methods. The University of California at Los Angeles requires Facts, Clients, and Lawyers (product-liability and fact investigation). The University of Chicago requires Elements of the Law (legal reasoning and the relationship between law, social, economic, and political issues). The University of Pennsylvania requires Labor Law

---

[4]International law is a growing field that is particularly relevant for those with foreign language skills and familiarity with another culture.

and offers the student a choice of one of four courses: American Legal History, Economics of Law, Income Security (welfare, Social Security), or Legal Philosophy. The University of Pennsylvania has a public service requirement: "all second- and third-year students perform a total of 70 hours of public service as a condition of graduation." One of the more recent innovations in law school curricula is the addition of courses, sometimes multidisciplinary, on *cyberlaw*: Legal issues involving the Internet (Harmon 1998).

University law schools frequently draw upon faculty from other disciplines—business, economics, history, psychology, and sociology—to present separate courses or to team teach such courses as family law, antitrust law, and criminal law. Some observers see this as obeisance to scholarly traditions rather than a genuine liberal arts commitment on the part of law schools. The emphasis remains on professional training rather than scholarship and is reflected by greater student interest in courses that promote career preparation than those of more scholarly interest. Professional legal training emphasizes advocacy, while scholarship implies truth-seeking (Kronman 1993).

One important innovation in the direction of scholarship (and legal realism/sociological jurisprudence discussed below) is the joint-degree program offered at a number of universities, combining law with a second discipline. For example, Columbia offers joint degree programs leading to a JD/MBA (Master of Business Administration), JD/MS (Journalism), JD/MPA (Master of Public Administration), JD/MFA (Master of Fine Arts), JD/MSW (Social Work), and JD/MS (Urban Planning). Michigan, in addition to a JD/MBA, offers joint degree programs in Law and Economics, Law and Modern Near Eastern and North African Studies, Law and Public Policy Studies, Law and Natural Resources, Law and Russian and East European Studies, and Law and World Politics. A number of universities combine a law degree with a doctorate in these and additional disciplines for a JD/PhD. There are about twenty law schools that offer a Doctor of Juridical Science (S.J.D.) degree, and even more that offer a Masters Degree in some specific aspect of law, for example, an LL.M. in taxation (Van Alstyne, Julin, and Barnett 1990).

Legal education appears to dampen a student's commitment to practicing law in the public interest in favor of the narrow interests of corporate America (Foster 1985; Granfield 1986). Robert Stover found a pronounced change between the first and last year of law school with respect to students' desire to work for social and political goals or to help persons or groups with whom they sympathized. "By the end of law school, students had downgraded the opportunities for altruism in public interest law, while upgrading them for business-oriented jobs" (1989: 34). Richard Kahlenberg (1992: 4) recalls his experience at Harvard: "We came to law school talking about using the law as a vehicle for social change, but when it was time to decide what we would do with our lives, we fell over each other to work for those law firms most resistant to change." Chris Goodrich (1991: 4) reflects on his first-year experience at Yale Law School: "Law schools commonly boast that they teach students to 'think like lawyers,' but I learned that some important things are lost, to both the culture and the individual, in the course of this transformation. Legal training doesn't create selfish, aggressive people—but it does provide the intellectual equipment with which recipients can justify and give force to beliefs and actions most people would wholeheartedly condemn." Law school teaching has also been criticized by female students at a number of elite institutions who have been alienated by the case-method approach[5] (E. Bernstein 1996; Guinier 1997).

STRATIFICATION OF LEGAL EDUCATION

Similarity of required courses does not mean that all law schools are equal. In fact, there is a great deal of stratification in legal education, and it reflects, and is reflected back, by stratification in the legal profession (discussed in Chapter 5). Of the approximately 175 schools approved by the ABA, about two dozen are consistently referred to as the most prestigious law schools in the United States. It is largely irrelevant whether these schools actually provide a superior education—some argue that Harvard actually provides, instead, elitism and fraternalism (Granfield and Koenig 1992)—what matters is that they are perceived by those who employ law school graduates, particularly national law firms, corporations, and investment bankers, as being superior. In this case, perception creates its own reality. Most of these schools are private institutions that are part of equally prestigious universities: Chicago, Columbia, Cornell, Duke, Harvard, New York, Northwestern, Pennsylvania, Stanford, Yale. Some are church affiliated: Georgetown, Boston College. And state universities are also prominent on any list of elite schools: California at Berkeley and Los Angeles, Michigan, Texas, Virginia (see Figure 4–1). There is a certain amount of homogeneity across elite schools, since their faculties are generally graduates of elite law schools (American Bar Association 1980).

FIGURE 4–1   STRATIFICATION OF LEGAL EDUCATION

STRATUM I
Elite law schools

STRATUM II
National law schools

STRATUM III
Regional law schools

STRATUM IV
Local law schools

---

[5]Women account for about half the students at elite law schools (Glater 2001).

Entry into these institutions requires an exceptionally high undergraduate grade point average (GPA) and score on the Law School Aptitude Test (LSAT).[6] Harvard, for example, receives more than 8,000 applications each year and admits about 800;[7] Yale about 5,000, while admitting about 350; Stanford more than 5,000 and admits about 450; Columbia receives more than 6,000 and admits about 900; the University of California at Berkeley, over 5,000 applications and about 800 admissions. (In each case, the number that actually enrolls is considerably smaller than the number of admissions; many top students are admitted to several schools.) "Because of variations from college to college in academic standards, law schools tend to favor applicants from undergraduate schools whose marks have proved reliable in the past. At law schools like Harvard, that means a continued influx from the Ivy League colleges, with smaller and lesser-known schools at a disadvantage. The sole leveler is the LSAT—the only measure common to all applicants" (Turow 1977: 28).

Next in the law school stratification system are national law schools that are part of a state or private university, and a number of them are church affiliated. These schools draw their student body from the nation as a whole. Then there are regional law schools whose students are primarily from the geographic region in which the school is located. At the bottom of the stratification system are law schools that are not part of a doctorate-granting university, the commuter schools that tend to educate local students for a local practice. Graduates of these schools are overrepresented in the ranks of solo practitioners and local government. There are also law schools that have not been approved by the ABA,[8] but whose graduates can be admitted to the practice of law in eight states if they pass the bar examination (Holmes 1996). California, for example, has experienced a growth industry in such schools since it has a very liberal policy with respect to qualifications for taking the bar examination.

CRITICISMS OF LEGAL EDUCATION

Langdell's career at Harvard coincided with an era of unbridled growth for American capitalism. The wheels of industry were greased with the labor of waves of immigrants: men, women, and children whose welfare was not a governmental concern. Positivism and social Darwinism (see Chapter 3) were popular among the educated classes, and the theories of Herbert Spencer provided an aura of science to doctrines that were inimical to the interests of the "huddled masses yearning to breathe free." Like biological evolution, case law was an evolutionary process that placed the brakes on legislatures' statutory interventions into natural legal processes. The preoccupation with judicial decisions and opinions of the past meant that

---

[6]Prior to the 1960s, most law schools did not rely on the LSAT, but accepted everyone who applied. They also typically dismissed many more students than they do today (Law School Admission Council 1995).

[7]In 2001, of the nine members of the U.S. Supreme Court, five were graduates of Harvard Law School; two graduated from Stanford; one from Yale; and one from Northwestern.

[8]In 1996, the ABA reached a settlement with the Department of Justice, which had accused the association of anticompetitive practices in its accreditation practices. Among other practices, the ABA dropped its policy of denying accreditation to "for-profit law schools" (Holmes 1996).

The LSAT and Law School Admissions

The Law School Aptitude Test (LSAT) is a post-World War II addition to the law school admissions process, administered by the Law School Admission Services (LSAS) four times a year. This standardized examination comprises five 35-minute multiple-choice sections—reading comprehension, analytical reasoning, logical reasoning (two sections), and an experimental section (the examinee does not know which section is experimental). There is also a 30-minute writing sample. The experimental section and the writing sample are not included in the scoring. The writing sample is sent to each law school to which the LSAT score is reported for the school's own use, if any. A candidate's score is based on the number of questions answered correctly—no penalty for guessing—and through a statistical calculation it is then equated with other LSAT tests, resulting in a scale that ranges from 120 to 180. The average (mean) score is about 150, while more than half of those taking the test score above (the median of) 151. According to the LSAS, the exam "is designed to measure skills that are considered essential for success in law school: the reading and comprehension of complex texts with accuracy and insight; the organization and management of information and the ability to draw reasonable inferences from it; the ability to reason critically; and the analysis and evaluation of the reasoning and argument of others."

Typically, a law school will use a formula that combines the LSAT score and the applicant's GPA into an index. Law schools will frequently use a minimum index score as a screening device. Those below the minimum will not ordinarily receive further consideration. Those meeting or surpassing the minimum are then judged by an admissions committee which, in addition to the index score, will consider extracurricular activities and a host of nonacademic variables. Most law schools require applicants to submit personal statements whose specifications vary from school to school. The Law School Admission Council advises students that a broad liberal arts curriculum is the preferred preparation for law school: "Enrolling in courses that are designated as part of a prelaw curriculum or major tends to be a less effective means of preparing for law school than enrolling in a diverse college program."

this legal science, generally referred to as *legal formalism*, would be distinctly conservative, and it was bitterly criticized by the proponents of sociological jurisprudence and legal realism.[9]

Sociological Jurisprudence and Legal Realism[10]

About the time of the First World War, some national law schools began to revise their curricula in a way that challenged the case method of instruction. Instead of the exclusive use of cases, which focused only on the *ratio decedendi* of appellate court decisions, a number of law schools, most notably Yale and Columbia,

---

[9]The conservative nature of the case method is offset by legal education's stress on the adversarial method. The legal profession's ethic of zealous advocacy serves to expand the reach of precedent and renders the case law approach more flexible.
[10]Gregory Alexander (n.d.) connects sociological jurisprudence and legal realism to the Amercian Progressive movement and its aftermath, the late nineteenth century until the New Deal.

introduced courses on legislation, comparative law, and the social sciences. This represented an attempt to "understand the law in terms of its factual context and economic and social consequences" (Kalman 1986: 3).

The changes had wide implications. Well known jurists and legal scholars asserted that deciding cases on the narrow grounds of precedent was both reactionary and illogical. Critics, such as Oliver Wendell Holmes, Jr. (1841–1935) and Benjamin N. Cardozo (1870–1938), both justices of the Supreme Court, became known as legal realists who favored a sociological jurisprudence—expanding the study of law beyond the case method to include social realities. The realists were critical of the proposition that judges are simply engaged in law-finding, that they merely apply the facts as presented by litigants to known and certain principles of law. Instead, realists argued, judges exercise considerable discretion in rendering decisions. Legal realists "asserted, with varying degrees of emphasis, that judges make law rather than find it" (Schur 1968: 43).

The realists had no patience for "the attempt by traditional jurists to reduce law to a set of rules and principles, which they insisted guided judges to their decisions" (Kalman 1986: 3). It is one of the curious features of Anglo-American case law, states Richard Wasserstrom, "that regardless of the way in which a given decision is actually reached, the judge apparently feels it necessary to make it appear that the decision was dictated by prior rules applied in accordance with the canons of formal logic" (1961: 17). Even when a judge decides to overrule a previous case—to disregard precedent—he or she often finds it necessary to confine the case to its particular facts—to *distinguish away*, a legal device that allows the judge to ignore precedent without stating that the previous decision was incorrect. To do this, the judge finds that the case whose precedent is being urged is not similar enough to the case at hand for the precedent to be relevant.

Realists argued that this is simply an effort to protect the dogma of the infalli-bility of the courts. The skillful judge will not be bound by the past, but will use precedent to maximize freedom of decision-making (Llewellyn 1951). Judges "need to find a way to impose their own views on the text without thinking of themselves as doing so, and they disguise their role by attributing what they say not to who they are but to what they read" (Frug 1986: 28). Posner notes that case citations can make "an opinion look more solid than it really is" (1990: 93).

Holmes and Cardozo argued that the proposition that judges merely find law was ludicrous—judges, they argued, choose between competing political, social, and economic values. Law, they concluded, is not a pure doctrine uncontaminated by practical affairs, nor can it be separated from social forces. Instead, law acts as a controlling and stabilizing force in a changing society. Thus, law has to be under-stood in the context of the social sciences: sociology, political science, economics, and history. "The realists did not object to legal rules and concepts per se; they believed that they could be useful in predicting judicial decisions. But they found other factors equally relevant to their understanding of the judicial process" (Kalman 1986: 6). *Social* justice must be recognized alongside the older *legal* justice (LaPiana 1994).

The realist position is that judges, in effect, *create* law (Murphy and Pritchett 1986). Indeed, the judge, as lawyer, is schooled in disregarding precedent that does not support his or her case, while citing in capital letters cases that do (Llewellyn

1951). Roscoe Pound (1870–1964), who received a Ph.D. in botany before becoming dean of the Harvard Law School (1916–1936), argued for a sociological jurisprudence that complemented the realist critique:

> Often formulas are conveniently elastic so that they may or may not apply. Often rules of contrary tenor overlap, leaving a convenient no-man's-land wherein cases may be decided either way according to which rule the court chooses in order to reach a result arrived at on other grounds. Occasionally a judge is found who frankly acknowledges that he looks chiefly at the ethical situation between the parties and does not allow the law to interfere therewith beyond what is inevitable. (Pound 1975: 59–60)

The legal realists, particularly legal scholar Karl Llewellyn (1893–1962) and Judge Jerome Frank (1889–1957), believed that judicial decisions are not controlled by prior rules of jurisprudence, but are simply value-laden choices of the judges. Rather than search for precedent to determine the outcome of a case, Frank (1970) reasons that judges arrive at a decision first, no matter how tentative, and then seek the justification for it. If sufficient justification cannot be found, that decision will be dropped, unless that judge is arbitrary or mad, and the process of seeking a justifiable decision continues. Conclusions determine a judge's reasoning and, according to Frank, the stimuli that lead a judge to justify a particular decision are what need to be studied and explained. In addition to variables such as the economic and political background of the judge (items stressed by judicial realists), Frank pointed to individualistic elements: the personality factors that influence a judge's decisions, an idiosyncratic jurisprudence: "By attributing the cause of their actions to others, these lawyers and judges establish legal rules without taking responsibility for what they are. They hide—even from themselves—the extent of their own role in choosing what these rules are. And by presenting themselves as experts, they reinforce the average reader's sense that only a professional can make legal judgments" (Frug 1986: 28). Frank states that personality factors that can influence a decision are usually beyond discovery except by the judge's own introspection—psychoanalytic jurisprudence: "The conscientious judge will, as far as possible, make himself aware of his biases . . . and by that very self-knowledge, nullify their effect" (1970: xxiii).[11]

The legal realists urged a system of law based on the social sciences and designed to meet the needs of contemporary society. They "hoped to force students to see the interrelationship between law and policy and to make them want to reform the law" (Kalman 1986: 68). Instead of organizing and teaching law along conceptual lines that emphasized "black letter" rules and legal principles, they stressed law in action. According to this view, law would be organized along the lines of factual situations, for example, building and construction contracts as opposed to mutual assent and consideration. "They tried, however inadequately, to integrate law with the social sciences, adopt the functional approach, and make legal education more clinical" (Kalman 1986: 52).

Appellate court justices, cognizant of the realists' critique, often provide reasons for the policies that underlie the legal rules they fashion and use (Feeley 1984). David Kairys points out, however, that "*stare decisis* neither leads to nor requires

---

[11]For a more recent attempt to apply a psychoanalytic approach to the legal process, see Shaibani (1999).

any particular results or rationales in specific cases. A wide variety of precedents and a still wider variety of interpretations and distinctions are available from which to pick and choose. Social and political judgments about the substance, parties, and context of the case guide such choices, even when they are not the explicit or conscious basis of decision" (1982: 14). As Posner points out: "We now know that if we give a legal problem to two equally distinguished legal thinkers chosen at random we may get completely incompatible solutions" (1987: 767).

Harold Berman (1958: 373; edited) places the arguments of those who stress the importance of precedent and the legal realists in perspective:

> Not only is *stare decisis* not absolute but it also has no clear meaning. The *ratio decedendi* of a case is never certain. Moreover, the doctrine of precedent has different values in different fields of law. In dealing with questions of property law or commercial law, a court is reluctant to overturn the holdings of previous cases, since the community relies upon the stability of court decisions in making property or business transactions. In dealing with questions of tort law, on the other hand, courts have less reason to be reluctant to overrule precedent or to "distinguish away" past cases; presumably if a driver of a car proceeds carelessly through an intersection when another careless driver is approaching from the opposite direction, he does not do so in reliance on a rule that the contributory negligence of the other driver will bar the latter's recovery. Nevertheless, predictability of judicial decision is a factor to be considered in tort cases as in any other, if only for the reason that the lawyers for the parties rely on past decisions in bringing suit or in defending.

The impact of legal realism is ambiguous; while it succeeded in pointing out that law and lawyers need more than "pure" law when seeking answers to legal problems, it failed to significantly affect the way lawyers are educated (Cosgrove 1987). While the notion of sociological jurisprudence was increasingly accepted, it proved to have little content, and "proved virtually meaningless for legal education" (LaPiana 1994: 156). Columbia University's attempt to expand legal education with an infusion of legal scholarship and the social sciences failed. Yale University was unable to create a sociological jurisprudence. While Pound expounded the view that law should be treated as one of the social sciences and, as such, a tool for social reform, as dean of the Harvard Law School (1916–1936) "he never attempted to meet the demands of his own sociological jurisprudence"; rather, Pound subscribed to the method established by Langdell (Kalman 1986: 46). By the 1930s and the New Deal, Pound had moved away from his earlier "radical" view of law, becoming increasingly conservative, a defender of the status quo in

*P*RECEDENT AND *P*ROPERTY

Judicial adherence to precedent is particularly important to the law of property: "Without certainty as to rules and their application, owners could not determine what they have acquired, how they can use it, and what they might convey. Without adherence to precedent, these private determinations could not be made; instead there would be constant litigation, resulting in significant costs to the interested parties and to the entire community" (Becker 1998; 856).

both law and politics, and even admired Adolf Hitler (Stevens 1983). While Fascism and Nazism were gaining strength in Europe, proponents of natural law attacked the realists because of their advocacy of *legal relativism*" . . . the Realists had difficulty articulating a consistent ethical and moral position; instead, with each situation a different set of facts influenced the course of the law" (Hall, Wiecek, and Finkelman 1991: 469). By the end of the Second World War, legal realism as a "movement" was history, although its impact on legal education remained. According to Stevens, the primary contribution of the legal realists "was to kill the Langdellian notion of law as an exact science, based on the objectivity of black-letter rules. When it became acceptable to write about the law as it actually operated, legal rules could no longer be assumed to be value-free. This change inevitably caused the predictive value of doctrine to be seriously questioned" (1983: 156).

The *Yale Law Bulletin* (YLB) notes that in some areas "the appellate opinion as the exclusive source of 'case' material was found to be too limited a vehicle for learning about legal rules, much less about the legal system." The bulletin points to the realists' effort to make the "science" of law more useful "by infusing it with the social sciences, locating law and legal institutions in the context of the entire social process, with attention not only to courts but also to legislatures, administrators, and the consumers of law—the people" (1985–1986: 16). An American Bar Association publication on law schools also describes the realists' challenge: "The movement infused certain law schools with intellectual excitement. At Yale and Columbia, particularly, inquiring and challenging minds were busy comprehending the function of law and evaluating its effects. The Columbia law faculty, reflecting the pragmatic, technological orientation of this era undertook the Herculean task of reorganizing its entire curriculum along functional lines with the goal of teaching law as an integral part of the social sciences" (1980: 7).

"Since World War II," notes the *Yale Law Bulletin*, "there has been a development of casebooks made up of 'cases and materials' where once there were only appellate opinions. There have been efforts to blend sociological and realist views, to move them on to 'policy science,' or to portray law in terms of context and process" (1985–1986: 16). In addition, as noted earlier, there has been an expansion of the law school curriculum, adding social science faculty and courses on jurisprudence, legal history, and legal philosophy, although curricula remain skewed toward the needs of business.

"Legal education in most law schools today focuses upon private rather than public conflict. Its emphasis is on private practice of law in a firm. Law school downplays legislation, public service, judicial or administrative law" (Gerber 1989: 38). Ted Gest (1993) reports, however, that in the 1990s, an increasing number of students have been motivated to enter the field of public service, and about 50 law schools have started programs to ease the debt burden of graduates who enter legal services or government agencies. Several states have created loan forgiveness programs that pay off some or all of a lawyer's student loans if they are employed in low-paying public service positions (Kendall 1991). Law schools have been slowly modifying the basic curriculum to cover problems of the poor.

CRITICAL LEGAL STUDIES

A more recent attack on legal education (and legal formalism) in the United States is known as critical legal studies (CLS), which became popular during the 1970s, a time when Americans were struggling with issues of civil rights and the Vietnam War. Allan Hutchinson (1989) dates the "official birth" of CLS to a conference in 1977 at the University of Wisconsin in Madison. The CLS movement is an attempt to revive the legal realist claims that *law is politics* (Manza 1990).

Many who take the CLS approach view law from a neo-Marxian perspective. Law, they argue, is part of an ideological system that legitimates the social order "by presenting existing social relationships [capitalism] as normal, desirable, and just" (Newman 1983: 19). Laws and their application are, thus, not neutral but represent the interests of a dominant elite to the disadvantage of the less powerful masses. CLS stalwarts ("crits") challenge the ability of the judicial system to dispense "true justice." They point to the prevailing probusiness climate of the nineteenth century, when judges interpreted tort law governing cases of personal injury in a manner that clearly favored business and industry at the expense of the public, and the routine use of courts to harass and weaken the ability of workers to organize and strike (discussed in Chapter 3). Instead of being neutral, the courts allowed corporate America to reign free from legal liability in their quest for profits, while workers were kept under strict legal control (Michalowski 1985).

CLS goes against the formalist view of law, pointing to the uncertain nature of meaning in language as the source of the indeterminacy of deciding cases. Thus, legal rules are so far from clear regarding where and how they should be applied that there is no possibility of their being applied consistently or objectively (McCormick 1999). Not only is the law inconsistent, but radically indeterminate, capable of producing opposite results in similar cases depending on the outcome the judge desires or the system requires. Furthermore, legal principals are not neutral, but biased in favor of certain economic and social arrangements that are themselves neither inevitable nor just—the law is not apolitical but in fact the instrument and enforcer of the ideology of liberal capitalism (Menand 1986). By pretending that legal outcomes are the product of apolitical and neutral modes of argument rather than the imposed preferences of those with wealth and power, the rule of law legitimizes current political and economic arrangements (Hutchinson 1988): *legal elites protecting monied elites*. The case law system "legitimates things by seemingly withdrawing matters of substantial ideological controversy from legislative and political debate. Fundamental issues are instead put into courts where they are translated into less apparent vocabulary that conveys the basic rightness of the status quo (Paul 2001: 714).

The elite law schools, in particular, have been criticized for turning out narrowly educated technocrats dedicated to the perpetuation of corporate interests at the expense of the urban and rural poor, workers, farmers, consumers, and the environment. A leader in the critical legal studies movement, Duncan Kennedy of Harvard, refers to legal education as "ideological training for willing service in the hierarchies of the corporate welfare state" (1982: 40). He offers a critical description of the lessons of today's law school:

[Students] learn to retain large numbers of rules organized into categorical systems (requisites for a contract, rules about breach, etc.). They learn "issue spotting," which means identifying the ways in which the rules are ambiguous, in conflict, or have a gap when applied to particular fact situations. They learn elementary case analysis, meaning the art of generating broad holdings for cases so they will apply beyond their intuitive scope, and narrow holdings for cases so that they won't apply where it at first seemed they would. And they learn a list of balanced, formulaic, pro/con policy arguments that lawyers use in arguing that a given rule should apply to a situation despite a gap, conflict, or ambiguity, or that a given case should be extended or narrowed. These are arguments like "the need for certainty," and "the need for flexibility," "the need to promote competition," and "the need to encourage production by letting producers keep the rewards of their labor." (1982: 45)

David Margolick points out, "For many students, law school has become more a conduit to lucrative positions in large law firms than an opportunity to ponder the larger questions about law and justice" (1983: 21). To Derek Bok, a president of Harvard University and an attorney, the overwhelming preference among top law graduates for such positions represents "a massive diversion of exceptional talent into pursuits that often add little to the growth of the economy, the pursuit of culture or the enhancement of the human spirit" (1983: 573). As noted earlier, many law schools are offering courses designed to broaden the education of their students, and there are law clinics through which students receive a more realistic legal experience and sometimes have the opportunity to serve the interests of the poor. However, the bulk of legal education is narrowly focused to meet the needs of business, not the public interest, and the heavy recruitment at the elite schools by national law firms tends to provide reinforcement for the status quo.[12] (For a further discussion of CLS, see James Boyle 1992; Cardarelli and Hicks 1994. For an in-depth critique, see Whitehead 1999.)

LAW AND ECONOMICS

At the other end of the political spectrum from critical legal studies is the law and economics movement, according to which "the overriding goal of law, as of economics, should be that of efficiency" (Schwartz 1993: 201)—a *consequentialist* approach. Economics as a scholarly discipline has impacted on the study and teaching of law as evidenced by specialized journals and the founding of the American Association of Law and Economics. The law and economics movement received its impetus at the University of Chicago when Edward H. Levi teamed with an economist to teach his course in antitrust law (Lewis 2000). Indeed, the law and economics perspective is sometimes referred to as the "Chicago School." Levi, who would become the dean of the law school, president of the University of Chicago, and

---

[12]Despite their criticism of the legal profession, the "crits" generally do not support opening up the practice of law, something supported by many political conservatives who want to break the legal profession's monopoly over the practice of law. "The rise of the paralegal," notes Posner, "has demonstrated that much of the traditional work of lawyers can be done by nonlawyers" (1995: 66).

attorney general of the United States in 1975, founded the school's *Journal of Law and Economics* in 1958 (Lewis 2000). The law and economics perspective argues that while common law judges feign obeisance to common law principles, in practice they decide their cases "as though they were trying to bring about the outcome that a free market would have produced (MacFarquhar 2001: 87).

The development of a legal focus determined by economics is, of course, not surprising; Chapter 1 noted that modern/rational law is intertwined with capitalism. Anthony Kronman states that "in almost every area of law a working knowledge of economics is now required to keep abreast of scholarly developments" (1993: 166). He sees this as an extension of the Langdellian view of law as a scientific endeavor—law as amoral. Of all of the various social sciences, why economics? Kronman points to the discipline's abstractness and "indifference to the content of human interests" (1993: 228)—it is closest in appearance to the ideological neutrality of the natural sciences. While the law and economics movement "can be regarded, in crude terms, as the right wing of modern American Jurisprudence, critical legal studies being its left" (Kelly 1993: 436), this would be an oversimplification: "The libertarian inclinations of most law-and-economics scholars place them to the right of most Americans on economic issues, but to the left on social questions. Cultural conservatives and Republicans of any stripe are a decided minority" in the law and economics movement (Glendon 1994: 216).

One of the foremost proponents of the economic approach to law is Richard Posner (1986), a federal appellate judge and law professor at the University of Chicago. Wealth maximization, Judge Posner argues, should be the guiding principle in common law adjudication. Issues should be stripped of their ideological or ethical implications and, instead, legal decisions should be based on "the costs to be incurred and the benefits to be reaped from alternative courses of action" (1995: 16). The common law, Posner states, serves to maximize wealth by imbuing judges with concern for promoting efficiency.[13] A failure to promote efficiency results in appeals and/or new legislation that conforms to the dictates of productivity. Thus, laws and legal decisions can be subjected to economic analysis along the lines of wealth maximization. Common law judges, he argues, are especially well equipped to promote prosperity: "The rules of the common law that they promulgate attach prices to socially undesirable conduct," thereby creating incentives to avoid such conduct (1990: 359). Instead of stare decisis, however, law and economics, like the discipline of economics, discards theories that are falsified by data—it is pragmatic (Posner 1995). Law and economics studies have influenced a number of legal subjects, most importantly, antitrust law—Judge Posner was a key player in the Microsoft antitrust case of 1999–2000.

The economic view of human behavior presumes that the pursuit of self-interest will guide decisions ranging from purchases and production to whether to break the law (Blackstone and Bowman 1999). Law and economics views human behavior as rational, driven by incentives to which people respond in accord with their own self-interest. This is the basis of rational choice theory, the presumption that individuals act to maximize their self-interest. Accordingly, legal rules which create incentives

---

[13]For a discussion of intricacies of applying cost–benefit analysis to policy issues, see Adler and Posner (2000); Sunstein (2000b)

or disincentives for people to act should conform to the goal of wealth maximization. However, while sound legal policy must recognize these incentive effects and be responsive to them, there is a great deal of evidence indicating that individuals frequently act in ways that are incompatible with the assumptions of *rational choice theory* (Korobkin and Ulen 2000).

And, of course, some legal issues are beyond the pale of economics—not all issues that arise in law can be recast as economic questions. Economics has difficulty, for example, with cases involving sexuality and reproduction (Posner 1995: 22). "The costs of forcing a woman to bear an unwanted child are readily analyzed within an economic framework, but what of the costs to the fetus of being aborted?"[14] Furthermore, "some legal rules are defensible even if they are shown to impose costs and inefficiencies," as do a host of due process requirements (Winick 1997: 191).

THERAPEUTIC JURISPRUDENCE

Like law and economics, therapeutic jurisprudence (TJ) is concerned with consequences. While law and economics favors an analysis along the dimension of efficiency, a cost–benefit analysis, TJ prefers to focus on consequences as either enhancing or detracting from psychosocial well-being. Originating in the early 1990s in the area of mental health law, TJ "seeks to apply social science to examine the law's impact on mental and physical health of the people it affects" (Winick 1997: 187). According to one of its primary proponents, Bruce J. Winick (1997: 188), TJ "suggests that, *other things being equal*, positive therapeutic effects are desirable and should generally be a proper aim of law, and that antitherapeutic effects are undesirable and should be avoided or minimized." "TJ doesn't necessarily dominate, but rather informs and in so doing provides insight and effective results. Such considerations enter into the mix to balance when considering a law, or a legal decision, or course of legal action" (Schma 2000: 1).

This would include those matters that come before the courts as well as those consigned to the lawyer's office and his or her responsibilities as a counselor for the client's *total* welfare (Stolle et al. 1997). According to Winick (1997), the types of cases that can incorporate this approach are quite broad, ranging from personal injury to domestic violence, to discrimination to estate planning. David Wexler (1999: 4) notes the types of questions TJ can address: "How the criminal justice system might traumatize sexual battery victims, how workers' compensation schemes might create the moral hazard of prolonging work-related injury, how a fault-based (rather than a no-fault) tort compensation scheme might enhance recovery from personal injury, and how the current law of contracts might operate to reinforce the low self-esteem of disadvantaged contracting parties."

> Legal rules, legal procedures, and the roles of legal actors (such as lawyers, judges, and often therapists) constitute social forces that, like it or not, often produce therapeutic or antitherapeutic consequences. Therapeutic jurisprudence proposes that we be sensitive to those consequences, rather than ignore them, and that we ask whether the law's antitherapeutic consequences can be reduced, and its therapeutic consequences

---

[14] For a discussion of the varied traditions that make up Law and Economics, see Mercuro and Medema (1997).

enhanced, without subordinating due process and justice values. Therapeutic jurisprudence does not suggest that therapeutic considerations should trump other considerations; therapeutic considerations are but one category of important considerations, as are autonomy, integrity of the fact-finding process, and community safety. Therapeutic jurisprudence also does not purport to resolve the value questions; instead, it sets the stage for their sharp articulation. (Wexler 1999: 4)

Judge William Schma (2000: 1) provides some examples. In busy dockets, he notes, it is common for judges to accept *nolo contendere*—no contest—pleas in sex offense cases in lieu of a guilty plea. A TJ approach asks the judge to consider the therapeutic effects that may follow as a consequence of such a plea. A *nolo* plea can reinforce a process of denial that will frustrate the offender's rehabilitation. "If the offender does not have to admit the crime to the judge, he or she may more easily deny it later to a probation officer or sex abuse counselor. Anti-therapeutic consequences such as frustration of rehabilitation and return to abusive behavior may result from the judge's acceptance of the plea."

Judge Schma continues: Consider the role of apology in tort law. In medical malpractice cases many plaintiffs only want an apology from their health care provider for the adverse outcome they experienced. A lawsuit is the furthest action on their mind. "And for negligent care providers, an apology for a regrettable mistake would be a therapeutic event." However, insurance companies usually prohibit an insured from having any contact with a patient who may file a claim. And, while there is a sound legal basis for this practice–fear that a nonprivileged admission could adversely impact the case–the anti-therapeutic result is that the patient is deprived of what the patient may want most, and the health care provider cannot take necessary steps to cleanse his or her mind and return to productive work. Moreover, because the provider is forced by the law into a position of denial, the likelihood of reoccurrence increases. Now that we have reviewed legal education, in the next chapter we will examine bar associations and the practice of law.

INTERNET CONNECTIONS

Legal sites on the Web: *ih2000.net/ira/legal.htm*
Emory Electronic Reference Desk: *law.emory.edu/LAW/refdesk/toc.html*
Legal journals on the Web: *usc.edu/dept/law-lib/legal/journals.html*
Meta-index for legal research: *gsulaw.gsu.edu/metaindex*
Law links: *washlaw.edu*
International Network on Therapeutic Jurisprudence: *law.arizona.edu/upr-intj*

REVIEW QUESTIONS

1. What are the Inns of Court?
2. How were most lawyers trained in colonial America?
3. Why was law as a course of study at an institution of higher learning not universally accepted in the early decades of the nineteenth century?

4. What factors led to the incorporation of private law schools by universities?

5. How did Christopher Columbus Langdell influence legal education in the United States?

6. What did Langdell mean when he described the study of law as a "science"?

7. Why is law not a science?

8. What is the case method of legal education?

9. How does the case method place the burden of learning on the student?

10. What are the advantages of the case method in legal education?

11. What are criticisms of the case method in legal education?

12. Why is the case method a very conservative approach to law?

13. How did the shift from apprenticeship to academic education bring about unanticipated consequences?

14. What are the advantages of having legal education standardized throughout law schools?

15. How is legal education stratified in the United States?

16. What did the legal realists advocate with respect to legal education?

17. What was the legal realists' critique of *stare decisis* as the commanding concept in rendering legal decisions?

18. What are the criticisms leveled at legal education and the practice of law by the advocates of critical legal studies (CLS)?

19. What was the primary contribution of the legal realists?

20. According to the law and economics view, what should be the basis of legal analysis?

21. What are the aims of therapeutic jurisprudence?

5

THE LEGAL PROFESSION AND THE PRACTICE OF LAW

In the last chapter we looked at the development of law schools and legal education. In this chapter, we will examine the parallel development of the practice of law, bar associations, and the stratification of the legal profession. We will then discuss federal legal services and public interest law firms.

LAWYERS IN REVOLUTIONARY AMERICA

Throughout the colonial era, there was hostility toward lawyers. Some colonists had had negative experiences with lawyers in England, and the poor often viewed lawyers as part of the ruling merchant and propertied class. There was also opposition to lawyers from the landed gentry of the South and the clergy of the North, both of whom saw attorneys as competitors for power and influence (Pound 1953). Legislation hostile to the practice of law was enacted in many colonies (Schwartz 1974). "In most societies at most periods," notes Grant Gilmore, "the legal profession has been heartily disliked by all non-lawyers: a recurrent dream of social reformers has been the law should be (and can be) simplified and purified in such a way that the class of lawyers can be done away with. The dream has never withstood the cold light of waking reality" (1977: 1).

A majority of colonial lawyers appear to have sided with the king and either left America for Canada or England or were forced to retire from practicing law after the Revolution. In some states, a loyalty oath was required before an attorney was permitted to practice law. The loyalty test required by the state of New York in 1779 resulted in so many attorneys retiring from practice "that the bar of the state Supreme Court had almost ceased to exist" (Chroust 1965: 10). Kermit Hall refers to the conflict between the colonists and the Crown as a conservative revolution under the influence of lawyers: "No heads rolled in America; loyalists were tarred and feathered but not hung. Patriot leaders permitted them to flee with their lives and they confiscated their lands only after proper legislative and judicial proceedings" (1989: 50). Many of those who left because of the Revolutionary War were the better trained lawyers, so the postrevolutionary bar was one of limited ability. And most judges were as unfit by training and education as the lawyers who practiced before them (Pound 1953).

Ambitious young men flocked to the practice of law as the dislocation of the Revolution expanded the need for attorneys at a time when the number of attorneys had dwindled. However, "a large segment of the young American bar was made up of men who had but a sketchy acquaintance with the law and with the standards required of an honorable profession" (Chroust 1965: 35). Yet, even those with little formal education were frequently quite literate. Patrick Henry was admitted to the practice of law in Virginia at age twenty-four, and "what law he knew was self-taught" (Handlin and Handlin 1982: 71); Alexander Hamilton's preparation for the bar consisted of three months of law reading (Ferguson 1984).

Economic disarray was widespread in the years following the Revolution, and the lawyer was despised in debtor areas as a tool of monied interests. A major part of his (there were no female lawyers) practice typically involved legal action against debtors, many of whom were Revolutionary War veterans who had left their farms and businesses unattended to serve in the military. They quickly found that patriotism had an economic price: Unable to pay their debts, veterans found their property foreclosed and sold at auction by the sheriff. If this was insufficient to pay off the debt, the debtor was imprisoned (Chroust 1965). In 1786, these conditions brought about a farmers' rebellion in western Massachusetts led by Revolutionary War veteran Daniel Shays (Hurst 1950). The newspapers regularly castigated lawyers, and legislation was proposed in a number of states to curtail the practice of law or otherwise open it up to anyone who wished to practice (Chroust 1965).

In spite of the antagonism against lawyers, the profession thrived. Anton-Herman Chroust notes that "highly effective in the gradual conquest of public opinion and the common mind was the consistent and clever barrage of self-serving propaganda which lawyers levied in their own behalf" (1965: 30). The portrait presented to the public was that of the noble lawyer eager to assist those who could not afford his services. They were also great exponents of the republic whose "voice and pen served both culture and country in a seemingly endless stream of works instructing and strengthening the American people in the meaning of republicanism" (Ferguson 1984: 26).

"The lawyer's status in this period was determined by his effort to rise above the level of a trade and reach that of a profession. The effort ran into opposition from those forces in American life which wanted no part of the specially trained and specially privileged elites who were trying to map out for themselves a broad control over society. . . . At the same time, the egalitarian 'folk' ethos gave way to the realities of a complex society where the lawyer's skills and discipline were needed. With its usual disregard for consistency, the public, while deprecating practitioners of law for inattention to truth and fairness, continued to bestow upon them offices of trust" (Haar 1965: 12–13).

Thus, despite the low status of the bar, lawyers continued to be prominent in American government. In fact, lawyers were the most prominent members of colonial legislatures and the Continental Congress. Of the 56 signers of the Declaration of Independence, 25 were lawyers. Of the 55 members of the Constitutional Convention, 31 were lawyers, as were 10 of the 29 senators and 17 of the 56 representatives of the first Congress[1] (Schwartz 1974); 13 of the first 16 presidents were lawyers (Ferguson 1984). Being aligned with the merchant and propertied class was obviously not a political handicap. "Economic necessity stimulated a demand for skilled interpreters of the labyrinth of provincial and local economic regulatory legislation" (Hall 1989: 23). Lawyers were articulate and active in community affairs, available to help with the myriad of increasingly complex issues affecting the newly independent United States. "If lawyers were an evil, they were, however, a necessary evil" (Friedman 1973: 83).

ADMISSION TO THE BAR

In colonial times, each colony set its own standards for admission to the bar, and requirements usually involved a long period of apprenticeship. Traditional English differences between solicitors and barristers, for all practical purposes, did not exist. In some colonies each court admitted attorneys to practice before it, and admission to the higher courts was more difficult than admission to the lower courts. In others, admission by one court granted an attorney the right to practice in all courts of the colony. In some colonies admission to practice was centralized through the royal governor or an examining body appointed by the court (Pound 1953). "Bar associations created by the leading lawyers soon gained the approval of the colonial legislatures, themselves increasingly penetrated by members of the legal profession. Bar examinations went hand in hand with licensing examinations by judges, the result of which was a more influential profession as well as a more English one" (Hoffer 1992: 66).

However, lawyers were extremely unpopular in the years following the Revolution and particularly during the era of Jacksonian democracy (1828–1836). Strong democratic feelings and concurrent opposition to monopolization of legal practice led to the demise of standards for entry into legal practice. During the first third of the nineteenth century, there was a legislative breaking down of educational and training requirements necessary to be admitted to the practice of law (Pound 1953). In 1800, a definite period of preparation for admission to the bar was prescribed in 14 of the 19 states or organized territories that made up the Union. By 1840, it was required in only 11 out of 30 jurisdictions. In New Hampshire (in 1842), Maine (in 1843), Wisconsin (in 1849), and Indiana (in 1851), any citizen and voter could enter into the practice of law with no other evidence than that of having good character. By the eve of the Civil War, only 9 of 39 jurisdictions had

---

[1]The 105th Congress (1996) had 53 senators and 172 representatives who listed their primary occupation as lawyers.

standards, and they were usually quite low: "Good natured lawyers gave certificates of 'regular and attentive study' liberally to the asker with little or no inquiry," thus qualifying the person for admittance to the bar (Pound 1953: 230).

Standards remained lax in most states during the nineteenth century, and not at all uniform from state to state; government control of occupations remained weak. An open-ended bar attracted ambitious, if not talented, persons. By 1850, there were more than 20,000 lawyers in the United States, when the population was at 23 million, a ratio of 1 to 1,150. However, according to the Census Bureau, by 1880 there were more than 64,000 lawyers for a population of 50 million, a ratio of 1 to 781; by 1900, there were 108,000 lawyers for a population of 76 million, a ratio of 1 to 703; and by 1910, there were more than 115,000 lawyers for a population of almost 92 million, a ratio of 1 to 800. In some areas lawyers formed guilds (bar associations) to restrict the entry of new practitioners by holding down the number of apprentices, and this may have served to lessen the rate of increase.

GROWTH OF BAR ASSOCIATIONS

While a variety of bar associations existed by the early part of the nineteenth century, these groups were not very effective. They failed to exert any real control over who was admitted to the practice of law. After 1870, bar associations became vigorous in their fight to limit entry into the practice of law, primarily by way of raising standards. This movement to limit entry into the practice of law coincided with Christopher Columbus Langdell at Harvard (discussed in Chapter 4) and the rise of the case method in legal education: "The two movements went hand in glove" (Friedman 1973: 536). The case method served to define the practice of law as a distinct and scientific discipline that required extensive education and training. There was now justification for a monopoly of practice.

In some cities, such as New York (where the Association of the Bar of the City of New York was founded in 1870), bar associations were "motivated in large part by the reformist intent of established patrician lawyers," a response to rampant judicial corruption (Powell 1988: 9). This reformist bent was tempered by self-interest— elite lawyers, in reforming the system, institutionalized the advantage of their most important clients: corporate America. Reform was also intertwined with nativism; striking a blow against the "blackguard Celtic tyrants," Irish machine politicians who dominated urban politics and thus the courts in metropolitan areas (Powell 1988).

The bar association movement was a characteristic feature of the turn of the century. Lawyers, in common with doctors, "flocked into professional associations whose growth—the number of bar associations jumped from 16 in 1880 to more than 600 by 1916—expressed the impulse for professional cohesion in a fragmented society undergoing rapid change" (Auerbach 1976: 62–63). As bar associations became more effective, standards for practice were raised. By 1890, nearly half of the states required some preparation for practice, and after 1890, more and more states began requiring stringent levels of training and/or education. By 1928, every jurisdiction except Indiana had a compulsory bar examination, and there were training and/or educational requirements in order to qualify (Stevens 1983). However, as late as 1927, 32 of 49 jurisdictions had no prelegal educational requirement, and an additional 11 required only high school graduation (Abel 1989).

Bar Examination.   Some conflict occurred between bar associations and law schools over the *diploma privilege*. Beginning with Virginia in the 1840s, several states agreed to admit the graduates of leading law schools to the bar without further examination. By 1870, nine schools in seven states had this privilege. Diploma privilege made it possible for law schools to attract increasing numbers of students who desired to avoid the bar examination. The bar leadership, however, "was not pleased with the diploma privilege, which it felt took control of entry into the profession away from practitioners and gave it to legal educators" (Stevens 1983: 26). Bar associations were successful in their efforts against the diploma privilege, and statewide boards of examiners slowly became the norm; by 1917, they existed in 37 jurisdictions (Stevens 1983). Standards for admission to the bar are still regulated by each state and differ accordingly.

All states except California require a college degree or at least three years of undergraduate education (Abel 1989).[2] Most, but not all, states require a candidate to have graduated from an accredited law school (seven states allow an apprenticeship alternative), show evidence of "sound character," and pass an examination testing their knowledge of the law and skill in legal reasoning.[3]

While it varies from state to state, the typical bar examination requires the candidate to analyze hypothetical cases and set forth proposed solutions and the applicable laws. It is heavily weighted toward business subjects (Smith 1997). Given in February and July, the exam lasts two days (except in California, three days, and Texas, two and a half days). The first is devoted to the National Conference of Bar Examiners (NCBE) multistate, a 200-question, multiple-choice exam that is computer graded, with questions on constitutional law, contracts, criminal law, evidence, real property, and torts. On the second day is a test of applicable state laws and practices that is typically a mix of multiple-choice and essay questions. (The National Conference has also developed a multistate essay exam.) Forty-seven states and the District of Columbia require candidates to take the NCBE Multistate Professional Responsibility Examination, which consists of 50 multiple-choice questions.

New York University law professor Harry Subin states that "even the most competent law student in the country probably cannot pass [the bar exam] without taking a two-month cram bar review course" (1990: 10). Christopher Smith argues: "If you give any group of lawyers, including law professors, a bar exam as an unannounced 'pop quiz,' virtually all would fail," and "passing a bar exam does not mean that an attorney possesses lawyering skills or knows anything about various areas of law" (1997: 74).

Despite the trend toward standardization in testing, each state sets its own passing grade. Once admitted, a lawyer may practice only in the state where he or she is a member of the bar, although many states have reciprocal agreements and will admit lawyers from reciprocating states who have practiced law for a certain number of years. "The state-based system of bar admission is anachronistic. Ours is an era of multistate, even international, law firms. The practice of law is frequently multistate,

---

[2]Some law schools allow early entry—after completing three years of college—for students with outstanding grades and high LSAT scores.

[3]Under diploma privilege, graduates of the University of Wisconsin Law School and Marquette University Law School do not have to take the Wisconsin bar examination to practice law in the state as long as their schools certify their legal competence and the Board of Bar Examiners certifies their character and fitness for the practice of law.

but bar admission still occurs one state at a time" (Gerber 1989: 65–66). In 1999, 73,970 persons took bar examinations and 66 percent passed. States vary considerably in the percentage of persons passing the bar examination, ranging from 48 percent in California to 64 percent in New York, to 75 percent in Texas. States with a smaller number of persons taking the exam typically have a higher number who pass; for example, Montana, 85 percent, Nebraska, 88 percent, and New Mexico, 87 percent (National Conference of State Bar Examiners). Interestingly, graduates of elite law schools generally do not do as well as those from less selective schools.

In 1913, Herbert Harley founded the American Judicature Society as a vehicle for judicial reform, including compulsory membership in bar associations. In labor-management relations this is referred to as the closed shop; Harley chose the more positive-sounding term *integrated bar* (McKean 1963). Thirty states have an integrated bar, which is mandated by the legislature or that state's highest court. Every lawyer must pay dues and subject him- or herself to its rules or forfeit the right to practice law in that state. Mandatory membership in the bar association has been upheld by the Supreme Court (*Lathrop* v. *Donohue* 1961).

For most of their existence, bar associations represented a distinct part of the legal profession—white, male, mostly Protestant, and devoid of the latest immigrant groups. Throughout the nineteenth century the organized bar fought "to keep the law in the hands of the profession and to keep the profession in the hands of the legal elite" (Hobson 1986: 57). Around the time of the Great Depression (1929 to

ATTORNEY'S OATH OF ADMISSION

I do solemnly swear:

- I will support the constitution of the United States and the Constitution of my State;
- I will maintain the respect due to courts of justice and judicial officers;
- I will not counsel or maintain any suit or proceeding which shall appear to me to be unjust, nor any defense except such as I believe to be honestly debatable under the law of the land;
- I will employ for the purpose of maintaining the cause confided to me such means only as are consistent with truth and honor and will never seek to mislead the judges or jury by any artifice or false statement of fact or law;
- I will maintain the confidence and preserve inviolate the secrets of my client, and will accept no compensation in connection with this business except from him or with his knowledge and approval;
- I will abstain from all offensive personality, and advance no fact prejudicial to the honor or reputation of a party or witness unless required by the justice of the cause with which I am charged;
- I will never reject, from any considerations personal to myself, the cause of the defense-less or oppressed, or delay any man's cause for lucre or malice, so help me God.

Note: The American Bar Association commends this form of oath for adoption by the proper authorities in all the States and Territories.

the Second World War), in some urban areas this actually led to the formation of competing bar associations—one for lawyers who represented solo practitioners and small firms, another for those who represented banks and corporate clients (Glick 1983).

AMERICAN BAR ASSOCIATION

The idea of a national association of lawyers originated in 1878 at a meeting of the Connecticut Bar Association, during which a motion was passed to have a committee consider the establishment of an association of American lawyers.[4] The committee of prominent members of the Connecticut bar subsequently reported in favor of the idea. A circular signed by prominent attorneys from throughout the United States issued a call for a meeting on August 21, 1878. The place was Saratoga Springs, a vacation spa just north of Albany, New York, famous for its mineral water and gambling. Although the invitation for the gathering had been circulated to 607 names drawn from 41 states, territories, and the District of Columbia, only 75 persons from 21 states and the District of Columbia were in attendance (Carson 1978). The South was well represented—many lawyers apparently saw the meeting as an opportunity to escape the southern heat. The American Bar Association (hereafter ABA) chose as its first president James O. Broadhead, a Virginian who had moved to Missouri, where he sided with the Union. The delegates met amidst the background of Reconstruction and the scandals of Ulysses S. Grant's second term as president.

Within a year, the ABA had 284 members in 21 states. From 1878 to 1889, the ABA met annually or in alternate years in Saratoga Springs. Until 1902, meetings alternated between Saratoga Springs and other cities. By 1909, the ABA had 3,716 members; by 1924 it had 22,024. The increase was the result of a reorganization that established a state director and 11 district directors to tie local associations closer to the national. In 1936, the ABA established a federalized system of governance; the ruling body is the House of Delegates, whose membership is selected by state and local bar associations. The ABA now has more than 375,000 members and is headquartered in Chicago.

In its earlier days, the ABA supported conservative business values that were threatened by majoritanism: "Irrational passion and ignorance might sweep through the majority, but if those committed to the rule of law could only prevail, social order could be reasserted through peaceful and institutional means" (Hobson 1986: 34). The association exhibited considerable nativism, racism, antisemitism, and sexism—for the first 40 years, the ABA had no female members (Margolick 1994a). In 1969, the ABA elected a Jewish president; in 1994, the association elected a woman president. Today the ABA commissions studies on a variety of matters important to the legal profession and recommends reforms on various issues such as uniform state laws, reciprocity for attorneys in one state to practice in others, maritime law, criminal law and procedure, patents, and trademarks.

---

[4]Robert Stevens ascribes the founding of the ABA to meetings of the American Social Science Association in 1876 and 1877, during which the creation of a national lawyer's group was urged: "The creation of the American Bar Association (ABA) in 1878 was largely the result of these meetings" (1983: 27).

In 1900, the ABA's Section on Legal Education organized a meeting of law school delegates in Saratoga Springs. At this meeting the Association of American Law Schools (AALS) was established for "the improvement of legal education in America, especially in the Law Schools" (Sunderland 1953: 47). To be eligible for membership in the AALS, law schools had to comply with admission and length of study requirements (not fewer than two years prior to 1905, and three years thereafter). Schools that failed to maintain the requirements were dropped from the AALS. There was friction between the teachers of law and the practitioners: "To generalize, teachers tended to view law as an instrument of social change; practitioners saw it as a means of social control" (Auerbach 1971: 570). In 1914, after the ABA shifted its annual meeting from August to October, an inconvenient time for teachers, the AALS ceased to have any organizational connection to the ABA.

The accreditation of law schools, however, is the responsibility of the Council of the Section of Legal Education and Admissions to the Bar of the ABA, and a few law schools that are not members of AALS are among the more than 175 law schools accredited by the ABA. Accredited law schools require three years of full-time study and passage of examinations in order to qualify for a *Juris Doctor* (J.D.) As noted in Chapter 4, the stratification of legal education is reflected in the stratification of the legal profession.

STRATIFICATION OF THE LEGAL PROFESSION

The legal profession can be conceived of as having three strata. *Stratum I* attorneys are partners in the national law firms; in *Stratum II* are certain government and corporate attorneys; and *Stratum III* contains all other attorneys (see Figure 5–1). Before the

---

FIGURE 5-1   STRATIFICATION OF THE LEGAL PROFESSION

STRATUM I

National law firms

STRATUM II

Corporate counsel for leading companies
Select government attorneys

STRATUM III

Solo practitioners
Small law firms
Attorneys for small corporations
Government attorneys

Civil War, the most prominent lawyers made their reputations in courtrooms and often went into politics—they were great litigators and orators. By the close of the nineteenth century, while most lawyers still went to court, "the Wall Street lawyer, who perhaps never spoke to a judge except socially, made more money and had more prestige than any other lawyer" (Friedman 1973: 549). At the time of the founding of the ABA, the "legal profession was changing rapidly with the railroad lawyer and the businessman-lawyer emerging as the dominant type, keeping step with the emerging interpretation of the due process clause of the Fourteenth Amendment" in support of business "and the needs of the corporate form of organization in the new industrial age" (Carson 1978: 11–12). By the turn of the century, the ABA was headed by railroad and corporate attorneys, and a pattern of stratification was emerging, a situation strengthened by development of the large law firm, a response to the modern large corporation (Hobson 1986), and the advent of the Cravath system.

The Cravath System and Stratum I Attorneys

In 1906, Paul D. Cravath (1861–1940), a graduate of Columbia Law School (at the top of his class), became the head of a Wall Street law firm that had been founded in 1819. He recruited associates right out of law school, thus avoiding experienced lawyers who had developed "bad habits." The ideal candidate was a Phi Beta Kappa and law review editor from Harvard, Columbia, or Yale. (The firm continues to recruit most of its lawyers from these three schools and New York University.) The Cravath system provided an internship for new recruits that was designed to supplement Ivy League law school study with a practical postgraduate induction into the world of corporate law and lawyering (Smigel 1964). Long hours and hard work were demanded; those unable to meet the Cravath standard were not retained. Other firms quickly followed the Cravath lead.

The "Cravath lawyer" is expected to be wholly devoted and loyal to a client. Each lawyer-intern does general work for several years, usually for a number of the firm's partners, before being placed in an area of specialization. Responsibilities increase with improved competence, and before the tenth year the question of partnership becomes relevant. An employee either becomes a partner or leaves the firm for other work. Partnership is a mark of success in legal practice: "It brings the lawyer into the ownership circle of the firm, enhances earnings, and opens further avenues for career advancement" (Kay and Hagan 1998: 728):

> The process begins with an intensive period of supervision. As associates enter the firm, they are assigned to work on specific matters by supervising senior partners. First assignments are typically in research, requiring work very similar to that already undertaken in law school; the partner wants a memorandum on a particular point of law or a particular fact situation. He outlines his problem and, in the process, points the associate in the direction of an answer. . . . Inevitably, of course, a certain number of mistakes will be made by younger attorneys. But even mistakes have their uses: they become opportunities for further teaching. Eventually, the associate will be producing satisfactory memoranda and will then go on to other tasks. . . .
>
> Once associates have passed through the apprenticeship stage, supervision is converted into consultation. Associates begin to work with increased autonomy. First they are encouraged to handle small matters on their own. Soon associates may even be allowed their

own less important clients. Then they join in the recruitment activities of the firm and in the training of younger associates. Eventually, they become members of the teams handling the largest and most sophisticated deals and cases in the office. When this happens in an orderly progression, associates can expect to be made partners. (Spangler 1986: 46)

Steven Kumble (with Lahart) provides a more stark description: "Top firms take a lot of lawyers out of law school, work them unmercifully, and over time, weed out those who are not going to make it" (1990: 23). "Making it" is in large part determined by hours billed (Kronman 1993).

The growth of the large law firm (in excess of 200 lawyers) is a post-Second World War phenomenon "feeding on the ever-increasing intervention of government in what had once been private business—complicated tax codes, aggressive antitrust enforcement, antidiscrimination laws, environmental requirements, questions of corporate governance, and securities issues" (Linowitz 1996: 100–101). However, the traditional Cravath-type tutelage system has given way to current economic realities: "Tutelage consumes valuable time of partners, as well as associates, that cannot be billed to clients. Thus it is hardly surprising that one-on-one sessions became shorter and formal continuing education programs were established in firms as competition for clients intensified in the 1980s. The mentoring system received another blow when starting salaries shot upward in 1986 as firms competed for top law graduates" (Glendon 1994: 27). Instead of the generalist training of the Cravath system, today's young associates are trained narrowly so they can be productive very quickly–specialization is the rule (Linowitz 1996). If the attorney's specialty is no longer lucrative—due to a change in market conditions, for example—he or she may face a career dilemma.

Into the 1960s, "most large firms ran with an egalitarian system of partner compensation that, except for a small bracket of 'name partners' or 'senior partners,' gave an equal share of annual profits to all those with the same seniority at the firm" (Linowitz 1996: 102). Today the field of corporate law is dominated by "rainmakers"—partners with client contacts "are generally more heavily rewarded than those whose labors buttress the firm's reputation for quality" (1996: 32). Another pattern set by Cravath—attorneys totally dedicated to the interests of their wealthy clients expending an unlimited amount of time and effort on their behalf—has also changed; legal expenses have ballooned and cost-cutting has become a feature of the corporate practice of law. And the focus on profits has reportedly made firm loyalty a quaint practice of yesteryear: successful partners (with their clients) are being lured away by competing firms offering greater rewards (Parsa 1999).

A Stratum I firm "is ordinarily divided into departments (corporate, banking, real estate, litigation, etc.) or working groups. Various specialists coordinate their efforts on the problems of the client" (Galanter and Palay 1991: 2). These law firms generally provide counseling, negotiation, and representation services, as opposed to trial advocacy. For these national law firms litigation generally represents failure—the firm practices preventive law and the goal is to avoid the uncertainty of trial courts. In fact, "much of what lawyers do involves planning a client's activities so that disputes are not likely to arise or can be settled advantageously if they do arise (dispute anticipating)" (Burton 1985: 19).

In the recent past, when litigation was inevitable, national law firms often recruited expert litigators from outside their traditional sources, from government service, for example (Hoffman 1982). This has changed. About one-third of

Cravath, Swaine, and Moore work now involves litigation: "The winds of change that have swirled through corporate America in recent years—the mega takeovers, the class-action suits, the rise of leveraged buy-outs and other complex financial transactions—have placed corporate litigators more and more in positions of power" (Reich 1986: 24). In fact, the Cravath reputation for handling litigation led to a contract from the Federal Deposit Insurance Corporation to help that agency recoup money from the savings and loan debacle (Margolick 1991a). Even at the local level, prosecution of corporate defendants has increased dramatically (Benson, Cullen, and Maakestad 1993).

Many national law firm attorneys, however, are simply "paper litigators," taking depositions and exchanging motions: "Most have only a fraction of the courtroom experience of legal aid lawyers who are half their age and one-twentieth as well compensated" (former Federal Judge Harold R. Tyler, quoted in Margolick 1988a: 19). Such persons can be inadequate to the task of trying a case before a jury. As a result, many blue chip firms recruit trial lawyers from the ranks of federal prosecutors whose caseload usually includes corporate crime (Goff 1989).

The clients of such firms, of course, must be in a position to pay for dedication; accordingly, national law firms represent corporate America, not individuals. They recruit graduates with good grades from the elite law schools—highly competitive individuals eager to advance into partnership. Traditionally, qualifications included lineage—the "right social background," which had the effect of keeping out many Catholics and Jews, and virtually all blacks, few of whom graduated from prestigious law schools. In fact, when more Jews began qualifying for elite law schools, they were met with quotas that artificially restricted their numbers. "This exclusion began to break down after the Second World War. Jewish associates were hired and some moved up the ladder to partner. Cravath appointed its first Jewish partner in 1959" (Galanter and Palay 1991: 25).

Partners in law firms representing blue chip corporations are overwhelmingly white males, and even in recent years the top firms have been slow in promoting minority lawyers to partner status (Glater 2001b). When African-Americans do become partners they find their social background a handicap in client development—finding firms capable of paying substantial billing rates requires networking of a type that traditionally has excluded persons of color (Keeva 1993). Women account for 13 percent of the partners at the 1,160 largest law firms (Buchholz 1996) and an increasing number are being hired as associates.[5] In 1999, Baker and McKenzie of Chicago with 2,330 lawyers and 535 partners, 91 percent of whom are men, chose a woman to be the firm's chairperson. At least 5 of the top 100 American law firms have chosen women to lead them (Peterson 1999). Women will continue to face a major hurdle, however, if they try to balance marriage and children with the long hours required of associates who are on a partnership track. Many settle for—or are forced into—the "mommy track," which allows them to remain with the firm without reaching partnership-or-out status. A 1996 report by the ABA revealed bias against female lawyers in the private sector has caused deep inequities of pay, promotion, and opportunity (N. Bernstein 1996a).

---

[5]Women constitute about 25 percent of the legal profession and nearly half of the law school population (N. Bernstein 1996a; Glater 2001).

Anti-semitism, Sexism, and Wall Street Law

In an interview, prominent defense attorney, author, and Harvard University law professor Alan Dershowitz recalled: "I was graduating from Yale law school. I was first in my class, editor of the Law Journal, but I was rejected when I applied for jobs with Wall Street firms" ("Q & A" 1991: 6). Ruth Bader Ginsburg, upon being nominated to the Supreme Court, recalled experiencing similar discrimination with respect to her gender.

While there is not a simple one-to-one relationship between size and prestige, the most prestigious law firms have over 200 lawyers—Cravath has over 350. About 50 firms in the United States have more than 200 lawyers, and about half qualify as "elite." The three largest firms have a total of more than 4,500 lawyers and thousands of support staff including paralegals, administrators, and librarians. While most of these firms are in New York, several can be found in Chicago, Cleveland, Dallas, Houston, Los Angeles, Philadelphia, and San Francisco. Many New York law firms have offices in Washington, D.C. and Los Angeles, gateway to the Orient and in many respects the nation's second city in commerce and finance.

These law firms represent the corporate elite, companies found on the *Fortune* 500 list. For example, Skadden, Arps represents 175 of the *Fortune* 500 companies, 18 of the world's 25 biggest banks, and 23 of the 25 largest investment banks (Lyon 1991). Exxon is represented by Baker and Botts of Houston; General Motors is represented by Well, Gotshal, and Manges of New York; Cravath, Swaine, and Moore represents IBM, Texaco, and CBS. "Only such clients can afford the elite corporate law firms and the kind of practice for which the firms pride themselves—one in which no stone is left unturned, no matter how seemingly insignificant, and with virtually no regard for time or money" (Stewart 1984: 14).

Washington law firms became particularly important during the New Deal era (1932–1941), when dramatic increases in government programs led to a corresponding increase in government attorneys.[6] This, in turn, led to a greater need for attorneys in Washington to represent business interests before Congress and regulatory bodies. These firms are often staffed by attorneys who previously worked for the government. Many Washington law firms practice influence rather than law. Thus, prestigious firms operating in the District of Columbia frequently have former members of Congress, cabinet officials, and White House staff as partners because of the access these persons presumably have to government decision makers. "Lawyer-lobbying" has proven very lucrative for about a dozen law firms who work for corporate interests: "They want a regulation changed, a law passed, amended or, more commonly, stopped. They thrive on contacts in government and the voracious appetite in Congress for campaign contributions" (Lewis 1989b: 26; McGuire 1993). While the firms often match members of Congress with political action committees (PAC), a few have established their own PACs, contributing directly to members.

---

[6]For an examination of the role of elite lawyers in the New Deal, see Shamir (1995).

There are also "Washington lawyers" who specialize in the Supreme Court:

They are former members of the solicitor general's staff who now utilize their enormous Supreme Court expertise in private practice. They are former clerks to the justices who have seen the Court from the inside. They are the well-educated, talented litigators who work in some of the nation's largest, most prestigious law firms and who represent a sophisticated clientele in the Court. They are counsel to any number of organized interests that have established offices throughout the neighboring streets of the capital community and that use appellate litigation to further their policy goals. These lawyers position cases in the lower courts for possible appeals. They file briefs at the agenda stage and argue cases on the merits. They strategize with amici curiae [friend of the court briefs] and consult with less experienced counsel. (McGuire 1993: 21-22)

An increasing number of major firms have expanded into global concerns with offices in major cities throughout the world. Baker and McKenzie of Chicago, for example, has offices in 32 countries, and less than a third of its attorneys are in the United States (Labaton 1988b; Feder 1993). New York's Skadden, Arps, Slate, Meagher and Flom, with about 1,000 attorneys, has offices on several continents. About two dozen law firms have opened offices in Brussels, capital of the European Community.

Elite firms have been establishing new (for them) areas of specialization, for example, corporate crime. Ironically, the persons hired for this specialty are the ones responsible for creating the need—U.S. attorneys who have been active prosecuting corporations and their executives. National law firms have also been establishing subsidiaries handling nonlegal business: real estate, banking, insurance, lobbying, health care and environmental consulting, and economic research. A number of firms—not necessarily "elite"—are providing "one-stop-shopping," diversifying into a broad array of non-legal services that were once entirely independent: investigations and money management, for example. This raises two troubling concerns. First, clients utilizing the non-legal services of a law firm may not be fully aware that they are not protected by attorney–client privilege. Second is a potential conflict of interest, the risk that lawyers will steer clients to their own business services rather than objectively laying out a range of options (Hines 2001a). The profusion of antitrust activities, leveraged buyouts, and mergers has also resulted in spinoffs from traditional law firms: firms managed by attorneys but that specialize in the economic analysis of legal issues (Margolick 1988b). Law firms faced with increasing technological complexity hire attorneys with science backgrounds, and there are nonlawyers with doctorates in scientific disciplines who work as in-house advisors.

At most big firms there are associates and partners. The former work for the latter; in fact, the partners earn profits largely on hourly billings of the salaried associates, and the more associates the greater the profits. The profits of the firm are typically shared by the partners in proportion to the amount of work brought in and their seniority. Most large firms have two or three associates per partner, and an associate should bring in three times his or her salary: one-third for the associate, one-third for overhead, and one-third for the firm (Lewin 1983). "Among larger firms it is common for name partners (the 'finders') to sign up the cases, then hand the actual work over to junior associates (the 'grinders')" (Grutman 1990: 79). Because of increased competition, some firms are basing their billings on the size of the transaction and case success, rather than hours exerted (Freitag 1989; Slade 1993).

In competition for students from elite law schools, some New York firms provide summer internships for third-year students at salaries of about $1,000 a week. Annual starting salaries with bonuses for students right out of law school hired as associates at elite firms range up to $160,000. In 2000, Craveth awarded a year-end bonus of $40,000 to its first-year associates, bringing the total compensation for the class of 1999 to $165,000.

Any number of firms have initiated two-tier hiring practices: Second tier associates on a nonpartnership track (sometimes called staff attorneys) are drawn from less prestigious law schools and are paid considerably less than tier one associates (Galanter and Palay 1991). They provide low-cost legal help for the firm's more routine, but labor-intensive, work such as reviewing documents in a complicated commercial litigation case—a chore most lawyers disdain. While many work on yearly renewable contracts, others become permanent employees of the firm. These nonpartner-track attorneys permit the firm to offer clients cheaper hourly rates (Lewin 1987a). Cravath, Swaine and Moore has created a middle-step "for senior associates who did not make partner; they have become 'permanent associates'" (Cherovsky 1991: 63).

Systemized recruitment patterns channel the legal talent flow into corporate law firms that provide comprehensive services to a restricted clientele (Auerbach 1976). In fact, these firms typically screen their prospective clients. Thus, with respect to an elite firm such as Sullivan and Cromwell with over 400 lawyers, it is only somewhat easier to become a client than a partner. Partners "have to follow an elaborate procedure for introducing new clients to the firm. Even lawyers' relatives have to be approved by the new client committee, which meets every Thursday" (Lisagor and Lipsius 1988: 283). Of course, "the main criterion for becoming a Sullivan and Cromwell client is wealth" (1988: 284). Keenly aware of the criticism leveled at them, national law firms typically provide pro bono (an abbreviation for *pro bono publico*—"for the public good") legal services. As part of their apprenticeship period, associates are often required to serve public interest groups such as those involved in civil liberties, civil rights, consumer, and environmental issues. During the politically volatile period of the 1960s, in order to recruit desirable law school graduates, prestigious law firms often found it necessary to promise prospective associates that they could work on public interest issues on company time. While some continue this tradition, it appears to be declining. In 2000, it was reported that many of the nation's largest firms were being inundated with so much work that they cut back significantly on pro bono work (Winter 2000),

Partners in national law firms are sometimes called upon for government service, usually at the federal level. This represents a temporary financial loss that can frequently be more than offset by the contacts and exposure resulting from a highly visible federal position.

Elite Lawyers

"These lawyers perform very significant work for very significant clients in every significant area of business and governmental activity" (Cherovsky 1991: 21).

Stratum II Attorneys

The most prominent attorney categories in Stratum II are a select few employed by the federal government and those employed by large corporations. A relatively small number of government attorneys, for example, federal judges, U.S. attorneys, cabinet officials such as the attorney general, legal advisor to the president, and the solicitor general, are in Stratum II. Numerically, most Stratum II attorneys are employed by corporations.

> Prior to World War II, the general counsel of a company was likely to be its outside law firm, and in those cases where there was a full-time house general counsel, he was likely to be in charge of a small staff that did the repetitive scutwork. Not infrequently, such an inside general counsel would do double duty, serving as corporate secretary, a cognate activity, or in some more remote function such as personnel director.
>
> As time passed, regulations proliferated, and the tax code grew, no single outside lawyer could answer the chief executives' questions about how some piece of law or regulation was going to affect the business. The lawyers who could answer the questions about regulations and specialized procedures at administrative agencies might well have the company's most feared competitors on their client roster. Many top executives were uncomfortable with the idea that they were getting advice on key decisions from the same people who were advising their rivals. (Linowitz 1996: 82-83)

Thus, in addition to retaining national law firms as outside counsel, large corporations employ salaried attorneys, often persons recruited from national law firms, as in-house counsel. Corporations prefer to hire experienced lawyers (Abel 1989). Since the 1970s, there has been a rapid growth in both the importance and size of corporate legal offices and the size of some corporate legal staffs exceeds that of many national law firms. They may train their own lawyers and compete with law firms in recruiting from elite law schools. This trend "is consistent with the general pattern of vertical integration—it is one more instance in which the corporation becomes an employer rather than a buyer of some element necessary to its production process, with all the enhanced control that such a move implies" (Spangler 1986: 72). The American Corporate Counsel Association, founded in 1982, represents more than 11,500 persons in 42 chapters in the United States and western Europe.

The legal division of major corporations is headed by the general counsel (a senior management official). Beneath the general counsel are deputy or associate administrators who supervise staff attorneys typically distributed throughout the ranking system established by corporate policy. While they may be physically dispersed and work for different divisions within a corporation, staff attorneys are directly responsible to their superiors in the law department, which is a self-contained entity for purposes of evaluation and advancement. "This arrangement is designed to protect not only the autonomy of the law department but, more important, the corporation's long-term interests in having its executives' business practices adequately monitored" (Spangler 1986: 76). For corporate counsel, the corporation—not its officers and directors—is the client (Gillers 1996). Seniority considerations play a central role in advancement for corporate attorneys.

The office of the general counsel does not usually represent the employer; rather, in-house counsel is involved with a myriad of legal concerns that are part of modern corporate activity. In-house counsel may:

- Assist with strategic planning whenever there are important legal implications, for example, providing a legal analysis to the board of directors and an evaluation of available options.
- Monitor business activities to ensure compliance with statutory and regulatory requirements, for example, securities, civil rights, and employee health and safety regulations.
- Provide continuing in-service education to ensure that corporate personnel understand compliance requirements.
- Serve as the corporation's liaison to the national law firm on retainer to the corporation.

Corporate attorneys "pride themselves on doing preventive law by advising on the structure of a business deal as it evolves" (Spangler 1986: 78). "While law departments formerly confined themselves to processing routine corporate legal matters and left major transactions and litigation work to outside counsel, they are now undertaking more work that once would have gone to outside lawyers. Some in-house counsel now conduct some or all of their own litigation" (Galanter and Palay 1991: 50). Although corporate counsel does not enjoy the prestige or income of a partnership in a national law firm, the environment is more relaxed, hours are more limited, and the position has considerably more prestige than that enjoyed by most Stratum III attorneys.

Stratum III Attorneys

"No nation has the lawyer population ratio of that found in the United States; none even comes close. With only 5 percent of the world's population, Americans have nearly two-thirds of the world's lawyers" (Stumpf and Culver 1992: 63). Since 1950, the number of attorneys has grown twice as fast as the population; by 1984 one out of every 364 people was a lawyer (Curran 1986), three times the ratio in England and more than nine times that in France. In 1991, there were 281 attorneys for every 100,000 persons in the United States; Germany had 111; England and Wales, 82; and Japan, 11 (Margolick 1991b). The U.S. has about 900,000 attorneys; each year, more than 50,000 persons are admitted to the bar. New York (more than 7,000) and California (about 6,000) lead the nation in new admissions, while five states (Florida, Illinois, Massachusetts, New Jersey, and Texas) admit more than 2,000 annually.

Derek Bok (1983), a former Harvard Law School dean, has been critical of the apparent overproduction of lawyers in the United States: "A nation's values and problems are mirrored in the ways in which it uses its ablest people." We graduate too many lawyers and not enough engineers. "In Japan, a country only half our size, 30 percent more engineers graduate each year than in all the United States. . . . It would be hard to claim that these differences have no practical consequences. As the Japanese put it, 'Engineers make the pie grow larger; lawyers only decide how to carve it up.'"

According to the American Bar Association, Washington, D.C., has the highest ratio of lawyers to population: 1 for every 25 persons. Wilmington, Delaware, where most major corporations are incorporated, has 1 for every 64 persons; the ratio in New York City is 1 for 177, below those of Harrisburg, Pennsylvania (1 to

JAPAN

While Japan produces only about 350 new lawyers a year, thousands of additional professionals who do not necessarily correspond exactly to the American lawyer perform important legal services (Sanders 1996). Moreover, the civil side of the Japanese legal system is much weaker than its counterpart in the United States. For example, there are no product liability laws, class action lawsuits, or punitive damages. The system reflects a government preference for conciliation and, accordingly, limits the number of persons who can enter law school and, thus, the number of lawyers and judges. Japan also has far fewer judges per capita than the United States (Goozner 1992; Sanders 1996). This results in overcrowded court dockets, making it difficult for a case to actually reach trial—about 40 percent longer than in a U.S. district court—encouraging settlements in which the weaker party is often denied "fair" compensation (Chira 1987; see Haley [1991] and Sanders [1996] for an examination of the legal system in Japan)."Japanese courts are notoriously slow and indifferent to the complaints of individuals." As a result, would-be plaintiffs hire gangsters—yakuza: "Essentially, the yakuza have taken on the role of lawyers-cum-negotiators" (Seymour 1996: 202).

57), and Olympia, Washington (1 to 65). Over 70 percent of American lawyers are in private practice, and half of the attorneys who practice law are in solo practice or two-lawyer firms; about 30 percent of those who have been admitted to the bar have non-law related jobs. Lawyers in firms of 4 to 10 lawyers account for about 20 percent of those in practice, and firms of 11 or more attorneys account for the remaining private practitioners. About 10 percent of all practicing attorneys are employed by government agencies on the federal, state, county, or municipal level.

While the prestige of Stratum III attorneys is considerably less than that of their Strata I and II colleagues, income is not the decisive factor. In fact, there are some Stratum III attorneys whose income surpasses that of most of those in Strata I and II. The nation's top litigator, Joseph Jamail of Houston, known as "king of the torts," earns up to 25 million annually (Jennings 1989). This is due to the contingency fee (discussed in Chapter 12). Because tort judgments can be quite substantial, Stratum III attorneys who practice personal injury law on a contingency basis can earn incomes well in excess of those earned by most Stratum I attorneys. Indeed, there is an organization of attorneys, the Circle of Advocates, whose members have all won at least one $1 million judgment. But millionaire trial lawyers are the rare exception among the tens of thousands found in Stratum III.

The solo attorney who predominates in Stratum III is typically identified by lack of a prestigious legal education and a social background that has kept him or her out of the circles of power and wealth that lawyers from the national law firms routinely frequent. The solo practitioner does not have the readily available research and investigative resources of a large law firm. By default, most solo lawyers end up doing the "dirty work" of the bar (Ladinsky 1963). Instead of depending on contacts with the world of big business, the solo practitioner depends on family, neighborhood, ethnic group, and local political contacts for clientele. He or she generally works for individuals, and the nature of the work may be distasteful. "Divorce work involves emotionally charged, embarrassing personal situations . . . personal injury work deals with grisly facts and with claimants who are badly maimed; and criminal work often requires the lawyer to associate with persons who are less than pleasant" (Heinz and Laumann 1982: 93). There is also the rural bar, strikingly homogeneous, whose practitioners work alone or with fewer than five partners, representing a broad range of clients (Landon 1990).

While there is not a strong relationship between the prestige of a particular field of law and a lawyer's income, there is a high correlation with the prestige of clients: "Fields that serve corporate, wealthier, more 'establishment' clients are accorded more deference within the profession than are those that serve individual, poorer clients" (Heinz and Laumann 1982: 331). There are also types of law practice whose prestige ranking is somewhat ambivalent. "For example, the practice of labor law (for both unions and management) involves considerable financial stakes, but it also involves association with blue-collar workers or their representatives. Similarly, the lawyers who represent defendants in personal injury cases usually work for high status clients, since those defendants are typically insurance companies, but their work also involves unsavory fact situations" (Heinz and Laumann 1982: 331). In any event, "contrary to the impression that television drama gives, with its emphasis on courtroom battles, most lawyers generally practice 'preventive law.' They help people discover ways to reduce their taxes or write valid wills and contracts. They study complex insurance policies and bank loan agreements. Such efforts reduce the probability of conflict. Most lawyers usually play a planning role. They help people create their own 'private laws,' laws governing their personal affairs and no more" (Carter 1984: 4).

There is also the private practice of law as part of a franchise law firm that offers "no frills" or "discount" legal assistance. Some firms have more than a hundred such offices throughout the country; their services are promoted by heavy advertising. They are typically housed in storefronts in retail business districts or shopping malls. They earn their profits by handling a large volume of relatively uncomplicated cases such as uncontested divorces, simple wills, and bankruptcies or personal injury claims where the total dollar amount is relatively small. On the fees that are typically charged, these firms cannot easily engage in full-scale litigation and they have been criticized for "settling too quickly for too little" (Gould 1986: F15). There is a great deal of lawyer turnover in these firms, and this can affect continuity of service in more complex cases, such as contested divorces, which can take several years to complete (see Van Hoy 1997 for a discussion of these firms).

The difficulty experienced in securing affordable legal services has spawned a variety of self-help firms that provide the documents for *pro se* (for oneself) representation. Some are franchised "do-it-yourself" businesses operated by nonlawyers who serve a function similar to that long-performed by paralegals working for law firms—primarily filling out forms. Typical cases involve bankruptcy, uncontested divorce, living trusts, wills, and incorporation. These firms are prohibited from offering legal advice, but some have attorneys available—usually by telephone—to answer legal questions. Bar associations have been vociferous in their opposition to these establishments, arguing that they are practicing law without a license and/or are misleading consumers into believing they can handle matters beyond their competence (Hines 2001b).

In Chapter 10 we will examine the practice of law in the criminal justice system. In this chapter, we will turn to the practice of law in the nonprofit sector of the civil system.

LEGAL AID

While a criminal defendant, in virtually all instances, is entitled to be represented by competent counsel, persons with civil grievances or defendants in a noncriminal action have no such constitutional entitlement (Ritchey 2001). Justice has a price that most Americans cannot afford to pay (unless there is a contingency fee): "Throughout most of our history, few of the poor have been able to turn to the courts for redress of their grievances and participate in judicial development of law and policy" (Lawrence 1990: ix).

The European Convention of Human Rights recognizes the right to counsel in civil cases as a fundamental human right, and all Western democracies furnish counsel for those who cannot afford their own in civil litigation. According to English law, "no one needing the protection of an English Court should be denied this for lack of means," and "the courts can fulfill their function of administering the law effectively, [only] through the parties coming before them on equal terms, irrespective of their financial resources" (Ritchey 2001: 333).

In the United States, in the years just before and immediately after World War I, there was fear of civil unrest that intensified with the Bolshevik Revolution in Russia. Immigrants who had fueled the Industrial Revolution were now seen as potential revolutionaries. Strikes and mass demonstrations for higher wages, better working conditions, and a 40-hour work week were viewed as the forerunner of radical upheavals. The American Bar Association argued that the influx of foreigners who lacked an understanding of American values and not class injustice was at the heart of the problem. It was important to educate these alien elements, to show them that they had a stake in the American system. Law and courts, not strikes and violence, are the American way, said the ABA. The bar had a responsibility, a *noblesse oblige*, to promote justice under law (Auerbach 1976).

Legal Aid Societies

The Legal Aid Society in New York was founded by German-Americans in 1876 to assist their compatriots, many of whom were being preyed upon by confidence men. The society subsequently expanded its services generally to the poor, and other cities followed the New York example. A society was formed in Chicago in 1886 to aid young women being lured into prostitution with duplicitous offers of legitimate employment. By the turn of the century, there were legal aid societies in six cities, and in 1909, the first bar association-sponsored legal aid society was established. Most societies, however, were supported by private contributions, and expansion of legal aid was primarily the result of the efforts of Arthur von Briesen, a Prussian immigrant who served the Union during the Civil War. He warned potential contributors that the alternative to legal aid was civil strife and political disorder—given the times, a very realistic approach to raising money. As fear of social unrest increased, so did the expansion of legal aid societies. Although there were only 15 by 1910, that number increased to 41 in the next decade, and by 1923 there were 61. In 1914, Reginald Heber Smith, a young Harvard Law School graduate, became the head of the newly formed Boston Legal Aid Society. He was appalled by the lack of legal services for the poor. Traveling on a Carnegie Foundation grant, Smith toured the United States visiting legal aid societies and courts. The result was a book, *Justice and the Poor* (1919). Because of his efforts, the National Organization of Legal Aid Organizations was formed, and the ABA established a standing committee on legal aid.

Legal aid societies limited their assistance to the "deserving poor," those who were employed, and cases accepted were those too petty for any private attorney—the societies wanted to avoid competing with the private bar. They did not involve themselves in law reform, rarely engaging in the appellate process. The continuing inability of legal aid even to begin to address the issue of equal justice under law eventually led to the establishment of the Legal Services Corporation and public interest law firms.

Federal Legal Services

In 1965, as part of President Lyndon B. Johnson's "War on Poverty," Congress authorized funding for legal aid for the poor in civil and criminal cases under the Office of Economic Opportunity (OEO). The program came in the wake of urban riots, much as the impetus for earlier legal aid was the unrest a half century earlier. Legal services had the support of the president of the ABA, Lewis F. Powell, Jr., who was later appointed to the Supreme Court by President Nixon. Bar groups, however, wanted assurance that the legal services attorneys would not compete with local private practitioners. Under OEO legislation, neighborhood law offices were opened by local groups with federal funding. Soon after the first offices were opened, legal services lawyers were swamped by more needy clients than they could properly represent (E. Johnson 1974).

A review of program goals led to the conclusion that the funding being provided by the federal government could not meet the needs of the poor. A new strategy was developed. Instead of handling the problems of the poor simply on an individual basis, legal services attorneys would work for law reform that could affect large numbers of poor persons—the instrumental use of law. The legal services lawyer would move from a client server role to that of a law reformer:

> Prior to the establishment of the Legal Services Program, the Court had seldom addressed the civil claims of the poor. There is a very simple explanation for this. The de facto assistance of counsel requirement had prevented those poor whose legal claims did not fit into an interest group's litigation strategy from bringing their cases to the Court. The philosophy of the legal aid societies produced a set of lawyers representing the poor who had little interest in litigation and even less in appellate advocacy. The poor's claims were rarely placed on the Court's jurisdictional agenda. (Lawrence 1990: 149)

As a result of legal services litigation, the Supreme Court focused on poverty issues outside the criminal justice process, using the due process and equal protection clauses to supervise the state's interaction with the less fortunate.

The goal of law reform was advanced by the quality of attorney attracted to the legal services program; law school graduates who would normally be destined for corporate practice were energized by the prospects of social action through law. During the entire history of the legal aid society, no staff attorney had ever taken a case to the Supreme Court, but between 1967 to 1972, legal services attorneys took 219, 136 of which were decided on their merits, and 73 of these were won (E. Johnson 1974). Federal legal services impacted dramatically on legislative and executive branch policy. Casebooks on poverty law were published and law schools began presenting courses on poverty law (Lawrence 1990).

By 1973, there were over 900 legal services offices around the country employing close to 5,000 lawyers. They initiated class-action suits (discussed in Chapter 12) against powerful interests. Without an overall national strategy, they forced federal and local governmental agencies to pay benefits to poor persons as mandated by welfare legislation; they forced the public schools to admit children of illegal aliens; they forced public hospitals to provide free abortions to indigent women; and they initiated litigation to force officials to improve jail conditions. The legal services attorneys upset business and farming communities by litigating to enforce state and federal statutes with respect to wages and working conditions. In addition to its efforts on behalf of farm workers, California Rural Legal Assistance forced the state to increase Medicaid and other welfare payments. (For a discussion of major legal services cases and strategies, see Lawrence 1990.) Then-Governor Ronald Reagan was unsuccessful in his efforts to cut off funding for the group.

In 1974, President Richard Nixon signed legislation creating the Legal Services Corporation (LSC) to insulate the activities of legal services lawyers from increasing political pressures. Soon after Ronald Reagan was elected president, however, he moved to abolish the program, asking Congress to cut out all appropriations. Congress refused, although funding was cut back 25 percent and significant restrictions were placed on the types of cases legal services lawyers could handle. The 1974 legislation provided for a governing board of 11 members appointed by the president, and in his continuing efforts to destroy the program, President Reagan nominated opponents of legal services to the governing board. In the first three years of his presidency, he nominated 26 people for the board, all opponents of legal services, none of whom were confirmed by the Republican-controlled Senate. Under President George Bush, this policy continued. Both Reagan and Bush resorted to recess appointments in order to delay Senate confirmation and over a period of a decade they were successful in stacking the board with legal services opponents. Two presidents of the American Bar Association, in 1986 and 1988, called for the removal of the chair of the Legal Services Corporation because of his hostility toward the mission of the very agency that he was chosen by the president to head (Raven 1988). The LSC chairman, a former aide to Senator Jesse Helms (R–NC), hired an attorney to draft a brief contending the corporation unconstitutional, and he hired lobbyists to convince Congress to cut the corporation's budget (Lewis 1989a).

The battle over the role of government in providing legal assistance for the poor continues, with the ABA on the side of continued funding and many political conservatives and the U.S. Chamber of Commerce in opposition. The latter have accused the LSC of being antibusiness and "part of a political movement that views the American free enterprise system as a grand conspiracy" (DiLorenzo 1988: 3). Maggie Gallagher, an editor of the conservative *National Review*, referred to the LSC as "a $300-million cornucopia for rebel lawyers with a cause. In the guise of helping the poor," she argues, "taxpayers' money goes to radical legal think-tanks, strategy sessions, and class-action lawsuits that have sought, in many cases successfully, to expand the welfare state and undermine bourgeois social values" (1988: 42).

With the election of Bill Clinton, a new board with members committed to the concept of Legal Services was chosen—Hillary Rodham Clinton, the president's wife, headed the LSC board during the presidency of Jimmy Carter. Nevertheless, in 1996 a Republican-controlled Congress succeeded in slashing the program's budget by 30 percent, from $400 million to $278 million for the fiscal year. (The figure was $330 million for the 2001 fiscal year.) Republican lawmakers also enacted a ban on Legal Services lawyers bringing class-action lawsuits (discussed in Chapter 12), an important tool in policy-oriented litigation (N. Bernstein 1996b).

Many of the most far-reaching legal services lawsuits had involved welfare cases, so the 1996 Congress "also prohibited the lawyers from taking part in any cases challenging the administration of welfare laws" (Greenhouse 1996b: E5). In addition, the legislation limited the freedom to represent client interests before legislative and administrative bodies. In 2001, the Supreme Court, in a 5–4 decision, ruled that this legislation violated the First Amendment by denying legal services attorneys the right to act as advocates (*Legal Services Corporation* v. *Velasquez*), But the irony continues: America has a glut of lawyers and an absence of affordable legal services.

PUBLIC INTEREST LAW

Public interest law is the name given efforts to provide legal representation to interests that historically have been unrepresented and underrepresented in the legal process (Council for Public Interest Law; hereafter CPIL 1976). Along with civil rights and civil liberties organizations, public interest lawyers "share an enthusiasm for using the legal system to redress social and economic injustices" (Aron 1989: 3).

There are two kinds of public interest law programs:

1. Programs with a "focus on policy-oriented cases, where a decision will affect large numbers of people or advance a major law reform objective." Test cases are selected because they have the potential to extend beyond the particular litigants, e.g., those involving the environment or civil rights (CPIL 1976: 7). The interest group controls the arguments advanced in an attempt to impact on policy. Instead of direct representation, public interest firms may submit *amicus curiae* briefs.

2. Programs "designed to provide legal services to underserved groups on matters of immediate concern only to the parties directly involved," such as those provided by legal aid societies, public defenders, and neighborhood legal services offices (CPIL 1976: 7).

    The first type of public interest law is of rather recent vintage. As noted in Chapter 3, historically, the judicial branch often thwarted legislative efforts designed to improve the situation of disadvantaged portions of our population: blacks, workers, children, mentally ill, the poor. While those on the left of the political spectrum advocated legislative remedies, those on the right found comfort in the courts. Over the years, however, the legislative branch became increasingly tolerant of activities that often denied equal protection and due process to less powerful elements in society. The Supreme Court headed by Earl Warren gave impetus to those seeking to use the judicial branch to advance liberal causes that had failed in the legislative branch. Policy-oriented public interest law emerged from this perspective and the political activism of the civil rights and Vietnam War era. "Influenced by the activism of the antiwar, civil rights, feminist, and environmental movements of the late 1960s and early 1970s, public interest lawyers have developed a common set of goals: to make government more accountable to the public and more responsive to the concerns and needs of unrepresented persons; to increase the power of citizens' groups; to insist on a place at the bargaining table; and to ensure that the development of public policy is open to public scrutiny" (Aron 1989: 3–4).

The public interest law firm is generally an independent, tax-exempt corporation operating under a board of trustees and funded chiefly by foundation grants and individual contributions. These firms usually combine traditional legal activities with research, publication, organizing, and public education. One of the best known public interest firms is the Legal Defense Educational Fund of the National Association

NATIONAL ASSOCIATION FOR THE ADVANCEMENT OF COLORED PEOPLE

Founded in 1909, the NAACP was originally a lobbying and educational group. It gradually increased its activities to include litigation through its Legal Defense Educational Fund (LDEF), which became independent in 1939. By 1921, the NAACP had won court cases on voting, housing, and grand juries; it was the LDEF (with lead attorney and later Supreme Court justice Thurgood Marshall) that litigated the issue of school segregation culminating in the decision of *Brown* v. *Board of Education*. The strategy used by the NAACP to challenge segregation was based on two major points, which are described by Rosemary Salomone: "First sue for equal schools [as per the *Plessy* decision] on the theory that the cost of maintaining a dual system would prove so prohibitive as to speed the abolition of a segregated system. Second, pursue desegregation on the university level where it was likely to meet the least resistance. Then proceed incrementally to the elementary and secondary level" (1986: 41).

The CPIL (1976) lists the elements of the model developed by the LDEF:

- It used full-time, salaried staff attorneys.

- It avoided routine service cases and took on those that affected issues beyond the immediate concern of individual litigants.

- It assumed a proactive posture, seeking out cases with issues that could bring about changes in the ways in which political and social institutions dealt with blacks.

- It raised funds from widespread membership efforts.

- It rejected the accumulation of big cases in favor of incremental victories that built a favorable legal climate and fostered a positive public and legislative climate that could be converted into changed behavior patterns.

- It created a network of private attorneys to follow up on court victories and convert the rights won in court into practical substantive benefits.

for the Advancement of Colored People (NAACP): "Virtually all subsequent public interest legal endeavors have followed in some respects the early example of the NAACP" (CPIL 1976: 34).

Public interest law firms usually specialize in a particular area of advocacy and litigation. The Trial Lawyers for Public Justice (TLPJ), a Washington-based public interest law firm, seeks damages on behalf of victims of government and corporate misconduct. Cases accepted by the firm must have a far-reaching effect on public interest litigation and set precedents for similar actions. Such cases generally have the potential for large monetary damage awards to alleviate the suffering of the victim and punish the wrongdoer. The cases must involve unique legal issues that demonstrate a creative use of law for the public good. The firm has brought suit against a number of companies on behalf of persons harmed from exposure to toxic chemicals and against government officials for failing to protect persons from contaminated water. TLPJ has utilized the federal Clean Water Act, which allows citizens to file suit against companies to force compliance with federal law. This is designed to improve water quality through punishing polluting companies with steep fines. The firm's activities are supported by private contributions, settlement fees, and pro bono work by numerous attorneys. TLPJ attorneys have been fighting against legislative efforts to limit the size of awards in personal injury cases (discussed in Chapter 12).

The Washington-based Center for Law and Social Policy was established in 1969 by four attorneys in the District of Columbia in order to work on behalf of the poor and the physically and mentally disabled. In addition to its advocacy efforts, the center sponsors a law school clinic, for which approximately 20 law school students a year receive academic credit. Equal Rights Advocates of San Francisco specializes in cases involving employment and employment-related discrimination against women. The firm chooses cases that will have an impact—either because of the number of people who will be affected by the results or because of the legal principle that will be established—with respect to pay equity, sexual harassment, access to nontraditional jobs, or pregnancy-based discrimination. The Center for Public Representation (CPR) is headquartered in Madison, Wisconsin, where it operates a clinical program with the University of Wisconsin Law School. CPR specializes in issues relating to health care cost containment, particularly for senior citizens. Founded in 1972, the Bazelon Center for Mental Health Law (BCMHL) is a public interest law firm that litigates on behalf of children and adults with mental disabilities. BCMHL litigation has improved conditions for persons confined to institutions and resulted in the establishment of community care for those inappropriately confined. The Washington-based center is supported by foundation grants, government contracts, sales of publications, and income from an endowment,

With the establishment of the Pacific Legal Foundation in 1973, a new development in the field of public interest law emerged—firms with expressly conservative or probusiness agendas. They hold the more traditional public interest legal firms largely responsible for overregulation of business "and see themselves as a balance to the influence such groups exercise over public policy" (Aron 1989: 74). The Washington Legal Foundation (WLF) was established in 1976 to promote "free enterprise and economic growth." WLF actively opposes the efforts of "so-called public legal advocates" who have "sought more judicial intrusion into our lives and marketplace, and more protection for dangerous criminals at our expense" (*WLF Annual Report* 1984: 3).

According to its Web site, the Washington Legal Foundation defends and promotes the principles of free enterprise and individual rights by

- Shaping public policy through aggressive litigation and advocacy
- Publishing timely legal studies
- Educating policy-makers and the public through extensive communications outreach

"WLF successfully counters the activities of well financed, anti-business, pro-criminal activists like the ACLU [American Civil Liberties Union], Ralph Nader and the Environmental Defense Fund who seek to implement a political agenda which they could not possibly achieve at the ballot box" (*WLF Annual Report* 1985: 1). The National Chamber Litigation Center (NCLC) was founded in 1977 as a public policy law firm for the U.S. Chamber of Commerce. The NCLC represents the business community in issues of national concern before the courts and regulatory agencies. The Mountain States Legal Foundation is a public interest legal center, which, according to its Web site, is "dedicated to individual liberty, the right to own and use property, limited government and the free enterprise system."

Conservative public interest law firms receive most of their financial support from corporations or corporate foundations.

Now that we have examined legal education and the practice of law in the United States, in the next chapter we will examine the places most attorneys do their work—the federal and state courts.

INTERNET CONNECTIONS

National Conference of Bar Examiners: *www.ncbex.org*

American Corporate Counsel: *acca.com*

American Bar Association: *abanet.org*

Nolo Self-Help: *nolo.com*

Washington Legal Foundation: *wlf.org*

Trial Lawyers for Public Justice: *tlpj.org*

Bazelon Center for Mental Health Law: *Bazelon.org*

Equal Rights Advocates: *equalrights.org*

Center for Law and Social Policy: *clasp.org*

Center for Public Representation: *law.wisc.edu/pal*

REVIEW QUESTIONS

1. Why was popular opinion in colonial America opposed to lawyers?

2. What were the characteristics of the postrevolutionary bar?

3. How did the introduction and popularity of the case method assist bar associations in their attempt to limit entry into the practice of law?

4. What were the characteristics of the early positions of the American Bar Association?

5. What was the diploma privilege, and why did it end?

6. What is an integrated bar?

7. What is the Cravath System?

8. How did the Cravath system help to stratify the practice of law?

9. How is the prestige of an attorney measured within the legal profession?

10. How does the role of a corporate attorney differ from that of attorneys working for a national law firm?

11. How does the stratification of the legal profession tend to support corporate America?

12. How does the relatively small number of attorneys in Japan impact on that society?

13. What are the characteristics of Stratum III attorneys?

14. How can the income of Stratum III attorneys surpass those who are partners in elite law firms?

15. What led to the expansion of legal aid services around the time of the First World War?

16. What was the impetus for the creation of federal legal services?

17. How did the success of federal legal services undermine their continued existence?

18. What is meant by public interest law?

19. How do public interest law firms usually go about trying to achieve their goals?

6

THE STRUCTURE AND ADMINISTRATION OF STATE AND FEDERAL COURTS

In the United States there are two parallel systems of courts: federal and state. Each is divided into trial courts and appellate courts. There are more than 200 statewide general and limited jurisdiction trial court systems in the United States, the District of Columbia, and Puerto Rico, and more than 130 appellate courts on the state and federal levels. State appellate courts range in size from five to nine judges—most have a state court of last resort with seven members (Rottman et al. 2000).

As noted in Chapter 2, in the United States (as opposed to inquisitorial systems) trial courts differ rather markedly from their appellate counterparts. The trial court has criminal and civil—that is, noncriminal—parts, something rare at the appellate level except in Oklahoma and Texas, which split final appellate review between criminal and civil parts (Rottman et al. 2000). The trial court has responsibility for settling the issue at hand and need not interest itself in wider issues such as the precedential value of its decisions. Cases are disposed of in trial courts by negotiation, plea bargaining, bench trials, and (except in equity cases) jury trials. Whatever the outcome, trial court judges rarely draft elaborate explanations of their decisions. With the exception of the United States Supreme Court, courts—trial and appellate—are limited by their jurisdiction.

JURISDICTION

Jurisdiction is basic to understanding the organization of a court system. It is the geographic area, subject matter, or persons over which a court can exercise authority. The area of geographic jurisdiction is referred to as *venue*, and it can be limited to a particular district, city, or county. Venue in criminal cases is relatively simple—it is where the crime is alleged to have taken place. In civil cases, however, venue can be based on a number of factors, such as where the cause of the action arose, where the defendant resides or conducts business, or where the plaintiff resides.

A mistake in venue can result in a case being overturned on appeal. The issue of court jurisdiction—the authority to adjudicate a case—can be quite complex, since it has many dimensions:

1. *Venue* is the area of geographic jurisdiction of a court and can be limited to a particular district, city, or county.

2. *Subject jurisdiction* refers to the category of cases the court is authorized to consider, e.g., criminal (misdemeanors or felonies), civil, juvenile, or matters of equity.

3. *Personal (in personam) jurisdiction* refers to authority over the defendant; without it the court cannot proceed.

4. *In rem jurisdiction* is the result of the presence of tangible or intangible assets within the court's venue.

5. *Original jurisdiction* refers to the authority to hear or act upon a case from its beginning to its conclusion.

6. *Appellate jurisdiction* refers to the authority to review decisions made by a lower court, to hear cases on appeal.

7. *Limited jurisdiction* means that the court has original jurisdiction in only a limited number of narrowly defined cases (e.g., only misdemeanors or civil cases where the money in dispute is below a specified sum, or only traffic cases).

8. *General jurisdiction* refers to the authority of a trial court to hear any type of case, civil or criminal, misdemeanor or felony, those involving small or unlimited amounts of money.

9. *Concurrent jurisdiction* occurs when two or more courts at the same time have the ability to hear and decide a particular case.

10. *Diversity jurisdiction* arises when litigants are from different states.

The jurisdiction of a state court never extends beyond that state's borders. However, various states have *long arm statutes* providing jurisdiction over nonresident persons or corporations if they have ties to that state by virtue of business transactions such as the supplying of goods or services, or if the cause of action is local and affects local residents. These statutes are used to exercise jurisdiction over nonresident motorists involved in motor vehicle accidents. The issue of state court jurisdiction over out-of-state defendants is filled with controversy, particularly when it involves the liability of foreign corporations whose products are sold in a particular state as part of the "stream of commerce."

In only one case is the jurisdiction of a court established by the U.S. Constitution. Article III, Section 2 states: "The judicial power of the United States shall be vested in one supreme Court, and in such inferior Courts as the Congress may from time to time ordain and establish." Similarly, state courts derive their authority from state constitutions and legislative enactments. The jurisdiction of the unitary federal court system often overlaps that of state courts (*concurrent jurisdiction*). Because issues of jurisdiction are sometimes blurred, a litigant may have a choice of bringing a case to one or more state courts or a federal court. However, the equitable doctrine of *forum non conveniens* allows a lawsuit to be dismissed, even when the court has jurisdiction, because it is inconvenient to the defendant(s) and/or witness(es) to try the case so far away, provided the plaintiff has an alternative forum available (Maag 2001). Some states, e.g., Texas, have abolished this doctrine, so if jurisdiction exists the judge is obligated to exercise it.

Diversity Jurisdiction

Because of our dual system of courts, a major question arises when litigants are from different states—*diversity jurisdiction*. In cases of diversity jurisdiction, based on Article III, Section 2 of the Constitution and the Judiciary Act of 1789, a plaintiff may choose either the state or federal courts. If the action is brought in the plaintiff's state, the defendant has a right to remove the case from state court in favor of federal court. The federal court, however, must review the circumstances to determine if it will apply federal or state law. Federal courts must follow state law, including state case law, except where the Constitution, federal statutes, or treaties provide otherwise (*Erie R.R.* v. *Tompkins* 1938). If the federal court is to defer to state law, however, it must determine which state law controls. Although these are typically complex legal issues, they often involve relatively small amounts of money. As a result, in 1958, Congress set $10,000 as the minimum amount being litigated before a federal court will assume jurisdiction in a diversity case; it has been raised to $75,000 in order to further reduce overburdened federal dockets. Such cases "often involve mortgage foreclosures, debt collections and commercial disputes far less rarified than the constitutional and Federal questions that judges prefer, and many Federal judges have long complained of being burdened by low-stakes cases that could more easily be decided in state courts" (Wiehl 1989a: 22). Federal courts will not consider domestic relations or probate cases even if there is diversity—lawyers sometimes attempted to get into federal court by appointing guardians or executors of estates from other states in order to satisfy the requirement for diversity jurisdiction. This practice was curtailed in 1988 by the Judicial Improvements and Access to Justice Act.

Controversy exists over the reasons for diversity jurisdiction. Some scholars claim that its purpose is to protect commercial interests from hostile state legislatures that might pressure state courts. Others see it as a way of protecting out-of-state defendants against the possibility of prejudice by state courts ("home cookin'"). While federal judges favor abolishing diversity jurisdiction, trial lawyers have been in opposition: The choice of courts provides an additional element in their legal strategy. The principal effect, notes federal appellate judge Frank Coffin, "is to allow large nonresident corporations that are sued in state courts to remove their case to federal court. The results are to burden federal courts with one-fourth of their caseload and one-half of their jury trials, to require federal judges to engage in arcane efforts to guess what state law might be, to flout the basic idea of federalism, to foster the idea that state courts are second-rate, and to remove any incentive for the influential segment of the bar representing nonresident corporations to work for the improvement of state courts" (1994: 64–65).

Some crimes (e.g., bank robbery and drug trafficking) violate both federal and state laws. In such cases, providence (who arrests the defendant—federal or local officers) or agreements between state and federal authorities determine jurisdiction. The jurisdiction of the federal courts has been expanded by congressional enactments on such matters as organized crime, commerce, civil rights, and taxation. Thus, a black litigant could opt to bring a civil rights action based on the Civil Rights Act of 1964 in federal court rather than in a state court in the South. The Racketeer Influenced and Corrupt Organizations (RICO) section of the Organized Crime Control Act of 1970 authorizes prosecution in federal court for the violation of certain *state* laws if the violations were committed in a certain pattern defined as "racketeering" (see Abadinsky 2000). Thus, in Cook County, Illinois, beginning in 1985, a number of state (circuit) court judges were successfully prosecuted in federal court under RICO for accepting bribes (although most of these cases had nothing to do with organized crime).

STATE COURTS

While there are systems of trial and appellate courts in each state, most are not at all systematic. As noted in Chapter 3, the history that shaped our judicial systems has mitigated against uniformity. Consequently, it is difficult to generalize about state courts. Some states, such as Illinois, have created unitary court systems with relatively simple structures (Figure 6–1). Other states, such as Texas, present a confusing system of courts, often with overlapping jurisdiction (Figure 6–2), while Washington fits somewhere between these two extremes (Figure 6–3).

The 50 state court systems present a complex array of structures: No two state court systems are alike. There are two basic types of courts: those that try cases (trial courts) and those that consider cases only on appeal (appellate courts) from a trial court or a lower appellate court. In some states, for example Washington (Figure 6–3), a trial court of general jurisdiction may hear appeals from courts of limited jurisdiction. These courts are known by a confusing variety of names in different states, so generic titles will be used in this chapter (see Figure 6–4):

INTERSECTING AND OVERLAPPING COURT SYSTEMS

"The two realms of our dual court system are not entirely separate and independent; they intersect and overlap in a number of important ways—ways which require of the skilled practitioner a knowledge of the workings of both state and federal courts" (Coffin 1994: 46).

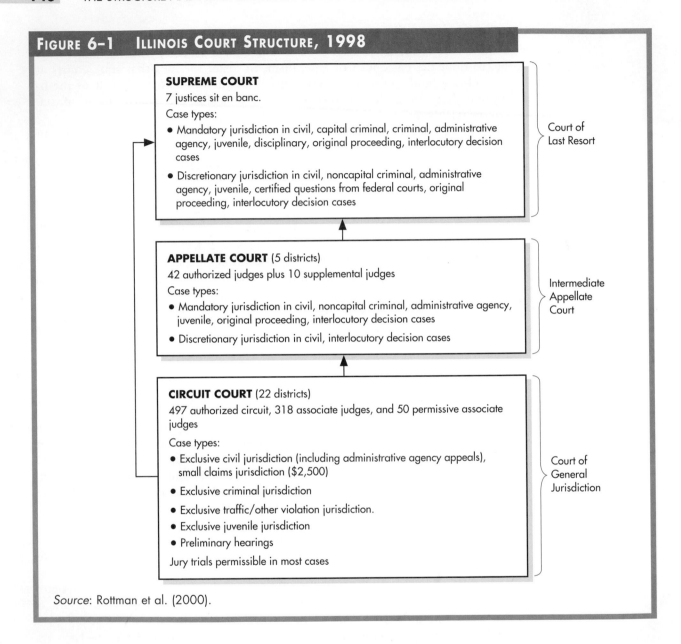

FIGURE 6-1   ILLINOIS COURT STRUCTURE, 1998

SUPREME COURT

7 justices sit en banc.

Case types:

- Mandatory jurisdiction in civil, capital criminal, criminal, administrative agency, juvenile, disciplinary, original proceeding, interlocutory decision cases

- Discretionary jurisdiction in civil, noncapital criminal, administrative agency, juvenile, certified questions from federal courts, original proceeding, interlocutory decision cases

Court of Last Resort

APPELLATE COURT (5 districts)

42 authorized judges plus 10 supplemental judges

Case types:

- Mandatory jurisdiction in civil, noncapital criminal, administrative agency, juvenile, original proceeding, interlocutory decision cases

- Discretionary jurisdiction in civil, interlocutory decision cases

Intermediate Appellate Court

CIRCUIT COURT (22 districts)

497 authorized circuit, 318 associate judges, and 50 permissive associate judges

Case types:

- Exclusive civil jurisdiction (including administrative agency appeals), small claims jurisdiction ($2,500)

- Exclusive criminal jurisdiction

- Exclusive traffic/other violation jurisdiction.

- Exclusive juvenile jurisdiction

- Preliminary hearings

Jury trials permissible in most cases

Court of General Jurisdiction

Source: Rottman et al. (2000).

- *Lower Court:* limited jurisdiction (there are more than 13,500)
- *Superior Court:* general jurisdiction (there are more than 2,600)
- *Intermediate Court of appeals:* appellate jurisdiction (not used in all states)
- *Supreme Court:* appellate jurisdiction of last resort

Lower Court

The lower court is composed of criminal and civil parts. (Lower courts are absent in six states, e.g., Illinois; see Figure 6–1.) Soon after a person is arrested by the police, he or she is usually brought to the criminal section of a lower court where

FIGURE 6-2   TEXAS COURT STRUCTURE, 1998

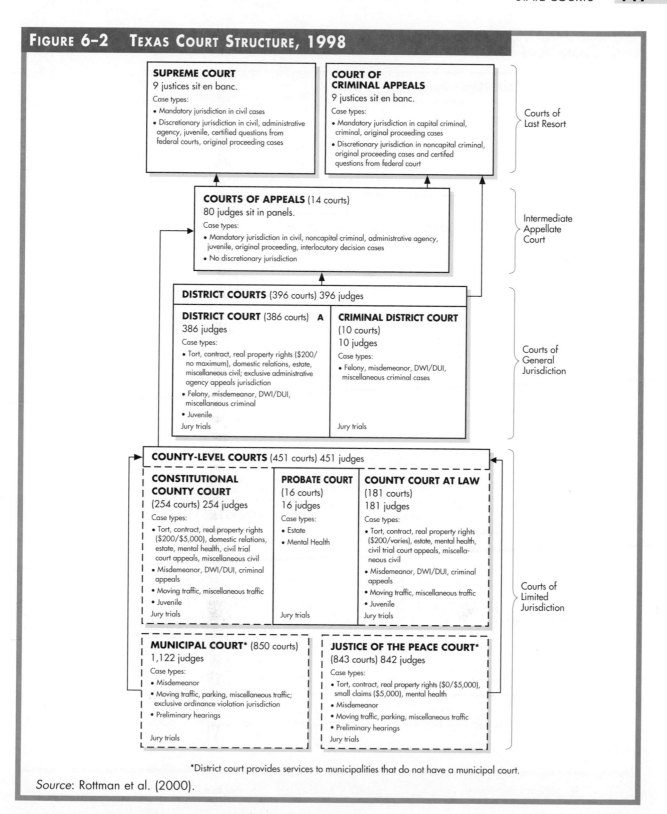

SUPREME COURT
9 justices sit en banc.
Case types:
• Mandatory jurisdiction in civil cases
• Discretionary jurisdiction in civil, administrative agency, juvenile, certified questions from federal courts, original proceeding cases

COURT OF CRIMINAL APPEALS
9 justices sit en banc.
Case types:
• Mandatory jurisdiction in capital criminal, criminal, original proceeding cases
• Discretionary jurisdiction in noncapital criminal, original proceeding cases and certifed questions from federal court

Courts of Last Resort

COURTS OF APPEALS (14 courts)
80 judges sit in panels.
Case types:
• Mandatory jurisdiction in civil, noncapital criminal, administrative agency, juvenile, original proceeding, interlocutory decision cases
• No discretionary jurisdiction

Intermediate Appellate Court

DISTRICT COURTS (396 courts) 396 judges

DISTRICT COURT (386 courts) **A**
386 judges
Case types:
• Tort, contract, real property rights ($200/ no maximum), domestic relations, estate, miscellaneous civil; exclusive administrative agency appeals jurisdiction
• Felony, misdemeanor, DWI/DUI, miscellaneous criminal
• Juvenile
Jury trials

CRIMINAL DISTRICT COURT (10 courts)
10 judges
Case types:
• Felony, misdemeanor, DWI/DUI, miscellaneous criminal cases

Jury trials

Courts of General Jurisdiction

COUNTY-LEVEL COURTS (451 courts) 451 judges

CONSTITUTIONAL COUNTY COURT (254 courts) 254 judges
Case types:
• Tort, contract, real property rights ($200/$5,000), domestic relations, estate, mental health, civil trial court appeals, miscellaneous civil
• Misdemeanor, DWI/DUI, criminal appeals
• Moving traffic, miscellaneous traffic
• Juvenile
Jury trials

PROBATE COURT (16 courts)
16 judges
Case types:
• Estate
• Mental Health

Jury trials

COUNTY COURT AT LAW (181 courts)
181 judges
Case types:
• Tort, contract, real property rights ($200/varies), estate, mental health, civil trial court appeals, miscellaneous civil
• Misdemeanor, DWI/DUI, criminal appeals
• Moving traffic, miscellaneous traffic
• Juvenile
Jury trials

Courts of Limited Jurisdiction

MUNICIPAL COURT* (850 courts)
1,122 judges
Case types:
• Misdemeanor
• Moving traffic, parking, miscellaneous traffic; exclusive ordinance violation jurisdiction
• Preliminary hearings
Jury trials

JUSTICE OF THE PEACE COURT* (843 courts) 842 judges
Case types:
• Tort, contract, real property rights ($0/$5,000), small claims ($5,000), mental health
• Misdemeanor
• Moving traffic, parking, miscellaneous traffic
• Preliminary hearings
Jury trials

*District court provides services to municipalities that do not have a municipal court.

Source: Rottman et al. (2000).

FIGURE 6-3 WASHINGTON COURT STRUCTURE, 1998

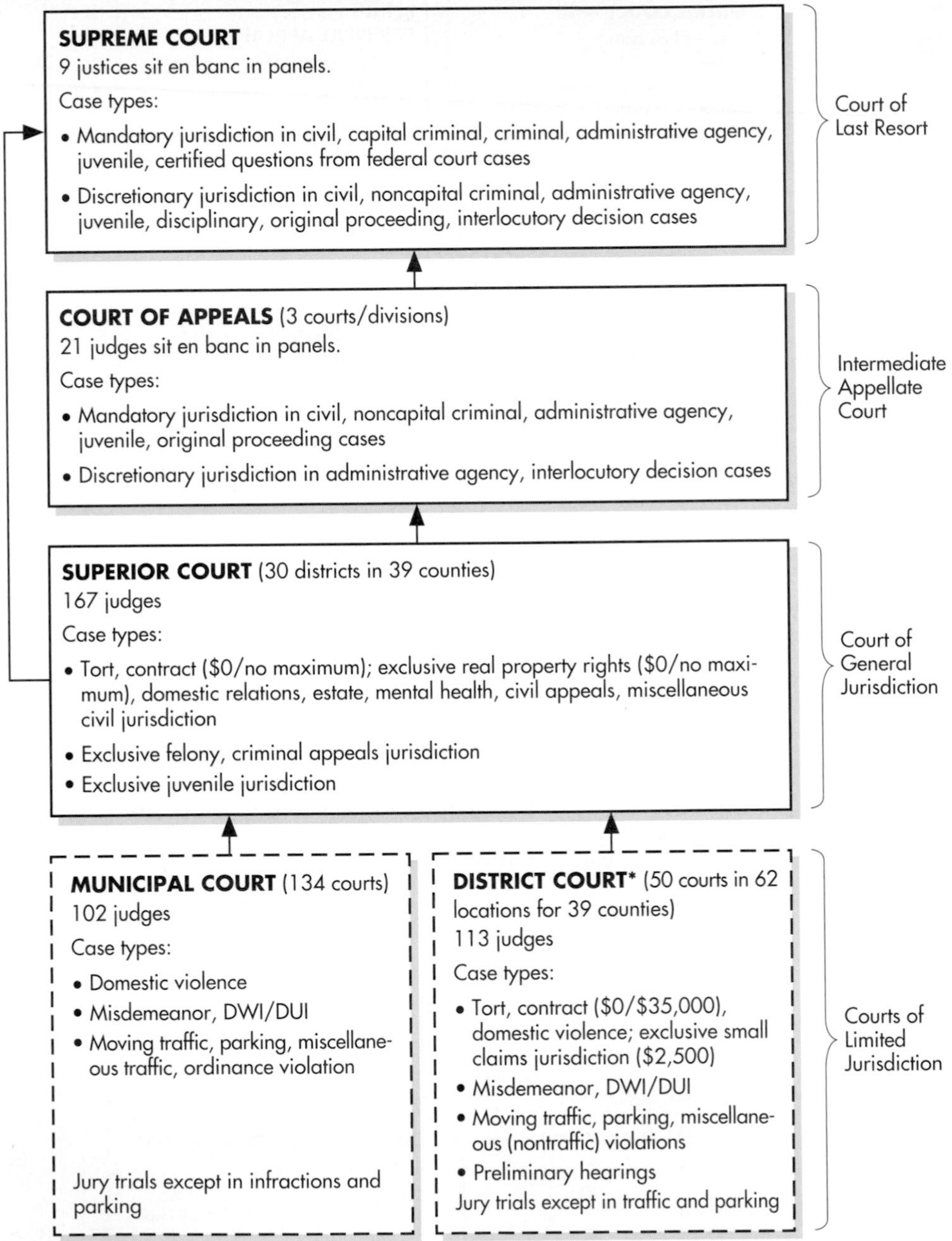

SUPREME COURT
9 justices sit en banc in panels.

Case types:

• Mandatory jurisdiction in civil, capital criminal, criminal, administrative agency, juvenile, certified questions from federal court cases

• Discretionary jurisdiction in civil, noncapital criminal, administrative agency, juvenile, disciplinary, original proceeding, interlocutory decision cases

> Court of Last Resort

COURT OF APPEALS (3 courts/divisions)
21 judges sit en banc in panels.

Case types:

• Mandatory jurisdiction in civil, noncapital criminal, administrative agency, juvenile, original proceeding cases

• Discretionary jurisdiction in administrative agency, interlocutory decision cases

> Intermediate Appellate Court

SUPERIOR COURT (30 districts in 39 counties)
167 judges

Case types:

• Tort, contract ($0/no maximum); exclusive real property rights ($0/no maximum), domestic relations, estate, mental health, civil appeals, miscellaneous civil jurisdiction

• Exclusive felony, criminal appeals jurisdiction

• Exclusive juvenile jurisdiction

> Court of General Jurisdiction

MUNICIPAL COURT (134 courts)
102 judges

Case types:

• Domestic violence

• Misdemeanor, DWI/DUI

• Moving traffic, parking, miscellaneous traffic, ordinance violation

Jury trials except in infractions and parking

DISTRICT COURT* (50 courts in 62 locations for 39 counties)
113 judges

Case types:

• Tort, contract ($0/$35,000), domestic violence; exclusive small claims jurisdiction ($2,500)

• Misdemeanor, DWI/DUI

• Moving traffic, parking, miscellaneous (nontraffic) violations

• Preliminary hearings

Jury trials except in traffic and parking

> Courts of Limited Jurisdiction

*District court provides services to municipalities that do not have a municipal court.

Source: Rottman et al. (2000).

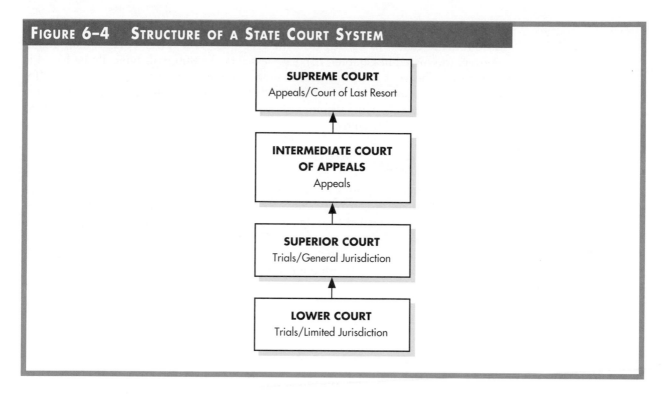

FIGURE 6–4   STRUCTURE OF A STATE COURT SYSTEM

SUPREME COURT
Appeals/Court of Last Resort

**INTERMEDIATE COURT
OF APPEALS**
Appeals

SUPERIOR COURT
Trials/General Jurisdiction

LOWER COURT
Trials/Limited Jurisdiction

the charges against the person are read, a determination is made about the appointment of an attorney (can he or she afford to hire one?) and, if the case is a felony, bail will be set. If the charge is a misdemeanor or less (an offense or violation), it can be dealt with immediately or at a later date (in which case bail will be set). Some jurisdictions may use a justice of the peace or, as in Connecticut, part-time magistrates for processing minor cases without a jury. After initial processing in lower court, felony cases must be transferred to a superior court. Search warrants are also the responsibility of the lower court.

Depending on the state, the lower courts can include juvenile or family court (discussed in Chapter 13), probate or surrogate court, county or municipal court, traffic court, and justice of the peace or police court. At this level there may also be other specialized courts, such as housing court (New York), tax court (Oregon), or water court (Colorado). Some observers point out that specialized courts are advantageous since "they have specific rather than general expertise over legal issues. A typical trial court whose caseload largely involves divorce matters will rarely have familiarity with the intricacies of the law in water rights disputes. The argument against most specialized courts is that they simply add another layer to the judicial bureaucracy and to the administrative problems that already plague the courts" (Stumpf and Culver 1992: 21).[1]

---

[1]There are also more than 450 justice forums among the 556 federally recognized tribes in the United States (Rottman et al. 2000).

In civil matters, if the money at issue is less than a specific amount (e.g., $5,000), the case will be heard in the civil part of a lower court. Small-claims matters (discussed in Chapter 12), e.g., less than $1,000, will typically be heard in a court that bears that title or is sometimes known as *pro se* court. *Pro se*, or "for oneself," refers to a court in which litigants represent themselves rather than use lawyers. Matters involving disputes above a certain dollar amount are heard in the civil part of a superior court.

Superior Court

Superior courts have criminal and civil parts. While this court is authorized to try any type of case, the criminal part typically deals only with felony cases. In some instances it may hear cases appealed from lower court, which can sometimes result in a trial *de novo* (a new trial) in superior court. The civil part of the superior court can hear cases involving noncriminal disputes, but cases considered are usually limited to those involving a minimum dollar amount or issues of equity. There are more than 2,600 superior courts in the United States. They are called circuit courts in 16 states; 15 states call them district courts; 13 states and the District of Columbia call them superior courts; two states use other names; and four states use a combination of names.

Intermediate Court of Appeals

The decision of a superior court in criminal and civil cases can be appealed (by the defendant in criminal cases; by either litigant in civil cases) to the appellate court. Thirty-nine states divide this court into an intermediate court of appeals and a court of last resort or supreme court. Those states without an intermediate court of appeals have relatively small populations, such as Maine, North Dakota, and Wyoming (Court Statistics Project 1999). States assign their intermediate courts of appeal to between five to fourteen locations, and "some are limited to civil or criminal appeals" (Coffin 1994: 57). California, for example, has six appellate districts, and a decision made by one district appellate court is not binding on any other district. Intermediate courts of appeal are usually called the court of appeals, although in some states they may have other names. The state of Texas has two courts of last resort: a supreme court and a court of criminal appeals (Figure 6–2).

In general, intermediate courts of appeal have mandatory jurisdiction—they must consider all appropriate cases—and cases are typically heard by panels of three judges (Flango and Flango 1997). But "there are wide variations in rules and patterns of practice" (Coffin 1994: 58). The intermediate court of appeals was designed to reduce the workload of the court of last resort, although in many instances the result appears otherwise; that is, it appears to encourage more appeals.

Supreme Court

In states without an intermediate court of appeals, the supreme court, except in West Virginia, must consider virtually all appeals. (Most states refer to their court of last resort as the "supreme court.") In other states, although rules vary from state to state, the supreme court usually has some discretion over the cases it will consider: "Almost everywhere the highest state court is not required to hear every appeal brought to it. The bigger the state and the higher the volume of litigation, the lower the likelihood that the state's highest court will decide any particular lawsuit" (Neely 1985: 34). Criminal cases involving the death sentence are automatically appealed to the supreme court and, in some states, those involving constitutional issues. "In courts having wide discretionary jurisdiction a major part of a judge's job is deciding which cases the court will hear. The litigant who lost below must apply for leave to appeal, or certiorari as it is called in some courts, and must file a brief [sometimes called a petition] supporting the application" (Marvell 1978: 17).

The supreme court generally sits in the state capital, but may hear cases in other cities. Supreme courts hear cases en banc; that is, all of the justices—none has more than nine—of the court sit in judgment. The decision of a supreme court is binding throughout the state, and the line of appeal from a state supreme court is directly to the

An Example: The Minnesota Court System[2]

Minnesota's court system is organized into three levels:

1. *District Court.* The 257 judges serve in trial courts in each of Minnesota's 87 counties. The trial courts are organized into 10 judicial districts for administrative purposes.
2. *Court of Appeals.* Created in 1983 to handle some of the increasing workload of the Supreme Court, most cases appealed from the district court go directly to the Court of Appeals. The 16 Court of Appeals judges divide into three-judge panels and travel to cities throughout Minnesota to hear cases. The court has authority to reverse (overrule), remand (send back to the lower court), modify or affirm the decision of the district court.
3. *Supreme Court.* Consisting of seven judges who are called justices, the Supreme Court hears appeals from the Court of Appeals, the Workers' Compensation Court, and the Tax Court. All first-degree murder convictions are reviewed by the Minnesota Supreme Court. Disputes about legislative elections also go directly to the Supreme Court.

The Supreme Court is the rule-making body for all of the state's courts. Although local courts enact some rules of practice, these rules must not be in conflict with those established by the Supreme Court. In addition, the Supreme Court has administrative responsibility for operation of the state court system. It also has a supervisory responsibility over the practice of law, including attorney disciplinary matters.

There are also special courts not in the judicial branch. The Tax Court and Workers' Compensation Court of Appeals are executive-branch agencies created by state law to deal with only one technical area of the law. The three Tax Court judges must be knowledgeable about taxes, but need not be lawyers. The five judges on the Workers' Compensation Court of Appeals, who must be attorneys, hear workers' compensation cases that are appealed from compensation hearings or that are transferred from district court.

---

[2]Minnesota Court Information Office, 1999.

United States Supreme Court—*the* court of last resort. The decisions of appellate courts, particularly those of a supreme court, are often elaborate legal treatises that provide material for the case method and the rule of precedent, or *stare decisis*.

While the court system of every state approximates the pattern of organization just outlined, in states without a unitary system there is often a confusing maze of overlapping courts and jurisdictions, a situation that potential litigants may find quite dismaying but that knowledgeable lawyers may use to their advantage. Court organization has "demonstrated little logic or planning, because adding certain new courts serves various political goals" (Glick 1983: 41). (Efforts to simplify the structure of state court systems will be discussed later in this chapter.)

FEDERAL COURTS

The federal court system in the United States got off to a slow start. The Constitution provides federal jurisdiction for only two crimes: piracy and counterfeiting. The Supreme Court ruled early that there were no common law crimes in the federal courts, and therefore no criminal prosecutions could be heard unless an act of Congress criminalized certain conduct. The federal trial courts had no "federal question" jurisdiction until 1875—if an individual wished to bring a lawsuit claiming that a right secured him by the federal constitution had been violated, that lawsuit had to be brought in state court. The Supreme Court of the United States could review a decision by the highest court of a state which decided a federal question, but the lower federal courts were not involved. Thus for nearly the first century of their existence, the staple of the business of the lower federal courts was admiralty cases and cases in which jurisdiction was based on diversity of citizenship. This distribution of business between the state court systems and the federal courts changed dramatically after the so-called Civil War amendments to the Constitution were adopted. In particular, the Fourteenth Amendment has been a prolific source of federal judicial activity (Rehnquist 1996).

Until the Judiciary Act of 1875, federal courts had jurisdiction over only a few matters (Coffin 1994). That act gave federal district courts federal question jurisdiction. Furthermore, the increasing pace of the Industrial Revolution, the rapid spread of the railroad, and the increasing size of manufacturing enterprises all provoked calls for regulation of what was increasingly a commerce which went well beyond state borders. The general view that the federal government's role should be limited to providing for the common defense, coin money, carrying the mails, and paying for itself by collecting customs duties, was changing.

Before the turn of the twentieth century, Congress had passed the Interstate Commerce Act, giving a federal commission some control over railroad rates and practices, and the Sherman Anti-Trust Act, forbidding conspiracies in restraint of trade. As we moved into the twentieth century, the coming of the automobile and the airplane continued the transportation revolution. The pace of increase in federal regulation continued, driven partly by the interstate nature of so much of the country's business, and partly by a number of reform movements seeking to ameliorate the plight of those who did not share in the generally rising tide of prosperity. The typical pattern was for reform movements to originate in the states, only to discover that the practices which they sought to prohibit or limit could not be prohibited or limited to their satisfaction without the intervention of the federal government (Rehnquist 1996).

First came concern about wages and hours worked in factories, and child labor there. States adopted maximum hour and minimum wage laws, and laws prohibiting child labor. But as often as not the manufacturing plants which would be effected by these laws would pick up and move to a state which did not have such laws. Congress, viewing this phenomenon with dismay, finally itself enacted federal prohibitions against child labor, and later a federal maximum hour and minimum wage law. This pattern has continued in various areas of the law (Rehnquist 1996).

Today, federal courts enjoy rather extensive jurisdiction over five types of cases:

1. Those in which the United States is a party

2. Cases involving foreign officials

3. Those involving parties from different states if more than $75,000 is involved

4. Cases involving the U.S. Constitution and federal laws

5. Those concerning specialty matters such as patent, copyright, customs, and bankruptcy

The state courts share jurisdiction with federal courts in categories 3 and 4, while the federal courts exercise exclusive jurisdiction in all other cases. "Only those state-court decisions involving the federal Constitution and laws may be appealed to the federal courts" (Wheeler and Levin 1979: 12). In the unitary federal system there are two basic classes into which courts may be classified: legislative and constitutional.

LEGISLATIVE COURTS

Courts created by Congress under Article I (legislative branch) of the Constitution are referred to as *legislative courts* because they may perform functions that are nonjudicial: "Legislative courts, unlike their constitutional [Article III—judicial branch] counterparts often have administrative and quasi-legislative as well as judicial duties. Another difference is that legislative courts are often created for the express purpose of helping to administer a specific congressional statute. Constitutional courts, on the other hand, are tribunals established to handle litigation" (Carp and Stidham 1993: 48).

Legislative courts "focus on disputes between individuals and the federal government" (Smith 1997: 40). They include the Court of Military Appeals, Tax Court, Court of Veterans Appeals, and the Territorial Courts of Guam, Virgin Islands, Puerto Rico, and the Northern Mariana Islands. The Court of Military Appeals was established in 1950. Its three judges provide civilian review of military courts martial. The 19 members of the Tax Court hear appeals on Internal Revenue Service rulings; the Court was originally an administrative (Article II—executive branch) court. The Court of Veterans Appeals, established in 1988, is the nation's newest federal court. Its seven judges review decisions of the Board of

Veterans Appeals concerning veterans' claims against the government. All legislative court judges are nominated by the president, confirmed by the Senate, and (except those of Territorial Courts, who serve 4 to 8 years; or Puerto Rico's federal judges, who enjoy lifetime tenure) serve terms of 15 years (instead of the lifetime appointments of all Article III judges).

To further complicate distinctions between these courts, some formerly legislative courts have been redesignated by Congress as constitutional courts. The Court of Claims was established by Congress in 1855 as a Constitutional (Article III) court, but declared a legislative (Article I) court by the Supreme Court in 1933, only to have it reestablished by Congress in 1953 as a constitutional court. In 1982, Congress created the Claims Court, replacing the Court of Claims as the "keeper of the nation's conscience," where citizens and corporations, foreign or domestic, can sue the government in those areas where Congress has waived sovereign immunity.

CONSTITUTIONAL COURTS

In addition to the U.S. Supreme Court, there are five categories of courts established by Congress under Article III of the Constitution (see Figure 6–5):

1. *Magistrates and Bankruptcy:* limited jurisdiction
2. *District Court:* general trial jurisdiction
3. *Specialized (Constitutional) Courts:* specialized jurisdiction
4. *Court of Appeals:* intermediate appellate jurisdiction
5. *Supreme Court:* appellate jurisdiction of last resort

Magistrate and Bankruptcy

The Judiciary Act of 1789 created a system of federal trial courts, permitting federal criminal cases to be tried in the newly established circuit and district courts. But matters of arrest and bail were left to be governed by state law and handled by state judicial officers. It became apparent soon after passage of the Judiciary Act of 1789 that, because of resistance in some states to federal policies, federal criminal process

UNITED STATES TAX COURT

Congress created the Tax Court under Article I to provide a judicial forum in which affected persons could dispute tax deficiencies determined by the Commissioner of Internal Revenue prior to payment of the disputed amounts. Composed of 19 presidentially appointed members who have expertise in the tax laws, the Court is physically located in Washington, but the judges travel nationwide to conduct trials in various designated cities. Trials are conducted before one judge, without a jury, and taxpayers are permitted to represent themselves if they desire. The vast majority of cases are settled by mutual agreement without the necessity of a trial. However, if a trial is conducted, in due course a report is ordinarily issued by the presiding judge setting forth findings of fact and an opinion.

FIGURE 6-5   STRUCTURE OF THE FEDERAL COURT SYSTEM

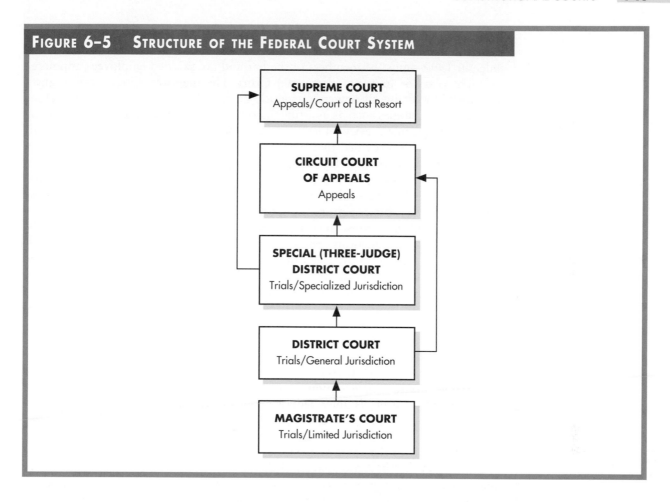

could not rely solely upon state judicial officers. In 1793, Congress authorized the federal circuit courts to appoint persons to take bail in federal criminal cases. In 1817, Congress officially named them commissioners of the circuit court and extended to them the authority to take depositions in civil cases. In 1842, Congress authorized circuit court commissioners to exercise general criminal process in federal cases by issuing arrest warrants and holding persons for trial (Foschio 1999).

The jurisdiction and role of the commissioners was repeatedly expanded throughout the nineteenth century, reflecting the rapidly changing social and economic needs of the country. In 1896, Congress renamed the office of commissioner of the circuit court to "United States Commissioner" and established a four-year term, subject to removal by the district court at any time. There were no minimum qualifications, compensation was determined under a uniform fee schedule, and there was a prohibition against holding other federal, civil or military offices (Foschio 1999).

In 1968, Congress authorized a system of magistrates to replace United States commissioners. Magistrates are appointed by majority vote of the active district judges of the district court to exercise jurisdiction over matters assigned by statute as well as those delegated by the district judges. The number of magistrate judge positions is determined by the Judicial Conference of the United States. While commissioners did not need to be attorneys and worked part-time on a fee-for-service basis, the approximately 500 magistrates—whose title was changed to magistrate judge in 1990—must be members of the bar and are salaried employees appointed for eight-year (or four-year part time) terms. The magistrate judge was granted authority to exercise all powers previously exercised by the commissioners, along with additional duties such as assisting district judges in the conduct of pretrial and discovery proceedings, review of habeas corpus petitions, and acting as special masters. The 1968 act also provided that magistrates could be given authority to perform other duties not contrary to law or the Constitution (Foschio 1999).

By statute, judges may assign a wide variety of pretrial work to magistrates. However, the Federal Judicial Center notes, "What is actually assigned to a magistrate depends upon a district's procedures for handling pretrial matters" (1985: xi). Typically, in criminal cases, magistrates conduct pretrial hearings—reading of the charges, bail, appointment of counsel—and, if both sides agree, try misdemeanors. In 1989, the Supreme Court ruled that magistrates do not have legal authority to preside over jury selection in felony cases without the defendant's consent (*Gomez* v. *United States*). If the charge is a felony, the case will be sent to the district court. Magistrates are authorized to consider civil matters when the amount in dispute is less than $10,000 or when both parties agree to have the magistrate decide the case with or without a jury.

In many districts, magistrates preside over pretrial case conferences and pretrial motions, although the final decision may be reserved for a district court judge based on a report and recommendation from the magistrate. Magistrates may deal with Social Security cases and habeas corpus petitions from prisoners, although this may involve only submitting a report and recommendation to the district court. Depending on local rules, the decisions of a magistrate can be appealed to the district court or directly to the court of appeals.

Federal courts have exclusive jurisdiction over bankruptcy cases. Bankruptcy judges, known as referees prior to 1973, while adjuncts of the district courts, are appointed by the courts of appeals for terms of 14 years. The number of bankruptcy judges is determined by Congress. As their title indicates, they handle the increasing number of bankruptcy cases entering the federal system (about one million a year). The decision of a bankruptcy judge can be appealed to the district court or a panel of bankruptcy judges, at the option of the district court or court of appeals.

District Courts

In 1789, Congress divided the nation into 13 judicial districts, and in the early 1790s, some states were divided into multiple districts. The president was authorized to appoint a federal marshal and U.S. attorney for each district. As new states entered the union, Congress created additional districts. Today, there are 94 federal district courts with more than 650 judges plus senior judges.[3] Each state, the

---

[3]The status of "senior judge" was established by Congress in 1919 and permits federal judges who meet the "Rule of 80" (reached the age of 65 and served as active judges for at least 15 years or reached the age of 70 and served for 10 years) to reduce their caseload while still receiving full-time salaries. Among a variety of responsibilities, they may fill in for absent judges, deal with specialized issues, and provide judicial services in areas that have no permanent federal judge. More than 15 percent of the federal courts' caseload is handled by senior judges.

Commonwealth of Puerto Rico, the District of Columbia, the Virgin Islands, Guam, and the Northern Mariana Islands, have at least one district, while three states (New York, California, and Texas) have four. With the exception of the District of Wyoming, which includes Idaho and Montana portions of Yellowstone National Park, no district cuts across a state line. Between one and twenty-eight judges are assigned to each district, the largest being the Southern District of New York, head-quartered at Foley Square in the Borough of Manhattan. The district court usually tries civil cases (more than $10,000) and criminal cases (misdemeanor trials and felonies), and deals with issues involving certain federal agencies. In the three territorial districts, the court also exercises local jurisdiction.

Federal district courts were established by Congress in 1789 with a great deal of ambivalence. While such courts were favored by those who supported a strong national government, there was the question of states' rights. The Supremacy Clause (Article VI of the Constitution) stipulates that "the Authority of the United States, shall be the supreme Law of the Land; and the Judges in every State shall be bound thereby, any Thing in the Constitution or Laws of any State to the Contrary notwithstanding." Thus, it was argued, since state judges are required to enforce the Constitution, federal courts would be redundant.

Early district courts served as the federal trial court for admiralty and maritime, as well as for some minor civil and criminal cases. Gradually, over the nineteenth century, Congress expanded the jurisdiction of the district courts. However, it was not until the Judiciary Act of 1875 that district courts were empowered to hear civil suits involving at least $500 (if the dispute arose "under the Constitution, laws, or treaties of the United States"). In recent times, new statutes have expanded the juris-diction of federal district courts, resulting in an increase in district court cases on such subjects as environmental protection, job discrimination, education of the handicapped, and (heretofore state) crime. About three-quarters of the civil cases, however, involve disputes between private individuals and businesses, and the United States is a party in the other 25 percent.

Appeals from a ruling by a district court go to the court of appeals, although in certain exceptional cases they may be appealed directly to the Supreme Court (e.g., injunctions against state laws).

Specialized (Constitutional) Courts

Specialized courts include a three-judge panel consisting of two district court judges and one judge of the Court of Appeals. Since 1976, the use of the special three-judge tribunal has been limited to congressional and legislative apportionment cases and issues involving the Voting Rights Act of 1965 and the Civil Rights Act of 1964. Appeals from the decision of a special district court ruling go directly to the Supreme Court.

Other specialized (constitutional) courts include the Court of International Trade, which adjudicates tariff and related disputes and the Court of Appeals for the Federal Circuit. The latter hears patent appeals from all district courts, appeals from the Court of International Trade, the U.S. Claims Court, and appeals from various administrative bodies. Like all other constitutional (Article III) judges, the nine members of the Court of International Trade serve life terms. Unlike other federal constitutional courts, no more than five members may be from the same political party. While these courts have constitutional status, "they nevertheless still occupy a special niche in the federal system" and "still perform, or at least may be viewed as performing, certain quasi-legislative and quasi-administrative functions" (Abraham 1998: 164–165).

Specialized courts (legislative or constitutional) provide several advantages: Judges with expertise in a technical field offer "the opportunity for a single court in a field to avoid legal conflicts that develop among courts or courts of appeals, and reducing the caseloads of generalist courts" (Baum 1994: 39). However, specialized courts may become unduly influenced by an interest group that the court deals with continuously—"repeat players." Support for the creation of a specialized court may reflect rather parochial interests: that the court would "rule more favorably toward them than would the district courts or courts of appeals" (Baum 1994: 39). The transfer of jurisdiction from generalist courts to specialized ones can produce fundamental changes in judicial policy.

Court of Appeals

The Judiciary Act of 1789 established a system of circuit courts—eastern, middle, and southern circuits—with both trial and appellate jurisdiction. Circuit courts served as trial courts for most federal criminal cases, for diversity cases, and for suits initiated by the United States; they also exercised appellate jurisdiction over civil cases originating in the district courts. The circuit had no judges of its own, but consisted of panels of two justices of the Supreme Court—reduced to one in 1793—and the local district court judge. The circuit is an English concept, transported to America in the colonial period. It allowed efficient use of judges by having them "ride circuit," traveling to several locations to hold court when no single location had enough judicial business to justify the appointment of a full-time judge for that court (Wheeler 1992).

As the country grew, the size of the Supreme Court was increased to provide a justice for each circuit. By 1869, faced with a sharp increase in federal litigation, Congress created a judgeship for each of the nine circuits then in existence. The circuit judge, the designated Supreme Court justice, the district judge, or some combination of two of them, presided over the circuit courts.

Until 1891, each Supreme Court justice would ride one of the federal circuits during recess and sit as a circuit court judge to hear appeals. This system, however, proved to be insufficient. After the Civil War, the phenomenal growth of the American economy led to an increase in government regulatory activity and, coupled with judicial activism on behalf of business and industry, produced a virtual breakdown in federal appeals by the 1880s (Howard 1981). In 1891, Congress created the Circuit Courts of Appeals, although the position of circuit judge lingered on until 1911. The 1891 legislation (Evarts Act) gave the courts of appeals jurisdiction over the great majority of appeals from the federal courts and greatly limited the categories of cases that could routinely be appealed to the Supreme Court. The Judiciary Act of 1925 continued this trend and by 1930, the court of appeals also had jurisdiction over administrative appeals of decisions by federal regulatory agencies.

The name of the court was officially changed to the U.S. Court of Appeals in 1948, even though the judges are often referred to as circuit judges. Today, the 13 appellate courts have about 180 judges. Although the courts of appeals were designed "to help the Supreme Court enforce the supremacy and uniformity of federal law" (Howard 1981: 3), in a number of respects, this purpose remains to be accomplished.

Although in theory the federal judiciary is organized into a typical pyramidal structure, in practice federal judicial power is widely diffused among judges who "are insulated by deep traditions of independence, not only from the other branches of government but also from each other" (Howard 1981: 3). Local rules and customs distinguish one court of appeals from another. Some rely on oral argument in every case, while others allow it in only a small portion of the cases they consider; some provide long opinions with their decisions, while others, due to caseload pressures, frequently utilize summary dispositions—decisions without opinions or very brief orders. In only two circuits (District of Columbia and the Seventh in Illinois) do judges of the court of appeals work in the same courthouse. Geographic dispersion, coupled with "rotation of panel membership, large caseloads, and ideological differences, can contribute to inconsistency *within* a court of appeals, limiting the courts' ability to produce uniformity in national law and increasing the burden on the Supreme Court" (Wasby 1993: 57). Regionalism remains a source of disparity and conflict among the circuits that can be resolved only by the Supreme Court (Howard 1981).[4]. But the Supreme Court reviews only about one out of every two hundred cases decided by the court of appeals, undermining the federal judicial system's capacity to promote uniformity in national law (Strauss 1990).

The defendant in a criminal case and the losing side in a civil case can appeal to the court of appeals in whose circuit the district court lies. There are 12 courts of appeals (if the Court of Appeals for the Federal Circuit, discussed above, is included, there are 13) in 11 numbered circuits and the District of Columbia, with between four and 28 judges. Each circuit, except the District of Columbia, encompasses at least three states (see Figure 6–6). A court of appeals sits in three judge panels, although in exceptional cases the court may sit en banc—most or all of the judges in the circuit hear the case. There are more than 200 appellate judges and senior judges assisting on circuit panels.

The jurisdiction of a court of appeals includes all of the cases decided by federal courts in its circuit and those of a number of federal administrative and regulatory agencies such as the Federal Communications Commission and the Environmental Protection Agency. An appeal from the decision of a court of appeals must be taken to the Supreme Court. Under certain conditions, a case can be appealed from district court directly to the Supreme Court. This will occur, e.g., when the case has been decided by a three-judge district court, or when a federal statute has been declared unconstitutional and the government is appealing, or when the issue is one of substantial national importance, such as the matter of the Nixon tapes.

Each circuit is assigned a Supreme Court justice, with the two most senior justices assigned to two circuits. This is a link to the earlier era before the appeals courts were established as separate intermediate-level courts (Goldman and Jahnige 1985).

---

[4]For example, in 1997 the Supreme Court agreed to hear a case (*Sacramento County* v. *Lewis*) involving a dispute over the rights of persons injured or killed in high-speed police chases, in this case the accidental death of a passenger on a motorcycle whose driver was fleeing the police. The Ninth Circuit in Sacramento (CA) had ruled that all that is required is proof of police conduct showing a "deliberate indifference" or "reckless disregard." Other federal circuits, however, adopted a higher standard: that the police action must also "shock the conscience."

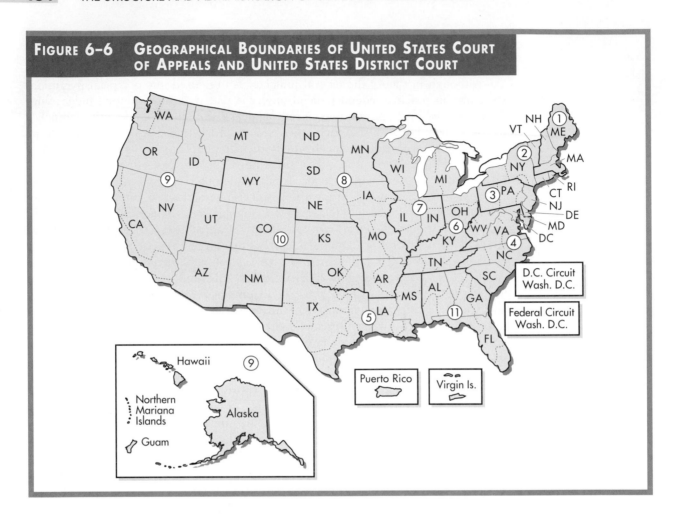

FIGURE 6-6 **GEOGRAPHICAL BOUNDARIES OF UNITED STATES COURT OF APPEALS AND UNITED STATES DISTRICT COURT**

On occasion, Supreme Court justices are asked to act on emergency petitions from their circuits when the Supreme Court is not in session. These petitions often involve cases of capital punishment, and a justice can order a stay of execution until the Court convenes. The courts of appeals must consider all cases brought to them.

Some circuit courts, by virtue of law or their geographic location, become magnets for certain types of cases. Certain appeals involving federal agencies must be brought in the District of Columbia, the site of agency headquarters, while others have a choice: that is, the action may also be brought in the circuit where the controversy developed. Because of its location in the financial capital of the United States, the Second Circuit (New York) is the site of a great deal of commercial litigation.

The Supreme Court

The Constitution, which provides for a Supreme Court, does not state how many members it is to have. The Judiciary Act of 1789 established a Supreme Court with one chief justice and five associate justices. As already noted, the size of the Court was increased to accommodate the establishment of new circuits to which each justice was attached; it reached nine in 1837. In 1863, a tenth justice was added, but in 1866, Congress reduced the number to seven. Legislation in 1869 provided for a justice for each of the nine circuits, and the number has since remained the same. The nine-member bench has become such a strong tradition that in 1937 even an overwhelmingly Democratic Congress refused to increase its membership at the request of President Franklin Roosevelt (discussed in Chapter 3).

The Supreme Court has three fundamental responsibilities (Freund 1961):

1. To resolve disputes between states, which often involve boundaries or the apportionment of interstate waters.

2. To provide for the uniformity of federal law. The Court has ultimate authority in the event of conflicting decisions by lower courts.

3. To maintain the constitutional order. The Court determines if executive or legislative actions conform to the Constitution.

Once an institution of little consequence, the Supreme Court is now an equal of the other branches of government. The decisions of the Court affect the lives of every person in the United States (and sometimes persons beyond its borders). Since the historic precedent in an otherwise unimportant case, *Marbury v. Madison*, the Supreme Court has enjoyed the power to declare a statutory enactment (or executive action) void because it is unconstitutional. The Supreme Court became the interpreter of the law not because the delegates at the Constitutional Convention declared it so, but because things worked out that way. In 1907, three years before his appointment to the Supreme Court, Charles Evans Hughes, then governor of New York and later becoming chief justice, stated: "We are under a Constitution, but the Constitution is what the judges say it is" (Harrell and Anderson 1982: 11).

Each associate justice of the Court is entitled to employ up to four law clerks (the chief justice is entitled to more), who traditionally serve terms of one year. Recently, some justices have been keeping clerks on for a second year, and the Court has also hired some career law clerks to provide expertise and continuity. The selection of law clerks is up to each justice, and the position is quite prestigious. It usually goes to the top graduates of elite law schools, based on recommendations from law professors or former clerks. The Court has declared itself immune from charges of employment discrimination, and its law clerks, as the justices themselves, have been mostly white males. During the Court's 1999–2000 term, among the new class of 35 law clerks were two African Americans and 12 women. The law clerks examine and summarize petitions, review briefs, conduct research, and draft opinions. They often play a key role in selecting cases for certiorari consideration.

The importance of the role of clerks for members of the Supreme Court is not without controversy: "In a perfect legal world," notes Bernard Schwartz (1988: 16), "the law clerk would perform the functions of an associate in a law firm, that is, research for senior members and assistance generally in the firm's work. But the tasks assigned clerks at the Supreme Court depend solely on the view of the job held by the individual Justice for whom they are working." Indeed, "the scope of the clerk's responsibility expands in inverse ratio to the caliber of the Justice." Thus, "it may be doubted that the great Justices, such as Oliver W. Holmes or Louis Brandeis, used their clerks as more than research assistants. More run-of-the-mill Justices have given their clerks a larger share of responsibility, including (in some cases) the writing of opinions."

JUDICIAL ADMINISTRATION AND REFORM

In the United States, the judicial branch is characterized by a lack of specialization. Judges are often confronted by case issues about which they have little knowledge or experience. A judge whose legal practice involved civil cases is found in criminal court, a criminal lawyer is found on the bench of juvenile court, and both may have to preside at a divorce hearing, antitrust case, or a case involving highly technical scientific issues. Judges are also responsible for administrative duties for which they usually have no training. Judges prize independence, and traditions of civility and camaraderie associated with the legal profession mitigate against a chain of command and formal rules of interaction among judges. Until the 1980s, judges typically avoided the advice of professional managers and proceeded without the benefit of modern techniques of careful research, planning, evaluation, and training (Cannon 1982). In many courts, judges were often slow to heed the advice of professional managers and continued to rely on intuitions and predilections born of legal training and disposition to follow precedents.

While operational agencies in the executive branch of government are organized bureaucratically, with day-to-day operations managed by a chain of command and carried out on the basis of a highly specialized division of labor, the judicial branch has resisted bureaucratization. What would be routine for an executive branch agency is often slow and inefficient in the judicial branch. While executive-branch operations are under the control of administrators who are more or less trained and experienced in management, the judicial branch is under the control of judges who may have little or no experience, and even less interest, in such mundane matters as providing adequate lighting, heating and cooling, clean washrooms, and bulletin boards for posting the daily court calendars. There is also the pressing problem of case management, promulgating calendars, assigning judges, court security, and maintaining and safeguarding case files. Legal education provides no exposure to court administration.

Administration of Federal Courts

At the beginning of this chapter, it was noted that no two state court systems are exactly alike, and the administration of each also varies. While the federal system has some administrative responsibilities vested in the Supreme Court, there is no ministry of justice, a centralized system that exists in other democratic countries. A major difference between most state court governance structures and the federal system is the role of the jurisdiction's highest appellate court. Supreme courts dominate governance in most states. Other than the activities of the Chief Justice, however, the U.S. Supreme Court's only significant role in federal judicial governance is in approving procedural rules developed by the Judicial Conference and sending them to Congress for review.

The Court has no other significant role in court governance, in part because of Chief Justice Charles Hughes' (1930–1941) reaction to executive–judicial conflicts in the 1930s, and the difficulties that federal court administration had caused the Justice Department. The chief justice wanted the Court free from contamination by bureaucratic infighting and inevitable charges of poor or even corrupt administration in faraway courts, about which the Supreme Court could know very little (Wheeler 1992). In 1938, Congress transferred the management of the federal judiciary from the Department of Justice to the federal judges themselves. However, because of Hughes' opposition, managerial control was not lodged in the Supreme Court. Instead, it is distributed throughout the federal judiciary (Howard 1981).

The Supreme Court promulgates rules for the lower courts, but its control over budgetary matters and policy-making is minimal. Each federal circuit has a circuit judicial council, and in each of the federal districts there is a chief judge who has administrative responsibilities. But the chief judge's ability to carry out policies is based more on the level of cooperation in a district than on any real powers that he or she can exercise—each judge is independent and appointed for life. In 1971, Congress passed the Circuit Executive Act, establishing an executive for each federal circuit to provide managerial expertise in budgeting, information systems, personnel and training, facilities, furnishings, and supplies, research, and public relations.

A Judicial Conference, established in 1922 as the Conference of Senior Circuit Judges, serves as the chief administrative policymaker for the federal judiciary. Chaired by the chief justice of the Supreme Court, the conference has 26 members, including the chief judges of the courts of appeals, a district judge from each circuit except Washington, D.C., and the chief judge of the Court of International Trade. The members meet twice a year, and the six-member executive committee acts for the conference between meetings. A variety of specialized committees conducts much of the work of the conference: rules of evidence and procedure, intercircuit transfers, need for additional judges to handle increasing caseloads, ethical standards for judges and other court personnel, qualifications for court personnel, and the budget for the federal judiciary. Lawyers serve on advisory committees, and lawyer representatives attend annual circuit judicial conferences. The Judicial Conference as a whole votes on committee recommendations and makes legislative recommendations for congressional action.

The Administrative Office of the United States Courts is headed by a director appointed by the Chief Justice in consultation with the Judicial Conference. The director serves as the chief administrative officer of the federal courts and is responsible for carrying out the policies of the Judicial Conference. The office provides staff support and counsel to the Judicial Conference and its committees, collects and reports judicial branch statistics, develops budgets, conducts surveys and assessments of judicial operations and programs, provides technical assistance to the courts, develops training programs, and fosters communication within the judiciary and with other branches of government and the public.

The Federal Judicial Center provides training and research for the federal judiciary in a wide range of areas including court administration, case management, budget and finance, human resources, and court technology. The center's operations are overseen by a board of directors consisting of the Chief Justice, the Director of the Administrative Office, and seven judges chosen by the Judicial Conference. The center develops orientation and continuing education programs for judges and other court personnel. It conducts studies of judiciary operations and makes recommendations to the Judicial Conference for improvement of the administration and management of the federal courts (Federal Judicial Center Information).

Administration of State Courts

While court administration can affect the level of justice dispensed in a system, judicial management has typically been the most primitive of governmental services. The judicial branch was the last to take advantage of the revolution in information management that resulted from the use of computers. David Saari points out that the courthouse has a natural aversion to change; the lawyers who dominate its operations "are not interested in working in a typical executive type of bureaucratically dominated, centralized atmosphere, which they will resist by keeping courts locally controlled to suit their own professional interest. Thus the politically favorable, localized power and the professionalism trends [of the legal profession] join together to preserve that historical design concept of the judiciary from excessive bureaucratization that has overrun other institutions of society, especially executive-branch organizations and large businesses. This antibureaucratic strain of courts seems to explain many local examples and variations where the public and courts have rejected reform aimed toward centralized control" (1985: 32–33).

At the top of a state court system is the chief judge of the court of last resort, who usually has certain statewide administrative responsibilities. There may also be a judicial conference or similar entity that promulgates rules for the entire state judiciary and helps to resolve disputes. The supreme court or the conference will have authority to remove judges for judicial misconduct. The day-to-day operations of a judicial district are the responsibility of the chief or presiding judge, who may gain the position by election (the judges in the district make the choice from among their colleagues) or by tradition (e.g., the judge with the most seniority who is not yet 65).

> His or her primary responsibilities are to keep the cases flowing in as efficient a manner as the administration of individual justice permits. [He or she will pressure judges to "move cases" whenever a backlog develops.] The other functions of this chief judicial officer vary depending upon local tradition and preferences but most perform the following tasks: (1) assign judges to various courts, (2) initiate disciplinary action against members of the bench, (3) act as spokespersons for bench to bar and general public, (4) preside over functions involving the bench, (5) serve as ex officio members of various

New York

The state constitution provides that the chief judge of the court of appeals is the state's chief judicial officer who, with the advice and consent of the administrative board—chief judge and the presiding justices of the four appellate divisions—appoints the chief administrative judge of the courts. The chief judge establishes statewide standards and administrative policies after consultation with the administrative board and promulgates these after approval by the court of appeals. The chief administrative judge is responsible for supervising the administration and operation of the trial courts and for directing the Office of Court Administration. The chief administrative judge appoints administrative judges in each jurisdiction who are given significant administrative latitude to carry out policy and address local issues.

committees within the court system, (6) decide administrative matters such as vacations and retirements of court members, and (7) plan and execute continuing education projects. (Wice 1985: 52–53)

Headed by the state court administrator, every state has a central office responsible for the day-to-day administrative responsibilities for the judicial branch. The administrator is typically an appointee of the chief justice of the highest court. The size of his or her office is a reflection of the degree to which there is centralization of key judicial functions (Rottman et al. 2000). Important managerial aspects of any court system are the responsibility of the clerk of the court. In some systems, the chief or presiding trial court judge is assisted by a court manager, a professional who is responsible for many of the nonlegal aspects of the court system.

Clerk of the Court. The duties and the title of clerk of the court vary from state to state. In about one-third of the states, there is a distinct elected office called county clerk. In other states, the functions of this official are performed by officers entitled clerk, circuit clerk, recorder of deeds, registrar of deeds, or even auditor. The clerk of the court may be elected or appointed and is responsible for maintaining the written records of the court and for supervising the work of the assistant clerks who attend

ADMINISTRATIVE OFFICE OF PENNSYLVANIA COURTS

Pennsylvania's Constitution invests in the state Supreme Court general supervisory and administrative authority over all of the Commonwealth's courts. The Constitution also establishes the office of Court Administrator of Pennsylvania, who is appointed by the Supreme Court. The court administrator heads the Administrative Office of Pennsylvania Courts (AOPC), whose supervisory, administrative and long-range planning duties include:

- reviewing practices, procedures, and efficiency at all levels of the court system and in all related offices
- developing recommendations to the Supreme Court regarding improvement of the system and related offices
- representing the judicial system before legislative bodies
- examining administrative and business methods used by offices in or related to the court system
- collecting statistical data
- examining the state of the dockets and making recommendations for expediting litigation
- managing fiscal affairs, including budget preparation, disbursements approval, and goods and services procurement
- supervising all administrative matters relating to offices engaged in clerical functions
- administering human resource systems, including personnel and benefits counseling and management
- conducting education programs for system personnel
- receiving and responding to comments from the public

all court sessions. According to the *Dictionary of Criminal Justice Data Terminology* (1981: 56), "The typical duties of the court clerk are receiving documents to be filed in the court record, assigning case numbers, scheduling cases on the court calendar [docketing], entering judgments and orders in the court record, preparing writs and warrants [for the judge's signature], and keeping the court records and seal," which must be affixed to all court documents if they are to be official. In some jurisdictions, the clerk of the court prepares the court budget, oversees jury selection, and collects court fees (Stout 1986; Rottman et al. 2000).

Court Managers.   Court management is a relatively new profession, dating only from the 1960s. But it has expanded rapidly. In 1970, there were fewer than 50 persons in court administrative positions who had management training. By 1980, that number was over 500 (Solomon 1987). There are a number of universities that provide graduate degrees in court management. The University of Denver, e.g., offers a Masters of Science in Legal Administration (M.S.L.A.), which includes preparation for law office management and judicial administration. Practitioners oversee the administrative functions of the court under the general direction of the chief judge. In practice, the judges of the court play the role of a board of directors: The chief judge serves as chairman of the board, and the court manager is the administrator or executive officer. Under this system, the judges determine policy that is implemented by the court manager. Many of the functions performed by a court manager are traditionally the duties of the chief judge. While the duties of court managers vary with the location and size of the court that employs them, their basic functions, according to the National Association for Court Management, include the following:

- *Personnel Management:* administration of wage and salary systems; recruiting, selecting, training, developing, evaluating, counseling, and disciplining nonjudicial administrative staff; and facilitating personnel matters for judicial staff.
- *Fiscal Management:* preparation of court budgets; administering accounting, purchasing, payroll, and financial control functions; guiding the budget through state and local government review processes.

CLERK OF THE FULTON COUNTY, GEORGIA, SUPERIOR COURT

The clerk of the Superior Court is elected by the citizens of Fulton County to serve a four-year term. The clerk maintains a comprehensive record of all civil and criminal actions of the Superior Court and prepares and records accusations, indictments, and the disposition of cases. Records are prepared for the Georgia Court of Appeals and the Georgia Supreme Court. The clerk also provides each Superior Court judge, senior judge, and visiting judge with a calendar clerk to prepare the court calendar and otherwise assist the courts.

Additionally, the clerk is responsible for recording deeds related to the sale of real property, personal property liens, maintaining the chain of title to all property in the county, and collecting real estate transfer taxes. Other records include suits, pleadings, charters, contracts, professional licenses, trade name registrations, and notary public appointments. All records maintained by this office are arranged to facilitate research and review by lawyers, real estate agents, and others.

- *Caseflow Management:* analysis and evaluation of pending caseloads; preparing and implementing recommendations for effective calendar management.

- *Automated Office Management:* analysis, evaluation, implementation of management information systems to assist the court (computers, telecommunications equipment, microfilm and microfiche devices and techniques).

- *Jury Management:* management of the jury system in the most efficient and cost-effective manner.

- *Space and Equipment Management:* planning for physical space needs; purchasing and managing equipment and supplies.

- *Records Management:* creating and managing uniform record-keeping systems.

- *Information Management:* collecting and providing management information for all departments and branches of government; publishing data on pending and completed judicial business and internal functions of the court system.

- *Court Liaison:* acting as a liaison to other courts, public and private agencies, governments, and attorneys to promote the work of the court.

- *Public Relations:* acting as a clearinghouse for the release of information to the media and the public; educating the public about the work of the court.

- *Research and Advisory Services:* identifying problems; recommending procedural and administrative changes to the court.

The role of court managers differs from the more conventional role of a business manager because the environment in which they work is considerably different from that of a more routinized business organization. Clear hierarchical lines of authority are absent. Judges enjoy considerable autonomy, and they "share professional interests and values with lawyers, who, for the most part, function outside of traditional types of organizations" (Stott 1987: 22). The courts more closely resemble hospitals and universities, large partnerships, and professional groups than business organizations. This setting means that strain caused by role ambiguity is inherent in the position of court manager.

ADMINISTRATIVE REFORM

Suggestions for reform at the federal level include adding additional judges to handle the increasing federal calendars, geographic realignment to better effect a balancing of court caseloads, delegating court management to professional managers, diverting certain cases for arbitration, and transferring mandatory jurisdiction over certain cases, e.g., diversity of citizenship, to the state courts. There have also been proposals for the establishment of additional specialized federal courts (similar to the U.S. Court of Tax Appeals) and pressure for the creation of another level of appeals courts in the federal system. But, in the assessment of J. Woodford Howard (1981), none of these proposals can respond to the problems created by the decentralized nature of the federal judiciary.

The three major administrative reforms for state court systems, advocated by such groups as the American Bar Association and the American Judicature Society, come under the heading of court unification: structural unification, administrative centralization, and unified budgeting.

COURT UNIFICATION

Court unification has three interrelated components:
1. Simplified state trial court structure
2. Judicial system policy- and rule-making authority covering practice, procedure, and administration vested in the supreme court or judicial council with system governance authority vested in the chief justice of the supreme court
3. Funding of all or a substantial portion of the judicial system, with a unified judicial system budget prepared by the administrative office of the courts

Source: Bureau of Justice Assistance (1988)

Structural Unification

Structural unification includes consolidating and simplifying existing trial courts and forming a single superior court on a countywide basis; lower courts cease to exist. While the consolidated superior court has specialized divisions, such as juvenile court, civil court, chancery court, small-claims court, misdemeanor court, and felony court, in exemplary unification all judges are equal and selected in the same manner—appointment, election, or merit (discussed in Chapter 9). Thus, the salary and authority of each trial judge is the same and, accordingly, judges can be allocated to whatever courts are in need during any particular period of time. With court unification, the neglect of the lower courts caused by judges aspiring to a superior-court bench would no longer be relevant.[5] In 1964, Illinois became the first state in the nation to adopt a unified court system.

Administrative Centralization

Administrative centralization places statewide authority for court policy and administration in the supreme court or judicial council. Governance responsibility is vested in the chief justice of the highest court or the position of chief administrative judge is established. "Centralized management provides the state's highest court with the power to make rules, appoint managerial personnel, assign judges and nonjudicial staff, and prepare and execute a centralized, state-financed yearly budget" (Stout 1986: 206). Under this system, there is a degree of uniformity rarely reached in more decentralized systems, and judges can be moved across counties on temporary assignments to reduce case backlogs. For example, in Illinois, which has unification and centralization, judges from downstate counties, which have a reduction in their court calendars during the summer months, are transferred to Cook County (Chicago) to help reduce calendar backlog there.

---

[5]"One-tier court systems," however, "tend to re-create a limited jurisdiction court by establishing an unofficial lower level of judges and staff who process routine, high-volume cases" (Rottman and Hewitt 1996: 83). In some jurisdiction these judges are part time; in Illinois, they are associate judges appointed by the elected trial judges.

In New York, the court system is centralized under the state's chief judge, who appoints a chief administrator for the courts; the administrator operates under policy and standards approved by the court of appeals, the state's highest court. The chief administrator is responsible for the day-to-day operations of the state's more than 3,500 judges and 9,000 support personnel. He or she estimates the financial needs of the courts, designates administrative judges for the trial courts, transfers judges to balance workloads, hires nonjudicial personnel, prepares reports of the activities of the courts, and makes recommendations for legislation affecting the courts.

Thomas Henderson and his colleagues summarize the arguments for and against court unification and centralization: "A simplified court structure and strong central direction . . . will increase uniformity of justice and enhance the managerial capability of the courts. Opponents of unification have countered that such changes will lead to a large central bureaucracy which will be insensitive to local concerns. In their view, rigidity will be substituted for individualized justice" (1984: 5).

Unified Budgeting

Unified budgeting "means that the budget for the court system is prepared at the state level, regardless of the source of funds, and that the executive branch does not have the authority to modify the budget request," since this would encroach upon the separation of powers. There are 27 states in which the primary responsibility for funding the trial courts is unified (Stout 1986: 206). Since the ability to prepare and implement the budget is a prime feature of the exercise of power, unified budgeting and court centralization are closely related, if not necessarily intertwined.

Obstacles to Reform

The options for restructuring a court system are limited by the constitutional requirements of separation of powers and the judicial norms of the adversary system. Simplification and centralization available to other organizations may be inappropriate for the courts. Furthermore, many court-related functions have been relegated by law to other organizations such as the prosecutor, public defender, sheriff, corrections department, county commission, and clerks (Henderson et al. 1984). Lawyers and court personnel, ranging from bailiffs to judges, are socialized into a particular system, and the familiar is often the most comfortable setting in which to spend one's working days. Private attorneys who have learned to negotiate the system enjoy certain advantages, and they are loath to give them up in the name of reform or efficiency—"If it ain't broke, why fix it?"

Those who have the most to gain from greater efficiency, the public, are rarely exposed to the judicial system on any regular basis. Litigants and defendants are only peripheral players, whose time-limited participation in the judicial system has little or no impact. The very inefficiency of the system is often a basis for additional personnel needs that provide patronage for the politicized judiciary. Court reform is usually opposed by Stratum III attorneys "who deal almost daily with local courts [and] become accustomed to and dependent on existing court organization, procedures, and personnel. Their intimate knowledge of how local courts operate is an important key to their legal success. Changes in court structure disrupt their routine and create new uncertainties about how courts will behave. Justice delayed is not necessarily justice denied, since delay may be part of a legal strategy to reach a negotiated settlement, to prepare a case more carefully, or to permit a lawyer to take on a larger volume of business than he or she can handle at one time" (Glick 1982: 23). Trial lawyers frequently form associations to protect their legislative interests. Rural and small-town lawyers also oppose court reform, particularly the streamlining of state courts, if it means that the local judges will be transferred to a larger city (Glick 1982).

As we might expect, lawyers usually found in the forefront of efforts at court reform are from Stratum I, attorneys seldom found in court, particularly the state courts. In general, like the clients they represent, Stratum I attorneys are Republicans working in urban areas dominated by Democrats, and the clash over court reform often becomes embroiled in highly partisan politics.

The most significant impetus for a major reform, improving case management in criminal court, has been the Fifth Amendment's guarantee of a speedy trial and legislation based on court interpretations of this amendment.

> In jurisdictions which had a strict speedy trial rule (i.e., the required dismissal of the charges against any defendant whose trial and dispositions had been unreasonably delayed beyond a fixed time period, such as 90, 120, or 170 days) and where there was public pressure on the judiciary to avoid any such dismissals, the various court organizations worked together to expedite the flow of cases. The incentive in such courts apparently was not the goal of general improvement in the administration of justice, but the avoidance of the very visible public outcry seen in jurisdictions where a defendant is released and his case dismissed, not because he was found not guilty, but because of delays in the processing of his case through the court. This incentive is particularly effective in those jurisdictions where the judiciary faces periodic elections. (Kreindel et al. 1977: 35)

Some are also concerned that speedy trial legislation may serve to force criminal defendants to trial before they are fully prepared. While the government may have been gathering evidence and preparing a case for a long period of time, particularly on the federal level, defendants can be forced to go to trial 70 days after indictment.

In the next chapter, we will examine the appellate process and judicial review.

INTERNET CONNECTIONS

Administrative Office of the U.S. Courts: *uscourts.gov*
Federal Judicial Center: *fjc.gov*
Council for Court Excellence: *courtexcellence.org/links.html*
National Association for Court Management: *nacm.ncsc.dni.us*
Nation's Court Directory: *courts.net*
State Justice Institute: *statejustice.org*
National Center for State Courts: *ncsc.dni.us*
Mid-Atlantic Association for Court Amendment: *maacm.org*

REVIEW QUESTIONS

1. What are the various elements that determine a court's jurisdiction?
2. What is diversity jurisdiction?
3. How do the responsibilities of a lower court differ from that of a superior court?
4. What was the purpose of creating an intermediate court of appeals?
5. Why is it necessary to have a federal court system in addition to one for every state?
6. In the federal system, what distinguishes legislative (Article I) courts from constitutional (Article III) courts?
7. What are the responsibilities of a federal magistrate?
8. In the federal system, what are "senior judges" and the "Rule of 80"?
9. What are the main components of judicial reform?
10. What are the obstacles to judicial reform?
11. What is the role of the court manager in the judicial system?

7

THE APPELLATE PROCESS AND JUDICIAL REVIEW

In this chapter we will review the appellate process and examine the role of judicial review. We examine the related issues of legitimacy and problem of implementing appellate judicial decisions.

THE APPELLATE PROCESS

Instead of witness testimony that determines outcome in trial courts, appellate courts decide cases based on written material:

- *Petition:* appellant's request or "prayer" for a certain action
- *Briefs:* written explanations and versions of the case prepared by opposing attorneys
- *Case Records:* written documents, including the transcript, from the court whose decision is being appealed

and sometimes after oral arguments from both sides. New testimony is not permitted: "The appellate court cannot stray outside the 'record' (the pleadings, exhibits, and transcript of the proceedings in the court below)" and these "are wholly the product of the parties' lawyers working in a strongly adversarial manner" (Hughes 1996: 22). During oral arguments the appellate court judges often assume an inquisitorial role with probing questions to the attorneys. There may also be *amicus curiae* ("friend of the court") briefs with or without oral arguments. "*Amici curiae* are organizations or, rarely, individuals not a party to the appeal but likely to be affected by the precedent created. They are then, interested in the lawmaking aspects of deciding appeals, and not the case-deciding aspects" (Marvell 1978: 80).

The justices and their law clerks read the briefs submitted by each side, *amicus curiae*, and research previous decisions that can have a bearing on the case at issue. Appellate court judges (as well as all federal and many state trial judges) are assisted by law clerks and sometimes by staff attorneys. The clerks are usually recent law school graduates who perform research and may even draft initial, if not final, opinions. They bring with them their recent exposure to outstanding law professors (Coffin 1994), and typically serve for one or two years. Cynics sometimes remark that the literary style of some judges appears to change with the same frequency as their law clerks. A great deal of competition takes place among federal judges seeking to secure the brightest candidates from among recent law school graduates (Margolick 1989a).

Anthony Kronman is critical of a "growing tendency of appellate judges to work by editing draft opinions prepared for them by their clerks instead of writing opinions themselves." Editing, he states, "does not in general make as strong a demand on the imagination as original composition," and editors tend to feel diminished responsibility for the writings they produce even when it is their name the writings bear. There is also the "increased tendency to defer to the judgment of the original author; and the temptation, to which every editor is liable, to view his primary task as one of stylistic improvement only" (1993: 331). This trend, he notes, has led to increasing both the length of decisions and the number of footnotes they contain, an indication of clerks' insecurity, a feature of their relative inexperience. Kronman argues there is a vicious circle at work: "The opinions that law students read have been written by law clerks, that is, by other beginners like themselves" (1993: 351).

A typical appellate decision contains (Re 1975b: 11–13):

- An introductory statement or paragraph setting forth the nature of the case and the appeal
- The question presented in the appeal: What is the court being asked to decide?

ELEMENTS OF THE APPELLATE PROCESS

- Reliance on a closed lower court record
- Deferential review of a prior heat-tested—via the adversarial method—decision
- Graduated, sequential decision-making, carefully applying precedent
- Collegial decisions
- Substantial (though not complete) reliance on the oral and written presentations of adversaries
- The restraint of professional legal conventions and rules
- The discipline of justifying a decision in writing

Source: Coffin (1994)

A Rational Appellate Court

In his classic, *The Common Law Tradition*, Karl Llewellyn (1960) provides 14 points against which to measure an appellate court:

1. *Law-conditioned officials.* The personnel must be trained and experienced lawyers who come to the appellate bench with years of active legal work.
2. *Legal doctrine.* There must be an accepted body of legal doctrines that are to be used in deciding specific cases. These doctrines serve to restrain appellate decisions.
3. *Known doctrinal techniques.* The legal doctrines must be used in a standard and generally accepted fashion.
4. *Responsibility for justice.* The justices must have an ingrained sense of duty to bring about a just result.
5. *One single right answer.* While there can often be in fact several answers, justices must act with an urge to find one answer alone that is the right one.
6. *An opinion of the court.* The decision must be made with a published opinion that "reaches far beyond the case in hand; the opinion has as one if not its major office, to show how like cases are properly to be decided in the future" (1960: 26).
7. *A frozen record from below.* The facts that the appellate court must consider should be largely the immutable record of the trial court.
8. *Issues limited, sharpened, and phrased in advance.* Lawyers must submit briefs that provide the justices with a basis for a decision.
9. *Adversary argument by counsel.* An appellate decision must be rendered only after written and oral arguments are presented by trained counsel. This assists in the predictability of outcome.
10. *Group decision.* "A group all of whom take full part is likely to produce a net view with wider perspective and fewer extremes than an individual . . . and continuity is likely to be greater with a group" (1960: 31).
11. *Judicial security and honesty.* The justices must be immune from personal or political retribution for their decisions.
12. *A known bench.* The appellate court establishes a way of looking at things that can be known to those who follow the court's decisions. This forms a tradition to which new justices are socialized.
13. *The general period-style and its promise.* A way of thought and writing must be closely associated with the court during particular periods. This enhances predictability—an inarticulate court produces excessive appeals by a confused or speculative bar.
14. *Professional judicial office.* The justices are full-time office holders who must not allow personal predilections to keep them from their responsibilities to the court.

- The essential or salient facts
- The judicial discussion of the pertinent authority (precedent) that resolves or decides the question or issues presented (*ratio decedendi*)
- The precise disposition of the appeal

The decision-making process of appellate courts is shrouded in secrecy; during deliberations, even clerks are rarely if ever present. "All internal communications about the cases (draft opinions, talk, and memoranda) are confidential. Until the decision is announced, no outsider is supposed to know which judge is writing on a case or how a case will be decided" (Marvell 1978: 7–8). Secrecy encourages the free flow of information between judges and allows for a change of mind without being subjected to question or criticism. Knowledge of the outcome of a case might also provide someone with a financial advantage (Marvell 1978).

JUDICIAL REVIEW BY THE SUPREME COURT

According to the Constitution, the Supreme Court has original jurisdiction "in all Cases affecting Ambassadors, other public Ministers and Consuls . . . [and] to Controversies to which the United States shall be a Party" (Article III, Section 2). In theory, the Court will also consider disputes between states, or between a state and the federal government, but in practice, it rarely does. Original jurisdiction is seldom exercised; by 1984 the Supreme Court had issued full opinions in only 164 such cases (Goldman and Jahnige 1985). In cases of original jurisdiction where the Court cannot reach a decision on the pleadings of the litigants, a senior district judge is usually appointed to hear testimony and make a finding and recommendation upon which the Court can act.

The Constitution is not explicit in stating the jurisdiction of the Supreme Court other than making it "appellate." Therefore, its jurisdiction is subject to congressional modification. Originally, the Court was required to hear all cases that came before it on a writ of error; under common law, an order from an appellate court directing a trial court to send up its record of a case for review. In 1914, the Court was granted certiorari jurisdiction, according to which it could deny consideration to any petition that was not supported by four justices. This discretion was at first limited to certain state decisions—those favoring rights claimed under federal law— but in 1916, all cases involving alleged denials of federal rights were shifted to the Court's certiorari jurisdiction.

The so-called Judges' Bill, the Judiciary Act of 1925, was drafted and promoted by members of the Supreme Court at the request of Congress to deal with the Court's growing caseload. It fundamentally redefined the Supreme Court's role by repealing much of the mandatory jurisdiction of the Court. According to the Act, which finalized the Court's power to pick the cases it would consider, some cases are technically outside the Court's certiorari jurisdiction. These include:

THE "WITHOUT COMMENT" DISPOSITION

In cases without obvious precedential value, an appellate court can render a "disposition without comment," a terse, not-for-publication opinion or a disposition without any comment whatsoever. While rendering a decision on the merits of the case, these dispositions do not make law—they have no precedential value. This approach is similar to the code systems (discussed in Chapter 2) in which case law does not play a central role (Gulati and McCauliff 1998).

- A case coming from a state supreme court when a federal law or treaty has been declared unconstitutional or when a state law or provision of a state constitution has been upheld against a challenge that it is in conflict with a federal law, treaty, or the Constitution
- Cases from a U.S. court of appeals when a state law or provision of a state constitution has been ruled unconstitutional
- Cases from any federal court when a federal law has been held unconstitutional and the United States—officers or agencies—is a party
- Cases required to be considered by a three-judge special district court which has granted or denied an injunction

In practice, however, the Court has exercised considerable discretion over "mandated" cases, frequently dismissing them for "lack of a substantial federal question" or "want of jurisdiction." Even when an appeal was accepted for review, the Court frequently disposes of it without any oral arguments, simply affirming the decision of the court below (Goldman and Jahnige 1985). Instead of overruling decisions originating in state courts, as a matter of policy, the Court typically remands the case to the state supreme court for "further proceedings not inconsistent" with their opinion (Spaeth 1979). In 1988, Congress eliminated all mandatory appeals except those few cases involving the special categories decided by three-judge federal district courts (Baum 1989).

The Supreme Court is also empowered to receive cases for *certification*. In this instance, a lower court—federal district court or court of appeals—requests (certifies) that the Court rule on a legal question in a pending case that it cannot resolve. If the Court accepts the certificate, the justices answer the question, which is then applied by the lower court in deciding the case. The procedure is rarely utilized. Even more rare is the use of Court authority to intervene in the activities of a trial court with an extraordinary writ ordering the judge to perform some act (*writ of mandamus*) or forbidding him or her from doing so (*writ of prohibition*).

According to Supreme Court rules, a *petition for certiorari* should be no longer than 30 pages, contain a copy of the lower-court decision that the defendant wants reviewed, a statement of the legal question(s) that the case presents. Since 1980, Court rules have required that petitions list the questions presented by the case on the first page and a statement of the reasons why the Court should consider the case. The page limitation does not include appendices, which can run hundreds of pages and may be more important than the actual petition (Baum 1989; Perry 1991). Many petitions come to the Court from prison inmates who do not have attorneys to see to it that legal papers are submitted in proper form. Often only a page or two, they rarely conform to any legal specifications and are placed in a special group (in *forma pauperi*s—brought by paupers) and examined by the chief justice's law clerks. In other courts, these papers would typically be rejected for lack of proper form. Since the Court grants certiorari in relatively few of the cases that are appealed, a lawyer who declares that he or she will take a case all the way to the Supreme Court is usually engaging in rhetorical excess. The Court does not give reasons for turning down a case (nor, for that matter, why a case is accepted for review). Most cases heard by the Court, however, result in reversals of the lower-court decision.

*S*UPREME *C*OURT *R*ULE 10:

CONSIDERATIONS GOVERNING REVIEW ON WRIT OF CERTIORARI

Review on a writ of certiorari is not a matter of right, but of judicial discretion. A petition for a writ of certiorari will be granted only for compelling reasons. The following, although neither controlling nor fully measuring the Court's discretion, indicate the character of the reasons the Court considers:

(a) A United States court of appeals has entered a decision in conflict with the decision of another United States court of appeals on the same important matter; has decided an important federal question in a way that conflicts with a decision by a state court of last resort; or has so far departed from the accepted and usual course of judicial proceedings, or sanctioned such a departure by a lower court, as to call for an exercise of this Court's supervisory power;

(b) A state court of last resort has decided an important federal question in a way that conflicts with the decision of another state court of last resort or of a United States court of appeals;

(c) A state court or a United States court of appeals has decided an important question of federal law that has not been, but should be, settled by this Court, or has decided an important federal question in a way that conflicts with relevant decisions of this Court. A petition for a writ of certiorari is rarely granted when the asserted error consists of erroneous factual findings or the misapplication of a properly stated rule of law.

For about a decade, the Court decided about 150 cases each term with full opinions, less than 4 percent of all petitions filed, with about half granted a hearing, that is, oral arguments by attorneys for both sides of the question. By 1993, that number had fallen to little more than 100 cases, with two one-hour oral arguments a day instead of the usual four (Greenhouse 1993b). When the Court opened its 1994–1995 term, it granted certiorari to none of the more than 1,600 cases that had been submitted over the three-month summer recess (Greenhouse 1994). In its 1999–2000 term, the Court decided 73 cases, the fewest of any term since the 1950s (Greenhouse 2000). Of those receiving a full hearing, about 85 percent are subjected to a detailed opinion written by one of the justices voting in the majority (to which dissents and concurring opinions can be attached). The remaining cases and those for which no oral arguments were conducted are typically disposed of by a *per curiam* opinion (in which the Court states its opinion, but the author is not revealed), or by a brief memorandum order such as "dismissed," "vacated" (render void), or "reversed and remanded" (overturn the decision and send the case back to the lower court for further consideration). The Court can also choose to affirm the judgment of the court below, which means the lower court decision stands, although this type of decision does not serve as a precedent.

U.S. Supreme Court Rules

Although some rules of the Supreme Court are published, "most of the internal procedures are by consensus, are unpublished, and are frequently unknown" (Perry 1991: 17). Several rules were outlined by Justice Louis D. Brandeis in a concurring decision (*Ashwander* v. *Tennessee Valley Authority* 1936):

1. Cases must not be presented in a friendly, nonadversarial proceeding (to get an advisory opinion, for example); the dispute must be a real one.[1]
2. The Court will not anticipate a question of constitutional law in advance of the necessity of deciding it.
3. The Court will not formulate a rule of constitutional law broader than is required by the precise facts to which it is to be applied.
4. If a case can be decided on constitutional grounds or on the grounds of statutory construction or general law, the Court will rule only on the latter.
5. The Court will not decide the validity of a statute upon the complaint of a person who fails to show that he or she is injured by its operation (has "standing").
6. The Court will not pass upon the constitutionality of a statute at the request of a person who has benefitted from it.
7. Whenever possible, the Court will avoid making a determination of the validity of an act of Congress.

Supreme Court Procedures

The annual term of the Supreme Court begins on the first Monday in October and is known by the year in which it starts; the term ends toward the end of June. More than 4,000 petitions are received each year; most are reviewed and summarized by clerks for the justices, and the present Court has a "cert pool" of clerks from various justices who collectively divide up the petitions for review and summary. They are voted upon by the justices at weekly conferences closed to the public.

Certain "cues" make a case stand out, thereby improving its chances for review: the reputation of the lower appellate judges; written dissents in the lower courts indicating controversy; the U.S. government being a party to the case and seeking review; and the presence of race relations, civil liberties, or a variety of economic issues. Other elements being equal, the more cues, the greater the likelihood of review (Glick 1983; see Perry 1991 for an examination of agenda setting in the Supreme Court). When a case is rejected for review, the decision of the lower court stands.

ACT OF CONGRESS

"When the validity of an act of Congress is drawn into question, and even if a serious doubt of constitutionality is raised, it is a cardinal principle that this Court will first ascertain whether a construction of the statute is fairly possible by which the question may be avoided."

—Charles Evans Hughes, *Crowell v. Benson* (1932)

---

[1]Some state constitutions provide for advisory opinions at the request of the governor or legislature.

In some cases, usually those involving important public issues, oral arguments will be scheduled and opposing attorneys will be given an opportunity to appear before the Court, which meets en banc. Between the granting of certiorari and oral arguments, briefs must be filed by the parties according to particular specifications as to size of print, size of pages, and cover color: petitioners must use a blue cover; respondents must use red; *amici curiae* briefs must have a green cover. These colors make it easier for justices to find particular briefs. An index of cases or authorities cited must be included, and briefs cannot exceed 50 pages; *amici curiae* briefs cannot exceed 30 pages (Rehnquist 1987). At the oral sessions, each attorney is usually permitted half an hour to present his or her case[2] and must be prepared to answer the often probing questions of the justices, some of whom may pepper the attorney with queries. The justices do not wait until the attorney is finished but often interrupt with questions.[3] Written presentations are discouraged, although a lawyer may use notes. "Showmanship is disfavored; when an inexperienced lawyer makes a florid presentation, a chill almost visibly settles on the bench" (Greenhouse 1993a: 84). Not only do the justices ask questions, they also make statements and suggest positions not raised by the lawyers (Wasby 1993). The purpose of a justice's questions and statements is often to influence his or her colleagues. There is some doubt as to the effect of oral arguments: "The arguments come after the opposing sides have filed long written briefs that state their cases in far more detail than can be done in 30 minutes of oral advocacy amid frequent interruptions from the bench." However, in close cases, where one or more justices may not have made a definite decision, "an especially good oral argument or an especially bad one may make a difference. A justice who is on the fence may be swayed" (Taylor 1986a: 12). In some cases someone who is not a party to the case—interest groups or the U.S. government represented by the solicitor general (see Chapter 9)—may, with the permission of the Court or the litigants, file an *amicus curiae* brief advocating a particular outcome. (Such briefs may also be submitted when the Court is considering certiorari.) Stephen Wasby notes that although the *amicus curiae* may at first have been thought to serve the court as neutral participants, "over time, there has been a shift in *amicus* participation from neutrality, actually being a friend of the court, to advocacy, being a friend of one of the parties" (1993: 153).

In order to appear before the Court, attorneys must be members of the bar of the Supreme Court, although temporary admission (*pro hac vice*) is usually granted if requested by another lawyer or agency employing the attorney. Membership requires the lawyer to have been a member of the bar in his or her home state for at least three years, have two sponsors, and to pay a small fee. Very few applications are rejected, and the rejections are usually based on disciplinary violations back

---

[2]Chief Justice Rehnquist writes: "In the fifteen years that I have been on the Court, the presentation of each side of a case has been limited to one half hour except in cases of extraordinary public importance and difficulty. Three hours were allowed in *United States* v. *Nixon* in 1974" (1987: 274). In this case, President Richard M. Nixon argued that he did not have to release the "Watergate Tapes" based on a claim of executive privilege—the Court ruled otherwise, and the president subsequently resigned.

[3]Justice William J. Brennan, Jr., states that he prepared for oral arguments by using his law clerks to help pick "to pieces every single case, the record, and briefs" (Taylor 1986c: 10). A Bench Memo submitted by law clerk Harlan Stone to Justice Oliver Wendell Holmes appears on page 176 (Stone would later become a justice of the Supreme Court).

*S*UPREME *C*OURT *R*ULE 28: *O*RAL *A*RGUMENT

1. Oral argument should emphasize and clarify the written arguments in the briefs on the merits. Counsel should assume that all Justices have read the briefs before oral argument. Oral argument read from a prepared text is not favored.

2. The petitioner or appellant shall open and may conclude the argument. A cross writ of certiorari or cross-appeal will be argued with the initial writ of certiorari or appeal as one case in the time allowed for that one case, and the Court will advise the parties who shall open and close.

3. Unless the Court directs otherwise, each side is allowed one-half hour for argument. Counsel is not required to use all the allotted time. Any request for additional time to argue shall be presented by motion under Rule 21 no more than 15 days after the petitioner's or appellant's brief on the merits is filed, and shall set out specifically and concisely why the case cannot be presented within the half-hour limitation. Additional time is rarely accorded.

4. Only one attorney will be heard for each side, except by leave of the Court on motion filed no more than 15 days after the respondent's or appellee's brief on the merits is filed. Any request for divided argument shall be presented by motion under Rule 21 and shall set out specifically and concisely why more than one attorney should be allowed to argue. Divided argument is not favored.

5. Regardless of the number of counsel participating in oral argument, counsel making the opening argument shall present the case fairly and completely and not reserve points of substance for rebuttal.

6. Oral argument will not be allowed on behalf of any party for whom a brief has not been filed.

7. By leave of the Court, and subject to paragraph 4 of this Rule, counsel for an *amicus curiae* whose brief has been filed as provided in Rule 37 may argue orally on the side of a party, with the consent of that party. In the absence of consent, counsel for an amicus curiae may seek leave of the Court to argue orally by a motion setting out specifically and concisely why oral argument would provide assistance to the Court not otherwise available. Such a motion will be granted only in the most extraordinary circumstances.

home. Lawyers who have no intention of practicing before the Supreme Court may request admission for status reasons. Every attorney who does practice before the Court receives a souvenir–two quills. Admissions may be revoked, which was the fate of several Watergate defendants in the 1970s.

After the en banc session, the justices go over the cases with their law clerks and tentatively decide on which way to vote. Prior to a final vote, justices may distribute memos indicating their thinking and try to influence their colleagues. They meet in conference—with only justices present—to discuss the cases under consideration. The chief justice speaks first, and the discussion continues according to seniority. Justices usually do not participate (*recuse*) in a case when they know the parties, in cases in which they were involved prior to their appointment to the Court, or when they have even a small, indirect financial interest, usually stock ownership.[4] When a consensus develops, a vote is taken in reverse order of seniority (to prevent the more senior justices from exerting too much influence). In the Rehnquist Court, at the end of the discussion, the chief justice announces how he is recording the vote, and members then have an opportunity to dispute the count if they believe he is mistaken. According to Chief Justice Rehnquist:

> If a case is a relatively simple one, with only one real legal issue in it, it will generally be very clear where each member of the Court stands on that issue. But many cases that we decide are complex ones, with several interrelated issues, and it is simply not possible in the format of the conference to have nine people answering either yes or no to a series of difficult questions about constitutional law. One justice may quite logically believe that a negative answer to the very first of several questions makes it unnecessary to decide the subsequent ones. . . . But if a majority answers the first question in the affirmative, then the Court's opinion will have to go on and discuss the other questions. (1987: 293)

The chief justice, if part of the majority, may write the decision him/herself, or choose an associate justice from the majority side to write the opinion of the Court; otherwise, the opinion is written by the senior justice in the majority or his/her designate. The chief justice assigns opinions when the decision is unanimous. The only exception is the tradition of allowing a new member of the Court to choose the first opinion he or she will write (Abraham 1998). A draft of the opinion is circulated to the other justices so they can offer changes that, if accepted, require a redraft and recirculation. Members may add their dissenting opinions to the final opinion, and sometimes a member of the majority will also provide a separate but concurring opinion in the case, agreeing with the outcome but, e.g., not the reasoning behind it. If five or more justices agree on the outcome but several submit concurring opinions, it may be difficult or impossible to ascertain the *ratio decedendi*. Some memorable dissents subsequently became majority decisions, such as that of Justice John M. Harlan in *Plessy* v. *Ferguson*. His arguments against "separate but equal" in 1896 became a unanimous decision in *Brown* v. *Board of Education* in 1954 (Abraham 1998).

The written opinion is often as important as the actual vote, since it provides the material for case law. Sometimes members use footnotes as a way of "dissenting" while casting a concurring vote (Toch 1982). The opinion of the Court is a closely guarded secret until announced and copies of the judgment are sent to the lawyers and the printer—leaks are rare. The Court has the final word if it affirms the decision of the lower court; otherwise, the case may be sent back for further judicial action, often a retrial.

---

[4]A 1974 statute requires all federal judges to disqualify themselves in any case in which their "impartiality might be reasonably questioned." Custom requires recusal whenever a judge has a financial interest in the case, personal knowledge of the dispute, or a blood relationship with a lawyer representing any party. There is some concern that Supreme Court justices, who typically do not explain their recusals, may be withdrawing from cases unnecessarily, and this could place a burden on the Court and its ability to render meaningful decisions (Greenhouse 1989a).

BENCH MEMO ON *MEYER* v. *NEBRASKA* TO BE ARGUED
February 23, 1923

FROM HARLAN STONE, Law Clerk, to Justice Oliver Wendell Holmes

QUESTION PRESENTED

Does Nebraska's Siman Law, which prohibits the teaching of foreign languages to children in the primary grades, violate the 14th Amendment due process clause rights of parents, teachers and students?

LOWER COURT HOLDING

The Supreme Court of Nebraska held that the Siman Law does not violate students', teachers' or parents' 14th Amendment rights because it is not arbitrary but is rationally related to the state's purpose of educating children to become good citizens in a democracy.

STATUTES, CASES, AND AUTHORITIES

- Amendment XIV: "Nor shall any state deprive any person of life, liberty, or property, without due process of law."
- The Siman Law, Nebraska Code 2567 (1919) (prohibiting teaching of foreign languages, with the exception of Greek and Latin, to children below eighth grade in private and public schools).
- *Adams* v. *Tanner*, 244 U.S. 590 (1917) (striking down law prohibiting employment agencies from charging fees).
- *Muller* v. *Oregon*, 208 U.S. 412 (1908) (upholding law limiting hours of work for women).
- *Lochner* v. *New York*, 198 U.S. 45 (1905) (striking down law regulating hours and working conditions of bakers as violating 14th amendment liberty of contract).
- Puffendorf, Le Droit (European philosopher, explicating a theory of natural law).

FACTS

Nebraska, following World War I and during a period of "Americanization," passed a statute prohibiting the teaching of any modern foreign languages to students who had not completed the eighth grade. Meyer, a schoolteacher in a rural Lutheran church school, was charged with violating that law. He appealed his conviction to the Supreme Court of Nebraska and lost. He is joined by parents and teachers alleging the law infringes their constitutional rights as well.

DISCUSSION

The petitioners argue that the law infringes the 14th Amendment liberty of (1) teachers to pursue a lawful occupation (teaching languages); (2) parents to control the education of their children and; (3) pupils to learn. They contend that the legislation is based on anti-German sentiments and that no legitimate purpose is served by the law since the study of languages is harmless. The law serves not to Americanize but to standardize children.

Nebraska counters that the law is a rational way of accomplishing a legitimate state purpose. The purpose is to promote civic unity and make English the mother tongue of all citizens. This purpose is no less legitimate than bringing light into dark tenements and is comparable to compulsory education and vaccination, provisions which the Court has upheld in the past. They point out that all kinds of supposedly private activities may properly be subjected to regulation by the states under their "police powers" without infringing federal constitutional rights.

Aside from cases about economic liberties, there is very little precedent in this area. The Court has not yet stated what, if any, family liberties are protected under the 14th Amendment Due Process Clause. Petitioners suggest that the rights to marry and raise a family and to acquire useful knowledge are within the liberties protected by the 14th Amendment. These claims are really substantive due process arguments, similar to those made in cases like *Adams* v. *Tanner*, and *Lochner* v. *New York*. These cases might provide precedent for striking down the state law, at least if we equate the freedom to raise one's children with the freedom to enter into a lawful profession and conclude that states may not infringe such liberties without some very weighty justification.

However, there are also conflicting precedents, such as *Muller* v. *Oregon*, holding that the state has broad "police powers" to pass legislation for the public good, including wage, education and labor laws. In *Muller*, the state's interest in protecting women from the rigors of long hours and heavy labor outweighed the freedom of employers to contract and of women workers to exploit their property rights in their own labor.

The crux of the case presented here is whether the Constitution should constrain states from making decisions regarding local matters such as education, absent some specific textual hook which explicitly limits state and local powers. Arguments can be made on both sides. Puffendorf is often cited for the proposition that parents possess natural rights to control and custody of their children which the framers never imagined could be invaded by man made laws. Your dissent in Lochner, however, illustrates the danger that the judiciary may misuse the Constitution to displace democratically enacted legislative judgments with their own personal value judgments.

RECOMMENDATION

Affirm. This is the thin edge of the wedge of federal courts' veto power over virtually any kind of local activities under the guise of protecting 14th Amendment liberties. If the Court recognizes this expansive version of the 14th Amendment, no legislation about families or education will be safe. Laws about marriage, about child labor, about health, and so on, will be challenged as impinging on 14th Amendment rights. Parents will be free to control their children's lives (preventing them from learning English, for example) even if it is not in the best interest of the child. The idea that parents liberties include the freedom to control another person seems antithetical to the notion of liberty and evokes the shades of Dred Scott.

If you decide to reverse and strike down the Siman Law, consider basing your vote on the antidiscrimination principles of the Equal Protection clause or perhaps on the children's intellectual liberty, as opposed to the parents' rights of custody and control. Why not use this as the opportunity to interpret the 14th Amendment as incorporating freedom of religion as well as freedom of speech?

SUGGESTED QUESTIONS

For Meyer

The state says that keeping children from exposure to English is as dangerous to their future development as keeping them in dark and unsanitary houses. How will the children in Zion church make their way in the world? Don't the children have any rights to a useful education?

For Nebraska

If the purpose of your Law is to insure children learn English without any other linguistic distractions, can you explain why only modern languages are banned by Nebraska? Why not Latin and Greek? Isn't the Law simply an excuse to go on harassing German Americans and their religious practices by prohibiting the language they use in their homes and church schools?

LEGITIMACY

It is important to recall that the judiciary is the "least dangerous branch," having no powers of enforcement beyond that offered by the other branches of government. The precedential effect of most court decisions can be nullified by subsequent legislation. Even decisions based on the Constitution can be nullified, albeit with great difficulty, by constitutional amendment (Burton 1985). The judicial branch is dependent on a perception of legitimacy surrounding its decisions, and it uses a variety of symbols to perpetuate the myth that judicial decision-making is neutral and objective: black robes and elevated benches alongside a formal, solemn courtroom environment "more akin to religious institutions and ceremonies than any other setting in American society" (Smith 1993a: 14).

Under our system of case law, the courts are not free to impose their own version of social arrangements; instead, they are constrained by four fundamental principles (Eisenberg 1988):

1. *Objectivity*. The courts derive their legitimacy in large measure from a perceived adherence to objectivity. That is, judges will be impartial and devoid of ties to disputants. Objectivity also requires the court to avoid ad hoc justice, that disputes be resolved not through the application of rules that are peculiar to the case at hand but according to universal rules applicable to all similarly situated cases. (*Rational law*, as discussed in Chapter 1.)

2. *Support*. The universal rules applied by a court must be supported by general societal standards or the particular standards of the legal system. This is necessary so that claimants can utilize the courts to uphold a claim of

a right based on existing standards. Changes in existing standards are the province of legislative bodies whose enactments govern the future and may be deliberately designed to alter existing standards. This approach, Melvin Eisenberg points out, presents a fairness dilemma: "How can it be fair to resolve a dispute concerning a past transaction by applying a legal rule that is articulated after the transaction occurred?" (1988: 10). Requiring judges to reach decisions based on existing standards helps to alleviate this problem; it is reasoned that the disputants knew or had reason to know at the time of their transaction that standards not previously officially recognized were applicable.

3. *Replicability*. In a complex society, it is desirable that lawyers be able to apply their skills of judicial reasoning in order to predict the likely outcome of a particular dispute. This enables legal advice to substitute for litigation. When the outcome is clear, disputes can be settled without recourse to formal judicial proceedings and the costs they can incur. This facilitates transactions since the parties involved, acting on "sound legal advice," can anticipate the likely outcome of any disputes arising out of the transaction. Furthermore, replicability ensures that the parties in dispute will be able to pursue the case with knowledge of the types of proofs and arguments that the courts will attend in reaching a decision.

4. *Responsiveness*. The courts are obligated to be responsive not to the citizenry at large but to the legal profession. As such, they are responsive to, but not obliged to follow, the briefs and oral arguments, material in law reviews, treatises and monographs, the decisions of sister courts, and addresses by legal scholars and practicing lawyers at bar associations or other professional conferences.

To the extent that courts do not adhere to these principles, they undermine a rational system of law and move in the direction of *kadi* justice (discussed in Chapter 1); and they erode the legitimacy of the judicial decision. "It is far fetched," states Steven Burton (1985: 189), "to think that the American people in any sense have consented or would consent to be governed in significant measure by the personal value preferences of judges, rather than by law." In a democratic society, it is hard to imagine why "the people should consent to such unbridled power in any office that is not politically responsible to the electorate at frequent intervals. If judicial decisions were a matter of personal value preferences, there would seem to be no good reason why the preferences of judges should prevail over the preferences of elected representatives of the people or, in the absence of a clear political expression of majoritarian preferences, the autonomous decisions of individuals."

This is why judges exercising the power to invalidate legislation as unconstitutional insist that their rulings simply give effect to the law set forth in the Constitution—they are not empowered to substitute their own policy judgments for those of democratically elected legislators (George 2000). A sound, "legitimate," judicial decision is supported by accepted legal reasoning and consideration of legislative prerogatives. The response to a judicial decision and its subsequent implementation are related to issues of legitimacy.

IMPLEMENTATION OF JUDICIAL DECISIONS

Judicial decisions are not self-implementing. While lower-court responses to most controversial decisions have been immediate and implementation by other government agencies almost complete, such as the 1973 abortion decision in *Roe* v. *Wade*, compliance was not forthcoming in the 1954 desegregation decision of *Brown* v. *Board of Education*—several federal court judges in the South, in fact, refused to implement the decision (Abraham 1998). And the 1963 decision prohibiting prayer in public schools (*Abington School District* v. *Schempp*) was implemented to varying degrees across the country. In 1986, segregation was again litigated in Topeka, Kansas, to force greater compliance with *Brown*, and in 1989, a federal appeals court ruled that while the Topeka school board was not resisting desegregation, it still had not fully carried out the Supreme Court mandate ("Court Allows Challenge to Bias Ruling to Continue" 1989). And, of course, the issue of school prayer is still being subjected to litigation in various parts of the country.

In some cases, it is necessary for judges to retain jurisdiction after immediate legal issues have been settled in order to monitor the implementation of a court decree (Lieberman 1981). For example, in 1987 the federal district judge monitoring the 1981 settlement of a lawsuit against the Texas prison system held the state in contempt of court for failing to carry out court-ordered reforms. The same day, a judge of the Massachusetts Superior Court ruled that the state welfare department had ignored his order to provide a standard of assistance that would allow welfare recipients to rear their children at home. Accordingly, he ordered a 30 percent increase in welfare benefits (*New York Times*, Jan. 6, 1987, p. 7). In 1976, a federal judge took control of the Cleveland, Ohio public schools for failing to end segregation. In 1998, a federal judge agreed to free the school district from court supervision because he said the district had done as much as it could to meet the court-imposed standards for integration.

While some judicial decisions lack the clarity necessary for easy implementation (as attempts to define pornography have proven), others have been subjected to one of three forms of opposition: defiance, avoidance, and limited application (Johnson and Canon 1984):

1. *Defiance*. Overt defiance is a relatively rare and highly unprofessional response in which a lower court judge refuses to follow the decisions of a higher court. Examples of defiance were seen in the South when some judges refused to uphold and implement the decision in *Brown*. Defiance may also take the form of simply ignoring the higher court's policy. This is more easily done in cases decided by trial courts, since appellate tribunals promulgate written decisions that are available to the public.

2. *Avoidance*. Procedural or technical considerations can be used in order to avoid having to implement unacceptable higher-court policy. A judge may also separate out the repugnant language of a decision as *dicta*, or commentary outside of the *ratio decedendi*. Such tactics serve merely to delay implementing judicial policy.

3. *Limited Application*. Since this is a normal response to many judicial decisions, a judge can distinguish away the precedent from the case at issue.

Edward Hartnett (1999: 127) points to differences between an *opinion* and a *judgment*: The latter is a judicial order applied to a specific case, while an opinion is the explanation for the judgment. "It is the judgment," he contends, "not the opinion, that settles authoritatively what is to be done." Indeed, a court can issue a judgment without providing an opinion, while judicial opinions may lack the degree of clarity and specificity necessary to implement them. Vague decisions, such as those concerning obscenity or *de facto* segregation, often result in numerous interpretations, which may encourage lower-court judges who oppose the decisions to resort to avoidance or limited application. Confusion over what is required by a decision may also result in multiple interpretations throughout a state, a federal circuit, or, in the case of the Supreme Court, the entire country. With respect to state courts, the U.S. Supreme Court "has no power to make a *final determination* in any case in which it reviews state court judgments. All it can do in these instances is to decide the federal issue and remand it to the state court below for final judgment 'not inconsistent with this opinion.' Because the state courts possess the power to raise new issues—issues based on 'independent and adequate state grounds'—after they receive the case back from above, they are provided with an opportunity to evade the substantive effects of the reversal by the Supreme Court in a number of ways" (Abraham 1998: 252).

In the next chapter, we will examine issues surrounding the role of the judicial branch in interpreting both statutes and the Constitution, and the related matter of the policy-making role of the judicial branch.

INTERNET CONNECTIONS

Legal Information Institute (Cornell University). *Law.cornell.edu*
Legal sites on the Web: *ih2000.net/ira/legal.htm*
Emory Electronic Reference Desk: *law.emory.edu/LAW/refdesk/toc.html*
Legal journals on the Web: *usc.edu/dept/law-lib/legal/journals.html*
Meta-index for legal research: *gsulaw.gsu.edu/metaindex*

REVIEW QUESTIONS

1. How does the judicial branch response to an issue differ from that of the legislative branch?
2. What is an *amicus curiae* brief?
3. What are the seven elements of the appellate process?
4. What is the controversial role of clerks in the appellate process?
5. What are the three fundamental responsibilities of the U.S. Supreme Court?
6. What is meant by the certiorari jurisdiction of an appellate court?
7. What is the role of Supreme Court clerks?
8. What are the cues that increase the chances of a case being granted certiorari by the Supreme Court?

9. What are the rules governing the Supreme Court's review of cases?

10. Why is the issue of legitimacy especially important for the judicial branch?

11. How does the judicial branch use a variety of symbols to perpetuate the legitimacy of judicial decision-making?

12. What are the three methods courts use to avoid implementing a judicial decision of a higher court?

8

$\mathcal{J}$UDICIAL $\mathcal{I}$NTERPRETATION AND $\mathcal{P}$OLICY-$\mathcal{M}$AKING

In Chapter 7, we looked at the appellate process and the role of judicial review. In this chapter we will examine the related issue—interpreting statutes and the Constitution, both of which involve the judicial branch in making policy. We will look at the contrasting views of those who stress legislative intent and plain meaning as the basic theoretical approaches to the interpretive process.

LEGISLATIVE INTENT VERSUS PLAIN MEANING

Statutory ambiguity is inevitable. No statute, writes Edward Levi, no matter how clearly written and intended, "can be completely unambiguous and applied as intended to a specific case" (1955: 5). On what basis is the judicial branch to interpret—for the purpose of application—the actions of the legislative branch? One approach is to determine *legislative intent* with respect to each specific case; another entails using the *plain meaning* of the statutory words, no matter how absurd the outcome.

Legislative Intent

When a statute is unclear with respect to a particular question, lawyers and courts generally commence their search for statutory meaning by asking the question: Did the legislature intend this particular statutory provision to cover this particular fact pattern? (Lane 1999). "The resort to legislative intent may be helpful in some cases, but reconstruction of the historical process of framing and expressing intent in a forum as complex as a representative legislature is a very risky enterprise. In a surprising number of cases, the legislative history will show that the legislature did not foresee the problem facing the judge and consequently had no intent concerning it" (Merryman 1985: 44).

Adrian Vermeule (2000) presents the choices with respect to using legislative history:[1]

- Judges should not consider legislative history.
- Judges may consider legislative history as a "persuasive," but not "authoritative," source.
- Judges should consider legislative history only if the statute is so ambiguous as to lack a plain meaning.
- Judges may always consult legislative history according to a hierarchy of relevance: committee reports, sponsors' statements, floor debate.

Determining legislative intent may entail a review of the committee reports, debates, or earlier drafts of the final bill. On the federal level, deciding on legislative intent may be quite difficult because the *Congressional Record* often contains remarks never made on the floor of either house, while omitting remarks that are made but which the speaker wants deleted (Spaeth 1979). Furthermore, when attempting to determine the legislative intent of an act of Congress, there are several difficult questions, including how much weight, if any, should be given to different participants: "Are the thoughts of some—for example, those who spoke, or spoke most often, in the debates—more important than the thoughts of others? What about the executive officials and assistants who prepared the initial drafts? What about the president who signed the bill and made it law? Should his intentions not count more than any single senator's?" (Dworkin 1986: 318).

Historically, reference by the courts to legislative intent has been the subject of intense critical analysis. Such criticism argues that judges frequently use legislative intent to trump statutory language the judges disfavor. In other words, if they do not like the outcome effected by the statutory language, they declare that a favored outcome was required by legislative intent (Lane 1999).

Twentieth century theories of statutory interpretation in the United States have emphasized the *original* meaning of statutes (Eskridge 1994). However, a legislator originally voting for a statute might have a different interpretation than contemporary lawmakers. "Over time, the gaps and ambiguities proliferate as society changes, adapts to the statute, and generates new variations on the problem initially targeted by the statute. The original meaning of the statute or the original intent of the legislature has less relevance for figuring out how the statute should apply to unforeseen circumstances" (Eskridge 1994: 9–10). In fact, the "Supreme Court often interprets statutes in ways that reflect statutory purpose or current values instead of original legislative intent" (1994: 15).

---

[1]Nearly two dozen states permit citizen ballot initiatives, whereby statutes are enacted without legislative approval. The courts are often required to clean up these laws without resort to legislative intent. The plain meaning of these laws may be confusing, since they have not been subjected to the normal legislative honing process.

Plain Meaning

In addition to the difficulties inherent in determining legislative intent, some oppose the practice on ideological grounds. They argue for the supremacy of plain meaning, noting that "ours is a government of laws, not persons, so law should be based on the objective import of statutory language rather than the unenacted intent of legislators." Once enacted, they argue, "a statute becomes the domain of the executive officers and judges charged with its enforcement and application, rather than remaining somehow tethered to the unenacted intentions of legislators" (Farber and Frickey 1991: 90). But the plain meaning may be unclear—as a result of careless drafting, statutes sometimes contain grammatical errors and words are omitted. The courts are "reluctant to follow statutory language when the result would be absurd or contrary to the statute's obvious purpose" (1991: 91). For example, the state of Illinois enacted a law to benefit a firm that was licensed to manufacture machine guns. The intent was clearly to make it easier to move the weapons for shipping. Instead, because of careless drafting, the final statute legalized the possession of such weapons by state residents—how should the courts rule?

In Illinois, for the first time in more than 25 years, the legislature and the governor's office were in Republican hands, and they sought to repeal a law that business interests called an expensive relic. That law permitted injured construction workers to sue for job-related injuries in addition to collecting workmen's compensation. In 1996, the legislature passed and the governor signed a bill halting the practice. The bill's *preamble* clearly stated that it was the intent of the legislature that all pending suits continue until resolved—only new suits were barred. Case law in Illinois holds that if a statute is repealed without a clause exempting pending lawsuits, then the repeal applies to all lawsuits that have not reached final judgment, and a preamble is to be considered *only* when the law is ambiguous. Four thousand cases involving millions of dollars hinged on the judicial interpretation of this law. In 1997, the Illinois Supreme Court, using the concept of legislative intent, "saved the lawmakers from further embarrassment" by exempting pending lawsuits (Armstrong and Fegelman 1996; Armstrong 1997: Sec. 2: 6).

The court has an advantage over the legislature, access to information generated by parties to a dispute: "The legislature passes a rule, thinking it knows what the effects will be, but cannot have a precise understanding of them in advance of the actual application of the rule. The judge has the advantage of seeing the rule in

"PLAIN MEANING"

In 1994 the Supreme Court was faced with ruling on a statute so carelessly written that its plain meaning rendered it unconstitutional. A misplaced word—"knowingly"—in the Protection of Children Against Sexual Exploitation Act left the Court with a dilemma: Interpret the law in the way Congress intended—in effect, rewrite the statute—or respond to it as written, the plain meaning? By a vote of 7–2 the Court voted to "rewrite" the law (*United States* v. *X-Citement Video*).

operation, and he can deal with problems of application that the legislature did not foresee" (Posner 1985: 5). "Case law rules can be more readily modified at the point of application (if judges so wish) so as to minimize the gap between rules themselves and substantive rationales and purposes" (Atiyah and Summers 1987: 97). While statutes are devoid of facts, judges make their determinations in light of the facts before them (and, it is hoped, without the untoward influence of lobbying and politics).

Obsolete, outdated, or anachronistic statutes that legislative bodies have simply failed to amend or repeal—legislative inertia—are another problem. In such cases it may be left to the courts to interpret them into harmlessness or strike them down on constitutional grounds (Atiyah and Summers 1987; see Calabresi 1982 for a discussion of this issue).[2] Or, as time passes and a statute must be applied in changed circumstances, judges may be confronted with having to enforce the original statute with the meaning it has always had or covertly amending the statute to make it current. In complex societies, "many issues will arise in cases that do not attract the substantial public or political attention needed to move a legislature to act. The avenues to legal change by the more democratic branches of government may be too broad to notice, in a timely way, small matters of significance in their cumulative effect. Incremental change by judicial decision keeps the law up to date on a case-by-case basis in a way that augments the more democratic avenues of legal change" (Burton 1985: 231). Thus, while there is a clear separation of powers in theory, in practice there is an overlap and dynamic tension between the legislative and judicial branches, with the courts often involved in policy-making.

THE POLICY-MAKING ROLE OF THE JUDICIAL BRANCH

Policy can be conceived of as deciding among alternative choices of action, particularly in the allocation of resources, "where the chosen action affects the behavior and well-being of others who are subject to the policymaker's authority" (Spaeth 1979: 19). As noted in Chapter 2, courts in civil law systems are distinguished from those in the United States by their lack of involvement in government policy. In the United States, it is the responsibility of the judicial branch to interpret the law and

JUDICIAL "LEGISLATING"

When a legislature enacts a statute, "it necessarily does so without full knowledge of the circumstances in which the rule might be invoked in the future. When the unforeseen circumstance arises—it might be the advent of the motor vehicle or of electronic surveillance, or a change in attitudes toward religion, race, or sexual propriety—a court asked to apply the rule must decide, in light of information not available to the promulgators of the rule, what the rule should mean in its new setting. Realistically, it is being asked to make a new rule; in short to legislate" (Posner 1995: 231).

---

[2]At times, legislative and administrative bodies include "sunset" provisions—expiration dates—in their statutes and rules.

to provide a public forum—courts—for resolving legal disputes. In every case the court must determine the facts and their legal significance. If the court determines their legal significance by applying an existing rule of law unchanged (finding law), it is engaged in pure dispute resolution. "But if to resolve the dispute the court must create a new rule or modify an old one, that is law creation" (Posner 1985: 3) or lawmaking: "lawmaking aspects create precedent that can be applied to other disputes"(Marvell 1978: 216). This constitutes the policy-making function of the judicial branch.

The policy decisions of the judicial branch of government affect virtually all areas of life in the United States. Our complex system of government, with over-lapping branches and territories, "ensures that disputes will arise among the branches and between the states and the central government" (Lieberman 1989: 20). The American "proclivity to think of social problems in legal terms and to judicialize everything from wage claims to community conflicts and the allocation of airline routes makes it only natural to accord judges a major share in the making of social policy" (D. Horowitz 1977: 12). "In spelling out limitations on the power of government, the Constitution preordained that issues which in other countries would be labeled political would in America be resolved in court" (Lieberman 1989: 20).

In the decades following the Second World War, the courts have been called upon to deal with a variety of issues that heretofore were the province (attended or unattended) of the legislative and executive branches (D. Horowitz 1977). Susan Lawrence (1990) points out that while courts in general, and the Supreme Court in particular, will not consider questions of policy, skillful attorneys can transform almost any policy issue into at least an arguably relevant judicial issue. (In order to do this, however, one obviously needs access to skillful attorneys.) Thus, "we have a two-track system where issues stuck in Congress can now jump off that track into the courts." But the attorneys who promote this legal activism are not answerable to the public (Meier 2000: WK 3).

The Supreme Court has revolutionized race relations, altered forever the manner in which legislative districts are drawn, overhauled the procedures of the juvenile court, dramatically increased the rights of accused criminals, prohibited prayer in public schools, overturned laws prohibiting abortion and the destruction of the American flag, and provided due process rights to welfare recipients. State and federal courts have overturned minimum-residency requirement laws for welfare recipients and expanded welfare eligibility, causing states to increase their welfare budgets. They have established elaborate standards for all aspects of prison life and have ordered some prisons closed, and they have done the same for mental institutions. The courts have ordered the equalization of school expenditures and established procedures for the handling of school discipline. Using the powers of equity, they have enjoined the construction of roads and bridges as damaging to the environment and have ordered the Forest Service to stop the clearing of timber. They have ordered the U.S. Army Corps of Engineers to maintain America's nonnavigable waterways and have eliminated the requirement of a high school diploma for a firefighter's job. Judges have taken over the operation of the entire state prison system in Alabama to end unconstitutional conditions (*Pugh* v. *Locke* 1976) and public schools in Boston (*Morgan* v. *Hennigan* 1974) to achieve desegregation. They have ordered sharp increases in property taxes in order to pay for school desegregation in the Kansas City school district (upheld by the Supreme Court in *Missouri* v. *Jenkins* 1990). The only policy area in which the judicial branch has not involved itself, at least since the Civil War, is foreign policy (Spaeth 1979). (For a discussion of judicial involvement in foreign affairs, see Franck 1992.)

Cases in which courts make policy determinations usually involve government, the Fourteenth Amendment, and the use of equity (discussed in Chapter 2), although "we have seen an increase in recent decades of policy oriented suits in private law cases" (Cooper 1988: 13). For example, "product liability suits and personal injury litigation have been used not merely to recompense persons hurt by industrial practices, but also in an attempt to change the business policy of these private firms." Even when the plaintiff's goal is compensatory, a significant damage award can shock private firms or government agencies into developing new policies (Smith 1997). Since units of government and their officials generally enjoy immunity from damage claims (states are immune from damage suits under the Eleventh Amendment), and monetary awards in some cases may not be relevant (e.g., protecting mental patients or prison inmates) equity is the remedy most often used against governmental violations of law. Relief through equity can be negative and/or affirmative: "The plea for negative relief is generally a request that the judge declare past actions illegal and enjoin the government from any further practices. . . . The affirmative relief requested is for a decree with provisions which attempt, by directing changes in structure or practice, to undo the damage done to the plaintiffs and others similarly situated" (Cooper 1988: 14). In public law policy cases, both negative and affirmative relief are often requested.

In some cases, the legislative branch fails to act, leaving important areas of law in a void for varying periods of time: "During the interim, the courts may have no realistic choice but to make law in the political vacuum or allow disorder or injustice to prevail," e.g., the area of copyrights. In 1909, Congress enacted a copyright act that was not revised until 1978. For almost 70 years the courts had to deal with an outdated copyright law as it applied to changing audio and visual technology (Burton 1985: 232). The Internet has added a complicated mix to the issue of intellectual property rights.

However, judges cannot impose their views until someone brings a case to court, often as a last resort after complaints to unresponsive legislators and executives (Wasby 1993). Plaintiffs must be truly aggrieved, or have *standing* (discussed in Chapter 12). The judicial response is focused sharply on the questions presented and "not related matters that a legislator might take up" (Lieberman 1989: 29): specific acts of discrimination perpetrated by particular actors, e.g., as opposed to remote but related issues, such as the causes of sexism or racism. The independence of the judicial branch, particularly at the federal level where judges are appointed for life, permits the courts to act as champions of those who do not command financial resources, large amounts of votes, or a positive public profile, to those who would otherwise receive no (or negative) attention from other branches of government. (Of course, a lifetime appointment can also lead to arrogance and petty tyranny.) The ability of appellate courts in general and the Supreme Court in particular to choose the cases it will decide strengthens the judicial branch's ability to enter policy areas.

ADMINISTRATIVE AGENCIES AND JUDICIAL POLICY-MAKING

A great deal of the judicial branch's policy-oriented decisions have been based not on the Constitution but on federal statutes concerning the rights of the disadvantaged, consumers, and the environment: "such litigation results from the need to have judges interpret and enforce vague and ambiguous statutory provisions and the regulations developed to implement the statutes" (Wasby 1993: 5).[3] Congress has been accused of creating administrative agencies with vague mandates in areas of controversial public policy (e.g., environmental protection) so as to avoid taking the political heat that more specific legislation can generate (Lieberman 1981).

Prior to the 1960s, the courts were reluctant to consider suits that called for more vigorous or extensive enforcement by regulatory agencies. The courts typically deferred to administrative discretion except when litigants were entitled to an application of the law in their own personal cases. Since administrative agencies, by definition, are composed of experts, judges typically deferred to their expertise. Beginning in the 1950s, however, there was concern that any number of these agencies had been "captured" by the very industries they were supposed to regulate (Shapiro 1988). Furthermore, when the appointees of more conservative executives, particularly President Richard Nixon and California's governor (and later President) Ronald Reagan, began to wield this discretionary power, liberal policy activists and public interest law firms (discussed in Chapter 5) initiated litigation to force agencies to comply with regulatory duties as seen by the plaintiffs. The courts granted standing to interest groups whose claims were general, rather than the individual and personal interest typically required of plaintiffs (Rabkin 1989). These efforts were furthered by Congress, which enacted legislation allowing citizen lawsuits when certain federal regulatory agencies, such as the Environmental Protection Agency (EPA), fail to perform a specific act or duty as required by statute. Thus, under the Clean Air Act, the Sierra Club was allowed to sue the EPA.

Entry of the judicial branch into the arena of administrative policy, in response to public interest group litigation, is not without controversy, as the title of a book by Jeremy Rabkin implies: *Judicial Compulsions: How Public Law Distorts Public Policy* (1989). Rabkin decries the courts' assumption of an oversight role for which they are not prepared: "Courts are entirely unequipped to act as ongoing, freestanding guardians of administrative performance. Our entire judicial system has developed on the assumption that courts will simply be deciding cases about property rights or personal rights, in the traditional sense" (1989: 20). Why should the judiciary recognize the policy preferences of plaintiffs purporting to represent the interests of the general public? Why should "factional interests be allowed to make preemptive claims on public policy?" (1989: 73) Furthermore, in the criminal sphere, private parties cannot compel the initiation of a prosecution; yet the courts have allowed parallel action when it involves regulatory agencies. Advocates of

---

[3]Administrative law is discussed in Chapter 2.

public interest law state that judicial intervention was necessary to keep appointees of the Reagan administration from subverting the historical mission of their agencies: "Much of public interest litigation," they argue, "aims simply to enforce existing laws" (Aron 1989: 100).

The policy-making role of the judicial branch is intertwined with the issue of judicial restraint versus judicial activism.

INTERPRETING THE CONSTITUTION: JUDICIAL RESTRAINT VERSUS JUDICIAL ACTIVISM

In order for a statute to be applied, it requires interpretation. Application also requires that the constitutional significance, if any, be determined. Interpretations of the Constitution by judges can effectively deprive the people of the right to resolve disputed issues in accordance with the normal procedures of democratic self-government, that is, in the political, as opposed to the judicial arena (George 2000). "Little did the Framers dream that the judicial power would be construed as a license to supersede the exercise of power by the other branches." Thus, according to Raoul Berger, the Supreme Court "has invaded the exclusive jurisdiction of a sister branch; it has violated the injunction of the separation of powers." It has done this in the name of a self-created doctrine—*substantive due process*, under which courts examine the reasonableness of government policy[4]—based on a concept as vague and self-serving as natural law (1977: 249–250). Judges "were not authorized to revise the Constitution in the interests of 'justice' " (1977: 299), to usurp the

DUCKS

"SITTING JUDGES"

Writing in a journal of the conservative Heritage Foundation, Dennis Shea (1997: 62) states: "In case after case, federal judges are expressing contempt for democracy, overturning laws passed by state legislatures or adopted directly by the people through the initiative process." The House Republican whip expressed his view—"They have thrown out the Constitution to advance their own political views"—when he announced an effort to impeach several federal judges (Seelye 1997: 13). The Constitution (Article II: 4) , however, provides for impeachment only in the case of "high Crimes and Misdemeanors." Shea (1997) suggests that Congress consider breathing new life into its own impeachment authority. Judges, of course, are constrained from engaging in public debate over their decisions; they cannot explain them at press conferences, nor do they have call-in radio and television programs at which to defend their rulings.

---

[4]The conventional interpretation of the due process clause is that government must follow certain procedures before taking a person's life, liberty, or property.

JUDICIAL RESTRAINT

View that appellate decisions should be based on precedent, rather than on the basis of achieving some public benefit, since that is a role delegated to the legislative branch.

JUDICIAL ACTIVISM

Appellate court disregard of precedent in an effort to achieve some public benefit, thereby usurping the legislative function.

policy-making authority of the legislative branch. Instead, *strict constructionists* argue, justices "must take the Constitution as they find it, and not make things up as they go along. Even if the Justices are appalled by the results this method produces, or believe that the Constitution's literal commands are severely out of step with the times, it is not their job to rewrite it. That prerogative belongs to the Congress and the President—and ultimately to the people, who retain the power to *amend* the Constitution" (Tribe 1985: 42; emphasis in original).

In contemporary times, it is common to portray those who argue for judicial restraint as "conservatives," and those who support judicial activism as "liberals." However, as we have seen in Chapter 3, American history does not support this view: During the later decades of the nineteenth century, for example, *judicial activism* protected property rights while *judicial restraint* ignored the civil rights of African-Americans.

While in the last few decades the charge of usurpation by the judicial branch has usually been leveled by conservatives, in the decades before the Great Depression, activist courts effectively restrained organized labor and legislative efforts designed to aid workers. And, during the administration of Franklin Roosevelt, when it was the liberals whose programs were found unconstitutional, conservatives defended the Supreme Court's activism (George 2000). In a March 9, 1937 "Fireside Chat," President Roosevelt argued in favor of "a Supreme Court that will enforce the Constitution as written—that will refuse to amend the Constitution by the arbitrary exercise of judicial power—amendment by judicial say-so." Roosevelt argued that the Court had usurped the legislative function by "reading into the Constitution words and implications which are not there, and which were never intended to be there." The president promised to appoint justices "who will act as justices and not as legislators." During his campaign for the presidency, Texas Governor George W. Bush made a similar assertion: "I don't believe in liberal activist judges; I believe in strict constructionists, and those are the kind I will appoint." To which his opponent, Vice-President Al Gore responded: "In my view the Constitution ought to be interpreted as a document that grows with the—with our country and our history" (quotes from the presidential debate of October 3, 2000).

Many of the Constitution's limitations on government are couched in obscure language so that the judicial branch, sooner or later, must deal with potentially explosive cases on important social issues, such as those involving schools or prisons (Lieberman 1989). The judiciary, particularly at the federal level, is insulated from the political pressures that typically affect legislators; thus, the courts are often in a better position to attend to the problems of persons who do not represent an important political constituency, a source of votes, or campaign funds. Of course, judges rendering policy decisions can also be viewed as undemocratic legislators, a position expressed by Gary McDowell.

McDowell (1982) decries the expansive use of equity (discussed in Chapter 2), with its inherent discretionary prerogatives, arguing that judicial activism under the guise of equity has been ignoring its history and distorting its purpose; equitable remedial powers have been used to impose a particular brand of liberal policy on society. The courts have done this, he argues, by denying or ignoring the great tradition of equitable principles and precedents, which have always been viewed as the inherent source of restraint in rendering equitable dispensations. "When the framers of the Constitution assigned the authority to decide legal 'cases in law and equity,'" states Jeremy Rabkin, "they understood themselves to be entrusting a rather more modest power to the courts because they took for granted much more modest notions about the proper ends of law" (1989: 118). Indeed, according to Christopher Wolfe, "equity is not the correction of mistakes made by the lawgiver in enacting the law in question, but rather corrections of the law that the legislator would have wanted had he been able to foresee the defects that would necessarily result from its generality. The purpose of equity is not to frustrate the will of the legislator but to effect it" (1986: 19).

Should a judge's personal preferences influence his or her decision? Should a judge uphold a legislative enactment that he or she finds personally objectionable, such as requiring students to salute the flag or face expulsion? This question was central to the historic confrontation between two giants of the Supreme Court: Hugo Black and Felix Frankfurter. Frankfurter answered in the negative (see Simon 1989). Should a judge—using the power of equity—vote according to conscience or support an offensive outcome that is, nevertheless, constitutional? Robert Bork refers to this dilemma: "In law, the moment of temptation is the moment of choice, when a judge realizes that in the case before him his strongly held view of justice, his political and moral imperative, is not embodied in a statute or in any provision of the Constitution. He must then choose between his version of justice and abiding by the American form of government" (1989: 1). For a judge to give in to "temptation," Bork argues, is to usurp the legislative prerogative (1989: 1), a position that is an anathema to judicial positivists such as Bork, persons who believe that a judge should not stray beyond the written word of a statute or precedent.

The view expressed by Judge Bork can be found in the work of Blackstone, who cautioned: "The liberty of considering all cases in an equitable light must not be indulged too far, lest we destroy all law, and leave the decision of every question entirely in the breast of the judge [*kadi law*]. And law, without equity, though hard and disagreeable, is much more desirable for the public good than equity without law; which would make every judge a legislator, and introduce most infinite confusion; as there would then be almost as many different rules of action laid down in our courts, as there are differences of capacity and sentiment in the human mind" (quoted in Wolfe 1986: 19).

In practice, a judge "can have his cake and eat it too," because words often lack clarity and can be given more than one interpretation, and nearly all of the Constitution's most important phrases—such as "unreasonable searches" and "due process of law"—"are deliberate models of ambiguity" (Tribe 1985: 42; see also Tribe and Dorf 1991). Thus, "the text does not always provide a definitive answer to a question(s) before the judge. The due process, equal protection, free speech, and antiestablishment clauses are scarcely self-defining in the same way that the clause giving each state two senators is" (Bond 1987: 10). The ambiguity in the Constitution provides opportunity "for judicial officers from both ends of the ideological spectrum to assert their authority and shape public policy" (C. Smith 1993b: 6). Take, for example, the emotionally-laden debate over the meaning of the Second Amendment (1791): "A well regulated Militia, being necessary to the security of a free state, the right of the people to keep and bear arms shall not be infringed." Does "the right of the people to keep and bear arms" provide authority for individuals to possess firearms, or does this right apply only to a "well regulated Militia"? While most modern court decisions have held that the Second Amendment refers to a state militia—the National Guard, this interpretation has been vigorously contested in and out of legal circles (Glaberson 2000e).

When there is ambiguity in applying a constitutional provision to specific cases, strict constructionists argue that judges should utilize the concept of original intent (Polin 1986). Only through a search for original intent can the courts be faithful to the central tenet of our democratic system, the rule of law (Berger 1987). Ronald Dworkin describes two basic schools of thought on this issue:

> One side argues that in spite of the difficulties every effort must be made, with the resources of history and analysis, to discover what the collective intention of the constitutional Framers was on disputed matters of interpretation. They believe that dogged historical study will reveal important and relevant original intentions. . . .The other side argues that any effort to discover the original collective intention of the Framers will turn out to be fruitless, or even perverse. It will end in the discovery that there are no, or very few, relevant collective intentions, or perhaps only collective intentions that are indeterminate rather than decisive one way or another, or perhaps intentions so contrary to our present sense of justice that they must in the end be rejected as a guide to the present Constitution. (1985: 38–39)[5]

Toward Kadi Justice?

"As more judges began to taste and enjoy the once-forbidden fruits of emancipation from the constraints of statute, precedent, Constitution, or tradition, the classical ideal associated with modesty, impartiality, restraint, and interpretive skill has been rivaled by an image of the good judge as bold, creative, compassionate, result-oriented, and liberated from legal technicalities." (Glendon 1994: 152)

---

[5]For a history of the issues surrounding ratification of the Constitution and the issue of *originalism*, see Rakove (1996).

Former Attorney General Edwin Meese stated that it was Ronald Reagan's intention during his presidency to appoint to the federal courts persons who had a traditional approach to the judiciary, who were not judicial activists; that is, persons whose deliberations and decisions would be in accord with what was intended by the framers of the Constitution: "Where the language of the Constitution is specific, it must be obeyed. Where there is a demonstrable consensus among the framers and ratifiers as to a principle stated or implied by the Constitution, it should be followed. Where there is ambiguity as to the precise meaning or reach of a constitutional provision, it should be interpreted and applied in a manner so as to at least not contradict the test of the Constitution itself" (1986: 38).

Federal appellate judge Irving R. Kaufman (1986) states there is a paucity of material on which to make a determination of original intent. The minutes of the Constitutional Convention and James Madison's notes of the proceedings (edited by Madison 20 years after the convention and first published in 1840; Farrand 1967) are very cursory, particularly with respect to the role of the judicial branch. And Madison himself rejected the doctrine of original intent: "As a guide in expounding and applying the provisions of the Constitution, the debates and incidental decisions of the Convention have no authoritative character" (quoted in Levy 1988: 1). "If the Framers, who met in executive sessions every day of their nearly four months of work, had wanted their country and posterity to construe the Constitution in the light of their deliberations," states Leonard Levy, "they would have had a stenographer present to keep an official record, and they would have published it" (1988: 2). In fact, he argues, the "Founders of the national government and its early officers simply did not think in terms of the original intent at Philadelphia" (1988: 6–7). Several years after it was ratified, those most associated with the document—Hamilton, Madison, Jefferson—were already clashing over the meaning of the Constitution on the issue of a national bank (Wolfe 1986).

The first major dispute over an interpretation of the Constitution occurred shortly after its ratification, when Alexander Hamilton proposed a national bank that was opposed by Thomas Jefferson. At issue was Article I, Section 8, which authorizes Congress "to make all laws which shall be necessary and proper for carrying into execution the foregoing Powers." Hamilton argued that Article I implied powers necessary for the proper implementation of the constitutional mandate, while Jefferson cited the Tenth Amendment, which reserves powers not delegated to the federal government to the states. The bank was established and, as noted in Chapter 3, Hamilton's position was eventually upheld by the Supreme Court (*McCulloch* v. *Maryland* 1819). Another dispute arose over the purchase of the Louisiana Territory, and this time positions were reversed. The Federalists adopted

*O*RIGINAL *S*OURCES

"Not only do Madison's notes and other sources allow us to track the daily progress of the deliberations at Philadelphia, but the records of the ensuing ratification debate reveal the range of meanings that the American political nation first attached to the proposed Constitution" (Rakove 1996: 7).

*O*RIGINAL *I*NTENT

"It is hard enough to ascertain the intention of a living person. It is harder still to determine the intention of a group of living individuals like a legislature or a Congress. The difficulty is compounded when the group of individuals is two centuries removed in time and the evidence of their thoughts and purposes is scattered, fragmentary, ambiguous, and conflicting. And the task is made almost impossible when the relevant intention pertains to questions which in all probability never occurred to the group of individuals and which are meaningful only in light of circumstances that would to them be inconceivable" (Post 1995: 33–34).

the strict constructionist argument that the Constitution did not authorize the president to purchase territory. President Jefferson argued that this power is implied by Article II, Section 2, which provides that the president "shall have Power, by and with the Advice and Consent of the Senate, to make Treaties."

The Founders were not saints writing a sacred text; they were, in the final analysis, politicians (Shaman 1992). Of the 55 delegates to the convention, only 39 signed the Constitution, and any number of them may have been casual in their attendance. We also know that the final document is the result of many compromises. "Moreover, many delegates (and still more state legislators, and even voters) clearly intended nothing at all about particular provisions but rather simply preferred the whole constitutional package to what they must have viewed as the likely alternative" (Kelman 1987: 216). The Constitution was drafted and ratified by persons who were certainly not representative of the people as a whole, given that a majority of Americans were ineligible to vote: blacks, women, Native Americans, and the poor. "Nor was democracy sufficiently advanced, even by the time of the post-Civil War amendments, to provide a democratic argument of fairness for taking the legislators' concrete opinions as good evidence of public opinion at the time" (Dworkin 1986: 364). The homogeneity of the Founders certainly does not reflect the diversity of contemporary America. With every passing year, the Constitution becomes more remote (Posner 1990).

In addition, since the Constitution required ratification by the state legislatures, does their intent also need to be considered? In fact, argues Judge Kaufman, many provisions in the Constitution were left deliberately vague; when the framers had a clear intent, they were explicit: "Article II, for example, specifies a minimum Presidential age of 35 years instead of merely requiring 'maturity' or 'adequate age'" (1986: 59). Meese (1986) responds that the period of the creation of the Constitution was alive with pamphlets, newspapers, and books on the great issues of the day. Furthermore, the disputes and compromises of the Constitutional Convention were carefully recorded, and the minutes of the Convention are a matter of public record. Edward Levi, also a former Republican U.S. attorney general, states that when it comes to a constitution, a change of mind from time to time is inevitable: "There can be no authoritative interpretation of the Constitution. The Constitution in its general provisions embodies the conflicting ideals of the community" (1955: 41). And what about equity: Should people be governed "by the detailed political convictions of officials elected long ago, when popular morality, economic circumstances, and almost everything else was very different?"(Dworkin 1986: 364). Punishment prohibited by the Eighth Amendment, for example, has obviously changed with modern definitions of what is "cruel and unusual."

At the investiture of William H. Rehnquist as chief justice and Antonin Scalia as associate justice (September 26, 1986), President Reagan stated that he had appointed these men to the Supreme Court because their opinions had demonstrated that they adhered to the concept of "judicial restraint." But, in fact, "judicial activism has characterized the Supreme Court from its early history" (Levy 1988: 56). There was a period of negative activism from 1898 to 1938, when "it seemed as though no progressive social or economic legislation was constitutionally permissible." During this period, the Court invalidated some 50 acts of Congress and about 400 state laws, as compared to 12 and 125, respectively, from the period 1874 to 1898 (McDowell 1988: 3). Since 1954, states McDowell, judicial activism has been far more positive in its assertions, as the federal judiciary, with the Supreme Court leading the way, has taken upon itself to achieve what the Court majority holds to be fair, decent, and humane, regardless of constitutional text, original intent, or judicial precedent, *acting more like legislators than judges*. For example, in *Griswold* v. *Connecticut* (1965), rather than leave its resolution to the legislature and the political arena, the Court majority overturned an objectionable statute (prohibiting physicians from providing birth control information to married persons) by invoking the "right to privacy," an allusion to natural law that is not mentioned in the Constitution. But the intentions of the framers of the Constitution "were indissolubly connected with the philosophy of natural rights and natural law expressed in the Declaration of Independence." Accordingly, any attempt to find original intent only in the Constitution is misguided (Jaffa 1988: 40).

While the legislative branch "can make a thousand detailed tradeoffs and produce a complex code that articulates no general principle but reflects moral intuitions, political pressures, and compromises," it is not the function of the judicial branch to decide what is good for us (Bork 1989: 81). Berger (1987) concludes that many of the Supreme Court's recent decisions represent an ongoing revision of the Constitution and, thus, a usurpation of the amendatory function that is reserved to the people by Article V. As we saw in Chapter 3, in 1937, President Franklin Roosevelt argued that the Court had usurped the legislative function by "reading into the Constitution words and implications which are not there" and he promised to appoint justices who would act as judges and not legislators. Conservative appointees selected by Presidents Reagan and Bush, however, have proven to be just as "active" as their liberal counterparts in distinguishing away, overturning precedent, and reaching for new legal doctrines. As the title of an article by Stuart Taylor, Jr., indicates: "The 'Judicial Activists' Are Always on the Other Side" (1988: E5).

The "Courts headed by Chief Justice Warren Burger and now by Chief Justice William Rehnquist, while perhaps less relentlessly adventurous than the Warren Court, displayed a strong affinity for legislating policy in the name of the Constitution" (Bork 1989: 101). For example, in a 5–4 decision (*Wards Cove Packing* Co. v. *Atonio* 1989) the Court ruled against its own precedents in cases brought under the Civil Rights Act of 1964. In 1971, the statute had been interpreted as placing the burden of proof on employers to prove that they had not deliberately engaged in unlawful discrimination whenever statistical evidence revealed a discriminatory

*T*EXTUALISM

Antonin Scalia (1996), who apparently relishes the role of legal scholar/iconoclast, supports a "plain meaning" approach to interpreting the Constitution and statutes; he is critical of those who revert to "intentions," either of the Constitution's Framers or legislators, as the basis for interpretation.

I belong to a school, a small but hardy school, called "textualists" or "originalists." That used to be "constitutional orthodoxy" in the United States. The theory of originalism treats a constitution like a statute, and gives it the meaning that its words were understood to bear at the time they were promulgated. You will sometimes hear it described as the theory of original intent. You will never hear me refer to original intent, because as I say I am first of all a textualist, and secondly an originalist. If you are a textualist, you don't care about the intent, and I don't care if the framers of the Constitution had some secret meaning in mind when they adopted its words. I take the words as they were promulgated to the people of the United States, and what is the fairly understood meaning of those words.[6]

According to Thomas Jefferson, however, "the true key for the construction of everything doubtful in a law is the intention of the law-makers. This is most safely gathered from the words, but may be sought also in extraneous circumstances provided they do not contradict the express words of the law."—Letter from Thomas Jefferson to Albert Gallatin, 1808. (University of Virginia Online Resources).

impact on women or minorities (*Griggs* v. *Duke Power*). In *Wards Cove*, the Court reinterpreted the statute and reversed the burden of proof. The Court majority in *Rust* v. *Sullivan* (1991) was taken to task by Associate Justice Sandra Day O'Connor, a Reagan appointee, for judicial activism: "It is a fundamental rule of judicial restraint," she noted, "that this Court will not reach constitutional questions in advance of the necessity of deciding them." The 5–4 decision upheld administrative restrictions on abortion counseling for agencies receiving federal funding. Justice O'Connor argued that this decision needlessly addressed constitutional issues when an interpretation of legislation would have been sufficient.

In its 1991 term, the Court overturned five of its own precedents, leading the editorial board of the *New York Times* (June 30, 1991) to decry the easy manner in which the new "conservative" majority was "recklessly reversing precedents." Their editorial argued, "that is not the role assigned to the Supreme Court." During the term of Chief Justice Earl Warren (1953–1969), the liberal Court overruled precedent in 63 cases. During Warren E. Burger's tenure (1969–1986), precedent was overruled 61 times (Greenhouse 1991b). The Court headed by William Rehnquist has not hesitated to overturn precedent in support of the government's position. For example, in a 1997 decision (*Agostini* v. *Felton*), the Court overturned a 1985 ruling that prohibited public employees from providing services in religious schools. And in

---

[6]For an analysis of the views of Justice Scalia, see Gutman (1998).

$\mathcal{S}$OFT AND $\mathcal{H}$ARD $\mathcal{O}$RIGINALISM

For the hard originalist, the meaning of the Constitution is settled by asking how those who ratified the relevant provision would have answered very specific questions. Does the free speech principle include commercial advertising, a particular kind of libelous statement, or sexually explicit movies? . . . For soft originalists, things are different. For them, the historical inquiry is necessary not to obtain specific answers to specific questions, but instead to get a more general sense of goals and purposes; it is these more general goals and purposes that matter in constitutional interpretations. For the hard originalist, the goal of originalism is to discover rules; for the soft originalist, the goal is to discover constraining but nonetheless flexible standards. (Sunstein 1996: 173)

what probably will be the Court's most controversial decision, a five-member majority determined the outcome of the 2000 election for President using the favored tool of judicial activists—the Fourteenth Amendment. The title of an article by Linda Greenhouse (1991c) noted: "Conservatively Speaking, It's An Activist Supreme Court." Long-time Court observer, journalist Stuart Taylor, Jr. (2000: 50) pointed out that all nine justices, despite their liberal or conservative labels, are "activists who boldly use federal judicial power to displace decisions by elected officials and state courts that offend their personal, philosophical or political values."

In the next chapter, we will examine how the key actors in the legal system are selected for their roles.

INTERNET CONNECTIONS

Emory Electronic Reference Desk: *law.emory.edu/LAW/refdesk/toc.html*
Legal journals on the Web: *usc.edu/dept/law-lib/legal/journals.html*
Legal Information Institute (Cornell University): *Law.cornell.edu*
Meta-index for legal research: *gsulaw.gsu.edu/metaindex*

REVIEW QUESTIONS

1. Why does the judicial branch in the United States often get involved in policy or political issues?
2. Why is judicial involvement in policy issues controversial?
3. What led to the entry of the courts into administrative agency operations?
4. What is the controversy surrounding this entry?
5. What is meant by strict constructionism and original intent?
6. How does textualism (associated with Justice Antonin Scalia) differ from originalism?

7. What are the arguments for and against "original intent" to interpret the Constitution?

8. What are the problems encountered when determining legislative intent?

9. In what way did President Franklin Roosevelt in the the 1930s express opinions similar to today's critics of the Supreme Court?

10. How can the Rehnquist Court be characterized as "conservatively activist"?

9

$\mathcal{J}$UDGES, $\mathcal{P}$ROSECUTORS, AND $\mathcal{C}$RIMINAL $\mathcal{D}$EFENSE $\mathcal{A}$TTORNEYS

At the center of the judicial system are the lawyers—judges, prosecutors, and attorneys who represent criminal defendants and plaintiffs and defendants in civil cases. They share a common education—law school—and, given the nature of the practice of law in the United States, are interchangeable: that is, many judges were at one time prosecutors and/or defense attorneys. Private defense attorneys, particularly those in criminal practice, have often served as prosecutors or public defenders. Lawyers who graduate from the elite law schools are seldom found among the ranks of these key actors, particularly those who practice in state courts. One reason is the salaries, which are not competitive with those of a partner in a national law firm. Another is the need for political connections of a type typically shunned by those practicing in large law firms. Furthermore, lawyers working for the government (e.g., judges or prosecutors) are quite limited in the type of additional remunerative work they may perform, with teaching and lecturing offering the least risk of a conflict of interest.

JUDGES

Reflective of our system of courts, there are two basic types of judges: the appellate judge who determines issues of law on appeal and the trial judge who, under our adversarial system of justice, is a referee responsible for enforcing rules that govern criminal and civil cases. When carrying out these responsibilities, the judge has total immunity from any legal action arising out of his or her decisions (*Mireles* v. *Waco* 1991). The judge has no interest in the outcome of a case before him or her, but must ensure that it has been accomplished fairly, according to codes of procedure, applicable statutes, and case law. In a trial court, when a jury is used the judge determines issues of law, and the jury determines issues of fact (the truthfulness and relevance of evidence). When there is no jury, the judge determines both issues of law and of fact. Since judges commonly come to the bench after years of litigation practice, it is vital that they be able to quickly change hats—to make the transition from advocacy to neutrality. In contrast to judges in continental Europe (civil law countries), judges in the United States receive no formal training before they assume their positions (although there is training available at state and national institutes). Their training is primarily "on the job."

Judges in the United States are generalists whose education and experience in non-legal areas are typically quite limited. This led to the establishment of specialized courts—for such matters as patents and taxes—and agency tribunals for particular technocratic concerns, such as the environment and communications. Nevertheless, judges are frequently required to deal with scientific issues for which they have little or no background, such as those of molecular biology and genetics. "To do their jobs well, modern judges must know the difference between DNA and RNA, and be able to evaluate the predictive value of a genetic test" (Blakeslee 1996: B7). And rapid changes in computer technology require judges to make determinations on matters they do not fully comprehend. In response, some jurisdictions are providing science and technology seminars for the purpose of bringing judges up-to-date information on matters they are likely to encounter in the courtroom.

A judge's behavior on the bench is subject to few controls, the most important being the possibility of a reversal by an appellate court—a blow to the professional standing of any trial judge. In states using some form of election, a judge can also suffer at the hands of the electorate. Trial judges actually preside over few trials— most criminal and civil (noncriminal) cases are settled without a trial. The role of the judge when bringing about these settlements varies from jurisdiction to jurisdiction, but mediation and conciliation skills are often as important, if not more so, than trial skills for the average judge (discussed in Chapters 11 and 12). A judge's action in chambers with parties to an action may be more important than what he or she does in the courtroom. A trial judge also has courtroom administrative responsibilities and, in criminal courts, may issue search warrants, impose sentences on defendants, and conduct probation revocation hearings. How are persons with all the talents required of a judge selected for their positions?

SELECTING JUDGES

The qualities generally voiced as necessary for a "good" judge (e.g., being fair minded, having personal integrity and judicial temperament) are so vague and devoid of objective measurement, as to be irrelevant. Even judicial experience may be of questionable value—many outstanding justices of the Supreme Court never held judicial office. Most important is the recognition of the judicial system as a rich source of political patronage. Accordingly, there are important political implications in any method used to select judges, of which there are four, with a number of variations in each: (1) appointment by a chief executive; (2) election; (3) merit system; and (4) selection by the legislature[1] (not discussed in this text). General jurisdiction trial court judges are selected through nonpartisan elections in about 18 states and through partisan elections in about 10 states; in 15 states, they are selected by the governor; and they are appointed by the state legislature in 3 states. Fewer than half the states select their appellate judges by gubernatorial appointment and 3 by legislative appointment. Fourteen use nonpartisan elections and eight partisan elections (Rottman et al. 2000).

Many states use a mixed system, with different judges selected through different systems. In New York, for example, all judges are elected except those serving on the court of appeals (court of last resort), who are appointed by the governor for terms of 14 years, and some serving in courts of limited jurisdiction, such as the New York City Criminal Courts, who are appointed by the mayor. In Illinois, all judges are elected, but the judges of the circuit court (general jurisdiction) appoint associate judges, who enjoy the same authority as (but less salary than) their elected colleagues (and serve for only four years instead of six). The Constitution provides for the presidential nomination of Supreme Court justices, but does not provide a method for selecting other federal judges.

Appointment

Appointment by a chief executive—a mayor, governor, or the president—is used in some states and is the method by which all federal judges are selected. In the federal system, all (constitutional) judges are appointed *by the President for life terms* (for legislative judges, see Chapter 6). Whenever there is a vacancy on a district court bench, the President (actually, officials in the Department of Justice) consults the senior U.S. senator from the state involved if he or she is a member of the President's party. Otherwise there is consultation with the junior senator. If neither senator is of the same party as the President, consultation involves the senior member of the House of Representatives from that state who is a member of the President's party, or the chair of the President's political party in the particular state, or even the governor. The official(s) consulted is asked to submit a list of candidates to the Department of Justice. Each candidate fills out an extensive questionnaire that is used as the basis of a background investigation conducted by the Federal Bureau of Investigation.

At some point, the final list of prospective candidates is reviewed by the Standing Committee on the Federal Judiciary of the American Bar Association (ABA). It was not until after the Second World War that the ABA became a major influence on the selection of federal judges. Almost immediately upon its establishment, the ABA committee was invited by the chairman of the Senate Judiciary Committee to make recommendations on each nomination. The ebb and flow of ABA influence coincided with different administrations, reaching something of a

---

[1]In Virginia, for example, judges are elected by a joint vote of both houses of the General Assembly and are commissioned by the governor for a term of six years (district court), eight years (circuit courts and court of appeals), or twelve years (supreme court). The Governor can make interim appointments when the General Assembly is in recess. There are also magistrates appointed by the chief judge of the circuit court for terms of four years.

crest in 1958. Under President Dwight D. Eisenhower (1952–1960), the U.S. attorney general agreed to refer to the ABA committee for informal evaluation the name of every potential candidate for a federal judgeship, followed by a formal submission of potential nominees for official evaluation and recommendation (Grossman 1965). This procedure has generally been followed by succeeding administrations.

The 15 members of the committee are chosen by the ABA president and serve for three years, which is considered to be quite prestigious within the legal community. For each judicial nomination, members of the committee conduct confidential interviews with dozens of lawyers and judges who are familiar with the candidate.

> The first step is to submit a detailed questionnaire, often running 15 to 20 pages and covering some 30 points of inquiry. One of the questions asks the candidate's judgment and evaluation of the ten "most significant" cases at constitutional law the candidate has litigated. A candidate is interviewed at length by a Committee member, normally one from the candidate's own judicial circuit base. Through interviews with lay and professional individuals—including all pertinent federal judges in the candidate's area, top state judges, local law school deans, lawyers, and certain non-lawyers—the Committee member presumably becomes generally familiar with the candidate's qualifications and character, rendering a useful and reliable appraisal of his ability. (Abraham 1990: 63)

The committee votes on a rating: (1) exceptionally well-qualified, (2) well-qualified, (3) qualified, or (4) not qualified. A rating may also note that a majority of the committee found the candidate minimally qualified, while a minority found him or her unqualified; this rating is "qualified/unqualified." The committee chair receives the information and submits a report to the full committee and the attorney general, who must decide if he/she wishes the ABA to present a full report. The ABA committee considers how long the candidate has been a member of the bar (not fewer than 15 years); the amount of trial experience (particularly for a district court appointment); reputation among the bar; scholarship (particularly for a court of appeals position, for example, publication of law journal articles and quality of any appellate decisions drafted by the candidate); and a rather vague quality known as "judicial temperament." While the nominee's ideology is not part of the evaluation process, as stated in its literature, the committee considers "extreme views" that "might bear on judicial temperament or integrity." The ABA Committee's Supreme Court procedures are somewhat different, including the use of teams of law school professors, practicing lawyers, and former Court clerks who examine the candidate's writings.

The president is under no compulsion to accept an ABA rating, but it can carry a lot of weight with the news media and with U.S. senators who must act upon any judicial nomination. Very few candidates are publicly declared "unqualified" by the ABA, but such a rating can kill an appointment. Richard Nixon, until the last days of his presidency (1968–1974), would not nominate any person rated "not qualified" by the ABA committee. However, during his last full day in office, he nominated Thomas Meskil, governor of Connecticut, to the Court of Appeals, despite an ABA rating of "not qualified," and Meskil was confirmed by the Senate.

The importance of the ABA in the selection process has at various times come under attack from liberals and conservatives. Liberals were critical when the committee supported Nixon Supreme Court nominees who failed to receive Senate ratification. Conservatives reacted when, in 1987, the committee gave Reagan Supreme Court nominee Robert H. Bork, a distinguished, albeit "original intent" conservative, federal judge and former solicitor general, a split decision in favor of his confirmation, which helped to deny him ultimate Senate approval. At the beginning of his term, President George Bush, for the first time since the administration of Dwight D. Eisenhower (1952–1960), refused to send prospective judicial nominees to the ABA for evaluation because of the ABA's handling of the Bork nomination. In testimony before the House Judiciary Committee, Attorney General Dick Thornburgh stated, "The [ABA] committee has extended its inquiry into areas which I believe are more properly left to the administration and the legislative branch. That is, into the ideological or political views of prospective nominees for the Federal bench" (Johnston 1989b: 12).

In response, the ABA agreed to drop from its list of criteria references to political or ideological philosophy "except to the extent they may bear upon the other factors" such as temperament, integrity, or competence, and the administration agreed to resume submitting judicial candidates to the ABA for evaluation (Johnston 1989b). Later that year, in the face of conservative opposition, Robert Fiske, a former U.S. attorney in Manhattan, had to withdraw his candidacy for the number two position in the Department of Justice. Fiske had served as chairman of the ABA Standing Committee on the Federal Judiciary from 1984 to 1987, a time when the committee had criticized some Reagan judicial nominees (Wines 1989). Shortly after he took office in 2001, President George W. Bush ended the ABA role in the judicial selection process (Lewis 2001). Later in the year, when the Democrats took control of the Senate, they began submitting the names of nominees to the ABA and agreed to wait for the group's rating before acting on a candidate.

In 1989, the Supreme Court ruled 8–0 that the ABA committee did not have to comply with the Federal Advisory Committee Act requiring open public meetings and records (*Public Citizen* v. *United States Department of Justice*).

The practice of "senatorial courtesy" requires the President to solicit nominations from the senior senator of the President's party in the state where a district court vacancy exists. According to the unofficial, yet binding, rules of the Senate, which in many ways is a "gentlemen's club," failure to follow this tradition will be viewed as "personally obnoxious" and Senate colleagues will not vote to confirm. A senator from either party can use the "blue slip blackball:" A senator who opposes a nominee from his or her state deliberately fails to return the blue—the color of the—slip of approval to the chairperson of the Senate judiciary committee. This can effectively kill a nomination.[2] Thus, in practice, while the President legally makes the nomination, the appointment process is not dominated by the President. A number of senators utilize advisory commissions to aid their judicial appointment decisions. During the administration of Bill Clinton (1992–2000), the Senate was controlled by Republicans who made it a practice of stalling the confirmation process whenever the President nominated judicial candidates who they considered "too liberal" or "too activist." As a result many federal judicial vacancies went unfilled, some for several years. When George Bush was elected President, the Senate was evenly split between Republicans and Democrats, and Democrats threatened to use the same tactics.

---

[2]Thus, the appointment of Federal District Court Judge J. Skelly Wright of New Orleans to the Fifth Circuit Court of Appeals was vetoed by Louisiana's senators using senatorial courtesy. Judge Wright's firm stand in desegregation cases had made him quite unpopular among southern politicians. He was eventually appointed to the Court of Appeals for the District of Columbia, a circuit outside the power of southern senators.

Each federal appellate circuit (except the District of Columbia and territorial circuits) includes several states. Court-of-appeals judgeships are informally allocated among the states of the particular circuit in rough proportion to the number of court-of-appeals cases that arise in each state. In this case, power over the appointment process is reserved for officials of the state to which the judgeship in question has been allocated (Posner 1985). A presidential nomination is referred to the Judiciary Committee, which conducts its own investigation and holds public hearings on all nominees. The committee then votes on whether to send the nomination to the full Senate for confirmation. In most instances, judges are routinely approved by both the Judiciary Committee and the Senate. For appointments to the Supreme Court, the process is the same, but no senator enjoys senatorial courtesy. For appointments to a state bench, it is the governor who makes the nomination and senatorial courtesy is customary in only six states. In New Jersey, for example, the practice allows senators to block judicial (and other) appointments from their county without giving a reason (Gray 1993).

Because the only formal qualification for federal judicial positions is that a district court appointee must live in the state where the vacancy exists (Supreme Court justices need not even be lawyers), presidential nominees have only infrequently been voted down by the Senate. In 1986, the Republican-controlled Judiciary Committee refused to vote out the nomination of a candidate for a district court judgeship in Alabama—the second judicial nominee in nearly half a century to suffer such a fate. The first candidate in 43 years, nominated by President Jimmy Carter for a North Carolina district court, was rejected in 1980 (when the Judiciary Committee went against the wishes of the Democratic senator from North Carolina, whose candidate had been found "qualified" by the ABA).

In addition to passing investigative screening and securing an ABA rating of "qualified," becoming a candidate requires political connections and often ideological compatibility with the appointing authority. While somewhat less important on a state level, ideological compatibility can be crucial in the case of federal judgeships. Democratic presidents tend to nominate liberals, and Republicans conservatives. Presidents Nixon and Reagan ran on pledges to appoint only conservatives—"traditionalists"—to the federal courts. During the Reagan years (1980–1988), the issue of judicial selection and the responsibility of the Senate regarding confirmation of presidential nominees received considerable attention. Liberals argued that Ronald Reagan was out to remake the federal judiciary generally, and the Supreme Court in particular, in his own image and that his Justice Department "used an ideological 'litmus test' in screening candidates for judicial appointments. Conservatives, on the other hand, argued that those who opposed Reagan's nominees were injecting partisan politics into the confirmation process and guilty of distorting the degree to which this president, like all of those who preceded him, was merely attempting to appoint men and women to the federal courts who espoused a judicial philosophy similar to his own" (McDowell 1990: xiii–xiv). In his campaign, Bill Clinton pledged to appoint judges whose views were similar to his own, particularly concerning the issue of abortion.

Geographic balance can also play a role in a federal district or circuit court nomination: "At the district level there is pressure on senators to "balance" the judicial process geographically. Accordingly, a senator may feel obligated to allocate a judicial vacancy to a particular congressional district, especially where that position had traditionally "belonged" to a particular district. There is also the need to balance rural and urban areas, eastern and western or northern and southern parts of a state. One arcane kind of turf fighting among states and senators that occurs only at the Court of Appeals level is the allocation of circuit court judgeships among the states of a given circuit. Some try to allocate judgeships among the states in a given Circuit by looking at the percentages of caseload originating from each state compared to the total caseload of the circuit, and/or similar comparison based on a state's percentage share of population within the circuit (Friend of the Constitution 1990).

As with other federal judicial posts, Supreme Court nominations also tend to involve religious and, more recently, racial, gender, and ethnic considerations. Geographic considerations have also played a role; presidents attempt to have all regions of the country represented on the Court. Because of the importance of the Supreme Court, nominees are subjected to greater scrutiny, although there have been infrequent vetoes by the Senate—two when Richard Nixon was president. In 1969 the Senate rejected, 55–45, Clement E. Haynsworth, a federal appellate court judge from South Carolina, over questions of judicial ethics (he had participated in a case involving a company in which he had a one-seventh interest) and strong opposition from labor and civil rights groups. In the 1970 vote on G. Harold Carswell, a little-known federal judge, the Senate floor manager for his nomination, Roman Hruska (R–NE), responded to critics who accused Carswell of having mediocre legal qualifications. "Even if he is mediocre," the senator argued, "there are a lot of mediocre judges and people and lawyers. They are entitled to a little representation, aren't they, and a little chance? We can't have all Brandeises, Cardozos, and Frankfurters, and stuff like that there." His argument was not persuasive; the nomination was defeated by the rather slim margin of 51–45 (Lewis and Peoples 1978). It was only the third time in the twentieth century that a nominee had been rejected. In 1987, the Senate rejected Judge Bork by the largest margin ever cast against a Supreme Court nominee—58 to 42. (For opposing views of this case, see Bork 1989; Pertschuk and Schaetzel 1989; and Bronner 1989.)

One of the more recent and controversial elements in the Senate confirmation process involves Judiciary Committee scrutiny. The practice of questioning nominees dates back to the 1930s, but the questioning was usually perfunctory. Now hearings are televised and receive widespread media attention. Nominees are asked about specific political issues and cases, often raising serious questions about judicial integrity. Robert Bork (1993: 11) refers to the proceedings as "televised inquisitions concerning every thought a nominee ever had about the minutiae of constitutional law." The purpose, Bork argues, is to use the answers against the nominee or, perhaps worse, to elicit commitments on future votes.

Elections

Prior to the Jacksonian era, most judges were appointed by the governor or the state legislature. Jacksonian democracy (1829–1837) led to the popular election of judges. Today, judges are elected in 42 states at some level and more than 80 percent of appellate judges face election (Glaberson 2000a). This raises the question of judicial accountability—to whom and for what should a judge be accountable? Elected officials should be held accountable for their decisions: This furthers the ends of a democratic society. But does holding judges accountable to the electorate for their decisions further the ends of justice? Indeed, the legal profession values judicial independence and abhors judicial partisanship and pandering to a (legally) unsophisticated electorate.

State judges may be elected in a partisan election, in which there is a party primary and the candidates are listed as Democrats or Republicans (or with some local party affiliation) in the general election, or in a nonpartisan election, in which candidates are not listed by any political affiliation. The nonpartisan election was largely an unsuccessful effort to remove judicial selection from the control of often corrupt political organizations. In theory, the electoral system for selecting judges is clearly the most democratic, and it is the way we select most important public officials in the other branches of government. But the nature of judicial office makes the electoral process controversial.

The attorney-as-advocate must leave that role behind when becoming a judge. As a candidate for judicial office, an attorney is, accordingly, restrained by a canon of ethics from taking positions on partisan issues (see Figure 9–1). While a candidate for legislative office is free to state a position on a host of controversial issues ranging from taxes to abortion, a candidate for judicial office is constrained from taking positions on such issues. A violation of the code of professional conduct (promulgated by the state supreme court and, in 47 states, based on a model ABA code of judicial conduct) can lead to the loss of office (by a successful candidate) and even to disbarment. In California, for example, Canon 5 of the *Code of Judicial Ethics* warns: "A candidate for election or appointment to judicial office shall not make statements to the electorate or the appointing authority that commit or appear to commit the candidate with respect to cases, controversies, or issues that could come before the courts." The *Indiana Code of Judicial Conduct* [Sec. 5A(3)(d)] has similar cautions: Judicial candidates "shall not make pledges or promises of conduct in office other than the faithful and impartial performance of the duties of office; make statements that commit or appear to commit the candidate with respect to cases, controversies or issues that are likely to come before the court." Thus, while campaigns for legislative and executive positions can be quite exciting, judicial elections are characteristically dull. These restrictions have been challenged on First Amendment/free speech grounds in a number of states, and courts have rendered conflicting decisions. At the end of 2001, the Supreme Court agreed to consider the issue (*Republican Party of Minnesota* v. *Kelly*).

The electorate is typically faced with a list of judicial candidates about whom little is known, and what is known usually has little or no bearing on the candidate's qualifications for judicial office (e.g., ethnic background, race, religion, and, in partisan elections, party affiliation). The outcome of a judicial election, particularly for the appellate bench, may depend on the ability of a candidate to promote his or her candidacy through advertising. The source of campaign funds raises questions of judicial independence. Trial lawyers, insurance companies, the gambling and medical care industries, unions, energy and natural resources companies have all been substantial contributors to judicial candidates. In 2000, the United States Chamber of Commerce announced their intention of spending more than $1 million for advertising in state supreme court races. What do they expect for their investments?

In addition to money, three often overlapping variables control an election for judicial office: (1) political party support, (2) ethnicity, race, and religion, and (3) position on the ballot. Let us look at these in reverse order of importance.

**FIGURE 9-1   CANON 7 OF THE AMERICAN BAR ASSOCIATION
CODE OF JUDICIAL CONDUCT**

A Judge Should Refrain from Political Activity Inappropriate to His Judicial Office

A. Political Conduct in General

(1) A judge or a candidate for election to judicial office should not:

(a) act as a leader or hold any office in a political organization;

(b) make speeches for a political organization or candidate or publicly endorse a candidate for public office;

(c) solicit funds or pay an assessment or make a contribution to a political organization or candidate, attend political gatherings, or purchase tickets for political party dinners, or other functions, except as authorized in subsection A(2).

(2) A judge holding an office filled by public election between competing candidates, or a candidate for such office, may, only insofar as permitted by law, attend political gatherings, speak to such gatherings on his own behalf when he is a candidate for election or reelection, identify himself as a member of a political party, and contribute to a political party or organization.

(3) A judge should resign his office when he becomes a candidate either in a party primary or in a general election for a nonjudicial office, except that he may continue to hold his judicial office while being a candidate for election to or serving as a delegate in a state constitutional convention, if he is otherwise permitted by law to do so.

(4) A judge should not engage in any other political activity except on behalf of measures to improve the law, the legal system, or the administration of justice.

B. Campaign Conduct

(1) A candidate, including an incumbent judge, for a judicial office that is filled either by public election between competing candidates or on the basis of a merit system election:

(a) should maintain the dignity appropriate to judicial office, and should encourage members of his family to adhere to the same standards of political conduct that apply to him;

(b) should prohibit officials or employees subject to his direction or control from doing for him what he is prohibited from doing under this Canon; and except to the extent authorized under subsection B(2) or B(3), he should not allow any other person to do for him what he is prohibited form doing under this Canon;

(c) should not make pledges or promises of conduct in office other than the faithful and impartial performance of the duties of the office; announce his views on disputed legal or political issues; or misrepresent his identity, qualifications, present position, or other fact.

(2) A candidate, including an incumbent judge, for a judicial office that is filled by public election between competing candidates should not himself solicit or accept campaign funds, or solicit publicly stated support, but he may establish committees of responsible persons to secure and manage the expenditure of funds for his campaign and to obtain public support from lawyers. A candidate's committees may solicit funds for his campaign no earlier than [90] days before a primary election and no later than [90] days after the last election in which he participates during the election year. A candidate should not use or permit the use of campaign contributions for the private benefit of himself or members of his family.

(3) An incumbent judge who is a candidate for retention in or reelection to office without a competing candidate, and whose candidacy has drawn active opposition, may campaign in response thereto and may obtain publicly stated support and campaign funds in the manner provided in subsection B(2).

Position on the Ballot.   The position of a candidate on the election ballot (or voting machine) is governed by election law and can be determined in several ways. In some states, the position of all candidates is determined by a lottery drawing, at least in the party primary. In the general election, it may depend on the number of

*E*LECTING *J*UDGES IN *C*OOK *C*OUNTY, *I*LLINOIS

In the 1994 Cook County (Chicago) Democratic primary, voters were faced with a ballot that, in addition to statewide candidates for the Appellate Court, listed 85 candidates vying for 14 countywide vacancies, and 166 candidates running for election to one of the 15 sub-circuits into which the county is divided. Voters chose 16 candidates who were considered unqualified by the four local lawyers' groups who evaluate judicial candidates. In 1996, Cook County voters elected six judges who had not submitted information about their backgrounds to any of the local bar groups. One had been licensed to practice law in Illinois for under two years—beyond that, nothing was known about her background. In 1998, in Cook County there were 178 candidates running for election to the appellate and circuit courts. In the 2000 general election, there were 77 judges seeking retention in office which requires a "yes" vote of 60 percent—all were retained. At the same election, all of the Democratic candidates for the Circuit Court had no opponents.

votes for governor cast at the last general election; the party receiving the highest number of votes gets the first position on the ballot. This position is preferred, because in jurisdictions that have a long ballot with dozens of usually unknown candidates running for a wide array of offices, many voters have a tendency to vote only for the first few candidates. In some states, the names of candidates are randomly rotated from election district to election district—obviously the fairest method.

Ethnicity, Race, and Religion.   In judicial elections, voters are usually faced with a list of names of persons about whom they know little or nothing. Under such circumstances (as every politician recognizes), the voter is likely to vote for names with which he or she identifies on the basis of ethnicity or religion. Thus, Irish voters may vote for Irish-sounding names, and the same would hold for Italian, Jewish, German, Polish, Bohemian, and other identifiable groups. Judges are often nominated and elected on the strength of their ethnic surnames. In some jurisdictions, candidates utilize middle and/or (hyphenated) maiden names to increase voter ethnic appeal. In Cook County, for example, L. Michael Getty was defeated in the 1984 Democratic Party for the Circuit Court; he changed his name to Michael Brennan Getty and was elected in 1988.

Political Party Support.   A circuit court judge in Chicago, "who had spent more time with a bottle of blended whiskey than with a volume of revised statutes," says political reporter David Axelrod, "offered a surprisingly candid self analysis: 'You know, I may not be much of a judge, but I'm one hell of a precinct captain'" (1983: 4). In order for an aspiring candidate for judicial office to appear on the election ballot, he or she must secure the signature of hundreds, sometimes thousands, of voters on nominating petitions. The circulating of petitions is usually accomplished by the precinct captains of a political party. These persons also have responsibility for getting out the vote for the party ticket. More organized political groups, those with active precinct captains, usually dominate judicial elections.

In partisan systems, a primary election is required to determine who will have the right to appear on the ballot in the general election with a particular party affiliation. In most areas, the primary election is controlled by a particular dominant political organization, Republican or Democrat. The leaders ("bosses") of such organizations select party candidates who, particularly for judicial office, are usually successful in the primary election. Since only a minority of eligible voters usually vote in any primary and still fewer actually cast votes for judicial offices, party leaders are able to dominate the election of judges by the discipline they can exert on party loyalists. In practice, it is the party leadership that typically determines who is elected to judicial office.

In some areas, the election of judges does not provide the electorate with a choice, because the elections are uncontested. In general elections, it is not unusual for candidates, judicial and otherwise, to be unopposed in districts where there is an absence of a viable two-party system. Thus, for example, judicial candidates in Chicago on the Democratic ticket usually run unopposed in the general election, while the same is true of Republican candidates in suburban and more rural downstate areas. From 1974 to 1984, for example, 71 percent of Circuit Court judgeships in Chicago were filled by candidates who ran unopposed in both the primary and general elections (Aspen 1987).

In New York City, Democratic candidates for judicial office frequently run unopposed, while in some suburban and upstate areas the same is true of Republican candidates. A study in New York found that in six consecutive elections for supreme court (superior court) judges, 87 percent were either uncontested or noncompetitive. Either an opposition candidate did not appear on the ballot or the leaders of the Democratic and Republican parties made a deal to cross-endorse the same candidates (a frequent occurrence in New York City) rather than leave it up to the electorate. Another study found the identical situation with respect to the election of civil court (lower court) judges in New York City (Fund for Modern Courts 1986). An editorial in the *New York Times* (October 25, 1986: 14) referred to this system as a "form of election fraud" that "is perpetrated every time New Yorkers cast votes for judges."

In most states, no matter how the judge is initially selected, he or she must submit either to re-election or to a nonpartisan retention or confirmation ballot after a certain amount of time on the bench. In Illinois, for example, after a circuit court judge (general jurisdiction) serves for six years and a supreme court judge (appellate jurisdiction) has served ten years, the judge's name will appear on the ballot of a general election, providing voters with an opportunity to vote for or against retention.

The Peculiar Americans

"Of all those parts of the world entitled to be called civilized, the States of our Union . . . are the only places where judges are elected" (Zane 1998: 284). As we saw in Chapter 2, in civil law countries judges are career civil servants and judges in England are chosen by, or on the recommendation of, the Lord Chancellor, a member of the prime minister's cabinet.

*f*INANCING *j*UDICIAL *E*LECTIONS

Concerned with the specter of judges taking campaign contributions from lawyers, businesses, and others who have a financial stake in the outcome of cases, a committee of the ABA recommended public financing of judicial elections (Bendavid 2001).

California, which has the largest judicial system in the country (about 1,500 judgeships), uses a nonpartisan election system for trial court judges and executive appointment for appellate court justices. The governor submits nominees for the Supreme Court and Courts of Appeal to the Commission on Judicial Appointments which consists of the chief justice of the Supreme Court, the attorney general, and the senior presiding judge on the Court of Appeals. The commission holds public hearings to receive comments on the nominee's qualifications before voting on whether to confirm the governor's choice. If they approve of the nominee—and they almost always do—the person serves until the next election, but not less than one year, at which time the judge's name appears on a retention ballot for a full 12-year term. At the end of their 12-year terms, justices are again subjected to a retention ballot.

In 1986, a successful campaign effort was launched by two political consulting firms against the retention of Rose Bird, chief justice of the California Supreme Court, and two associate justices, based on claims that they had refused to uphold the death sentence against scores of convicted murderers. "For the first time since retention elections were adopted for the state's appellate justices in 1934, the public not only rejected a chief justice, but defeated two other justices" (Wold and Culver 1989: 323). Noted legal scholar Karl Llewellyn (1960) disapproved of the retention vote, arguing that appellate court justices must be immune from personal or political retribution for their decisions. (It is the reason federal judges enjoy life terms.) In 2000, a member of the Idaho Supreme Court was defeated by a trial court judge who campaigned on the issue of evolution: "could not possibly be true," the victor argued. Less idiosyncratic issues such as school financing, abortion, health care, and liability laws with caps on torts have led to increased contributions to judicial campaigns from interest groups whose involvement threatens judicial independence. Judicial elections have become bitter, with attack ads and thinly veiled advertising by which candidates express opinions on issues which, as judges, they may have to rule (Glaberson 2000a). And "across the country, judges are being fined, censored and even threatened with removal for practicing that venerable political art: exaggerating or outright lying during a campaign" (Glaberson 2000c: 1). In 2000, 15 of the most populous states organized a summit of chief justices in response to abuses arising out of electoral contests for judicial office (Glaberson 2000d).

Merit System

Efforts to reform the way judges are chosen have taken a number of forms. The most notable is the Missouri Plan, adopted in Missouri in 1940. The politics of Missouri were influenced for many years by the often corrupt activities associated

A Political Judiciary

"The courts are often thought to be less 'political' than the other branches of government. This popular view is probably too much influenced by the workings of the Supreme Court. The justices of Supreme Court, cloistered, unelected, and appointed for life, are free to ponder and ruminate on the grand issues of jurisprudence. The judges in a state court are more constrained. Elected judges know they rule at the discretion of the voters, and, like politicians, they rule accordingly" (Tabarrok and Helland 1999: 187). "Since most plaintiffs are in-state voters and many defendants are out-of-state nonvoters, elected judges have an incentive to service their constituency by aiding plaintiffs. A particularly low-cost method of aiding plaintiffs is to transfer wealth from out-of-state business defendants to in-state plaintiffs. Campaign contributions from trial lawyers are also likely to increase the proportion of 'high aware' judges in elected states" (1999: 186).

with the Pendergast machine of Kansas City (see Dorsett 1968). The selection of judges by popular election suffered accordingly, and the leadership of the Missouri bar, with the support of the press, was successful in instituting a unique way of selecting some judges (originally proposed by Albert Kales of the American Judicature Society in 1914 [Stumpf and Culver 1992]). The system has three basic features:

1. *Nominating commission.* There is a nominating commission for each level of courts to which the plan applies (some local courts continue to use popular election) made up of lawyers (elected by the attorneys residing in each jurisdiction); laypersons whose only legal qualification is residency in the jurisdiction and who are appointed by the governor; and the chief justice of the supreme court, who is the ex officio chairman.

2. *Governor's selection.* When there is a judicial vacancy in any applicable court, the nominating commission sends a list of three candidates to the governor, who is required to pick one of the three.

3. *Retention ballot.* After one year of service, each judge appointed under the system appears on a retention ballot: "Shall Judge _____ be retained in office?" If a majority of those casting votes on the question say yes, the judge remains in office for the full term (either six or twelve years, depending on the court). If the judge does not receive a majority of yes votes, the office is declared vacant, and the nominating commission drafts a new list for the governor.

Currently there is a national trend toward using some form of merit system. In 1960, only four states utilized merit systems based, in whole or in part, on the Missouri Plan; by 1997 almost one-half of the states had done so (Abraham 1998). Most use a modified form of the Missouri system, the salient feature being a nominating commission of lawyers and laypeople. More than half the states have established judicial nominating commissions that review candidates for all of the courts. Some have different nominating commissions for each court level, and in a few, a commission reviews candidates only for certain courts—such as the court of last resort in New York and the general and limited jurisdiction courts in North Carolina. All of these states permit laypersons to serve on the commissions. In Connecticut, the commission provides a list of nominees to the legislature, not the governor, which makes the appointment.

STRENGTHS AND WEAKNESSES OF THE METHODS FOR CHOOSING JUDGES

The appointment of judges by a chief executive places the decision in the hands of a highly visible public official. This system provides the greatest level of accountability. A president or governor will be praised or criticized for his or her judicial appointments, a factor that can encourage the appointment of qualified candidates. On the other hand, governors and presidents have at times shown a willingness to appoint persons of dubious ability or questionable background, public criticism notwithstanding. The appointment process removes the public from any direct participation in the judicial selection process, weakening the quest for legitimacy (discussed in Chapter 7).

The electoral method receives support from political party leaders with whom the power of judicial selection is largely vested. They argue that it is "democratic," that all other important public officials are elected by the people. The best defense of this position had been put forward by Edward Costikyan (1966), a reform leader of the Democratic party of Manhattan ("Tammany Hall"). He asserts that the collective decision-making of district or ward party leaders is superior to appointment by one person, a chief executive. He notes that judicial candidates selected by party leaders because of their political activity have had experience with the human problems that make up a large part of the court caseload, particularly in the lower courts. However, the electoral method of selecting judges receives little support from political scientists, bar associations, and newspaper editorial boards, because it places too much power in the hands of party officials. Furthermore, these party officials, who in reality select the candidates, are able to avoid accountability because judges are officially put into office by the electorate.

Judicial candidates in contested elections (or those facing retention elections) must raise funds for their campaigns and attempt to win over blocks of voters; either can compromise judicial independence. Most of those who contribute to judicial campaigns are attorneys (who else would be interested enough to contribute their money?) whose practice will bring them into the courts of the very judges they help to elect. Judge Samuel Rosenman states: "I learned first hand what it means for a judicial candidate to have to seek votes in political club houses, to ask for the support of political district leaders, to receive financial contributions for his campaign from lawyers and others, to make nonpolitical speeches about his own qualifications to audiences who could not care less—audiences who had little interest in any of the judicial candidates, of whom they had never heard, and whom they would never remember" (Task Force on Administration of Justice 1967: 66–67).

The Journal of the American Judicature Society ("Editorial" 1964: 124–125) referred to the nonpartisan election of judges "as the worst of all the traditional methods." Under this system, "having the same name as a well-known public figure, a large campaign fund, a pleasing TV image, or the proper place on the ballot are far more influential in selecting judges than character, legal ability, judicial temperament or distinguished experience on the bench."

In the 1973 election for chief justice of the New York Court of Appeals (court of last resort), the successful candidate spent more than $1.2 million and defeated a highly respected appellate judge. As a result, the legislature passed a merit system law for the state's highest court. Now a commission of lawyers and laypeople draws up a list of candidates, and the governor makes the final selection. In 2000, a spirited campaign for the Ohio Supreme Court pitted a candidate favored by organized labor against one favored by business in which both sides spent millions of dollars for advertising to influence the outcome (Glaberson 2000b).

The merit/Missouri system has many supporters among editorial writers, the ABA, and the American Judicature Society, who favor taking the courts "out of politics." "At the very least," states U.S. District Court Judge Marvin Aspen, "merit selection will broaden the pool of potential judicial applicants to include many fine lawyers who have little hope of serving on the bench under present election procedures" (1987: 17). However, under this system accountability is almost completely absent because the selection process is diffused among a commission, the governor, and, finally, the electorate (and there is a great deal of voter disinterest in retention elections).

The laypeople appointed to commissions are usually closely aligned with the governor and support the governor's preferences. And governors often covertly influence commission deliberations by conveying their preferences for a judicial vacancy. "As a result," states Alan Tarr (1999: 70), "under merit selection governors may exercise as much control [with a great less accountability] as they do under a system of gubernatorial appointment." Furthermore, in the appointed and electoral systems, political leaders are concerned with fulfilling political commitments—patronage. In the lawyer-dominated merit system, the focus is on the expected judicial attitudes and policies of potential candidates, a more personal and, perhaps compromising, concern. Henry Glick notes that all of the research on the selection of state judges reveals that "while there are some differences among state judges, differences do not result from the particular selection system used and the Missouri plan does not produce judges with superior formal credentials for office" (1983: 89; see also Stumpf 1988). And retention elections can easily become focused on the decisions of judges, something the Founding Fathers wanted to keep out of the political arena.

REMOVING JUDGES

Russell Wheeler and A. Leo Levin point out the issues and delicate balance involved in dealing with judicial discipline. There is a "need to preserve judicial independence and need to deal with the judge who cannot or will not properly discharge the functions of office. Moreover, the problems of defining unfitness are subtle and complicated: what some may perceive as judicial incompetence—such as comments to witnesses and attorneys that are seen as rude or insensitive—others may perceive as conduct well within the bounds of discretion that judges must have for the effective movement of cases" (1979: 3).

Four basic methods are used to impose judicial discipline and removal, the first being the only one used in the federal system.

1. *Impeachment and conviction.* Removing a federal judge involves the cumbersome and infrequently invoked impeachment process. Impeachment refers to the bringing of charges; it is analogous to an indictment in the criminal process. Even federal judges who are convicted of crimes can be removed from office only by impeachment. Thirteen federal judges have been impeached: seven were convicted and removed and one resigned. A federal judge impeached and removed from office in 1989 was subsequently elected to Congress.

   The process begins in the House of Representatives, whose members vote on articles of impeachment. The articles are prosecuted in the Senate by members of the lower house chosen by their peers; they act as prosecutors before the Senate, which serves as judge and jury. According to the Constitution (Article I), "The Senate shall have the sole Power to try all Impeachments." In order to avoid tying up the entire Senate, this is usually handled by a panel chosen by the Senate leadership. The panel hears the evidence and makes a recommendation to the full body. The Constitution (Article I) provides that "no person shall be convicted without Concurrence of two thirds of the Members present." All states have provisions for the impeachment of public officials, and the procedures generally follow the federal model.[3]

   In 1980, Congress enacted the Judicial Councils Reform and Conduct and Disability Act, which provides for the judicial council in each of the 13 appellate circuits to consider allegations about the personal conduct, mental, and physical condition of federal district court judges. If the council finds that a judge has engaged in conduct that is grounds for impeachment, it can request that the Judicial Conference[4] refer the matter to the House of Representatives for impeachment proceedings. Short of that, the council can censure or reprimand an offending judge, publicly or privately. Before such sanctions can be imposed, however, the judge has the right to appeal to a three-member panel of the Judicial Conference. The procedure has been closed to outside scrutiny and judges rarely, if ever, receive public reprimands (Margolick 1989b).

2. *Legislative resolution.* More than half the states permit the removal of a judge by a concurrent two-thirds vote of both houses or by the governor with the concurrence of a majority vote of both houses.

3. *Recall.* Seven states, mostly in the West, have constitutional provisions for the recall of elected officials, including state judges. Recall requires circulating a petition. If enough valid signatures are secured, the name of the official appears on the ballot at the next general election; the electorate votes *yea* or *nay* with respect to continuing the official in office.

4. *Commission system.* In 1960, California became the first state to establish a permanent commission charged with the regulation of judges' conduct. By 1981, by constitutional amendment, statute, or by court rule, all states

---

[3]For a cross-national comparison of procedures for judicial misconduct, see Volcansek (1996).
[4]The Judicial Conference is discussed in Chapter 6.

established commissions on judicial conduct empowered to investigate, prosecute, and adjudicate allegations of judicial misbehavior. Though the commissions vary widely in structure, composition, and procedure, they are typically authorized either to recommend or impose sanctions on a continuum that extends from private reprimand to removal from office. Most are composed of about 5 to 15 members and include judges, lawyers, and laypersons (Rottman et al. 2000). Moreover, nearly every state has also adopted a version of the Model Code of Judicial Conduct, which sets mandatory standards for both official and off-the-bench conduct (Lubet 1998).

PROSECUTORS

In British common law, a crime was viewed not as an act against the state, but as a wrong inflicted upon the victim, who was responsible for the arrest and prosecution of the offender. The common law courts would adjudicate the matter "much as they would a contract dispute or a tortuous injury" (Kress 1976: 10). The origin of the public prosecutor in the United States is in doubt. Some trace it to the Dutch experience in New York, where the sheriff acted as a prosecutor; some see its roots in the French *procureur publique*, who operated under an inquisitorial system; others see its origin in the English post of the king's attorney (Kress 1976). In colonial America, the prosecution of cases was the responsibility of a district attorney (the title varied), usually appointed by the governor and assigned to a particular county or region. "In this respect colonial practice diverged from the custom in England, where private prosecutors handled all but the most important cases" (Walker 1980: 22). By the end of the American Revolution, all states had enacted legislation establishing the office of public prosecutor, who was usually an elected county official. In the federal system, the Judiciary Act of 1789 provided for a United States attorney to be appointed by the president in each court district. Since then, the prosecutor has become the most powerful figure in the criminal justice system, exercising enormous discretion, the decision to prosecute being "one of the most solitary and unfettered exercises of power in the American political system"[5] (Stewart 1987: 10). Indeed "the prosecutor's decision to institute criminal charges is the broadest and least regulated power in American criminal law" (Gershman 2002: 57).

Federal Prosecutors

Since U.S. attorneys must be confirmed by the Senate, a senator's influence over the appointment of a U.S. attorney (USA) is similar to his or her influence in the appointment of a district court judge. In 1870, Congress created the Department of Justice (DOJ) with the attorney general as its head. The attorney general supervises USAs and their assistants (who are generally not political appointees), and investigative agencies, such as the Federal Bureau of Investigation and the Drug Enforcement Administration.

---

[5]For a discussion of prosecutorial immunity, see Chemerinsky (1998).

REMOVING JUDGES

ILLINOIS

The two-tiered discipline process provided for by the Illinois Constitution began in 1971 and is typical of many states: There is a Judicial Inquiry Board with nine members; two are circuit (superior) court judges selected by the supreme court and seven are appointed by the governor—three lawyers and four nonlawyers. The board has authority to receive or initiate complaints concerning judges and file them with the Court Commission. "The Board shall not file a complaint unless five members believe that a reasonable basis exists (1) to charge the Judge or Associate Judge with willful misconduct in office, persistent failure to perform his duties, or other conduct that is prejudicial to the administration of justice or that brings the judicial office into disrepute, or (2) to charge that the Judge or Associate Judge is physically or mentally unable to perform his duties."

The Judicial Inquiry Board prosecutes the complaint before the Court Commission: one supreme court judge, two appellate court judges, and two superior court judges. With the concurrence of three members, the Commission has the final authority to remove the judge from office, suspend without pay, or censure.

NEW YORK

The New York State Commission on Judicial Conduct consists of 11 members—four appointed by the governor, three by the chief judge of the court of appeals, and one each by the speaker of the assembly, the majority leader of the senate, and the two legislative minority leaders. At least two of its members must be nonlawyers and four must be judges. Members serve staggered four-year terms, and they appoint an administrator who is charged with the day-to-day operations of the commission.

The commission receives or initiates complaints about the conduct, qualifications, fitness to perform, or performance of official duties of any judge in the state and conducts an investigation and a hearing, both of which are confidential until complete. If the commission finds cause for disciplinary action against a judge, its findings are made available to the public through the clerk of the court of appeals; the commission publishes an annual report of its activities. The commission has the power to admonish, censure, remove, or retire a judge based on its findings.

CALIFORNIA

The Commission on Judicial Performance, a constitutionally created independent agency, was the first in the United States established to monitor judicial conduct and has served as a model for most other states. The commission is composed of two appellate justices, two superior court judges, and one municipal court judge, appointed by the state Supreme Court; two lawyers selected by the state bar; and two nonlawyers appointed by the governor. Members serve four-year terms.

The commission receives and investigates all complaints of judicial misconduct and can recommend to the Supreme Court admonishment, censure, or removal. The commission can recommend involuntary retirement in the event of a permanent disability that interferes with the performance of judicial duties.

*R*EMOVING *J*UDGES *(continued)*

VIRGINIA

The Judicial Inquiry and Review Commission has seven members consisting of three judges, two lawyers, and two citizen members who are not lawyers. The members are elected by the Virginia General Assembly for four-year terms. The Commission employs a staff to assist in the investigation of complaints of misconduct against all state court judges.

Following the investigation, the Commission may consider the complaint informally or it may conduct a formal hearing. If the Commission determines there has not been an ethical violation, the complaint will be dismissed. If there has been a violation, the Commission may summon the judge and advise the judge of its findings. Charges that are sufficient to require the retirement, censure or removal of the judge may be filed by the Commission in the Supreme Court of Virginia. The Commission may conclude the complaint after counseling with the judge. It may reprimand the judge privately, or place the judge on a period of supervision subject to terms and conditions, or refer the matter to the Virginia Supreme Court. The Supreme Court may dismiss the complaint or it may retire, censure, or remove the judge.

The position of U.S. attorney holds a great deal of prestige and public visibility; the names of USAs are frequently mentioned in the local news media. Service as a USA can lead to a higher office (e.g., a federal judgeship) or can be a springboard for elected office. Although part of the DOJ, a USA enjoys considerable autonomy and a great deal of discretionary authority. Subject only to being overruled by the attorney general (an infrequent occurrence), the USA decides which cases will be investigated and prosecuted. Observers have noted that a U.S. attorney's relationship with the judges of the district is actually more important than the USA's relationship with the DOJ (Wasby 1993; Goldman and Jahnige 1985). The ability of the attorney general to hire and fire a USA depends on his or her influence with the President—the President appoints and only the President can fire a USA (Eisenstein 1978). When a new president takes office, incumbent USAs (but not assistant USAs) usually submit their resignations, even if their appointment has not expired. In a few cases, USAs may serve several administrations (Stewart 1987).

The U.S. attorney receives cases for prosecution from a variety of federal law enforcement agencies in several departments, primarily Justice and Treasury, but also Transportation, Interior, Agriculture, Defense, Education, and the Postal Service. (For an interesting look at the work of justice department attorneys, see McGee and Duffy 1996.)

A solicitor general in the DOJ handles cases to be taken before the Supreme Court.

SOLICITOR GENERAL

The office of solicitor general was created by the Judiciary Act of 1870: "There shall be an officer, learned in the law, to assist the Attorney General." The Solicitor General is nominated by the president and confirmed by the Senate. As an officer of the

PRIMARY FEDERAL LAW ENFORCEMENT AGENCIES

DEPARTMENT OF JUSTICE

Drug Enforcement Administration
Federal Bureau of Investigation
Immigration and Naturalization Service
Marshals Service

DEPARTMENT OF THE TREASURY

Bureau of Alcohol, Tobacco and Firearms
Internal Revenue Service
Customs Service
Secret Service

Department of Justice, with a staff of 5 deputies and about 20 assistant solicitors, the solicitor general decides what cases the government should ask the Supreme Court to review and represents the United States in all cases before the Court. The United States is involved in about two-thirds of all the cases the U.S. Supreme Court decides on the merits each year. The Office also reviews all cases decided adversely to the government in the lower courts to determine whether they should be appealed and, if so, what position should be taken. The Solicitor General determines whether the government will participate as an amicus curiae, or intervene, in cases in any appellate court.

While the solicitor general's primary office is in the building of the Department of Justice, there are also permanent chambers in the Supreme Court Building. The Office of Solicitor General reviews every case in which the government was a losing litigant and determines whether or not to appeal. When the solicitor general appears before the Supreme Court, he or she has a distinct advantage over other attorneys: "Partly because his client is the Government, partly because his office has a reputation for professional excellence and a measure of independence, his arguments have usually carried special weight with the Court" (Taylor 1986b: 8). While the Court hears less than 4 percent of all petitions, more than 70 percent of those filed by the solicitor general receive hearings, and of those, the office has won a comfortable majority in every term since 1935–1936. While most lawyers appear in business suits, tradition requires the solicitor general to be attired in a morning coat and striped pants (Taylor 1986b).

The justices of the Supreme Court "turn to the SG for help on legal problems that appear especially vexing, and two or three dozen times a year they invite him and his office to submit briefs in cases where the government is not a party. In these cases especially, the justices regard him as a counselor to the Court" (Caplan 1987: 7). The Court provides the solicitor general with a special dispensation to file a brief as a friend of the court without the permission of the parties to the suit. Consistent with this special role, the solicitor general "confesses to errors." That is, when the government wins on grounds that appear to the solicitor general to be unjust, he or she recommends to the Supreme Court that the decision be overturned. (For an examination of the work of the Solicitor General's Office during the Reagan administration, see Fried 1991.)

STATE PROSECUTORS

Like his/her federal counterpart, the prosecutor in a state system (sometimes called district attorney, county attorney, commonwealth attorney, state's attorney) receives a great deal of media attention and, in most states, enjoys complete autonomy. In all but a few states, the prosecutor is an elected county official answerable only to the electorate. In Alaska, Connecticut, and Delaware, criminal prosecution is the responsibility of the state's attorney general, and in New Jersey the governor appoints a prosecutor for each county (Dawson 1992). In those states that elect prosecutors, the aspiring candidate, if he or she is to be successful, obviously needs the support of a political organization and campaign contributors. The office of prosecutor has served as an important source of political patronage, and it can investigate political enemies while protecting political friends. Being a prosecutor has often been seen as a stepping stone to higher public office. Most prosecutors aspire to higher office, and many important public officials were at one time prosecutors.

A prosecutor's office decides which cases are to be prosecuted, and for what criminal charges. While a prosecutor's office cannot control intake—it is dependent on the police to bring cases—prosecutors can decide not to prosecute and legally need not provide any reason, although politically it might be a necessity in highly publicized cases. The prosecutor's office can decline to prosecute a case, dismiss it, accept a plea of guilty to a reduced charge, or prosecute it to the fullest extent allowable by law. The enormous discretion enjoyed by the prosecutor provides the basis for much of the plea bargaining in criminal courts (which will be discussed in Chapter 11).

Like a U.S. attorney, a prosecutor employs assistants[6] who do most of the actual trial work (in large counties they do it all). In practice, as we shall see in later chapters, there are relatively few trials in either the criminal or civil courts. Most assistant prosecutors are recent law school graduates who use the prosecutor's office as an opportunity to gain trial experience. A typical assistant prosecutor works for three or four years and then enters private practice, often to do criminal defense work. The prosecutor's office, then, is characterized by a great deal of turnover, sometimes due to electoral politics, but often as a result of assistants leaving for more lucrative opportunities in private legal practice. In Illinois, for example, more than 83 percent of assistant state's attorneys serve fewer than five years (Parsons 2000). As noted in Chapter 5, the legal profession is highly stratified with only limited mobility. "One's final position in the status hierarchy of the profession is heavily determined by the status position of one's first job as a lawyer. That, in turn, is influenced by the prestige of one's law school which, in turn, is influenced by the prestige of one's

---

[6]There are more than 22,000 working for about 2,350 prosecutor's offices (DeFrances, Smith, and van der Does 1996).

college which, in turn, is influenced by one's family socioeconomic background. Being an assistant prosecutor as the first job in one's legal career does little to enhance one's occupational mobility" (Fishman 1979: 252).

Most assistants are not graduates of prestigious law schools, although there are some exceptions. The New York (Manhattan) County District Attorney's Office has had an outstanding reputation ever since Thomas E. Dewey was elected to the position in 1937. Dewey, a Republican, became governor and was succeeded by his first assistant, Frank S. Hogan, a Democrat who remained district attorney until he retired 34 years later. The nonpolitical nature of the office, its reputation for excellence, and jurisdiction attract many law school students who might otherwise enter corporate practice upon graduation. The office receives more than 1,500 applications for the approximately 50 annual vacancies.

In some jurisdictions, the decision to charge a suspect is left to the police (usually detectives), and the prosecutor's office receives the case only after charges against the subject have already been filed. In other jurisdictions, the charging decision is controlled by the prosecutor from the beginning: An assistant prosecutor decides what, if any, charges should be filed. In still other jurisdictions, if a felony is to be charged by the police, the prosecutor must first give permission; the police can usually charge misdemeanors without any consultation.[7]

Early screening keeps weak and petty cases from overburdening the system (see Figure 9–2). For example, the Los Angeles County District Attorney's Office, which has about 1,000 prosecutors, handles approximately one million cases annually. However, it can also result in faulty decisions since there may not be a great deal of information available about the case and/or the suspect so early in the process.

The prosecutor's office may be organized to handle cases horizontally, vertically, or in a combination of the two methods.

1. Horizontal prosecution. This is the predominant mode of handling cases in more populous jurisdictions—each assistant prosecutor is assigned to handle a different step in the judicial process. (See Chapter 10 for these steps.) For example, the Cook County, Illinois, State's Attorney's Office, the country's second largest, employs over 900 assistant prosecutors assigned to eight bureaus. In every prosecutor's office, assistants are assigned to receive and screen cases as they enter the system; some will be assigned to the lower courts to deal with bond hearings, probable-cause hearings, and misdemeanor cases. If a felony case is sent to the grand jury or superior court, it will be managed by assistants assigned to those bodies. If a case is appealed, it will be handled by assistants who specialize in appeals. (Those who are familiar with basketball will recognize this method as the *zone defense*.) Horizontal prosecution in felony cases means that a victim or complainant may have to deal with a different assistant prosecutor at each stage of the judicial process. The victim may feel tossed about, receiving little personal attention, and this can be costly in terms of cooperation.

---

[7]In many states, "city ordinances duplicate state misdemeanor provisions, and minor offenses therefore may be prosecuted under state law or under the local ordinances" (Kamisar, LaFave, and Israel 1986: 26). Local ordinances are typically prosecuted by the city attorney who often has the title of corporation counsel.

FIGURE 9-2 DIFFERENCES IN HOW PROSECUTORS HANDLE FELONY CASES IN FOUR JURISDICTIONS

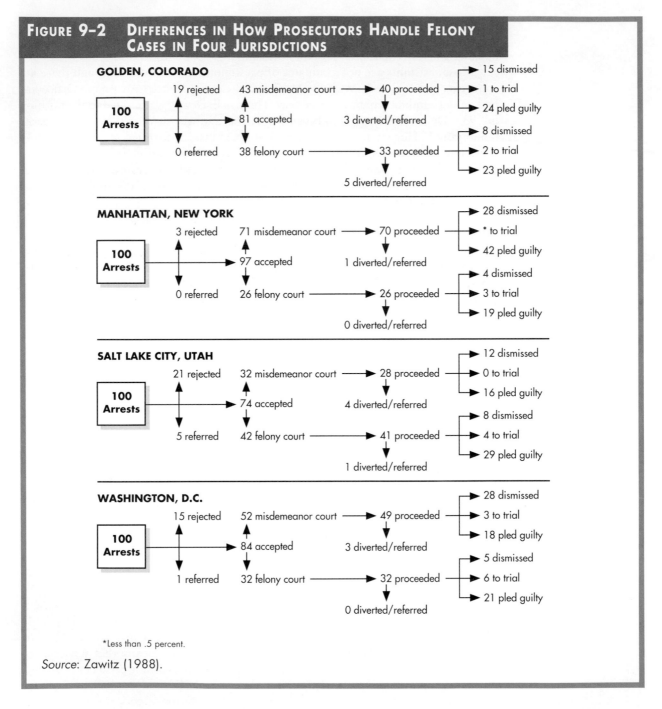

*Less than .5 percent.

Source: Zawitz (1988).

2. *Vertical prosecution.* This system is used in smaller jurisdictions where the prosecutor's office is not overburdened by the mass of cases that characterize most metropolitan areas. Each assistant prosecutor is assigned a caseload (a number of specific cases) for which he or she has total responsibility. The assistant picks up the case after the decision to charge has been made and stays with it until the final disposition. (Those familiar with basketball will recognize this method as the *man-to-man defense*.) The victim has the comfort of one assistant throughout the entire judicial process; he or she does not have to discuss the case anew with each new assistant. This method can be quite costly in terms of personnel. It is often difficult to gather all of the primary and secondary actors in court at the same time, with the necessary files and exhibits needed for the case to move forward. Quite often, an assistant prosecutor will find that he or she is prepared for trial but other actors or records are either missing or not prepared, and the case will be rescheduled for another date. With horizontal prosecution, the clerk will call the next case and the prosecutor will deal with that one; with vertical prosecution, the entire day may be wasted.

3. *Mixed prosecution*. This system takes advantage of the strengths inherent in horizontal and vertical prosecution. Most routine cases will be handled in a horizontal (cost-effective) manner, while certain targeted cases (e.g., murder, those involving organized crime, or serious repeat offenders) will be subject to vertical prosecution. When using this mixed method the prosecutor may set up special bureaus such as a homicide bureau, a rackets bureau, or a serious repeat offender bureau with assistants and investigators who have special training or experience in dealing with these types of cases.

Like the police, a prosecutor is responsible for enforcing the law, and as such acts in the name of "the people" (actually, in the name of the United States of America or the State of _____). Unlike the police, however, a prosecutor has an additional responsibility: *justice*. A police officer who has the minimum level of evidence necessary to effect a lawful arrest (probable cause) must, in the case of a felony, arrest the suspect. The prosecutor needs a much higher level of evidence—beyond a reasonable doubt. (Differing levels of proof play an important role in plea bargaining, which will be discussed in Chapter 11.) As an officer of the court, the prosecutor must be concerned with the possibility of prosecuting a person who is innocent or a person against whom the evidence is not sufficient to justify a verdict of guilty; to prosecute under such circumstances would be unjust. This explains why prosecutors will often dismiss cases or declare *nolle prosequi* (or simply "nol pros"), a formal entry on the record by the prosecutor that he or she will not prosecute the case any further. According to legal ethics scholar Monroe Freedman, a prosecutor cannot properly go forward with a case unless satisfied beyond a reasonable doubt that the accused is guilty. "A prosecutor should be professionally disciplined for proceeding with a prosecution if a fair-minded person could not reasonably conclude, on the facts known to the prosecutor, that the accused is guilty beyond a reasonable doubt" (1975: 88).

While the police are sensitive to immediate demands for crime control, prosecutors must be sensitive to the legal constraints on governmental action (McDonald et al. 1982). In addition to having different evidentiary concerns, there are social and educational differences between police officers and prosecutors. While a number of jurisdictions have increased educational standards, qualifications for the position of police officer do not go beyond a bachelor's degree. While prosecutors conceive of their positions as a point of entry to private practice or some other public service, police are likely to see their job as a career. In order to reduce some of the distance between police officers and prosecutors that can hinder effective

AMERICAN BAR ASSOCIATION GENERAL STANDARDS FOR PROSECUTORS

- The duty of the prosecutor is to seek justice, not merely to convict.
- A prosecutor should not institute, cause to be instituted, or permit the continued pendency of criminal charges in the absence of sufficient admissible evidence to support a conviction.

REALITY ACCORDING TO THE *CHICAGO TRIBUNE*

"With impunity prosecutors across the country have violated their oaths and the law, committing the worst kinds of deception in the most serious of cases. They have prosecuted black men, hiding evidence that the real killers were white. They have prosecuted a wife, hiding evidence that her husband committed suicide. They have prosecuted parents, hiding evidence their daughter was killed by wild dogs. They do it to win. . . . They have done it to defendants who came within hours of being executed only to be exonerated" (Armstrong and Possley 1999: 1).

prosecution, several jurisdictions have established special cooperative programs to have prosecutors work directly with the police on specialized (e.g., drug or gang crime) investigations.

CRIMINAL DEFENSE ATTORNEYS

In civil matters, neither plaintiff nor defendant is constitutionally entitled to an attorney. However, in criminal cases the complainant is represented by a government attorney—the prosecutor—and the defendant has a constitutional right to be represented by "competent" counsel. Criminal justice in the United States is based on an adversarial model, and the defense counsel is one of its cornerstones. Within this adversarial system of justice, the attorney for the accused has a singular purpose: As an advocate, he or she must use every lawful means to exonerate the accused or, failing that, to mitigate punishment. Questions of justice, of guilt or innocence, which should concern the prosecutor, are not the responsibility of defense counsel—at least not in the United States. Freedman (1975) notes that in some totalitarian countries, such as China or Cuba, it is the responsibility of the lawyer not to argue that his or her client is innocent but to determine if the client is guilty, and if so, to seek the sanction necessary to best provide rehabilitation—even if that means execution. They may be aided in this endeavor by Chinese judges who under communism are considered agents of the state who frequently lack legal training (Kynge 2001). At least three attorneys who defended protesters involved in the 1989 Tiananmen Square incident have been suspended by the People's Republic for trying too hard on behalf of their clients (Schmetzer 1991). Lon Fuller argues that under our adversarial system, an attorney who refuses to defend a client because the attorney thinks he or she is guilty "is wrongfully usurping the office of judge and jury" (1961: 34).

In the United States, only agents of government must be dedicated to truth-finding. Defense counsel is under no comparable obligation; his or her role is to defend the client whether innocent or guilty. In fact, defense counsel is required to throw up roadblocks in the face of the truth, to prevent admission of evidence that may be wholly reliable, such as a murder weapon seized in violation of the Fourth Amendment or a truthful but involuntary confession. "Our interest in not convicting the innocent," notes Justice Byron R. White, permits counsel "to put the State's case in the worst possible light, regardless of what he thinks or knows to be the truth" (*United States* v. *Wade* 1967). Freedman says that in the adversary system, "it is not the role or function of the advocate to act upon conclusions of ultimate facts such as guilt or innocence. That function is assigned to the judge or jury, which bases its decision on the adversaries' presentation of their clients' cases. Thus, the fact of guilt or innocence is irrelevant to the role that has been assigned to the advocate" (1975: 57).

A public defender writes: "It is an axiom of criminal defense practice that you represent your guilty clients as zealously as you do your innocent ones (not that you can always tell the difference). [A] client who you really believe is innocent . . . does not happen very often. In fact, it happens rarely enough to be considered remarkable. One of the awkward truths about being a public defender is that you are in the practice of representing people who are, indeed, guilty as charged" (Bellows 1983: 8).

The right to counsel existed in colonial America, although often in practice rather than by law. In Connecticut it has been the custom since 1750 to appoint counsel for defendants who requested attorneys, although there was not a statutory provision until 1818. As early as 1701, Pennsylvania and Delaware provided all criminal defendants with the same privilege of counsel as their prosecutors, and South Carolina did the same in 1731. Most states made the provision regarding the right to counsel in their postrevolutionary constitutions (McDonald 1983). The Sixth Amendment provides that "in all criminal prosecutions, the accused shall enjoy the right . . . to have the assistance of counsel for his defense." In 1932, the Supreme Court ruled (*Powell* v. *Alabama*) that an indigent defendant accused of a capital offense in a state court is entitled to counsel at public expense. In 1928, the Court (*Johnson* v. *Zerbst*) ruled that an indigent defendant is entitled to counsel in a federal criminal prosecution. In 1963, the Court ruled (*Gideon* v. *Wainwright*) that all indigent defendants accused of felonies are entitled to counsel at state expense; and in 1972,

AMERICAN BAR ASSOCIATION GENERAL STANDARDS

The basic duty the lawyer for the accused owes to the administration of justice is to serve as the accused's counselor and advocate with courage, devotion, and to the utmost of his or her learning and ability and according to law.

the Court (*Argersinger* v. *Hamlin*) extended the right to counsel for indigent defendants accused of misdemeanors for which the penalty includes possible imprisonment. These decisions established lawyers as a cornerstone for criminal justice. They asserted the value of the legal profession for ensuring equality in the midst of gross inequalities (McDonald 1983).

In the United States today, there are three ways to accomplish the right to counsel: (1) engaging a private attorney, (2) public defender systems, and (3) assigned counsel.

Private Defense Attorney

Relatively few lawyers in private practice handle criminal cases on a regular basis, and most of them are solo practitioners or work within law firms of fewer than four partners or associates. The professional and private lifestyle of the criminal attorney usually falls far short of the glamorous portrayals in books, movies, and on television. Paul Wice (1978) presents a portrait of the private criminal attorney that is, instead, rather depressing. He (very few are women[8]) must be concerned about continually securing clients, and in some jurisdictions this requires unlawful kickbacks to other attorneys or persons working in criminal justice (such as clerks, police officers, bailiffs) for referrals. He must worry about being paid, because criminal defendants usually are poor and may refuse to pay when a case is over. The hours are long, and a great deal of time is spent simply waiting in, or traveling to, courthouses. The private criminal lawyer is usually at the office for an hour or two prior to his morning court appearance and will return there in the late afternoon for a few additional hours. He may also be found in his office on weekends and on those rare days when no court appearances are required. For the bulk of the day, however, the criminal lawyer will be in the courthouse, roaming hallways, waiting for appointments, chatting with fellow practitioners over rancid coffee, and occasionally carrying out professional responsibilities before a judge (Wice 1978). The daily routine of famed Bronx, New York, criminal defense attorney Murray Richman is typical: "Despite the frentic pace of his daily calendar, a great part of Richman's working life is spent idling, waiting out the inevitable delays in court, or in jail, for something that's supposed to happen, or someone who's supposed to appear. . . " (Gourevitch 2001: 163).

The private practice of criminal law not only is physically demanding, but also has significant social and psychological costs. Attorney Murray Richman states that people ask him "How can you represent people like this?" (Gourevitch 2001: 164). "The private criminal lawyer obviously suffers from guilt by association. The public reflexively links the client with his attorney and fails to appreciate the professional and constitutional responsibility which the latter must exercise. The public seems to reason that if a lawyer chooses to defend a guilty man, then the lawyer must himself also be tainted with some guilt" (Wice 1978: 91).

Because his clients are poor financial risks, the private criminal attorney usually requires at least part of his fee in advance—"upfront money." In many cases this is the only fee he can expect to receive. Since the fee any single client can afford to pay is relatively low, the criminal attorney must substitute quantity for quality. That is,

---

[8]A noted exception is Leslie Abrahamson, who has been the defense attorney in a number of high-profile cases. She has written about her experiences (Abrahamson with Flaste 1997).

he must have numerous clients to maintain a profitable criminal practice, and he cannot spend too much time on any single case since the fee is inelastic and extra time will not necessarily result in additional payment. Federal court of appeals judge Frank Easterbrook suggests that defendants who prevail at or before trial be reimbursed for the market cost of legal assistance. "Just as the promise of compensation attracts able counsel to antitrust and civil rights litigation, so it would attract counsel to criminal litigation" (1992: 1974). For defense attorney Richman, "Reasonable doubt begins with the payment of a reasonable fee" (Gourevitch 2001: 160).

It is not unusual for an attorney to find him- or herself prepared for a hearing that fails to take place, because, e.g., the defendant, complainant, or other principal fails to appear or records have been misplaced. Because of the likelihood that any one case scheduled for a court hearing on a particular day will result in a continuance, private attorneys, like airlines, usually overbook (airlines may book more passengers for a flight than the plane has seats, under the assumption that not everyone will actually show up for the flight, and every empty seat represents lost income).[9] Case management becomes a preoccupation as the attorney rushes from courtroom to courtroom juggling his cases, frequently requesting continuances. In New York City, e.g., one study found that 43 percent of the criminal cases were adjourned at least once due to defense counsel trial-scheduling conflicts (Jacobs and Chayet 1986). Since the prosecutor can object to a continuance, and a judge need not grant one, the attorney needs to maintain good relations with the other key actors. This has implications for plea bargaining (Chapter 11).

Public Defender

The public defender is a counterpart of the prosecutor; that is, he or she is a government official. Instead of representing "the people," however, the public defender represents the interests of indigent defendants. Unlike most prosecutors, the public defender is typically not an elected official, but is usually appointed by the judiciary or county board. The reason for using an appointment system is quite simple: On what would an aspiring candidate for public defender base his or her campaign? "If I am elected, more criminal defendants will go free, and others will serve less time in prison"? While a candidate for prosecutor can engage in a great deal of law-and-order rhetoric and posturing, promising to be "tough on criminals," the aspiring public defender is limited in what he or she could possibly do to attract votes. The public defender is an anomaly, "paid by the state to befriend those whom the state believes are its enemies and to question—and, whenever possible, to thwart—the prosecution of those whom the state suspects are criminals" (McIntyre 1987: 1).

A victorious public defender raises the specter of unfairness or incompetence since it can only mean that "(1) the defendant was actually innocent and ought not have been arrested in the first place and prosecuted in the second, or (2) the police and/or prosecutor failed to properly handle the case such that a conviction could be won" (McIntyre 1987: 72). Conventional wisdom in criminal justice

---

[9]Barry Mahoney points out that courts also overbook: "Almost always, courts 'overset' their trial calendars, scheduling more cases for trial on a given day or week than they could possibly try if some did not settle" (1988: 81).

holds that if everyone is doing his or her job properly, the public defender does not win cases. For this reason, public defenders do not usually broadcast their successes for public consumption.

There are statewide and local public defender systems: "Under statewide public defender systems, an individual is designated by statute as the State public defender and is charged with developing and maintaining a system of representation for each of the counties in the State. In such systems, there is usually a governing board that shares responsibility with the State public defender for the operation of the program. Most statewide systems are part of the executive branch, but others may operate as part of the judicial branch, as independent State agencies, or as independent nonprofit organizations" (*Criminal Defense Systems* 1984: 3).

Local public defenders are usually part of county government and are often appointed by the county legislature on a recommendation from the judiciary. An independent nonprofit organization is used in New York City, where the Legal Aid Society represents all indigent criminal defendants except those accused of murder. The society is governed by a board of directors "that's a *Who's Who* of prominent lawyers, businessmen, and educators" (Pileggi 1982: 30). It was founded in New York City in 1876 as *Der Deutscher Rechts-Schutz Verein*, an association to help German immigrants. This limitation and the German name were soon dropped in favor of helping the poor of all nationalities (Brownell 1951). As opposed to public defender offices, which handle only criminal matters, the Legal Aid Society has a civil division.

While public defenders are the primary providers of criminal defense services in only about 35 percent of all counties in the United States, they serve almost 70 percent of the nation's population. More than 40 percent of the largest 50 counties in the nation are served predominantly by a public defender program (*Criminal Defense Systems* 1984; DeFrances and Litras 2000). Like the prosecutor's office, a public defender's office may be organized horizontally ("zone defense"), vertically ("man-to-man defense"), or a combination of the two ("mixed system"). Like the prosecutor, the public defender employs assistant or deputy defenders, who may be full- or part-time, and investigative personnel. Like the prosecutor's office, that of the public defender suffers from a great deal of personnel turnover. The position of an assistant is attractive to lawyers who are interested in gaining a great deal of criminal trial experience in a relatively short period of time. However, the public defender suffers from a lack of "respect" in the legal community and the community at large, a failure to acknowledge the individual public defender's legitimacy as a "real" lawyer (McIntyre 1987).

Like providers of other forms of welfare, the public defender may be resented by the recipients of his or her services. In addition to this attitude toward receiving a necessary beneficence, there is the common folk wisdom that "you only get what you pay for!" Jonathan Casper points out:

> What attracts defendants to private lawyers is, for a large number of them at least, the notion that, because of the financial exchange between lawyer and client, the lawyer will be more committed to the defendant's interests. It is money that provides a sense of control, the leverage to insure that lawyers will listen to their clients, take instructions from their clients, and generally exert themselves on their clients' behalf. Moreover, not only does the client fail to pay, and thus lack this leverage over public defenders, but someone else does. And that someone else is "the state"—the very same institution

that is proceeding against the defendant. Thus, the public defenders suffer not only from the fact that they are imposed upon defendants rather than being selected, and from the absence of financial exchange, but they are employed by the enemy. (1978: 4)

There does not appear to be any significant difference in the conviction rates of defendants represented by private or publicly financed attorneys. However, of those found guilty, "higher percentages of defendants with publicly financed counsel were sentenced to incarceration" (Harlow 2000: 1).

Wice contrasts the public defender with the private criminal attorney. He notes that, by developing a reputation as a successful advocate, a private criminal attorney can improve his or her economic condition. "Public defenders," he writes, "will receive their salaries regardless of the outcome of the case, but private attorneys know that their economic worth is directly related to how well they satisfy their clients." Private attorneys "are motivated to offer several benefits usually unavailable at the public defender's office. Although these advantages may not be related to the ultimate disposition of the case, they nevertheless do heighten the prestige of private criminal lawyers in the eyes of their clientele" (Wice 1983: 41). There are two major advantages of private lawyers:

1. They can provide personalized attention, sometimes referred to as "hand-holding." The large caseloads typical of a public defender's office results in cases being handled horizontally—clients are represented by different attorneys at various stages of the judicial process. Clients do not have their own attorney and cannot drop in for a review of their case in a secluded office. In addition, among criminal clientele, there is prestige in having one's own attorney.

2. Private lawyers are more willing to take an aggressive stance toward both the judge and the prosecutor on behalf of the client. Private criminal attorneys have been found to be much more willing to risk contempt citations and other forms of judicial anger than public defenders, who are often assigned to a specific judge for a length of time; confrontations with the judge could make things quite difficult for the public defender. Some observers, however, have found the opposite—that private attorneys are more willing to compromise, and public defenders are more aggressive. This issue will be looked at again when plea bargaining is discussed in Chapter 11.

But public defenders have advantages, too. As opposed to most attorneys in private practice who handle criminal cases, they have access to their own law libraries and at least limited use of investigators. "Additionally, the public defender is clearly a criminal specialist" and, "because of his continued involvement with the prosecutors and judiciary, the public defender can frequently develop a working relationship in which the exchange of favors, so necessary to greasing the squeaky wheel of justice, can directly benefit the indigent defendant" (Wice 1985: 65). Lisa McIntyre is more cynical; to her, the public defender merely serves to provide legitimacy for the criminal justice system: "The role of the public defender is not justice, but is to strengthen the perception that justice is being done, to make the system appear more legitimate" (1987: 52). Since all indigent criminal defendants are entitled to legal representation, without public defender systems large urban jurisdictions would be unable to process their enormous criminal caseloads. One study found that private attorneys, as opposed to public defenders, received more favorable plea bargain offers for their clients. Thus, "persons unable to afford the services of a private attorney must face more punitive or severe conditions as part of their plea bargain agreements" (Champion 1989: 262).

Assigned Counsel

One study (Smith and DeFrances 1996) revealed that about three-fourths of the inmates in state prisons and about half in federal prisons received public defender or assigned counsel for the offense for which they were serving. About 60 percent of the counties in the United States use court-appointed private attorneys as the primary method for providing legal representation for indigent criminal defendants. These are primarily rural counties with small populations; their limited number of cases do not justify a salaried public defender system. Even in counties that use a public defender system, many defendants are represented by private attorneys assigned by the trial judge.

There are two reasons for this. First, when public defenders are unable to handle their caseloads adequately, especially during certain peak seasons, judges supplement them by appointing private counsel. Second, the court will appoint attorneys when there is a conflict of interest because one attorney or a single law firm (the public defender's office fits this definition) would be representing codefendants. There is always a potential conflict of interest between codefendants, because one may testify against the other(s) in return for leniency or to exculpate him- or herself.

Private attorneys in most jurisdictions are assigned by individual judges on an ad hoc, case-by-case basis. In some areas, however, the assignment of private counsel is more systematic and involves an administrator who oversees the program and develops standards and guidelines. In a few jurisdictions, responsibility for appointment is given to the public defender or clerk of the court. In a growing number of jurisdictions, there are contract services: Private attorneys or a law firm are under contract to provide legal services for indigent criminal defendants. This system has been criticized (much like HMOs—health maintenance organizations) for placing cost containment before quality representation and creating incentives to plead cases rather than go to trial (Spangenberg et al. 2000).

In most jurisdictions, a list of attorneys who have requested to be considered for appointment provides the basis for assigning private counsel. Compensation for assigned counsel is usually based on a fee schedule for in-court and out-of-court hours spent on a case. The hourly fee varies with the jurisdiction and sometimes with the complexity of the case. Hourly fees are considerably less than what an attorney would normally expect for representing a private client—but payment is guaranteed.

Some jurisdictions, such as New York City, have a difficult time finding attorneys who will accept assignments to represent indigent defendants, and salary explains why: in the year 2001, the rate was $40 per hour for work performed in court and $25 per hour for work performed out of court. (By way of contrast, Colorado pays $50 and $40.) As a result, trials in serious cases—murder, rape, and robbery—are repeatedly delayed because overloaded assigned counsel are often on trial in other cases on virtually a continual basis. When criminal cases are delayed this long, prosecutors often have great difficulty securing their witnesses for trial and criminal defendants are

Justice v. Assigned Counsel

In New York City, "underpaid, ill-prepared, virtually unsupervised private attorneys some-times represent hundreds of defendants per year, leaving little time or incentive for them to master the facts, prepare and argue the cases or file appeals of dubious convictions" ("Drive-by Legal Defense" 2001: 26).

denied a speedy resolution of the charges against them. An investigation found that in New York City assigned counsel were woefully inadequate (Fritsch and Rohde 2001a, b). In 2001, lawyers in New York City refused to take Family Court assignments, causing a due process crisis in that court. Meanwhile, criminal cases continued to back up because of a shortage of attorneys for indigent defendants.

Assigned private attorneys suffer from much the same negative client perception as do public defenders. One study found that "attorneys with public clients labor in the shadow of the 'public defender' stereotype. Whether they actually work as public defenders makes no difference, their clients give them little respect and distrust them" (Flemming 1988: 230).

In the next chapter, we will examine criminal justice and the jury trial.

INTERNET CONNECTIONS

National Institute of Justice: *ojp.usdoj.gov/nij*

National Criminal Justice Reference Service: *ncjrs.org*

Legal Resource Center: *crimelynx.com/research.html*

National Judicial College: *judges.org*

Council for Court Excellence: *courtexcellence.org/links.html*

National District Attorneys Association: *ndaa.org*

American Judges Association: *aja.ncsc.dni.us*

American Judicature Society: *ajs.org*

REVIEW QUESTIONS

1. Why are the graduates of elite law schools seldom found as trial judges or prosecutors in the state courts?

2. What are the roles and responsibilities of a trial judge?

3. How can the conciliation skills of a trial judge be as important as his or her trial skills?

4. What are the four basic systems for selecting judges?

5. What are the advantages and disadvantages of three of these systems?

6. What is the role of the U.S. Senate in the selection of a federal district judge?

7. What is the role of the American Bar Association in the selection of federal judges?

8. Why is the American Bar Association role in the judicial selection process controversial?

9. What is the Missouri Plan, and how does it operate?

10. How are judges removed in the federal system?

11. What are the methods for disciplining judges in state systems?

12. What is the role of the Solicitor General?

13. What are the powers of a prosecutor that make him or her the most powerful person in the criminal justice system?

14. What are the advantages and disadvantages of early case screening by a prosecutor's office?

15. What are the advantages and disadvantages of vertical ("man-to-man") prosecution?

16. What are the advantages and disadvantages of horizontal ("zone") prosecution?

17. Why does the role of criminal defense counsel require a disregard for "justice"?

18. Why do relatively few attorneys in private practice accept criminal cases?

19. Why are most public defenders appointed, while prosecutors are typically elected?

20. Why do criminal defendants usually prefer private counsel to representation by a public defender?

21. Why is it necessary to have assigned counsel when there is a public defender's office in operation?

10

CRIMINAL JUSTICE

In the last chapter we examined the key actors in the legal system, all of whom are attorneys, and in previous chapters we looked at the role of attorneys in the appellate process. In this and the two chapters that follow, we will look at the public stage upon which attorneys are the stars, and at the scenarios of criminal trials, plea bargaining, and civil trials. The trial brings together two opposing attorneys whose combat in an adversarial system is refereed by a judge. In some cases, the judge also acts as a finder of fact; in other cases, this responsibility is left to a jury. In this chapter we will be concerned with the criminal jury trial[1] (see Figure 10–1).

AMERICAN CRIMINAL JUSTICE

The administration of criminal justice in the United States reflects the highly decentralized nature of our governmental structure. While policing is basically a municipal responsibility, there are also county and state police agencies. A county may have dozens of police agencies—more than 135 in Cook County (Chicago), Illinois—and a single municipality may have specialized police agencies for public housing and/or

---

[1]For a criminal attorney's intimate look at a jury in New Jersey considering a 1982 murder case, see Wishman (1986). For a detailed look at another jury trial, also involving a murder, see Heymann and Kenety (1985). Valerie Hans and Neil Vidmar (1986) have produced a lively and informative look at the American jury system using as examples highly publicized cases such as those involving John DeLorean, Joan Little, Jean Harris, and John Hinckley.

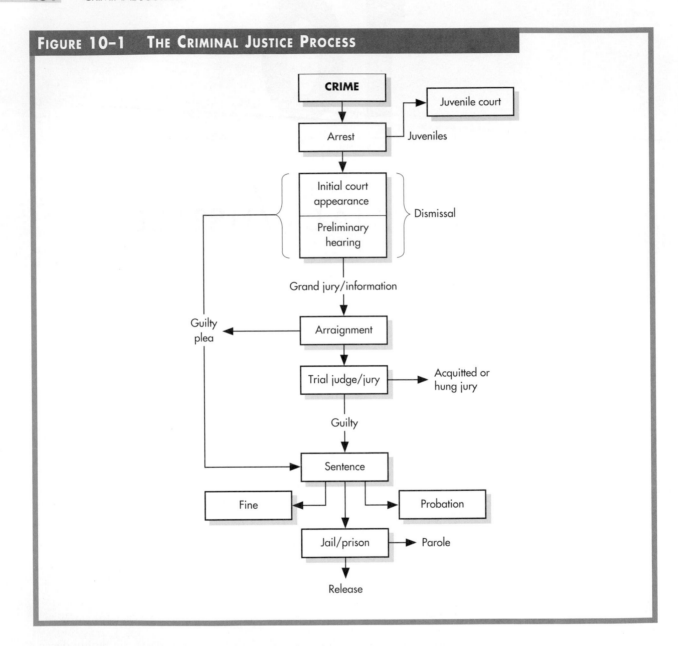

FIGURE 10-1   THE CRIMINAL JUSTICE PROCESS

mass transit. Federal law enforcement agencies such as the Federal Bureau of Investigation and Drug Enforcement Administration have responsibilities that often overlap with those of state, county, and municipal police.

Research has revealed that most crimes are not reported to, or discovered by, the police, and of those that are reported, about one in five is cleared by an arrest. Thus, persons entering the criminal justice system represent the least skilled criminals and/or those whose sheer number of offenses has sufficiently enhanced the probability of detection and arrest.

The prosecutorial function, as discussed in Chapter 9, is usually a county responsibility, but New York City has an elected district attorney in each of its five boroughs. The jail is usually a responsibility of the county sheriff, but many large municipalities (and any number of counties) have their own department of corrections. Probation may be administered at any level of government, in either the judicial or executive branch, while prisons and parole are a state responsibility. And, of course, there is a separate federal system of criminal justice.

CORPUS DELICTI

Basic to criminal process is the rule of *nullum crimen sine lege*: "No crime without a law." The Constitution (Article 1, Sec. 9) prohibits the passage of an *ex post facto* law and (case law) requires "fair warning" (*McBoyle* v. *United States* 1931) that the behavior is proscribed: "Courts have no jurisdiction in criminal cases unless there is a statute specifically making the defendant's act a crime" (Berman and Greiner 1980: 133). When statutory jurisdiction exists, the state must prove the *corpus delicti* ("the body of the crime"), referring to the substance (or body) of the alleged violation of the criminal law. It includes two elements that must be proved in order to sustain a criminal charge: *actus reus* and *mens rea*.

Actus reus means a wrongful act or deed; it refers to the need to prove that a violation of the criminal law—a crime—actually occurred. *Actus reus* consists of a description of the criminal behavior and evidence that the accused acted accordingly. For example, according to the criminal law of Illinois (Chapter 38: 19-3a), "A person commits residential burglary who knowingly and without authority enters the dwelling place of another with intent to commit therein a felony or theft." Thus, it must be proved that the defendant entered the dwelling place of another without permission of the legal occupant for the purpose of committing a felony, harming the occupant, for example, or taking something of value. The defendant's fingerprints found inside a dwelling, to which he had never been given legal access, may be sufficient as proof of actus reus—i.e., burglary—while possession of jewelry belonging to the occupant, which the defendant had not been given permission to possess, would constitute evidence of *mens rea*: intent to commit theft.

Mens rea, "guilty mind," is a legal standard referring to the question of *intent*—the mental state accompanying an illegal act. In order to prove the *corpus delicti*, the prosecutor must show that the defendant had a wrongful purpose—willfulness—in carrying out the *actus reus*. Thus, a person lawfully employed by a moving company who mistakenly entered the wrong apartment and mistakenly removed household items was devoid of *mens rea*. *Mens rea* may also be absent as a result of infancy or mental incapacity. (This issue is related to free will versus determinism, discussed later in this chapter.) However, a person who injures or kills another by accident has (general) mens rea if he or she was acting in a reckless manner, for example, driving under the influence of alcohol or drugs. Behavior that is a gross deviation from the standard of care expected of a reasonable person may constitute *mens rea* if it involves a conscious and unjustifiable risk of harm to others: for example, backyard target practice in an urban area. "Intent" may be general or specific. All crimes require general intent, but certain crimes, for example, assault with intent to rape, require evidence of specific *mens rea*.

Some offenses do not require a showing of general or specific *mens rea*. In cases of *strict or absolute liability*, the intentions of the perpetrator are irrelevant. If the law prohibits possessing a concealed firearm, a claim of ignorance—not knowing that it is illegal in that jurisdiction—is not an acceptable defense. Persons accused of violating federal environmental protection laws can be prosecuted without regard to intent.[2] Except in drug, weapons, and certain pollution cases, however, the penalties in strict liability cases are usually fines and not imprisonment.

A defendant can also raise an *affirmative defense:* He or she can claim self-defense or entrapment, that government trickery induced him or her to commit a crime that he or she was otherwise not independently predisposed to commit. Prosecutors, however, have wide latitude in demonstrating an "independent predisposition," and it is one of the exceptions to the hearsay rule (discussed later).

DUE PROCESS

Due process is one of the rare legal terms that is meant to be understood literally: the process that is due; procedures to which a person is entitled. Due process was originally derived from English common law dating back to the twelfth century. The concept serves to restrain government from arbitrarily depriving a person of life, liberty, or property (Abraham 1972). The Supreme Court has ruled that a high school student is entitled to some sort of hearing before being suspended from school (*Goss* v. *Lopez* 1975), and students at a *public* university also have rights based on the due process clause of the Constitution. At private schools, however, student disciplinary procedures typically afford few of the rights that attach in criminal cases, and this has been a source of increasing controversy. Students at private colleges can often be expelled on the basis of flimsy evidence and they usually are not permitted to be represented by counsel at disciplinary hearings (Pérez–Peña 1994a; see Stevens 1999 for a discussion of this issue). The amount of due process required in a particular setting is dependent upon what is at stake: While a college student's challenge to a course grade is entitled to only minimal due process, a criminal defendant can lose liberty or even life and is thus provided with the maximum amount of due process available under our system of justice.

In a criminal action, the state is arrayed against an individual defendant. This inherent inequality requires that certain specific procedures be followed, or the defendant cannot be found guilty and punished according to law. There is an inherent tension between society's desire for security and safety and the value we place on liberty. Herbert Packer (1968) refers to this as a conflict between two conceptual models of criminal justice: crime control and due process. (A conceptual model is a way of representing an idea that allows for discussion and understanding of the reality represented by the model.)

---

[2]In civil cases, strict liability dispenses with the need to prove fault. In tort cases involving extremely hazardous activities, such as the lawful use of explosives, the actor is accountable for any reasonably related injuries, even in the absence of a showing of negligence. For an examination of strict liability, see Vandall (1989).

The *Crime Control Model* "is based on the proposition that the repression of criminal conduct is by far the most important function to be performed by the criminal justice process" (Packer 1968: 158). The stress is on achieving the greatest amount of societal security and safety. Effective crime control requires a high level of efficiency: The system must be able to apprehend, prosecute, and convict a large proportion of criminal offenders. However, the system must respond to these cases with only limited resources. Consequently, efficiency demands that cases be handled speedily, with a minimum of formality and without time-consuming challenges. This efficiency can be accomplished only by a presumption of guilt: "The supposition is that the screening processes operated by the police and prosecutors are reliable indicators of probable guilt" (1968: 160). To maximize crime control after this screening, the system must move expeditiously to conviction and sentencing. The crime control model is characterized by a high level of confidence in the ability of police and prosecutors to separate the guilty from the innocent. It is a model that tends toward an inquisitorial system of justice and conflicts with the due process model.

The *Due Process Model* stresses the need to protect individual liberty. It assumes that the criminal justice system is deficient and stresses the possibility of error (1968: 163): "People are notoriously poor observers of disturbing events—the more emotion-arousing the context, the greater the possibility that recollection will be incorrect; confessions and admissions by persons in police custody may be induced by physical or psychological coercion so that the police end up hearing what the suspect thinks they want to hear rather than the truth; witnesses may be animated by a bias or interest that no one would trouble to discover except one specially charged with protecting the interests of the accused (as the police are not)."

Due process confronts crime control and its need for efficiency and speed with an obstacle course of formalities, technicalities, and civil rights: "Power is always subject to abuse—sometimes subtle, other times, as in the criminal justice process, open and ugly. Precisely because of its potency in subjecting the individual to the coercive power of the state, the criminal justice process must . . . be subjected to controls that prevent it from operating with maximal efficiency" (1968: 166). The

CRIME CONTROL VERSUS DUE PROCESS

The conflict between the crime control and due process models of criminal justice can be conceived of as a zero-sum continuum: Court decisions or legislation that move criminal justice toward one model do so at the expense of the other. Exceptions to the exclusionary rule, e.g., while they may increase police efficiency in certain instances, also lessen the ability of the courts to control police misconduct.

Crime Control   **Due Process**

←--→

Efficiency   Liberty

due process model requires the system to slow down until it "resembles a factory that has to devote a substantial part of its input to quality control" (1968: 165)—due process guarantees.

Due Process Guarantees

A finding of guilty requires a level of certainty referred to "as beyond a reasonable doubt," as opposed to the standard in a civil case of "preponderance of the evidence" (something over 50 percent). While this legal concept cannot be quantified, it would certainly be far in excess of 50 percent: The juror must be fully satisfied or entirely convinced of the defendant's guilt. In *Sandoval* v. *California* (1994), the Supreme Court defined *reasonable doubt* as "not a mere possible doubt . . . [but] that state of the case which after the entire comparison and consideration of all the evidence, leaves the minds of the jurors in that condition that they cannot say they feel an abiding conviction, *to a moral certainty*, of the truth of the charge." If a juror cannot conclude, based only on the evidence presented and admitted at trial, beyond any reasonable doubt that the defendant committed the crime alleged, the juror must vote for a verdict of "not guilty." In 1993, the Supreme Court (*Sullivan* v. *Louisiana*) ruled that if a judge failed to instruct the jury properly on this issue, a guilty verdict is invalid (it is not a "harmless error").

There is a series of guarantees that are part of the Constitution or Supreme Court rulings (case law) based on the Constitution. While the Constitution provides a number of due process rights, particularly in the first 10 amendments (Bill of Rights), these were not automatically applicable to the states, although many states have similar provisions. Slowly, over a considerable period of time, the Supreme Court has applied many of these rights to the states, usually through the vehicle of the Fourteenth Amendment (discussed in Chapter 3).

While the Supreme Court determines the minimum level of due process to which a defendant is entitled, states have the sovereign power to provide rights beyond those embodied in the U.S. Constitution, and most states provide additional rights by statute or a result of judicial interpretation of a state constitution. Thus, while the Supreme Court has ruled that six-person juries and less than unanimous decisions by 12-member juries are constitutional, most states require unanimous decisions by 12-member juries. In New York, the state's highest court (Court of Appeals) has ruled in more than a dozen cases that the state constitution extends protections to individuals beyond those granted by the U.S. Supreme Court. "The Court of Appeals

REASONABLE DOUBT

While criminal statutes, e.g., Illinois (Ch. 38: 3–1), typically declare "no person shall be convicted of any offense unless his guilt thereof is proved beyond a reasonable doubt," the term reasonable doubt is not defined. Like other legal standards, reasonable doubt defies quantification. It infers a degree of certainty that is conclusive and complete. It is however, less than certainty—no possibility of error—since that would be an impossible standard to expect of a human tribunal.

has ruled, e.g., that the state demands a more stringent standard for searching a car or closing an adult bookstore" (Kolbert 1990: 12). "Over the past decade, state courts increasingly have been interpreting state constitutions more broadly than the U.S. Supreme Court interprets the federal Constitution" ("State Courts Providing Broader Constitutional Protections" 1993: 1), a process known as *judicial federalism* (Jones 1997). This has been particularly true in the area of criminal due process (Coffin 1994).

Right to Remain Silent.   According to the Fifth Amendment, a person cannot "be compelled in any criminal case to be a witness against himself." Thus, the government must prove the allegation beyond a reasonable doubt, and the defendant is protected from having to assist in this endeavor. The basis for providing this protection is the long history of coerced confessions which undermined justice in a number of respects, the most obvious of which is that coercion encourages torture. The innocent may falsely admit guilt; in addition to the obvious moral dimension, this permits the guilty to escape sanctions. The Fifth Amendment, however, protects only against verbal testimony. The government may compel a defendant to provide blood, hair, voice, and handwriting samples, participate in a lineup, or put on articles of clothing. Even a defendant's diary can be used against him or her.

In 1966, the Supreme Court interpreted the Fifth Amendment (*Miranda* v. *Arizona*) to require that before a suspect can be questioned by the police, he or she must be informed of the right to remain silent as well as the right to counsel during any questioning. Since that time, however, the Court has restricted the application of *Miranda* in a number of ways. In 1984, the Supreme Court, in a 5–4 decision (*New York* v. *Quarles*), ruled that "overriding considerations of public safety" may justify questioning a suspect in custody without providing the warnings contained in *Miranda*. The public safety exception was the result of a woman's complaint to two New York City police officers that she had been raped and that the suspects had entered a nearby supermarket. The officers entered the store and apprehended one of the suspects, who was found to be wearing a shoulder holster. One of the officers asked whether he had a gun. The suspect nodded toward a pile of boxes and said, "The gun is over there." The Court ruled that the unattended firearm represented an immediate danger to public safety, and the gun and the statement were admitted into evidence.

In 1985, the Court handed down a decision in the case of *Oregon* v. *Elstad* that affected the *Miranda* decision. Pursuant to an arrest warrant, the police went to the home of an 18-year-old suspect and explained to him that they thought he was

Miranda v. Arizona

"The current [1966] practice of incommunicado interrogation is at odds with one of our nation's most cherished principles—that the individual may not be compelled to incriminate himself. Unless adequate protective devices are employed to dispel the compulsion inherent in custodial surroundings, no statement obtained from the defendant can truly be the product of his free choice."

involved in a burglary. He responded, "Yes, I was there." An hour later at the police station, the officers informed the suspect of his *Miranda* rights. He indicated that he understood and gave a full confession. On appeal the Court ruled that the statement "I was there" was inadmissible; however, the Court ruled that the second confession was valid despite defense arguments that it was an extension of the original inadmissible confession and was thereby tainted.

In a 1986 decision (*Moran* v. *Burbine*), the Court ruled that a suspect's *Miranda* rights were not violated when the police misled his attorney. Brian Burbine had been arrested for the brutal murder of a woman. An assistant public defender telephoned the police station where Burbine was being held and was told that there would be no questioning until the next day. The suspect was not informed of the call. About an hour later, Burbine was advised of his rights and confessed to the murder. The Court ruled that "events occurring outside of the presence of the suspect and entirely unknown to him, surely can have no bearing on the capacity to comprehend and knowingly relinquish a constitutional right." In that same year, the Court ruled (*Colorado* v. *Connelly* 1986) that confessions of mentally ill defendants are admissible: A criminal suspect's "perception of coercion flowing from the 'voice of God,' however important or significant such perception may be in other disciplines, is a matter to which the United States Constitution does not speak."

In 1990, the Court upheld a murder confession given by an inmate to an undercover police officer posing as a fellow inmate. In an 8–1 decision the Court ruled that the *Miranda* decision prohibits *coercion*, not *deception*. In this case, the inmate confessed to an unsolved murder for which he had not been charged (*Illinois* v. *Perkins*). In a 6–2 decision that went in the other direction, the Court ruled that once a suspect in custody has asserted his right to an attorney, the police may no longer question him unless counsel is actually present. The decision overturned a murder conviction based on questions asked of the suspect after he had consulted with an attorney (*Minnick* v. *Mississippi* 1990). The following year, in a narrow (5–4) decision (*Arizona* v. *Fulminante*), the Court held that even when a confession is coerced or involuntary, its admission into trial can be a "harmless error" that need not reverse a finding of guilty if the remainder of the evidence was sufficient beyond a reasonable doubt. In addition to Supreme Court decisions limiting the application of *Miranda*, there are reports that police tactics are routinely chipping away at the Fifth Amendment rights of suspects (Hoffman 1998a, 1998b). In 2001, the Court on such an issue (*Texas* v. *Cobb*). In this case, the defendant was free on bail for burglary and denied knowing anything about two apparent murders. After confessing to his father that he had committed the murders, the defendant was arrested and questioned by the police, who obtained a written confession in the absence of counsel. The Court ruled 5–4 that the right to counsel is "offense-specific." That is, police can question a suspect without his or her lawyer present even if the suspect is being represented by counsel in a closely related crime. In 2000, the Court affirmed the *Miranda* decision by a vote of 7–2 (*Dickerson* v. *United States*).

Right to Counsel.   At the time of the American Revolution, defendants in England were not entitled to be represented by counsel, even at their own expense, except in cases of treason (McIntyre 1987). The right to counsel became part of the Constitution through the Sixth Amendment, which guarantees the accused "the assistance of Counsel for his defence." But it was not until 1963 that the Supreme Court ruled that states must provide counsel for all indigent defendants in felony cases (*Gideon* v. *Wainwright*). In the opinion of Justice Hugo Black: "That government hires lawyers to prosecute and defendants who have the money hire lawyers to defend are the strongest indications of the widespread belief that lawyers in criminal courts are necessities, not luxuries. The right of one charged with a crime to counsel may not be deemed fundamental and essential in some countries, but it is in ours."[3] Subsequently, this right was extended to misdemeanor cases where imprisonment might result (*Argersinger* v. *Hamlin* 1972). The right to appointed counsel is not limited to court, but extends to any time the police wish to ask a suspect questions (*Miranda*).

While the criminal defendant has an absolute right to counsel, the question of attorney competency is not as clear. Defendants often challenge their convictions by arguing on appeal that they were represented by ineffective counsel. In general, for the defendant to prevail, he or she must show that counsel made errors that were so serious as to deny the constitutional right to representation; and that the deficient performance prejudiced the defense (*Strickland* v. *Washington* 1984).

Right to Bail.   As noted in Chapter 8, the Constitution is vague on a number of important issues; one of them is bail. While the Eighth Amendment prohibits "excessive bail," no definition of "excessive" is provided. For a person without means, a bail of even $25 can be excessive, while some major drug dealers find no difficulty raising $1 million for bail. In 1987, the Supreme Court ruled that defendants found to constitute a danger to public safety may be held without the setting of bail (*United States* v. *Salerno*), and persons charged with murder are generally held without bail. In some states, bail bondsmen, who are privately licensed entrepreneurs, provide a defendant's bail for a fee, generally 10 percent of the bond. If the defendant fails to return to court as required in the bail agreement, the bond is forfeited. Bail bondsmen employ skip-tracers ("bounty hunters") to apprehend bail jumpers. Jumping bail is an additional criminal offense for which a judge issues an arrest warrant providing law enforcement agents (and bounty hunters) with authority to arrest the wayward defendant.

Many defendants are released without the need for a cash bond or its equivalent (e.g., title to a car or house); known as release on recognizance (ROR), this is an unsecured pledge to return to court on the appointed date to stand trial. In some jurisdictions there are programs designed to maximize the number of persons who can qualify for ROR. The best known of these programs, the Manhattan Bail Project, was developed by the Vera Foundation in New York City and has been copied by many jurisdictions. Defendants are interviewed by pretrial investigators (who are sometimes law students) and the results are entered on a point scale form (see Figure 10–2). "A number of items dealing with the defendant's ties in the community (e.g., employment, residence, and family ties) and relevant criminal justice factors (such as prior record, current charge, or prior bail violations) are included in the scale. Normally a defendant is given plus or minus points for each item. The information obtained in the interview is then verified by referring to records, employers, and family members. If the defendant has attained a certain number of points, a recommendation is made to the court for release" (Kirby 1977: 1).

---

[3]Plaintiff Clarence Gideon, of course, was indigent. He was represented by Abe Fortas, who was appointed by the Supreme Court to act pro bono.

FIGURE 10-2 ORIGINAL VERA POINT SCALE—MANHATTAN BAIL PROJECT

To be recommended, defendant needs:

1. A New York area address where he can be reached and
2. A total of five points from the following categories.

Interview	Verified	
		Prior Record
1	1	No convictions
0	0	One misdemeanor conviction
−1	−1	Two misdemeanor or one felony convictions
−2	−2	Three or more misdemeanor or two or more felony convictions
		Family Ties (in New York area)
3	3	Lives in established family home and visits other family members (immediate family only)
2	2	Lives in established family home (immediate family)
		Employment or School
3	3	Present job 1 year or more, steadily
2	2	Present job 4 months or present and prior 6 months
1	1	Has present job which is still available OR unemployed 3 months or less and 9 months or more steady prior job OR unemployment compensation OR welfare
3	3	Presently in school, attending regularly
2	2	Out of school fewer than 6 months but employed, or in training
1	1	Out of school 3 months or fewer, unemployed and not in training
		Resident (in New York area steadily)
3	3	1 year at present residence
2	2	1 year at present and last prior residence or 6 months at present residence
		6 months at present and last prior residence or in New York City 5 years or more
		Discretion
+1	+1	Positive, over 65, attending hospital, appeared on some previous case
−1	0	Negative—intoxicated—intention to leave jurisdiction

Total Interview Points _____

Interview Verified _____

Recommended _____

Not Recommended _____

Source: Kirby (1977).

Persons who are unable to effect a release on bail are held in custody in a jail. This subjects legally innocent persons to punishment; separates them from family, friends, and employment; limits them in assisting their attorneys in the defense process; and adds to the severe overcrowding that is characteristic of most jails.

While incarceration is always an unpleasant experience, it is even more so in a jail. Most provide few opportunities for recreation, and they are usually understaffed and overcrowded, subjecting the inmates to the possibility of physical and/or sexual assault by other prisoners.

The basic purpose of bail is to guarantee a defendant's return to court, but it is often used as a form of preventive detention. When there is strong belief that the defendant will return to crime, a judge, often on the recommendation of the prosecution, will set bail at a level that is impossible for the defendant to make. The use of bail in this manner, while not illegal, is controversial. It involves predictions of future behavior, always a questionable undertaking with important moral and legal dimensions. The judge's bail decision is influenced by the defendant's previous criminal record, previous behavior while out on bail, roots in the community, the attitude of the prosecutor, and publicity that the case may have generated. Some jurisdictions are using house arrest with electronic monitoring in "bail or jail" decisions.

Right to a Speedy and Public Trial.   Again we are confronted with constitutional vagueness. The Sixth Amendment guarantees that "In all criminal prosecutions, the accused shall enjoy the right to a speedy and public trial, by an impartial jury." But the term "speedy trial" is not defined in the Constitution. In 1972, the Supreme Court (*Barker* v. *Wingo*) ruled that determination of whether a particular defendant has been denied a speedy trial is to be made on a case-by-case basis, and the Court established several tests by which to judge the delay: (1) length of the delay, (2) reasons for the delay, (3) timely assertion of the right to a speedy trial, and (4) prejudice to the defendant as a result of the delay. The Court indicated an interest in preventing oppressive pretrial incarceration, minimizing the anxiety and hardship of the defendant, and avoiding hampering the defense. Delay that hampers the defense can result in the denial of a fair trial, which violates the Fifth and Fourteenth amendments. In response to *Barker*, states and the federal government enacted statutes specifying the amount of time allowed from arrest to trial. The *U.S. Code* (Sec. 3161) provides that "In any case in which a plea of not guilty is entered, the trial of a defendant charged in an information or indictment with the commission of an offense shall commence within seventy days from the filing date (and making public) of the information or indictment, or from the date the defendant has appeared before a judicial officer of the court in which such charge is pending, whichever date last occurs." In Illinois, statutes require that the defendant be brought to trial within 120 days if incarcerated, or 160 days if free on bail; otherwise, the case must be dismissed.

While the Sixth Amendment protects criminal defendants from being tried in secret, can a defendant waive this right or demand a closed trial?[4] In 1986, the Court ruled that the First Amendment's freedom of the press cannot be overcome by a defendant's assertion that a public trial will be prejudicial. In 1986 (*Press-Enterprise Company* v. *Superior Court of California*), the Court ruled that judges may bar the press and the public from pretrial hearings in criminal cases only as a last resort to assure a fair trial, and only after stating why it is necessary to conduct the hearings in secret. Chief Justice Warren E. Burger, writing for the majority, pointed out that "one of the important means of assuring a fair trial is that the process be open to

---

[4]This is an issue only for criminal trials, because the public has no constitutional right to attend a civil trial.

neutral observers." In addition to the trial itself, in 1984 the Court ruled unanimously that trial judges must also ordinarily permit the public and news media to attend jury selection proceedings (*Press Enterprise* v. *Superior Court*).

The televising of trials has also added new meaning to the term "public." Almost all states permit television coverage of at least some of their judicial proceedings, and the federal courts experimented with broadcasting civil cases for three years. Although no problems had been reported, in 1994 the Judicial Conference of the United States Courts voted to end the practice. On July 1, 1991, cable television introduced "Court TV," which offers a continuous variety of trials, some taped, some live, to interested viewers. During trial breaks, guest attorneys present their views of the proceedings. These broadcasts provide the public with more accurate versions of the justice process, often in stark contrast to the stylized and summarized portrayals on television dramas.

Right to Confront Witnesses.

The Sixth Amendment requires that the defendant "be informed of the nature and cause of the accusation; to be confronted with the witnesses against him; to have compulsory process for obtaining witnesses in his favor." Thus the defendant can subpoena a witness to testify in his or her defense and has the unlimited right to cross-examine adverse witnesses (discussed later in this chapter).

Double Jeopardy Prohibited.

The Fifth Amendment forbids double jeopardy, stating that no person shall "be subject for the same offence to be twice put in jeopardy of life or limb." Once a defendant has been acquitted (not guilty), he or she can never be tried again for the same crime. Jeopardy attaches when the jury is impaneled and sworn, and in a bench trial when the judge begins to hear evidence. (Jeopardy issues are not relevant in civil or administrative proceedings.) The Court has permitted separate trials in federal and state courts based on the same act (e.g., murder in a state court and civil rights violations based on the murder in federal court), and in more than one state. In the case of four Los Angeles police officers accused of beating Rodney King, they were acquitted in state court and tried again in federal court for civil rights violations based on their actions in the same incident.

In *Heath* v. *Alabama* (1985), the Court ruled that two states may prosecute a defendant for the same criminal act without violating the Fifth Amendment. Larry Heath was sentenced in Alabama and Georgia for hiring two men to kidnap and kill his pregnant wife. She was kidnapped from their home in Alabama and shot to death in Georgia. In order to avoid a possible death sentence, Heath pled guilty in Georgia to a noncapital crime. He was subsequently tried and convicted of the same charges in Alabama and sentenced to death. The Court ruled that because each state is sovereign, the defendant had committed separate offenses against the law of each and, therefore, the convictions were an exception to the double jeopardy clause.

The double jeopardy clause also prohibits multiple punishment for the same offense. However, in 1997, the Court ruled 9–0 in favor of the imposition of both criminal and civil sanctions on an offender for the same behavior. *Hudson et al.* v. *United States* involved three bank officers who had agreed to pay civil fines to the government for making illegal loans from banks they had run in the 1980s. The government subsequently indicted them, which the Court, reversing a precedent established eight years before (*United States* v. *Halper*), ruled permissible.

Exclusionary Rule

This legal principle, sometimes referred to as the "poisoned fruit doctrine," is based on the Fourth and Fourteenth Amendments and prohibits evidence obtained in violation of the Constitution from being used at trial—if the tree (the search) is poisoned, so by logical extension is its fruit (the evidence). Thus, even evidence proving a defendant's guilt beyond a reasonable doubt cannot be entered into evidence if it was secured in an unconstitutional manner (*Weeks* v. *United States* 1914; *Mapp* v. *Ohio* 1961). The exclusionary rule is the Court's way of controlling the behavior of law enforcement agents: It renders certain improper activities not worth the effort (since the results will be inadmissible). A great deal of criticism has been leveled at the exclusionary rule, particularly by persons in law enforcement and political conservatives. They have argued that the proper remedy for unconstitutional activity by the police is a tort, not the suppression of evidence; to paraphrase Justice Cardozo, why should the criminal go free because the police blundered? Supporters of the rule contend that a tort action is an awkward mechanism for controlling police behavior, and it assumes that the victim of police misconduct will be able to secure adequate legal assistance. On the other hand, personal liability may actually prove too great a restraint on police activity, police officers being reluctant or unwilling to act even when they have lawful authority.

Since the Court's decision in *Mapp*, a series of (often confusing) cases has limited its application without overturning its basic premise—controlling police behavior. In 1968, the Court ruled that with "reasonable suspicion" a police officer is permitted to

MAPP v. OHIO

In 1914, the Supreme Court ruled (*Weeks* v. *United States*) that if federal agents seize evidence in violation of the Fourth Amendment, it can be (on a motion by the defense) excluded from use at trial. For more than 40 years, this exclusionary rule did not apply to state officials.

On May 23, 1957, three Cleveland police officers arrived at the home of Dollree Mapp and demanded admittance because they believed that a fugitive, as well as a large amount of illegal lottery paraphernalia, was being hidden in the house. After telephoning her lawyer, Mapp refused to let the police into her house. The officers conducted a surveillance, and three hours later, with additional officers, they forced their way into the house. Mapp and her attorney, who had arrived at the scene, demanded to see the search warrant. One of the officers held up a piece of paper. Mapp seized the paper and was arrested and handcuffed. The entire house was thoroughly searched, and police discovered obscene materials. No evidence that a search warrant had ever been issued was presented at the subsequent trial. Despite this apparent violation of the Fourth Amendment, Mapp was convicted of possessing obscene materials.

On appeal, the Supreme Court held that "the State, by admitting evidence unlawfully seized, served to encourage disobedience to the Federal Constitution which it is bound to uphold." The Court concluded, "The ignoble shortcut to conviction . . . tends to destroy the entire system of constitutional restraints on which the liberties of the people rest." Through the Fourteenth Amendment, the Court applied the exclusionary rule to the states.

stop and frisk a suspect even in the absence of probable cause—for the officer's protection (*Terry* v. *Ohio*). In 2000, the Court ruled (*Illinois* v. *Wardlow*) that flight at the mere sight of a police officer is sufficient to justify a stop-and-frisk search. Later that year, however, the Court ruled (*Florida* v. *J. L.*) unanimously that an anonymous tip that a person is carrying a gun, absent any further sign that the information is reliable, is not sufficient to justify a stop and frisk.

In 1984 (*United States* v. *Leon*) the Court ruled that when the police act on a defective search warrant, the exclusionary rule need not apply, since its purpose is to control the behavior of the police, not of judges (who issue warrants). In the same year, the Court established the doctrine of *inevitable discovery* as an exception to the exclusionary rule in *Nix* v. *Williams* (a continuation of a famous 1977 case, *Brewer* v. *Williams*). Robert Williams was suspected of killing a 10-year-old girl, and 200 volunteers combed the Des Moines, Iowa, area searching for her body. The police promised the suspect's attorney that they would not question Williams, but as they were driving Williams across the state, they asked him to think about the fact that "the parents of this little girl should be entitled to a Christian burial" for their daughter. His led police to the victim's body.

In the 1977 case decision, the Court ruled that the "Christian burial" speech had violated the suspect's constitutional rights by inducing him to incriminate himself outside his lawyer's presence. Williams was tried again, and the prosecutors did not offer into evidence any incriminating statements of the defendant, nor did the state attempt to show that Williams had directed police to the body. The trial judge admitted the prosecution's evidence as to the condition of the body and related physical evidence on grounds that the prosecution had shown that, even if Williams had not been improperly interrogated, the victim's body would nevertheless have been found by the search party. In its decision, the Court gave recognition to the principle of inevitable discovery.

In *Colorado* v. *Bertine* (1987), the Court created an inventory exception to the exclusionary rule when it stated that police need not secure a search warrant to look into closed containers found in a confiscated vehicle. Police found illegal drugs in a closed backpack after a drunk-driving arrest. The Court ruled that police were following standardized procedures by opening closed containers and listing their contents during a vehicle inventory. The Court noted that knowledge of the precise nature of property found in vehicles for which the police have a responsibility helps to guard against claims of theft, vandalism, or negligence.

In *Maryland* v. *Garrison* (1987), the Court established a *reasonable mistake* exception to the exclusionary rule. Police officers in Baltimore, acting on a valid search warrant, entered the wrong apartment in a multiunit dwelling, where they found illegal drugs. The Court ruled that under the circumstances—two apartments on a floor that the police reasonably believed contained only one apartment—the Constitution had not been violated. Later in 1987 the Court appeared to move in a different direction. In *Arizona* v. *Hicks*, the Court ruled that police officers acting on a warrant to search for illegal weapons could not move stereo equipment suspected of being stolen to check the serial numbers.

In 1989, the Court ruled that without a warrant, a police helicopter could hover over a home at an altitude of 400 feet and take pictures without violating the owner's rights. The decision (*Florida* v. *Riley*) did not indicate how low the helicopter could fly before it engaged in an impermissible search. A 1990 case dealt with a longstanding exception to the exclusionary rule: prosecutors have been allowed to use illegally obtained evidence to impeach the testimony of a defendant (*Harris v. New York* 1971). In an Illinois case, that state's highest court ruled that even when a defendant chooses not to testify, illegally secured evidence could be used to impeach the testimony of defense witnesses. The Supreme Court, in a 5–4 decision, refused to allow the Illinois exception (*James v. Illinois* 1990). In 1990, the Court ruled 6–3 that the Constitution does not prohibit American law enforcement agents operating outside the United States from warrantless searches and seizures of property owned by foreigners. The decision appears to prohibit similar searchers of property owned by American citizens in other countries (*United States v. Verdugo-Urquidez*). In 1991, in a 7–2 decision, the Court held that evidence, such as drugs, discarded by a fleeing suspect, can be admitted into trial even in the absence of evidence that police had a sufficient basis for their original suspicion leading to the pursuit. The Court ruled that a chase is not a seizure within the meaning of the Fourth Amendment (*California v. Hodari D.*). In 1995, in a unanimous decision (*Wilson v. Arkansas*), the Court ruled that the police must "knock and announce" their presence when executing a valid search warrant, or evidence discovered will be suppressed. Unless there are specific exigent circumstances—e.g., imminent peril or destruction of evidence—the Court found that the Fourth Amendment does not permit a "no knock" entry. In a 5–4 decision, in 2001, the Court ruled that absent a search warrant, law enforcement officers could not point a heat sensing device at a home to detect evidence of illegal activity—marijuana growing. The decision, *Kyllo v. United States*, was written by Justice Scalia who based it on his view of *original intent* (discussed in Chapter 8): Technology allowing intrusion into space that would have otherwise necessitated physical entry, requires a warrant. To rule otherwise, he argued, "would leave the homeowner at the mercy of advanced technology."

Joinder of Offenses

An issue related to double jeopardy occurs whenever a defendant is alleged to have violated several statutes based on the same act, or several acts that are somehow connected: "Most often, local law grants the prosecutor the option to bring either separate prosecutions or a single prosecution when the several charges arose from the same criminal episode" (Israel and LaFave 1980: 31). However, a prosecutor who opts for separate prosecutions runs the risk of crossing the somewhat nebulous line that constitutes double jeopardy and, in any event, state law and court decisions will typically bar cumulative sentences: "the maximum sentence will be limited to that available for the highest offense on which a conviction is obtained" (1980: 34). At times the court will order two or more indictments or informations to be tried together (joined) if they could have initially been the subject of a single indictment/information. In 1992, however, the Court ruled 9–0 that the Fifth Amendment is not violated by successive prosecutions for committing a crime and then for conspiring to commit that crime. *United States v. Felix* involved prosecutions for the illegal manufacture of methamphetamine and for *conspiracy* to manufacture and distribute the drug.

Conspiracy

Conspiracy is an agreement between two or more persons to commit a criminal act; it is the agreement that becomes the *corpus* (body) of the crime. Conspiracy requires proof (beyond a reasonable doubt) that two or more persons planned to violate the law and (in many but not all jurisdictions) that at least one overt act in furtherance of the conspiracy was made by a conspirator, e.g., the purchase of materials to aid in the transportation or dilution of the drugs. There are several different types of conspiracy (see Abadinsky 2000).

PRETRIAL PROCEDURES

Before we look at the steps in the process used in the adjudication of criminal defendants, we need to note that its details vary from state to state and even between jurisdictions in the same state. Therefore, this chapter will present a generalized version of the criminal trial process that may not match exactly that of every jurisdiction, as shown in Figure 10–3.

Criminal cases usually begin with a summary arrest (that is, an arrest without a warrant) by a police officer acting on his or her own—having seen a crime committed—or on behalf of a civilian complainant, usually the victim of a crime. In either event, the evidence needed to effect a lawful arrest is known as *probable cause:* "That set of facts or circumstances based on reliable information or personal knowledge or observation by an officer which reasonably show and would warrant an ordinary prudent man in believing that a particular person has been guilty of, is threatening, or is about to commit some offense against the law" (Texas Criminal Justice Council 1974: 161). Less frequently, an arrest is made pursuant to a warrant issued by a judge based on information provided by police or an indictment by a grand jury.

Once arrested, the perpetrator, except in some minor offenses (usually involving a motor vehicle), will be transported to a police facility, fingerprinted, photographed, and given the opportunity to make one or more telephone calls. (At this point the procedures vary, and the following are those most frequently encountered.) If the charge is a misdemeanor, a lesser crime for which most jurisdictions provide a penalty of no more than one year of imprisonment, the suspect may be allowed to post bond and appear in court on a subsequent date. If the subject is unable to post bail, or if the charge is a felony, that is, a crime punishable by more than one year of imprisonment, he or she will be transported to a lower court for an initial appearance or (in misdemeanor cases) arraignment usually within 24 hours after the arrest: The charges will be read, the need for assigned counsel considered (in a misdemeanor case a plea is entered), and bail will be set. In misdemeanor cases, the charge(s) may be disposed of at this stage in a process often referred to as *rough justice.*

FIGURE 10-3   THE FLOW OF FELONY CASES

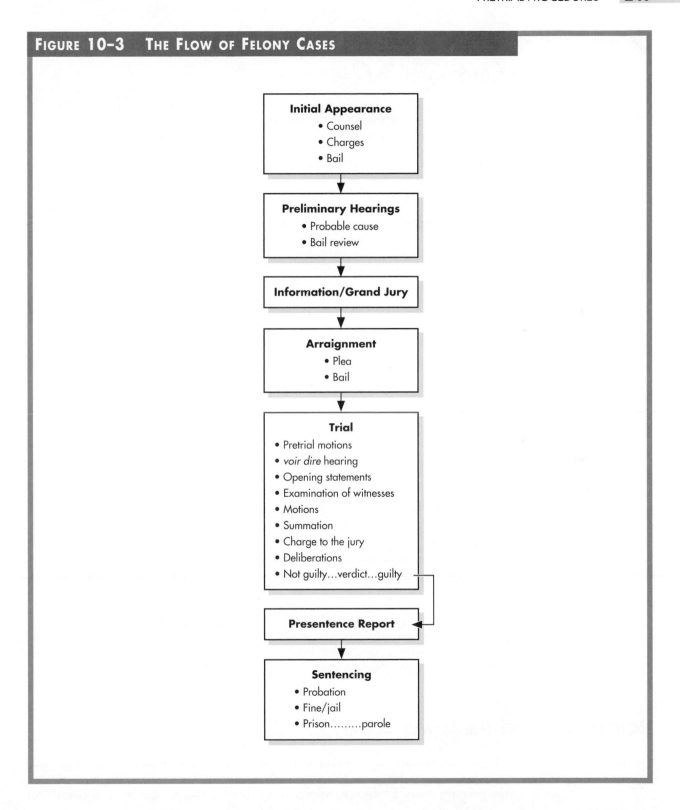

Initial Appearance
- Counsel
- Charges
- Bail

Preliminary Hearings
- Probable cause
- Bail review

Information/Grand Jury

Arraignment
- Plea
- Bail

Trial
- Pretrial motions
- *voir dire* hearing
- Opening statements
- Examination of witnesses
- Motions
- Summation
- Charge to the jury
- Deliberations
- Not guilty…verdict…guilty

Presentence Report

Sentencing
- Probation
- Fine/jail
- Prison………parole

$\mathcal{F}$ELONY $\mathcal{C}$ASES IN $\mathcal{O}$HIO

When a police officer determines that there is probable cause to believe that a crime has been committed by the suspect, an **arrest** will be made. The suspect is "booked" upon arriving at the police district station house. This is essentially an administrative process of acquiring identification information on the suspect and entering it into the arrest log.

The **initial arraignment** is the first court hearing for all persons charged with a criminal offense. The purpose is to inform the defendant of the nature of charge(s) against him or her, to establish the identity of the accused, to have the bail set by the judge, and to have the defendant enter a plea to the charge (for homicide, a plea of not guilty must be entered).

A **preliminary hearing** is held to determine "probable cause" that a crime has been committed and that the accused has committed it. Bond may be re-evaluated and raised or lowered by the judge. The prosecutor will present evidence and witnesses to show probable cause for the arrest charge and for further prosecution of the defendant. The defendant and the defense attorney are present; the attorney will cross examine the state's witnesses and may call defense witnesses. If probable cause is determined, the case is "bound over" to the grand jury; if no probable cause is found, the case is dismissed.

The purpose of the **grand jury** is to determine probable cause. The prosecutor presents "prima facie" (on the face) evidence to the grand jury, but evidence to the contrary is disregarded at this stage. The case is presented through witness testimony and physical evidence is introduced. Grand jury hearings are closed to the public and witnesses called in to testify do so individually. The defendant and the defense attorney are not present—only the prosecutor's side of the case is presented. The grand jury will either decide to indict (prosecute further) or to ignore (dismiss) the case. The grand jury reports these decisions three or four days after the hearing.

The purpose of the (post grand jury) **arraignment** is the same as the initial arraignment—to read the charge(s) against the defendant, to re-evaluate bond, and to have the defendant enter a plea. The defendant and the defense attorney are present, along with the prosecutor and judge.

At a **pretrial hearing**, usually including defense attorney, prosecutor, and judge, the case is usually discussed along with the possibility of a plea bargain. Neither the defendant nor witnesses are present.

The **trial** is the final hearing to determine guilt or innocence of the accused. The defendant has the choice between a trial by jury or by judge. Both prosecution and defense may present witnesses and evidence in their behalf. The jury or the judge then determines guilt or innocence.

If the verdict is guilty, oftentimes a judge will postpone sentencing until a presentence investigation is done. This is a short background history of the defendant written up by the probation department. The probation officer will evaluate the defendant's background, criminal record, employment position, family relationships and ties to the community, etc. If the defendant is found guilty, he or she has the right to **appeal** the conviction.

ROUGH JUSTICE IN THE LOWER COURTS

Most criminal cases begin and end in the lower courts. Because of the large volume of cases entering this part of the criminal justice system, efficient case processing is the primary focus. Efficiency requires speed, but the various due process guarantees to which every criminal defendant is entitled slow down the process considerably. In an effort to avoid delay, judges in the lower courts typically disregard the niceties of due process, and they are assisted in this process by both prosecutor and defense counsel. Defendants may be processed collectively, or at such high rates of speed that individualization is virtually impossible. Dismissals and pleas of guilty predominate, and to the casual or uninformed observer the scene is confusing and not at all resembling popular portrayals of justice—it is rough justice (Feeley 1979). A study by the chief administrative judge in New York revealed that, on average, lower court judges in that city spend a mere 3.4 minutes on each case ("No Trial—and No Punishment Either" 1986). An editorial in the *New York Times* (August 18, 1986: 22) referred to the lower courts in New York as dispensing "cattle car" justice. In Chicago (where I worked for the sheriff), processing occurs so swiftly that defendants are often unaware of the fact that their cases have been dismissed—the inconvenience of being housed in dank and often foul-smelling police and court lockups being viewed as sufficient punishment for innocent and guilty alike.

In order to avoid legal complications that cause delay, the key actors must gain the cooperation of the defendant. This is accomplished by treating him or her in a lenient manner. Thus, defendants who waive their rights and who do not object to the speedy processing receive an outcome considerably more lenient than that to which they might otherwise be entitled. The rare defendant who insists on the full array of due process rights will get them, but there is often a price. Such defendants may be viewed as disruptive, as lacking in any show of contrition and, therefore, deserving of more severe treatment. If convicted they will receive sentences in excess of the norm, and, in the meantime, they may be subjected to relatively high bail and

Nightmare Justice

After an arrest, in New York City a defendant will spend time in a police or court holding pen. For persons unfamiliar with the criminal justice system, the experience can be a nightmare. These cells were originally built to hold persons for a few hours, and they are too small for the numbers they now handle. Detainees are without mattresses, bedding, clean clothing, or showers. Toilet bowls along the walls are encrusted and often overflowing. They are cold in the winter, stifling in the summer, and the stench can be overpowering. Residents may be violent and dangerous; some are sick, suffering from the effects of drugs or alcohol (Glaberson 1990b). In 1991, the Supreme Court ruled that detention prior to appearance before a judicial officer may not exceed 48 hours (*Riverside* v. *McLaughlin*).

But the Supreme Court is not in a position to oversee its mandates, as a Maryland case dramatizes. A homeless man charged by the police with automobile arson spent 13 months in the Baltimore jail without ever appearing before a judge—correction officers failed to take him to court and a warrant was issued for his failure to appear. Despite his protestations, the man remained in jail until a statistician with the state's attorney's office discovered the case on a computer printout. It was later discovered that several other inmates—as many as 100—were also being held without a court appearance (Associated Press, August 13–15, 1991).

a stay in jail awaiting trial. It is no small irony that offenders who raise no objections and quickly plead guilty are often able to avoid incarceration, while those who insist on their innocence may be incarcerated, even if only for a short period of time. A former assistant district attorney in Manhattan reports: "For the down and out, even a hundred dollars' bail guaranteed their waiting in Rikers Island Prison for a trial that might easily be six months away. The message was loud and clear: take my reasonable offer of five days or you're going to rot in Rikers fighting the issues. . . . Strong-arming defendants into a plea was rough justice, but it kept the number of dispositions up, the numbers of 'bodies in the system' down, and sped cases along to a conviction" (Heilbroner 1990: 58).

FELONY CASES

In felonies, the prosecutor may send a case to the grand jury or present evidence at a preliminary (probable-cause) hearing and file an information setting forth the details of the alleged offense, such as date, time, and place.

Grand Jury

The use of a grand jury dates back to King Henry II in twelfth-century England, when it was called the "accusing jury." The king used it to seize jurisdiction of cases handled by the church and baronage, enhancing the royal treasury by claiming fines and forfeitures that flowed from the jury's proceedings. The grand jury was also used to terrorize political enemies (Armstrong 1998). Over the centuries it remained an arm of the king, part of his law enforcement and prosecutorial authority.

In the American colonies, however, grand juries were not an arm of executive power and routinely defied governmental authority. As revolution approached, these juries were generally sympathetic to those resisting British rule; they refused, for example, to indict opponents of the Stamp Act. It was during this period that the grand jury gained a reputation as a protector of the individual against unwarranted prosecution and, as a result, was incorporated into the Fifth Amendment: "No person shall be held to answer for a capital, or otherwise infamous crime, unless on a presentment or indictment of a Grand Jury." England, which originated the grand jury, abolished it in 1933, and the Supreme Court has ruled that this Fifth Amendment requirement does not apply to the states (*Hurtado* v. *California* 1884). Thus, while the federal government operates under the grand jury requirement, states differ in their use of this body.

" . . . What You Pay For"

Public defenders faced with excessive caseloads perform triage: Defendants facing serious felony charges receive primary attention, whereas defendants facing misdemeanor, juvenile delinquency, or lower-level felony charges receive much less" (Spangenberg Group 2001: 4).

In 14 states, the grand jury is required for all felony crimes; in others, it is required in cases of capital and/or life imprisonment cases (Rottman et al. 2000). Many states follow the federal practice of requiring that indictments be used to charge serious crimes but allowing informations (or complaints) to be used to bring charges for lesser felonies and misdemeanors. In 25 states, the use of indictments is a prosecutor's option. Connecticut and Pennsylvania abolished the use of grand juries to return indictments, but kept the investigating grand jury. Even where the use of a grand jury for bringing charges is optional,

> under certain circumstances prosecutors may prefer to use the grand jury or be forced to do so by events outside their control. For example, a grand jury indictment may be used to file charges when the defendant cannot be located and the time limits allowed for prosecution under the statute of limitations are about to be exceeded. Similarly, the secrecy of the grand jury may allow defendants to be charged and taken into custody before they can pose potential danger to a witness's safety or flee from the jurisdiction. In addition, the need to protect the identity of undercover agents, the ability to test a witness before a jury, or the opportunity to involve the community in case screening may be contributing factors. (Emerson 1983: 13)

In the federal system, a grand jury is a body of 23 citizens empowered to operate with a quorum of 16; 12 votes are required for an indictment. In the 50 states, however, while the minimum varies considerably, nowhere does the maximum number of grand jurors exceed 23. While some states adhere to the federal rule of 12 for an indictment, in others the range is anywhere from 4 to 9. Like those serving on a petit or trial jury, grand jurors are generally selected from the voting roles. Because grand jury terms usually last 18 months or more, they tend to include more retired persons. A panel may have no meetings for lengthy periods when prosecutors have no need for them. Sometimes, a grand jury may be involved in more than one case at a time.

The members of a grand jury meet in secret sessions in a court building to consider evidence presented by the prosecutor in the absence of a judge, defendant, or defense attorney. Secrecy prevents subjects from escaping before arrest or tampering with witnesses, and encourages witnesses to speak freely without fear of retaliation. Testimony is recorded by a court stenographer and the transcript can be used at trial if the witness dies or cannot be called to testify for some other reason. If the witness testifies at trial, but says something different than what he or she said before the grand jury, the prosecutor or defense attorney can use the transcript to impeach trial testimony.

A presiding judge convenes the grand jury, usually at the request of the prosecutor, selects the jurors, and rules on any motions that are brought by witnesses who do not want to testify. The judge will also rule on any other legal matters and, at the request of the prosecutor, will provide immunity from prosecution in order to compel testimony that would otherwise be barred by the Fifth Amendment. While a witness can refuse to reply to any questions if the answers may be incriminating, he or she can be granted immunity and, under the threat of being jailed for contempt, be required to answer all questions.

There are two types of immunity:

1. *Transactional immunity* provides blanket protection against prosecution for crimes about which a person is compelled to testify.

2. *Use immunity* prohibits the information provided by a person from being used against him or her, but the person can still be prosecuted using evidence obtained independently of his or her testimony before the grand jury.

Since the members of a grand jury (at least in theory) are not agents of the government—they act as representatives of the citizenry—the extensive due process rights typically enjoyed by a criminal defendant are not relevant to grand jury proceedings. The grand jury meets in secret and its activities and hearings can be kept secret until its term (e.g., 18 months) expires. (In 1990, the Supreme Court ruled in *Butterworth* v. *Smith* that statutes prohibiting grand jury witnesses from ever making their testimony public violate the First Amendment.) Sixteen states permit the subject of a grand jury inquiry to have an attorney present at the hearing, but counsel is permitted only to give advice. In the other states and the federal system, an attorney is not even permitted to accompany his or her client at the hearing. There is no right to present evidence or to cross-examine adverse witnesses.

In most jurisdictions, the grand jury can receive virtually any type of information, even that which would not be admissible at trial, such as certain types of hearsay and evidence that was secured in violation of the Fourth Amendment—the exclusionary rule does not apply to the grand jury (*United States* v. *Calandra* 1974). If a majority of grand jury members vote in support of an indictment, they return a true bill; a failure to indict (no true bill) is a relatively rare event, since jurors have only heard the prosecutor's version of the case.

In every state and the federal system, the grand jury may also be used for investigation. The California constitution, for example, requires that each county impanel a grand jury every year. Such grand juries have the power to, among other things, investigate and report upon the conduct of local government. Investigative grand juries typically have broad investigative authority, including the power to subpoena persons (*subpoena ad testificandum*) and documents (*subpoena duces tecum*). In those states where statutes permit and in the federal system, the grand jury is used to investigate the operations of law enforcement and other government agencies (particularly when corruption is suspected) and the activities of organized crime. In addition to handing down indictments, a federal grand jury (impaneled under the Organized Crime Control Act of 1970) and those of several states are permitted to issue reports. Federal organized-crime grand juries have the power to publish reports at the completion of their terms on certain types of noncriminal misconduct by public officials, although on the state level the practice varies. "Many states prohibit grand jury reports, and those that permit them commonly circumscribe the grand jury's power. Grand juries are generally prohibited from commenting on purely private activity, and reports criticizing publicly elected officials tend to be allowed only where statutory authority exists. Finally, as a rule, grand jury reports may be disclosed only with court approval" (Frankel and Naftalis 1977: 32). While grand jury reports cannot command any particular performance, the widespread publicity they receive usually encourages action by government officials.

The original purpose of the grand jury in the United States was to protect a person from being subjected to prosecution in absence of sufficient evidence. Since the grand jury hears only one side of the case, however, it seldom votes for no true bill, and

Virginia Grand Jury

There are three types of grand juries in the commonwealth: regular, special, and multi-jurisdiction. A regular grand jury is convened at each term of the Circuit Court of each city and county, to attend to the usual matters needing grand jury action. On infrequent occasions a court will convene a special grand jury to investigate some particular matter. Multijurisdiction grand juries involve more than one jurisdiction and are primarily used to investigate drug law violations.

there are many observers who feel that its original purpose has been distorted into being a tool of the prosecutor. The former chief judge of New York State called the requirement for a grand jury indictment a waste of scarce resources. In addition to grand juror fees, he argued, are untold additional and duplicative expenses borne by the taxpayers for court officers, police officers and prosecutorial resources diverted from other activities. Furthermore, he notes, the public often equates an indictment with guilt because it is ignorant of the difference between grand and petit juries, notwithstanding the constitutional presumption of innocence (Wachtler 1990). And, as noted, the subject of a grand jury inquiry is not entitled to the due process guarantees that are normally attach in any other judicial proceeding, such as a preliminary or probable cause hearing. Indeed, federal—and most state—prosecutors are not required to disclose exculpatory evidence to the grand jury (Brenner 1995).

Preliminary/Probable Cause Hearing

If the grand jury is not used, the lower court judge will have witnesses sworn and hear testimony from both prosecution and defense. This process is similar to, but more informal than, the trial process, since its only purpose is to allow a judge to determine whether there is enough evidence (probable cause) to justify continuing the case. In effect, this hearing reviews the sufficiency of evidence used by the police officer to justify an arrest. If no probable cause is found (an infrequent occurrence), the subject is released. If probable cause is found, the prosecutor will file an information, an accusatory document detailing the charges, and the defendant will be arraigned in superior court. In a few jurisdictions, such as Ohio (see box, p. 250), both a preliminary hearing and a grand jury indictment are required before a case can be transferred to superior court (Boland et al. 1988).

Arraignment

After a probable cause hearing and the filing of an information and/or a grand jury indictment, an arrest warrant is issued, and the subject is brought before a judge in superior court for arraignment. He or she is informed of the charges and, if indigent, an attorney will be appointed; bail is set or (if previously set) reviewed; and the subject enters a plea: (1) not guilty, (2) not guilty by reason of insanity, (3) guilty but insane (12 states), (4) guilty, or (5) *nolo contendere*. Literally meaning "I choose not to

Judge's Charge to a Grand Jury, Mississippi

As members of the Grand Jury, you are a part of the judicial branch of state government and have the power of indictment or presentment in a crime and the additional authority to issue reports. The grand jury is the means, not only of bringing to trial persons accused of crime, but also to protect persons from unfounded accusations whether presented by legal officers or by others who may be motivated by public clamor or private malice. Your duty is to allow or to deny issuance of an indictment. There are from 15 to 20 members of a grand jury and 12 members must agree before you can approve an indictment. You will hear only one side of a case. It is not your duty to decide the guilt or innocence of the accused. It is your duty to determine whether there is sufficient evidence or probable cause to require an accused to stand trial. If the evidence establishes a probability that a crime was committed and that the defendant committed the crime, then you should return a "true bill." If the evidence fails to establish a probability that a crime was committed and that the defendant is guilty of that crime, then you must refuse to return a "true bill."

You are cautioned that rumor and hearsay testimony are unreliable. Also, that no person may be compelled to be a witness against himself/herself. A witness who testifies about his/her own participation in crime must first be advised in your presence of his/her constitutional rights by the prosecuting attorney(s) before you may accept such evidence. You determine what witnesses you will permit to appear and testify before you. It is the duty of the prosecutor to be present with the grand jury in the room to present the evidence, to examine the witnesses, and to give advice on any matter of law which may be raised. You are entitled to the legal advice of the prosecutor on matters of law unless you are instructed to the contrary by the court. You are, however, the sole judges of the facts and the prosecutor may not influence you as to whether an indictment will be approved. After the testimony is taken and you are discussing what action you will take, the prosecutor will withdraw from your jury room. Prosecutors are not permitted to be present during your deliberations nor when a ballot is taken and they may not influence your decision on any question of fact. You may request the advice and assistance of the attorney general of the state. You are also at liberty at any time to call for further instructions from the court. You are an independent body. You, as well as the prosecutor, have the right to require the clerk of this court to issue subpoenas for witnesses to be brought before you to testify.

The oath is your promise that you will keep secret what takes place in the grand jury room. A grand juror, except when called as a witness in court, shall not disclose any proceedings or action in relation to offenses brought before it for six months after the adjournment of the grand jury upon which the juror served. A grand juror shall not disclose the name or testimony of any witness who has been before the grand jury. Any disclosure of secrets within the six-month period is punishable by fine or imprisonment for contempt of court.

dispute," and commonly referred to as "no contest," *nolo contendere* pleas are allowed in all federal courts, but in state courts in only about half the states, and both the prosecutor and the judge must agree to the plea. A *nolo contendere* plea has the same effect as a plea of guilty, but it cannot be used as evidence of a criminal conviction at any subsequent civil trial related to the criminal act (Precker 1996).

Persons who plead "guilty but insane" are sentenced as would be any other defendant guilty of the same offense. They do receive mental health attention and treatment if necessary. Persons who refuse to enter a plea have a plea of not guilty automatically entered for them. In practice, many pleas at arraignment are "guilty," since there has often been an agreement to enter a plea of guilty in exchange for some form of leniency. (Plea bargaining is discussed in Chapter 11.) Defendants who plead not guilty or not guilty by reason of insanity are ready to be tried. (Those who plead guilty or *nolo contendere* are ready for a sentencing hearing.)

The (Petit) Jury

The origins of the jury system date back to the early Middle Ages and the *inquisitio*, "which consisted in having the inhabitants of an area interrogated under oath by royal agents. It mainly related to questions of landed property in which the king or the church had an interest" (Van Caenegem 1994: 26). The use of citizens summoned by the Crown to render verdicts became popular after Pope Innocent III in 1215 prohibited ecclesiastical officiation at trials by combat and ordeal. "This step effectively undermined the existing procedural alternatives to the jury and opened the way for its rapid expansion" (Landsman 1993: 26). At first, juries were composed of knowledgeable witnesses who relied on their own knowledge. Gradually, the jury became a disinterested body of laypeople that was to draw its own conclusions based solely on testimony provided by witnesses. As these changes occurred, so did other aspects of legal procedure. Factual questions were strictly separated from legal questions, "so a juror would address only those questions he could comprehend" (Llewellyn 1989: 34).[5]

Juries were available in virtually all civil and criminal cases in Virginia no later than 1624, and they were specifically provided for in the 1641 Massachusetts Body of Liberties (Landsman 1999). In the years prior to the Revolutionary War, the Crown prosecuted American colonists for revenue violations in admiralty courts without juries, rather than risk an acquittal in common pleas courts. Trials for treason were conducted in England, thus removing them entirely from the scrutiny or participation of colonists, practices which helped precipitate the revolution. Even before the Declaration of Independence, each of the 12 states that had adopted a written constitution included the right of the accused to a jury trial (King 1999).

The jury trial was eventually made part of the Constitution for criminal cases by Article III, Section 2, and the Sixth Amendment; but no details were provided. As a result, for nearly two centuries, judges interpreted the jury provisions in Article III and the Sixth Amendment to govern only prosecutions in federal courts for violations of federal criminal law. However, most crimes are state offenses and only a tiny fraction of all criminal prosecutions takes place in federal court. Even though every state guaranteed the right to a jury trial for at least some criminal charges, state law differed as to what that right entailed. This patchwork system of justice, with the state and federal courts following separate laws, sometimes resulted in striking differences in jury procedures. It was not until 1968 (*Duncan* v. *Louisiana*) that the Supreme Court applied the Sixth Amendment's right to a jury trial to the states (King 1999).

The Supreme Court has interpreted the Constitution as requiring a jury trial only when the possible sentence is imprisonment for six months or more, although some states provide jury trials for all criminal defendants. In 1898, the Supreme

---

[5]In England, devoid of a constitution, "the nature and extent of the right to trial by jury are governed by ordinary parliamentary statute, which can be altered by a simple act of Parliament" (Lloyd–Bostock and Cheryl Thomas 1999: 11).

Court ruled (*Thompson* v. *Utah*) that a jury must be "composed of not less than twelve persons," but this was not applied to the states. While most states and the federal government use 12-person juries, the Supreme Court has determined that the number 12 was an "historical accident" and has ruled that juries with as few as six persons are constitutionally permissible except in cases involving a capital crime (*Williams* v. *Florida* 1970). The state of Florida uses six-member juries and in California, if both sides agree, a six-person jury is permitted.

The Court ruled against a five-person jury even in misdemeanor cases (*Bellew* v. *Georgia* 1978). In 45 states, jury decisions (verdicts) are required to be unanimous (Zawitz 1988); otherwise, the result is a hung jury and a retrial or dismissal of the charges. The Court has ruled that jury verdicts of 10–2 (used in Oregon) and 9–3 (used in Louisiana) are constitutionally permitted (*Apodaca* v. *Oregon* 1972; *Johnson* v. *Louisiana* 1972). All states require unanimity in capital cases (Zawitz 1988), and the Supreme Court has ruled that if six jurors are used, the decision must be unanimous (*Burch* v. *Louisiana* 1979). In a small number of criminal trials, when evidence admissible against one defendant is inadmissible against another, two juries may be utilized. Both juries are present only during testimony admissible against both defendants.

The jury selection process involves seven steps (see Figure 10–4).

1. *First master list.* The voting roles, by their very nature, contain the names of citizens over the age of 18. In some jurisdictions, the rolls of the motor vehicle bureau or tax rolls are used because some persons choose not to register to vote in order to avoid jury duty.

2. *First juror list.* Names are selected at random from the master list.

3. *Questionnaires.* Persons on the first juror list are mailed questionnaires to determine if they are qualified. Most jurisdictions require that the jurors be citizens of at least 18 years of age who are able to read, write, and understand the English language, have been residents of the court's jurisdiction for at least one year, and are free of felony convictions and physical or mental handicaps that would make them unable to render jury service. Otherwise qualified persons may be exempted for a variety of reasons, depending on the statutes and customs of the jurisdiction, e.g., law enforcement officers, doctors, lawyers, and mothers of infants. More than two dozen states have eliminated all automatic exemptions—those summoned can be excused on a case-by-case basis. Persons may also receive a temporary postponement based on a hardship that is time-limited (e.g., teachers during the school year or farmers during the harvest season).[6] Evasion of jury service is a significant problem in the United States, and sometimes trial courts have to shut down because not enough of those summoned appear for service—another reason for prosecutors to avoid a jury trial in favor of negotiation.

4. *Second master list.* Based on the questionnaires, a second master list is developed, and jury service summonses are sent out. Those responding are screened as disqualified, exempt, excused, or qualified.

---

[6]In 1999, the mayor of New York, a former federal prosecutor, was selected as a juror in a civil case.

FIGURE 10-4   THE JURY SELECTION PROCESS

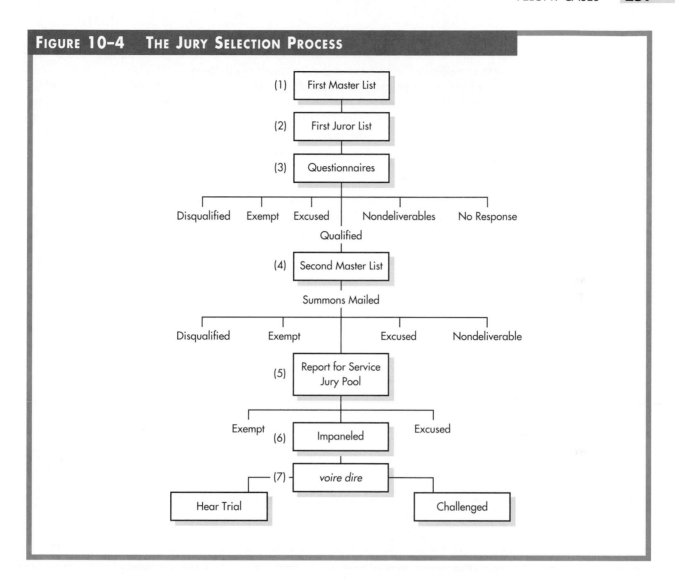

5. **Report for service.** Those who are qualified are directed to report to a central jury room, where they constitute the jury pool.
6. **Impaneled.** The members of the jury pool are sworn in as jurors.
7. **Voir dire.** A panel of jurors is brought into a large courtroom in which the key actors are present in addition to the defendant. Each member of the panel is questioned by the judge, prosecutor, and defense counsel. (In some jurisdictions, only the judge questions the jurors, although attorneys may submit questions to the judge.)

There are two purposes for the *voir dire* (pronounced vwor deer—an Old French term meaning "say the truth") hearing: first, to determine if a juror is unfit to serve on this particular jury, e.g., if he or she is familiar with the defendant or victim, is prejudiced, or has heard a great deal about the case as a result of pretrial publicity; and second, to allow the attorneys for the prosecution and defense some discretion in determining who will serve on the jury. These goals are achieved by use of the challenge for cause and the peremptory challenge.

Either attorney can argue that a juror is not fit to serve based on certain information that is revealed as a result of the questions asked by the judge or the attorneys. A challenge for cause must be upheld by the judge, in which case the juror is excused. Peremptory challenges can be used by either attorney to excuse any juror without having to state a reason. Their number is limited from two to 26, depending on the statutes and the seriousness of the charges. Some jurisdictions (and England) do not permit peremptory challenges. The hearing continues until a jury is chosen and impaneled, which means they are administered an oath by the court clerk "to well and truly try the case." In many jurisdictions, one or two additional, or alternate jurors, are chosen in the event a regular juror becomes ill or cannot serve for some other reason.

In 1986, the Supreme Court ruled that prosecutors may not use their peremptory challenges to exclude blacks from juries because they believe that such persons may favor a black defendant. In *Baston* v. *Kentucky*, the Court overruled a 1965 decision on the same issue. The Court determined that "Although a prosecutor ordinarily is entitled to exercise permitted peremptory challenges 'for any reason at all, as long as that reason is related to his view concerning the outcome,' the Equal Protection Clause [Fourteenth Amendment] forbids the prosecutor to challenge jurors solely on account of their race or on the assumption that black jurors as a group will be unable to impartially to consider the state's case against a black defendant."

The decision also made it easier for a defendant to raise the issue. The Court's decision noted, "Once the defendant makes a *prima facie* [sufficient on its face] showing [that black jurors were excluded], the burden shifts to the state to come forward with a neutral explanation for challenging black jurors." This decision may hasten the move to abolish the peremptory challenge, a position that was supported by Justice Thurgood Marshall in his concurring opinion. In *Griffith* v. *Kentucky* (1987) and *Brown* v. *United States* (1987), the Court ruled that the decision in *Baston* would apply retroactively. (The ruling for retroactivity represents a significant shift from the Court's previous approach to rulings on criminal procedure.) In 1992, the Court ruled 7–2 that the defense, also, cannot exclude jurors based on race (*Georgia* v. *McCollum*). In a 1994 case that involved paternity and child support issues (*J.E.B.* v. *T.B.*), the Court extended the prohibition in *Baston* to include gender. Later that year, however, the Court refused to grant certiorari in a case that involved the prosecutor's removal of a juror because he was a Jehovah's Witness (*David* v. *Minnesota*).

In 1990, the Court ruled 5–4 against a white defendant's claim that he was denied the right to an impartial jury because the prosecutor used peremptory challenges to remove the only two members of the jury pool who were black. The decision (*Holland* v. *Illinois*) states that the Sixth Amendment requires an impartial, not a representative, jury. In 1991, the Court, by a vote of 7–2, extended the defendant's right to object to the prosecution's use of peremptory challenges based on race. In this case (*Powers* v. *Ohio*), the defendant was a white man accused of murdering two white people; the excluded jurors were black. Writing for the majority, Justice Anthony Kennedy stated that race cannot be a criterion, regardless of the race of the defendant or the jurors.

The Court has ruled that prospective jurors who state that they could not under any circumstances vote for imposition of the death penalty could be excluded for cause. In *Lockhart* v. *McCree* (1986), the Court stated that the so-called death-qualified jury, "unlike the wholesale exclusion of blacks, women or Mexican-Americans from jury service, is carefully designed to serve the state's concededly legitimate interest in obtaining a single jury that can properly and impartially apply the law to the facts of the case at both guilt and sentencing phases of a capital crime." (In most states that authorize the death penalty, the jury first decides on guilt, and then, after a hearing, determines whether the death sentence should be imposed.)

Scientific Jury Selection and Trial Consultants

Scientific jury selection refers to the use of tools of the social sciences to assist attorneys in the jury selection process. A number of "sociologists, psychologists, market researchers and others use public opinion surveys, in-depth interviews, computer analyses correlating jurors' backgrounds and attitudes and laboratory simulations of impending trials to help lawyers select jurors likely to favor their side, exclude those likely to be hostile to it, and present their cases in ways psychologically designed to benefit from the unconscious needs and motives of the jurors" (Hunt 1982: 70). Consultants are used in about 6,000 mostly civil trials annually. The American Society of Trial Consultants has over 400 members, some of whom are employed by companies that offer jury consultation services (Gavzer 1997).

Social scientists attempt to identify the type of person most likely to be favorable to their side, as well as those most likely to be hostile, for use at *voir dire* hearings. In some programs, a simulated jury selection process is conducted and the "jurors" selected are paid to participate in a mock trial that helps to prepare attorneys for the actual case being litigated. After the mock trial, the "jurors" are interviewed to

In Support of the Peremptory Challenge

Peremptory challenges will make the verdict more acceptable to the losing party while assuring the public that the case has been decided based on the evidence, not the personal biases of the jurors.

Because there are limits on the use of challenges for cause, some jurors, even though biased, will otherwise remain on the jury because the attorney is unable to prove that the juror is not impartial. The peremptory challenge enables the screening out of suspected, but unprovable, bias.

Peremptory challenges are also essential in order to protect effective *voir dire*. An attorney does not know, until he or she asks questions, if a particular juror is biased. While questioning may reveal suspected bias, there may not be sufficient proof of bias to satisfy a challenge for cause. However, by questioning of a potential juror's impartiality, an otherwise impartial juror may be insulted and develop a bias against the attorney. Without peremptory challenges, such persons could not be excluded. Therefore, an attorney may opt to refrain from asking potentially offensive questions rather than risk insulting a prospective juror (Henley 1996).

determine the best trial approach, the one most likely to convince a real jury—what questions should be asked, how to speak, what clothes to wear—all in an effort to enhance the attorney's influence on the prospective jury, to provide an "edge." They may also assist attorneys in preparing questions for potential witnesses and evaluate pretrial statements.

A number of firms will provide this service, and it is expensive. For that reason, except in isolated cases, social scientific assistance usually occurs only in civil cases where the outcome can involve millions of dollars. The best known criminal case where this approach was used (by the defense)—it would be too costly for the prosecution—(the O.J. Simpson case being a noted exception) involved a 20-year-old black female inmate, Joan Little. In 1974, while being held in the rural Beaufort, North Carolina, jail on a burglary charge, Little stabbed a white, 62-year-old night jailer to death with an ice pick. Little claimed that the jailer had used the ice pick to force her to commit an act of oral sodomy, and while there was conclusive evidence of a sex act, it could not be determined if the jailer had perpetrated a rape or had been lured to his death.

Because of racial and gender implications, Joan Little received assistance that she would not have otherwise been able to afford. Social scientists conducted a public opinion poll among residents in the counties of the Beaufort area, and the degree of prejudice uncovered caused the court to grant a change of venue to Raleigh (Wake County). Subsequent surveys of a sample of Wake County voters revealed a profile of friendly and unfriendly jurors that assisted lawyers at the *voir dire* hearing. The five-week trial ended with a jury deliberation that lasted only 78 minutes—Joan Little was acquitted. The cost of the scientific jury services contributed to the Little defense was estimated at $300,000 (1974 dollars). The potential for exacerbating already existing inequities in our system of justice is obvious.

In addition to firms that provide jury selection services, the American Society of Trial Consultants reports there are more than 250 trial consultants in the United States. These persons, most frequently psychologists and a few lawyers, usually work for defendants at fees of about $150 an hour: "Under the guidance of jury consultants, lawyers are increasingly checking people's body language and asking questions aimed at eliciting open-ended answers that will reveal hidden biases" (Gollner 1994: B11).

Instructions to the Jury

The members of a jury are given specific instructions by the judge about their responsibilities as jurors. They are cautioned against discussing the case with anyone, including fellow jurors, and against reading or listening to anything pertaining to the case. They are directed to report any person who attempts to discuss the case with them, since this may constitute a crime—jury tampering. In particularly sensitive cases, or when there is a great deal of news coverage of a case, the jurors may be sequestered. This can happen from the time the jury is impaneled or after the trial is over and they are sent to deliberate. In such cases, jurors are held in a form of protective custody in a hotel or motel guarded by court officers, bailiffs, deputy sheriffs, or marshals. What they read or view on television is monitored and subject to censorship, and their telephone conversations with family or friends are restricted accordingly. Each court day they are transported by a special bus to and from the courthouse under guard. The sequestering continues until the jury reaches a verdict or until they are dismissed by the judge if they are a *hung jury*—unable to reach a verdict.[7]

Under our system of adversarial justice, members of a jury are observers who, until they begin deliberations, must remain silent and passive. However, in selected cases in about 30 states, including New York and California, civil and criminal jurors are being allowed to question witnesses and inform judges when they want more information. Juror participation is an extension of the growing restlessness of trial judges, who have frequently interrupted lawyers to question witnesses directly—inquisitorial in style. Generally, jurors are permitted to ask questions when opposing lawyers agree and only after they are finished questioning a witness. "The guidelines sent to participating judges suggest that jurors submit written questions to lawyers on both sides and that a lawyer submit any evidentiary objections in a handwritten note to the judge" to avoid slighting a juror (Wiehl 1989b: 20). This might help keep jurors interested in the case—or at least keep them awake, something that has become a problem at marathon trials (Pallasch 1998).

Evidence

Evidence secured in an unconstitutional manner cannot be admitted at trial (exclusionary rule). Jurors must also be protected from evidence that may be misleading or prejudicial. This includes *hearsay*: an assertion made by a testifying witness about a statement made out of court by someone else. Hearsay is generally considered unreliable, if not prejudicial, because opposing counsel does not have an opportunity to test the reliability of the evidence by cross-examining the person who allegedly made the original statement. "The speaker may have been joking, or guessing, or even deliberately lying" (Friedenthal, Kane, and Miller 1985: 464). The jury, after all, is made up of laypeople, and it is the responsibility of the judge, acting on motions or objections from counsel, to prevent improper testimony from being entered as evidence. There are many exceptions to the general prohibition against hearsay evidence, over 30 in the *Federal Rules of Evidence*.

There are two fundamental types of evidence, direct and indirect:

1. *Direct evidence* is testimony provided by an eyewitness (which in law also includes hearing and the senses of taste, smell, and touch). An example of eyewitness evidence would be a statement such as, "I observed the defendant exit the liquor store with a firearm in his right hand and a paper bag in his left hand."

2. *Indirect or circumstantial evidence* does not prove a proposition directly. An example is a bullet recovered from the body of the victim that matches those fired from a revolver owned by the defendant. Jon Waltz states that

---

[7]There has been concern over jurors selling, or offering for sale, their experiences on highly publicized trials—fear that jurors will be influenced in favor of a case outcome that has greater commercial appeal. It became known that in at least one case, the "Howard Beach trial," which concerned a racially motivated killing in New York, a juror attempted to sell the story even while deliberations were in progress. For an examination of various aspects of this issue, see Cunningham (1989), Nagel (1989), Lomasky (1989).

Hearsay

The following are not excluded by the hearsay rule in the *Federal Rules of Evidence* if the declarant is unavailable as a witness:

- *Former testimony.* Testimony given as a witness at another hearing of the same or a different proceeding, or in a deposition taken in compliance with law in the course of the same or another proceeding, if the party against whom the testimony is now offered, or, in a civil action or proceeding, a predecessor in interest, had an opportunity and similar motive to develop the testimony by direct, cross, or redirect examination.

- Statement under *belief of impending death.* In a prosecution for homicide or in a civil action or proceeding, a statement made by a declarant while believing that the declarant's death was imminent, concerning the cause or circumstances of what the declarant believed to be impending death.

- *Statement against interest.* A statement which was at the time of its making so far contrary to the declarant's pecuniary or proprietary interest, or so far tended to subject the declarant to civil or criminal liability, or to render invalid a claim by the declarant against another, that a reasonable person in the declarant's position would not have made the statement unless believing it to be true. A statement tending to expose the declarant to criminal liability and offered to exculpate the accused is not admissible unless corroborating circumstances clearly indicate the trustworthiness of the statement.

- *Statement of personal or family history.* (a) A statement concerning the declarant's own birth, adoption, marriage, divorce, legitimacy, relationship by blood, adoption, or marriage, ancestry, or other similar fact of personal or family history, even though declarant had no means of acquiring personal knowledge of the matter stated; or (b) a statement concerning the foregoing matters, and death also, of another person, if the declarant was related to the other by blood, adoption, or marriage or was so intimately associated with the other's family as to be likely to have accurate information concerning the matter declared.

circumstantial evidence "is frequently far more persuasive than direct evidence" (1997: 12). Evidence such as fingerprints and hair samples are often more reliable than that provided by an eyewitness, particularly when the latter is based on the testimony of an untrained civilian, often the victim. Persons who are threatened or otherwise subject to the trauma of a crime are notoriously poor observers (Engelhardt 1999). "Witnessed events often occur under less than optimal viewing conditions. Moreover, witnesses to crimes often experience high levels of stress or emotional arousal" (Stanny and Johnson 2000: 359). "The major problem is that people are not very good at recognizing other people. Especially strangers. Especially strangers of a different race. Especially strangers of a different race seen briefly under stress" (Uviller 1996: 55). In studies of persons wrongfully convicted, but later exonerated by DNA testing, the most common cause was eyewitness error (Gawande [2001]; see Cutler and Penrod [1995] for a discussion of this issue; also Huff, Rattner, and Sagarin [1996] for a discussion of the issue of "convicted but innocent").

These two types of evidence come in three basic forms (Waltz 1997):

1. *Testimonial evidence* is that presented orally by a witness in court and under oath, although occasionally it takes the form of a sworn pretrial written deposition, common in civil cases. Six states do not require a court order for taking depositions in criminal cases; 38 allow such depositions only if a witness will not be available for trial; and six other states allow them with a court order (S. Johnson 1991).

2. *Tangible evidence* is any physical exhibit, which can be:
   (a) *Real evidence*, such as the actual murder weapon, fingerprints, drugs; or
   (b) *Demonstrative evidence*, usually a visual aid such as a drawing of the crime scene or an anatomical model.

3. *Judicial notice* refers to those matters that are subject to common knowledge or certain verification through reference to such highly reliable sources as calendars or medical dictionaries. Such matters need not be proved, but the judge will instruct the jurors to take them as fully established without any necessity of witnesses or exhibits.

Court Personnel

Before proceeding to the trial, we should note the presence of persons other than the key actors. There will be one or more bailiffs (deputy sheriffs, court officers, marshals) responsible for maintaining order, security, and guarding prisoners. There will be a clerk who maintains records and may call cases. There will be a court reporter who records all proceedings in the courtroom, especially testimony of witnesses. The reporter uses a small, typewriter-like stenographic device, which in the hands of a skilled operator permits simultaneous recording at about 250 words per minute. The stenographic record is transcribed and becomes the official record of the trial. In some jurisdictions, a tape recorder may be used in addition to the court reporter.

THE TRIAL

The centerpiece of the adversarial process is the trial, a highly structured battle between two attorneys accomplished in accord with established rules of procedure under the stewardship of a judge.

Pretrial Motions

Before the jury is brought into the courtroom to hear opening statements and presentation of evidence, the defense attorney has an opportunity to make pretrial motions—oral and/or written pleadings. The most common are:

- *Motion to dismiss*. This motion is routinely made and routinely denied. Defense counsel claims that the information or indictment is insufficient to justify a trial.

- *Motion for a change of venue*. The defense argues that a fair trial is not possible in the current jurisdiction because of the amount of pretrial publicity. If the judge agrees, the trial will be moved to another jurisdiction.

- *Motion for a bill of particulars.* This motion is an attempt by the defense to obtain details of the prosecution's charges and of the occurrences to be investigated at trial. The defense is then able to place limits on evidence offered by the prosecution; it must be material (that is, clearly related to the items in the bill of particulars), or it will be excluded as immaterial on an objection by defense counsel.

- *Motion for discovery.* This is a request for access to the evidence the prosecution plans to use at trial, allowing counsel to prepare his or her defense. While statutes and practices governing discovery differ considerably between states, and in the federal system (Middlekauff 1994), in many, if not most, jurisdictions, discovery is informal and opposing counsel is routinely allowed to review evidence, which facilitates plea bargaining. The deliberate withholding of exculpatory evidence by a prosecutor is an unconstitutional denial of due process (*Brady* v. *Maryland* 1963). The state, however, is obligated to disclose only that evidence for which there is a reasonable probability that the trial outcome would have been different had the defense obtained the evidence in time for trial (*United States* v. *Bagley* 1985).

- *Motion to suppress.* This motion seeks to invoke the exclusionary rule. If successful, it often leaves the prosecution without important evidence and requires a *nolle prosequi* or dismissal of the charges.

- *Motion for severance.* Defendants charged with multiple counts may move to have them severed—require separate trials for various offenses that can be bundled together in a logical manner—or request separate trials (rejoinder) for two or more defendants.

Side-Bar

At times during a trial, the prosecution or defense will approach the bench and request a side-bar, a private conference with the judge. This is usually done at the side of the bench away from the jury, and opposing counsel must be present because any *ex parte* discussion (having only one party present) with the judge is considered improper. This brief conference conducted out of hearing of jurors usually involves the question of admissibility of certain evidence, or it may be used to inquire if certain questions can properly be asked of a witness. If the issue cannot be decided quickly, the judge will have the jury removed and hear arguments in open court on the matter.

Opening Statements

Before any evidence is presented, each side is allowed to address the jury in the form of a general outline of the case he or she intends to present. The prosecutor formally introduces him- or herself (and any colleagues) to the court and states his or her intentions and the nature of the evidence to be relied upon: "Ladies and gentlemen of the jury, the state intends to prove that on . . ." The defense may decline to present an opening statement; it is up to the prosecution to prove the defendant guilty beyond a reasonable doubt, and the defendant has no corresponding responsibility. An opening statement also provides advance notice to the opposition of the line of prosecution or defense. There is no time limit for an opening statement; it is at the discretion of the judge. Defense may object to any overstatements by the prosecution, or the prosecutor's opening statement may be used by the defense at summation to bring the prosecution's credibility into question for failing to prove what was set forth in the opening statement. At the conclusion of opening statements, it is time for the prosecutor's case-in-chief: the presentation of evidence.

Presentation of Evidence

Evidence must be presented by a witness who is called, sworn in by the court clerk or bailiff, and directed to take the witness stand, a raised chair at the side of the judge's bench. A witness may testify on matters he or she saw, heard, or has knowledge of by one or more of the senses. Third party testimony is hearsay. For example, a witness who testifies, "I was told by the defendant's girlfriend that he robbed . . . " will not normally be permitted to continue because defense counsel cannot test the reliability of the girlfriend's statement. As noted earlier, however, there are many exceptions to the hearsay rule (e.g., hearsay evidence is admissible in conspiracy cases for the purpose of tying together defendants who comprise the combination or confederation that is the basis for the criminal allegation). In general, a witness cannot offer an opinion or conclusion unless it has been established that he or she is an "expert." However, lay opinion with respect to matters such as duration of time, height, weight, or the speed of a vehicle is commonly allowed into evidence. Expert witnesses—scientists, medical doctors, handwriting analysts—can offer their professional opinions and conclusions, or they can be asked to respond to a hypothetical question that has a bearing on the case.

Witnesses, particularly police officers, are used to identify physical (or forensic) evidence such as documents, photos and diagrams of the crime scene, fingerprints, bloodstains, and weapons. Without such identification, an item cannot be admitted into evidence as "Exhibit A" or "B" or "C." This involves the *chain of custody*: The prosecutor must be able to prove that the piece of forensic evidence being presented to the jury is without any doubt the same item that was retrieved at the scene of the crime or during a subsequent investigation. This is not as easy as it may sound. The trial usually occurs months, if not years, after the crime. The evidence has passed through a number of hands—the police officer(s) who responded to the scene; the technician(s) who analyzed it; and other police officers or clerks involved in transporting, filing,

TYPES OF WITNESSES

There are two main types of witnesses in a criminal (or civil) trial:

- *Witness of fact.* Using the senses, this person has heard, seen, felt, or smelled something that has a bearing on the matter being litigated.
- *Expert witness.* Persons who by virtue of education, training, and/or experience are able to form an (expert) opinion that is beyond the scope of the average person.

and storing for use at the trial. Each person handling the evidence must record that fact by writing out his or her name, the date, time, and purpose. It must be shown that the evidence was properly secured, that only authorized persons had access to it, and that they properly recorded every time they had custody of the item. Each person in the chain can be required to testify, and any broken link can render the evidence inadmissible. Poor police practices (e.g., failing to properly secure the crime scene from the public and/or other police officers) can raise doubts about evidence. If many police officers were walking around the crime scene, each can be called to testify by the defense. This can be problematic for the prosecution because the jury can grow quite bored, and the more officers, the greater the chances of contradictory testimony.

When introducing physical/forensic evidence, the attorney shows the evidence to the judge and opposing counsel and asks that it be marked (by the clerk) for identification (e.g., "Prosecution's Exhibit A"). The attorney then shows the marked evidence to the witness for proper identification: "Officer, do you recognize this firearm marked as 'Prosecution's Exhibit A?'" A positive response will result in the attorney asking the witness to identify the firearm for the court and then requesting that it be admitted into evidence. Opposing counsel can object to the offering. The witness is then asked a series of questions about the evidence. (In some jurisdictions, these questions come before moving to have the evidence admitted.)

In the adversarial system of justice used in this country (as opposed to an inquisitorial system), the examination of a witness involves a series of questions. The questions and their responses must be narrow enough for opposing counsel to have the opportunity to object—to claim that the jury is about to hear testimony that is inadmissible. If such testimony does occur and the attorney objects, the judge will order it stricken from the record and instruct the jury to disregard it, which may be easier said than done. Questions cannot be *leading*, that is, queries that suggest their own answer, such as "Isn't it true that the defendant owned a firearm?" as opposed to the more permissible question, "To your knowledge, did the defendant own a firearm?" The exceptions are preliminary questions to establish some basic facts, e.g., "You reside at 1492 Columbus Avenue?" or "Is it correct that you are employed as a manager by the Howell Strident Corporation?" During a side-bar, counsel may request permission from the judge to ask a leading question and state the reason for wanting to ask such a question—to help the witness remember an item, for example. In any event, direct questioning has as its purpose getting the witness to tell a story without wandering.

Opposing counsel can object to any question or answer on grounds the attorney is leading the witness or for any other procedural defects (e.g., that it is immaterial and irrelevant or that it requires an opinion or conclusion that only an "expert" witness can offer). The judge determines whether to uphold the objection or to overrule. If the objection is sustained, opposing counsel may make an offer to prove, which is dictated to the court reporter out of hearing of the jury. If an objection is overruled, the attorney may make "an exception," which has the effect of arguing that the court made an error, thereby preparing the record for a possible appeal. Lawyers must not only seek to win their cases at trial, but must do everything they can to generate a record of the trial that will convince an appellate court that justice did or did not prevail. Since an appellate court can only consider the formal record generated at trial, attorneys must be careful to create a complete and accurate record of the trial. An action to which an objection was not raised at trial is not preserved for appellate review. "Appellate courts, except in cases of egregious error that led to fundamental injustice, take the position that any issue not timely raised in the earlier proceedings has been lost by 'procedural default'" (Hughes 1996: 22). This process is an effort to foreclose on a strategy of avoiding objections at trial, when they should be made, in order to use them as a weapon on appeal. It would also open the floodgates to indeterminate appeals (Coffin 1994).

Cross-Examination

After the prosecutor has completed the direct examination of a witness that he or she has called, the defense has an opportunity to cross-examine. During this phase of the trial, the attorney can ask leading questions: "Isn't it true that on the night of December 30th, you consumed at least five glasses of alcoholic beverages?" Cross-examination has several purposes. It is used to challenge a witness' testimony (e.g., by questioning his or her memory or vision). The attorney may attempt to impeach the credibility of the witness (e.g., by asking questions about any criminal record, history of mental illness, or alcoholism, any information that will tend to blemish the reputation of the witness in the eyes of the jury). The attorney may ask for details of any previous relationship with the defendant. As

PERJURY

Perjury is a crime committed when a person, under oath in a judicial proceeding, willfully makes a false statement in a material (that is, relevant to the issue) matter. The statement may be oral (e.g., court testimony) or written (e.g., an affidavit). Some jurisdictions use a broader concept, false swearing, in which case the falsehood need not be in a judicial matter or even material. According to the *U.S. Code* (Sec. 1621): "Whoever (1) having taken an oath before a competent tribunal, officer, or person, in any case in which a law of the United States authorizes an oath to be administered, that he will testify, declare, depose, or certify truly, or that any written testimony, declaration, deposition, or certificate by him subscribed, is true, willfully and contrary to such oath states or subscribes any material matter which he does not believe to be true; or (2) in any declaration, certificate, verification, or statement under penalty of perjury as permitted under. . . [law] willfully subscribes as true any material matter which he does not believe to be true; is guilty of perjury and shall, except as otherwise expressly provided by law, be fined under this title or imprisoned not more than five years, or both." This section is applicable whether the statement or subscription is made within or without the United States.

The Bible contains only one instance of *lex talionis*, the literal carrying out of "an eye for an eye," in the case of the "false witness," in which case "ye shall do unto him, as he had purposed to do unto his brother" (*Deuteronomy* 19: 19). For a false witness presenting exculpatory testimony, the penalty was 40 (in practice 39) lashes. In Illinois, perjury is a Class 3 felony punishable by a term of imprisonment for two to five years.

with direct examination, the prosecutor can object to any questions. In some states, "rape shield laws" have placed restrictions on the type of personal questions that can be asked of a victim.

Re-Direct and Re-Cross-Examination

After defense counsel has had an opportunity to cross-examine an adverse witness, the prosecution can ask additional questions of the witness about any new matters that have been brought out during the cross-examination, in an effort to reestablish the testimony or rehabilitate the witness. Questions that go beyond those new areas raised on cross-examination can be objected to by defense counsel. After the prosecution has completed redirect examination, defense counsel can re-cross-examine. This process can continue until both sides have no further questions or the judge intervenes.

After all prosecution witnesses have been subjected to direct and cross-examination, redirect and re-cross-examination, the state rests; the prosecution's case-in-chief has been presented. At this point, defense may ask for a *directed verdict*; the jury is removed from the courtroom, and the judge is requested to render a verdict of not guilty based on insufficient evidence having been presented by the prosecution. Rarely does a judge agree to a directed verdict; the motion usually is made to preserve some legal rights on appeal. The judge, however, may dismiss certain counts of a multicount indictment or information based on insufficient evidence, but the trial will continue on the remaining counts.

In many jurisdictions, particularly if defense counsel declined to make one earlier, he or she may now present an opening statement summarizing evidence that will be used to counter the prosecution's case. Defense counsel now has an opportunity to present witnesses, who may or may not include the defendant. According to the Fifth Amendment, a defendant cannot be forced to testify and this cannot be used against him or her when considering the question of guilt or innocence; this will be explained to the jury by the judge.

If the defendant decides to testify, the defendant-as-witness can be subjected to vigorous cross-examination by the prosecutor, who will attempt to impeach his or her credibility. As part of the impeachment process, questions about past criminal behavior, as well as alcohol or drug abuse, which would not ordinarily be permitted, are relevant and permissible. As a witness on his or her own behalf, the defendant can refuse to answer any question. But such a refusal can be used as evidence, an issue the prosecution will usually stress to the jury during closing arguments. Having a defendant with a serious criminal history testify is, obviously, a calculated risk for the defense. In most cases, the defendant's criminal history will be placed before the jury during direct examination by his or her attorney in order to blunt the issue.

Witnesses called by the defense are questioned by direct examination and subjected to cross-examination by the prosecution. Redirect and re-cross-examination continue as with the witnesses called by the prosecution. After the defense has rested, the prosecutor is permitted to call further witnesses for the purpose of rebuttal, testimony designed to refute the testimony of defense witnesses. If prosecution has introduced new evidence or has delved into new matters, defense is entitled to a rejoinder, testimony restricted to new defense evidence to refute the prosecutor's rebuttal. In practice, however, a judge seldom allows a rejoinder. On the rare occasions when there is a surprise witness, it is during rebuttal or rejoinder that he or she is usually called to testify.

Final Motions and Closing Arguments

After both sides rest, and without the jury present, defense can renew the motion for a directed verdict of acquittal, a pleading that the prosecution has not provided sufficient evidence—e.g., failed to prove the *actus reus*) to allow the case to be decided by the jury. If the motion is sustained, the trial is over and defendant acquitted. If denied by the judge, summations or closing arguments are in order.

The prosecutor is allowed to address the jury, presenting remarks that summarize the case he or she has presented, usually highlighting important testimony. Summations are not evidence, and the jury is informed of this by the judge. The defense is provided with the same opportunity, typically stressing the weakness of the state's case and the need to find a defendant guilty beyond a reasonable doubt. Attorneys for the state and for the defendant are allowed considerable leeway during summations, which can sometimes be quite dramatic. However, improper remarks by the prosecutor (e.g., those that are inflammatory) can provide a basis for appealing an adverse jury decision. After the defense closes, the prosecutor is permitted a rebuttal. This is typically limited to those areas discussed by the defense in summation; new lines of argument are not permitted. In some states, if the defense has not called any witnesses, he or she is entitled to first and last closing arguments. There are no specific time limits for closing arguments, which may last only a few minutes or, in complex cases, run for a few days.

Charge to the Jury

The judge now charges the jury—explains their responsibilities and the options they have as jurors.[8] In a multiple-count indictment or information, e.g., in addition to a verdict of guilty or not guilty, they can find the defendant guilty on some counts and not guilty on others. The judge will carefully cover the law applicable in the case, stating the issues and defining terms that may be unfamiliar to a layperson. This task can be difficult—terms such as reasonable doubt, malice aforethought, and mayhem are not exemplars of clarity even for lawyers (Tiersma 1999). In many states, attorneys are permitted to submit suggestions to be included in the instructions to the jury, and the judge will indicate those that are acceptable and those that are not. Defense counsel may object to any ruling on suggestions, which is recorded by the court reporter, providing the basis for an appeal in the event of an adverse verdict.

The judge instructs the jurors in two areas:

> First, the judge informs the jurors what their task consists of during deliberation and what procedures they should employ in reaching a verdict. The procedures defined by the judge generally include the instruction that the juror is to regard the defendant as innocent until proven otherwise; that the burden of proof is on the prosecution; that the juror's task is to determine the facts on the basis of credible evidence; that certain information may be regarded as evidence, such as direct testimony of witnesses, charts and exhibits, observations of the witnesses, and reasonable inferences drawn from the testimony; that other information may not be regarded as evidence, such as statements and questions posed

---

[8]In some jurisdictions, such as Missouri, the judge reads instructions to the jury *before* closing arguments.

by the attorneys, or race and background of defendant; how to assess the credibility of testimony, such as each witness' opportunity to observe, possible bias, character, and contradictions in testimony; what constitutes a reasonable inference as opposed to unwarranted speculation; and what is the meaning and application of the standard of proof, namely beyond a reasonable doubt, in assessing the truth of allegations. The second portion of the judge's instructions defines for the jurors a complete set of possible verdicts, of which they must choose one. (Hastie, Penrod, and Pennington 1983: 17)

As in the English system, in some jurisdictions, particularly federal district courts, the judge is permitted to comment on the evidence, although the judge's opinion is not binding on the jurors. Most jurisdictions, however, prohibit judges from commenting on witness credibility.

Jury Deliberations

The jury retires to the jury room and elects a foreperson (unless the trial takes place in one of the states where the foreperson is automatically the first juror chosen). The room is guarded by a bailiff, and no one is permitted to enter without an explicit request from the foreperson, via the bailiff, to the judge. At times, jurors may request the court reporter to read some testimony or to review some forensic evidence. The manner in which the jury proceeds is not governed by law or custom; each jury is independent and not bound by precedent. Deliberations may take less than an hour or a few days. As noted earlier, jurors may be sequestered, or they may leave at the end of the court day, even when they have not reached a verdict.

If all jurors agree on a verdict, it is signed by the foreperson and read aloud in court by the foreperson, the bailiff, or the court clerk. The jurors may be polled, each asked by the judge if this is his or her decision. After the verdict is read, the jury is dismissed by the judge "with thanks." Jurors are now free to discuss the case with anyone they choose—the press, the prosecutor, or defense attorneys. (Five states and 18 federal districts prohibit trial lawyers from speaking with jurors at the end of a trial.) In a Connecticut rape case in which the jury was deadlocked, the defense attorney hired a member of the jury to act as a consultant at the retrial. The attorney was interested in finding out what arguments had been most effective. Nevertheless, the defendant was convicted at the second trial (Johnson 1986).

If, despite repeated encouragement from the judge, jurors cannot reach a unanimous decision, it is a hung jury. The prosecutor must decide if he or she wishes to retry the case. This often depends on the number of jurors who voted for a conviction. For example, an 11–1 vote for conviction would almost invariably result in a retrial (or plea bargain).

SENTENCING

If the defendant is found guilty, he or she enters the sentencing stage. Sentencing in the United States can be *determinate* or *indeterminate*—a rules versus standards issue (discussed in Chapter 2). Determinate sentencing is a rule-based system that evolved out of a classical approach to crime and criminals; indeterminate sentencing represents a standard based on a positive approach to crime and criminals. While the classical school is based on philosophy and law, the positive school is based on empiricism.

Positive School

"Positivism," as formulated by Auguste Comte (1798–1857), refers to a method for examining and understanding social behavior. Comte argued that the methods and logical form of the natural sciences—the "scientific method"—are applicable to the study of man as a social being, hence "social sciences." Social phenomena, Comte stated, must be studied and understood by observation, hypothesis, and experimentation in a new discipline he called sociology. The positive approach to the study of crime became known as criminology.

The positive school places emphasis not on the crime but on the criminal. It contradicts the theory of free will and substitutes a chain of interrelated causes and, at its most extreme, a deterministic basis for criminal behavior: The criminal could not do "otherwise." Since criminal behavior is the result of social and psychological, if not physiological, conditions over which the offender has little to no control, he or she is not culpable so punishment is inappropriate because the offender lacks *mens rea*. (For a discussion of free will versus determinism in law, see Honderich 1993.)

Nevertheless, a criminal does represent a threat to society and, therefore, must be "treated," "corrected," or "rehabilitated" (or, according to early positivists, separated from society, perhaps castrated or executed). In practice, the change in emphasis from punishment to correction did not result in a less severe response to criminal offenders. Some modern critics contend that rehabilitation opened the door to a host of questionable schemes for dealing with offenders under the guise of "treatment" and "for their own good." The American Friends Service Committee notes: "Retribution and revenge necessarily imply punishment, but it does not necessarily follow that punishment is eliminated under rehabilitative regimes" (1971: 20). In any event, positivism provides a philosophical basis for the indeterminate sentence.

Indeterminate or Indefinite Sentencing. While the indeterminate sentence can be traced back to the nineteenth century (see Abadinsky 2003), contemporary use dates back to the years following the Second World War. Toward the end of the war, Governor (and later Chief Justice) Earl Warren of California, responding to a prison scandal, instituted a new approach to penology: corrections. Instead of punishing criminals, the California system would attempt to rehabilitate offenders using the latest scientific approaches: Prisons became correctional institutions, wardens became superintendents, and guards became correction officers. "Treaters" (psychiatrists, social workers, teachers) were sent to the correctional institutions. Since it is not possible to know in advance how much time will be needed to "correct" a specific offender, the indeterminate sentence was instituted and became the cornerstone of the corrections approach.

Under the indeterminate sentence, an offender is sentenced to a minimum and a maximum number—the judge sets the parameters—of years. For example, a sentence might be three years to nine years—written 3-0-0/9-0-0. It is the parole board, not the judge, who determines when the offender is to be released from prison (correctional facility) in 3-0-0, or 4-0-0, or 5-0-0, all the way up to 9-0-0. Members of the parole board review an inmate's record, efforts at rehabilitation, past criminal history, and future plans and make a release decision within the parameters set by the judge's sentence. Inmates not paroled become eligible for release prior to the expiration of their sentence through the mechanism of "time off for good behavior," usually one-third off the maximum. Thus, an inmate serving 3-0-0/9-0-0 could be paroled after serving three years, but in any event, assuming good behavior, the inmate would be released after six years (6-0-0). Persons paroled or released on good time come under the supervision of a parole officer for the remainder or a portion of the unserved sentence.

The California system of corrections spread to every state in the nation. It was criticized by those on the right of the political spectrum for releasing criminals before the expiration of their sentence. But critics on the left argued that the indeterminate sentence actually kept persons in prison longer than they would have been made to serve if punishment had been the sole basis of incarceration. Critics pointed out that under the indeterminate sentence, persons sent to prison for crimes of similar severity would not all serve the same amount of time—some would be paroled before others—which amounts to unequal justice. Furthermore, parole boards often returned offenders to prison for violating the conditions of their release, meaning the rules of parole (see Figure 10–5). By the mid-1970s, criticism increased as research into rehabilitative efforts failed to reveal any significant level of success in preventing recidivism (a reversion to criminal behavior). By 1980, a number of states, including California, had switched back to a classical philosophy and determinate sentencing, and that trend continues.

Classical School

Concern for equality before the law can be found in the Bible: "You shall not respect persons in judgment; ye shall hear the small and the great alike" (*Deuteronomy* 1: 17; and 16: 18). The issue again came to the fore as part of the classical school, an outgrowth of the Enlightenment period of eighteenth century Europe (sometimes referred to as the "Age of Reason"). During this period, philosophers such as Charles-Louis de Secondat, Baron de La Brede et de Montesquieu (1689–1755), and Francois-Marie Arouet Voltaire (1694–1778) spoke out against the French penal code and punishments that were both inhuman and inequitable. Jean Jacques Rousseau (1712–1778) and Cesare Bonesana, Marchese di Beccaria (1738–1794), argued for a radical concept of justice based on equality. At a time when laws and law enforcement were unjust and disparate and punishment often brutal, they demanded justice based on equality and punishment that was humane and proportionate to the offense. This revolutionary doctrine—equality—influenced the American Revolution with the declaration "all men are created equal" and the French Revolution, in which the "Declaration of the Rights of Man and Citizen" (1791) emphasized the equality of all citizens.

Basic to classical thought is the notion of a *social contract*, a mythical state of affairs wherein each person agrees to a pact (social contract) that stipulates conditions of law are the same for all—all men being created equal: "The social contract establishes among the citizens an equality of such character that each binds himself on the same terms as all the others, and is thus entitled to enjoy the same rights as all the others" (Rousseau [1762] 1954: 45). Rousseau asserts, "One consents to die—if and when one becomes a murderer oneself—in order not to become a murderer's victim" (1954: 48). In order to be safe from crime, we have all consented to punishment if we resort to crime.

FIGURE 10-5   COLORADO CONDITIONS OF PAROLE

1.   **RELEASE:** (if applicable) Upon arrival from the sending state, Parolee shall report
     to: _____

2.   **RESIDENCE:** Parolee shall establish a residence of record and shall reside at such
     residence in fact and on record shall not change this place of residence without the
     consent of his Parole Officer; and shall not leave the area paroled to nor the State
     paroled to without the permission of the Parole Officer.

3.   **CONDUCT:** Parolee shall obey all State and Federal laws and Municipal ordinances
     at all times. Parolee shall follow the directives of the Parole Officer.

4.   **REPORT:** Parolee shall make written and in-person reports as directed by the Parole
     Officer and shall permit visits to place of residence as required by the Parole Officer.
     a. Parolee further shall submit urinalysis or other tests for narcotics or chemical
         agents upon the request of the Parole Officer, and is required to pay for all tests.
     b. Parolee further agrees to allow the Parole Officer to search his person, or his
         residence, or any premises under his control, or any vehicle under his control upon
         request.

5.   **WEAPONS:** Parolee shall not own, possess, nor have under his control or in his
     custody firearms or other deadly weapons.

6.   **ASSOCIATION:** Parolee shall not associate with any person with a criminal record
     without the permission of the Parole Officer.

7.   **EMPLOYMENT:** Parolee shall seek and obtain employment or shall participate in a
     full-time education or vocational program, unless waived by the Parole Officer.

8.   **ALCOHOL/DRUGS:** Parolee shall not abuse alcoholic beverages or uses illegal drugs.

9.   **ADDITIONAL CONDITIONS:**

     I have read the foregoing document or have had it read to me and I have full and
     intelligent understanding of the contents and the meaning thereof, and I have
     received a copy of this document.

     I hereby affix my signature of my own free will and without reservation or coercion.

     _____   _____
     Parole Officer   Parolee

                                          _____
                                          Date

Source: Colorado Board of Parole.

Contrary to the manner in which law was being enforced, the classical school argued that law should respect neither rank nor station—all men are created equal—and punishment is to be meted out with a perfect uniformity. This premise was given impetus by Cesare Beccaria (1963) who, in *An Essay on Crimes and Punishments* (1764; English edition, 1867), states that laws should be drawn precisely and matched to punishment intended to be applied equally to all persons regardless of class or rank. The law, he argued, should stipulate a particular penalty for each specific crime, and judges should mete out identical sentences for each occurrence of the same offense. Punishment, he stated, must be "the minimum possible in the given circumstances, proportionate to the crime, dictated by the laws" (Maestro 1973: 33).

According to the classical position, punishment is justified because the offender who violates the social contract is rational and endowed with free will. This concept holds that every person has the ability to distinguish and choose between right and wrong, between being law-abiding or criminal. Behavior that violates the law is a rational choice made by a person with free will, and as such has *mens rea*. The classical school argues, however, that since human beings tend toward hedonism (seek pleasure and avoid pain), they must be restrained from pleasurable acts that are unlawful by fear of punishment. Accordingly, the purpose of the criminal law is not simply retribution, but also deterrence. In sum, the "individual is responsible for his actions and is equal, no matter what his rank, in the eyes of the law" (Taylor, Walton, and Young 1973: 2).

The approach of the classical school, note Ian Taylor, Paul Walton and Jock Young (1973), supported the interests of a rising eighteenth-century middle class, which was demanding legal equality with the privileged noble class, as well as protection from the predations of the lower class. There remains a contradiction between the defense of equality and the emphasis on maintaining an unequal distribution of wealth and property. Free will is an oversimplification, since one's position in society determines the degree of choice with respect to committing crimes: "A system of classical justice of this order could only operate in a society where property was distributed equally," where each person had an equal stake in the system (Taylor, Walton, and Young 1973: 6). It is irrational for a society, which in too many instances does not offer a viable alternative to crime, to insist that criminal behavior is simply a matter of free will. As noted by Anotole France: "The law, in its majestic equality, forbids both the poor man and the rich man to sleep under bridges, to beg in the streets, and to steal bread" (1927: 91).

In sum, there are seven basic tenets of classicalism:

1. Human beings are rational.
2. All persons are created equal.
3. All persons have an equal stake in society and, thus, an equal stake in preventing crime.
4. Free will endows each person with the power to be law-abiding or a criminal.
5. People tend toward hedonism.
6. The purpose of punishment is deterrence.
7. Punishment must be meted out fairly, with absolute equality and in proportion to the offense. (Taylor, Walton, and Young 1973)

Since, no matter the sentencing system used, classical philosophy provides the basis for our system of justice, its pictorial representation often appears on many courthouses and documents in the form of a woman—"Justice"—carrying scales and wearing a blindfold. The classical view provides the basis for the determinate or definite sentence.

Determinate or Definite Sentencing. In response to criticism of indeterminate sentencing and parole boards, a variety of so-called flat or definite sentence schemes have been adopted. While each requires the setting of a specific sentence—no minimum or maximum—they differ according to the amount of discretion left to the judge. Used in about a dozen states, determinate sentencing requires a judge to impose a specific number of years for each particular crime, e.g., nine years (9-0-0) for robbery. The offender is required to serve the entire sentence minus time off granted for good behavior in prison (usually a maximum of 50 percent off the sentence; much less in the federal system). In practice, no state has adopted a strict classical approach. Instead, determinate sentences can be classified according to the amount of discretion enjoyed by the judge.

- *Definite sentence/wide discretion.* The legislature provides for a range of sentences for each level of offense. For example, a Class 2 felony would be punishable with a sentence of between 3-0-0 to 9-0-0. Under this system the judge retains discretion to sentence a Class 2 offender to 3-0-0, or 4-0-0, or more all the way up to 9-0-0. The sentence imposed is definite, for a specific number of years, but the judge's discretion is quite wide.

- *Presumptive/narrow discretion.* The legislature limits discretion to a narrow range of sentences for each level of offense. For each level there is a presumed sentence from which the judge cannot deviate except if there are aggravating or mitigating circumstances, and then only in a very limited manner. If a defendant is convicted of a Class 2 felony, the judge would be required to set a sentence of (for example) 5-0-0. Upon a showing of aggravation by the prosecutor, however, the judge could increase the presumptive sentence to (for example) 6-0-0; upon a showing of mitigation by the defense, the judge could decrease the presumptive sentence to (for example) 4-0-0. In some states, e.g., Minnesota, the presumed sentence is increased by a fixed amount based on the severity of any prior convictions (see Figure 10–6).

- *Presumptive/wide discretion.* As in the presumptive sentence with narrow discretion, the legislature provides three possible terms for each class of felony. However, while each class has a presumptive sentence, the judge may decrease (for mitigation) or increase (for aggravation) by significant amounts, a few months or several years (depending on the class of offense). A departure from the presumptive sentence usually requires a written statement of factual findings and reasons for the departure.

The rationale behind determinate sentencing was to reduce judicial discretion and promote less disparity in sentences for crimes of equal severity. As noted already, however, determinate sentencing schemes often maintain wide discretion and even those with narrow discretion cannot control the prosecutor's role in determining the charges. A study of federal determinate sentencing found great variation in

FIGURE 10-6 MINNESOTA SENTENCING GUIDELINES GRID

PRESUMPTIVE PRISON SENTENCE LENGTHS IN MONTHS

Less Serious ◄————————————————► More Serious

SEVERITY OF OFFENSE (Illustrative Offenses)	CRIMINAL HISTORY SCORE						
	0	**1**	**2**	**3**	**4**	**5**	**6 or more**
Sale of simulated controlled substance	12*	12*	12*	13	15	17	19 *18–20*
Theft-related crimes ($2,500 or less) Check forgery ($200–$2,500)	12*	12*	13	15	17	19	21 *20–22*
Theft crimes ($2,500 or less)	12*	13	15	17	19 *18–20*	22 *21–23*	25 *24–26*
Nonresidential burglary Theft crimes ($2,500 or less)	12*	15	18	21	25 *24–26*	32 *30–34*	41 *37–45*
Residential burglary Simple robbery	18	23	27	30 *29–31*	38 *36–40*	46 *43–49*	54 *50–58*
Criminal sexual conduct 2nd degree	21	26	30	34 *33–35*	44 *42–46*	54 *50–58*	65 *60–70*
Aggravated robbery	48 *44–52*	58 *54–62*	68 *64–72*	78 *74–82*	88 *84–92*	98 *94–102*	108 *104–112*
Criminal sexual conduct, 1st degree Assault, 1st degree	86 *81–91*	98 *93–103*	110 *105–115*	122 *117–127*	134 *129–139*	146 *141–151*	158 *153–163*
Murder, 3rd degree Murder, 2nd degree (felony murder)	150 *144–156*	165 *159–171*	180 *174–186*	195 *189–201*	210 *204–216*	225 *219–231*	240 *234–246*
Murder, 2nd degree (with intent)	306 *299–313*	326 *319–333*	346 *339–353*	366 *359–373*	386 *379–393*	406 *399–413*	426 *419–433*

☐ At the discretion of the judge, up to a year in jail and/or other nonjail sanctions can be imposed instead of prison sentences as conditions of probation for most of theses offenses. If prison is imposed, the presumptive sentence is the number of months shown.

☐ Presumptive commitment to state prison for all offenses.

Notes: 1. Criminal history score is based on offender's prior record and seriousness of prior offenses. 2. Numbers in italics represent the range of months within which a judge may sentence without the sentence being deemed a departure from the guidelines. 3. First degree murder is excluded from the guidelines by law and carries a mandatory life sentence.

* One year and one day.

sentences for crimes of equal severity (Lacasse and Payne 1999). Determinate sentencing has been criticized for failing to deal adequately with the issue of disparity due to the influence of a prosecutor in determining the sentence via plea bargaining (discussed in Chapter 11). It has also led to the demise of rehabilitative programming in many prisons and may exacerbate problems arising from overcrowding.

Determinate sentencing systems usually include a provision for "good time" in order to promote prison discipline and keep down the prison population. It generally consists of one day for every day served—50 percent off the sentence. If a defendant were sentenced to a determinate sentence of 5-0-0, he or she would be released (presuming good behavior) after 2-6-0. In practice, good time is deducted in advance, when the offender is first received at the institution; misbehavior results in time being added. In some states, an inmate may be entitled to additional time off the sentence for exemplary performance: "meritorious good time" or "industrious good time"; in Illinois, this can amount to as many as 180 days. Enhanced good-time schemes are usually a response to court orders that flow from prison overcrowding. Good time provisions have come under severe political assault and many public officials are advocating or enacting "truth in sentencing laws," which reflect the actual amount of time each sentenced offender will serve—or provisions requiring the serving of at least 85 percent of the sentence. Of course, this will increase prison overcrowding, requiring larger expenditures, new schemes for releasing inmates early, or placing more offenders on probation.

Presentence Investigation Report

In some states, before imposing a sentence, the judge is required to order a presentence investigation (PSI) report; in other jurisdictions, it is discretionary. The presentence report has several purposes: Most important, it serves as a guide for the judge in the exercise of sentencing discretion, especially when a sentence of probation instead of imprisonment is being considered. In most jurisdictions, the report is given to the judge, prosecutor, and defense counsel and becomes a subject at the sentencing hearing. (The PSI also assists correctional authorities to classify prisoners and probation and parole agencies to supervise offenders.)

In some jurisdictions (e.g., Illinois) the judge has very wide discretion, and therefore the presentence report may be quite important. In other states, such as California, the judge has limited discretion, which renders the presentence report relatively unimportant. Most cases end not with a trial, but with a negotiated plea of guilty. This makes the presentence report unnecessary, although in some jurisdictions a similar (pre-plea) report is submitted to provide a basis for plea bargaining.

Sentencing Hearing

In some states, sentencing authority rests with the jury in all serious criminal cases, and in a few others that authority is restricted to particular types of cases. In 37 states and the federal system, sentencing is the prerogative of the trial judge, and "in most states no person can be put to death unless the jury, through its verdict, says that he or she deserves to die" (Hans and Vidmar 1986: 220).

*C*LASSICALISM	*P*OSITIVISM
Equality/punishment	Discretion/rehabilitation
Determinate sentencing	**Indeterminate sentencing**
(specific term of years, e.g., 5-0-0)	(minimum/maximum, e.g., 3-0-0/9-0-0)

PRESENTENCE INVESTIGATION REPORT

The primary purpose of the probation department's presentence investigation (PSI) is to assist the judge in rendering a sentencing decision based not only on the criminal record but on the social and psychological background of the offender (see Abadinsky 2002). The PSI report typically contains information on the following items:

- Offense
    - Official version
    - Statement of police officer, complainants, victims
    - Defendant's version
- Prior juvenile and criminal record
- Family history
    - Defendant
    - Parents and siblings
    - Spouse and children
- Education
- Health
    - Physical
    - Mental
- Employment history
- Financial condition
- Victim impact statement
- Evaluation and summary
- Recommendation

The Supreme Court has ruled that a defendant who has been convicted has a right to be represented at sentencing by an attorney. Counsel can muster facts and present them in a manner most likely to benefit the defendant in his or her attempt to win some form of leniency from the court. The prosecutor and the defense are permitted to address the court, each advocating an outcome in this final scene of the long adversarial process. The judge's degree of discretion varies depending on the statutes and the particular sentencing scheme used, indeterminate or definite. Generally the judge can impose a fine and/or, if the subject is eligible, a sentence of probation. The judge can impose a sentence of incarceration in the county or the local jail (for terms of one year or less) or in a state prison for felony convictions. For some offenses in various jurisdictions, there is a mandatory sentence for certain crimes.

APPEALS

The American system of justice is unique in the extensive post-conviction review procedures to which a defendant is entitled. A convict may petition the trial court for a new trial or take an appeal to the state's intermediate appellate court, and if unsuccessful there, can still appeal to the state court of last resort. If unsuccessful in state court, he or she can petition the U.S. Supreme Court for certiorari. The convict can also attack the conviction "collaterally" (using indirect means by way of a writ of *habeas corpus*) claiming that his or her constitutional rights were violated in some way by the state court conviction. Habeas corpus requires authorities holding a prisoner to produce him or her and justify custody. Having exhausted direct and indirect appeals in state courts, he or she can move over to the federal courts claiming again that the conviction was unconstitutional, usually on grounds of lack of due process.

The appeal of a guilty verdict requires submitting a notice of appeal and elaborate documents, including a trial transcript. In 1963 (*Douglas* v. *California*), the Supreme Court ruled that an indigent defendant is entitled to state-appointed counsel on the first appeal following a felony conviction. Court rulings in 1990 curtailed the right of state prison inmates to appeal in federal courts using favorable rulings that have been issued since their own convictions (*Butler* v. *McKellar*; *Saffle* v. *Parks*).

An appeal—criminal or civil—is a separate proceeding, rather than a continuation of the trial. The appellate court cannot act as a trial court (i.e., receive new evidence concerning facts already established at the original trial). It is limited to addressing new theories or legal arguments regarding the law applicable to these facts or challenges to a verdict based on errors of procedure—applying the rules of evidence, for example. As noted above, in order to preserve the right to appeal, defense counsel is required to raise objections to errors committed at trial, objections that allow problems to be corrected immediately by the trial judge. These objections become part of the trial record upon which the appeal is based. While, in general, appellate courts will review only those claims that were properly presented at trial, there are a number of exceptions designed to protect defendant rights (Israel and LaFave 1980). The appellate court (as noted in Chapter 7) can uphold the verdict, overturn it, or order it reversed and remanded to the trial court for a new trial.

PROBATION AND PAROLE

Persons sentenced to probation and those released from prison by a parole board or based on time off their sentence for "good behavior" typically come under the supervision of a probation or parole officer. The former is usually part of the judicial branch; the latter is always part of the executive branch, although some states combine probation and parole (P/P) in the same agency under the executive branch (see Abadinsky 2003). P/P officers have responsibility for enforcing the rules and regulations by which a probationer or parolee/conditional releasee is required to abide. If the P/P officer alleges that the rules have been violated, an administrative process will be implemented.

At the beginning of this chapter, it was learned that the amount of due process required is dependent upon what is at stake. Persons on probation and parole have already been convicted and, therefore, are not entitled to the same rights as a criminal defendant. But while supervision in the community curtails freedom, it is valuable—less restrictive than incarceration. This provides a "liberty interest," and therefore due process rights before probation or parole can be revoked. For probation violations, a preliminary hearing (as per *Gagnon* v. *Scarpelli* 1973) will take place before a judge—if possible, the one who imposed the original sentence of probation.

At the preliminary hearing, the judge will determine if there is sufficient evidence (probable cause) to indicate that the probationer violated one or more of the conditions of probation in an important respect. If so, the probationer can be held in custody for 60 days pending a revocation hearing. At the preliminary and revocation hearings, the probationer will have an opportunity to confront and question adverse witnesses, be represented by counsel, and provide evidence on his or her own behalf. At the revocation hearing, the judge considers the probationer's entire record while under supervision (e.g., employment record) in addition to the rule violations, and makes a decision (based on the preponderance of the evidence) whether to continue probation or revoke supervision and order the offender to serve his or her sentence in jail or prison.

For parole violations, the process is similar, except that the hearing is not part of the judicial system; rather it is held under the administrative authority of the parole board (as per *Morrissey* v. *Brewer* 1972). The preliminary hearing is usually conducted by a hearing officer, and the revocation hearing by members of the parole board. At the revocation hearing, members of the parole board determine whether the violation is serious enough to warrant returning the parolee to prison.

EXECUTIVE CLEMENCY

All states and the federal government (Article II of the Constitution) have provisions for clemency. In 31 states and the federal government, the chief executive holds the final clemency power, and in most of these states, the parole board or a clemency board appointed by the governor investigates clemency applications at the request of the governor. Clemency consists of the reprieve, the commutation, and the pardon. A reprieve is a temporary suspension of the execution of sentence. Its use today is quite limited and usually concerns cases in which capital punishment has been ordered. In such cases, a governor or the president of the United States can grant a reprieve—a stay of execution—to provide more time for further legal action or other deliberations. A commutation is a modification of sentence to the benefit of an offender. Commutation has been used when an inmate provided some assistance to the prison staff, such as during prison riots. It may also be granted to inmates with a severe illness, like AIDS or cancer. Laws governing commutation differ from state to state, and it is traditionally granted at Christmas time. A pardon is an unconditional forgiveness for any crimes committed and, in addition to a release from a prison sentence, can restore civil/legal rights lost as a result of a criminal conviction.

Now that we have examined the criminal trial process, in the next chapter we will examine how most criminal cases are adjudicated, through negotiation and a plea of guilty.

INTERNET CONNECTIONS

National Institute of Justice. *ojp.usdoj.gov/nij*
National Criminal Justice Reference Service: *ncjrs.org*
Legal Resource Center: *crimelynx.com/research.html*

Criminal justice links: *lawguru.com/ilawlib/96.htm*

American Bar Association Criminal Justice links: *abanet.org/crimjust/links.html*

U.S Department of Justice links: *usdoj.gov/02organizations/02_1.html*

American Society of Trial Consultants: *astcweb.org*

Criminal justice links: *statesnews.org/other_resources/law_and_justice.htm*

American Probation and Parole Association: *APPA.org*

National Association of Pretrial Services: *napsa.org*

Probation departments: *cppca.org/link.html*

Parole links: *tbcnet.com/~salsberry/Parole%20Sites.htm*

Parole boards: *crimelynx.com/stateparole.html*

REVIEW QUESTIONS

1. What is meant by the need to prove the *corpus delicti* in a criminal case?

2. How does strict liability effect *mens rea*?

3. How can there be *mens rea* when harmful behavior is committed by accident?

4. How does the crime control model differ from the due process model in criminal justice?

5. What are the basic due process guarantees to which every criminal defendant is entitled?

6. How does the exclusionary rule control police behavior?

7. What is the "reasonable mistake" exception to the exclusionary rule?

8. How have Supreme Court decisions effected specific due process guarantees?

9. What is meant by the concept of "probable cause"?

10. Why are the lower courts referred to as dispensing "rough justice"?

11. What is the purpose of a grand jury?

12. What are criticisms of the grand jury?

13. What is the purpose of a preliminary hearing?

14. What is the purpose of a *voir dire* hearing?

15. How does "scientific jury selection" operate?

16. How is direct evidence distinguished from indirect or circumstantial?

17. How can circumstantial evidence be more reliable than direct evidence?

18. What is the purpose of a prosecutor's opening statement in a jury trial?

19. How does the Fifth Amendment right to confront adverse witnesses affect the manner in which evidence must be presented in a trial?

20. What is the chain of custody?

21. How does a defense attorney prepare the trial record for a possible appeal?

22. What is the purpose of a defense attorney's cross-examination?

23. What rules govern a jury's deliberations?

24. What does the classical approach recommend with respect to sentencing?

25. What does the positive approach recommend with respect to sentencing?

26. How can determinate sentencing schemes be differentiated according to discretion?

27. Why is it necessary to have a parole board in a system that uses indeterminate sentencing?

28. What is the primary purpose of a presentence report?

29. Why would a presentence report not be important in sentencing schemes based on a classical approach?

30. What are the different types of executive clemency?

11

NEGOTIATED JUSTICE: PLEA BARGAINING

Most court cases in the United States, criminal and civil, are settled not by trial but by negotiation (or dropping of the action). Only about 3 to 4 percent of all civil filings and criminal cases are disposed of by trial. In the federal system, jury trials account for 4.3 percent of criminal cases and 1.5 percent of civil cases (Glaberson 2001). In the criminal justice system, negotiated settlements are referred to as plea bargaining, an ad hoc exchange between a defendant who agrees to plead guilty to a criminal charge and a prosecutor who offers leniency in return. The degree of leniency depends upon a variety of factors that are the subject of the first part of this chapter.

PLEA BARGAINING

Plea bargaining in the United States dates back more than 100 years (Friedman 1979) and "appears to have become fairly well entrenched in a number of United States jurisdictions by the 1880s" (Sanborn 1986: 134). In New York City, for example, guilty pleas composed as much as 85 percent of the total number of convictions during the last two decades of the nineteenth century (Sanborn 1986). At this time, "judges found themselves confronted by an onslaught of new, and newly complex, civil suits brought on by the ravages of industrial machinery," and they embraced the expediency of negotiating outcomes in civil and criminal cases (Fisher 2000: 1074).

In the 1920s, plea bargaining was criticized as a device for enabling politically connected defendants to gain preferential treatment; when it emerged as an issue again during the 1950s, however, its condemnation centered around the coercion involved in "forcing" a defendant to plead guilty (Nardulli 1978). In more recent

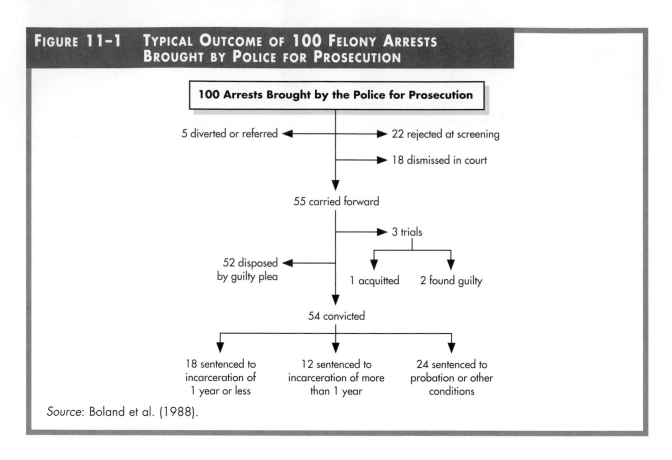

FIGURE 11-1   TYPICAL OUTCOME OF 100 FELONY ARRESTS BROUGHT BY POLICE FOR PROSECUTION

100 Arrests Brought by the Police for Prosecution

5 diverted or referred ◄——————► 22 rejected at screening

————► 18 dismissed in court

55 carried forward

————► 3 trials

52 disposed by guilty plea ◄——————

1 acquitted   2 found guilty

54 convicted

18 sentenced to incarceration of 1 year or less

12 sentenced to incarceration of more than 1 year

24 sentenced to probation or other conditions

Source: Boland et al. (1988).

debates, plea bargaining has been criticized for providing criminals with excessive leniency and coercing defendants to waive their constitutional rights to a trial. Nevertheless, in more than 90 percent of felony cases the defendant pleads guilty, and this is most likely to be the result of some sort of plea bargain, explicit or implicit (Dawson 1992).

Plea bargaining occurs "when a defendant enters a guilty plea with the reasonable expectation of receiving some consideration from the state" (McDonald 1985: 6). In some jurisdictions, however, a trial can be more like a plea bargain than the adversarial proceeding it is supposed to symbolize: "Defendants learn that if they agree not to contest the trial they will receive more lenient sentences than they might if they challenge the cases against them." Although such cases are essentially plea bargains, they are counted as trials and help maintain the appearance of a trial system. Paul Wice notes that consideration from the state can take two forms, "being charged with a less serious crime, which will usually result in a lighter sentence, or receiving the minimum punishment allowable for the originally charged offense" (1985: 24).

Plea bargaining is often criticized as an abuse of discretion that results in leniency for serious criminals. On the other hand, it is also criticized as unfair to defendants who must either waive their constitutional rights or run the risk of a substantially higher sentence if found guilty after a trial: The significant sentencing differences between guilty pleas and jury trials support the idea that the defendant who plea bargained got away with something (Guidorizzi 1998). Popular perceptions of plea bargaining, however, fall far short of reality. In order to better understand the reality of plea bargaining, we will examine two opposing views.

THE NEGATIVE VIEW

Critics argue that plea bargaining is a symptom of a system operated to further the needs of principal actors rather than the needs or interests of justice or the public. Heavily funded police departments bring an abundance of cases into a judicial system that does not have the resources necessary to provide individualized justice. Justice requires a deliberately slow and exacting concern for due process; it is a luxury the system cannot afford—cases resulting in trials take about twice as long as cases disposed of by guilty pleas (Bureau of Justice Statistics 1986). In response to this dilemma, the key actors—judges, prosecutors, defense attorneys—disregard the goal of justice and, instead, tailor their activities to enable the system to function with a minimum of difficulty or disruption.

In the United States, justice is ensured through the adversarial method, an ideal characterized by a vigorous prosecutor for the state who is opposed by an equally vigorous advocate for the defendant in a courtroom battle staged before judge and jury. In the view of Abraham Blumberg, the requirements of the judicial system have led to an abandonment of the adversarial ideal—and thus justice, the practice of criminal law being reduced to a *confidence game.* "Organizational goals and discipline impose a set of demands and conditions of practice on the respective professions in the criminal court, to which they respond by abandoning their ideological and professional commitments to the accused client, in the service of these higher claims of the court organization. All court personnel, including the accused's own lawyer, tend to be coopted to become agent-mediators who help the accused redefine his situation and restructure his perceptions concomitant with a plea of guilty" (1967: 19–20).

How does the system "help" defendants "redefine" their situation in a manner that induces a plea of guilty? The scenario begins with criminal statutes that prescribe lengthy terms of imprisonment for many felony crimes. Although these sentences are rarely imposed, they serve to generate a great deal of fear in a defendant. This fear is aided by police and prosecutors who engage in overcharging, vertical and horizontal. *Vertical overcharging* means charging a single offense at a higher level than the cir-

POLITICS OF PLEA BARGAINING

"Demagogues seek to establish that they are tough on crime and that others are not, thereby harnessing for themselves the tremendous public emotion that the crime issue generates. It is thus in the self-interest of entrepreneurial politicians to portray the criminal justice system as worse than it is—and to preach against plea bargaining as a particularly odious part of that system" (McCoy 1993: xvi).

cumstances in the case would appear to support, such as charging murder in a case where the evidence seems to indicate manslaughter, or charging as a felony the kind of case routinely disposed of as a misdemeanor. *Horizontal overcharging* means charging the arrestee with every conceivable crime even remotely related to his or her actions, even though the actual sentence will usually be limited to that available for the highest offense on which a conviction is obtained (see *joinder of offenses* in Chapter 10). Twenty-five years later, David Lynch, who served as both a public defender and a prosecutor, supported Blumberg's assertions: "It has been my experience that judges, lawyers, and even police officers often love plea bargaining. They love it not because it prevents the breakdown of the criminal justice system but because it helps them avoid work and stress" (1994: 122).

What about Blumberg's charge that defense counsel is, in effect, a "double agent"? In his investigation of the charge, Rodney Uphoff (2002: 88) found that low income defendants who do not qualify for public defender or assigned counsel often cannot obtain adequate legal representation. They are advised by defense counsel that the meager retainer paid will only cover a negotiated plea. "The economic realities of the system, not the defense lawyer's lack of zeal, frequently pressure the defendant to accept a plea." He concludes that "unless we give defense lawyers the necessary resources and incentives to challenge the state, our adversarial system indeed will drift further toward the co-optative system Blumberg described" (2002: 98).

In order to better manipulate the client, Michael Cox points out, the defense counsel is assisted by the prosecutor:

> Prosecutors have great leverage; they draft the charges and generally make recommendations on sentencing. These prosecutorial prerogatives put the defendant at a disadvantage. A prosecutor may "overcharge," either horizontally (e.g., in a bad check case charge uttering, obtaining by false pretenses, and forgery, even though they may overlap and be multiplicious for sentencing), or vertically (e.g., always charge homicides as first degree murder). Through overcharging, an accused is immediately put on the defensive. If the case is tried on the merits, a jury will often react by thinking (even if only subconsciously), "There are so many charges and they are so serious; the defendant must be guilty of something." The number of charges/specifications and the "degree" [e.g., robbery in the first degree or burglary in the second degree] are at the heart of plea negotiations. As an added incentive to deal, a prosecutor may threaten to recommend a high sentence if conviction is obtained after a trial on the merits. (1975: 34)

Thus, at their first meeting the defense counsel tells the defendant that if convicted on the highest count or on all of the counts alleged by police, he or she will be ready for Social Security before being released from prison. The unsettling prospect of a lengthy prison term signals the beginning of a softening up process. As a part of this, overcharging results in higher bail, which can cause the defendant to remain in jail while awaiting adjudication. Even when compared to prisons, most jails are unpleasant places, leaving defendants desperate to get out.

If the system is to function efficiently, the occasional recalcitrant defendant must be made to serve as an example for others who might be contemplating a jury trial. Thus, "after Ron Baker was arrested for robbery, prosecutors offered him probation in return for a guilty plea. The public defender assigned to handle his case urged him to accept the offer. But Baker, a delivery man with no criminal convictions, pleaded innocent and asked for a chance to prove it in a jury trial. Eventually he was convicted, and the same judge who had earlier approved the probation offer sentenced

*P*LEA *B*ARGAINING AS *D*ISASTER

"Constitutional and doctrinal objections aside, plea bargaining seriously impairs the public interest in effective punishment of crime and in accurate separation of the guilty from the innocent" (Schulhofer 1992: 1979). For a response to Schulhofer, see Gorr (2000).

Baker to six years in prison" (Tybor and Eissman 1985: 1). In another county, a defendant refused to be intimidated by the judge into accepting a plea bargain, and lost at trial. "He received a 30-year sentence, one so harsh (though perfectly legal) for the crimes committed that attorneys reacted with stunned disbelief about it. . . . That was the last time any defense attorney dared to have a trial before that judge for a long, long time" (Lynch 1994: 120).

In Tulsa, Oklahoma, the 38-year-old defendant declined a plea bargain for sentences totaling 10 years for marijuana possession. After a trial, he was convicted. Noting that the defendant had rejected plea negotiations that would have allowed a much lighter punishment, the judge imposed prison sentences totaling 93 years (Braun 1997). The judicial attitude behind such treatment is summed up in the statement: "He takes some of my time; I take some of his" (Uhlman and Walker 1980).

If the defendant is able to secure private counsel, in addition to being concerned about the outcome of the case, he or she must be concerned about paying legal fees. As noted in Chapter 9, criminal attorneys depend on quantity rather than quality and demand "upfront money" because their clients are generally poor and unreliable. In most cases this will not be sufficient for the hours typically required for a jury trial. "Most attorneys who specialize in criminal cases depend on a high turnover of clients who can afford only modest fees. Without high volume and the investment of a modest amount of time in each case, many a private defense counsel would go broke" (Jacob and Eisenstein 1977: 26). Most work for a flat fee paid in advance. "Since court rules usually prohibit defense counsel from withdrawing once an appearance has been entered, a retained attorney is obliged to take her case to trial if settlement negotiations fail, and in that event, her additional services are rendered free of charge" (Schulhofer 1992: 1988). Under such circumstances, a private defense counsel is likely to recommend that the client plead guilty in exchange for leniency. For a defendant facing the prospect of a lengthy term of imprisonment, this may appear to be sound advice. Summarizing the purpose of these plea bargaining practices, Albert Alschuler states that "overcharging and subsequent charge reduction are often the components of an elaborate sham, staged for the benefit of defense attorneys. The process commonly has little or no effect on the defendant's sentence, and prosecutors may simply wish to give defense attorneys a 'selling point' in their efforts to induce defendants to plead guilty" (1968: 95).

Public Defender

While private defense counsel must depend on client fees, the public defender is a salaried employee who is paid regardless of how many cases he or she handles. Nevertheless, "public defender organizations charged with representing all indigent

"Let's Make a Deal"

"Once people are arrested, and when the number of arrests start skyrocketing, the court system itself becomes jammed. There simply aren't enough judges and there isn't enough time for each defendant to get a trial. Especially when someone has been arrested and been convicted before, he faces a particularly daunting choice.

"In certain states, like California, where the legislature has passed mandatory sentencing for certain crimes, insisting on a trial could mean a life sentence. Both prosecutors and defense attorneys are acutely aware of that pressure. Hence, the attraction of the so-called plea bargain. Avoid the trial altogether. Accept a relatively mild sentence of, say, six to eight years in prison, and live to walk the streets again. Except that what gets lost in the shuffle is the case of the occasionally innocent defendant who takes the deal rather than face the prospect of what will happen if he loses at trial. And that . . . actually happens more often than you might like to believe." Ted Koppel, "Let's Make a Deal," ABC News, May 12, 2000.

defendants prefer a quick disposition because their manpower barely suffices to handle their case load" (Jacob and Eisenstein 1977: 26). A report for the City Bar Association revealed that indigent defendants in New York City were not being adequately represented; legal aid lawyers in the criminal division were seeking to process as many cases as possible instead of providing vigorous advocacy for clients. The report stated that "barely .5 percent of the cases handled by society attorneys resulted in a trial and more complex cases were referred to court-appointed counsel, many of whom were incompetent, if not senile" (Margolick 1985: E4).

While the public defender is a salaried employee, he or she may experience pressure from trial judges concerned with disposing of as many cases as possible and as quickly as possible. Trial judges are under pressure from the chief administrative judge anxious to move cases so they do not exceed speedy trial requirements and thus require dismissal. In 1999 in Baltimore, for example, a judge dismissed first-degree murder charges against four men who had been awaiting trial for almost three years. The delay was a result of a massive backlog in the criminal courts because of aggressive policing designed to reduce the rate of homicides (Janofsky 1999).

Pressure from a trial judge may begin with a judge's suggestion that a certain plea agreement would be fair and if a defender accepts this suggestion, the matter is at an end. Defenders who resist judicial suggestions too often, however, are frequently forced to endure abusive remarks from the bench:

"You're a quasi-public agency. You should be interested in justice."
"Haven't you got any client control?"
"You spend too much time on hardened criminals."
"No private attorney would take this case to trial."
"You must be awfully eager for experience."
"When will you guys bend to reality?"
"You guys believe your clients too much."
"You're acting like a private lawyer." (Alschuler 1975: 1237)

The counsel for the defense—whether private, public defender, or assigned—shares a great deal in common with prosecutors and judges: a similar educational, professional, and often political background. Defense attorneys are socialized into a closed system, and they learn that a price must be paid for failing to understand and abide by system norms. Milton Heumann describes how this socialization takes place: "In the process of handling their cases, new defense attorneys learn that the reality of the court differs from what they had expected; through rewards and sanctions, they are taught to proceed in a certain fashion" (1978: 57). In particular, he points out, they learn to avoid legal challenges that can gain the enmity of both prosecutors and judges and may be seen as frivolous. "The hostility of prosecutors and judges to these time-consuming motions is communicated to the new attorney. First, the prosecutor or judge may simply call the defense attorney into his office and explain that the motions are needless formalities. If this advice is insufficient to dissuade the newcomer, sanctions such as 'hassling' the attorney by dragging the case out over a long period of time, closing all files to the attorney, and even threatening to go to trial on the case, ensue" (1978: 62). Lynch states that many defense attorneys fear trials because they lack trial experience, and this fear "not only causes attorneys to talk clients into plea bargaining when their clients really want to go to trial but also can negatively affect their ability to negotiate, since they know in their hearts that they fear going to trail" (1994: 1270).

Conformity is rewarded; attorneys who cooperate, who do not raise time-consuming motions or engage in frivolous behavior, can expect to build "credit" that can be drawn upon in time of need, as one public defender points out: "Everybody, by virtue of being a good guy, has so many chips a year that he can cash in. You go in to a judge and you say, 'Look, judge. I'm busting my buns every day in this dang court, and I need a break on this case.' It has nothing to do with justice, nothing to do with law. I need a break. Okay! You get so many chips a year that you can cash in" (quoted in Eisenstein et al. 1988: 30).

The prosecutor can keep a private attorney hopping by objecting to continuances when the lawyer overbooks. Usually, if counsel requests a continuance, and the prosecutor does not object, it will be routinely granted. If the prosecutor objects, however, and the judge is also opposed, an attorney with several cases scheduled for the same day is in serious trouble. The prosecutor can make the defense attorney's life pleasant or miserable, "by agreeing to or opposing continuances; by opening or closing files for discovery; by waiving or insisting on technical requirements; by recommending or denigrating the attorney to prospective clients; by being generally agreeable or disagreeable" (Dershowitz 1983: 355).

Thus, defense attorneys are forced to abandon their adversarial stance in favor of accommodation. Alschuler states that the system of plea bargaining "leads even able, conscientious, and highly motivated attorneys to make decisions that are not really in their clients' interests" (1975: 1179). Defendants are finessed or coerced, sometimes both, into cooperating with a system that not only is seeking to inflict punishment on them, but also lacks the resources to ensure that the innocent do not plead guilty. Prosecutors whose cases pass initial screening have no option other than to ignore claims of innocence: They have an incentive to avoid any reduction in the penalty for the possibly innocent that might lead to strategic behavior—"I'm innocent and deserve a break"—by guilty defendants (Scott and Stuntz 1992).

THE BENIGN OR POSITIVE VIEW

When asked to explain the existence of plea bargaining, even informed observers point to the amount of cases that threaten to overwhelm the judicial system; they say, "Nobody likes plea bargaining, but it's the only way the system can survive." Candace McCoy argues that the "caseload pressure" explanation is a ploy by court workers to avoid blame for the perceived leniency of plea bargaining: "No court worker wants to be blamed for sentencing leniency, and the caseload hypothesis shifts the blame from criminal justice decisionmakers to their supposedly overloaded working conditions" (1993: 69). Malcolm Feeley (1997) refers to this as the "functional fallacy," and Milton Heumann (1978) points out that guilty pleas have been the outcome of most criminal cases for almost 100 years, even when courts were not overburdened with too many cases. Indeed, trials have not been the central means for resolving criminal or civil cases for more than a century. In New York, for example, in 1839, guilty pleas were 25 percent of convictions; by 1869, that figure had jumped to 70 percent, and they increased every year until leveling off to around 90 percent in the 1920s (Guidorizzi 1998). It was similar in New Haven, Connecticut, during roughly the same period (Feeley 1997).

Heumann states that defense and prosecution have a preference for guilty pleas because they "recognize the factual culpability of many defendants, and the fruitlessness, at least in terms of case outcome, of going to trial. From these perceptions flows the notion that if the obviously guilty defendant cops a plea, he will receive some reward. Whether the defendant believes this results from his show of contrition, or, more prosaically, from saving the state time and money," is irrelevant. "Similarly, prosecutors and judges do not believe that they accord this reward simply to 'move the business.'" By rewarding the defendant who pleads guilty, prosecutors believe they are furthering their own professional goals by sorting serious cases from nonserious ones and obtaining certain prison time in serious cases—it is not simply an expedient to dispose of onerously large case loads (1978: 156).

William McDonald (1985) corroborates this view. His research indicates that, contrary to popular belief, prosecutors are not concerned with the question of case backlog or caseload when they evaluate what to do with specific cases. With respect to overcharging, he points out that it is considerably easier to drop or reduce charges than to add or increase them. Police are likely to charge up not simply to provide room for bargaining, but because the amount of information available early in a case is often limited. (It should also be noted that the credit received by an officer who makes an arrest is dependent on the seriousness of the charges, another reason for charging up.)

Lynch points out that in the suburban county in which he worked, the "evidence against most defendants was overwhelming, and many defendants, realizing this, probably would have pled guilty eventually without a bargain. To go to trial when the evidence is overwhelming would invite public humiliation." But more important, it would indicate an obvious lack of remorse to the judge, who presides not only at the trial but at the sentencing. "Defendants who had little hope of winning at trial generally recognized that trials were not in their best interests and correctly guessed that judges would usually reward a plea of guilty (even one entered without a bargain) with a greatly reduced sentence" (1994: 118).

Malcolm Feeley (1979) explains the prevalence of plea bargaining by noting that one of the norms of the legal profession is a preference for events that have a relatively high level of *predictability*. (This is not unique to lawyers; in most businesses, from grocery stores to auto manufacturers, uncertainty is problematic.) But the trial process lacks predictability; it requires professionals (prosecutor and defense counsel) to relinquish control over the outcome of a case to a jury, a panel of 12 persons (typically) without any legal training. Whether it is a civil or criminal matter, lawyers do not normally find this situation appealing. Research by Celesta Albonetti revealed that "prosecutorial screening following felony indictment is influenced by decision makers' attempts to avoid uncertainty" (1986: 640).[1]

The prosecutor has additional concerns. First, the longer a case takes, the greater the likelihood of an outcome in favor of the defendant. Witnesses may fail to appear, die, or forget important facts, and files are sometimes misplaced or lost. Gathering necessary elements for the trial, including the defendant and witnesses, all at the same time in the same courtroom, can be troublesome. In Los Angeles County, California, for example, the sheriff's office must move more than 1,000 defendants a day from their cells to various courthouses scattered throughout this very large county (Shuster 2001). Nancy Jacobs and Ellen Chayet found that in New York City "trouble in delivering an incarcerated defendant, while not a regular occurrence, consumes nearly two months, on average, when it is a factor. Witness production problems, for either the prosecution or defense, typically adds an average of a month to case processing time" (1986: 15). And producing physical evidence is sometimes a problem. In Chicago, for example, the police department's Evidence and Recovered Property section has a history of losing evidence, including millions of dollars in narcotics and thousands of dollars in jewelry (Ferkenhoff 2001; Hanna and Ferkenhoff 2001).

Another reason for preferring the certainty of plea bargaining is that the gathering of physical evidence at the crime scene and crime lab shortcomings can undermine a prosecutor's case, as dramatically portrayed in the criminal case against O.J. Simpson. In 1985, the state of Illinois ordered the shutdown of a laboratory that regularly botched tests involving drug and drunk-driving cases (Franklin 1985). A study by the Chicago Crime Commission in 1986 revealed that failure to complete tests on suspected contraband drugs substantially hampered prosecution of drug cases in that city (Tybor and Eissman 1986). A three-year study of 240 government-operated crime laboratories at the federal, state, county, and municipal levels revealed that 70 percent failed to perform even a simple blood test correctly (Grunson 1983). "Unlike clinical laboratories which perform tests for hospitals and doctors' offices, the nation's crime laboratories are exempt from regulation and external review," and "there are no minimum certification requirements for lab personnel" (Giannelli 1994: E15). As if to underscore this problem, in 1994 authorities arrested a forensic chemist for falsifying evidence that led to the conviction of dozens of persons in several states, some of whom have already been freed from

---

[1]P.S. Atiyah and R.S. Summers state that "in England the gradual decline in the civil jury over the last fifty years is itself partly due to the fact that barristers actually prefer trial by judges to trial by jurors in civil cases. And this in turn is due to the fact that barristers prefer more rational, and less emotional, fact-finding procedures, and have greater confidence in the fact-finding ability of judges" (1987: 166).

prison as a result of disclosures of impropriety (Associated Press 1994). In 1997, the forensic laboratory of the FBI, long considered exemplary, was criticized by the Department of Justice inspector general for lax procedures in handling evidence (Johnston 1997; Navarro 1997).

Investigations of the medical examiner's offices in New York and Chicago revealed numerous errors in determining the causes of death. And in some counties investigations into the causes of death are conducted by nonphysician elected coroners. As a result, an undetermined number of deaths are misdiagnosed, leading to acquittals for the guilty and convictions for the innocent (Baden and Hennessee 1989). In 1992, a Texas pathologist was convicted of faking autopsies—at least 20 death penalty convictions were obtained with the aid of his testimony (Giannelli 1994). Research indicates that prosecutors are less likely to agree to plea bargain when forensic evidence strongly associates the defendant with the crime (Peterson 1987).

The norms of the legal profession require cordiality between adversaries. As in the case of professional boxers, attorneys are expected to (at least figuratively) shake hands before and after a bout, an act that does not reduce their efforts to emerge victorious. David Neubauer explains that "if defense and prosecution are on good terms, this does not mean the adversary process has broken down. It may be only a reflection of the normal rules of conduct expected of lawyers. The 'cooperation' of defense and prosecution is a product of such general expectations about how lawyers should conduct themselves" (1974: 78).

Although defense attorneys, private or public defenders, are typically on good terms with their counterparts in the prosecutor's office, each is a professional who is expected by the other, as well as by the rest of their legal peers, to behave in a professional manner. And the norms of professionalism require a lawyer to engage in vigorous advocacy; anything less can lead to a loss of respect that can devastate a legal career. And reputation among the principal players is an important dynamic in maintaining respect: "Members of the criminal defense bar are in constant contact with local prosecutors. Reputations are valuable in markets characterized by repeat dealing. A good part of the practice of many defense lawyers, especially in the period before indictment, is supplying information to prosecutors. Prosecutors take seriously information coming from reputable counsel. Guilty defendants cannot copy the signal of innocence sent

Botched Evidence

A prosecutor in Arkansas who admitted the FBI tested the wrong strand of hair from the 1991 murder of a schoolgirl, said he will drop charges against the suspect. Prosecutors originally said DNA testing done on a hair tested by the FBI had linked the defendant to the victim. But they later determined that the tested hair had been taken from the girl during her autopsy, rather than from the defendant's car during the investigation. That left no physical evidence to link the defendant to the death of the 9-year-old (Associated Press 2000a).

THE BENIGN OR POSITIVE VIEW

DREAMWORLD OF PLEA BARGAINING

"Critics of plea bargaining commit the Nirvana Fallacy, comparing an imperfect reality to a perfection achievable only in imaginary system" (U.S. Court of Appeals Judge Frank Easterbrook 1992: 1976).

by careful, honest lawyers. . . . Lawyers with the best evidence of innocence secure the dismissal of charges (or attractive pleas) even though they do not succeed in 'proving' innocence" (Easterbook 1992: 1971–1972).

In place of a trial as the epitome of the adversarial ideal, private plea negotiation has evolved, and as Suzann and Leonard Buckle (1977) argue, plea negotiation is adversarial. In place of two opposing attorneys meeting in a highly dramatic and time-consuming courtroom confrontation, they negotiate in private settings such as the judge's chambers. Each attorney reviews the case, pointing out the strengths of his or her position as opposed to the weaknesses of his or her opponent's position. The process continues until an agreement—a "deal"—can be struck; it is like a mini-trial without the time-consuming formalities required in a courtroom.

During plea bargain conferences with prosecutors in a California municipal court, defense attorneys presented case narratives that highlighted salient characteristics that were advantageous to clients. In effect, they were rehearsing their likely courtroom presentations for the benefit of the prosecutor. Through this approach, attorneys attempted to gain the best possible outcome for clients by portraying their cases as strong relative to the evidence available to the state (Maynard 1988; Emmelman [1996] found a similar approach in the county she studied).

In Alameda County, California, Pamela Utz (1979) found that early discussion between defense and prosecution was encouraged by an informal discovery process during which both sides reviewed the case together before the preliminary hearing. It was understood that cases that were not prison material should not go to trial, while serious cases with good evidence were inappropriate for plea bargaining—nonnegotiable cases. The prosecutor met with the defense attorney as a fellow professional, rather than as an adversary, ready to share in reviewing and evaluating cases. "Using the facts of the case, including what is known about the offender, the two sides try to determine 'what really happened,' and what is an equitable disposition for the particular defendant." According to the unwritten policy that evolved, "the parties must assess the evidence according to the norms of rational inquiry, and each side is there to hold the other accountable. Thus, negotiation continues to presume vigorous advocacy, although the assessment binds both sides who must refrain from threatening a trial. If, after settling the facts, the defendant is judged guilty, the seriousness of the offense is judged according to community interests and a penalty that is realistically related to seriousness and case worth is jointly decided on the basis of established norms" (Utz 1979: 112). In the jurisdiction she studied, Debra Emmelman (1996) found that public defenders frequently used veiled or explicit threats of going to trial as part of their negotiating techniques.

Does the prevalence of plea bargaining indicate that the adversarial method has been abandoned in favor of expediency in the attempt to reduce uncertainty? Feeley states an emphatic no! "To infer the lack of an adversarial stance and the existence of bargained settlements—for the pure purpose of administrative convenience—from the absence of trials is to ignore altogether the importance of these other 'truth testing' and highly combative processes. . . . . [In other words] combativeness—short of trial—does in fact exist" (1979: 29).

THE PROCESS AND THE LAW

The accomplishment of a plea bargain depends on many factors, particularly the prosecutor's assessment of the case and agreement among judicial actors about the appropriate charges. When a prosecutor receives a case from the police, its strengths and weaknesses are evaluated. This is usually done by an assistant prosecutor assigned to an intake (screening) unit. A prosecutor's office frequently has to deal with dozens of state, county, and municipal police agencies (and even more in some metropolitan areas). As would be expected, some agencies perform better than others. Some police officers are well trained and conscientious; some are poorly trained and lack motivation. The prosecutor receives cases from them all.

Rather than waste scarce resources prosecuting petty or weak cases, prosecutors employ a screening system that generally follows a scheme with four categories for rating cases (outlined in Figure 11–2):

Category I. A case in which the charges are not serious and the evidence is weak will usually not be prosecuted.

Category II. A case in which the charges are not serious but the evidence is strong is a good candidate for plea bargaining.

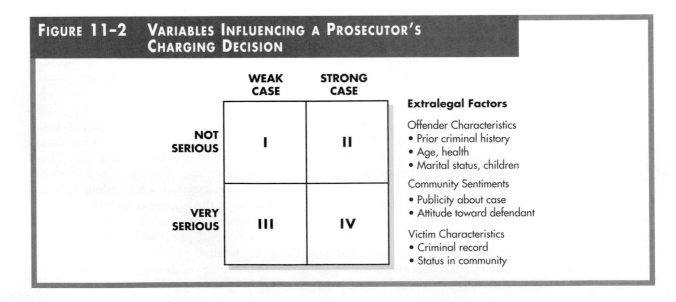

FIGURE 11-2   VARIABLES INFLUENCING A PROSECUTOR'S CHARGING DECISION

	WEAK CASE	STRONG CASE
NOT SERIOUS	I	II
VERY SERIOUS	III	IV

Extralegal Factors

Offender Characteristics
• Prior criminal history
• Age, health
• Marital status, children

Community Sentiments
• Publicity about case
• Attitude toward defendant

Victim Characteristics
• Criminal record
• Status in community

Category III.   A case in which the charges are serious but the evidence is weak is a good candidate for rejection, dismissal, or plea bargaining.[2]

Category IV.   A case in which the charges are very serious and the evidence is strong is a candidate for vigorous prosecution.

One research effort found that in cases in which the prosecutor believes the defendant to be guilty but the legally admissible evidence does not support successful prosecution, "using the threat of a prison or jail sentence as a lever, the prosecutor may bargain with defense counsel and defendant for a reduced charge or a suspended sentence in return for a plea of guilty" (Winfree and Kielich 1979: 176). Another researcher found "an overwhelming propensity to moderate the harshness of plea bargain terms to defendants if the government had a weak case against them" (Champion 1989: 257).

In addition to legal factors that influence a prosecutor's charging decision, there are extralegal factors such as the defendant's prior criminal record, age, health, marital status, and work history; publicity about the case; and the background and status of the victim. Donald Black refers to the social structure of a case: Are the differences in *social status* between perpetrator and victim upward or downward? Is there a low status defendant and high status victim (more favorable to the prosecutor), or vice versa? What is the relationship, if any, between victim and perpetrator? And what about the probable judge and jury? In one study, for example, white judges were found "more likely than black judges to convict defendants of serious crimes (felonies). White judges handling black defendants have the highest conviction rate, and black judges handling white defendants have the lowest conviction rate. A comparison of sentencing in two cities indicates that judges of northern European ancestry and those from a middle-class background are more legalistic and severe than ethnic judges (such as Jews and Italian-Americans) and those from a low-income background" (Black 1989: 16). An experimental study revealed that white jurors were more likely than black jurors to find a criminal defendant guilty, and even more likely to do so when the defendant is black (Black 1989). Another study found that "a defendant's socioeconomic condition influences his/her chances regarding plea bargain agreements," and that "prosecutors appear to be most sensitive about who represents an alleged offender" (Champion 1989: 262). In some cases the defendant will assist police or the prosecutor, such as by providing information about other criminals. These factors combine with evidentiary aspects of a case to determine the charging decision.

The degree of case screening accomplished by a prosecutor's office differs from jurisdiction to jurisdiction. A jurisdiction that subjects cases to an early and vigorous review "increases the degree of confidence we can have that the guilty plea process is convicting probably guilty defendants" (McDonald 1985: 46). Where such screening is not used, guilty pleas may be made without those "values associated with ideas about legality and the requirement of proof beyond a reasonable doubt." On the other hand, vigorous screening programs "reject cases that could have been convicted through plea

---

[2]According to the Bureau of Justice Statistics, "evidence-related deficiencies and witness problems account for more than half the rejections by prosecutors at screening. In most jurisdictions, evidence and witness problems are also the most common reasons for dismissals in court" (1985: 14).

bargaining. For those who believe that a little bit of punishment for a lot of offenders, regardless of the seriousness of their crimes or their prior records, deters more crime than the selective prosecution of a smaller number of serious offenders, rigorous screening is not regarded as positive reform" (McDonald 1985: 46–47). There exist many difficulties when evaluating prosecutorial performance on the basis of a conviction rate since "it may be a sign of excellent prosecutorial performance or a sign of overly conservative charging policies" (Feeney, Dill, and Weir 1983: 243).

Strong cases are built on quality investigations—all the available evidence has been gathered and all of the witnesses have been found and interviewed. Cases brought in by police may fail to meet the evidentiary standard necessary to justify prosecution and are rejected at screening. A high rejection rate "may be a sign of lax performance by either the police or the prosecutor, illegal or highly aggressive police work" (Feeney, Dill, and Weir 1983: 243). Research indicates that only a small fraction of police officers (8 to 19 percent) account for about half of the arrests that end in convictions. These officers are apparently more adept at gathering evidence than their peers (Boland et al. 1983).

Serious cases that appear strong at intake can begin to weaken as time passes. They are either dropped after charges have been filed or negotiated down to secure a guilty plea. The Vera Institute of Justice found the main reason that many of the cases that begin as felonies are not prosecuted as felonies is because "a high percentage of them, in every crime category from murder[3] to burglary, involve victims with whom the suspect has had prior, often close relations. Logically, suspects who are known to their victims are more likely to be caught than strangers because they can be identified more easily by the complainants. And this very fact of a previous personal relationship often leads a complainant to be reluctant to pursue prosecution through adjudication" (1977: 134). This reluctance can be the result of tempers that cool with the passage of time; or informal mediation, conciliation and/or restitution may have been effective; or the complainant may have been intimidated.

Because criminal conduct is often the explosive spillover from ruptured personal relations among neighbors, friends, lovers, and spouses, prosecutors are sometimes reluctant to prosecute as full-scale felonies cases that erupted from quarrels between persons with close prior relationships. Often the primary purpose of an arrest in such situations is to defuse a potentially violent situation, and these cases are frequently candidates for rejection at screening or subsequent dismissal in court (Vera Institute 1977). (Increased awareness and concern with the problem of domestic violence may alter this picture.)

Prosecutors who utilize a more intensive case-screening policy drop fewer charges after filing: "One effect of a rigorous screening policy is that crimes that are in essence private disputes are prevented from taking up costly court time and resources. Studies have shown that many crimes against persons involve individuals who had some kind of prior relationship. At the time of the incident, police intervention may be necessary to quell a potentially explosive situation. But by the time the case is brought to court, the victim often no longer wants to prosecute. With experience, prosecutors learn to identify such cases and can prevent them from getting into the

---

[3]A study by James Fox revealed that of all the homicides committed between 1980 and 1987 in which the perpetrator was known, less than 24 percent were committed by strangers (Malcolm 1989).

court system only to be dropped later in the proceedings" (Boland et al. 1983: 6). An overwhelming majority of assault cases investigated in New York City "were alleged to have occurred between friends and relatives." These cases were usually treated quite leniently (Bernstein et al. 1977: 374).

Plea bargaining may result from a prosecutor's perception that the case is unlikely to be won at trial due to the failure of a complainant to cooperate because of intimidation, or "because the burden of further cooperation exceeds his ebbing anger, or his sense of civic duty, or his tolerance of the treatment he received in court. He . . . may live far from the courthouse, and his presence is required on a great many occasions along the enforcement route—when he files the complaint, at the preliminary hearing, before the grand jury, and finally at trial. While not all cases travel the whole route, some of these occasions require repeated appearances because of unforeseen adjournments and other managerial obstacles" (Zeisel 1982: 27). These adjournments may be the result of a paucity of attorneys to represent indigent defendants. As noted in Chapter 9, some jurisdictions have a difficult time finding attorneys who will accept assignments to represent indigent defendants, because of the low compensation. As a result, cases are repeatedly delayed because assigned counsel are overloaded with cases that are scheduled for trial.

Reduced charges, however, often are "not the result of negotiations between prosecutor and defense counsel but, rather, reflect the unilateral decision on the part of the prosecutor that the appropriate conviction charge should be a less serious crime than the initial arrest or court charges" (Boland and Brady 1985: 18; also Winfree and Kielich 1979). Such decisions are normally made early in case processing.

NORMAL CRIMES

The outcome of cases not screened out at intake or dropped after charges have been filed is usually a guilty plea, the result of some form of negotiation, implicit or explicit, based on one of two models:

1. *Concessions model* "emphasizes explicit bargaining over the terms of the agreement, haggling in the style of a middle-eastern bazaar."
2. *Consensus model* "likens agreement to a shopper's acceptance of a super-market's posted prices. Once the nature of the item is known, the posted price, the 'going rate,' prevails" (Eisenstein, Flemming, Nardulli 1988: 243). This approach can be seen in a discussion of "normal crimes."

While the guilty plea is most often a result of some form of exchange, the actual process may be so simple that it cannot be accurately described as "negotiation." David Sudnow (1965) explains such transactions by introducing the concept of *normal crimes*: those that have common features (the ways they usually occur, the characteristics of persons who commit them, as well as the typical victims) and can be classified as "normal." For example, a "normal burglary" involves a nonprofessional violator who is black or Latino, no weapons, low-priced items, little property damage, and a lower class victim. However, possession of firearms, harm to the occupants, victims who are not lower class, indications of professional criminality (see Abadinsky 1983), or organized crime (see Abadinsky 2000), for example, would remove the incident from the category of "normal burglary." If the defense attorney and prosecutor agree that a burglary is a normal one, custom and precedent provide for a settlement without the need for negotiation. Although the statutes provide a penalty for each crime, judicial actors have established their own unwritten penalties for each "normal crime," which, because they mitigate statutory penalties, serve to encourage pleas of guilty and thus ensure a penalty for the perpetrator at a minimum expenditure of scarce legal resources.

This procedure is made possible by the reality that "core members of the [court] community usually develop a common understanding of what penalties ought to be attached to which crimes and defendants" (Eisenstein et al. 1988: 203). "[T]hrough daily wrangling, court workers generally agree on a baseline, expected sentence for each category of crime" (McCoy 1993: 55). During his research, Dean Champion found "considerable agreement among prosecutors concerning the going rate for various offenses" that facilitated plea bargain agreements (1989: 256–257). Serious crimes, however, especially those likely to be tracked by the news media, are less likely to fall into a "going rate" category—cases that Sudnow might view as not "normal." Most defense attorneys will candidly admit that virtually all of their felony clients are undoubtedly guilty, and the cases against them are usually conclusive. Under such conditions, forcing a trial makes little sense. As one Cook County assistant public defender comments: "You get a guy who was caught red-handed with the proceeds, with the stuff, and he's already confessed. . . . The state's attorney offers a good deal, and my guy's happy with it. As long as my client is happy with it, and especially as long as I can't see how by pushing it we could do better, then I tell him go ahead and cop, and take the plea. So, essentially the case is over. It maybe only took a half hour; hell, it maybe only took five minutes. But why should I spend any more of my time on it? Sometimes I pick up maybe fifteen cases like that in one morning. Sometimes more" (McIntyre 1987: 64).

Emmelman (1996) found that cases are often not immediately subjected to plea bargaining, and some involve multiple episodes of plea bargaining in which the negotiations entail a wide array of formal litigation proceedings. The public defenders "generally believe that unless an initial offer is better than average, offers for guilty pleas will not get any worse and could become more favorable to the defendant further along in the adjudication process. They explain that this occurs because either the prosecutor loses witnesses or better evidence eventually turns up on behalf of the defense" (1996: 42–43). Sometimes they miscalculate: the prosecution's case gets stronger "and the prosecutor will offer a defendant less incentive to plead guilty than previously" (1996: 343).

A study of the Los Angeles Superior Court found that public defenders (PDs) determined which cases to settle without a trial based on predictions of case outcome:

> In making these predictions, PDs investigated their client's version of what happened, the arrest report made by police, the transcript of the preliminary hearing, testimony of possible witnesses, any physical evidence, and other pertinent information. There was a staff of investigators for attorneys in the public defender's office to help check out evidence and interview witnesses, and the PDs themselves had one day a week with no cases assigned to allow them time for investigations in the field. The PDs then evaluated all of the strengths and weaknesses in each case against perceived judge and jury behavior on the issue of reasonable doubt. (Mather 1988: 256)

The majority of felony cases, however, were "dead bang" with little chance of an acquittal. Cases won at trial were usually the result of sloppy prosecution.

When presented with the same hypothetical cases, "prosecutors and defense counsel were in remarkable agreement in their estimates of the probability of conviction in those versions of the cases where the evidentiary strength of the case was strong" (McDonald 1985: v). In weaker cases, however, there were significant differences between them.

In order to facilitate plea bargaining, judges, prosecutors, and defense attorneys must constitute a *workgroup* (Jacob and Eisenstein 1977). This cooperation requires regular players who interact frequently and share the common goal of disposing of cases with a minimum of resource expenditure and uncertainty. Only a stable workgroup can develop the patterns necessary to make behavior predictable. Judicial systems in which personnel (judges, assistant prosecutors, defense attorneys) are shifted frequently lack the stability necessary for the formation of workgroups and plea bargaining will be more difficult to accomplish.

THE ROLE OF THE JUDGE

The role of the judge in plea bargaining differs from jurisdiction to jurisdiction and may depend on the type of sentencing scheme used (discussed in Chapter 10) and rules governing their behavior. Federal district court judges are prohibited by the *Federal Rules of Criminal Procedure* from participating in plea negotiations. In Mississippi, while "the prosecuting attorney is encouraged to discuss and agree on pleas which may be entered by the defendant," Rule 8.04 also adds that "the trial judge shall not participate in any plea discussion." In Illinois, however, circuit court judges are routinely involved in plea negotiations. In states where judges exercise a great deal of discretion in the sentencing process, they tend to be more involved in plea negotiations. Where judges have only limited options, their role is less important. For example, Illinois utilizes a determinate sentencing system in which the judge has wide discretion. The charging decision, which is controlled by the prosecutor, does not carry with it a specific sentence. Therefore, before a prosecutor can offer a sentence to the defendant in return for a plea of guilty, the judge must be in agreement. A pre-plea conference must be requested by defense counsel. When agreement is reached, a sentence is conveyed to the defendant by his or her counsel. If the defendant accepts, the principals return to the courtroom and formalize the agreement on the record. In many cases, the judge will request from the probation department a pre-plea report, which provides background information—social, psychological, and criminal—on the defendant, before agreeing to a particular sentence.

In 1984, when federal legislation established a system that significantly reduced the sentencing discretion of judges, the prosecutor gained de facto sentencing power by determining the charges which are linked to specific sentences. Plea bargaining shifted accordingly, from *sentence bargaining* to *charge bargaining* (Nasheri 1998): "By assigning a narrow range of sentencing options to virtually every criminal violation and by giving judges only limited power to impose a sentence below that range, guideline systems have invested prosecutors with the power to dictate almost every sentence by choosing one set of charges over another" (Fisher 2000: 1072).

A Minneapolis study found that plea negotiations did not involve the prosecutor, who is present but merely as a "third party" witness. Instead, the judge led discussions centering on the sentence, not the charges. The same situation obtained in

Pittsburgh, where negotiations centered on the sentence, instead of the charges, and typically involved the judge and defense counsel (Levin 1977). In the county she studied, Emmelman (1996: 338) found that judges encourage case settlements, so when both sides agree on the terms of plea bargains, judges generally accept those terms. "When the attorneys encounter problems in reaching agreements, however, the judges act as arbiters. In this arbitration, the judge typically exerts pressure on, or makes promises regarding sentencing to, either attorney in order to reach a settlement."

In some jurisdictions, there is a "plea court," an arrangement whereby one or more judges who specialize in "moving cases" preside at calendar hearings; their purpose is to dispose of as many cases as possible by pleas of guilty. In New York City, Judge Harold J. Rothwax of the Supreme Court (a trial court) developed a reputation for moving cases, usually one every two to ten minutes. As each case is called, an assistant district attorney hands him a sheet indicating the details of the crime, the recommended bail, and the plea offer. As an example of how the judge expedited the cases before him, reporter Sam Roberts provides this vignette: "Two repeat felons appear before Judge Rothwax, one without counsel. Instead of adjourning the case he assigns a lawyer sitting in the front row reserved for attorneys. The district attorney's offer was a sentence with a minimum of two years and a maximum of four years. "After today," the judge states, "it's three to six; after that it's four to eight." To the lawyer he states: "If they're ever going to plead, today is the time to do it" (1985: 13).

The wide discretion over sentencing enjoyed by judges in New York obviously facilitates plea bargaining. And without plea bargaining New York's system would quickly come to a halt: "The strain on New York City's system could be seen one morning in December [1998] in the Jury 7 courtroom of the sprawling Manhattan Criminal Courts building. At 9:30, Judge Robert A. Sackett tried to urge dozens of defendants and prosecutors into beginning trials or agreeing to plea bargains that would resolve the 64 cases on the docket that day. Five cases dated to 1996. Twelve dated to 1997" (Rohde 1999: 19).

The number of cases disposed of by a judge is one important indicator of productiveness. In Cook County, Illinois, judges are under scrutiny by the chief judge with respect to how many cases they dispose of every year; a "scorecard" is kept and judges strive to avoid coming in at the close of the year with a "low score." This typically results in a scramble to dispose of large numbers of cases in December, with judges pressuring prosecutors to speed up the plea bargaining process in order to clear their dockets before the new year begins. Prosecutors, fearful of jurors experiencing "holiday time mercy," also wish to avoid jury trials during the Christmas season. The need for judges to dispose of large numbers of cases is evidenced in Kings County (Brooklyn), New York, where in the first 11 months of 1989, judges assigned to the Supreme Court received 13,460 felony cases. A little over 6 percent ended in a trial (Glaberson 1990a).

LIMITING OR ABOLISHING PLEA BARGAINING

Attempts to limit or exclude plea bargaining from criminal justice have had mixed results. In New York, for example, laws passed at the behest of Governor Nelson Rockefeller, known locally as the "Rockefeller laws," severely limited the ability of prosecutors to plea bargain. According to the legislation, once charges were filed,

PLEA BARGAINING, FOR BETTER OR WORSE

"In all, the prevailing system of plea bargaining seems both better and worse than its popular image. It is better because by and large it neither cheapens crime by overgenerous allowances nor discriminates against the poor and friendless defendant. Whether it induces guilty pleas from the innocent is hard to say, but it is probably true that most of those who plead guilty would be convicted on trial. At the same time, the system is worse than its image because it unavoidably levies a tax on those who elect to exercise their constitutional right to trial by jury" (Uviller 1996: 198). There is no reason to believe that, absent plea bargaining, innocent defendants would be any better off (Scott and Stuntz 1992).

the prosecutor was quite limited in lowering them. The result was a substantial increase in the number of defendants demanding jury trials, and prosecutors and judges soon found ways to circumvent the law. They initiated *front-loading*—plea bargaining at an early stage of the criminal justice process, prior to the filing of formal charges (Joint Committee on New York Drug Law Evaluation 1977; Aaronson et al. 1977). This tactic brings with it all of the dangers of "justice" done in haste. In Alaska, on the other hand, when the attorney general (that state's chief prosecutor) issued an order prohibiting the state's district attorneys from engaging in plea bargaining, the number of defendants pleading guilty remained about the same. Prosecutors did not have to waste time on negotiations, and the system became more efficient. There were, however, unanticipated results of the policy:

- There was absolutely no change in sentences for cases involving violent crimes such as rape, robbery, and felonious assault.

- There was very little change in sentences for most serious property offenders, particularly those with prior felony convictions.

- The major change was longer sentences for less serious property offenders. (Rubinstein, Clarke, and White 1980)

Since the initial ban, plea bargaining returned to most areas of Alaska, although because of statutory changes—the state now uses determinate-presumptive sentencing (discussed in Chapter 10)—instead of bargaining over the sentence, it is likely to focus on the charges (Carns 1992). In 1993, the attorney general removed the ban on plea bargaining (Guidorizzi 1998).

Belinda McCarthy and Charles Lindquist (1985) found that robbery defendants in Jefferson County (Birmingham), Alabama, frequently pled guilty even in the absence of significant benefits. Levin (1977) found that in Minneapolis judges discouraged plea bargaining, but defendants pled guilty at a very high rate nevertheless. A study in Cook County (Chicago) revealed no significant difference between the penalties given to violent offenders who entered pleas of guilty and those convicted by judges at bench trials (Eissman and Tybor 1985). However, bench trials may actually be the result of the "slow plea." The defendant waives the right to a jury trial in exchange for an expected leniency and the case is recorded as a trial, providing considerable cover for prosecutors and judges (Guidorizzi 1998).

In California, voters in 1982 approved of Proposition 8, the "Victims Bill of Rights" to, among other things, curtail plea bargaining in cases of serious crimes. A study by Candace McCoy and Robert Tillman (n.d.) revealed, however, that this did not happen. Pursuant to a plea agreement, in felony cases defendants plead guilty in lower (municipal) court, and the case is then "certified" to superior court for review and sentencing. In practice, the superior court rarely overturns a certified (plea bargain) case. The 1982 proposition increased front-loading through the use of plea certification: "Court professionals learned to accept disposition of serious felony cases through guilty pleas to 'normal' sentences at much earlier stages of prosecution than had been usual before Proposition 8" (McCoy 1993: 131). As in the New York situation, however, front-loading has some distinct disadvantages: "Neither defense counsel nor prosecutors can fully examine the strengths of the case. Similarly, lower court judges have little information on legal points or on the defendant's background so as to inform the sentencing decision—and a sentencing decision it is, even though superior court later reviews it very quickly" (n.d.: 6).

LEGAL ISSUES

In general, plea bargaining has been supported by legal decisions basing their logic on contract law (Easterbrook 1992). Just as two parties are entitled to enter into a contractual relationship in a noncriminal matter, so too is plea bargaining supported as simply the criminal justice system's extension of this law of contract. "Just as there is no inherent conflict between a tort plaintiff's right to a day in court and his ability to trade that right in settlement negotiations, there is no inherent conflict between the right to a criminal trial and the ability to sell that right for sentencing concessions" (Scott and Stuntz 1992: 1916). Of course, contracts are invalid if they are the result of *duress*. While improper coercive behavior invalidates a contract, the mere fact that a person enters into a contract as a result of pressure or undesirable circumstances is not sufficient: people in financial distress may sell their homes or cars or settle a tort for less than the "fair value."

In order for a plea bargain agreement to be legally binding on a defendant, the trial judge is required to determine if the defendant understands the ramifications of a plea of guilty. The plea must be "informed," since information deficits can invalidate a contract (Scott and Stuntz 1992). The *Federal Rules of Criminal Procedure* require that a judge determine that the defendant understands:

MISSISSIPPI CODE: PLEA BARGAINING PROHIBITED

"Under no circumstances shall the party or the prosecutor engage in discussion for the purpose of agreeing to exchange concessions by the prosecutor for the party's admission to the petition."

- The nature of the charge to which the plea is offered, the mandatory minimum penalty provided by law, if any, and the maximum possible penalty provided by law including the effect of any special parole terms
- If the defendant is not represented by an attorney, that he or she has the right to be represented by an attorney at every stage of the proceeding against him or her and, if necessary, one will be appointed
- That he or she has the right to plead not guilty or to persist in that plea if it has already been made, and that defendant has the right to be tried by a jury and at that trial has the right to the assistance of counsel, the right to confront and cross-examine adverse witnesses and the right not to be compelled to incriminate him- or herself
- That if he or she pleads guilty or *nolo contendere* (no contest) there will not be a further trial of any kind, so that by pleading guilty or *nolo contendere* the defendant waives the right to a jury trial
- That if the defendant pleads guilty or *nolo contendere*, the court may ask questions about the offense to which he or she has pleaded, and if defendant answers these questions under oath, on the record, and in the presence of counsel, the answers may later be used against him or her in a prosecution for perjury or false statement

Figure 11–3 is an example of the kind of document used to prove that the judge has ascertained that the defendant understands the ramifications of a guilty plea.

In 1970, the Supreme Court ruled (*Brady* v. *United States* and *North Carolina* v. *Alford*) that a determination must be made as to the voluntary nature of a plea of guilty and, furthermore, the plea must be made knowingly and intelligently (*Boykin* v. *Alabama* 1969). Accordingly, federal Rule 11(d) provides that "The court shall not accept a plea of guilty or *nolo contendere* without first, by addressing the defendant personally in open court, determining that the plea is voluntary and not the result of force or threats or of promises apart from a plea agreement. The court shall also inquire as to whether the defendant's willingness to plead guilty or *nolo contendere* results from prior discussions between the attorney for the government and the defendant or his attorney." Figure 11–4 is an example of the document used by the judge to prove that a guilty plea is voluntary and intelligent.

In every case in which a plea agreement is reached, there must be a stipulation of a factual underpinning for the guilty plea—the defendant generally must state the details of his or her culpability in court for the record (Palermo et al. 1998).

If a defendant refuses a prosecutor's offer of leniency in return for a plea of guilty, can the prosecutor reindict the defendant on more serious charges? In 1978, the Supreme Court (*Bordenkircher* v. *Hayes*) said *yes*. In this case, Paul Hayes declined to plead guilty to a lesser charge in return for a sentence of 5 years. He was subsequently convicted of forgery and sentenced under Kentucky's "habitual offender" statute to a term of life imprisonment. The Court reasoned that since plea bargaining had been ruled constitutional in prior decisions, the Court must also accept the "simple reality that the prosecutor's interest at the bargaining table is to persuade the defendant to forego his right to plead not guilty." As long as procedural safeguards have been adhered to, charging the defendant with a more serious crime when he or she declines to plead guilty, does not violate the Due Process Clause of the Fourteenth Amendment.

FIGURE 11-3   AN EXAMPLE OF A DOCUMENT USED TO PROVE THAT A JUDGE HAS ASCERTAINED THAT A DEFENDANT UNDERSTANDS THE RAMIFICATIONS OF A GUILTY PLEA

GUILTY PLEA PROCEEDING

The defendant personally appearing before me, I have ascertained the following facts, noting each by initializing it.

Judge's Initials

_____ 1. That the defendant understands the nature of the charges against him.

_____ 2. That the defendant understands the range of possible sentence for the offenses charged, from a suspended sentence to a maximum of _____ and that the mandatory minimum (if any) is _____ .

_____ 3. That the defendant understands the following constitutional rights which he gives up by pleading guilty:
(a) His right to trial by jury, if any.
(b) His right to the assistance of an attorney at all stages of the proceeding, and to an appointed attorney, to be furnished free of charge, if he cannot afford one.
(c) His right to confront the witnesses against him and to cross-examine them as to the truthfulness of their testimony.
(d) His right to present evidence on his own behalf, and to have the state compel witnesses of his choosing to appear and testify.
(e) His right to remain silent and to be presumed innocent until proven guilty beyond a reasonable doubt.

_____ 4. That the defendant wishes to give up the constitutional rights of which he has been advised.

_____ 5. That there exists a basis in fact for believing the defendant guilty of the offenses charged.

_____ 6. That the defendant and the prosecutor have entered into a plea agreement and that the defendant understands and consents to the terms.

_____ 7. That the plea is voluntary and not the result of force, threats or promises other than a plea agreement.

On the basis of these findings, I conclude that the defendant knowingly, voluntarily, and intelligently pleads guilty to the above charges, and accept his plea.

_____   _____
Date   Judge

Certification of Defendant

I certify that the judge personally advised me of the matters noted above, that I understand the constitutional rights that I am giving up by pleading guilty, and that I desire to plead guilty to the charges stated.

_____   _____
Defense Counsel, if any   Defendant

In 1989, in an 8–1 decision, the Court ruled that when a defendant withdraws an initial plea of guilty and is convicted after a trial, the judge may impose a longer sentence than the earlier plea agreement had called for. In *Alabama* v. *Smith*, a plea agreement called for a sentence of no more than 30 years; after withdrawing his plea and being convicted for burglary, sodomy, and rape, the defendant was sentenced to 150 years. Can a defendant contest a plea agreement on the grounds that his or her

> **FIGURE 11-4** **AN EXAMPLE OF THE DOCUMENT USED BY A JUDGE TO PROVE THAT A GUILTY PLEA IS VOLUNTARY**
>
> **PLEA AGREEMENT:**
>
> The state of Arizona and the defendant hereby agree to the following disposition of this case:
>
> **Plea: The defendant agrees to plead guilty/no contest to:** _____
>
> Terms: On the following, understands terms and conditions:
>
> 1. That the defendant will receive a sentence no greater than _____ and no less than _____ and consistent with the following additional terms: _____
> 2. That the following charges are dismissed, or if not yet filed, shall not be brought against the defendant _____ .
> 3. That this agreement, unless rejected or withdrawn, serves to amend the complaint, indictment, or information to charge the offense to which the defendant pleads, without the filing of any additional pleading. If the plea is rejected or withdrawn, the original charges are automatically reinstated.
> 4. If the defendant is charged with a felony, that he hereby gives up his right to a preliminary hearing or other probable cause determination on the charges to which he pleads. In the event the court rejects the plea, or the defendant withdraws the plea, the defendant hereby gives up his right to a preliminary hearing or other probable cause determination of the original charges.
> 5. Unless this plea is rejected or withdrawn, that the defendant hereby gives up any and all motions, defenses, objections or requests which he has made or raised, or could assert hereafter, to the court's entry of judgment against him and imposition of a sentence upon him consistent with this agreement.
> 6. That if after accepting this agreement the court concludes that if any of its provisions regarding the sentence or term and conditions of probation are inappropriate, it can reject the plea, giving the defendant an opportunity to withdraw the plea.
>
> I have read and understood the above. I have discussed the case and my constitutional rights with my lawyer. I understand that by pleading (guilty) (no contest) I will be giving up my right to a trial by jury, to confront, cross-examine, and compel the attendance of witnesses, and my privilege against self incrimination. I agree to enter my plea as indicated above on the terms and conditions set forth herein. I fully understand that if as a part of this plea bargain I am granted probation by the court, the terms and conditions thereof are subject to modification at any time during the period of probation in the event that I violate any written condition of my probation.
>
> _____   _____
> Date   Defendant
>
> I have discussed this case with my client in detail and advised him of his constitutional rights and all possible defenses. I believe that the plea and disposition set forth herein are appropriate under the facts of this case. I concur in the entry as indicated above and on the terms and conditions set forth herein.
>
> _____   _____
> Date   Defense Counsel
>
> I have reviewed this matter and concur that the plea and disposition set forth herein are appropriate and are in the interest of justice.
>
> _____   _____
> Date   Prosecutor

lawyer was ineffective? In order to do so, the Supreme Court has ruled (*Hill* v. *Lockhart* 1985), there must be a reasonable probability that, but for counsel's errors, the defendant would not have pleaded guilty and would have insisted on going to trial—that he or she would have gotten a better deal is not sufficient. In fact, it may be impossible to distinguish between good and bad bargaining: "A two-minute conversation with the prosecutor in the hallway with only slight advance preparation may represent evidence of sloppiness and sloth. Or it may be that defense counsel, who has a great deal of experience in dealing with similar cases, knows the market price, realizes that investigation is extremely unlikely to lead anywhere, and understands how to get the best offer expeditiously" (Scott and Stuntz 1992: 1959). Presumably, the judge knows the "market price" and has discretion to revise the agreed-upon sentence accordingly. (For criticism of the *Hill* decision, see Rubin 1998.)

Does a prosecutor have to live up to the terms of a plea bargain? In 1971, the Supreme Court (*Santobello* v. *New York*) said *yes*. In this case, the assistant district attorney agreed to permit the defendant to plead guilty to a gambling misdemeanor charge that would carry a maximum prison sentence of one year. The prosecutor agreed to make no recommendation as to the sentence. After the plea of guilty was entered, a sentencing hearing was scheduled at which a different assistant district attorney appeared. In violation of the agreement, this district attorney recommended the maximum sentence. The Court ruled that "when a plea [of guilty] rests in any significant degree on a promise or agreement of the prosecutor, so that it can be said to be part of the inducement or consideration [to plead guilty], such promise must be fulfilled." State appellate courts have ruled that prosecutors violate plea agreements when they convey an impression that the sentence should be more severe than that called for in the plea agreement or indicate reservations about the plea agreement sentence recommendation (Palermo et al. 1998). In 1984, however, the Supreme Court (*Mabry* v. *Johnson*) ruled unanimously that a defendant has no constitutional right to enforcement of a proposed plea bargain that a prosecutor withdraws before it becomes official.

Now that we have completed our examination of plea bargaining, in the next chapter we will turn to the civil side of justice.

INTERNET CONNECTIONS

National Institute of Justice: *ojp.usdoj.gov/nij*
National Criminal Justice Reference Service: *www.ncjrs.org*

REVIEW QUESTIONS

1. What is meant by plea bargaining?
2. According to the critics of plea bargaining, what is its purpose?
3. According to critics, how does plea bargaining undermine due process?
4. What do critics mean when they describe plea bargaining as a "confidence game"?
5. How can the police assist in the plea bargaining scenario?
6. According to critics, what is the role of the defense attorney in plea bargaining?

7. How can the economics of private defense attorney practice influence plea bargaining?

8. How can the public defender be encouraged to plea bargain?

9. How can judges and prosecutors punish private attorneys who refuse to go along with the need for a speedy resolution of cases?

10. How do the norms of the legal profession encourage plea bargaining?

11. In addition to saving resources, why would a prosecutor engage in plea bargaining?

12. How can the adversarial process remain intact in plea bargaining?

13. How do the concepts of "going rate" and "normal crimes" promote plea bargaining?

14. What are the nonlegal elements that influence plea bargaining?

15. How does the quality of police activities influence plea bargaining?

16. How does the relationship between defendant and victim influence a prosecutor's decisions?

17. How does the type of sentencing used in a particular jurisdiction affect the role of the judge in plea bargaining?

18. What have been the results of efforts to do away with plea bargaining?

19. How does contract law justify plea bargaining?

20. What has the Supreme Court ruled with respect to plea bargaining?

12

CIVIL JUSTICE

In this chapter we will look at the procedures used to resolve civil disputes, issues surrounding the contingency fee, and class action lawsuits. It must be pointed out that, as in the criminal justice system, very few civil cases are adjudicated with a formal trial. About 90 percent of the approximately one million lawsuits filed each year are settled[1] at the earliest stages of the system, somewhere between filing a complaint or petition and the first scheduled appearance before a judge. In some jurisdictions, extensive activity takes place before a complaint is ever filed with the court, and the "case," usually a tort, is frequently settled or abandoned without any court involvement. In one 12-month period, jury cases were 2 percent of the 762,000 tort, contract, and real property cases disposed by state courts of general jurisdiction in the nation's most populous counties (DeFrances et al. 1995). In numerous cases, a trial is not the goal; instead, there is a need for a judicial declaration, for example, uncontested divorces or probate proceedings (Galanter 1989).

According to Herbert Kritzer, criticisms of settlement in the civil justice system neatly parallel those of plea bargaining. "Some people attack the deals that are made by way of settlement as evidence that victims of legally compensable injuries are forced (by delay, uncertainty, and the like) to accept resolutions far short of what the law entitles them to. Others see the civil justice process as a vehicle by which

---

[1]When parties settle, they will usually ask the court for a consent order: judicial recognition of the agreement which cannot then be nullified without the consent of both parties.

undeserving persons (and their contingent-fee lawyers) extort payments by filing frivolous lawsuits which defendants choose to settle because the cost of defending the case in court exceeds the amount that the plaintiff is willing to accept in settlement" (1991: 5).

CIVIL LITIGATION AND ADJUDICATION

While a criminal action can only be brought by government (municipal, county, state, or federal prosecutor), most civil actions are brought by private parties, although the government is sometimes a plaintiff or a defendant. Cases typically handled by the civil justice system involve:

- *Torts*. Injury that did not involve a contract.
- *Contracts*. Violation of an agreement (about a third of all civil trial cases).
- *Property*. Disputes relating to the exclusive right to possess, use, or dispose of an item. Real property refers to land and buildings (or crops) on that land; personal property is everything else.
- *Succession/estate*. Issues relating to the right to pass along property after death; inheritance; probate.
- *Family relations*. Issues related to marriage, children, and divorce.
- *Civil rights*. Violation of federal or state constitutions or statutes designed to protect individuals from the abuse of power by public and nonpublic officials.

There are common elements in a civil case:

[Each] involves a complaining party who demands a remedy from the courts for an asserted legal wrong. Every case involves a defending party who denies having a legal obligation in the matter, or at least contends that its legal obligation is different or less than the complaining party contends. In any particular case, the facts may be contested, compelling the tribunal to resolve conflicting evidence in making a determination of the facts. In addition, the meaning or application of the law may be contested, in which event the tribunal must resolve conflicting interpretations of the law. Many cases involve disputes of both fact and law. (Hazard and Taruffo 1993: viii)

Several important distinctions between civil and criminal justice exist. For example, the doctrine of *nullum crimen sine lege* (no crime without law; discussed in Chapter 10) is not applicable in civil litigation, and the *ex post facto* law prohibited by the Constitution (Sec. 1, Art. 9) is limited to criminal cases (*Calder* v. *Bull* 1798). Courts often accept jurisdiction in civil cases although the legislature has not specifically declared that the wrong allegedly committed by the defendant is the basis for a civil action; and (noncriminal) statutes and case law may be applied retroactively. One of the important guarantees that does apply—*res judicata*—is similar to the prohibition against double jeopardy. Once a plaintiff loses a suit, he or she cannot raise the same cause of action again even if there are new grounds for the claim. The defendant, likewise, is prevented from bringing a new action to defeat an adverse judgment. Plaintiff and defendant can of course, appeal an adverse decision. In Chapter 10 we discussed *joinder of offenses*; in civil actions there is a parallel device—*joinder of parties/claims*. Rules governing these devices allow the plaintiff to name as defendants any/all persons allegedly responsible in any way for injuries or damages. The joinder of claims allows the court to consolidate claims if they arose out of the same incident and are too complex/interdependent to be considered separately.

In addition to narrowly drawn conflicts, the courts are often called upon to decide broad issues of public policy, such as school desegregation, legislative reapportionment, and antitrust actions (discussed in Chapter 8). Civil litigation can accomplish three desirable goals (Lieberman 1981):

1. Provide for the compensation of those who have been injured
2. Serve to deter future harms or actions that are potentially harmful by the knowledge that some types of behavior can result in costly suits
3. Cause the termination of ongoing harms or the reformation of institutional systems that perpetuate them

The resolution of a dispute between private parties involves a lawsuit that has several key elements (Holland 1982):

- A lawsuit is a conflict about private rights motivated by self-interest. A typical civil action involves a tort, a lawsuit based on allegations of damages caused to the plaintiff by the defendant.
- The dispute is about events that happened in the past—events that disturbed a preexisting social harmony.
- A third party stands as a passive and impartial umpire who, after hearing arguments offered by each party in the presence of the other, resolves the dispute in accordance with preexisting legal rules.
- The court must hear the plaintiff's claim, and the parties initiate and control the definition of the issues, the development of facts, and the presentation of law.

"To prevail in a lawsuit, the plaintiff must prove both that the defendant committed an act that caused injury and that the act was a legal wrong" (Lieberman 1981: 18). However, modern litigation often involves the transformation of once lawful acts into legal wrongs: "Through a steady stream of legislative enactments and judicial pronouncements [case law], the citizen's right to redress has grown apace," replacing, for example, "the doctrine of *caveat emptor* (let the buyer beware) and related rules, with stringent duties of care on those who act," such as manufacturers, hospitals, and units of government (1981: 19).

The expansion of the role of the judiciary has also led to an increase in lawsuits whose primary purpose appears to be the harassment of opponents. In an effort to thwart these "frivolous" lawsuits, the federal judiciary toughened Rule 11 of the *Federal Rules of Civil Procedure* to ensure that every legal filing is grounded in fact and not designed "for any improper purpose such as to harass or to cause unnecessary delay or needless increase in the cost of litigation." If a judge finds that a lawyer has violated Rule 11, the plaintiff can be forced to pay the costs and legal fees expended by their opponents in defending against the improper action—an incentive to avoid cases that do not fit into established legal concepts. The amended Rule 11 requires attorneys to inquire into the merits of their cases before proceeding, invalidating a "pure heart, empty head" defense. Critics argue that the new rule has created just another means of harassing opponents through the use of civil litigation, increasing the amount of time required for litigation, generating a great deal of additional legal work, and thereby increasing costs accordingly—the opposite of what was intended. Indeed, the rule has spawned a new area of jurisprudence with treatises and newsletters on the subject (Labaton 1992). There is also fear that the possibility of sanctions for bringing a legal action may frighten off aggrieved parties with legitimate claims, while serving to keep attorneys from filing innovative cases with legal theories that require the passage of time before being accepted (Lewin 1986b).

THE CIVIL PROCESS

For the most part, the adversarial process used in criminal trials is also used in civil trials, with some important differences. "Judges are far more free in civil cases than in criminal cases to construe statutes broadly and to remedy wrongs not previously recognized as such" (Berman and Greiner 1980: 133). While the rules of evidence are generally the same, "the law of criminal evidence has more restrictions favoring the accused" (Hazard and Taruffo 1993: 132).

Standing

In a noncriminal case, a litigant must have *standing*—meaning he or she must have a personal stake in the outcome of the controversy so that the adversarial model will be fully operative. For example, in order to challenge the constitutionality of a particular statute or executive action, a litigant must be prepared to show that he or she has been or will be harmed—an *injury in fact*—unless the court provides a remedy. The party who seeks to invoke the court's authority must show that he or she has suffered, not in the abstract but personally, some actual or threatened injury as a result of allegedly illegal conduct on the part of the defendant (Schwartz 1988). In 1991, for example, a lawsuit filed by a group of Harvard law students accusing their school of discriminating against women and minorities in faculty hiring and promotion was dismissed in state court because the plaintiffs lacked standing—they could not show direct harm ("Judge Voids Suit on Harvard Hiring" 1991). Standing is particularly important when the case at issue may provide precedent, thereby influencing other disputes not before the court. It is generally believed in the legal community that a party with an immediate stake is more likely to present the court with a specific and well developed fact situation upon which law (that is, precedent) can be made (Marvell 1978).

Ideological opposition or a general grievance, for example, against a particular policy of government, is not sufficient to provide standing. Thus, a taxpayer who wanted a court to halt covert aid to contras fighting in Nicaragua on the theory that it is an unauthorized expenditure of taxpayers' money "may be told that, since the injuries he alleges are not personal to him, his suit will be dismissed for lack of standing." The Court "will not even examine the accusation that tax money is being illegally spent, although this may well be the case" (Lempert and Sanders 1986: 23–24). In 1923 (*Frothingham* v. *Mellon*), the Court ruled unanimously against taxpayer suits as a device for limiting the manner in which federal funds are spent; the Court stated that the plaintiff must show that he or she sustained "some direct injury." Being one of millions of taxpayers creates a minute, indeterminable, and remote

∫TANDING

"Have the appellants alleged such a personal stake in the outcome of the controversy as to assure that concrete adverseness which sharpens the presentation of issues upon which this court so largely depends for illumination of difficult questions? This is the gist of the question of standing."—William J. Brennan, Jr., *Baker v. Carr* (1962)

effect, and not interest sufficient to support standing. In 1968, however, the Court limited the application of *Frothingham* by recognizing standing in the case of a challenge to congressional funding that conflicts with a constitutional limitation, in this case (*Flast* v. *Cohen*) aid to parochial schools as a violation of the First Amendment. And, as noted in Chapter 8, the courts have granted standing to groups with generalized claims on behalf of the "public interest." Liberalizing the rules governing standing has been subjected to severe criticism by persons on the right of the American political spectrum, such as James Q. Wilson (1989, Chapter 15).

Jury Issues

In 1970, the Supreme Court upheld a Florida statute mandating six-person juries in criminal cases (*Williams* v. *Florida*), and in 1973, *Colgrove* v. *Battin* extended this ruling to federal civil trials. Accordingly, civil juries often have fewer than 12 members, and they are not sequestered. Thirty-four states do not require unanimity in civil verdicts (Zawitz 1988); in California, for example, only nine of out of 12 jurors have to agree on a verdict. In actions involving issues of equity (nonmonetary matters requesting specific performance—discussed in Chapter 2), there is not a constitutional right to a jury trial. The Seventh Amendment guarantees the right to a jury trial only in common law suits "where the value in controversy shall exceed twenty dollars." While the Seventh Amendment has not been made applicable to the states, almost all states have similar constitutional guarantees (Friedenthal, Kane, and Miller 1985).

As in criminal cases, *voir dire* remains an important aspect of the civil jury process. "Lawyer-conducted *voir dire* is the traditional American method of screening the members of the panel called for jury service. In some states, *voir dire* has been left so completely in lawyers' hands that the judge does not even preside at the sessions in which opposing lawyers question potential jurors" (Landsman 1999: 292).

Criticism over alleged lawyer abuse of *voir dire*—e.g., lawyers using the *voir dire* to indoctrinate the jury and to cultivate friendly relationships with individual jurors; lawyer-directed questioning veering into inappropriate areas touching on jurors' private lives and specific views about evidence they have not yet heard—has led various courts to impose restrictions on lawyer participation in the questioning process. In the federal courts, civil rules authorize judges to conduct the entire *voir dire* themselves. In many jurisdictions, lawyers are permitted to supplement the judge's questioning, making it possible to secure both the benefit of judicial restraint and lawyer probing. Sometimes an oral *voir dire* is supplemented with a written questionnaire answered by each potential juror (Landsman 1999).

MOOT CASES

If the outcome of a case will have no significant impact on the litigants, it is moot—"neither side would gain in the immediate dispute no matter how the court ruled"—and the case will generally be thrown out. Typically, the case begins with a real dispute, but changed circumstances have resolved the issue and the adversarial system will no longer be operative. At times, however, an appellate court will decide a moot case if the issue is one likely to come before the court again (Marvell 1978: 43). For example, in *Bowers* v. *Hardwick* (1986), the Supreme Court ruled that the Constitution does not prohibit a state from criminalizing homosexual acts between consenting adults, despite Georgia's decision not to prosecute Bowers, making the case moot.

Once *voir dire* has been concluded, each side is allowed to exercise its peremptory challenges—federal rules entitle each side to three, and states vary in their number. Peremptory challenges can be used by either attorney to excuse any juror without having to state a reason. In 1991, the Supreme Court ruled (*Edmonson* v. *Leesville*) that the prohibition against prosecutors using peremptory challenges to exclude blacks from juries because they believe that such persons may favor a black defendant (*Baston* v. *Kentucky* 1986) also applies to both the plaintiff and defendant in civil actions. When the complaining party makes a prima facie case of discriminatory challenges, the burden shifts to the party who exercised the peremptory strikes to articulate a "neutral explanation" for his or her selections. Then the trial court decides if unlawful discrimination has been proven.

Evidence

In civil cases, a finding for the plaintiff—the party bringing the action—is based on a *preponderance of the evidence* and, sometimes (e.g., for punitive damages in some states or for involuntary civil commitment), *clear and convincing evidence*, not the more stringent criminal standard of *beyond a reasonable doubt* (Figure 12–1). Many of the extensive due process guarantees that accrue to a defendant in a criminal case are not applicable in a civil proceeding, in particular:

FIGURE 12–1 LEVELS OF TRIAL EVIDENCE IN ORDER OF STRINGENCY

Evidence beyond a reasonable doubt
(all criminal cases)

Clear and convincing evidence
(some civil cases)

Preponderance of evidence
(most civil cases)

- Neither plaintiff nor defendant is constitutionally entitled to counsel; government has no legal obligation to provide an attorney to an indigent party involved in a civil action.

- There is no right to remain silent, and defendants are often called upon to testify.

- The right to cross-examine adverse witnesses is circumscribed in civil cases: In the absence of a witness, his or her deposition may be read into evidence. When a witness is outside of the jurisdiction of the court, the party seeking testimony can apply to the court for *letters rogatory*. This commission is directed to an official or attorney in the proper jurisdiction empowering him or her to take the witness's deposition and forward it to the court. In some states, court intervention is not necessary, only notice to opposing counsel of the intention to take a deposition.

Jurisdiction

There is a code of civil procedure that governs noncriminal disputes, and the first issue to be determined is jurisdiction, which can at times be quite complex (see Chapter 6). Is the case a proper one for federal or state court? What if the plaintiff and defendant live in different counties, different states, or even different countries? What if the damages occurred in a third county or state? Some actions are local, for example, mortgage foreclosure, and can be brought only in the county where the property is located. Other actions can be transitory, meaning they may be brought wherever the defendant is found and served with the summons, such as a tort action for personal injuries. There is also a variety of specialized courts such as domestic relations, chancery, and small claims. The plaintiff is required to establish that the court has jurisdiction to rule on the issue being presented. Under Article IV, Section 1, of the Constitution, a judgment rendered by a state court is enforceable in all states: "Full faith and Credit shall be given in each State to the public Acts, Records, and judicial Proceedings of every other State."

In 1998, the Supreme Court ruled 9–0 that despite Article IV, one state's court system cannot bind another's to an agreement barring particular testimony or evidence from a trial. In this case (*Baker* v. *General Motors*), as a result of a settlement, a former employee who had testified as an expert witness against General Motors agreed to an injunction barring him from testifying in further lawsuits against the company. A Michigan court issued an order putting the settlement into force. When the employee was subpoenaed to testify in a suit against General Motors in Missouri, the company invoked the Michigan injunction, but the trial judge invoked Missouri law and permitted him to testify. The plaintiffs—survivors of a woman who died when her Chevrolet Blazer caught fire after a crash—were awarded $11.3 million.

Jurisdiction can be exercised over the defendant: *in personam* jurisdiction empowers the court to issue judgments against the defendant personally, seizing the person's assets, for example, to satisfy a judgment. Or, jurisdiction can be exercised over things and status: *in rem* jurisdiction empowers the court to dissolve a marriage or adjudicate the disposition of real estate (Emanuel 2000b).

Filing a Civil Complaint

A typical civil case is either *ex delicto*, a tort or action alleging a wrong committed by the defendant against the plaintiff, or *ex contractu*, an action alleging a breech of a promise set forth in a contract. A civil action is known by the name of the plaintiff and the name of the defendant—*Smith* v. *Jones*; the plaintiff's name appears first. The case typically begins (Figure 12–2) when the plaintiff's attorney pays a fee and files a complaint or petition with the clerk of the proper court, setting out the facts on which the action is based, the damages alleged, and the remedy or relief being sought, generally called a *prayer*. The petition may consist of a simple court form requiring only that blanks be filled in; or long, typed documents. The clerk issues a summons, which is attached to a copy of the complaint or petition, and both are served on the defendant by personnel from the sheriff's office, a U.S. marshal, or a private process-serving agency.

FIGURE 12–2 THE FLOW OF CIVIL CASES

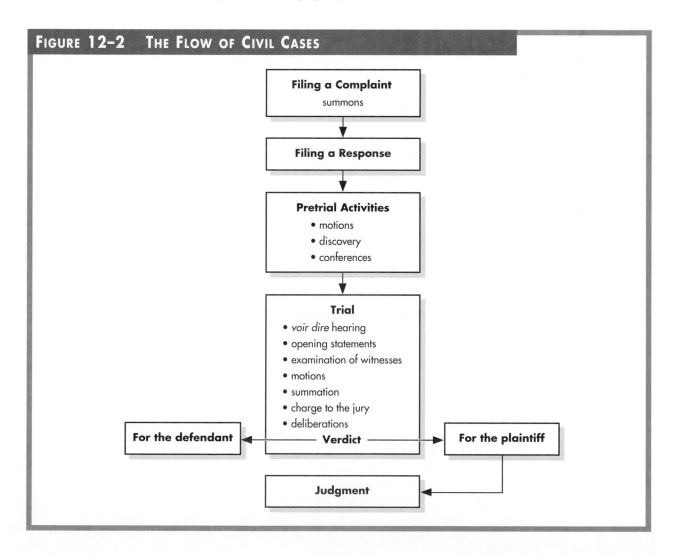

The summons directs a defendant to file a response—*pleading*—within a certain time, usually 30 days, or suffer a judgment of default. A default judgment requires that the defendant be served personally and not by proxy. There are some alternative methods, for example, registered mail accompanied by an announcement in the legal section of a newspaper or a copy affixed to the defendant's residence or business, a form of service known as "nail and mail." It is not necessary that the defendant actually have notice of the action being brought, so long as the method of service is reasonably calculated to give notice and an opportunity to defend (Berman and Greiner 1980). The defendant's attorney can now respond to the allegations, sometimes alleging wrongdoing on the part of the plaintiff (a counterclaim), moving to dismiss, or filing a claim against another party who he or she alleges should be held accountable.

PRETRIAL ACTIVITIES

Activities prior to a civil trial are extensive and, in practice, usually lead to an out-of-court settlement. Settlements have been aided by services available to attorneys. One firm, for example, provides computerized data on jury verdicts nationwide. The data is used to predict the statistical probability of a plaintiff winning a personal injury case and the likely award (Hinds 1994). The employment of specialized assistants has become routine. These persons, trained in a particular area of litigation (e.g., nurses who analyze medical records and interview victims) aid in analyzing the *value* of cases.

The delay after filing and preliminary motions may last several months, and roughly 75 percent of cases are resolved during that time without a trial. (An unknown number of cases are settled before any court filing actually occurs.) Depending on how cases are calendared in the particular jurisdiction, a judge may first become involved within two to four months after the complaint is filed, or the judge may wait until a certificate of readiness, at-issue memo, or similar document is filed by one or both of the attorneys signifying that the case is ready to be placed on the trial calendar (Mahoney 1988). In some jurisdictions, there may be an initial conference with the attorneys in order to set a schedule for future events in the case. In any event, there are usually pretrial conferences with the judge to facilitate a settlement. As opposed to criminal cases, the litigants, not the court, have primary responsibility for control of the case (speedy trial requirements apply only to criminal cases).

MOTIONS

A number of pretrial motions can be made by defense counsel:

- A *motion to quash* asks the court to void the summons as not having been properly served.
- A *motion to strike* asks the court to excise parts of the petition as irrelevant, improper, or prejudicial.
- A *motion to make more definite* asks the court to require the plaintiff to be more specific about the complaints that are alleged, for example, to describe the injuries in greater detail so the defense will be better able to respond.

- A *motion to dismiss* argues that the court lacks jurisdiction, or that the plaintiff has not presented a legally sound basis for a cause of action against the defendant even if, in fact, the allegations are true (known as a *demurrer*).
- A *motion for summary judgment* is based on a claim that there is no genuine issue of material fact and, therefore, the undisputed portion of the case should be eliminated from trial; if the undisputed issues are crucial, the entire case may be determined without a trial.

Additional motions may be made subsequent to discovery (discussed later), for example, adding another person/corporation as a defendant—*motion for permission to join*.

The defendant's response can be to deny the allegations, admit some and deny others, or admit them all and plead extenuating circumstances—an excuse. The defendant may also file a counterclaim, which may be part of the response (cross-claim) or filed independently (counterclaim). It asks for relief or damages from the plaintiff and sometimes from others. The plaintiff may then file any of the above motions against the cross-complaint, except the motion to quash. Either party can now file a reply in answer to any new allegations raised by the other party. The plaintiff's answer to the defendant's plea is referred to as a *replication*; the defendant's response to a replication is called a *rejoinder*.

Discovery

"In the early days of the American legal system, a party had to prove its case with evidence that it obtained on its own, without help from the other side" (Morrison 1996: 70). "The term 'discovery' encompasses the methods by which a party or potential party to a lawsuit obtains and preserves information regarding the action" which "should permit parties to obtain a fair understanding of all relevant evidence before the trial begins, thereby avoiding 'trial by ambush'" (Friedenthal, Kane, and Miller 1985: 380; Alliance of American Insurers 1987: 19). Since it is presumed that litigants act in their own self-interest, discovery rules "compel the disclosure of evidence that would not—were it not for the fact of pretrial discloser itself—emerge at trial . . . Discovery adds to the accuracy of outcomes not only by eliminating surprises about the evidence, but also by expanding the quality of evidence" (Hay 1994: 482; 498). Discovery seeks to make decision-making more accurate. It should help the parties avoid a trial and evaluate settlement conditions. Discovery rules empower judges to punish false or incomplete disclosure by attorney fee awards, contempt citations, and default judgments. Doctored evidence or false denials about the existence of relevant evidence exposes a litigant to civil and criminal liability; attorneys to professional discipline, disbarment, and prosecution (Hay 1994).

The discovery phase of civil litigation differs considerably from its criminal counterpart. The civil process utilizes extensive discovery procedures, whereas "even in 'liberal' jurisdictions, [criminal] attorneys can get only a fraction of the information that is routinely available in civil litigation" (Schulhofer 1994: 137)—noncriminal defendants have no Fifth Amendment protection against extensive requests for information. The discovery phase of litigation can be lengthy and costly, providing an advantage to those litigants who can afford to absorb such costs. "There are attorneys," notes Roy Grutman (with Thomas 1990: 60), "who are assigned to do nothing but create correspondence and bury the opposition in paperwork. The issues in the case become secondary." While rules of evidence require attorneys to prove the need for particular discovery information, this is rarely enforced by judges (Linowitz 1996). Some jurisdictions have limited the number of witnesses who can be deposed or the number of interrogatory questions that can be propounded, or the amount of documents required. "Thus, while discovery is often criticized because of the burdens it imposes, a reasonable amount of discovery is essential if informed decisions are to be made about settlement. The problem is drawing the line between reasonable and excessive discovery" (Morrison 1996: 73).

Discovery in a civil action includes interrogatories, depositions, and requests to produce, enter, or inspect documents

Interrogatories. If relevant answers are not forthcoming, either side can submit written questions (known as *interrogatories*) for the other side to answer under oath. While a respondent need not answer a question deemed improper, the interrogating party can seek a court order to compel an answer. In particularly acrimonious situations, the court can appoint a referee to handle the discovery phase. A variation of the interrogatory is the *request for admission:* Written statements of material facts or allegations at issue are submitted to opposing counsel for a response—admission or denial. Those that are admitted need not be proved at trail.

> Interrogatories are considered very useful for obtaining information from the other side, at quite modest cost, since the only expense is the writing of the questions. They are particularly useful when the other side is an organization, such as a corporation or government agency, because the rules require the organization to make reasonable inquiries to all persons in the organization who might have information about the subject, and it cannot reply based on one person's knowledge or lack of it. The principal difficulty in using interrogatories is that, if the question is not precisely phrased, clever counsel on the other side can respond in a way that, while literally true, does not provide information of the kind that requesting party was actually seeking and would have obtained if the question had been framed slightly differently. (Morrison 1996: 72)

Depositions. As part of the discovery stage, the civil process utilizes a legal device, the deposition, which is generally absent from criminal cases. (Most states allow criminal depositions only if a witness will not be available for trial.) The deposition is an out-of-court procedure whereby plaintiff, defendant, and any witnesses are placed under oath and asked questions by opposing counsel on matters not otherwise privileged and that relate to the pending case. The questions and their answers are recorded by a private court reporter engaged for this purpose. If a witness lives a considerable distance from where the case is being tried, typically one hundred miles or more, and is not a party to the dispute, that person cannot be subpoenaed to testify. A deposition, however, may be taken and read into the record, often by a professional deposition reader—there are firms that provide this service.

Depositions are particularly useful for narrowing down the issues involved, and they provide each side with an opportunity to evaluate the case and better prepare for trial (or settlement). The deposition can also be used in court as a basis for impeaching subsequent testimony in conflict with the sworn out-of-court record. While many of the rules that apply in court are in effect, a deposition is not a matter of public record and, thus, the press has no right of access until it is released by virtue of a court order. The process can be expensive, since both sides and their lawyers have a right to be present and the session must be recorded by a legal stenographer or on videotape.

Documents. Discovery may also involve the production and inspection of documents, such as a contract or lease, and may require the plaintiff to undergo an examination by a medical doctor chosen by the defendant or the court in order to substantiate claims of injury.

The *Federal Rules of Civil Procedure* require lawyers to furnish opponents with basic factual information at the onset of litigation, including relevant documents and lists of witnesses: "Litigants seeking information need do nothing but wait for it. The party possessing the information has the burden of marshaling the relevant documents and determining which witnesses have relevant information, and then producing this information to his or her opponent" (Koski 1994: 85). In addition to other penalties, the failure to disclose relevant information precludes its use at trial.

Pretrial Conference

After discovery, but before trial, the attorneys appear before the judge, usually without their clients, in order to agree on certain uncontested factual issues (*stipulations*) such as the date and time of the incident, photos, sketches, and other routine evidence. The purpose of stipulations is to make the trial process more efficient and cut down on the time necessary for completion. (Often, this part of the process can result in a settlement without the need for a trial.) The judge enters a pretrial order which may specify the witnesses to be called and the documents to be offered at trial. The order governs the conduct of the trial. "A pretrial conference is a regular procedure in federal courts, but many state courts hold pretrial conferences only in complex cases" (Hazard and Taruffo 1993: 122).

TRIAL

Civil and criminal trials (discussed in Chapter 10) are conducted in the same manner: selection of a jury/*voir dire*, opening statements, witnesses called by the plaintiff and then the defense, direct examination, cross-examination, re-direct, re-cross-examination, closing arguments, charge to the jury, deliberations, and verdict. A judge may preclude the case being sent to the jury by ruling in favor of a motion for a *directed verdict*—at the close of the presentation of the opponent's evidence, either defense or plaintiff can argue that the evidence is either so compelling or so weak that only one outcome would be proper. If the plaintiff fails to present sufficient evidence from which a jury could reasonably find a verdict for the plaintiff, the judge dismisses the case for *failure of proof*.

At the beginning of the trial, after seating the jury, the judge usually provides an orientation to the case, introducing the parties and their counsel, describing the general subject of the case, and outlining the duties of the jury, the judge, and counsel (Hazard and Taruffo 1993).The plaintiff's attorney typically makes the first opening statement and the final closing argument (paralleling the role of the prosecutor in criminal trials). Usually the plaintiff is a witness, and the defendant may also opt to testify or be called as a witness by the plaintiff. In closing arguments, the plaintiff's attorney summarizes the case in a manner that points to the defendant's liability and stresses the losses that the plaintiff has suffered. Defense counsel claims that the defendant is not responsible for the injury or loss, or that the compensation claimed is too high. The plaintiff's attorney is usually permitted a brief rebuttal. Closing arguments are typically limited by the judge depending on the complexity of the case.

Civil trials may involve complex legal and scientific matters (e.g., medical or engineering testimony) presented by expert witnesses, which needs to be simplified to be understood by the jury. (For a discussion of problems with civil juries, see Litan 1993.) Attorney Roy Grutman (and Thomas 1990: 117) recalls such a case, when Memorex sued IBM for unfair competition. "The billion-dollar lawsuit was a test of physical stamina as well as the jurors' grasp of economics, engineering and corporate psychology. The trial lasted three months, as jury members listened to eighty-seven witnesses, examined three thousand exhibits, and then spent nineteen days in deliberation before informing the judge they were too confused to reach a verdict."

Under such circumstances, the judge may utilize a legal device known as the special verdict. Instead of a verdict for or against the defendant, the jury responds to a series of written questions of fact posed by the judge. Based on the jury's answers, the judge determines the outcome of the case. A verdict in favor of the defendant by judge or jury ends the trial; a finding for the plaintiff requires a judgment. A trial judge may reduce a jury award that is excessive, order a new trial when the verdict goes against the clear weight of the evidence, or reverse a verdict that is unreasonable given the facts presented at trial and the legal standard to be applied (known as a *judgment notwithstanding the verdict*).

While some states require unanimity, the decision rule in others requires only a supermajority—5 out of 6 or 9 out of 12. "Research shows little effect of jury size or decision rule on outcomes" (Feigenson 2000: 35).

In the civil jury verdict, must all of the jurors agree on each of the issues? "Consider, for example, a personal injury action in which plaintiff alleges three separate factual bases for finding that defendant was negligent. Suppose that the jurors split eight to four against a finding of negligence on each of these bases, but as to every determination, different four jurors thought that negligence had been established. Thus, despite their disagreements on the specific factual issues, all twelve jurors find defendant at fault and return verdict for plaintiff" (Friedenthal, Kane, and Miller 1985: 461). The judge may become aware of this situation as the result of a post-verdict poll of the jury, and courts have split on the matter of letting the verdict stand. The trend seems to be in favor of upholding the verdict. "The result turns on whether the particular jurisdiction views the proper role of the jury merely to decide specific factual issues or to determine the overall outcome of the case" (1985: 461–462).

In cases of equity, or when both sides waive a jury trial, the judge will often interject his or her own questions to witnesses, and when all evidence is received, the judge may ask the parties for written briefs on issues of fact and law. The judge may reserve decision until he or she has had an opportunity to review the trial transcript (Hazard and Taruffo 1993).

Judgment

There is no sentence in a civil case; the next step is a determination by judge or jury of the remedy or damages to be assessed. Once the judge enters a judgment against the defendant, if appropriate, the plaintiff can ask to have the court clerk issue an order to execute the judgment. This document commands the sheriff or U.S. marshal to take possession of the defendant's property and sell it at auction to satisfy the judgment, or a lien (garnishment) can be placed against the defendant's salary and a certain amount of money taken out each payday by the employer for the plaintiff. If the defendant fails to carry out the provisions of the judgment, the plaintiff can ask for a contempt order that can result in arrest and imprisonment. In cases where there is concern that a defendant may move or otherwise dispose of his or her property prior to the outcome of a trial, the plaintiff can request an attachment preventing any disposition of property that may thwart satisfaction of an adverse judgment. In practice, enforcement of a judgment can be complex. For example, most states immunize some of the property of debtors from attachment or seizure, such as the debtor's home and a vehicle required for employment (Hazard and Taruffo 1993).

In the civil process, as opposed to the criminal process, there is a peculiar practice known as *vacating* a decision. Vacating typically refers to setting aside or rescinding a (faulty) judgment. In this case, it means that the losing party and the winning party have struck a deal, perhaps in exchange for extra compensation, asking the court to vacate the decision as if it never existed. The decision is stricken from the record and no longer available to serve as a precedent. While it doesn't actually disappear (the records can be found in the courthouse where the judgment was issued), few lawyers would ordinarily be aware of it (Kolata 1993).

SPECIALIZED COURTS AND ADMINISTRATIVE BODIES

The civil courts are handicapped by an oppressive caseload, and it is not unusual for a tort action to take as long as five years before reaching the trial stage. In the nation's largest court system, Cook County, Illinois, the average length of time it takes for a lawsuit to reach trial is six years. When plaintiffs have a choice of courts, they usually select the one with the least amount of delay, although travel considerations will also be taken into account; the court of choice may be located some distance from the plaintiff and his or her attorney. Efforts to deal with the problem of delay have included establishment of specialized courts and administrative bodies (as well as alternative dispute resolution, discussed in Chapter 14). The civil division of a state court system frequently has specialized courts for such matters as equity (chancery court), divorce (a family or domestic relations court), settlement of estates (probate court), cases of juveniles (discussed in Chapter 13), and small claims cases.

Small Claims Courts

Small claims courts have jurisdiction to decide cases when the money being contested is not above a certain dollar amount, depending on the statutes of the jurisdiction, ranging from $1,500 (Illinois) to $5,000 (California), to $10,000 (Tennessee). The first small claims court was established in 1913 by the Cleveland Municipal Court.

The simplified process required no pleadings, only a nominal filing fee, and participation of lawyers was discouraged. By 1920, other cities—Chicago, Minneapolis, New York, Philadelphia—had established small claims courts based on the Cleveland model. In that year, Massachusetts adopted a statewide small claims court; every lower court judge was required to establish special sessions for hearing all claims under $35 (Harrington 1985). Contemporary small claims courts siphon off less complex cases for handling in a less formal manner than is typical in most other trial courts. The court's rules of procedure and evidence are relaxed to make it easier for persons to represent themselves without hiring attorneys. Filing fees are low, usually under $25—less than $6 in New York, although $69 in Illinois—and a summons can often be served by certified mail or by the sheriff for a small fee. The plaintiff need not engage an attorney, and defendants are rarely represented by counsel. Some states, for example California, prohibit the use of attorneys.

Although these courts were supposedly designed for the "little man," the citizen whose case does not involve enough money to interest a lawyer on a contingency basis (discussed later), it has frequently been used by collection agencies, utility companies, and retailers as a relatively cheap and efficient way to move against persons allegedly owing small amounts of money. "No issue with respect to small claims court has evoked more controversy than the question of whether collection agencies should be permitted to use these courts" (Weller and Ruhnka 1978: 3). Some states, such as New York, have enacted legislation prohibiting this use of small claims courts.

Administrative Bodies

In addition to specialized courts, governmental agencies have established administrative bodies (a number of these were mentioned in Chapter 1) that have quasi-judicial authority to adjudicate certain types of cases. For example, a worker's compensation board determines whether an employee's injury was job-related, thus qualifying him or her for workers' compensation. Motor vehicle departments may have hearing boards that make determinations about revoking driving licenses, and many states have boards that rule on matters involving civil rights and cases of alleged discrimination.

Administrative agencies hold evidentiary hearings before administrative decisions that adversely affect private individuals are made. While procedures vary from agency to agency, these hearings follow most of the elements of civil trial procedure, including the calling and cross-examination of witnesses by opposing counsel, but they exclude juries. The agency must explain the basis for the decision it makes at the conclusion of the hearing (Schwartz 1996).

SMALL CLAIMS COURT, SAN JOAQUIN COUNTY, CALIFORNIA

Small Claims Court is a special court where disputes are resolved quickly and inexpensively. The rules are simple and informal. In Small Claims Court, you may ask a lawyer for advice before you go to court, but neither party can have a lawyer in court. Your claim cannot be for more than $5,000.

APPEALS

Within a specified length of time, usually 30 days, a losing litigant can appeal an adverse decision. However, under our adversarial system it is the obligation of the appellant's lawyer to draw the court's attention to relevant portions of the trial record in his or her brief. The appellate court does not independently search the record for trial court errors, "but leaves the decision of what needs review to the litigants" (Friedenthal, Kane, and Miller 1985: 601). In general, appellate review is limited to errors that were objected to by the aggrieved party's attorney at trial and, thus, appear in the trial record; attorneys cannot offer new evidence. "Errors that are not objected to before or arguments that are not raised at trial generally cannot be raised for the first time on appeal" (Friedenthal, Kane, and Miller 1985: 598). The appellate court must determine if the judge's ruling was incorrect and, if so, whether or not the error(s) was serious enough to justify a new trial or if it was a "harmless error" not affecting the outcome of the trial. In cases involving money damages, the defendant can also appeal the jury award: The court can lower the amount (*remittitur*) or order a new trial on the single issue of the amount of damages.

CONTINGENCY FEE

The contingency fee offers a partial answer to the problem of providing legal assistance to persons without financial means who have suffered a tort. In this scheme, plaintiff's attorney in a personal injury case receives no retainer (compensation paid in advance). If the case is lost, the lawyer receives no payment. If the lawyer is successful, the plaintiff shares a percentage, generally one-third, of the compensation with his or her attorney. Plaintiff's attorneys collect about $30 billion a year in contingency fees (Sherrid 2001).

The contingency fee was declared legal by the Supreme Court in 1877 (*Stanton v. Embry*). Nevertheless, the American Bar Association challenged it on grounds of propriety and recommended that contingency fees be supervised by the judiciary. Fees received by law firms from corporate interests would, of course, remain free of any scrutiny. Corporate lawyers argued that because contingency fees would cause spurious lawsuits instigated by shyster lawyers, contingency contracts required supervision. The same lawyers who argued that legislation providing a minimum wage or maximum hours of employment (e.g., a 40-hour work week) was an infringement on the freedom of contract found no contradiction with their stand on contingency contracts. Critics also argued that a lawyer should not have a personal, as opposed to a professional, interest in a client's case. Sol Linowitz argues that this was not a matter of class prejudice, but "was a rule the leaders of the bar applied to themselves in their corporate practice." Paul Cravath, for example, "forbade anyone who worked at Cravath, Swaine, and Moore from owning stock in any client corporation" (1996: 29). "One of the traditional criticisms of the contingent fee is that, by having an interest in the outcome of the cases, lawyers are hindered in providing the kind of dispassionate professional advice they should be rendering to their clients" (Kritzer 1991: 99). And, in some cases, "it is more beneficial financially for the lawyer to secure a quick settlement, even if the amount paid is much lower than what could be achieved by going to trial" (Kritzer 1991: 100).

In the personal injury area, plaintiff's lawyers may have a number of cases against a single insurance company; in this situation the lawyer may try to negotiate settlements for several cases at the same time. Given the lawyer's interest in maximizing the return from the complete set of cases, it may be expedient to forego a maximum return in any single case in order to achieve the best aggregate result (Kritzer 1990: 10): "Regular players in the system—attorneys who handle a great deal of personal injury litigation—may approach cases with a future orientation (such as relationships with other attorneys) rather than securing the best possible outcome for the instant case. A refusal to accept a settlement in a current case, while it may be in the best interest of a client, may harm future settlements."

"Tort Reform"

Of no small historical interest is the current controversy pitting trial lawyers and the contingency fee against the insurance industry and its clients. Both sides have sought to claim the high ground by using terms such as "reform," "justice," and "fairness." They typically attempt to mask the substantial self-interest inherent in their respective positions. Both sides have buttressed their arguments with dubious statistics and anecdotal evidence (Daniels and Martin 1995). In 1994, a number of prominent legal scholars urged reform of the contingency fee to prevent windfalls for what amounts to nothing more than routine legal services. In 1989, a soft-drink delivery truck crashed into a school bus killing 21 children and injuring dozens of others. Since fault was never really in doubt, insurance companies settled for $122 million, the plaintiff lawyers getting at least one-third, which amounted to $25,000 an hour. Lawyers are paid about $15 billion a year in contingency fees (Passell 1994).

The United States is a litigious society. In 1986, insurance companies began a vigorous lobbying campaign for a statutory cap on tort judgments, particularly for "punitive damages" that are supposed to serve as a deterrent. Punitive damages are typically those making headlines because of the dollar amounts imposed.[2] However, they account for only about five hundred cases a year and the amounts assessed are often reversed or cut back on appeal (Cohn 1991). The campaign to impose caps is supported by local governments and doctors, as well as a variety of business and charitable organizations, all of whom have to pay high insurance premiums.

Increasing rates have caused some local governments to drop their insurance coverage (and, correspondingly, public services). Insurance companies claim that the increase in rates is a result of defending against lawsuits and, most importantly, against judgments that are out of step with the tort concepts of fault and wrongdoing. They claim that judges and juries often hold "deep-pocketed" defendants liable simply because they have the resources to compensate plaintiff victims. However, a study of 9,000 trials throughout the country found that judges award punitive damages about as often as juries. Punitive damages are awarded in about 4 percent of the cases won by plaintiffs (Glaberson 2001b). Critics argue that fear of potential

---

[2]In 1997, for example, a jury awarded $2.5 billion dollars in punitive damages against the CSX Corporation for a railroad fire in New Orleans in 1987, this despite the fact that the federal National Transportation Safety Board determined that CSX had not caused the accident and no serious injuries had resulted (Salpukas 1997; Broder 1997).

CHAOTIC JUSTICE?

"Numbers have been, along with horror story anecdotes, one of the main tools used in the strategic representation of the civil justice system as a system in chaos. This is despite the limited amount of data actually available and the question of how to interpret them." And the "opponents of civil justice reform have not been idle. There is an antireform rhetoric that is equally problematic because of its use of horror stories, appeals to passion over reason, misuse of quantitative data, and so on" (Daniels and Martin 1995: 53; 246).

liability claims caused one company to shelve an asbestos substitute, and the American Medical Association complains that lawsuits have forced all but one pharmaceutical firm out of birth-control research (Gest 1989). By 1989, 23 states had enacted legislation placing caps on malpractice awards.

A 1989 report by the National Academy of Sciences revealed that frequent malpractice lawsuits against obstetricians have caused some of them to stop delivering babies, resulting in a shortage of obstetrical care in many rural and inner city areas where low-income women are more likely to experience high-risk pregnancies. Malpractice insurance premiums for obstetrics in some cities exceeds $100,000 per year ("Study: Obstetrics Suits Make Doctors Wary" 1989). The rising cost of malpractice insurance has impacted on health clinics, causing many to cut back or eliminate services for low-income patients. Clinics treat high-risk patients such as pregnant women whose circumstances may cause them to neglect prenatal care until problems become acute.

A study by the *New York Times* (Steinhauer and Fessenden 2001: 24) revealed that "many New York hospitals routinely hire and retain doctors with bad records—especially those who bring a lot of money." A comprehensive study by the New York State Department of Health revealed that while thousands of deaths and tens of thousands of injuries are tied to medical negligence each year, relatively few result in any court action (Sack 1990). The National Academy of Sciences reports that in addition to those permanently disabled by in-hospital medical errors, errors kill 44,000 to 98,000 people a year (Pear 1999), figures that have been challenged by the medical establishment. A study of lawsuits against physicians in New Jersey (Taragin et al. 1993) found that the defensibility of a case generally determines outcome: The researchers (medical professionals) found that in 25 percent of the cases physician error was clear and in over 90 percent of these cases judgments were (appropriately) for the plaintiffs. In the 62 percent of cases they considered defensible, physicians prevailed 80 percent of the time. In the remaining cases, it was not clear if physician care was defensible. They conclude: "Our findings suggest that unjustified payments are probably uncommon" (1993: 780). Another study revealed that out of 46 malpractice suits resolved after 10 years, in 13 cases where the records showed that there was no malpractice, litigants were nevertheless awarded an average of $98,192. In ten cases, where injuries to the patient were clearly caused by the underlying disease, litigants received an average of $28,760 each from insurance companies eager to avoid the costs of a trial (Reuters 1996).

The Drunk, the Train, the Award

In 1980, Francisco M. entered a New York City subway station. He was apparently intoxicated. A subway employee notified the police that an intoxicated man was on the platform. Before the police arrived, Mr. M. fell on the tracks, was hit by a train, and lost his arm. A jury awarded him $3.6 million, but this was dismissed by a state appeals court in 1996.

Trial lawyers argue that increases in tort litigation have been proportionate to the increase in population. "Sue the bastards" is apparently an old American tradition, and there are more lawyers than ever apparently eager to carry the tradition forward. Ironically, lawyers have increasingly become a target of malpractice suits, and many attorneys can no longer afford the cost of malpractice insurance (Talbac 1987). There are now firms whose entire practice is devoted to suing or defending attorneys in malpractice cases (Pérez-Peña 1994b). Personal injury lawyers, and those involved with securities and real estate syndication, have been the primary targets. The single most important factor in the increase of such suits is that lawyers are no longer seen as simply mere advocates, "but as advisers, deal makers and, in some instances, investors. And as they have become more versatile, they have also become more vulnerable" (Margolick 1988c: 25). But many malpractice lawsuits are the result of attorneys failing to meet filing deadlines and other routine matters (Pérez-Peña 1994b).

Some states have enacted legislation limiting pain-and-suffering awards, and congressional Republicans have endorsed "capping" legislation for the federal system. The cases of Harry Jordon and Agnes Mae Whitaker exemplify the difference that such legislation can make. Harry Jordon was a Californian with a malignant kidney. His Los Angeles surgeons accidentally removed the healthy one, relegating him to a short and painful life. The victim's award was reduced to $256,000 as the result of a California statute that limits pain and suffering awards (Quinn 1986). On the other hand, a jury in New York awarded Agnes Mae Whitaker, a victim of medical malpractice, a compensatory award of $7 million: Doctors had failed to diagnose an intestinal constriction that caused an infection requiring the removal of most of her small intestine. The jury also awarded Ms. Whitaker an additional $58 million dollars for pain-and-suffering (Editorial, *New York Times*, July 24, 1986: 22). New York subsequently enacted legislation that limits the amount of a single payment to a successful plaintiff to $250,000, with the remainder paid out over 10 years. In 1996, President Bill Clinton vetoed a bill that would have placed caps on the amount of money people injured by faulty products could win in lawsuits. (In 1995 the president vetoed a bill to make it harder for stockholders to file lawsuits against corporations for securities fraud. This veto was overridden by Congress.) In 1999, Alabama joined about two dozen states in placing a ceiling on punitive damages. This, after a jury awarded $581 million to a family that had been overcharged $1,200 for two satellite dishes. The Alabama law limits punitive damages in noninjury cases against large corporations to three times the compensatory damages or $500,000, whichever is greater. In injury cases, the caps are three times the compensatory

How Much Is a Death Worth?

While the controversy over "just" compensation for victims in tort cases continues, insurance companies are also concerned about the cost of "death compensation." Their attorneys argue that frequently "large jury verdicts include compensation for intangible non-economic injuries, like the decedent's pre-death fear or decedent's loss of enjoyment of life (hedonic damages) or for decedent's family's grief, anguish, mental distress, and loss of nurture, companionship and love. Without in any way questioning the significance of injuries, the fact is that money does not alleviate them." Therefore, "judges and juries should not be permitted to make financial awards for intangible non-economic losses [since] the law does not and cannot give juries and judges any legal principles or other useful yardsticks to determine how to evaluate these losses" (Craft 1989: 2).

Trial lawyers respond that "money can make family members who have suffered a grievous loss feel better. The recognition by the law that they have suffered such a grievous loss at the hands of a negligent defendant gives rise to an expectation of damages. The recovery of these damages does fulfill a psychological need. And while it is true that revenge and punishment are not parts of compensatory damages, the fact is that aggrieved family members do derive satisfaction that the negligent defendant has been caused to pay for the loss. Furthermore to deny the victims adequate damages would only reward the defendant's wrongdoing" (Kreinler 1989: 2).

damages or $1.5 million, whichever is greater (Firestone 1999). However, top state courts in more than a half-dozen states have struck down laws placing limits on liability awards as contrary to state constitutions (Glaberson 1999).

In 1987, the American Bar Association endorsed a controversial plan that would place some limits on the rights of injured parties to sue for damages, and the association endorsed greater discretion for trial judges to reduce awards they consider excessive. Some critics of the current system argue for the *English Rule*, a system in Great Britain that requires the losing side in a lawsuit to pay the winning side's attorney costs (Samuelson 1992).[3] In 1989, the Supreme Court ruled that unlimited awards for punitive damages do not violate the Eighth Amendment's prohibition against "excessive fines." In a 7–2 decision, the Court ruled that the limitation on fines applied only to government and not to private lawsuits. In this case, a jury awarded compensation of $51,146, but set punitive damages at $6 million (*Browning-Ferris Industries* v. *Kelco Disposal*). In 1991, the Court upheld a $1 million jury award to a poor woman with $3,800 in medical bills that an insurance company had refused to pay (*Pacific Mutual Life Insurance Co.* v. *Haslip*). In 1993, the Supreme Court ruled again on the issue of excessive punitive damages: in a 6–3 decision the Court refused to overturn a $10 million award for a $19,000 injury (*TXO Production* v. *Alliance Resources*). In 1994, however, the Court set aside a damage award of $5 million dollars for an Oregon man who was injured when his

---

[3]Contingency fees are illegal in England (Linowitz 1996: 175), which is offset by the "existence of more tax-supported legal assistance programs."

How Much Is Your Brain Worth?

Sylvia Richardson, 35, married with one daughter, went into a university medical center to have her wisdom tooth removed. The resident gave her ten times the intended amount of anesthesia resulting in a 10-day coma and brain damage—she requires around-the-clock care. Indiana, which limited malpractice awards to $500,000, no matter how serious the incident, increased the amount to $750,000 as a result of this case (Wilkerson 1990).

The man who successfully lobbied for the cap on damage awards in Indiana became the victim of medical malpractice that left him confined to a wheelchair and kept alive by a respirator. At age 49 and in constant pain, he was given less than two years to live. Like Mrs. Richardson, Frank Cornelius (1994) is limited to a damage award of $750,000—his medical bills are in excess of $5 million.

three-wheeled vehicle overturned on him. In *Honda* v. *Oberg*, the Court ruled 7–2 that punitive damages pose a risk of being arbitrary and, therefore, some judicial review of jury awards is constitutionally required—Oregon was the only state that failed to provide for such review. In 1996, in a 5–4 decision (*BMW* v. *Gore*), the Court ruled that punitive damages can be so "grossly excessive" as to be unconstitutional. Evidence had been presented that BMW repainted at least 1,000 cars sold as new, a violation of Alabama law, but not illegal in every state. An Alabama state court jury found the damage and repair diminished the value of the plaintiff's car's value by $4,000, and multiplied that by 1,000 to arrive at a punitive award (which was cut in half by the Alabama Supreme Court). The U.S. Supreme Court ruled that state courts could not use punitive damages for conduct that may be legal in another state. In an elaboration of *BMW* v. *Gore*, the Supreme Court ruled 8–1 (*Cooper Industries Inc.* v. *Leatherman Tool Group Inc. 2001*) that federal and state appellate court must give searching scrutiny when deciding if a jury award for punitive damages is excessive. The decision was seen as a victory for opponents of punitive damage awards (Greenhouse 2001).

In 1996, President Bill Clinton vetoed a bill that would have set limits on punitive damages in both state and federal courts, in cases involving product liability. The bill was part of a measure that had been included in the "Contract with America," the manifesto of Republican members of the House of Representatives (Lewis 1996).

An extensive research effort into medical malpractice, product liability, and punitive damage lawsuits concludes:

> The characterization of juries and the civil justice system animating the tort reform movement is at odds with the findings of systematic empirical research or is based on claims about things for which there is little or no systematic research. This is especially true in terms of systematic evidence for the causal connections linking the legal system to a host of social and economic ills. Consequently, we are skeptical of the efficacy of enacted reforms and concerned about the possible unintended consequences of those measures. Beyond the self-interest of those groups lobbying for reform, we can see little reason for continuing or endorsing this reform movement. (Daniels and Martin 1995: 249)

WHO IS CONCERNED WITH JUSTIN?

In 1985, when he was 26 months old, Justin was rushed to a Florida public hospital suffering an asthma attack. He has never left. By the following day, mistakes admitted to by the hospital left the boy with severe brain damage: He cannot walk, talk, breathe, and take nourishment without the aid of tubes. His mother wants Justin home, but she cannot afford to pay for the cost of care this would entail—Florida law limits the liability of state agencies to $200,000 (Navarro 1995). "Throughout America there are thousands of doctors—working in hospitals, clinics and private offices—who hurt and even fatally injure patients through incompetence or carelessness yet remain in active practice" (Gavzer 1996: 4) because they are often protected by caps on liability in the name of "reform."

Juries decide more than 10,000 tort cases per year and in about half the jury finds for the defendant. The median award is between $30,000 and $40,000 and less than 5 percent of plaintiffs win punitive damages (Litras, Gifford, and DeFrances 2000).

An additional element in this controversy is the mass tort or class action lawsuit.

CLASS ACTION LAWSUIT[4]

The class action lawsuit is traditionally used when there are many parties involved to prevent the inconvenience of a multiplicity of lawsuits. "An early but important principle applied to class actions was that judgment would apply to absentee class members who were not parties in the court" (Alliance of American Insurers 1987: 39). The current controversy over class action lawsuits is the result of a 1966 change in Rule 23 of the *Federal Rules of Civil Procedure*, which most states copied. This statute authorizes the filing of a lawsuit brought by one plaintiff or a small number of persons on behalf of a larger number of persons, which the plaintiffs believe themselves to represent, such as Vietnam veterans exposed to Agent Orange, industrial workers injured by exposure to toxic chemicals, or prison inmates, and more recently recipients of silicone breast implants. The 1966 revision did away with the requirement that all individuals seeking money damages with class action lawsuits need to "opt in": sign on affirmatively. Instead, those who the plaintiffs claim to represent are deemed to be part of the lawsuit unless they specifically "opt out": withdraw (Hensler et al. 1999).

Plaintiffs have standing as a group much as other recognized collectivities like labor unions and corporations, but without the need for organization. "*Interest* provides the substitute for individual initiative and consent; the class action justifies action that legally binds another without his consent by pointing out that his interest is represented in a situation in which it is inconceivable that he would not wish his interest to be so pursued" (Yeazell 1987: 15).

[4]For an excellent summary discussion of the class action lawsuit, see Hensler et. al (1999).

Too Little or Too Much?

A jury in Tampa, Florida awarded $3.3 million to a man whose doctor fused the wrong vertebrae in his neck during surgery (Associated Press 2000b).

But this presents a legal problem: Under our system of due process each individual is entitled to control the destiny of his or her own litigation. Generally, if the court certifies the lawsuit as a class action, all members of the class must be notified and given an opportunity to opt out of the class or lose the ability to bring an individual action. In some cases, however, notification is not required, and a person who may not be aware of the lawsuit loses the ability to bring an individual action at some later date.

Class action lawsuits are frequently brought by public interest groups on behalf of consumers or environmental concerns, and to protect minorities, women, the handicapped, and the elderly against discriminatory practices. In 1996, the Republican-controlled Congress banned class-action suits by the federally funded Legal Services Corporation, eliminating "the most effective tool at the disposal of legal services lawyers for attacking systemic problems in government institutions and benefit programs" (Greenhouse 1996b: E5). There are also class action cases brought for pecuniary reasons.

> There are a few nominal plaintiffs who are members of the class, but the suit is usually the entrepreneurial undertaking of a law firm for a contingent fee. In class action cases the most important decision the court must make is whether the alleged claims can be combined into one lawsuit. A decision that the claims cannot be combined will inevitably cause the whole matter to go away because no one plaintiff has enough at stake to justify bringing the suit. Certification of the class, on the other hand, may allow the aggregation of small claims to the tune of millions of dollars—and a 30 percent contingent fee interest in an award of that size definitely justifies some real care and attention by the plaintiffs' law firm. (Neely 1985: 45)

In many cases "opportunistic lawyers themselves initiated litigation and used the club of costly adversarial legalism to extract settlements that primarily benefited the lawyers themselves" (Kagan 1994: 42). A growing number of companies are taking advantage of class-action rules to immunize themselves against future litigation—they are initiating class-action lawsuits against themselves. The firms encourage the litigation which they subsequently settle with inflated legal fees. This enriches plaintiff attorneys while limiting the ability of those harmed from subsequently litigating claims against the company (Meier 1996).

In order for their claims to be accepted, "litigants must show that they are proper representatives for the class of persons they seek to champion, that the type of issues they wish to raise are common to the class, and they must be able to demonstrate how a remedy can be formed that will meet the needs of the class" (Cooper 1988: 15). If the class prevails in the tort, "it is entitled to a remedy that embraces all its members, even though only one or two have participated actively in the lawsuit" (Yeazell 1987: 1).

"WINNERS" AND LAWYERS

A real estate broker in Portland, Maine, discovered he had won $2.19 in a class action lawsuit brought against his bank, an action he knew nothing about until he spotted a $91.33 miscellaneous deduction from his escrow account—it went to pay an $8.5 million fee for "his" lawyers (Meier 1995). The broker brought a lawsuit against the lawyers, an action supported by the attorney generals of several states (Meier 1997). The case was dismissed in federal court and the Supreme Court refused to consider his appeal.

While Scott Baldwin (1984), president of the Association of Trial Lawyers of America, argues that the class action contingency fee is the only sure way to protect the "little guy," Stephen Case (1984), of the Wall Street firm of David Polk and Wardell, responds that plaintiff attorneys are grossly overcompensated in class action suits. Case notes that in every tort case two issues must be resolved: (1) Did the defendant commit a wrong? (e.g., market an unsafe product), and (2) How much money should the claimant receive? In mass torts there can be dozens, and sometimes hundreds or thousands, of claimants represented by a single attorney or small law firm. Contingency fees in such cases can range in the millions, although the work involved is not significantly more complex than in single-plaintiff cases.

Baldwin counters that references to the mass tort by attorneys representing corporate interests are merely a smokescreen to divert attention from the real damages, pain, and suffering inflicted upon real persons who, without the class action contingency fee, would not have the funds necessary to deal with the legal resources of corporate law firms. Trial lawyers involved in class action lawsuits often expend considerable resources over many years in a venture that may yield no profits. In cases such as those involving the Dalkon Shield, asbestos, and Rely tampons, there were thousands of clients and complex scientific questions that had to be dealt with (e.g., see Bacigal 1990). In some cases they required an investment by the lawyers of several million dollars. For example, in the "Agent Orange" case, five lawyers each contributed more than $250,000 to a common defense fund (Wagner 1986). A cap on judgments would make such cases not worth the gamble, leave injured parties without legal representation, and reduce the incentive to deal with the negligence that is at the root of personal injury judgments.

While class action lawsuits can provide impressive contingency fees for attorneys, individual claimants may actually derive very little, since the settlement has to be shared among so many persons. Without going to trial to fight for a better deal, class action lawyers can settle for a few cents on the dollar for their clients while earning millions of dollars in legal fees for themselves (Eichenwald 1993). In 1994, about a dozen law firms, serving as class action counsel, shared $22 million dollars in a settlement with a major securities company, while defrauded investors received about $679 each. Ironically, the lawyers originally settled for a lesser amount, which was rejected by the court. Those who opted out of the class action did considerably better in their settlements (Eichenwald 1994). For more than two decades, however, judges have usually employed the *lodestar formula* to determine attorney fees in class action cases.

In the lodestar method, "the court makes a determination of the number of hours that were 'reasonably' spent on the case by the plaintiff class attorney (usually a matter of some dispute) and multiplies this by the going hourly billing rate for lawyers of 'comparable' skills (another area of dispute). This product is called the 'lodestar' and reflects roughly what the lawyers would have received had they been paid contemporaneously on an hourly rate. The lodestar is then adjusted upward by various multipliers to reflect such factors as the risk of losing the case (in which event there would be no fee at all) and the delay between the effort and deferred compensation. The final result is the attorney fee award" (Lynk 1994: 187–188).

In the next chapter, we will turn to the justice system used for juveniles.

INTERNET CONNECTIONS

Legal sites on the Web: *ih2000.net/ira/legal.htm*
Law Guru: *lawguru.com*
'Lectric Law: *lectlaw.com/ref.html*

REVIEW QUESTIONS

1. What are the goals of law in civil cases?
2. Why is the issue of standing relevant to civil, but not criminal, cases?
3. What constitutional guarantees that apply to criminal trials are not applicable in civil cases?
4. Why are jurisdictional issues in civil cases more complex than those in criminal cases?
5. What pretrial activities typically used in civil cases are not generally used in criminal cases?
6. What is a "directed verdict," and why is it used?
7. How is a "special verdict" a response to technically complex civil trials?
8. What is the philosophy and purpose of small claims court?
9. How is the contingency fee a partial response to the problem of legal representation for poor persons?
10. What are the issues that have pitted insurance companies against trial lawyers?
11. What is a class-action lawsuit?
12. What is the legal problem to which a class-action lawsuit is a response?

13

$\checkmark$UVENILE $\checkmark$USTICE

Because the goals of juvenile justice and the procedures of the juvenile court are so different from both the criminal *and* civil processes, they are examined separately. We will review the historical development and legal foundations of juvenile justice, procedures of the juvenile court, and juveniles prosecuted in criminal court.

HISTORY AND PHILOSOPHY

In Europe, from Roman times to the late eighteenth century, children were routinely abandoned by their parents; the classical philosopher Rousseau, for example, boasted of abandoning five of his children to foundling homes (Boswell 1989). Abandoned children were subjected to extreme levels of deprivation and exploitation. English common law considered children as chattel, and a rather indifferent attitude toward children became characteristic of America, where children became creatures of exploitation. Child labor remained an important part of economic life into the twentieth century. Children of the poor labored in mines (where their size was an advantage), mills, and factories with unsanitary and unsafe conditions. As noted in Chapter 3, the Supreme Court reflected the prevailing belief in *laissez faire* capitalism and would not intervene—statutes prohibiting children under 12 from employment and limiting the workday of youngsters over 12 to 10 hours were ruled unconstitutional or routinely disobeyed. Increased immigration, industrialization, and urbanization drastically altered American society. The 10- and 12-hour work-day left many children without parental supervision, and family disorganization became widespread. Many children lived in the streets, where they encountered the disorder and rampant vice of the urban environment.

In the early days of colonial America, the family remained the mainstay of social control, "although by 1700 the family's inability to accommodate and discipline its young was becoming more apparent" (Mennel 1973: xxii). Numerous laws began to appear threatening parents for failing to properly discipline their children. Furthermore, the British practice of transporting wayward young to America for indenture, which often involved neglect, cruelty, and immorality, left many youngsters without supervision as they fled from these onerous circumstances. By the end of the eighteenth century, society began to realize that a "system of social control would have to be developed apart from the family which would discipline homeless, vagrant, and destitute children—the offspring of the poor" (1973: xxvii). This need led to the rise of houses of refuge.

The first house of refuge opened in New York in 1825 and was quickly followed by one in Boston (1826) and another in Philadelphia (1828). These institutions provided housing and care for troublesome children who might otherwise be left in the streets or, if their behavior brought them into serious conflict with the law, sent to jail or prison. The house of refuge was used "not only for the less serious juvenile criminal, but for runaways, disobedient children or vagrants" (Empey 1979: 25–26). Orphan asylums were used for abandoned or orphaned children, for the children of women without husbands, or for children whose parents were "unfit." These institutions "were established to inculcate children with the values of hard work, orderliness, and subordination and thereby ensure their future good behavior" (Mennel 1973: 8). To achieve these ends, however, discipline and punishments were often brutal, and the house of refuge in New York experienced group escapes and inmate uprisings.

Although these institutions were run by private charities, their public charters included the first statutory definitions of juvenile delinquency and provided the basis for the state to intervene in the lives of children who were neglected or in need of supervision, in addition to those youngsters who had committed crimes (Walker 1980). Within these charters was embodied a "medieval English doctrine of nebulous origin and meaning" (Schlossman 1977: 8) known as *parens patriae*, originally referring to the feudal duties of the overlord to his vassals and later the legal duties of the king toward his subjects who were in need of care, particularly children and the mentally incompetent. In its original form, *parens patriae* provided the Crown with authority to administer the estates of landed orphans (Sutton 1988). The legal system's exercise of jurisdiction over families and children in the United States is founded on principles of equity (National Council of Juvenile and Family Court Judges 1988).

"With the independence of the American colonies," states Herbert Lou, writing in 1927, "and the transplanting of the English common-law system, the state in this country has taken the place of the crown as the *parens patriae* of all minors" (1972: 4). This concept gave almost complete authority over children to the state—the Bill of Rights simply did not apply to children (*Ex parte Crouse* 1838)—and *parens patriae* became the legal basis for the juvenile court. While *parens patriae* has become identified with the rehabilitation of juvenile delinquents, it originally applied only to dependent children.

As the end of the nineteenth century approached, both immigration and urbanization continued unabated, and the specter of masses of undisciplined and uneducated children gave rise to the child-saving movement. Led by middle- and upper-class women of earlier American stock, the child-savers were influenced by nativist prejudices of their day and, later, by Social Darwinism (discussed in Chapter 3), in addition to more humane motivations. The juvenile court was the result of their efforts, although controversy surrounds the interests and motivations of the child savers.

Anthony Platt argues that these women, although they "viewed themselves as altruists and humanitarians dedicated to rescuing those who were less fortunately placed in the social order," were actually motivated by boredom and middle- and upper-class social, economic, and political interests (1974: 3). "The child-savers were concerned not with championing the rights of the poor against exploitation by the ruling class but rather integrating the poor into the established social order and protecting 'respectable' citizens from the 'dangerous classes'" of people, who might otherwise be drawn into social revolution, if not criminality (Platt quoted in Empey, 1979: 31). According to Platt, the juvenile court would serve to protect propertied and commercial interests from the predations of lower class youngsters while ensuring an adequate supply of disciplined and vocationally trained labor. In fact, however, many states had already separated juvenile cases from those of adults without establishing a distinct juvenile court. And the movement to establish a juvenile court was part of a larger program of social reform advocated by the Progressives of the late nineteenth and early twentieth centuries. David Rothman (in Empey, 1979: 37) places the issue in perspective: The juvenile court movement "satisfied [both] the most humanitarian of impulses and the most crudely self-interested considerations."

Something had to be done to save the children from their environment of ignorance and vice, or they would become progenitors of the same. The asylum, the house of refuge, and the reformatory were all part of this movement, but the most important accomplishment was the establishment of the juvenile court.

JUVENILE COURT

While common law did not differentiate between adults and minors, in most states a minor was 10 to12 years of age (McMillian 1999). While a minor might be sent to the house of refuge or the reformatory instead of jail or prison, he or she could be arrested, detained, and tried like any adult accused of a crime. A few jurisdictions modified their trial process for children in the decades after the Civil War in an attempt to separate them from adult offenders, but "it was left to Illinois to pass the first comprehensive law to create the first specially organized juvenile court" (Lou 1972: 19). That this occurred in Chicago was no coincidence. Chicago was the scene of rapid urbanization. From 1890 to 1900, the population increased almost 50 percent, with 70 percent of the residents being foreign born (Pettibone et al. 1981). In 1893, there was an economic panic, and as conditions of the poor continued to deteriorate, reforming juvenile justice became the primary goal of the child-savers, women who "were generally well-educated, widely traveled, and had access to political and financial resources" (Platt 1974: 77).

The first juvenile court was established in Cook County (whose county seat is Chicago) on July 1, 1899, the result of the Juvenile Court Act of April 14, 1899. In addition to children who were delinquent (persons under sixteen who violated the law), and consistent with the concept of *parens patriae*, the juvenile court was given jurisdiction over neglected and dependent children, and over children who presented "behavior problems" but who were not delinquent, truants and runaways. This special category became known as *status offenders*. Within thirty years, all but two states had a separate court for juveniles operating under the concept *parens patriae* (Finckenauer 1984).

Because the purpose of the juvenile court was to aid, not punish, children, the due-process guarantees of the adult criminal court were absent. With its informal and unstructured system of justice, the juvenile court quickly became the standard for similar courts established throughout the United States. The noncriminal nature of the proceedings even extended to the nomenclature used, as shown in Figure 13–1.

LEGAL DEVELOPMENTS

The nature of the juvenile court process remained unchanged into the 1960s, when the Warren Court began to pay increasing attention to questions of due process as indicated by decisions in the cases of *Gideon, Mapp*, and *Miranda* (discussed in Chapter 10). In 1966, the Court granted certiorari in the case of *Kent* v. *United States*. Morris Kent, age 16, had been convicted in criminal court of raping a woman in her Washington, D.C., apartment. He was sentenced to a term of 30 to 90 years in prison. Following federal statutes, the case had first been referred to the juvenile court where, over the objections of defense counsel, jurisdiction was waived to the criminal court. The Supreme Court ruled that before a juvenile can be tried in adult court, he or she is entitled to a waiver hearing with counsel and, if jurisdiction is subsequently waived, a statement of the reasons must be provided by the judge for the record.

While this decision had only limited application, the Court noted a problem in applying *parens patriae*. In past decisions, the Court had interpreted the Fourteenth Amendment to mean that certain classes of persons, such as juveniles, could receive less due process if accompanied by a compensating benefit—in the case of juveniles,

FIGURE 13-1   ADULT AND JUVENILE COURT TERMS COMPARED

Adult Criminal Court	Juvenile Court
defendant	respondent
information/indictment	petition
arraignment	hearing
prosecution	adjudication
verdict	finding
presentence report	predisposition report
sentence	disposition
parole	aftercare

greater concern for the youngster's interests. Noting that this benefit may not actually exist, the Court stated that the juvenile may receive the worst of both worlds: "neither the protection accorded to adults nor the solicitous care and regenerative treatment postulated for children." *Parens patriae* assumes that the state, "acting as a substitute parent, will act considerately and in the best interests of the child" and that "the interest of the state and the welfare of the child are in harmony" (McMillian 1999: 6). When this harmony is not present, when the state fails to fulfill its obligations under *parens patriae*, serious issues of due process emerge as the next case reveals.

Gault Decision

In 1967, the Supreme Court decided the most important case affecting the juvenile court when it agreed to consider a writ of *habeas corpus* in the case of *In re Gault*.[1] Gault was an Arizona case that reached the Court without benefit of a lower court review. In general, an appellate court will not consider a case unless all other remedies have been exhausted. However, Arizona law did not permit a review of juvenile court decisions, and furthermore, no record had been made of the juvenile court proceedings upon which to base an appeal. Gerald Gault, age 15 at the time, and a friend were arrested by police on the complaint of a female neighbor that they had made lewd and indecent remarks over the telephone. The youngster's parents were not notified of their son's arrest and did not receive a copy of the petition. Juveniles were not entitled to many due process guarantees in Arizona juvenile court proceedings, and Gerald was not advised of his right to remain silent or his right to counsel. At a second hearing, Gerald was declared to be a juvenile delinquent and committed to the state industrial school for a maximum of six years—until his twenty-first birthday. Had Gerald been over the age of 18, the maximum sentence would have been a fine of not more than $50 or imprisonment for up to 60 days. The complainant was not present at either hearing, the judge did not speak with her on any occasion, and no record was made of the court proceedings.

In its decision, the Supreme Court acknowledged the helping (noncriminal) philosophy that led to the establishment of the juvenile court. But it also revealed a sense of outrage over what had transpired in this case: "Under our Constitution, the condition of being a boy does not justify a kangaroo court." The Court ruled that a youngster being adjudicated in juvenile court is entitled to certain rights and procedures, which include the following:

1. *Notice*. The child and parents or guardians shall receive a notice "in writing, of the specific charge or factual allegations to be considered at the hearing, and . . . such written notice [shall] be given at the earliest practicable time, and in any event, sufficiently in advance of the hearing to permit preparation."

2. *Right to counsel*. This requires that "the child and his parents must be notified of the child's right to be represented by counsel retained by them, or if they are unable to afford counsel, that counsel will be appointed to represent the child."

---

[1]In states that do not provide an appellate process for juvenile court cases, such as Arizona, they are cited as In re (in the matter of), as opposed to the more conventional format of *Gault* v. *Arizona*.

3. *Protection against self-incrimination.* This guarantee "is applicable in the case of juveniles as it is with respect to adults." The Court added, "It would be surprising if the privilege against self-incrimination were made available to hardened criminals but not to children."

4. *Right to confront and cross-examine adverse witnesses.* This, like the right to remain silent, was found to be essential: "No reason is suggested or appears for a different rule in respect to sworn testimony in juvenile courts than in adult tribunals."

5. *Right to appellate review and transcripts of proceedings.* The Court held that this cannot be denied: "As the present case illustrates, the consequences of failure to provide an appeal, to record the proceedings, or to make findings or state the grounds for the juvenile court's conclusion may be to throw the burden upon the machinery for *habeas corpus*, to saddle the reviewing process with the burden of attempting to reconstruct a record, and to impose upon the Juvenile Judge the unseemly duty of testifying under cross-examination as to the events that transpired in the hearings before him."

Other Juvenile Justice Decisions

Twelve-year old Samuel Winship was charged with stealing $112 from a woman's purse in a store. No one actually saw him take the money, but he was seen running from the scene just before the woman noticed the money was missing. Because of the noncriminal nature of the juvenile court, instead of the proof-beyond-a-reasonable-doubt standard, the level of evidence required for a finding of delinquency was the civil standard of the preponderance of evidence. Based on that standard, Winship was adjudicated a delinquent and sent to a New York State training school. In 1970, the Supreme Court (*In re Winship*) overturned the adjudication and ruled that "the reasonable-doubt standard plays a vital role in the American scheme of criminal procedure. It is a prime instrument for reducing the risk of conviction resting on factual error." Accordingly, the Court determined that "the constitutional safeguard of proof beyond a reasonable doubt is as much required during the adjudicatory stage of a delinquency proceeding as those constitutional safeguards applied in *Gault*."

At age 16, Joseph McKeiver was charged with robbery, larceny, and receiving stolen goods. It was alleged that he and 20 to 30 youths chased 3 youngsters and took 25 cents from them. His lawyer requested a jury trial, which was denied by the juvenile court judge. McKeiver was adjudicated a delinquent and placed on probation. In 1971, in *McKeiver v. Pennsylvania*, the Court ruled that a juvenile court proceeding is not a criminal prosecution within the meaning of the Sixth Amendment and, therefore, a child is not entitled to a jury trial. Nevertheless, about a half-dozen states recognize a juvenile's right to a jury trial in delinquency cases either by law or court decisions (Possley 1999).

In 1975, the Court (*Breed v. Jones*) ruled on the issue of double jeopardy for juveniles. Gary Jones was 17 years old when he was arrested for armed robbery, and a juvenile petition alleging the original charge and two other robberies was filed. After taking testimony from two witnesses presented by the prosecutor and the respondent, the judge sustained the petition. At a subsequent disposition hearing, however, the judge ruled that the respondent was not "amenable to the care, treatment and training program available through the facilities of the juvenile court" and ordered that he be prosecuted as an adult. Jones was subsequently found guilty of armed robbery in superior court. In its decision, the Supreme Court held "that the prosecution of respondent in Superior Court, after an adjudicatory proceeding in Juvenile Court, violated the Double Jeopardy Clause of the Fifth Amendment, as applied to the States through the Fourteenth Amendment."

In 1984, in a strong affirmation of the concept of *parens patriae*, the Court upheld the constitutionality of a New York statute that permits the preventive detention of juveniles when there is a "serious risk" that the juvenile may commit an act before trial that, if committed by an adult, would constitute a crime. Gregory Martin, age 14, was charged with robbery, assault, and possession of a weapon after he and two other youths hit a boy on the head with a loaded gun and stole his jacket and sneakers. Martin was held in detention pending adjudication. Martin's attorney filed a writ of *habeas corpus*. In *Schall v. Martin*, the Supreme Court found that juveniles, unlike adults, "are always in some form of custody," and that by definition, they "are not assumed to have the capacity to take care of themselves."

Adhererence to almost all of the criminal justice system's due process guarantees has made the juvenile court—like its criminal counterpart—adversarial, helping to facilitate a dramatic shift away from the concept of *parens patriae* (what the juvenile needs) and toward a model based on *just deserts* (what the offender deserves—punishment) for juvenile offenders. While this clearly defeats the purpose of a separate court for juveniles where the *raison d'être* is help, not punishment, this movement has proven politically popular. While *parens patriae* is paternalistic and not inconsistent with the concept of punishment (Weisheit and Alexander 1988), the use of a punitive approach in juvenile court would make it simply a criminal court for children and therefore without grounding as a separate system of justice. At the same time, some states have relinquished juvenile court jurisdiction over status offenders. Jurisdictional modifications have narrowed "the scope of juvenile courts at the 'hard' end through the removal of serious juvenile offenders and at the 'soft' end through the removal of noncriminal status offenders" (Feld 1992: 59).

THE JUVENILE COURT PROCESS

The juvenile court process differs from state to state and jurisdiction to jurisdiction—even the name can vary—but all juvenile courts approximate the model presented in Figure 13–2

The definition of a juvenile is statutory, meaning the age of adulthood is determined by the legislature. In most states it is 16. The juvenile court has responsibility for four types of cases:

1. *Delinquency*, or behavior that, if engaged in by an adult, would constitute a crime. In the case of certain very serious criminal behavior (e.g., murder), the law may require a transfer of the case for prosecution in adult criminal court.

2. *Status offense*, or behavior that would not constitute a crime if engaged in by an adult, but that (based on *parens patriae*) provides the basis for governmental intervention in the life of a child, such as truancy, being

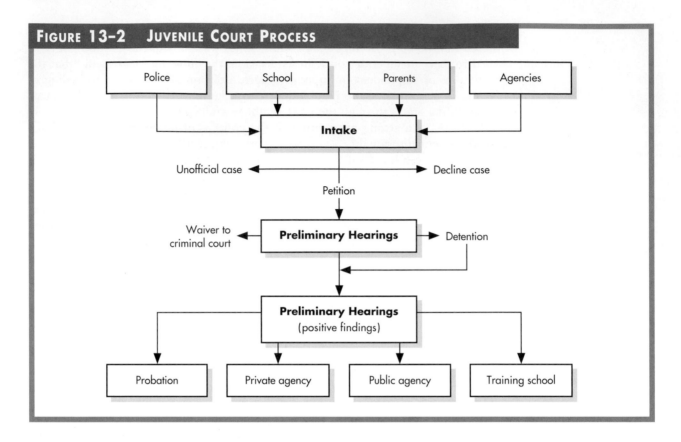

FIGURE 13-2 JUVENILE COURT PROCESS

beyond the control of parents, addiction to drugs or alcohol, running away from home, and sexual promiscuity (almost invariably referring to the behavior of girls).

3. *Neglect or abuse*, or the cases of children who are neglected or abused by parents or guardians.

4. *Dependency*, or the cases of children who do not have parents or guardians available to provide proper care.

Unlike adult courts, in most states juvenile proceedings are closed to the general public, and the records and transactions are confidential. In most states, the records of a juvenile court proceeding are sealed and access to them requires a court order. Juveniles are not routinely fingerprinted and photographed, and their names are usually not printed in newspapers. This confidentiality is now under severe attack, especially for more serious juvenile offenders. Until 1992, the FBI collected records only of juveniles tried as adults. In that year, however, new regulations gave the FBI's National Crime Information Center (NCIC) authority to receive juvenile court information. While states do not have to submit juvenile court records to the FBI, the NCIC can instantly transmit to law enforcement agencies, and within days to some employers, juvenile court records formerly kept confidential.

The juvenile court may be part of a division of superior court, but more frequently it is a lower court. Judges usually sit at a table, instead of the more traditional high bench, and they usually do not wear judicial robes.

Intake

Cases referred to the juvenile court enter by way of the intake section, which is usually staffed by probation officers (PO). The intake officer determines if the court has jurisdiction, if the case is to be referred to a courtroom for a hearing, or if services should be provided by another source. He or she will interview the child and the child's parents or guardians, and any other interested parties, for example, a victim or witness. The files of any previous court contact will be reviewed, and the intake officer will often consult (especially in serious cases) with the prosecutor's office before making a determination.

Most of the cases that come to the attention of the juvenile court involve delinquent acts (about 1.80 million annually), and referrals are typically made by police. About 20 percent of delinquency cases are dismissed at intake because they are not legally sufficient. Status offenders (about 160,000 annually—called MINS, Minors in Need of Supervision; or PINS, Persons in Need of Supervision, or CHINS, Children in Need of Supervision) are referred to juvenile court by police, school officials, and parents or guardians who complain that the subject is beyond their control (U.S. Office of Justice Programs statistics).

Most cases involving abused, neglected, or dependent children are referred to juvenile court by the department of child welfare after it has been notified by the police, neighbors, or certain responsible professionals. The law requires certain persons—such as medical doctors, nurses, teachers, and social workers—to report cases of suspected abuse or neglect to the child welfare agency for investigation. A caseworker may then draft a petition and refer the case to juvenile court, which has the authority to ensure the protection and treatment of the child through various judicial orders. In order to qualify for certain federal funds, states must appoint an attorney (*guardian ad litem*) to represent and act as an advocate on behalf of an abused or neglected child. A juvenile court judge may also appoint a special advocate to advise the court about the best interests of an abused or neglected child. Every state uses volunteer nonattorney advocates who investigate the child's situation and report back to the court with a recommendation. They may also be appointed to monitor compliance with court orders (*Court Appointed Special Advocates* 1997).

Instances of less serious delinquency and status offenses, neglect, abuse, or dependency that come to the attention of the authorities are often handled in a manner that does not involve the formal justice apparatus. School officials or police, for example, may refer such cases directly to public or private social welfare or child protective agencies without any juvenile court involvement. In less serious cases, a nonjudicial alternative is often the first choice, making it an unofficial case. If all parties are amenable, the child and parents/guardians will be referred to a social service agency, and/or the youngster may be placed on unofficial probation for 90 days.

If unofficial handling is not successful or if the case is too serious for such treatment, it will be sent to court by way of a petition—about 60 percent of delinquency cases are handled by petition. The petition sets out the allegations in the case, and filing results in a court hearing at which an assistant corporation counsel (municipal attorney) or assistant prosecutor represents "the people." Children whose families are unable to pay for legal services are represented by an assistant public defender.

*I*NTAKE IN *T*EXAS

It is 1:15 A.M. in Texarkana. James, 15 years of age, and an adult male have been arrested for aggravated robbery. Police are taking the juvenile to the detention center intake unit at the Bowie County Juvenile Probation Department. Harold Harlston, a probation officer on duty, has just been called to the intake office where he must decide if James will be detained or released. In checking the records, Harlston finds that James has a prior arrest for theft, but the initial police report suggests that this time James was influenced to participate in the robbery by the older man. Harlston awakens James' parents with a phone call. They are quite upset and head for the center. While continuing to interview James, the PO is interrupted by a call alerting him that the police are bringing in a girl involved in a street fight. She is being charged with assault—again. Harlston anticipates a long, busy night.

The girl being brought in is 14 and goes by her street name, "Decca." Street wise, she has learned to cover her vulnerability with a defiant attitude and abusive vocabulary. She fidgets nervously as she waits for her intake interview. A file check reveals that Decca lives with her mother and several siblings. The father does not live in the home and the family has a history of court referrals.

Harlston learns that James' parents have just arrived. He tells them their son will be held until his detention hearing, usually occurring within 48 hours. His parents express their disappointment; they would like to take James home tonight. The PO explains the serious-ness of the charges and the state law allowing juveniles to be tried in adult court for offenses as serious as aggravated robbery. If James is transferred to adult court, he could be sentenced to prison. The young man is lucky; his parents express their love and pledge to stand by him. Decca is not so fortunate. When her mother is contacted, she tells the probation officer: "Do whatever you want with her—I'm tired."

The night is young, and Harlston learns the police are bringing in two more youths. Detention center staff prepare for overcrowding by placing temporary cots in the dining area of the 10-bed facility.

Intake in the juvenile court is unique: it permits the court to screen cases not only on jurisdictional and legal grounds, but on social dimensions. The PO interviews the presenting agent, the young person, and the child's parents or guardians. The officer then reviews court files for previous records concerning the child. If the case involves a serious crime or child abuse and has not already been screened by the prosecutor, the PO consults with that office. At this stage, the probation officer has a dual function: legal and social service.

The *legal function* requires that the PO determine if the juvenile court has juris-diction and also requires that the child and parents be advised of the right to coun-sel and the right to remain silent during the intake conference. There is criticism that defense attorney participation at an intake conference is rare, waivers of rights tend to finessed, and the norm is for parents to encourage the child to discuss his or her participation in the alleged offense with the intake officer (Rubin 1998: 304; Feld, 1992). When defense attorneys are present in juvenile court, tension is inherent in their responsibilities to the client: "a choice between the traditional adversary role (or the procedural model that regulates professional behavior in the criminal court) and the historic treatment or rehabilitative concerns of the family [juvenile] court"

(Fabricant, 1983: 41). Barry Feld reports that even when juveniles are represented by counsel, "attorneys may not be capable of or committed to representing their juvenile clients in an effective adversarial manner. Organizational pressures to cooperate, judicial hostility toward adversarial litigants, role ambiguity created by the dual goals of rehabilitation and punishment, reluctance to help juveniles 'beat a case,' or an internalization of a court's treatment philosophy may compromise the role of counsel in juvenile court" (1992: 395). Indeed, he notes that the presence of counsel may actually be disadvantageous to the juvenile, those represented by attorneys tending to receive more severe dispositions. Nevertheless, Feld, a law professor, advocates legislation that mandates counsel and does not permit a waiver of this important constitutional right.

The *social service function* involves an assessment of the child's situation—home, school, physical, and psychological—and can provide the basis for *adjusting* the case, handling it informally without the filing of a petition. This happens in about one-half of the cases reaching the juvenile court, when the situation is not serious, when the matter can best be handled by the family, and when neither the child nor the public is in any danger. When the child is in conflict with parents or school officials, the worker may serve as a mediator.

If the young person and parents agree to informal processing, the juvenile can be placed under supervision of a probation officer, usually for a period of 90 days. Although this may save the young person and his or her parents from the trauma of court action, unofficial handling has its critics. Informal processing requires an explicit or tacit admission of guilt. The substantial advantages that accrue from this admission (the avoidance of court action) also act as an incentive to confess. This approach casts doubt on the voluntariness and truthfulness of admissions of guilt.

Preliminary Hearings

A preliminary hearing is held to inform parties of the charges in the petition and of their rights in the proceedings as per the *Gault* decision. If the case involves an abused, neglected, or dependent child, a guardian will be appointed to act as an advocate for the child, usually a social worker from a child welfare agency. If appropriate, the hearing will be used to determine whether an alleged delinquent child should remain in detention or custody. This custody hearing is usually held within 24 hours of the apprehension. If it is determined that there is an "urgent and immediate necessity" to continue detention, the judge issues a hold in custody order. Otherwise, the child is released to parents or guardians or to shelter care.

Dependent, neglected, or abused children and status offenders may be placed into foster care or a residential shelter. Within a few days, a shelter hearing is held at which a judge determines whether continued out-of-home placement is necessary. If it is, the judge will appoint a temporary guardian for the child, usually someone from a child welfare agency, but sometimes a relative or family friend. The judge may also issue an order of protection, which allows the penalties for contempt of court (summary imprisonment) if violated. An order of protection will usually contain specific restrictions on a potential abuser or assailant to refrain from further abuse and/or contact with the child or others in danger. During a custody or shelter hearing, probable cause must be established: that is, the judge must determine whether there is enough evidence to believe that the allegations stated in the petition justify an adjudicatory hearing.

Adjudicatory Hearings

The adjudicatory hearing parallels an adult trial. Its purpose is to provide the judge with a basis for determining whether the child should be made a ward of the juvenile court because he or she is delinquent, a status offender, abused, neglected, or dependent. There are three phases common to adjudicatory hearings:

1. A plea is entered in the form of an admission or denial of the allegations made in the petition.
2. If a denial is made, then evidence must be presented to prove beyond a reasonable doubt that a delinquent act was committed by the respondent—more than half of the cases result in a positive finding—or, in the case of a status offense, with a preponderance of the evidence that the child is a MINS (or CHINS or PINS), or abused, neglected, or dependent.
3. If the allegations are sustained, the judge enters a finding that the child is an adjudicated delinquent, a MINS (or CHINS or PINS), abused, neglected, or dependent and declares him or her to be a ward of the court (see Figure 13–3).

FIGURE 13-3   GUIDE TO THE MOST COMMON HEARINGS IN JUVENILE COURT

adoption: Custody hearings which grant custody to the prospective adoptive parents, and adoption hearings, which grant final adoption.

adjudication: (1) Hearing at which the minor enters a plea to one or more allegations of the petition and at which the judge pronounces the child a delinquent minor; (2) contested hearing (trial) at which witnesses testify and evidence is presented, at the conclusion of which the judge determines whether or not the child has been found to be a delinquent minor

advisory: Hearing for youth paper-referred to court at which the petition detailing the delinquent allegations is presented, a determination is made whether the minor qualifies for appointed counsel, and a trial review date is selected

detention: Hearing held within 24 hours of the filing of a petition for a detained youth at which counsel is appointed and the court considers whether the minor should be detained or released from custody

disposition: Hearing, analogous to the adult court sentencing, for which the probation officer prepares a comprehensive report of the adjudicated child's background and at which the judge determines what action(s) the court will take

restitution: Hearing at which the judge determines what restitution to a victim the child must pay to satisfy the conditions of probation

review: Review of the child's adherence to probation conditions to consider revising these conditions or terminating the minor from probation

revocation: Hearing to determine if the minor has violated probation by failure to adhere to the conditions of probation or by committing a delinquent act

transfer: Hearing to determine if the juvenile court should retain jurisdiction for the allegations set forth in the petition or whether the matter should be transferred for prosecution to the adult court

trial review: Hearing at which the child requests that the charges be set for a contested adjudication (trial), or at which he/she admits one or more allegations of the pending petition

Source: Pima County, Arizona, Juvenile Court

Despite its noncriminal nature, with the exception of a jury, the procedures of an adjudicatory hearing are the same as a criminal trial (discussed in Chapter 10).

Predisposition Report

The goal of the juvenile court is to provide services. To do so on the basis of the best available information, if the judge makes a positive finding, the probation department prepares a predisposition or social investigation report containing the social and psychological factors affecting the child and his or her family (it parallels the presentence report used in criminal court).

The probation officer who conducts the investigation will present his or her findings in a report that includes the sociocultural and psychodynamic factors that influenced the juvenile's behavior, providing a social history that is used by the judge to determine a disposition for the case. The report will typically include:

- Review of court records
- Review of school records
- Review of police records
- Interviews with the respondent
- Interviews with family members
- Interviews with teachers and school officials
- Interviews with employers, youth workers, and clergy whenever appropriate
- Interviews with complainant, police officer, or witnesses
- Results of any psychological or psychiatric examinations
- Recommendation, which should include the available treatment alternatives

Sometimes the recommendation of the PO is not included in the report, but is transmitted orally to the judge. The completed report should enable the judge to make the best disposition available based on the individual merits of the case and the service *needs* of the young person. One problem encountered at the disposition stage is the paucity of available alternatives for helping a youngster. A youngster will often be placed on probation because of a lack of feasible alternatives.

Disposition Hearing

The purpose of the dispositional hearing is to determine what outcome will best serve the interests of the child, his or her family, and the community. A number of different dispositions are available to a juvenile court judge, but some depend on the resources available in the jurisdiction. Basic to dispositions in the juvenile court is the concept of *least restrictive alternative*, meaning that a disposition should not be more restrictive than that which will adequately serve the needs of the child. In cases of delinquency, these include:

- *Commitment* to a state youth authority or the juvenile division of the department of corrections for children who are at least 13 and whose offense would be punishable with incarceration if tried under the criminal law. The period of this commitment is indeterminate, but may not last longer than the delinquent youth's twenty-first birthday. (The actual date of release is determined by youth authority or department of corrections juvenile officials.) A few states (e.g., Oregon, Wisconsin) have extended the age to 25 years (Torbet et al. 1996).

- *Probation* for adjudicated delinquent children of any age for a period not beyond the age of 21. A child placed on probation will be released to parents or placed out of the home and receive supervision and services by a probation officer. As a condition of probation, juveniles are usually required to obey their parents, attend school regularly, be home at an early hour in the evening, avoid disreputable companions and places, and refrain from alcoholic beverages and controlled substances. In some cases there will also be a requirement for restitution and/or community service.

- *Conditional discharge* and release to parents on the condition that no further delinquent acts will take place.

- *Out-of-home placement*, often in the form of a commitment to the child welfare agency, which will arrange for a foster home, group home, or residential treatment setting that can provide counseling and education to help the child to behave in a more constructive manner.

- *Referral* to a public or private agency with specialized services, such as a drug treatment program for children who are addicted to controlled substances or alcohol.

- *Detention*, usually for no more than 30 days, in a juvenile facility and then release to probation supervision, perhaps in combination with one of the other alternatives listed above. If appropriate, the judge may also order protective supervision of the parents or guardians to whose custody the child was released.

The dispositional alternatives for status offenders include probation supervision, out-of-home placement, referral, and emancipation of the child as a mature minor. The federal Juvenile Justice and Delinquency Act of 1974 states that in order to qualify for funding, juveniles not charged with acts that would be crimes for adults "shall not be placed in secure detention facilities or secure correctional facilities." For children who are abused or neglected, the court will choose the disposition that is best able to provide protection and overcome the ill effects of neglect or abuse. The dependent child is by definition without parents or guardians available to provide

Blended Sentencing

A relatively recent approach to juvenile dispositions is highlighted by legislation in Minnesota creating a new category of serious juvenile offender. They are tried as juveniles but given full due process protections, including the right to a jury trial. If convicted, they are given an adult sentence which is applied *only* in the event the juvenile does not satisfactorily complete the juvenile court disposition (Stevenson et al. 1996). In some states (e.g., California, Florida), the case is tried in criminal court, which has the authority to impose a juvenile or adult sanction (Torbet et al. 1996).

proper care, and dispositions are limited to an out-of-home placement with the assignment of a guardian or emancipation. As in cases involving other categories of children, the judge may also order protective supervision. In many jurisdictions, particularly those that utilize a family court, the court may also have jurisdiction over cases of adoption, child support, paternity disputes, and related "family" issues, in addition to cases of juveniles.

The family court operates in about 20 states and is a single forum in which all legal matters relating to children can be decided. The first family court was created by the New Jersey legislature in 1912, followed by Ohio in 1914, which created a Division of Domestic Relations in Hamilton County (Cincinnati). In addition to cases of delinquency, the Hamilton County court was given jurisdiction over matters involving divorce, alimony, dependency, neglect, and support. Today, family courts vary in the types of cases over which they have jurisdiction (Hurst 1999).

The disposition stage of the juvenile court process has typically been based on the concept of *parens patriae*. Distinctions between dispositions have been based on the needs of the child and not necessarily on the behavior that brought a case to the attention of the juvenile court—in other words, based not on justice but on rehabilitation, positivism rather than classicalism. Although the Supreme Court ruled that the juvenile court must adhere to due process, it continued to be a vehicle for providing social services to children in need. As noted earlier, in some states the line between adult criminal court and juvenile court has become blurred as the latter moves toward a justice (or classical) model (what the youngster *deserves*) and away from *parens patriae* (what the youngster *needs*). "The concept of *parens patriae* has largely disappeared from the political and public agenda. The delinquency courtrooms now work more like the criminal system that the juvenile court was supposed to counter" (Kiernan, 1997: 12).

Juvenile Court Dispositions

Basic to dispositions in the juvenile court is the concept of *least restrictive alternative*, meaning that a disposition should not be more restrictive than that which will adequately serve the needs of the child. The following dispositions generally follow this principle, progressing from the less to the more restrictive.

- Reprimand with unsupervised probation
- Probation with supervision
- Foster care with or without probation
- Community-based day treatment
- Group home
- Private school or residential treatment
- Community-based secure facility
- Training school

This disturbing trend is exacerbated by the lack of effective legal representation in most jurisdictions. Public defenders in juvenile court are unable to handle caseloads that are often in excess of 500 cases. Often, they have no time to meet with clients prior to the detention hearing. Resources are often inadequate to investigate the charges or gather critical information from families, schools, or social service agencies. Accordingly, there is a reduction in the accuracy of judicial decision-making, inappropriate disposition, and the unnecessary transfer of juveniles to the adult criminal justice system (Puritz and Shang 1998).

Juveniles are sometimes released in the custody of their parents for placement in private boarding schools, military academies, sanitoria, and so on. This disposition is most often limited to children from at least middle-income status, and Dale Mann notes: "One obvious effect is to guarantee that public institutions for juvenile offenders serve an underclass population" (1976: 12). Jerome Miller (1992: 5) refers to a "two-tiered system of residential care [that] has grown up across the country with a dramatic surge in short-term hospitalization in private psychiatric hospitals for recalcitrant, disobedient, or drug-abusing suburban adolescents. Whether or not this approach works, the effect is to spare these youngsters the correctional diagnosis and the labels which undermine hope—'psychopath,' 'sociopath,' 'unsocialized aggressive.' Such terms apply only to the children of the poor and the racial minorities who populate our youth correctional institutions."

Female offenders often receive harsher treatment in juvenile court because of the lack of alternative programs for them: "Although a sentencing judge may be willing to consider a variety of dispositional alternatives, he or she is often faced with only one program possibility—the state training school or reformatory" (Female Offender Resource Center, 1979: 13). In addition,

> once institutionalized, girls are afforded fewer services and program opportunities than boys. Boys, on the other hand, suffer from disadvantages which result from confinement in larger institutions which are filled to capacity. We can only speculate as to the reasons for these discrepancies. Some people in the juvenile justice system justify the differences in programs and services available in girls' institutions by arguing that it is cost effective to spend the limited funds which do exist on boys who commit more serious crimes and who outnumber girls in the system nearly four to one. (Female Resource Center, 1979: 13)

In many states, while a judge can order an adjudicated youth committed to the department having responsibility for institutional care, the judge cannot determine the type of institution to which he or she will be confined. In Idaho, for example, youth in Department of Juvenile Corrections custody go through an observation and assessment process to determine the best placement; a judge may not specify secure confinement or make any recommendations for placement of adjudicated youth.

JUVENILES IN CRIMINAL COURT

During the 1970s, there was increasing public concern over juvenile crime and the juvenile justice system, which was frequently attacked as too lenient. Enter Willie Bosket. His first contact with the juvenile system occurred at age 9 when his mother complained to the court that she could not control him. Willie remained in state agency placements for the next several years. At age 15, six months after being released from a maximum security youth facility, he shot and killed two New York City subway passengers. Labeled "the Baby-Faced Butcher," because he was 15 and subject only to juvenile court jurisdiction, the maximum sentence was a placement with the Division for Youth until he was 21.

In the midst of a tough campaign for reelection, New York's liberal governor called the legislature into special session to pass the "Willie Bosket law" which provides for the automatic transfer of children as young as 13 to criminal court if charged with murder; children as young as 14 would automatically be transferred if charged with various crimes of violence. Many states followed New York's lead and the jurisdiction of juvenile courts over serious crimes has been cut back in state after state (Klein 1998). "The pool of cases eligible for criminal court handling has been vastly expanded and critical decisionmaking power in this area has been shifted away from judges and toward prosecutors" (Torbet et al. 2000: 1).

It should be noted that the possibility of transfer to adult criminal court is not an invention of the late twentieth century. Since the establishment of the juvenile court, judges have retained the discretion to waive jurisdiction over serious young offenders and allow them to be prosecuted in criminal court. In Cook County, the juvenile court typically waived about 15 boys a year. These were usually juveniles age 16 or older arrested for violent crimes (Klein 1998).

Currently, all states allow juveniles to be prosecuted as adults in criminal court under certain circumstances. More than 40 states limit the juvenile court's jurisdiction over cases involving serious, violent, and chronic offenders, increasing the circumstances under which a juvenile can be tried in criminal court (as long as the process is in accord with the *Breed* decision). There are three basic mechanisms for accomplishing the transfer of a juvenile to criminal court:

1. *Legislative exclusion.* Three dozen states and the District of Columbia exclude certain categories of juveniles from juvenile court jurisdiction (Torbet 1996). Some states exclude only the most serious offenses against persons; in Illinois, for example, juveniles 15 years of age or older charged with murder, aggravated criminal sexual assault, or armed robbery with a firearm are automatically tried under criminal proceedings. Florida statutes mandate that juveniles charged with capital and life felonies be transferred to criminal court. In addition to the most serious crimes against persons, such as murder, New York excludes burglary, and some states exclude traffic, boating, fish and game and other minor violations. Eighteen states have enacted "once an adult, always an adult" provisions, requiring that once a juvenile has been prosecuted in criminal court, all subsequent cases involving the juvenile will be in criminal court (Torbet et al. 1996). To mitigate automatic transfer statutes, more than 20 states have *reverse waiver* provisions, whereby prosecutors in criminal court can move to have a juvenile case sent back to juvenile court (DeFrances and Strom 1997).

2. *Judicial waiver.* Virtually every state and the federal system permit juvenile court judges to "waive" (transfer) their jurisdiction over certain juvenile offenders. This discretion is limited by statutory criteria with regard to such factors as age, type of offense, prior record, amenability to treatment, and

dangerousness. About a dozen states have *presumptive waiver* provisions, according to which certain juvenile offenders must be waived to criminal court unless they can prove they are amenable to rehabilitation, shifting the burden from the prosecutor to the juvenile.

3. *Prosecutorial discretion.* About a dozen states empower prosecutors to charge juveniles in either juvenile or adult courts. This discretionary power may be limited by statutory criteria with regard to age and type of offense. The state of Florida, in a dramatic move toward a "justice model," enacted legislation in 1981 that provides prosecutors with almost unlimited discretion—"when the public interest requires it"—to transfer (direct file) 16- and 17-year-olds to criminal court. A study of transfer practices in Florida (Bishop, Frazier, and Henretta 1989) revealed that direct file provision cases have seldom been "the serious and chronic offenders for whom transfer is arguably justified." In fact, Donna Bishop and her colleagues found that relatively few cases are subjected to direct transfer provisions and that "many of those who are transferred seem inappropriate" (1989: 195).

Other researchers have reported a lack of any significant difference in sentence outcome for youngsters adjudicated in juvenile court and those tried in criminal court after statistically controlling for the severity of offense. They point out that "minors are likely to be looked upon as special persons by prosecutors, probation officers, and judges in the criminal courts. They are younger than the main population of defendants before the criminal courts. Even jurors may view the young person in criminal court differently." Thus, in the cases they examined, "there were more findings of 'not guilty' in the criminal court than in the juvenile court. The labeling process may be different in the two courts. While a minor may be looked upon as a hardened criminal in the juvenile court, (s)he may be viewed as a mere innocent youngster in criminal court" (Sagatun, McCollum, and Edwards 1985: 87). Only about 1.5 percent of petitioned delinquency cases are transferred to criminal court. Florida leads the nation in juvenile court transfers to criminal court, relying primarily on prosecutorial discretion while mandating direct file for certain repeat and violent offenders (Bishop et al. 1999).

*J*UVENILE *J*USTICE AND *P*OLITICS

"'Commit an adult crime, do adult time.' It rhymes and it sounds good in a political speech. Unfortunately, just because something rhymes does not necessarily make it good policy" (Klein 1998: 1). Nevertheless, the "traditional rehabilitative goals of juvenile sanctioning have been deemphasized in favor of straightforward adult-style punishment and long-term incapacitation, with few allowances for the individual circumstances and special needs of juveniles" (Torbet et al. 2000: 1).

$\mathcal{A}$DULT $\mathcal{C}$RIME, $\mathcal{A}$DULT $\mathcal{T}$IME

The Juvenile Medium Security Facility at Bordentown, New Jersey, is an unimposing two-story brick building that opened in 1983. It houses about 100 youngsters, mostly 16 to 18 years of age. Each inmate has a cell in which his or her movements can be watched, "schooling is minimal, therapeutic counseling has all but been abandoned, and solitary confinement for up to 30 days is the principal means of trying to change behavior" (Treaster, 1994: 1). The cost is more than $60,000 per inmate per year. Illinois operates a maximum security facility at Joliet for juveniles at a more modest cost: a little over $34,000; however, the facility is understaffed and overcrowded.

ISSUES OF CONTROVERSY

A great deal of controversy has been generated over juvenile justice, particularly with respect to the role of juvenile court judges, defense attorneys, status offenses, and treatment.

Judges

While a judicial post requires knowledge of law and legal procedure, the juvenile court judge also needs a working knowledge of several other disciplines, including psychology, sociology, and social work. Judges in general come to the bench without any special training for the position, and this can be a particular problem in juvenile court. Legal education provides very little in the way of training for practice in juvenile justice, and the judge typically comes to a juvenile court bench with a background in civil or criminal law and with little knowledge of the philosophy and practice of the juvenile court. Furthermore, many if not most judges have little or no experience with children of lower class groups, which are most likely to be found in juvenile court.

In many jurisdictions, the juvenile court is a bench with relatively low prestige. Those receiving juvenile court appointments often aspire to a higher court, one with more prestige (and perhaps a greater salary). This can have a destabilizing influence on the juvenile court (one that could be corrected by a unified court system; see Chapter 6). In order to deal with the other shortcomings, some states have mandated training for juvenile court judges. The National Council of Juvenile Court Judges sponsors a college located on the campus of the University of Nevada at Reno. Some jurisdictions are utilizing referees or masters, specialists trained in law and juvenile justice who hold hearings and make recommendations to juvenile court judges.

Defense Attorneys

The role of defense counsel in juvenile court can be fraught with ambivalence. In a criminal case, the role is clear: advocacy, bringing to bear all of one's professional skills to gain the best possible outcome for a client. The "best possible outcome" in juvenile court, however, is often a matter of opinion, and the role of the attorney in a *parens patriae* proceeding is not clear. Most children entering juvenile court are in need of help. Should defense counsel become an agent mediator between the court, the youngster, and his or her parents, so that the client receives this help? Or should the lawyer argue vigorously against the allegations in the petition in order to free the client of all judicial encumbrances? While the canons of legal ethics do not require an attorney to accept the client's view of a particular situation, how far can counsel go in disregarding the wishes of a youngster facing action in juvenile court?

For youngsters automatically transferred to adult criminal court, defense attorneys are often ill prepared. "They, like judges, prosecutors, and probation officers assigned to criminal courts, are generally untrained and inexperienced in recognizing the needs and characteristics of young defendants" (Young 2000: 1). Defense attorneys working with children encounter problems that their adult clients have compensated for or overcome. Many have suffered trauma or abuse, which may not have been diagnosed, and which may interfere with their ability to communicate, to aid in their own defense. "They often suffer from behavioral problems, family crises, poverty, learning disabilities, asthma or other health problems, alcohol or drug abuse, or emerging mental illness." Adequate representation requires attorneys to understand and explain a child's competency to waive his or her rights, to make an admission, or to confess. "An attorney representing a child must be able to explain how child development issues apply to the case as part of a defense." Yet most lawyers trained for practice in adult criminal court are unfamiliar with the field of child development (Young 2000: 4)

Status Offenses

Juvenile court jurisdiction over status offenders has long been controversial. In 1976, I argued against such jurisdiction, and similar positions have been taken by the National Council on Crime and Delinquency and the American Society of Criminology. Since, by definition, a status offender has not been accused of a crime, punitive intervention—arrest, detention, the court process, training schools—is inappropriate, and the stigma is potentially harmful. Edwin Schur states that an initial appearance in juvenile court can set in motion a potentially damaging series of events, "a complex process of response and counterresponse beginning with an initial act of rule-violation and developing into elaborated delinquent self-conceptions and a full-fledged delinquent career" (1973: 120). In Scandinavian countries and in Belgium, social agencies have responsibility for status offenders without the need for court intervention. As already noted, some states have relinquished juvenile court jurisdiction over status offenders.

Proponents of continued juvenile court jurisdiction over status offenders argue that these youngsters are not essentially different from those youngsters committing delinquent acts. They are all children in need of services, and without the intervention of juvenile court, they argue, these services would not be forthcoming. Indeed, in cases of delinquency a finding of status offense may result from "plea bargaining."

Treatment

In the field of juvenile justice there is general agreement that services for children are inadequate. Judges are often faced with few options at dispositional hearings, something that accounts for the frequent use of probation even when this is not in the best interests of the child and the community. Treatment facilities for children are quite expensive, especially residential facilities, where operating expenses can easily run to more than $35,000 per year per youngster. This unfortunate situation shows no signs of improving in the future.

In the next chapter we will examine alternative dispute resolution and therapeutic justice.

INTERNET CONNECTIONS

National Council of Juvenile and Family Court Judges: *ncjfcj.unr.edu*
American Bar Association Juvenile Justice Center:
   abanet.org/crimjust/juvjus/home.html
Office of Juvenile Justice and Delinquency Prevention: *ojjdp.ncjrs.org*

REVIEW QUESTIONS

1. What historical variables led to the establishment of the juvenile court?
2. What is the concept of *parens patriae* as applied to the juvenile court?
3. What rights did the *Gault* decision provide to juveniles?
4. What is the duel role of intake in the juvenile court process?
5. How does the juvenile court process differ from the criminal court process?
6. What is a blended sentence?
7. How has the move toward a "just deserts"/classical model undermined the original reason for a juvenile court?
8. Why is it more difficult to be a juvenile court judge than one in criminal court?
9. Why can the role of defense counsel in juvenile court be described as ambivalent?
10. What is a status offense, and what is the role of the juvenile court in such cases?

14

ALTERNATIVE DISPUTE RESOLUTION AND THERAPEUTIC JUSTICE

The complexity and formalism of American law and justice, as well as their attendant expense, have led to a search for alternatives, particularly for those matters that appear unsuitable for, or less relevant for adjudication by, traditional adversarial systems. This chapter will explore this issue by examining alternative dispute resolution and therapeutic justice.

ALTERNATIVE DISPUTE RESOLUTION (ADR)

ADR "is the resolution of disputes by means other than litigation" (Mills 1991: 1) and it often derives from dissatisfaction with the administration of justice in the United States: "The processes themselves are described as incomprehensible, the products of lawyers who profit from obfuscation and complexity so that the lay person is incompetent to seek redress in the courts without professional guidance" (Cooke 1982: 3). Even lawyers find the system problematic: "Attorneys more frequently are considering alternatives such as mediation in divorce cases, arbitration in commercial cases, and private courts or rent-a-judge programs in cases where there is a need for speedy resolution or confidential treatment of certain matters" (Alfini 1986: 252).

In practice, few persons make use of the entire process of justice; most cases, criminal or noncriminal (civil), are settled without resorting to trials. On the civil side, a trial can be painstakingly slow and expensive, and the outcome may create new problems for the principals. These outcomes are always zero-sum decisions:

that is, there is a winner and a loser. On the other hand, cases that do not go to trial—the minor cases, both civil and criminal—are typically given short shrift as part of the mass of cases that enter the justice system. For these reasons, Supreme Court Justice Sandra Day O'Connor urged that "the courts of this country should not be the places where the resolution of disputes begins. They should be places where the disputes end—after alternative methods of resolving disputes have been considered and tried" (quoted in Roehl and Ray 1986: 2).

While the adjudication of serious criminal behavior would be inappropriate for any forum other than the criminal court, civil disputes and interpersonal disputes that do not involve serious criminal behavior have been seen as candidates for alternative processing, that is, utilizing a forum other than the formal justice system. Alternative processing can also be beneficial in criminal cases, as David Aaronson and his colleagues (1977: 3) point out:

> A central thesis of the alternatives movement is that our criminal courts, patterned on an adversary model for the resolution of social conflicts, are an imperfect—and often inappropriate—societal response to the processing of many offenders, especially those charged with minor criminal offenses or offenses involving no substantial factual disputes. In many lesser criminal cases the process of conventional adjudication may be too time-consuming, too expensive, somewhat irrelevant to, or even inconsistent with, achieving effective dispositions. . . . Alternatives seek immediate relief for the overburdened criminal justice system: through simpler, less expensive, more effective and fairer dispositions.

The ADR movement is a response to "(1) criticism of lower courts for not providing procedural or substantive justice to minor offenders, and (2) the claim that courts cannot effectively address social demands expressed in complex disputes because such disputes require a more flexible negotiation process that involves the parties more directly in decision making" (Harrington 1985: 34). ADR can move beyond the symptoms of conflict, establishing "an outlet for the discussion of larger issues than can be covered in a court of law" (L. Kennedy 1990: 84). ADR programs have also been seen as a way of alleviating court delay by moving less serious cases out of the formal system: "An underlying premise of many of the programs has been that removing a significant volume of particular types of cases from the courts would help reduce backlogs and improve the speed with which the remaining cases are processed" (Mahoney 1988: 63, 66).

While dissatisfaction with the courts as a vehicle for adjudicating minor criminal matters is often due to the need to expedite the handling of such cases—rough justice, dissatisfaction in civil disputes is usually due to the inability of persons with grievances to afford access to the courts. Most people cannot manage the cost of litigation unless there is a provision for a contingency fee. In cases that do not promise a financial settlement or where the amount of money in dispute is relatively small, such as in tenant–landlord or consumer–merchant disputes, litigants have no easy way to gain satisfaction. The frustrations arising out of this reality can result in bitter resignation, alienation, or even violence.[1] In addition to the interpersonal level, ADR is used extensively at the corporate and government regulatory levels.

---

[1]Richard Posner states that the trial with all of its surprises and confrontations—adversary zeal—"all seem related to the function of judicial dispute resolution as a substitute for retribution" (1985: 6).

RESOLVING MINOR CRIMINAL DISPUTES

Ronald L. Olson, chair of the ABA Special Committee on Dispute Resolution, provides an example from Clay County, Alabama, of the need for alternate systems of dispute resolution.

The person who was accused of mule stealing apparently had been a tenant farmer on one of the largest farms in that part of the state, the landowner being a very rich and powerful individual who not only owned much land and had many tenants, but was responsible for getting the prosecutor elected and the judge appointed. When he discovered a mule was missing, it didn't take long for him to push the arm of the law into action. The prosecutor very quickly investigated and arrested one of the tenants. Of course the prosecutor vigorously prosecuted him. At the conclusion of the presentation by the prosecutor, the tenant decided it wasn't really worth his effort to take the stand.

The judge, knowing whose mule it was, issued some very harsh instructions and sent the jury off to deliberate. The jury came back after about five minutes or ten minutes of deliberations, and the judge asked, as is the custom, "Mr. Foreman, have you reached a verdict?"

"Yes, we have, your honor."

"What is that verdict?"

"We find the defendant not guilty, provided he returns the mule." Well that caused an uproar. The judge exploded from his seat. The prosecutor jumped up. The judge, red in the face, gave the jury a whole new set of instructions, more harsh than before, and sent them back to bring in a "proper verdict." . . . They came back in about a minute and a half:

"Have you reached a verdict, Mr. Foreman?"

"Yes, we have your honor."

"What is it?"

"We find the defendant not guilty and he can keep the mule." (Ray et al. 1983: 7)

Under an adversarial system of law, "the lawyer is not supposed to see the resolution of these disputes as a question of what might be best for the society as a whole. He is an advocate; his function is to see the possible resolution of a controversy in terms of his client's best interests (though he is not obliged to accept his client's view of what these best interests might be)" (Mayer 1969: 82). There are, however, systems of law whose goal is the resolution of disputes in terms of what might be best for the society as a whole, or at least what is best for both disputants: mediation and arbitration. The goal of both inquisitorial and adversarial systems is the determination of "truth" so that blame or guilt can be assigned. The outcome clearly favors one or the other side of the dispute—a zero sum outcome. Alternative dispute resolution, mediation and arbitration, on the other hand, has as its goal reconciliation between the disputants. In mediation, the disputants assign a neutral party who recommends a settlement after hearing from both sides. Arbitration is a similar process, but the decision of the arbitrator is binding on the parties. Mediation and arbitration are legal forms frequently found in preindustrial (e.g., tribal) societies or less developed countries (see, for example, Gluckman 1955; Elias 1956).

Alternatives to formal adjudication of civil and criminal disputes share a common goal, "trying to resolve the underlying problems that exist between parties in a manner that will result in an avoidance of future disputes" (DeLappa 1983: 9). While these systems, which focus on harmony as opposed to vindication, have predominated in preindustrial societies (e.g., Newman 1983), only since the 1970s have they been studied and adapted to industrial societies such as the United States. Support for mediation and arbitration has appealed to both conservative and radical instincts. Conservatives see a reaffirmation of the superiority of traditional values and their potential for establishing order within the community. Radicals see similarities with Comrades' Courts and People's Courts of China and Cuba, which conjure up visions of more collective, democratic and egalitarian modes of dispute resolution (Matthews 1988).

In some instances, the use of mediation has been established by law, such as the U.S. Mediation and Conciliation Service, which provides for the mediation of labor–management disputes arising out of the Labor–Management Relations Act of 1947. The Civil Rights Act of 1964 created the Community Relations Service of the Department of Justice to resolve disputes relating to discrimination based on race, color, or national origin. "The agency assists people in resolving disputes through negotiation and mediation rather than having them utilize the streets or the judicial system" (Moore 1986: 22). Although none existed as late as 1979, many jurisdictions now require mediation in domestic relations cases and custody and visitation dispute. "After an agreement is worked out, the contract is brought to the judge, who then issues a court order to make it enforceable" (Kassberg 1989: 4). North Carolina requires superior court litigants and their attorneys to participate in a settlement conference with a paid mediator before their case can be tried in court. In California, any case with claims less than $50,000 per plaintiff is eligible for referral or court order for mediation or arbitration. For claims that exceed $50,000, the parties can agree to participate in ADR voluntarily.

Expansion of ADR in the federal system occurred in 1988 when Congress authorized 10 district courts to implement mandatory arbitration programs and an additional 10 to establish voluntary arbitration programs. A further impetus came with the passage of the Civil Justice Reform Act of 1990, which requires all district courts to develop, with the help of an advisory group of local lawyers, scholars, and other citizens, a district plan to reduce cost and delay in civil litigation. ADR is one of the six civil case management principles recommended by the statute (Plapinger and Steinstra 1996). The federal Alternative Dispute Resolution Act of 1998 requires each district court to establish at least one ADR program. The statute also requires federal district courts to authorize the use of ADR in civil actions and bankruptcy adversary proceedings. Before their cases can proceed to trial, litigants must consider the use of court-based or private ADR.

MEDIATION

In our society, most disagreements are handled informally, sometimes through avoidance. When this is not possible, tensions may force action, formal or informal. Formal action ranges from filing complaints with administrative agencies to instituting a tort. Informal action includes unlawful coercion or violence. Formal action may be time-consuming and/or expensive; informal action is obviously dangerous to the persons involved and to society in general. No matter which course of action is utilized, there is a strong possibility that the outcome will leave a great deal of unresolved acrimony. Mediation provides an alternative avenue of resolving disagreements that is both informal and prosocial, and which strives to alleviate or obviate bitterness.

The mediation process utilizes an impartial third party to assist disputants in reaching a voluntary settlement of their differences. It is nonadversarial, devoid of any attempt to determine right or wrong. Lawrence Cooke notes that the most notable feature of mediation is "its dedication to the parties' self-resolution of their disagreement"; the mediator "encourages communication, assists in the identification of areas of disagreement, as well as agreement, and then works to bring both parties to a resolution, but a resolution reached and defined by the parties themselves" (1982: 5). The mediation process "attempts to discover and resolve the underlying cause of the dispute. This may result from consideration and airing of the feelings and attitudes of the individual disputants in addition to the facts" (DeLappa 1983: 8). Instead of the adversarial method wherein the product is "justice" (determining who is right and who is wrong), mediation has as its goal reconciliation, a more harmonious relationship between the parties. The role of a mediator "can range from minor involvement, in which an individual who is essentially a conciliator offers some advice to the disputants regarding a possible resolution, to highly structured interaction with disputants" (McGillis and Mullen 1977: 11).

The "assumption behind an outsider's intervention is that a third party will be able to alter the power and social dynamics of the conflict relationship by influencing the beliefs or behaviors of individual parties, by providing knowledge or information, or by using a more effective negotiation process and thereby helping the participants to settle issues" (Moore 1986: 14). It is the mediator's role to reconcile differences between the parties to the dispute.

The typical mediation process begins with an introduction by the mediator, who explains the procedures and attempts to establish some rapport with the two parties. The complaining party is then asked to present his or her story. The mediator takes copious notes, sometimes asking for restatement or clarification of material from the complainant. At the conclusion of the statement, the mediator summarizes the presentation, omitting any disparaging remarks, and determines if the responding

Mediation

"Mediation is the intervention into a dispute or negotiation by an acceptable, impartial, and neutral third party who has no authoritative decision-making power to assist disputing parties in voluntarily reaching their own mutually acceptable settlement of issues in dispute" (Moore 1986: 14).

Arbitration

Arbitration involves an agreement between (or requirement that) parties to submit their dispute to a person(s) chosen by them for determination.

party understands the complaining party's story. The second party is then asked to present his or her story, and the mediator once again takes notes, asks for restatement or clarification, and summarizes (Cooley 1986).

The mediator now attempts to clarify the underlying issues in the dispute by talking privately (ex parte) with each party (something not permitted in an adversarial process). In subsequent joint sessions, the mediator summarizes areas of agreement and disagreement, carefully avoiding disclosure of material given in confidence. The mediator then employs two fundamental principles of effective mediation: "creating doubt in the minds of the parties as to the validity of their positions on issues; and suggesting alternative approaches which may facilitate agreement" (Cooley 1986: 267). He or she continues meeting individually and collectively with the disputants to narrow the areas of disagreement and to urge a settlement with which each side can live more harmoniously.

The popularity of mediation has led to the establishment of mediation/ADR centers throughout the United States. Some have government sponsorship, others are attached to a university; some function under the aegis of the Better Business Bureau or similar entity, while others are independent not-for-profit corporations.

COMMUNITY MEDIATION MOVEMENT

Since the 1970s, there has been a movement to encourage the establishment of community mediation centers. The National Association for Community Mediation (NAFCM)[2] reports on the types of cases that are typically handled by such centers:

- *Neighborhood and community disputes* consist of cases involving neighbors or family members or others who have a fairly close relationship. They can range from noise complaints, landlord–tenant and consumer–merchant disputes, to assaults, threats, and harassment problems.

- *Family/custody disputes* are viewed broadly, beyond divorce/custody, to include grandparent visitation and disputes involving family members other than the husband and wife.

- *Juvenile and school mediation* seeks to address issues of conflict and violence in schools by establishing school conflict resolution programs. Most community mediation programs believe that the sooner people learn basic problem solving and communication skills, the sooner they can solve their own problems and improve their relationships.

- *Victim–offender* mediation programs offer an opportunity for victims and offenders to participate in a dialogue with each other (see, for example, Umbriet 2001). Most of these programs do not handle extremely serious cases such as rapes and armed robberies. This type of mediation is an effort to humanize the situation and increase sensitivity to the victim, thus creating the potential of restorative justice (discussed later).

---

[2]National Association for Community Mediation, 1527 New Hampshire Avenue, NW, Washington, DC 20036-1206; (202) 667-9700; Email: nafcm@nafcm.org.

- *Courts/legal system referrals to mediation* are the result of case referrals from court clerks, prosecutors, judges, and the police. These cases are generally referred for one of two reasons: either no law is being broken and the conflict involves quality of life issues (e.g., noise which does not rise to the level of a public disturbance but keeps a neighbor awake), or the referring agency recognizes that issuing citations or judgments might make the conflict worse.
- *Civil litigation mediation* is offered for those cases that have already entered the litigation process. Cases must be deemed appropriate for mediation and clients must be represented by an attorney. These mediations utilize an attorney-mediator who is skilled in the use of joint and individual sessions (Dispute Resolution Center of Travis County, Texas).

Beyond these types of cases, community mediation programs are involved in parent–child disputes and school conflicts including truancy and gang mediation. Programs throughout the country are involved in a wide, diverse variety of innovative applications involving such issues as construction sites, prison, AIDS, race relations, boycotts, migrant workers, agriculture, clean air/water rights, public policy, farm grazing rights, employment, religious disputes, community policing, and business/corporate disputes (NAFCM publications).

Dispute Resolution Programs, Texas.

During the 1980s, Texas enacted legislation authorizing each county to establish an alternative dispute resolution system. Its purpose, the peaceable and expeditious resolution of citizen disputes, had a special focus on disputes involving the parent–child relationship, including mediation of issues involving conservatorship, custody, and support of children, and the early settlement of pending litigation through voluntary settlement procedures.

The Dispute Resolution Center of Travis County (Austin), established in 1983 under this legislation, has a small paid staff, 150 volunteer mediators, several volunteer intake workers, and a volunteer board of directors. Mediators come from all parts of the community and from a wide variety of backgrounds—about 30 percent are attorneys. Approximately half of the center's revenue comes from the Travis County ADR Fund and the rest from training services, grants, fund raising, and client fees. Client fees, although nominal, help encourage the disputing parties' commitment to the mediation process. Fees are never a barrier to services and are reduced or waived when appropriate.

The center provides several training opportunities, such as a 5-day (40-hour) mediation training course offered to the general public several times each year. The course is designed to provide individuals with the skills and credentials they need to serve as a mediator under state law. Individuals actively participate in role plays following each lecture session, and certificates are provided to participants upon completion of the course. A 3-day (24-hour) family training course fulfills the Texas requirement for mediators doing court-ordered family mediation. The sessions include family law, family and child dynamics in a combined lecture and role play environment.

Dispute Resolution Programs, New York.

Established by the state legislature in 1981, the Community Dispute Resolution Centers Program (CDRCP) is a unit of the New York State Unified Court System. The program is a joint local/state effort to provide community forums for the resolution of disputes as an alternative to criminal, civil, and family court litigation in each of the state's 62 counties. The primary function of the CDRCP is to administer, fund, and oversee the statewide network of not-for-profit community-based dispute resolution programs. These centers serve as a community resource where individuals can discuss and resolve their interpersonal disputes. As a condition of receiving funding, community-based resolution centers are monitored for compliance with state program procedures.

CDRCP has more than 2,000 volunteer mediators and arbitrators as well as the paid staff at local dispute resolution centers. In 1999, centers conducted more than 23,000 conciliation, mediation, and arbitration conferences serving over 57,000 New Yorkers. Over 77 percent of cases that were mediated resulted in a voluntary agreement by the participants. Building on the success of the CDRCP, the New York State Unified Court System is developing a number of court-annexed ADR programs (discussed below). The state ADR Office was established in January 1998 to promote the use and development of court-annexed ADR and to expand the range of services provided through the CDRCP.

Dispute Resolution Programs, Oklahoma.

The Oklahoma Alternative Dispute Resolution System was established in 1985 and includes 12 community-based mediation centers centrally coordinated through the Administrative Office of the Courts. The centers are located throughout Oklahoma so that each of the state's 77 counties has a designated program to serve its residents. Salaried staff members do some work as mediators, but the majority of the mediation work is done by carefully selected, trained, state-certified mediators who donate their time as volunteers.

Dispute Resolution Programs, Michigan.

Since 1990, the Michigan Supreme Court State Court Administrative Office has administered the Community Dispute Resolution Program, through which 3,500 disputes are resolved annually through a network of 25 nonprofit organizations. Approximately one-half of the cases opened at the community dispute resolution centers are matters pending in Michigan's trial courts. Volunteer mediators receive 40 hours of training approved by the State Court Administrative Office.

Exemplary Program.

Funded by the City of New York, the *Crown Heights Community Mediation Center* is a neutral place where youths and adults from the racially and culturally diverse community of Crown Heights, Brooklyn, can come to air grievances and settle disputes. The mediation center, which operates out of a storefront, mediates interpersonal and group disputes.

The center trains its own mediators from the Crown Heights community. In addition to a 25-hour basic training, volunteer mediators attend supplemental workshops and are invited to a monthly Mediators Forum for continuing education. The mediation center also offers conflict resolution workshops to young people in schools. The center handles about 40 cases each month. Among the issues handled by the mediators are breach of contract, consumer–merchant disputes, coworker disputes, cross-cultural disputes, employer–employee conflicts, harassment, landlord–tenant disputes, noise complaints, and small claims. The center also provides family mediation, which deals with issues like truancy, acting out in school, power struggles within the family, special education needs, youth employment, and other parent/teen issues (Center for Court Innovation information).

Exemplary Program.   Established in 1983, the *Dispute Settlement Center of Durham* (DSCD), North Carolina, originally accepted only minor criminal cases referred by the district court. The center now provides family and divorce mediation, school and workplace mediation, and conflict resolution training. Specially trained mediators handle divorce cases, which typically require several sessions. At the initial meeting, which lasts about an hour, the parties present the general issues that need to be addressed. The parties are asked to bring relevant information for subsequent sessions designed to clarify issues in conflict and enable them to deal with property, custody, and visitation matters. The parties are asked to obtain legal counsel prior to signing the final agreement arising from mediation. All aspects of the hearings and agreements are confidential.

Housed in their own office building, DSCD volunteer mediators are trained by the American Bar Association. Typical minor criminal cases include harassment, assault, and related problems among relatives, neighbors, and acquaintances. Referrals come from a daily review of warrants issued at the court clerk's office and complaints received at the district attorney's office. The police department occasionally refers cases. In addition to interpersonal disputes, the center also handles worthless-check cases two days a month (McGillis 1998).

Exemplary Program.   The *Harrisburg, Pennsylvania, Neighborhood Dispute Settlement Program* (NDS) is an alternative dispute resolution tool for police, police administrators, and lower court judges for minor, but annoying and potentially volatile, incidents: usually harassment, excessively loud noise or music, a property boundary dispute, a barking dog.

Offending behavior between neighbors may fall just short of being criminal and/or be inappropriate for resolution through the criminal process. Police and other public authorities are usually limited by time-priority constraints in how they can respond to what are essentially private disputes early on. Calls to police and other local authorities are all too frequent responses from bickering neighbors—and perhaps the most perplexing matters to resolve. Too often, they have to wait until enough substantiation to support a charge exists before being able to intervene. Utilized properly, community mediation can provide another tool for public authorities to deal with neighbor conflict very early on and conserve limited, expensive resources.

NDS gives police officers another tool to address first-time and chronic disputes between neighbors and other individuals. The program is a front-end approach to community problems, in that it seeks to address incidents before anything is defined as a "crime" and anyone a "victim" or "offender." It serves as an alternative to issuing citations, or making an arrest, or canceling the call—when any of these is likely to leave the situation unresolved.

Upon responding, the officer explains the NDR process and the "complainant" (usually the person(s) who called the police) agrees to accept it as an alternative to prosecution for a minor offense or no prosecution for incidents where the officer otherwise may not be able to do anything. A three-part form is completed and one copy given to the "complainant" and one copy given to the "respondent" (usually the person(s) who is alleged to have offended); the third copy is provided to NDS. The form provides NDS with sufficient contact information on the parties and a brief summary of the incident(s) which occurred.

A respondent is required to contact NDS within five days and cooperate with arranging mediation; the complainant has the responsibility to follow through with trying mediation or the matter is entirely dropped. In this manner, both parties have some responsibility in attempting to reach a resolution through mediation. Once the cooperation of both sides is obtained, a mediation is scheduled at the site (church or other building) nearest the residences of both disputants. Two local mediators are arranged, scheduling letters sent to all concerned and reminder calls made the day before or day of the mediation, whichever is more appropriate. All parties within the disputants' households or neighbors who have experienced direct conflict with the other side, other than the principals themselves, are requested to attend; all involved should attend, as it may prevent flareups from surrogates acting on behalf of the original disputants. If not, too often one side will assert the other has violated an agreement, although the offender was not a party to the agreement, but was previously known to be affiliated with the principal(s).

If the parties reach an agreement that resolves the matter, a copy is provided to both sides. Both sides are informed that a copy will be retained by the NDS office and a copy sent to the referring police official/officer. This is the only document or information which is disclosed out of the mediation. A followup letter is sent to the police department to have any pending complaint canceled or initiated (if not resolved or no show), whichever is appropriate. If the mediators suspect that the disputants have not completely resolved the matter, they will often urge the parties to agree to reconvene in 30–60 days after some history with the agreement has developed. The NDS program has documented a reduction of calls for police service by more than 77 percent in chronic neighbor disputes (NDS Web site).

ARBITRATION

In the last quarter of the nineteenth century, many states enacted legislation governing arbitration, and by the end of the century it was a common practice in the United States (MacNeil 1992). The New York arbitration law of 1920 provided a basis for the model Uniform Arbitration Act of 1955, adopted by more than 30 states and the District of Columbia. The act provides legal recognition of the inclusion of arbitration provisions in a contract for resolving disputes arising out of the agreement. The 1925 United States Arbitration Act makes arbitration clauses in contracts specifically enforceable, and such provisions are standard in labor–management agreements (Leeson and Johnston 1988; for a history of arbitration law, see MacNeil 1992). The 1990 Administrative Dispute Resolution Act requires federal agencies to consider ADR for resolving disputes, and a 1991 executive order directs agencies to consider ADR as a method for improving civil justice. A number of agencies, many with the assistance of the Administrative Conference of the United States, have developed ADR programs for internal as well as external disputes (Stienstra and Willging 1995).

The arbitration process utilizes one or more (sometimes panels of three) persons whose decision is binding on both parties. Although arbitration is less formal than the judicial process, it is nevertheless "a formal proceeding following the standard adversary process, often involving rules of evidence and written briefs" (DeLappa

The Uniform Arbitration Act: Section 1

[*Validity of Arbitration Agreement.*] A written agreement to submit any existing controversy to arbitration or a provision in a written contract to submit to arbitration any controversy thereafter arising between the parties is valid, enforceable and irrevocable, save upon such grounds as exist at law or in equity for the revocation of any contract. This act also applies to arbitration agreements between employers and employees or between their respective representatives.

1983: 9). Arbitration promises a more speedy resolution of a dispute than could be expected in the judicial process. It is also conducted in private, an important advantage for parties who wish to preserve confidentiality.

The disputants must agree to arbitration and to the arbitrators. Directories from which arbitrators can be selected are produced by the American Arbitration Association, the Federal Mediation and Conciliation Service, the National Mediation Board, the Bureau of National Affairs, and Prentice Hall. These may be non- or for-profit firms, and fees range from several hundred dollars an hour to a flat charge of several thousand dollars. The American Arbitration Association is a nonprofit organization established in 1926. It has offices throughout the country and over 25,000 ADR specialists. Established in 1979, the nonprofit Legal Program of the Center for Public Resources (now known as the CPR Institute for Dispute Resolution) encourages and facilitates the use of ADR in business disputes (Sabatino n.d.; Stienstra and Willging 1995).

As in the handling of civil cases in the judicial process, there may be discovery, typically referred to as "information exchanges," prehearing conferences, submission of briefs, and oral arguments in an adversarial spirit. The Uniform Arbitration Act provides subpoena power for arbitrators. Arbitration rules typically disavow strict adherence to hearsay rules, but the arbitrator can bar certain hearsay testimony or simply disregard it (Sabatino n.d.). As opposed to the mediation process, *ex parte* conferences (i.e., with only one party present) are not permitted. At the conclusion of the arbitration process, the arbitrator(s) makes a decision orally and, usually, in writing. On occasion, these may be accompanied by lengthy opinions of the basis (*ratio decedendi*) for the decision (Cooley 1986), but other arbitrators are under no obligation to follow them. Courts have shown a reluctance to overturn voluntary arbitration awards, except when fraud or other unethical conduct is proven, and they generally enforce arbitration rulings as they would judicial judgments (Leeson and Johnston 1988).

Court-Annexed ADR

In some jurisdictions, all civil cases involving disputes under a certain fixed amount must be submitted to arbitration. In 1952, the Pennsylvania legislature granted trial courts the power to establish compulsory arbitration programs (Johnson 1977). In Philadelphia, for example, as of 1985, all cases (except real estate and equity) under $20,000 are referred to panels of three attorney–arbitrators. The panel awards are

ARBITRATION: THE CORPORATE VIEW

"Many businesses have suppliers and customers sign arbitration agreements as a condition of doing business. And now, even employment discrimination and sexual harassment claims are sometimes submitted to arbitration. One reason so many companies opt for arbitration is that it's both faster and cheaper than going to court. Instead of months of depositions, the process of discovery is normally limited to each side turning over requested documents. Arbitrating a dispute might be over in a few months rather than the several years a lawsuit often takes. And instead of trying to educate a jury, you present the case to arbitrators who are already familiar with your industry and with the issues involved—and less likely to issue a runaway verdict. . . .

On the other hand, because arbitration is less expensive than litigation, it's also easier for someone to file a claim against you. And if your arbitration policy commits your company to paying most of the expenses, you may in effect be inviting employees to initiate arbitration. Fortunately, this door swings both ways. It's also easier to defend a claim, so former employees and other people unhappy with your business are less likely to extort a settlement from you based on the cost of a lawsuit" (Bahls and Hauls 2000: 106).

binding unless the loser requests a trial, and the litigant whose trial does not improve the size of the award is penalized. "Other jurisdictions employ mandatory screening panels, in particular subject areas such as medical malpractice. These panels listen to informal presentations of both sides' cases and recommend settlements" (Marks, Johnson, and Szanton 1985: 31). At least 16 states have authorized court-ordered arbitration programs, as have a number of federal judicial districts.

In the federal system, the small percentage of cases that are tried indicates that ADR procedures serve primarily as alternatives to traditional forms of pretrial dispute resolution (see Chapter 12), and not as alternatives to trial. In administering a court-based ADR program, the court generally provides a roster of mediators who conduct the sessions, establishes criteria for inclusion on the roster, and adopts rules regarding such matters as case selection, methods for assigning mediators to cases, confidentiality guarantees, and guidelines for conducting the ADR session.

Some programs automatically refer certain types of cases to the ADR process, a so-called "mandatory" referral; the parties can request that their cases be removed from the program. In other programs, cases enter the ADR process only after referral by a judge or at the request of the parties. In all federal court ADR programs, the outcome is nonbinding (Stienstra and Willging 1995).

In 1978, the U.S. District Court for the Western District of Washington established a local rule that provides a mandatory mediation process for the designation of any civil case. In such cases, attorneys for all parties must meet at least once to engage in a good-faith attempt to negotiate a settlement without mediation within two months of notification. If the parties are unable to reach a settlement, they must agree upon a mediator, a volunteer attorney serving pro bono. Each side presents the mediator with a memorandum of contentions relative to both liability and damages, not to exceed 10 pages. The mediator may respond with a memorandum of settlement recommendations and meet with the parties individually and jointly to promote the settlement. If these efforts are unsuccessful, the plaintiff must file a certificate with the clerk of the court showing compliance with requirements of the mediation process. The court then convenes a conference of attorneys to consider appointment of an arbitrator. The arbitrator, also a volunteer attorney serving *pro bono*, is empowered to make a decision or award in the case. Unless the right to a trial has been waived beforehand, however, the losing party is entitled to a trial de novo—all of the mediation/arbitration proceedings being privileged (confidential) in all respects (Tegland 1984).

One of the earliest alternative dispute programs involving criminal cases was established in Columbus, Ohio, in 1971. The Night Prosecutor's Program (NPP) handles cases involving interpersonal disputes that are referred by the police or prosecutor's office. Respondents are informed by program staff that failure to appear for a hearing "may bring further legal action," and the notification is signed "by order of the police prosecutor." The NPP relies on mediation and utilizes law students who act as hearing officers. No record of the cases handled are kept on official documents, although records are maintained for statistical purposes and in the event the parties return. The hearings are informal; each side is allowed to tell his or her own story without interruption. The goal is to get the disputants to arrive at a mutual agreement on a solution for their problem. In order to emphasize that the program is unable to enforce settlements, no written resolutions are maintained by NPP. If requested, however, a summary is provided to the parties by the hearing officer (Palmer 1974; McGillis and Mullen 1977). The Night Proecutor's Program now operates in several Ohio jurisdictions.

A similar program for juveniles was established in 1973 in Anne Arundel County, Maryland: the Community Arbitration Project (CAP). There, police officers, in place of an arrest, were authorized to issue a juvenile citation for certain offenses. The citation is signed by the youngster and parent or guardian, and if there is a civilian complainant, he or she receives a copy of the citation. The citation directs the youngster and parents to appear for a hearing, which is conducted in a court-like setting. Instead of a judge, however, an arbitrator presides; he or she is authorized to close the case for insufficient evidence, to issue a warning, or to require the youngster to participate in a counseling and/or a community service project that may involve restitution. If appropriate, the arbitrator refers the case to the prosecutor's office for possible prosecution (Blew and Rosenblum 1977).

The National Council of Juvenile and Family Court Judges favors the use of ADR because it "is often capable of resolving much more than immediate conflict by teaching the participants how to resolve their own problems. By focusing on early intervention, and providing resources to preserve a child's ongoing relationships with family and society, ADR can facilitate a more effective and less disruptive solution than can be achieved through formal adversarial adjudication" (1989: 4).

In 1974, the American Bar Association provided grants for the establishment of programs that provide alternatives to the court system. One of these programs is sponsored by the Orange County (Florida) Bar Association with support from the city of Orlando. The Citizen Dispute Settlement Program (CDS) was established to provide "impartial hearings to residents of Orange County, Florida, who had complaints involving ordinance violations and misdemeanors" (Conner and Surette 1977: xiii). In addition to salaried staff, CDS utilizes volunteer attorneys who serve as hearing officers. Most of the complainants are referred by the police or prosecutor's office.

A citizen presenting a complaint to CDS is interviewed by the program staff. A hearing date is set, usually within the coming week. The other party involved in the dispute, the respondent, is notified by mail of the date, place, and purpose of the hearing. "Each hearing is unique. Some are as short as thirty minutes, others extend for two or three hours. The complainant, respondent, and a hearing officer are present at some hearings; at others, if it is permitted by the hearing officer, the complainant and respondent are joined by family, friends, and witnesses. If the parties reach an agreement, they sign a statement listing the terms of the agreement. Copies of the statement are given to both the complainant and respondent" (Conner and Surette 1977: 3). CDS now operates in many Florida judicial circuits.

The most extensive effort to provide alternative mechanisms for resolving interpersonal and civil disputes using mediation was initiated by the Law Enforcement Assistance Administration (LEAA). LEAA, a federal funding program for local justice agencies, was established by the Johnson Administration and discontinued during the administration of Jimmy Carter. Some of these Neighborhood Justice Centers (NJC) were sponsored (with federal funding) under private auspices, such as the American Arbitration Association, and others by public agencies such as the police or, in Columbus, Ohio, the city attorney's office. Some ended with the LEAA, while others continued their operations with local funding. Private sponsorship has the advantage of avoiding the stigma that attaches to official justice agencies such as the police department or the prosecutor's office: "Any project which is attached to criminal justice system agencies has the automatic problem of being viewed by some as presumptively biased in favor of the complainant" (McGillis and Mullen 1977: 47). However, those attached to public agencies have an automatic source of referrals and authority to compel appearances and even enforce settlements.

An evaluation of NJC projects in Atlanta, Kansas City, and Los Angeles found that they all operated quite well, handling large numbers of cases that were diverted out of the formal justice system within one or two weeks from intake, with about half the cases reaching an agreement through mediation. Most of the respondents indicated that they were satisfied with the program and the outcome of their cases and would return again should the need arise. After six months most of the settlements were still in place and being upheld. It was noted that the NJCs connected to justice agencies attracted and resolved more disputes than those programs without such referral sources. The researchers concluded that "Neighborhood Justice Centers appear to handle most minor interpersonal disputes more efficiently than the courts" (Cook, Roehl, and Sheppard 1980: 21).

Exemplary Program.   The *United States Court of Appeals for the District of Columbia Circuit Appellate Mediation Program* was created in 1987 to accommodate a dramatic increase in cases and to help parties curtail the expense involved in protracted appeals by providing a forum to stimulate the development of creative resolution options that are not likely to be achieved through a court order. Issues and positions are clarified in the mediation process so that, even if settlement is not achieved, the court benefits from more efficient briefing. Finally, mediation frequently saves time and money for the litigants themselves. It can also produce agreements that meet their needs more effectively than the relief that could be provided

A Sample CDS Case: A Neighbor's Barking Dogs

On Friday night, Mr. Merkle was awakened for the third time by the sound of barking dogs. A telephone call to his neighbor, Mr. Stearns, only resulted in a heated exchange, and the dogs continued to bark throughout the night. The next morning Merkle confronted Stearns about the dogs and about their phone conversation the night before. Tempers flared, but this time Stearns assaulted Merkle. Mr. Merkle stormed off to call the Orange County Sheriff's Department, while Mr. Stearns put the dogs inside his house. When the deputy arrived, he saw no barking dogs. Because Merkle did not want to press assault charges, the deputy referred him to the Citizen Dispute Settlement Program.

Mr. Merkle decided to visit the program office, where he explained his problem to the CDS staff. CDS then scheduled a hearing for the following Thursday night and sent Mr. Stearns a notice to come to the hearing. Both parties arrived at the local traffic court (where CDS hearings are held) that Thursday evening to attend the informal hearing. Mr. Trees, a local attorney who had volunteered to serve as their mediator, was introduced to them by the project director.

> *Trees:* Both of you gentlemen will have a chance to speak your piece so don't interrupt each other, please. I'll have some questions and we'll try to get a clear view of the issue. Now, this is not a trial and I'm not a judge; we're trying to avoid that. What transpires here is not legally binding on anyone, so it doesn't prevent anyone from pursuing the traditional legal process. But hopefully, you will take advantage of this opportunity. We'll try to reach some sort of a compromise agreement tonight.

Mr. Merkle started by stating that Mr. Stearn's dogs were keeping him awake at night. His bedroom window faced the yard where the dogs were kept. All he wanted, he said, was some peace and quiet at night.

Now it was Mr. Stearn's turn to tell his side of the story. He explained that he had gotten the dogs for protection because his house had been broken into several times. Mr. Stearns said that he had not heard the dogs barking. This only happened, he explained, when someone or something was in the yard. And, he added, no one is in the yard at night. Then the discussion started.

> *Merkle:* I hear them very clearly! You must be a heavier sleeper. Why should *I* have to listen to your dogs?
>
> *Stearns:* I have the right to protect my home!
>
> *Trees:* OK, listen. Would you agree that Mr. Merkle has a right to enjoy his home and not be disturbed by dogs at unreasonable hours? And would you, Mr. Merkle, agree that Mr. Stearns has a right to have pets?
>
> (Both nod in agreement)
>
> *Trees:* Good, then let's start working toward a solution where you can both enjoy your rights and live next to each other in relative peace.

Within half an hour both parties agreed that Stearns would keep the dogs in the enclosed porch at night in an effort to reduce the barking. Both parties also agreed to stop threatening and yelling at each other. At the conclusion of the hearing, these agreements were written down and signed by both parties as a sign of good faith; each party received a copy of the agreement. Before they left, Merkle and Stearns separately rated their satisfaction with their hearing, and both stated they were quite satisfied.

Source: Conner and Surette, 1977.

through judicial disposition. Mediation is offered at no cost to the parties. Cases are selected for mediation by attorneys in the Legal Division of the clerk's office. Screening occurs after dispositive motions have been decided. No criminal cases enter the program.

Mediators are senior members of the bar, academicians from local law schools, and attorneys with broad experience mediating complex civil cases. They are not paid for their services, but are reimbursed by the court for minor out-of-pocket expenses. The mediators protect the confidentiality of all proceedings and do not communicate with the court about what transpires during mediation sessions.

Within 15 days of the selection of a case for mediation, counsel are required to submit a position paper, not to exceed 10 pages, to the mediator. The position paper outlines the key facts and legal issues in the case and includes a statement of motions filed and their status. Position papers are not briefs, are not filed with the court, and need not be served on the other party unless the mediator so directs. The mediator sets the date for the initial mediation session and schedules followup sessions as needed.

The initial session is normally held at the court, although a mediator may decide to hold this or subsequent meetings in his/her office or at another location. All cases in mediation are subject to normal scheduling for briefing and oral argument. The court requires that counsel for parties attend all mediation sessions. All parties are also strongly urged by the court to attend each mediation session. Each party represented must have counsel or another person present with actual authority to enter into a settlement agreement during the session. In cases involving the United States government or the District of Columbia government, senior attorneys on either side of the case may attend mediation sessions so long as someone with settlement authority can be reached by telephone during conference sessions. If settlement is reached, the agreement is put into writing, and counsel files a stipulation of dismissal. If the case is not settled, it remains on the docket and proceeds as though mediation had not been initiated.

Mediation begins with a joint meeting attended by the mediator, counsel for the parties and, whenever possible, the parties themselves. The mediator explains how the mediation is to be conducted. After this introduction, each party is asked to explain to the other party or parties and to the mediator its views on the matter in dispute. The party who filed the appeal typically speaks first. The mediator is likely to refrain from asking questions or allowing the parties to ask questions of each other until all parties have had an opportunity to speak. Once the views of all parties have been stated in the joint session, the mediator usually caucuses individually with each of the parties. The purpose of these caucuses is to allow the mediator and the parties to explore more fully the needs and interests underlying their stated positions. It is also to help the parties begin thinking about settlement options that perhaps go beyond what could be accomplished in the court proceeding alone. The mediator encourages the parties to think broadly about the problem and helps them explore options for settlement. After the initial series of meetings, the mediator may convene followup sessions to help the parties continue to explore settlement possibilities. These discussions may take place in person or over the telephone, whichever the mediator thinks likely to be most beneficial under the circumstances of the particular case (Federal Judicial Center 1997).

OTHER MEANS OF DISPUTE RESOLUTION

Stephen Ware refers to two types of arbitration: (1) general and (2) intragroup. The first involves parties who share no membership in any small cohesive group and is more "lawyerized" and legalistic. For example, a variety of standard contracts contain clauses requiring the parties to submit disputes to general arbitration. The second "resolves disputes among members of a small, cohesive group"—it is only for members of the groups involved (1999: 1057). In cities with an organized Jewish community, there is often a rabbinical court (*bet din*) or mediation forums for the private resolution of personal disputes involving members of the community. Chinese communities have similar systems. A variety of other organizations provide mediation or arbitration in specific disputes; the Chamber of Commerce, Better Business Bureau, and trade associations may sponsor forums for settling certain types of consumer disputes. "Countless trade associations," Ware notes, "arbitrate disputes among their members. In many trade association arbitrations the parties have no lawyers representing them and the arbitrator is not a lawyer. The arbitrator may have a similar background to the parties, or be engaged in the same business; he is likely, then, to be familiar with the presuppositions and understandings of the trade" (1999: 1057–1058).

California enacted legislation in 1872 providing for a "private" judicial system, although it has only been since the 1970s that the law has been extensively utilized. Los Angeles uses dozens of retired superior court judges as arbitrators for civil litigants who opt for a more speedy resolution of their claims. In California, however, these arbitrators have judicial authority and their decisions are enforceable by the state (Chambers 1986). The arbitrators are paid by the parties involved, and they set their own fees, which can be about $200 an hour or $800 a day. That fee can hasten the settlement. The most famous of these "private justice" judges is Joseph Wapner, star of television's "The People's Court," which is limited to disputes in which damages do not exceed $1,500. In 1993, Connecticut authorized a similar system, except the mediators/arbitrators must be sitting judges and they work for the nonprofit Sta-Fed ADR, Inc. (Johnson 1993).

Attorneys are frequently turning to mediators to resolve family disputes over questions such as: Should an elderly relative be placed in a nursing home? What happens when three siblings inherit a piece of property? Should a child attend a private or public school? (Dullea 1986). In 1984, the ABA adopted "Standards of Practice for Lawyer Mediators in Family Disputes." The preamble states:

> For the purposes of these standards, family mediation is defined as a process in which a lawyer helps family members resolve their disputes in an informative and consensual manner. This process requires that the mediator be qualified by training, experience, and temperament; that the mediator be impartial; that the participants reach decisions voluntarily; that their decisions be based on sufficient factual data; and that each participant understand the information upon which decisions are reached. While family mediation may be viewed as an alternative means of conflict resolution, it is not a substitute for the benefit of independent legal advice.

One type of business ADR is known as the corporate mini-trial, a mix of the adversarial approach, mediation, and negotiation:

The mini-trial is a nonbinding settlement procedure structured to convert a legal dispute into a business problem. Lawyers make abbreviated presentations exposing the strengths and weaknesses of the case to an audience of business executives from both sides, rather than a judge or jury. These summaries are often heard by a neutral advisor, who may be a retired judge or an authority on the technical issues in the case. The neutral advisor presides at the hearing and may offer suggestions and opinions. After the attorneys for each party present their case, the business executives meet in private to negotiate an agreement. This meeting frequently resembles a practical business deal rather than a legal settlement. (Henry 1985: 114)

This approach can offer considerable savings on legal fees, while resolving issues that can easily drag out into several years of litigation. A similar approach, the *summary jury trial*, requires the parties make to make a condensed presentation of their evidence to a regular jury. The jury then delivers a verdict, but it is nonbinding. If the parties are unhappy, they can still have a regular trial. Summary jury trials encourage settlement because the parties can see how the jury evaluates the case.

CRITICISM OF ALTERNATIVE DISPUTE RESOLUTION

A less positive view of ADR centers is expressed by Stephen Schulhofer, who declares that, while the idea of neighborhood justice is appealing, "what we have learned about the operation of these centers does not afford much basis for an optimistic assessment of their potential" (1986: 86). According to Schulhofer, there are no significant differences in satisfaction levels expressed by those using an NJC and those resorting to the courts. "There is no evidence," he states, to indicate that "neighborhood mediation, when it occurs, has been more successful than adjudication in reaching the underlying causes of conflict. In practice, mediators have tended to deal only with the superficial aspects of disputes" (1986: 88). He points to the professionalization of mediators, who tend to be lawyers (the ABA is quite interested in mediation programs—they have a section on dispute resolution) and notes that dispute resolution is fast becoming another specialty for attorneys. Indeed, there are many lawyers on the Internet offering ADR services.

There is a problem of participation, of creating dispute processes in which both parties will participate. Whereas it is often the complainant who withdraws from participation in the lower criminal court, in the ADR programs, it is frequently the respondent who withdraws. Christine Harrington observes that "the coercion and authority of police, prosecutors, and judges are essential elements to the institutional existence of neighborhood justice centers" (1985: 170). One study found that when there was a criminal charge pending, compliance reached 86 percent; and without the threat of prosecution, 38 percent (Marshall 1988). The need to resort to these coercive elements "suggests that mediation reproduces the participation problems reformers sought to resolve with alternatives" (Harrington 1985: 170).

Some critics argue that informal justice systems merely widen the net without reducing the burden on formal systems; persons who would not have been subjected to litigation or prosecution find themselves involved in a similar, albeit informal, system. Indeed, a majority of cases in the neighborhood justice systems would not have received a hearing in the formal courts. In many instances, however, the alternative to informal justice may be a simmering dispute leading to interpersonal intimidation and/or violence (Matthews 1988). Tony Marshall responds that the "provision of dispute settlement services, just like social work or psychiatric services, can therefore be justified in terms of public good as well as compassion for human suffering. Moreover, it may not just be suffering that is saved, but also the resources of citizens released from debilitating and fruitless conflict" (1988: 42).

Other criticisms center on the question of disparity: forcing the poor to resolve disputes in lesser forums while the wealthy continue to have access to, and make use of, the formal systems of justice. "By diverting poor people's cases to less formal forums do we lessen the chance that the courts will be made fairer to poor people— as by requiring that adequate representation be provided to those who cannot afford to hire their own lawyers?" (Marks, Johnson, Szanton 1985: 52). On the other hand, there is also concern "that corporations and other major litigants will create 'luxury class justice' outside the courts." Freed from having to deal with cumbersome delays and the other shortcomings of formal justice, elite litigants will desert the courts, and "just as public schools deteriorate when affluent parents send their children to private schools, so the argument goes, court performance will deteriorate further when affluent litigants no longer have to face delays and costs which burden the rest of the litigating populace" (1985: 52).

Businesses have been inserting clauses into retail contracts mandating arbitration, "often in ways that are nearly invisible to all but the most conscientious consumers" (Meier 1997b: C7). They are frequently found in many routine transactions such as those involving computer purchases, doctor–patient relationships, and bank credit cards. These clauses require the consumer to give up the right to sue in favor of arbitration. Such clauses have long been routine in certain businesses, such as brokerage firms and health plans.

Corporations have added arbitration clauses to their employment contracts in order to ease the burden of discrimination lawsuits—more than 200,000 discrimination cases are filed each year. Federal employment law, such as the Americans with Disabilities Act of 1990 and the Civil Rights Act of 1991, have fueled a dramatic increase in employment-related litigation, particularly discrimination and wrongful discharge claims. "If you don't waive your right to sue, you don't get the job" (Kaufman and Underwood 1997: 48). Many of these mandatory arbitration clauses are heavily weighted in favor of the employer: for example, the employer can opt for court; the employer has the sole right to pick the arbitrator(s); employees are not permitted outside counsel; caps on punitive damages. Arbitrators are neither licensed nor regulated, and companies can choose anyone to serve in the position (Furchgott 1997). The Supreme Court has been generally supportive of these arbitration clauses in employment contracts (*Circuit City Stores* v. *Adams* 2001; Walsh 2001).

Another issue is that of uncertainty. As noted in Chapter 1, a rational system of law promotes commerce and industry, which require a high level of predictability— capitalists require a reasonable expectation of a particular outcome for the myriad transactions with which they are involved. Alternative dispute resolution mechanisms, often informal justice, render decisions on a case-by-case basis and not necessarily according to legal norms—"but mediate mutually acceptable agreements or apply common notions of justice to decide disputes" (Marks et al. 1985: 55). Contracts between buyers and Wall Street brokers, for example, require arbitration. Arbitration panels decide cases based on the information presented, without complex rules, and precedent is absent since the arbitrators do not have to explain their decisions (Fatsis 1990). Alternative dispute mechanisms represent a move toward *kadi* or ad hoc justice (discussed in Chapter 1) and may render outcomes less predictable. However, several law reporters are being published containing written opinions and arbitration awards made by labor arbitrators, and *stare decisis* is beginning to appear as arbitrators cite cases that are part of *ratio decedendi* for their decisions (Leeson and Johnston 1988).

An extension of the "alternatives" approach will be examined under the rubric *therapeutic justice*.

THERAPEUTIC JUSTICE (TJ)[3]

In recent decades, in addition to their traditional dispute-resolving function, there has been a trend toward using law and the courts as problem-solving entities. This is sometimes accomplished in traditional court settings, although specialized courts are proliferating. "The purpose of the new specialized courts is to qualitatively improve outcomes for litigants and society in cases involving individuals with underlying social and emotional problems" (Rottman 2000: 22). Domestic violence courts, for example, are an effort to provide a more comprehensive approach to this critical problem, beyond the traditional "order-of-protection" response (Tsai 2000). The TJ approach is seen as more appropriate and effective than the traditional adversarial process for these types of cases. Previously, specialized courts were intended to enhance efficiency by using differentiated case management techniques. In past decades, the juvenile court would clearly have been included under the rubric "therapeutic justice." However, as noted in Chapter 13, the juvenile court has moved in the direction of the criminal court, considerably lessening its therapeutic goals.

There is concern over the abandonment of adversarial justice—reminiscent of the pre-*Gault* juvenile court (discussed in Chapter 13)—often inherent in therapeutic justice where, in place of the adversarial configuration characteristic of a traditional criminal proceeding, the courts adopt an ethic of cooperation (Boldt 1998; Winick 1997). Indeed, so-called "youth courts," which are designed to move youngsters out of the juvenile court, are becoming quite popular. Staffed by youngsters who have themselves been through the juvenile court process, youth courts handle mostly cases involving minor transgressions—truancy, vandalism, shoplifting, fighting. Teenagers perform all of the tasks usually assigned to legal professionals—judge, prosecutor, and defense counsel—and a jury of peers determines "guilt" or innocence. Upon conviction, "sentences" usually consist of some combination of community service and restitution. A failure to comply with the process can result in the case being referred to the juvenile court for adjudication (Sengupta 2000).

While therapeutic justice would include the use of mediation and arbitration in court-annexed programs, it extends to a wide range of social problems that arise in a community, paralleling the move toward community policing. The impetus for this trend is societal change "that placed courts in the frontline of responses to substance

---

[3]The scholarly study of this applied area of law and justice is referred to as *therapeutic jurisprudence* (Winick 1997), which is discussed in Chapter 4.

abuse, family breakdown, and mental illness. Courts cannot restrict the flow of such problems into the courtroom, and often such problems stand in the way of effective adjudication of cases" (Rottman and Casey 1999: 13). Therapeutic justice "directs the judge's attention beyond the specific dispute before the court and toward the needs and circumstances of the individuals involved in the dispute." According to TJ, attending to the individuals as well as the issues involved in the case will lead to more effective dispositions (Rottman and Casey 1999: 14). The TJ court "is in a better position to mobilize and coordinate treatment and social service providers in a locality, providing the court with access to skilled resources" (Rottman 2000: 23). Among the approaches that fall under this trend are drug courts, restorative justice, and community courts.

DRUG COURTS

When the "war on drugs" policy of the 1980s (see Abadinsky 2001) exacerbated already overcrowded prisons and court dockets, new methods were devised to divert drug abusers from the criminal justice process and into treatment (Gebelein 2000). Judges increasingly made participation in drug treatment a condition of probation, as did parole boards. In 1989, treatment and punishment were melded in the form of a specialized "drug court" in Miami, Florida (Boldt 1998). This high-volume court expands on traditional drug-defendant diversion programs by offering a year or more of court-run treatment; defendants who complete this option have their criminal cases dismissed. Between 1991 and 1993, Miami influenced officials in more than 20 other jurisdictions to establish drug courts (*The Drug Court Movement* 1995). The 1994 Crime Act provides federal funding to establish or expand drug courts, and by the end of 1999 they were available in almost every state. In 1994, the National Association of Drug Court Professionals (NADCP) was formed by about a half-dozen judges; five years later, its annual training meeting drew 3,000 participants (Gebelein 2000).

Drug courts typically target nonviolent drug abusing offenders and in a "slow track process" retain jurisdiction over the case until the defendant satisfactorily completes the treatment or, if he or she fails, is returned to court for further processing—prosecution and possible incarceration. "Drug courts funded by the 1994 Crime Act may process only nonviolent offenders, but many drug courts that are wholly State funded or locally funded accept some violent offenders" (Gebelein 2000: 4).

The Madison County, Illinois, drug court was fueled by a 437 percent increase in drug arrests between 1988 and 1992. The program targets persons arrested on felony drug charges who are diagnosed with alcohol or drug dependence that could be treated on an outpatient basis. Those who successfully complete the program have their charges dismissed. The program provides job assistance, which includes vocational training and high school equivalency education. Initially, clients are scheduled for three to five intensive three- to four-hour counseling sessions per week. As they progress, the number and length of sessions is reduced. Depending on a client's progress, the program can be completed in about one year or less. Random drug tests are given, and failure to comply with program requirements results in prosecution for the original felony offense (Illinois Criminal Justice Authority 1999).

In Maricopa (Phoenix) County, Arizona, the goal of drug court is considerably different—to increase the number of drug cases entering the system. Using a catchy "do drugs, do time" slogan, law enforcement agencies targeted casual users to enforce a "zero tolerance" policy. Users are "held accountable" for their illegal drug use by a policy of arrest and threatened prosecution; those who accept the treatment option—which includes paying fees—avoid further court action (Hepburn, Johnston, and Rogers 1994).

RESTORATIVE JUSTICE

"*Restorative Justice is a problem-solving approach to crime which involves the parties themselves, and the community generally, in an active relationship with statutory agencies*" (Marshall 1998: 1). In the United States, criminal law views the state as victim, with the victim in fact placed in a passive and secondary (at best) role (Carlson 1993). Instead, a relatively recent perspective known as restorative justice (RJ) "views crime as a violation of one person by another, rather than against the state" (Maloney and Umbreit 1995: 43). Emerging during the 1970s as part of the victim's movement, restorative justice is the guiding philosophical framework for a new paradigm that seeks to promote maximum involvement of the victim, the offender, and the community (Bazemore and Maloney 1994). Instead of simply punishing those who commit crimes—*retributive justice*—the focus is on allowing the offender an opportunity to make amends to his or her victim (Wright 1991; Umbreit 2001).

While there is some variation, proponents of restorative justice agree on its core principles (Kurki 1999: 2):

- Crime consists of more than violation of the criminal law and defiance of government authority.
- Crime involves disruptions in a three-dimensional relationship of victim, community, and offender.
- Because crime harms the victim and the community, the primary goals should be to repair the harm and heal the victim and the community.
- The victim, the community, and the offender should all participate in determining the response to crime; government should surrender its monopoly over that process.
- Case disposition should be based primarily on the victim's and the community's needs—not solely on the offender's needs or culpability, the dangers he presents, or his criminal history.

RESTORATIVE JUSTICE: A DEFINITION

"*Restorative justice is a process whereby parties with a stake in a specific offense resolve collectively how to deal with the aftermath of the offence and its implications for the future*" (Marshall 1998: 1).

RESTORATIVE JUSTICE

"Crime is a violation of people and relationships. It creates obligations to make things right. Restorative justice involves the victim, the offender, and the community in a search for solutions which promote repair, reconciliation, and reassurance" (Zehr 1990: 181). "Restorative justice views crime as a violation of one person by another, rather than a violation against the state" (Umbreit and Carey 1995: 47).

As Jim Sinclair points out, the depersonalized mechanisms of criminal justice "fail to deliver the message to the offender that by his/her actions s/he has harmed another human being; and that part of the offender's habilation or rehabilitation should be geared toward making the victim whole again. The evolution of the criminal justice system in this country has resulted in a de-emphasis on the responsibility of the offender toward the victim(s) of his/her wrongful acts" (1994: 16). Thus punishment "may have several counterdeterrent effects on offenders, including stigmatization, humiliation, and isolation, that may minimize prospects for regaining self-respect and the respect of the community"; while a rehabilitation response provides little in the way of a message that the offender has harmed someone and should take action to repair damages to the victim (Bazemore and Umbreit 1995: 300).

Restorative justice offers a new way to look at the response to crime and criminal behavior beyond the traditional debate over punishment and rehabilitation. Instead of advocating more/better rehabilitation or greater punishment, the new model seeks systemwide change, a new philosophical framework in which the victim is at the center. RJ argues for not only bringing the victim back into the criminal justice system, but that all parties—victim, offender, community—should be included in the response to crime (Umbreit 2001).

Restorative justice is appealing to those on the left and the right of the political spectrum: The approach "is consistent with fiscal conservatism, the call for a reduced role for government and an emphasis on personal accountability. On the other hand restorative justice's reduced emphasis on physical punishment and call for accountability are consistent with traditional liberal values" (Kay 1998: 12).

RJ is accomplished by means of victim–offender mediation through which the parties are given a human face: "Facing the person they violated is not easy for most offenders. While it is often an uncomfortable position for offenders, they are given the equally unusual opportunity to display a more human dimension to their character. For many, the opportunity to express remorse in a very direct and personal fashion is important. The mediation process allows victims and offenders to deal with each other as people, oftentimes from the same neighborhood, rather than as stereotypes and objects" (Umbreit 1994: 9).

This is the basis of VORP—the *Victim/Offender Reconciliation Program*—a sentencing alternative popular in a number of communities, including Orange County, California where it is sponsored by the St. Vincent De Paul Center and handles both juvenile and adult criminal cases often referred by the probation department.

Mediators are trained volunteers who receive cases from a case manager, make the initial call to the offender, and meet with that person and his or her parents. If they are willing to participate, the mediator calls the victim and arranges a joint meeting during which each tells their story, expresses feelings, and discusses what might be done to make things right. After an agreement is reached, a contract is drafted and the case returned to the VORP office, where a staff person follows up on the execution of the agreed-upon conditions.

In meetings that last about an hour, victims typically ask "Why me?" "Were you watching us?" "Do you have any idea what this has done to me/us/our family?" This process is believed to hold offenders more directly accountable for their actions. Perpetrators must listen to the human side of the injuries they have caused and must begin to take some responsibility for repairing the damage they caused. In some cases, that might also include offering genuine expressions of remorse (Gehm 1998).

While this approach appears appropriate for less serious crimes and offenders (although Levrant et al. 1999 disagree), particularly when there is a prior relationship between victim and offender, it is with more serious crimes and more hardened criminals that RJ appears more complex. Restorative justice is about righting wrongs in a more healing and meaningful way. Therefore, according to Marty Price (1997), when a serious crime has been committed, the concept of mediator neutrality is not appropriate—the parties come to victim–offender mediation as a wronged person and a wrongdoer. While the mediator is neutral as to the individuals, respecting both as valuable human beings and favoring neither, the mediator is not neutral as to the wrong. For these reasons, as well as to guard against the possibility of revictimizing victims at the mediation session, programs seldom mediate with an offender unless the offender has admitted the wrongdoing. The process of facilitating meaningful accountability in offenders often requires the mediator to help offenders acknowledge their wrong and their responsibility for it. When either victim or offender is unwilling to participate, or when the offense is too heinous or the suffering too severe, the offender meets with other victims, often through victim advocate organizations, rather than their own victim(s) as a step toward assuming responsibility (Zehr 1990).

*R*ESTORATIVE *J*USTICE IN *V*ERMONT

In Vermont, restorative justice is statewide, mandated by statute. Persons convicted of non-violent offenses and placed on probation are required to appear before the local reparative board. Each town has its own volunteer board and larger municipalities have several. Victims and other affected parties are invited to appear and a reparative plan to be completed in 90 days is negotiated. The offender may listen to the victim's account or to the reactions of victims of similar offenses. He or she may be required to write an essay describing the harm that was done. The plan may include victim restitution, a letter of apology, and community service. Counseling and educational opportunities are offered to the offender with the goal of reducing the likelihood of reoffending (Karp 2001).

Victim rights advocacy groups have been critical of restorative justice, particularly those programs operated by community corrections—probation and parole—agencies "whose habits are offender focused." The RJ process "can cast victims as little more than props in a psychodrama focused on the offender, to restore him (and thereby render him less likely to offend again)." A victim "while engaged in restorative conferencing and feeling genuinely free to speak directly to the offender may press a blaming rather than restorative agenda." Attempts to script victim participation are destructive of the RJ process. And "restorative processes depend, case by case, on victims' active participation, in a role more emotionally demanding than that of complaining witness in a conventional prosecution—which is a role avoided by many, perhaps most victims" (M. Smith 2001: 5)

COMMUNITY COURTS/NEIGHBORHOOD JUSTICE

The courts have become distant from the public, both physically and psychologically. The lack of connection between public and courts results in the latter being seen by the former as irrelevant to solving the problems of pressing concern to most citizens (Rottman and Casey 1999). Without bypassing the traditional adjudicatory function of the courts, neighborhood justice is a collaborative problem-solving approach to quality-of-life offenses. It is a response to the fact that centralized courts focus resources on serious crimes and devote insufficient attention to quality-of-life offenses. As a result, low-level offenses like prostitution, street-level drug possession, and vandalism erode the quality of life and create an atmosphere in which serious crime flourishes (Sviridoff, Rottman, and Curtis 1997).

This approach has its parallel in policing in what has become known as the "broken windows" approach—leave one broken window unattended, and they will soon all be broken (see Wilson and Kelling 1982). There are more than two dozen community courts in a number of states, including Colorado, Connecticut, Maryland, Minnesota, and New York. Instead of the traditional adversarial system, neighborhood justice asks judges to play new roles, lessening their judicial detachment and actively engaging defendants, victims, and community members. But adversarial justice is not discarded—the district attorney prosecutes each case and each defendant is represented by counsel (Feinblatt, Berman, and Sviridoff 1998).

RESTORATIVE JUSTICE FOR JUVENILES

"A restorative sanctioning model could provide clear alternatives to punishment-centered sanctioning approaches now dominant in juvenile justice and could ultimately redefine the sanctioning function. Specifically, by shifting the focus of offender accountability or 'debt' from the state to the victim, restorative justice sanctions could meet the need of communities to provide meaningful consequences for crime, confront offenders, denounce delinquent behavior, and relay the message that such behavior is unacceptable—without primary reliance on punishment and incarceration" (Bazemore and Umbreit 1995: 302).

THE MIDTOWN COMMUNITY COURT MODEL

- Locating the court in the community, close to where crimes take place.
- Repaying a community damaged by low-level crime by requiring offenders to compensate neighborhoods through community service.
- Using the leverage of the court to sentence offenders to complete social services that will help them address problems such as drug addiction or involvement in prostitution.
- Bringing the court and the community closer by making the courthouse accessible, establishing a community advisory board, and publishing a quarterly newsletter.
- Using the court as a gateway to treatment and making social services available to offenders right at the courthouse (Lee 2000).

The first community court opened in New York in 1993. The Midtown Community Court seeks to honor the idea of community by making justice restorative and accountable to neighborhood residents. Offenders are sentenced to pay back the community through work projects such as caring for streets, trees, removing graffiti, cleaning subway stations, and sorting cans and bottles for recycling. The court also links offenders to drug treatment, health care, education, job training, and other social services in order to get to the root causes of their criminal behavior. The center staff includes a resource coordinator who serves as a link between the court, attorneys, and social service providers, keeping track of sentencing options and making sentencing recommendations to judges based on the results of defendant assessments carried out by the city's pretrial services agency (Feinblatt, Berman, and Sviridoff 1998).

After an arrest in the area covered by the Midtown Community Court (MCC), the individual is booked and either issued a desk appearance ticket to appear in court at a future date, or detained by the police and escorted to court. All arrestees are interviewed by the city's pretrial services agency to help create a detailed portrait. This information is bundled with the defendant's rap sheet and made available to the judge, defense attorney, and prosecutor through the court's computer system. Color-coded information highlights problems such as homelessness and drug use. Each defendant is interviewed by a public defender. The resource coordinator reviews the information and makes a recommendation to the judge. If the defendant makes a request for a particular service, drug treatment, for example, the coordinator will have the defendant interviewed by a court-based counselor.

When the defendant appears in an MCC courtroom, the judge already has considerable information about him or her. In 80 percent of the cases, the defendant pleads guilty and the judge is able to construct a sentence that takes into account personal circumstances, past criminal history, and compliance with prior sentences at Midtown Community Court. Approximately 70 percent of defendants receive community service or social service sentences; the rest are disposed of with jail or fines. Those sentenced to community and/or social services are immediately escorted by a court officer to the alternative sanctions floor devoted to the scheduling and monitoring of alternative sanctions and the provision of court-based social services.

They are interviewed by nurses from the city's health department, who provide referrals for health services and on-site testing for HIV, TB, and STDs. Community service clients are divided into those requiring low, medium, and high supervision, and includes cleaning streets, removing graffiti, and assignments under direction of the Salvation Army and similar service agencies. Social services are provided by a number of public and private agencies, all of whom have personnel on site (Center for Court Innovation n.d.).

The MCC approach has been replicated in a number of jurisdictions. The Harford Community Court (HCC) was established in 1998. HCC processes defendants accused of a wide range of nonviolent public nuisance and misdemeanor offenses that are often ignored or given low priority in other jurisdictions. About 80 percent of defendants are in court responding to a summons to appear and most do so without attorneys, although a public defender is available to provide counsel. Those who fail to appear become ineligible for the community court process. HCC places priority on providing social services to defendants.

Upon their arrival in court, defendants are interviewed by a bail commissioner who reviews criminal records and checks for outstanding warrants. The commissioner then verifies personal data and prepares a psychosocial report. If the defendant is under the influence of drugs or alcohol, or otherwise in an unstable condition, he or she can be sent immediately to an appropriate facility for evaluation. Defendants then negotiate in open court with a prosecutor who explains the specifics of their cases and the requirements for participation in the court, typically a conditional plea of guilty and sentence of community sentence in exchange for subsequent dismissal of the case. Some defendants are slated for mediation while others are referred to social services to which they are escorted by a sheriff's deputy. Satisfactory completion of a court-referred program results in a dismissal of the charges. Defendants claiming a justification or explanation for their behavior are given a continuance and an opportunity to provide documentation to support their claim (Goldkamp, Weiland, and Irons-Guynn 2001).

CONCLUSION

In summary, from more primitive and informal systems of justice we moved to the complexity and strictures of common law, which later gave rise to the need for a system of equity. In the United States, case law and the attendant system of adversarial justice have become so complex, time-consuming, and expensive that they have led to a renewed interest in more informal systems of resolving disputes: mediation and arbitration. We have come full circle in our examination of law and justice.

INTERNET CONNECTIONS

Community courts: *communitycourts.org*

International Network on Therapeutic Justice:
law.arizona.edu/upr-intj/intj-welcome.html

Center for Restorative Justice: *ssw.che.umn.edu/rjp/default.html*

Restorative Justice online: *restorativejustice.org*

Center for Problem Solving Courts: *problemsolvingcourts.com*

Twentieth Judicial Circuit of Florida Citizen Dispute Settlement: *courtadmin.cjis20.org/citizen.htm*

Harrisburg, PA, Neighborhood Dispute Settlement Program: *geocities.com/Eureka/Plaza/6502/ndsprog.html*

Center for Court Innovation: *courtinnovation.org*

REVIEW QUESTIONS

1. How do the goals of mediation differ from those of inquisitorial and adversarial systems?

2. How does mediation differ from arbitration?

3. What are the advantages of mediation over formal judicial mechanisms for resolving disputes?

4. What is the *corporate mini-trial*? The *summary jury trial*?

5. What are the criticisms of using alternative dispute mechanisms?

6. What are the goals of therapeutic justice?

7. What is the purpose of "drug court"?

8. What is "restorative justice"?

9. What is the purpose of establishing "community courts"?

10. What is therapeutic justice?

11. What are the types of programs established as "therapeutic justice"?

GLOSSARY

accord: When an agreement has been carried out, thus barring the right of further action.

acquittal: When a defendant is found not guilty.

action: Proceeding or dispute before the court.

action *in personam*: Legal action founded on personal liability.

action *in rem*: A legal action for the recovery of property possessed by another.

actus reus: Behavior that constitutes a specific crime.

adjournment: A delay in trial ordered by the judge, usually at the request of one of the lawyers.

adjudication: A judgment or decision.

adjudicatory hearing: Trial in juvenile court.

administrative law: Body of law created by administrative and regulatory bodies.

adversarial method: System of fact-finding used in American trials in which each side is represented by an attorney who acts as an advocate.

affidavit: A sworn, written statement of facts.

affirm: Uphold the decision of a lower court.

affirmative defense: Without denying the charge, defendant raises extenuating or mitigating circumstances such as insanity, self-defense, or entrapment.

alternative dispute resolution (ADR): Alternative to courtroom litigation such as mediation and arbitration.

amicus curiae: Latin, "friend of the court;" refers to allowing parties who are not litigants to participate in arguments before the court.

answer: Formal response by defendant to plaintiff's allegations.

appeal: Legal challenge to a decision by a lower court.

appellate jurisdiction: A court having authority to review and modify the decision of a lower court.

appellate review: The consideration of a case by a court of appeals.

arbitration: The submission of a dispute to a nonjudicial third party for binding judgment.

arraignment: Early stage in the judicial process when the defendant is informed of the charges and enters a plea of guilty, *nolo contendere*, or not guilty.

arrest: The physical taking into custody of a suspected law violator or juvenile.

arrest warrant: A document issued by a judicial or administrative officer authorizing the arrest of a specific person.

assumption of risk: Doctrine according to which a person cannot collect damages for injuries to which they voluntarily expose themselves.

atavism: Reversion or "throwback" to a primitive or prehistoric state.

at issue: The point in the civil pleadings when one side affirms what the other side denies; thus, the case is ready for trial.

attachment: An order by which a plaintiff can secure a lien on the property of the defendant prior to a judgment.

attorney of record: The attorney whose name appears on the permanent case files.

bail: Money or other security placed in custody of the court in order to ensure the return of a defendant to stand trial.

bankruptcy: Legal process by which persons or businesses that cannot pay their debts can seek the assistance of bankruptcy court.

bench trial: A trial conducted without benefit of a jury.

beyond reasonable doubt: Standard of proof required to find a person guilty of a crime or a delinquent.

bind over: To hold for trial or send to grand jury.

black codes: Statutes enacted by Southern states after the Civil War designed to deny blacks many of their basic rights.

blended sentence: A combination of juvenile and criminal sanctions given to young offenders.

bond, personal recognizance/release on recognizance (ROR): Document signed by a defendant in which he or she agrees to return to court at a subsequent date to stand trial.

bond hearing: An appearance before a judicial officer who determines the conditions of release—bail—pending trial.

booking: The process of photographing, fingerprinting, and recording of identifying data subsequent to a suspect's arrest.

Brandeis brief: An appellate brief that, in addition to conventional legal citations, contains extensive social and economic data.

breach of contract: Wrongful failure to carry out one or more promises in contractual agreement.

brief: Report prepared by an attorney and filed in court setting forth facts and applicable law in support of a case.

burden of proof: The need to establish a claim or allegation; in a criminal case, the state has the burden of proof.

calendar: A list of cases to be heard in a trial court on a specific date, containing the title of the case, the lawyers involved, and the case number.

case law: Previous decisions of appellate courts, particularly the Supreme Court.

case method: Teaching device using case law and the Socratic method to educate students in law school.

case reporter: Series of books containing court decisions of a particular court(s).

cause: Any question/action subject to litigation before court.

cause of action: Facts that give rise to a matter before the court.

caveat emptor: "Let the buyer beware"; relieves the seller of liability for a defective product.

certification: (1) Process of transferring a minor's case from juvenile to adult (criminal) court. (2) A request from a federal court asking the Supreme Court to rule on a legal question in a pending case that the federal court cannot resolve.

certiorari: Writ issued by an appellate court accepting a case for review; requirement that four justices agree to hear a case before it can be considered by the Supreme Court.

certiorari before judgment: Supreme Court rule that permits an immediate hearing upon a showing that the case is of such public importance as to require prompt resolution.

challenge: Legal objection raised by opposing attorney.

challenge for cause: Objection to using a prospective juror raised by counsel at a *voir dire* hearing.

chambers: Judge's office.

change of venue: Moving a trial to a county where the crime did not occur in order to avoid an unfair trial due to pretrial publicity.

charge: Accusation against the accused that he or she violated a specific criminal law(s).

charge to the jury: The instructions of a judge to the jury after the trial is complete and deliberations are about to begin.

chief judge: Judge who has primary responsibility for court administration.

child in need of supervision (CHINS): Status offender.

child-saving movement: Activities of middle- and upper-class women of the late nineteenth century to establish the juvenile court.

circumstantial evidence: Indirect evidence, such as fingerprints, from which an inference can be drawn.

citation: Reference to a legal authority; written directive to appear in court in place of arrest.

civil law: A system of law using statutes or codes in which precedent is absent as a legal concept; statutes and court decisions that involve noncriminal matters.

class action lawsuit: A tort action brought by one person or a small number of persons on behalf of a larger number of persons, of which the plaintiffs believe themselves to be representative.

classical theory: An outgrowth of Enlightenment philosophy that stresses free will and equality before law—"all men are created equal"—and provides a basis for determinate sentencing.

clear and convincing evidence: Standard of evidence for certain civil cases that exceeds preponderance of evidence but is lower than beyond a reasonable doubt.

clemency: A grant of mercy, such as a pardon, by a chief executive.

clerk of the court: Official responsible for managing the flow of cases and maintaining court records.

closing arguments: Summary statements to a judge or jury by opposing attorneys at the end of a trial.

code: A compilation of laws arranged by chapters.

collateral action: Challenging a judgment indirectly, rather than through direct action of an appeal.(e.g., claiming that the court lacked jurisdiction).

collateral estoppel: Rule that bars raising a claim in a judicial proceeding that has already been adjudicated in another proceeding.

comity: Without being bound by precedent, one court follows the decisions of another court in a similar case.

commit: Court order sending a person to an institution such as a prison, a hospital, or reformatory.

common law: A legal system inherited from England based on tradition or precedent rather than statutory law or fixed legal codes; law the result of judicial decisions as opposed to legislative enactment.

commutation: A shortening of sentence provided by a governor or president as part of the powers of executive clemency.

comparative negligence: A system whereby blame and therefore damages are apportioned on a percentage basis.

compelling government interest: Sufficient reason for government action that overrides otherwise fundamental rights.

complaint: Means of initiating a criminal or noncriminal case by setting out the cause of action.

concurrent jurisdiction: That shared by different courts.

concurrent sentence: Sentences for more than one time that are served simultaneously.

concurring opinion: Agreeing with the decision, but not the rationale.

conditional release: Release from prison based on the accumulation of time off for good behavior and requiring the releasee to abide by certain regulations.

consensual crime: An offense that has no complaining victim but has nevertheless been outlawed, such as the possession of heroin or certain sexual activities.

construction: The process of interpreting or determining the real meaning of a statute, legal document, or agreement.

contempt of court: A summary judgment holding that a person has willfully disobeyed a lawful order of the court.

contingency fee: A portion of the settlement in a tort action received by an attorney, generally one-third.

continuance: A delay in trial granted by the judge at the request of either attorney in a case; an adjournment.

contract: An agreement between two or more parties that creates an obligation to do or not do a particular thing.

contributory negligence: Plaintiff's failure to exercise care, which contributed to the damages he or she sustained.

conviction: Judgment of guilt against a criminal defendant.

corpus delecti: Proof that a crime has been committed: *actus reus* and *mens rea*.

corroboration: Supplementary evidence that tends to strengthen or confirm other evidence previously introduced.

counsel: Legal advice; attorney.

counterclaim: Claim made by defendant against plaintiff; counterlawsuit.

court: Government entity authorized to resolve legal disputes; used by judges to refer to themselves in the third person.

court of general jurisdiction: Trial court that can adjudicate any type of case.

court of last resort: Highest appellate court in a jurisdiction.

court of limited jurisdiction: Court that can only adjudicate certain minor cases.

court reporter: Skilled stenographer who makes a word-by-word record of what is said in court.

courtroom workgroup: The regular participants in the day-to-day activities of a particular courtroom: judge, prosecutor, defense attorney. Clerks and bailiffs may also be included.

court unification: Entails a simplified state trial court structure, rule-making centered in the supreme court or judicial council, system governance authority vested in the chief justice of the supreme court, and state funding of the judicial system with a statewide judicial system budget.

Cravath system: A method used by national law firms to train the graduates of elite law schools in the practice of corporate law.

crime: Any violation of the criminal law.

crime control model: A theoretical construct that emphasizes efficiency as a vital factor in the detection, apprehension, and conviction of criminal offenders and views due process as impeding this efficiency.

criminal intent: *mens rea*; necessary element to be proved in a criminal trial.

criminalistics: The science of crime detection; refers to the examination of physical evidence of a crime such as footprints, weapons, and bloodstains.

criminal law: Statutes defining certain acts of commission or omission as crimes.

criminal negligence: Crime based on failing to exercise the necessary degree of care.

criminology: The scientific study of criminal law, criminal behavior, and the system of criminal justice.

cross-claim: Lawsuit by co-defendants or co-plaintiffs against each other and not persons at the opposite side of the lawsuit.

cross-examination: The questioning of a witness by the attorney who did not call the witness; questions aimed at discrediting the courtroom testimony of an opposition witness.

cyberlaw: Legal issues involving the Internet.

damages: Compensation paid by defendants to successful plaintiffs in civil cases.

death-qualified jury: Jury panel whose members do not oppose the death penalty.

declaratory judgment: Judgment that expresses an opinion without the need for enforcement.

de facto: In fact; actual (as contrasted with *de jure*).

default judgment: Judgment in favor of plaintiff because the defendant failed to answer or appear to contest the plaintiff's claims.

defendant: Person accused of a crime or against whom the plaintiff brings suit.

definite sentence: *See* determinate sentence.

de jure: By law (as contrasted with *de facto*).

delinquent: A person found to have violated the law, but whose age prevents defining him or her as a criminal.

demurrer: A motion to dismiss based on the charge that, even if the facts alleged are true, the defendant's behavior does not constitute the basis for legal action.

de novo: Anew; for a second time.

deposition: The testimony of a witness not taken in open court; used extensively during the preliminary stages of a civil case.

derivative evidence: That derived from or obtained only as a result of other evidence.

determinate sentence: A term of imprisonment, imposed by a judge, that has a specific number of years, for example, 9–0–0 (nine years), as opposed to indefinite/indeterminate sentences.

determinism: A construct stressing the lack of choice, particularly the belief that one's behavior is "determined" by physiological or environmental variables, devoid of *mens rea*.

dictum: Explanatory comments in a ruling that are not part of the *ratio decedendi* and, thus, do not establish precedent.

diploma privilege: Admitting the graduates of law school to the bar without further examination.

direct evidence: That which stands on its own to prove an allegation; usually eyewitness testimony.

directed verdict: An instruction by the judge to the jury to return a specific verdict. In criminal cases, a judge may not direct a guilty verdict.

direct examination: Questions asked of a friendly witness by counsel at trial.

disbarment: Disciplinary action that disqualifies an attorney from practicing law.

discovery: A pretrial procedure allowing access to the information held by opposing counsel.

discretion: The lawful ability of an agent of government to exercise choice in making a decision.

dismissal: Termination of a case before trial.

disparate impact: Law or practice that, while apparently neutral in theory, has a differential and adverse impact in practice.

disposition: The decision of a juvenile court judge after a positive finding has been made (e.g., placing the respondent on probation).

dissent: A minority opinion in an appellate case.

distinguish away: To disregard an apparently relevant precedent by narrowly confining the case to its particular facts.

diversion: Permitting a person charged with an offense to avoid prosecution in exchange for participation in a rehabilitative or restitution program.

diversity of citizenship: Provides the basis of federal jurisdiction in disputes between citizens of different states and/or foreign nations.

docket: Log containing the complete history of each case in the form of a brief chronology.

double jeopardy: Trying a defendant a second time for the same offense after he or she has already been found not guilty.

dual federalism: Concept that federal and state governments are sovereign and each exercises its own authority.

due process: Those procedural guarantees to which every criminal defendant is entitled under the Constitution and its interpretation by the Supreme Court (e.g., the right to remain silent, to a trial by jury).

due process, substantive: *See* substantive due process.

due process clause: Fifth and Fourteenth amendments, which prohibit government from taking life, liberty, or property without due process of law.

due process model: A theoretical construct which brings into question the ability of law enforcement officials to correctly identify criminals; it stresses painstaking procedures to ensure that errors are avoided, that the innocent are not found guilty, and that the police do not abuse their authority. This restrictive approach places roadblocks in front of the efficiency of the crime control model.

Durham rule: A test of responsibility that maintains that a defendant cannot be held legally accountable if his or her criminal behavior was the product of a mental disease.

en banc: All of the judges of an appellate court collectively deciding a case.

English rule: Losing side in a lawsuit must pay the legal costs of the winner.

enjoin: Issue an injunction.

entrapment: The behavior of an agent of government that encourages the committing of a criminal act by a person who was not predisposed to do so. Constitutes an affirmative defense.

equal protection clause: That part of Section 1 of the Fourteenth Amendment prohibiting states from denying persons their right to equal protection of the law (discriminating).

equitable: Referring to civil suits in equity.

equity: Legal standard that refers to a concern for fairness of outcome. Often implemented through the use of injunctive relief and judicial review.

estate: Property left by the deceased.

estoppel: Acknowledgment of facts that bars making subsequent claims to the contrary.

estoppel doctrines: Application of equity to avoid unfair outcomes.

evidence, circumstantial: That from which something can be inferred (e.g., fingerprints).

evidence, direct: Eyewitness testimony.

exception: A formal objection to the action of the court during trial; provides the basis for an appeal.

exclusionary rule: A legal doctrine prohibiting evidence secured in an improper manner from being used at a trial.

ex contractu: Action alleging breech of a promise set forth in a contract.

ex delicto: A tort; an action alleging a wrong committed by the defendant against the plaintiff.

executive clemency: Refers to the power of a governor or president to grant pardons, commutations, and reprieves.

ex parte: Discussion having only one party present.

ex post facto **law:** After the fact; statute making an already completed behavior a criminal act.

expunge: Official erasure of court record in whole or part.

extradition: Surrendering a fugitive to another jurisdiction.

failure of proof: Basis for a dismissal when the plaintiff or (with affirmative defenses and counterclaims) defendant fail to present sufficient evidence.

family court: Court having jurisdiction over juvenile cases as well as issues such as divorce and custody.

Federal Register: Government publication containing all rules/regulations proposed and promulgated by federal agencies.

fellow servant rule: Doctrine according to which an injured employee cannot recover damages against an employer as the result of actions by another worker.

felony: The more serious of the two basic types of criminal behavior, usually bearing a possible penalty in excess of one year in prison.

fiduciary: The obligation of a trustee to act according to scrupulous good faith.

file: Place a document in official custody of the clerk of the court to enter into the files or records of a case.

finding: The verdict in a juvenile court.

flat sentence: *See* definite sentence.

forum non conveniens: A legal action that could be dismissed because it is inconvenient for the defendant and/or witnesses to try a case so far away, provided the plaintiff has an alternative forum.

free will: According to classical theory, each person has the opportunity to be law-abiding or criminal (*mens rea*) and, therefore, the person who opts to commit a crime is deserving of punishment commensurate with the offense.

full faith and credit: The constitutional requirement that the official judicial acts of one state will be respected by every other state.

garnish: Collecting a portion of the earnings of a debtor to satisfy a debt.

general jurisdiction: The ability of a trial court to hear any type of case.

good faith exception: Exception to the exclusionary rule that allows the admission of evidence based on the officer's reasonable, but mistaken, belief that his/her action was proper.

good time: A reduction of the time served in prison as a reward for not violating prison rules; usually one-third to one-half off the maximum sentence.

grand jury: A group of citizens, usually numbering 23, who are assembled in secret to hear or investigate allegations of criminal behavior.

guardian ad litem: Person appointed by a court to look after the interests of a minor during the course of a judicial proceeding.

guilty but insane: A legal concept according to which a person who is suffering from a mental illness is not relieved of criminal responsibility.

habeas corpus: A legal document challenging custody and designed to force authorities holding a prisoner to produce him or her and justify the custody. Often used as an alternate method of appealing a conviction.

harmless error: Error that does not affect that outcome of a judicial proceeding.

hearsay: Statement by a witness who did not hear or see the incident but heard about it from someone else; a statement whose veracity cannot be subjected to cross-examination and is therefore generally not admissible (although there are many exceptions).

holding: Principle which may reasonably be drawn from a case in the case law process.

hostile witness: A witness whose testimony is not favorable to the side that called him or her; can then be subjected to cross-examination by the party who called the witness.

hung jury: A jury that cannot reach a verdict.

immunity: Exemption from a civil or criminal action.

impaneling: The selection and swearing in of a jury.

impeachment: Official accusation against a public official brought by a legislative body seeking his or her removal; impunging the credibility of a witness at trial.

impeachment of a witness: An attack on the credibility of a witness during cross-examination.

inadmissible: Cannot be admitted under the rules of evidence.

in camera: In private, referring to a judge's chambers.

indefinite sentence: A sentence that has both a minimum and maximum term of imprisonment, the actual length determined by a parole board.

indeterminate sentence: Same as an indefinite sentence.

indictment: Formal criminal charge issued by a grand jury.

indigent: Unable to afford counsel.

indirect evidence: Circumstantial evidence, such as fingerprints, from which an inference can be drawn.

inevitable discovery: A legal doctrine that permits the use of evidence even though it was secured in an improper manner on the belief that it would have eventually been discovered anyway—an exception to the exclusionary rule.

infancy: A legal age at which a person cannot be held criminally responsible.

inflammatory remarks: Impermissible remarks by counsel at trial designed to inflame the jury.

in forma pauperis: Being able to bring an action without payment of legal fees.

information: Accusatory document, detailing the charges and filed by the prosecutor, which serves to bring a defendant to trial.

infraction: Minor violation of law not punishable by incarceration.

injunction: Court order prohibiting a threatened or continuing act.

in personam: *See* action *in personam.*

in re: In the matter of.

in rem: *See* action *in rem.*

insanity: In law, refers to lack of criminal responsibility.

insanity defense: Affirmative defense offered to avoid being held accountable for criminal behavior.

integrated bar: Membership in a state bar association is required (compulsory) in order to practice law.

intent: *Mens rea;* state of mind that must be proved in a criminal trial.

interlocutory appeal: An appeal raised prior to the completion of a trial alleging errors by the judge which must be corrected if the trial is to proceed in a just and proper manner.

interrogatories: In a civil case, written questions submitted to opposing counsel for answering out of court and under oath. While a respondent need not answer a question deemed improper, the interrogating party can seek a court order to compel an answer.

jail: A local, municipal or county, institution used to house those awaiting trial, those convicted of a misdemeanor, and those convicted of a felony and awaiting transfer to a prison.

joinder of claims: Allows the court to consolidate claims if they arose out of the same incident and are too complex/interdependent to be considered separately.

joinder of offenses: A single prosecution when the several charges arose from the same criminal episode.

joinder of persons: Allows a civil plaintiff to name as defendants any/all persons allegedly responsible in any way for injuries or damages.

judgment: Official decision of a court resolving the dispute.

judgment notwithstanding the verdict: A trial judge may reduce a jury award that is excessive, or order a new trial when the verdict goes against the clear weight of the evidence, or reverse a verdict that is unreasonable given the facts presented at trial and the legal standard to be applied.

judicial activism: Pejorative term referring to a court overstepping its authority.

judicial comity: A courtesy according to which the courts of one state defer to the laws and judicial decisions of another state. As contained in the Eleventh Amendment, serves to protect the independence of the state courts from federal intervention.

judicial conference: A body of judges established to provide uniformity of policy and to consider matters of judicial discipline.

judicial federalism: Refers to state courts providing due process rights beyond those required by the Supreme Court.

judicial restraint: Belief that judges should exercise power cautiously and within strict parameters set by precedent and/or deference to the other branches of government.

judicial review: The power of the judicial branch to declare acts of the executive and legislative branches unconstitutional.

jurisdiction: The authority to adjudicate a case based on a variety of factors such as geography, seriousness of the crime, or the value of the amount in dispute.

jurisprudence: Study of law and the structure of the legal system.

jury pool: Those persons who have been summoned and sworn to serve on a jury, but who have not yet been subjected to a *voir dire* hearing.

juvenile: Person who has not achieved an age set by law.

laissez-faire capitalism: Economic theory that argues against government intrusion in the marketplace.

law clerk: Law school graduates who assist judges with research.

law review: Legal journal edited by law school students.

leading question: During the examination of a witness at trial, a question that suggests an answer.

legal aid: Legal services provided by an agency to indigent persons.

letters rogatory: A court-issued document enabling a party in a civil action to secure testimony from a witness out of the court's jurisdiction; it empowers an official or attorney in the proper jurisdiction to take the witness's deposition and forward it to the court.

limited jurisdiction: Refers to a trial court that can only hear certain types of cases.

lodestar formula: A general procedure used by judges to determine attorney fees in class action cases.

long arm statues: Allows jurisdiction over nonresidents if they have ties to that state when the cause of the action is local and affects local residents.

magistrate: Judicial officer in a court of limited jurisdiction.

***mala in se*:** "Evil in itself"; behavior that is universally recognized as criminal.

***mala prohibita*:** Behavior that is wrong because the law defines it so.

malfeasance: Official misconduct.

mandamus: *See* writ of mandamus.

mandatory release: The release of an inmate at the end of his or her sentence minus any good time.

material: Relevant.

mediation: Submitting a dispute to a nonjudicial third party who attempts to get the parties to agree on an outcome.

***mens rea*:** The "guilty mind"—intent—necessary to establish criminal responsibility.

misdemeanor: Lesser of the two basic types of crime; usually punishable by no more than one year of imprisonment.

Missouri Plan: The "merit selection" of judges using a panel whose members are appointed by the governor or selected by the bar association; the panel submits a list of candidates to the governor, who must pick one for a judicial vacancy. After serving for one year, the judge must stand for retention at a general election.

mistrial: Trial declared invalid, the result of a fundamental error or jury deadlock.

M'Naghten rule: A test of criminal responsibility based on English common law; did the offender know that what he or she was doing was wrong?

moot: If the outcome of a case will have no significant impact on the litigants, it is moot—already resolved. Typically it will be dismissed, but in some cases an appellate court may render a decision on a moot case if the issue is likely to come before the court again.

motion: Application to the court for the invoking of a rule or order.

natural law: Belief that there is a code that is higher/supersedes positive (manmade) law.

natural rights: Inherent rights which cannot be abridged by government.

negligence: Failure to exercise ordinary care.

***nolle prosequi*:** A decision by the prosecutor declining to prosecute a particular defendant.

nolo contendere: A plea of "no contest" to criminal charges. Has the same effect as a plea of guilty, but cannot be used as evidence of a criminal conviction at any subsequent civil trial related to the criminal act.

normal crimes: A concept that recognizes that there are certain frequent and routine patterns that result in categories of crime being viewed as "normal" by prosecutors and defense attorneys.

notary public: Person authorized to administer oaths, certify signatures, and perform other minor official acts.

no true bill: Grand jury decision not to indict.

nullum crimen sine lege: "No crime without a law." The Constitution (Article 1, Sec. 9) prohibits the passage of an *ex post facto law*.

obiter dicta: Incidental statements contained in an appellate decision.

objection: The act of taking exception to a statement or procedure during a trial.

opening statements: Remarks made to the jury by attorneys at the start of a trial.

opinion: Written opinion by which judges explain the decision of the court.

oral argument: Opportunity for lawyers to summarize their position before the court and respond to the judge's questions.

ordinance: A statute enacted by a municipality or county.

organized crime: Refers to persons involved in ongoing criminal conspiracies whose goals are personal gain and who may persist indefinitely.

original intent: Doctrine that the Constitution and statutes should be interpreted according to what their authors intended.

originalism: *See* original intent.

original jurisdiction: Trial jurisdiction.

overcharging: A practice of alleging an excessive number of criminal violations when charging a suspect.

overrule: Judge's decision not to allow an objection; decision by a higher court that a lower court decision was in error.

pardon: An act of executive clemency that has the effect of releasing an inmate from prison and/or removing certain legal disabilities from persons convicted of crimes.

parens patriae: Common law concept that refers to the obligation of the state toward persons who are unable to care for themselves, such as children or the mentally ill.

parole: The release of a prison inmate prior to the expiration of sentence by a board authorized to make such a decision, followed by a period of supervision by a parole officer.

parole board: An administrative body whose members are chosen to review the cases of prisoners eligible for release on parole. The board has the authority to release such persons and to return them to prison for violating the conditions of parole.

pat-down: Refers to frisking, placing the hands about the body of a suspect in order to detect any weapons that he or she may be carrying.

per curiam: A decision in which an appellate court states its opinion, but the author is not revealed.

peremptory challenge: The right of opposing attorneys to excuse prospective jurors without having to state a reason.

perjury: Deliberately testifying falsely under oath about a material fact; a criminal offense.

personal recognizance: Pretrial release without the need for bail.

personam, in: *See* action *in personam*.

person in need of supervision (PINS): Status offender.

petition: Formal written request or "prayer" for action; form of complaint used in juvenile proceedings.

petit jury: Trial jury composed of six or twelve persons.

plaintiff: Person initiating an action in a civil case or on appeal.

plea: Criminal defendant's response to the charges.

plea bargain: A legal transaction in which a defendant pleads guilty in exchange for some form of leniency.

pleading: Written statements of contentions submitted by parties in a legal action, each responding to the other, until the points at issue are sufficiently narrowed to proceed to trial.

police powers: Authority of the state to enact law to further the public health, safety, and welfare.

positive law: Deliberately created law (as opposed to natural).

positivism: In criminology, the use of the scientific method to study crime; the belief that such methods will enlighten society about the nature of crime and criminals and that crime is not simply the result of free will.

precedent: Court decision in an earlier case that is relevant to subsequent cases, as per *stare decisis*.

preponderance of the evidence: Standard used to determine the outcome of a noncriminal action.

presentence investigation report: A document submitted by a probation department to a judge containing information about the offender upon which the judge can base his or her sentencing decision.

presumptive waiver: Provisions according to which certain juvenile offenders must be waived to criminal court unless they can prove they are amenable to rehabilitation, shifting the burden from the prosecutor to the juvenile.

pretrial release: Setting free a defendant without requiring bail; ROR (release on recognizance).

preventive detention: Holding a defendant in custody pending trial on the belief that he or she is likely to commit further criminal acts.

prima facie **case:** A case that is sufficient (i.e., has at least the minimum amount of evidence necessary to allow it to continue in the judicial process).

private law: Civil action between two parties that does not involve government as a defendant or plaintiff.

privilege: An exceptional right.

privity of contract: Liability limited to the immediate party to a contract and not extending to any third party (who may be the actual manufacturer).

probable cause: The minimum level of evidence needed to make a lawful arrest or secure certain warrants; a level of information that would lead a prudent person to believe that a crime was being, or had been, committed by a specific perpetrator.

probable cause hearing: A court hearing to determine if an arrest was justified—did the officer have probable cause?

probation: A sentence in lieu of imprisonment under which a defendant is supervised in the community by a probation officer.

probation officer: Public official authorized to accomplish presentence reports and supervise probationers.

pro bono: Lawyer working without compensation.

procedural law: Specific instructions for invoking substantive law.

pro se: Latin for "on one's own behalf"; presenting a case without a lawyer.

prosecutor: A public official who represents the state in a criminal action.

protective search: A search by law enforcement officers without the benefit of a search warrant to ensure that there are no weapons about that could endanger them, or to secure items in possession of a suspect who has been placed under arrest.

public defender: An attorney employed by government to represent indigent defendants.

public law: Noncriminal action in which government is either a plaintiff or defendant.

public safety exception: An exception to the exclusionary rule on the grounds that the action which resulted in securing evidence that would normally be suppressed was necessary to protect the public from some immediate danger.

punitive damages: Award in excess of the loss sustained in order to punish the defendant.

quash: To void or declare invalid; usually a summons or indictment.

ratio decedendi: The legal principle on which a case decision is based.

rational law: A system in which there is an application of general principles to specific facts.

reasonable doubt: Doubt that a reasonable person could have with respect to the evidence.

reasonable mistake exception: Legal argument raised to justify the admission of evidence that might otherwise be suppressed, as per the exclusionary rule.

rebuttal: The introduction of contradicting testimony.

recidivate: The repetition of criminal behavior.

recognizance: Obligation to perform some act, usually returning to court to stand trial.

recuse: A judge disqualifying him- or herself from a case because of some personal involvement or interest.

redirect: The questioning of a friendly witness after he or she has been subjected to cross-examination by opposing counsel.

rejoinder: Defense response to prosecutor's rebuttal; defense response to plaintiff's answer to the defense plea.

released on own recognizance: Releasing a defendant without the need to post bail; referred to as ROR.

remand: To send back, usually for a new trial or sentencing.

remedy: Means by which a court can enforce a finding.

remittitur: Procedure whereby the amount awarded by a civil jury is lowered, or a new trial on the issue of the amount of damages is ordered.

reprieve: A temporary stay of the execution of a sentence to allow more time for judicial review.

request for admission: Written statements of material facts or allegations at issue are submitted to opposing counsel for a response—admission or denial. Those that are admitted need not be proved at trial.

reserved powers: Those enjoyed by the state or the people under the Tenth Amendment.

res ipsa loquitur: "The thing speaks for itself"; if damages resulted, unless proven otherwise, negligence on the part of the defendant is assumed.

res judicata: A controversy that has already been adjudicated, thereby barring a new legal action.

restorative justice: Approach to criminal justice in which the victim is at the center.

retainer: An advance paid by a client to an attorney in order to engage the attorney's services.

reverse: Act of an appellate court setting aside the decision of a trial court.

rules of evidence: Standards governing the admission of evidence.

self-defense: Affirmative defense claiming that physical force was used to protect oneself or others in imminent danger.

self-incrimination: Forcing a suspect to provide evidence against him- or herself; prohibited by the Fifth Amendment.

senatorial courtesy: Tradition that allows a U.S. senator to veto the appointment of a federal official in his or her state.

sentencing disparity: The phenomenon of offenders committing similar crimes receiving vastly different sentences.

sentencing guidelines: An attempt to reduce sentencing disparity by providing judges with a structure to guide their decisions.

separation of powers: The division of government into three branches: executive, legislative, and judicial.

sequestering: Placing a jury in protective custody until they complete deliberations.

service of process: Delivery of writs or summonses to the appropriate party.

shelter: Temporary residential facility for children in need of emergency care.

sidebar: Conference between judges and attorneys in courtroom out of hearing by the jury.

small claims court: Court having jurisdiction to adjudicate civil claims below a certain amount without a jury and in which parties usually appear without attorneys (*pro se*).

social investigation: A study prepared by a probation officer in juvenile court to provide the judge with information on which to base a disposition.

sovereign immunity: Rule of law that a nation or state is exempt from a lawsuit (unless legislation specifically waives immunity).

special verdict: In civil trials, when the issues involve complex legal and scientific (e.g., medical or engineering) matters that need to be simplified in order to be understood by the jury, the jury responds to a series of written questions of fact posed by the judge instead of delivering a verdict for or against the defendant. Based on the jury's answers, the judge determines the outcome of the case.

specific performance: An order under equity compelling the fulfillment of the terms of a contract where damages would be inappropriate or inadequate.

standing: Having the right to bring a legal action by virtue of being personally harmed.

stare decisis (*Stare decisis et non quieta movere*): "Stand by the decision and do not disturb what is settled" is the basis for adhering to precedent in common/case law adjudications.

status offense: Actions that would not constitute a crime if the actor were an adult (e.g., truancy) but, in accord with *parens patriae*, can subject the youngster to the juvenile court process.

statute: Law passed by a legislature.

statute of limitations: Period of time fixed by law within which a lawsuit or prosecution must be commenced, or it will be barred forever.

statutory law: The enactments of legislative bodies.

stay: A court order that temporarily stops a legal proceeding.

stipulation: An agreement between opposing counsel on certain uncontested factual issues, such as the date and time of the incident, photos, sketches, and other routine evidence.

strict liability: The absence of a need to prove *mens rea* (criminal intent) in a criminal action or fault (e.g., negligence) in a tort case; absolute liability.

subpoena *ad testificandum*: A court order requiring a witness to appear and testify.

subpoena *duces tecum*: "Bring with you"; a court order requiring a witness to bring all relevant documents that might affect the outcome of legal proceedings.

substantive due process: A vague concept, based on the Fourteenth Amendment, that there are individual rights which cannot be unreasonably or arbitrarily interfered with.

summary decision: Made by an appellate court without benefit of briefs or oral arguments.

summary judgment: A judgment rendered by the court on a motion by the plaintiff or defendant who claims that there is an absence of a factual dispute requiring a verdict.

summons: Legal instrument used to notify a person that he/she is being named as a party in a legal action and requiring the defendant to appear and defend. Also used to notify a witness or juror to appear in court.

suppress: Forbid the use of evidence at trial because it was improperly obtained.

supremacy clause: Article VI, Clause 2, declares the federal Constitution and laws to be "the supreme Law of the Land," and provides the federal government powers that cannot be exercised by the states and which the states must heed.

sustain: Upholding an objection.

temporary restraining order: Judicial order in equity prohibiting a person from an action that is likely to cause irreparable harm that lasts only until a hearing can be held.

testimony: Oral evidence presented by witnesses.

textualism: Method of judicial interpretation that stresses the plain meaning of words as they were understood at the time they were promulgated, as opposed to seeking out the intent of those who enacted the law.

therapeutic jurisprudence: Study of the role of law as a helping/treating agent.

therapeutic justice: Use of law and courts for problem-solving.

tort: A private wrong that is the subject of a lawsuit; *ex delicto*.

transcript: Written word-for-word record of a judicial proceeding or oral deposition.

trial: A fact-finding process using the adversarial method.

trial *de novo*: A new trial in which the entire case is retried as if no prior trial had taken place.

true bill: The handing up of an indictment by a grand jury.

truth in sentencing: Statute requiring offenders to serve their entire sentence, usually with a small reduction for good behavior.

ultra vires: Acting beyond one's authority; typically applies to public officials and corporations.

unification: *See* court unification.

Uniform Commercial Code: Comprehensive laws relating to commercial transactions promulgated by the National Conference of Commissioners on Uniform State Laws and adopted by each state except Louisiana.

uphold: Appellate court agrees with the lower court.

vacating a decision: Setting aside or rescinding a faulty judgment or at the request of the winning litigant, usually for extra compensation to avoid making it part of the public record.

venire: Process by which jurors are summoned to service.

venue: Proper jurisdiction for considering a particular case.

voir dire hearing: The judicial procedure by which opposing attorneys have an opportunity to question and/or challenge prospective jurors.

waive: To give up a personal right (e.g., to remain silent as per the Fifth Amendment).

warrant: Legal document authorizing a search or arrest.

witness: A person called to testify in a judicial proceeding.

writ: A court order commanding certain action(s).

writ of certiorari: Order of the U. S. Supreme Court directing a lower court to transmit records for a case that it has agreed to hear on appeal.

writ of mandamus: From a Latin word meaning "to order": an extraordinary court order compelling a public official to perform his or her duty.

writ of prohibition: Extraordinary writ forbidding a public official from performing some act.

REFERENCES

Aaronson, David E.; Nicholas N. Kittrie; David J. Saari; and Carolina Cooper
1977 *Alternatives to Conventional Adjudication Guidebook for Planners and Practitioners.* Washington, DC: U.S. Government Printing Office.

Abadinsky, Howard
2003 *Probation and Parole: Theory and Practice,* 8th ed. Upper Saddle River, NJ: Prentice Hall.
2001 *Drug Abuse: An Introduction,* 4th ed. Belmont, CA: Wadsworth.
2000 *Organized Crime,* 6th ed. Belmont, CA: Wadsworth.
1983 *The Criminal Elite: Professional and Organized Crime.* Westport, CT: Greenwood.

Abel, Richard L.
1989 *American Lawyers.* New York: Oxford University Press.

Abel, Richard L., and Philip C. Lewis, eds.
1988 *Lawyers in Society: Vol. 2, The Civil Law World.* Berkeley: University of California Press.

Abraham, Henry J.
1998 *The Judicial Process: An Introductory Analysis of the Courts of the United States, England, and France,* 6th ed. New York: Oxford University Press.
1990 "Beneficial Advice or Presumptuous Veto? The ABA's Committee on Federal Judiciary Revisited." In *Judicial Selection: Merit, Ideology, and Politics,* edited by Henry J. Abraham, Eugene W. Hickok, Jr., and William Bradford Reynolds, pp. 61–78. Washington, DC: National Legal Center for the Public Interest.
1972 *Freedom and the Court: Civil Rights and Liberties in the United States.* New York: Oxford.

Abraham, Henry J. and Barbara A. Perry
1994 *Freedom and the Court: Civil Rights and Liberties in the United States.* New York: Oxford University Press.

Abrahamson, Leslie, with Richard Flaste
1997 *The Defense is Ready: Life in the Trenches of Criminal Law.* New York: Simon and Schuster.

Adler, Matthew D. and Eric A. Posner

2000   "Implementing Cost–Benefit Analysis When Preferences Are Distorted." *Law and Economics Working Paper No. 88*, University of Chicago Law School.

Albonetti, Celesta A.

1986   "Criminality, Prosecutorial Screening, and Uncertainty: Toward a Theory of Discretionary Decision Making in Felony Case Processings." *Criminology* 24 (Nov.): 623–644.

Aldisert, Ruggero J.

1989   *Logic for Lawyers: A Guide to Clear Legal Thinking.* New York: Clark Boardman.

Alexander, Gregory S.

n.d.   Property in the Two Legal Realisms." Cornell Law School Working Papers.

Alfini, James J.

1986   "Alternative Dispute Resolution and the Courts: An Introduction." *Judicature* 69 (Feb.–March): 252–253, 314.

Alliance of American Insurers (AAI)

1987   *Advancing Justice: May We Approach the Bench?* Schaumburg, IL: AAI.

Alschuler, Albert W.

2000   *Law Without Values: The Life, Work, and Legacy of Justice Holmes.* Chicago: University of Chicago Press.

1975   "The Defense Attorney's Role in Plea Bargaining." *Yale Law Review* 84: 1179–1314.

1968   "The Prosecutor's Role in Plea Bargaining." *University of Chicago Law Review* 36: 50–112.

Alter, Jonathan, with Howard Fineman and Eleanor Clift

1989   "The World of Congress." *Newsweek* (April 24): 28–34.

American Bar Association (ABA)

1980   *Law Schools and Professional Education:Task Force on Lawyer Competency and the Role of Law Schools.* Chicago: ABA.

1979   *Lawyer Competency and the Role of Law Schools.* Chicago: ABA.

American Friends Service Committee

1971   *Struggle for Justice.* New York: Hill and Wang.

Andreski, Stanislav, ed.

1971   *Herbert Spencer: Structure, Function and Evolution.* New York: Scribners.

Archer, Peter

1956   *The Queen's Courts: An Account of the History, Jurisdiction, and Procedure of the Various Courts and Tribunals Which Administer English Law.* Middlesex, England: Penguin.

Armstrong, Ken

1998   "The Verdict on the Accusers: Not So Grand." *Chicago Tribune* (September 27): Sec. 2: 1, 8.

1997   "Injured Construction Workers Regain Right to Seek Damages." *Chicago Tribune* (September 12): Sec. 2: 6.

1996a   "Spare the Rod, Spoil the Judge, Critics Argue." *Chicago Tribune* (June 23): 1, 8.

1996b   "Judicial Hopefuls Take Civic Liberties." *Chicago Tribune* (March 7): 1, 24.

Armstrong, Ken and Andrew Fegelman

1996   "Wayward Words Might Kill Workers' Suits." *Chicago Tribune* (December 13): B1, 2.

Armstrong, Ken and Maurice Possley

1999   "The Verdict: Dishonor." *Chicago Tribune* (January 10): 1, 1213.

Aron, Nan

1989   *Liberty and Justice for All: Public Interest Law in the 1980s and Beyond.* Boulder, CO: Westview Press.

Aspen, Marvin E.

1987   "Let's Select Judges on Their Merit, Not Their Politics." *Chicago Tribune* (Jan. 21): 17.

Associated Press

2000a   "Prosecutor Admits Botched Evidence." June 14.

2000b   "Jury Awards $3M in Botched Surgery." July 1.

1994   "Accused of Falsifying Evidence in Criminal Cases, Chemist Surrenders." *Chicago Tribune* (August 5): 14.

Atiyah, P. S., and R. S. Summers

1987   *Form and Substance in Anglo-American Law: A Comparative Study in Legal Reasoning, Legal Theory and Legal Institutions.* Oxford, England: Oxford University Press.

Aubert, Vilhelm
1983   *In Search of Law: Sociological Approaches to Law.* Totowa, NJ: Barnes and Noble.

Auerbach, Carl A.
1983   "Administrative Agency." In *Guide to American Law*, pp. 74–75. St. Paul, MN: West.

Auerbach, Jerold S.
1976   *Unequal Justice: Lawyers and Social Change in America.* New York: Oxford University Press.
1971   "Enmity and Amity: Law Teachers and Practitioners, 1900–1922." In *Law in American History*, edited by Donald Fleming and Bernard Bailyn, pp. 549–601. Boston: Little, Brown.

Axelrod, David
1983   "Judicial Bench No Place to Practice Party Loyalty." *Chicago Tribune* (August 28): Sec. 4: 4.

Bacigal, Ronald J.
1990   *The Limits of Litigation: The Dalkon Shield Controversy.* Durham, NC: Carolina Academic Press.

Baden, Michael M., with Judith A. Hennessee
1989   *Unnatural Death: Confessions of a Medical Examiner.* New York: Random House.

Baldwin, Scott
1984   "The Sure Way to Protect the 'Little Guy.'" *New York Times* (Dec. 2): F2.

Baudouin, Jean-Louis
1974   "The Impact of Common Law on the Civilian Systems of Louisiana and Quebec." In *The Role of Judicial Decisions and Doctrine in Civil Law in Mixed Jurisdictions*, edited by Joseph Dainow, pp. 1–22. Baton Rouge: Louisiana State University Press.

Bahls, Steven C. and Jane Easter Hauls
2000   "And Arbitrated Justice for All." *Entrepreneur* 28 (December): 106.

Baum, Lawrence
1994   *American Courts.* Boston: Houghton Mifflin.
1989   *The Supreme Court*, 3d ed. Washington, DC: Congressional Quarterly Press.

Bazemore, Gordon and Dennis Maloney
1994   "Rehabilitating Community Service: Toward Restorative Service Sanctions in a Balanced Justice System." *Federal Probation 58* (March): 24–35.

Bazemore, Gordon and Mark S. Umbriet
1995   "Rethinking the Sanctioning Function in Juvenile Court: Retributive or Restorative Responses to Youth Crime." *Crime and Delinquency* 41 (July): 296–316.

Beard, Charles A.
1913   *An Economic Interpretation of the Constitution of the United States.* New York: Macmillan.

Beccaria, Cesare
1963   *An Essay on Crimes and Punishments.* Indianapolis, IN: Bobbs–Merrill. (Originally published in 1764; English edition 1867.)

Becker, David M.
1998   "Debunking the Sanctity of Precedent." *Washington University Law Quarterly* 76: 854–974.

Beckerman-Rodau, Andrew
1999   "A Jurisprudential Approach to Common Law Legal Analysis." Internet. Originally published in the *Rutgers Law Review* 269 (1999).

Bellows, Randy I.
1983   "Notes of a Public Defender." Paper prepared for the Program on the Legal Profession, Harvard University Law School.

Bendavid, Naftali
2001   "Report: Public Should Finance Judge Elections." *Chicago Tribune* (July 23): 7.

Benson, Michael L., Francis T. Cullen, and William J. Maakestad
1993   *Local Prosecutors and Corporate Crime.* Washington, DC: National Institute of Justice.

Berger, Raoul
1987   *Federalism: The Founders' Design.* Norman: University of Oklahoma Press.
1977   *Government by Judiciary: The Transformation of the Fourteenth Amendment.* Cambridge, MA: Harvard University Press.

Berman, Harold J.
   1958   *The Nature and Functions of Law*. Brooklyn, NY: Foundation Press.

Berman, Harold J. and William R. Greiner
   1980   *The Nature and Functions of Law*, 4th ed. Mineola, NY: Foundation Press.

Bernstein, Emily M.
   1996   "Law School Women Question the Teaching." *New York Times* (June 5): B10.

Bernstein, Illene N., Edward Kick, Jan T. Leung, and Barbara Schultz
   1977   "Charge Reduction: An Intermediate Stage in the Process of Labeling Criminal Defendants." *Social Forces* 56 (Dec.): 362–384.

Bernstein, Nina
   1996a   "Equal Opportunity Recedes for Most Female Lawyers." *New York Times* (January 8): 12.
   1996b   "Curb on Class-Action Suits for the Poor Is Challenged." *New York Times* (August 1): 14.

Bishop, Donna M., Charles F. Frazier, and John C. Henretta
   1989   "Prosecutorial Waiver: Case Study of a Questionable Reform." *Crime and Delinquency* 35 (April): 179–201.

Bishop, Donna, Charles Frazier, Lonn Lanza-Kaduce, and Henry George White
   1999   *A Study of Juvenile Transfers to Criminal Court in Florida*. Washington, DC: Office of Justice Programs.

Black, Donald
   1989   *Sociological Justice*. New York: Oxford University Press.

Blackstone, Erwin A. and Gary W. Bowman
   1999   "Economics and the Law from Posner to Post-Modernism." *Atlantic Economic Journal* 27 (December): Internet.

Blakeslee, Sandra
   1996   "Genetic Questions Are Sending Judges Back to Classroom." *New York Times* (July 9): B7, 10.

Blew, Carol H., and Robert Rosenblum
   1977   *The Community Arbitration Project: Anne Arundel County*, Maryland. Washington, DC: U.S. Government Printing Office.

Blumberg, Abraham S.
   1967   "The Practice of Law as Confidence Game: Organizational Cooptation of a Profession." *Law and Society Review* 1: 15–39.

Blumrosen, Alfred W.
   1962   "Legal Process and Labor Laws." In *Law and Sociology: Exploratory Essays*, edited by William Evan, pp. 185–225. Glencoe, IL: Free Press.

Bok, Derek
   1983   "A Flawed System of Law Practice and Training." *Journal of Legal Education* 33: 570–585.

Boland, Barbara, and Elizabeth Brady
   1985   *The Prosecution of Felony Arrests, 1980*. Washington, DC: U.S. Government Printing Office.

Boland, Barbara, Catherine H. Conly, Lynn Warner, Ronald Sones, and William Martin
   1988   *The Prosecution of Felony Arrests, 1986*. Washington, DC: U.S. Government Printing Office.

Boland, Barbara, Elizabeth Brady, Herbert Tyson, and John Bassler
   1983   *The Prosecution of Felony Arrests, 1979*. Washington, DC: U.S. Government Printing Office.

Boldt, Richard C.
   1998   "Rehabilitative Punishment and the Drug Treatment Court Movement." *Washington University Law Quarterly* 76: 1205–1306.

Bond, James E.
   1987   *The Art of Judging*. New Brunswick, NJ: Transaction Books.

Bordenhamer, David J.
   1992   *Fair Trial: Rights of the Accused in American History*. New York: Oxford University Press.

Bork, Robert H.
   1993   "The Senate's Power Grab." *New York Times* (June 23): 11.
   1989   *The Tempting of America: The Political Seduction of the Law*. New York: The Free Press.

Boswell, John
   1989   *The Kindness of Strangers: The Abandonment of Children in Western Europe from Antiquity to the Renaissance*. New York: Pantheon.

Bouchoux, Deborah E.
2001   *Cite-Checker: A Hands-On Guide to Learning Citation Form*. Albany, NY: Delmar.

Boyle, James, ed.
1992   *Critical Legal Studies*. New York: New York University Press.

Boyle, Joseph
1992   "Natural Law and the Ethics of Traditions." In *Natural Law Theory*, edited by Robert P. George, pp. 3–30, Oxford, England: Oxford University Press.

Braun, Bill
1997   "Plea Offer Rejected, Defendant Given 93 Years." *Tulsa World On-Line*, February 28.

Brennan, William J., Jr.
1986   "Guaranteeing Individual Liberty." *USA Today* (Sept.): 40–42.

Brenner, Susan W.
1995   "The Voice of the Community: A Case for Grand Jury Independence." *Virginia Journal of Social Policy and the Law* 67 (Fall): Internet.
1992   *Precedent Inflation*. New Brunswick, NJ: Transaction Books.

Broder, John M.
1997   "Stares of Lawyerly Disbelief at a Huge Civil Award." *New York Times* (September 10): C1.

Bronner, Ethan
1989   *Battle for Justice: How the Bork Nomination Shook America*. New York: Norton.

Brown, Richard M.
1971   "Legal and Behavioral Perspectives on American Vigilantism." In *Law in American History*, edited by Donald Fleming and Bernard Bailyn, pp.103–144. Boston: Little, Brown.
1969   "The American Vigilante Tradition." In *The History of Violence in America: Historical and Comparative Perspectives*, edited by Hugh Davis Graham and Ted R. Gurr, pp. 154–226. New York: Bantam.

Brownell, Emery A.
1951   *Legal Aid in the United States: A Study of the Availability of Lawyers' Services for Persons to Pay Fees*. Rochester, NY: Lawyers Co-Operative Publishing Co.

Buchholz, Barbara A.
1996   "Slow Gains for Women Who Would Be Partners." *New York Times* (June 23): 10F.

Buckle, Suzann R., and Leonard Buckle
1977   *Bargaining for Justice: Plea Disposition in the Criminal Courts*. New York: Praeger.

Bureau of Justice Assistance
1988   *Court Unification*. Washington, DC: U.S. Government Printing Office.

Bureau of Justice Statistics
1986   *Felony Case-Processing Time*. Washington, DC: U.S. Government Printing Office.
1985   *Crime and Justice Facts*, 1985. Washington, DC: U.S. Government Printing Office.

Burt, Robert A.
1995   Alex Bickel's Law School and Ours." *Yale Law Journal* 104 (May): 1852–1873

Burton, Steven L.
1985   *An Introduction to Law and Legal Reasoning*. Boston: Little, Brown.

Calabresi, Guido
1982   *A Common Law for the Age of Statutes*. Cambridge, MA: Harvard University Press.

Caldeira, Gregory A.
1986   "Neither Purse Nor the Sword: Dynamics of Public Confidence in the Supreme Court." *American Political Science Review* 80 (Dec.): 1209–1226.

Calder, Norman
1993   *Studies in Early Muslim Jurisprudence*. New York: Oxford University Press.

Cannon, Mark W.
1982   "Innovation in the Administration of Justice, 1969–1981: An Overview." In *The Politics of Judicial Reform*, edited by Philip L. Dubois, pp. 35–48. Lexington, MA: D.C. Heath.

Cantor, Norman F.
1999   *Imagining the Law: Common Law and the Foundations of the American Legal System*. New York: HarperCollins.

Caplan, Lincoln
　1987　*The Tenth Justice: The Solicitor General and the Rule of Law*. New York: Knopf.

Cardarelli, Alpert P. and Stephen C. Hicks
　1994　"Radicalism in Law and Criminology: A Retrospective View of Critical Legal Studies and Radical Criminology." *Journal of Criminal Law and Criminology* 84: 502–553.

Cardozo, Benjamin N.
　1924　*The Growth of the Law*. New Haven, CT: Yale University Press.

Carlson, Jill M.
　1993　"Restorative Justice: Beyond Crime and Punishment." Master of science thesis, Mankato State University, Minnesota.

Carns, Teresa White
　1992　"Alaska's Ban on Plea Bargaining Reevaluated." *Judicature* 75 (April–May): 310–317.

Carp, Robert A., and Ronald Stidham
　1993　*Judicial Process in America*. Washington, DC: Congressional Quarterly.
　1985　*The Federal Courts*. Washington, DC: Congressional Quarterly.

Carson, Gerald
　1978　*A Good Day at Saratoga*. Chicago: American Bar Association.

Carter, Lief H.
　1985　*Contemporary Constitutional Lawmaking*. New York: Pergamon.
　1984　*Reason in Law*, 2d ed. Boston: Little, Brown.
　1983　*Administrative Law and Politics*. Boston: Little, Brown.

Carter, Lief H. and Christine B. Harrington
　2000　*Administrative Law and Politics*. New York: Longman.

Case, Stephen
　1984　"Lawyers Are Often Grossly Overpaid." *New York Times* (Dec. 2): F2.

Casper, Jonathan
　1978　*Criminal Courts: The Defendant's Perspective: Executive Summary*. Washington, DC: U.S. Government Printing Office.

Center for Court Innovation (CCI)
　n.d　*How It Works*. New York: CCI.

Central Office of Information
　1976　*The Legal System of Britain*. London, England: Her Majesty's Stationery Office.

Chambers, Marcia
　1986　"California's Private Courts Are Swift." *New York Times* (Feb. 24): 9.

Champion, Dean J.
　1989　"Private Counsels and Public Defenders: A Look at Weak Cases, Prior Records, and Leniency in Plea Bargaining." *Journal of Criminal Justice* 17: 253–263.

Chapin, Bradley
　1983　*Criminal Justice in Colonial America: 1606–1660*. Athens: University of Georgia Press.

Chemerinsky, Edwin
　1998　"Prosecutorial Immunity: The Interpretation Continues." *Trial* 34 (3): 80–83.

Cherovsky, Erwin
　1991　*The Guide to New York Law Firms*. New York: St. Martin's Press.

Chira, Susan
　1987　"If You Insist on Your Day in Court, You May Wait and Wait and Wait." *New York Times* (Sept. 1): 4.

Choate, Rufus
　1962　"The Positions and Functions of the American Bar." In *The Legal Mind in America, From Independence to the Civil War*, edited by Perry Miller, pp. 258–273. Garden City, NY: Anchor.

Chroust, Anton-Hermann
　1965　*The Rise of the Legal Profession in America, Vol. 2*. Norman: University of Oklahoma Press.

Coffin, Frank M.
　1994　*On Appeal: Courts, Lawyering, and Judging*. New York: Norton.

Cohn, Bob
　1991　"The Lawsuit Cha-Cha." *Newsweek* (August 26): 58–59.

Conley, John J.
1991 "Natural Law." Letter to the *New York Times* (August 2): 14.

Conner, Ross F., and Ray Surette
1977 *The Citizen Dispute Settlement Program: Resolving Disputes Outside the Courts—Orlando, Florida*. Chicago: American Bar Association.

Cook, Royer F., Janice A. Roehl, and David I. Sheppard
1980 *Neighborhood Justice Centers Field Test: Executive Summary*. Washington, DC: U.S. Government Printing Office.

Cooke, Lawrence H.
1982 "Mediation: A Boon or a Bust?" In *Mediation in the Justice System*, edited by Maria R. Volpe, Thomas F. Christian, and Joyce E. Kowalewski, pp. 3–17. Chicago: American Bar Association.

Cooley, John W.
1986 "Arbitration vs. Mediation—Explaining the Differences." *Judicature* (Feb.–March): 263–269.

Cooper, Philip J.
1988 *Hard Judicial Choices: Federal District Court Judges and State and Local Officials*. New York: Oxford University Press.

Coquillette, Daniel R., Mary P. Squiers, and Stephen N. Subrin
1989 "The Role of Local Rules." *ABA Journal* (Jan.): 62-65.

Cornelius, Frank
1994 "Crushed By My Own Reform." *New York Times* (October 7): 15.

Cosgrove, Richard A.
1987 *Our Lady, the Common Law: An Anglo-American Legal Community, 1870–1930*. New York: New York University Press.

Costikyan, Edward
1966 *Behind Closed Doors*. New York: Harcourt, Brace and World.

Cottrol, Robert J.
1996 "Outlawing Outcasts: Comparative Perspectives on the Differing Functions of the Criminal Law of Slavery in the Americas." *Cardozo Law Review* 18 (November): 717–752.

Council for Public Interest Law
1976 *Balancing the Scales of Justice: Financing Public Interest Law in America*. Washington, DC: Council for Public Interest Law.

"Court Allows Challenge to Bias Ruling to Continue"
1989 *New York Times* (June 6): 25.

Court Appointed Special Advocates: A Voice for Abused and Neglected Children in Court
1997 Washington, DC: United States Department of Justice.

Court Statistics Project
1999 *State Court Caseload Statistics, 1998*. National Center for State Courts.

Cox, Archibald
1987 *The Court and the Constitution*. New York: Houghton Mifflin.

Cox, Michael P.
1975 "Discretion: A Twentieth Century Mutation." *Oklahoma Law Review* 28: 311–332.

Craft, Randal R., Jr.
1989 "Put Limits on Death Compensation." *New York Times* (Oct. 8): Sec. 3: 2.

Criminal Defense Systems
1984 Washington, DC: U.S. Government Printing Office.

Cunningham, Richard F.
1989 "Selling of Jury Deliberations: Commentaries on the Issue." *Criminal Justice Ethics* 8 (Winter/Spring): 27–30.

Curran, Barbara A.
1986 "American Lawyers in the 1980s: A Profession in Transition." *Law and Society Review* 20: 19–52.

Currie, David P.
1990 *The Constitution in the Supreme Court: The Second Century, 1888–1986*. Chicago: University of Chicago Press.

1985 *The Constitution in the Supreme Court: The First Hundred Years: 1789–1888*. Chicago: University of Chicago Press.

Curtis, Michael K.
1986 *No State Shall Abridge: The Fourteenth Amendment and the Bill of Rights.* Durham, NC: Duke University Press.

Cutler, Brian L. and Steven D. Penrod
1995 *Mistaken Identification: The Eyewitness, Psychology and the Law.* New York: Cambridge University Press.

Damâska, Mirjan R.
1986 *The Faces of Justice and State Authority: A Comparative Approach to the Legal Process.* New Haven, CT: Yale University Press.

Daniels, Stephen and Joanne Martin
1995 *Civil Juries and the Politics of Reform.* Evanston, IL: Northwestern University Press.

Darnton, John
1993 "England's Judges (and Hiring System) Under Fire." *New York Times* (July 18): 3.

Darwin, Charles
1859 *On the Origin of Species by Means of Natural Selection.* London, England: Murray.
n.d. *The Descent of Man.* New York: Modern Library. Originally published in 1871.

Dawson, John M.
1992 *Prosecutors in State Courts, 1990.* Washington, DC: Bureau of Justice Statistics.

Dawson, John P.
1961 "The Functions of the Judge." In *Talks on American Law*, edited by Harold J. Berman, pp. 18–28. New York: Vintage Books.

DeFrances, Carole J. and Kevin J. Strom
1997 *Juveniles Prosecuted in State Criminal Courts.* Washington, DC: Bureau of Justice Statistics.

DeFrances, Carol J. and Marika F. X. Litras
2000 *Indigent Defense Services in Large Counties, 1999.* Washington, DC: Office of Justice Programs.

DeFrances, Carol J., Steven K. Smith, and Louise van der Does
1996 *Prosecutors in State Courts, 1994.* Washington, DC: Bureau of Justice Statistics.

DeFrances, Carol J., Steven K. Smith, Patrick A. Langan, Brian J. Ostrom, David B. Rottman, and John A. Goerdt

1995 *Civil Jury Cases and Verdicts in Large Counties.* Washington, DC: Bureau of Justice Statistics.

Degler, Carl N.
1991 *In Search of Human Nature: The Decline and Revival of Darwinism in American Social Thought.* New York: Oxford University Press.

DeLappa, Fred
1983 *Resolving Disputes: An Alternative Approach.* Chicago: American Bar Association.

Dershowitz, Alan M.
2001 *Supreme Injustice: How the High Court Hijacked Election 2000.* New York: Oxford University Press.
1983 *The Best Defense.* New York: Vintage Books.

De Tocqueville, Alexis
1956 *Democracy in America.* New York: New American Library. Originally published in 1835.

Dictionary of Criminal Justice Data Terminology
1981 Washington, DC: U.S. Government Printing Office.

DiLorenzo, Thomas
1988 *The Anti-Business Campaign of the Legal Services Corporation.* St. Louis, MO: Center for the Study of American Business.

Dold, R. Bruce
1989 "Law Firms Hiring Few Minorities." *Chicago Tribune* (May 8): 1, 8.

Dorsett, Lyle W.
1968 *The Pendergast Machine.* New York: Oxford University Press.

Draper, Israel
1989 *Crime and Punishment in the Ancient World.* Lexington, Massachusetts: DC Heath. Originally published in 1865.

"Drive-by Legal Defense"
2001 *New York Times* editorial (April 12): 26.

The Drug Court Movement
1995 Washington, DC: National Institute of Justice.

Dubois, Philip L., ed.
1982 *The Politics of Judicial Reform.* Lexington, MA; D.C. Heath.

1982   *The Analysis of Judicial Reform*. Lexington, MA: D.C. Heath.

Ducat, Craig R.
2000   *Constitutional Interpretation*, 7ed. Belmont, CA: West.

Dullea, Georgia
1986   "Using Mediators to Resolve Family Disputes." *New York Times* (April 21): 17.

Dworkin, Ronald
1986   *Law's Empire*. Cambridge, MA: Harvard University Press.
1985   *A Matter of Principle*. Cambridge, MA: Harvard University Press.

Earle, Edward M.
1937   "Introduction" to *The Federalist*. New York: New Modern Library.

Easterbrook, Frank H.
1992   "Plea Bargaining as Compromise." *Yale Law Journal* 101: 1969–1978.

"Editorial"
1964   *Journal of the American Judicature Society* 48: 124–125.

Edmunds, Palmer D.
1959   *Law and Civilization*. Washington, DC: Public Affairs Press.

Eichenwald, Kurt
1994   "Lawyers Receiving $22.6 Million of Prudential Settlement." *New York Times* (May 20): C2
1993   "Millions for Us, Pennies for You." *New York Times* (December 19): Sec. 3: 1, 12.

Eisenberg, Melvin A.
1988   *The Nature of the Common Law*. Cambridge, MA: Harvard University Press.

Eisenstein, James
1978   *Counsel for the United States: U.S. Attorneys in the Political and Legal Systems*. Baltimore, MD: Johns Hopkins University Press.

Eisenstein, James, Roy B. Flemming, and Peter F. Nardulli
1988   *The Contours of Justice: Communities and Their Courts*. Boston: Little, Brown.

Eissman, Mark, and Joseph R. Tybor
1985   "Plea Bargaining Declines." *Chicago Tribune* (Nov. 3): 1, 18.

Elias, Stephen
1989   *Legal Research: How to Find and Understand the Law*. Berkeley, CA: Nolo Press.

Elias, T. Olawale
1956   *The Nature of African Customary Law*. Manchester, England: Manchester University Press.

Emanuel, Steve
2000a *Constitutional Law*. Larchmont, NY: Emanuel Publishing Corp.
2000b *Civil Procedure*. Larchmont, NY: Emanuel Publishing Corp.

Emerson, Deborah D.
1984   *The Role of the Grand Jury and the Preliminary Hearing in Pretrial Screening*. Washington, DC: U.S. Government Printing Office.
1983   *Grand Jury Reform: A Review of Key Issues*. Washington, DC: U.S. Government Printing Office.

Emmelman, Debra S.
1996   "Trial by Plea Bargain: Case Settlement as a Product of Recursive Decision-Making." *Law and Society Review* 30 (No. 2): 335–360.

Empey, LaMar, ed.
1979   *Juvenile Justice: The Progressive Legacy and Current Reforms*. Charlottesville: University Press of Virginia.

Engelhardt, Laura
1999   "The Problem with Eyewitness Testimony: A Commentary on a Talk by George Fisher and Barbara Tversky." *Standford Journal of Legal Studies* 1 (December): 25–29.

Eskridge, William N., Jr.
1994   *Dynamic Statutory Interpretation*. Cambridge, MA: Harvard University Press.

Eskridge, William N., Jr., Philip P. Frickey, and Elizabeth Garrett
2000   *Legislation and Statutory Interpretation*. New York: Foundation Press.

Evan, William M., ed.
1962 *Law and Sociology: Exploratory Essays.* Glencoe IL: Free Press.

Fabricant, Michael
1983 *Juveniles in the Family Courts.* Lexington, MA: D.C. Heath.

Farber, Daniel A. and Philip P. Frickey
1991 *Law and Public Choice: A Critical Introduction.* Chicago: University of Chicago Press.

Farrand, Max
1967 *The Records of the Federal Convention of 1787* (three volumes). New Haven, CT: Yale University Press.

Fatsis, Stefan
1990 "Investor Challenges Arbitration Process on Losses." Chicago Tribune (Jan. 22), Sec. 4: 3.

Feder, Barnaby J.
1993 "The Unorthodox Behemoth of Law Firms." *New York Times* (March 14): Sec. 3: 1, 6.

Federalist, Papers The
1937 New York: New Modern Library. (Originally published in 1788.)

Federal Judicial Center (FJC)
1997 *Mediation and Conference Programs in the Federal Courts of Appeals: A Sourcebook for Judges and Lawyers.* Washington, DC: FJC via Internet.
1985 *The Roles of Magistrates: Nine Case Studies.* Washington, DC: U.S. Government Printing Office.

Feeley, Malcolm M.
1997 "Legal Complexity and the Transformation of The Criminal Process: The Origins of Plea Bargaining." *Israel Law Review* 31 (Winter–Summer): Internet.
1984 "Legal Realism." In *The Guide to American Law: Everyone's Legal Encyclopedia*, pp. 129–131. St. Paul, MN: West.
1979 *The Process Is Punishment: Handling Cases in a Lower Court.* New York: Russell Sage Foundation.

Feeney, Floyd, Forrest Dill, and Adrianne Weir
1983 *Arrests Without Conviction: How Often They Occur and Why.* Washington, D.C.: U.S. Government Printing Office.

Feinblatt, John, Greg Berman, Michele Sviridoff
1998 *Neighborhood Justice.* New York: Center for Court Innovation.

Feld, Barry C.
1992 "Criminalizing the Juvenile Court: A Research Agenda for the 1990s." In *Juvenile Justice and Public Policy: Toward a National Agenda*, edited by Ira M. Schwartz, 59–88. Lexington, MA: Lexington Books.

Feldstein, Thomas M., and Stephen B. Presser
1984 "David Dudley Field." *The Guide to American Law: Everyone's Legal Encyclopedia.* St. Paul, MN: West.

Female Resource Center
1979 *Little Sisters and the Law.* Washington, D.C.: U.S. Government Printing Office.

Ferguson, Robert A.
1984 *Law and Letters in American Culture.* Cambridge, MA: Harvard University Press.

Ferkenhoff, Eric
2001 "Cops Find, Then Lose Widow's Jewelry." Chicago Tribune (March 3): 1, 8.

Field, David Dudley
1965 "The Index of Civilization." In *The Golden Age of American Law*, edited by Charles H. Haar, pp. 30–47. New York: George Braziller.

Finckenauer, James O.
1984 *Juvenile Delinquency and Corrections: The Gap Between Theory and Practice.* New York: Academic Press.

Firestone, David
1999 "Alabama Acts to Limit Huge Awards by Juries." *New York Times* (June 2): 14.

Fisher, George
2000 "Plea Bargaining's Triumph." *Yale Law Review* 109 (March): 857–1086.

Fisher, William W., III, Morton J. Horwitz, and Thomas A. Reed, eds.
2000 *American Legal Realism.* New York: Oxford University Press.

Fishman, James J.
1979 "The Social and Occupational Mobility of Prosecutors: New York City." In *The Prosecutor*, edited by William F. McDonald, pp. 239–254. Beverly Hills, CA: Sage.

Flango, Victor E. and Carol R. Flango
1997 "A Taxonomy of Appellate Court Jurisdiction." *Caseload Highlights* 3 (July): 1–4.

Flemming, Roy B.
1988 "Client Games: Defense Attorney Perspectives on Their Relations with Criminal Clients." In *Criminal Justice: Law and Politics*, edited by George F. Cole, pp. 228–252. Pacific Grove, CA: Brooks/Cole.

Foschio. Leslie G.
1999 "A History of the Development of the Office of United States Commissioner and Magistrate Judge System." *Federal Courts Law Review* 4. Internet.

Foster, James C.
1985 "Legal Education and the Production of Lawyers to (Re)Produce Liberal Capitalism." *Legal Studies Forum* 9: 179–211.

France, Anatole
1927 *The Red Lily*. Trans. by Winifred Stephens. New York: Dodd, Mead.

Franck, Thomas M.
1992 *Political Questions/Judicial Answers. Does the Rule of Law Apply to Foreign Affairs?* Princeton, NJ: Princeton University Press.

Frank, Jerome
1970 *Law and the Modern Mind*. Gloucester, MA: Peter Smith. (Originally published in 1930.)

Frankel, Marvin E., and Gary P. Naftalis
1977 *The Grand Jury: Institution on Trial*. New York: Hill and Wang.

Franklin, Tim
1985 "State to Seek Funds to Replace Bungling Lab." *Chicago Tribune* (Aug. 18): Sec. 3: 1.

Freedman, Monroe H.
1975 *Lawyers' Ethics in an Adversary System*. Indianapolis, IN: Bobbs–Merrill.

Freitag, Michael
1989 "Law Firms Lift Income Aided by Takeover Fees." *New York Times* (July 6): 25.

Freund, Paul A.
1961 "The Supreme Court." In *Talks on American Law*, edited by Harold J. Berman, pp. 71–84. New York: Vintage Books.

Fried, Charles
1991 *Order and Law: Arguing the Reagan Revolution—A Firsthand Account*. New York: Simon and Schuster.

Friedenthal, Jack H., Mary Kay Kane, and Arthur R. Miller
1985 *Civil Procedure*. St. Paul, MN: West.

Friedman, Lawrence M.
1984 *American Law*. New York: Norton.
1979 "Plea Bargaining in Historical Perspective." *Law and Society Review* 7: 247–259.
1973 *A History of American Law*. New York: Simon and Schuster.

Friend of the Constitution
1990 "Congress, the President, and Judicial Selection: Lessons from the Reagan Years." In *Judicial Selection: Merit, Ideology, and Politics*, edited by Henry J. Abraham, Eugene W. Hickok, Jr., and William Bradford Reynolds, pp. 49–58. Washington, DC: National Legal Center for the Public Interest.

Fritsch, Jane and David Rohde
2001a "Lawyers Often Fail New York's Poor." *New York Times* (April 8): 1, 27.
2001b "Caseloads Push System to Breaking Point." *New York Times* (April 9): 1, 16.

Frug, Jerry
1986 "Henry James, Lee Marvin and the Law." *New York Times Book Reviews* (Feb. 16): 1, 28–30.

Fuchs, Joseph
1965 *Natural Law: A Theological Investigation*. New York: Sheed and Ward.

Fuller, Lon L.
1961 "The Adversary System." In *Talks on American Law*, edited by Harold J. Berman, pp. 30–43. New York: Vintage Books.

Fund for Modern Courts
  1986   *The Illusion of Democracy: New York City Civil Court Elections, 1980–1985*. New York: Fund for Modern Courts, Inc.

Furchgott, Roy
  1997   "Opposition Builds to Mandatory Arbitration at Work." *New York Times* (July 20): F11.

Gac, Edward J.
  1988   "The Socratic Method in Undergraduate Education: Overcoming the Law School Image." *Focus on Law Studies* 3 (Spring): 3, 5.

Galanter, Marc
  1989   "Adjudication, Litigation and Related Phenomena." In *American Court Systems: Readings in Judicial Process and Behavior*, edited by Sheldon Goldman and Austin Sarat, pp. 106–111. New York: Longman.

Galanter, Marc and Thomas Palay
  1991   *Tournament of Lawyers: The Transformation of the Big Law Firm*. Chicago: University of Chicago Press.

Gallagher, Maggie
  1988   "Legal Disservices: The New Serfs." *National Review* (August 5): 42–43, 56.

Gavzer, Bernard
  1997   "Are Trial Consultants Good for Justice?" *Parade* (January 5): 20.
  1996   "Why Some Doctors May Be Hazardous to Your Health." *Parade* (April 14): 4–7.

Gawande, Atul
  2001   "Under Suspicion: The Fugitive Science of Criminal Justice." *New Yorker* (January 8): 50–53.

Gebelein, Richard S.
  2000   *The Rebirth of Rehabilitation: Promise and Perils of Drug Courts*. Washington, DC: Office of Justice Programs.

Gehm, John R.
  1998   "Victim-Offender Mediation Programs: An Exploration of Practice and Theoretical Frameworks." *Western Criminology Review* 1 (1): Internet.

George, Robert P.
  2000   "Introduction." *Great Cases in Constitutional Law*. Princeton, NJ: Princeton University Press.

Gerber, Richard Allan
  1981   "The Reinterpretation of the Due Process Clause of Fourteenth Amendment in the Age of Industrialization." In *American Industrialization, Economic Expansion, and the Law*, edited by Joseph R. Frese and Jacob Judd, pp. 143–209. Tarrytown, NY: Sleepy Hollow Press.

Gerber, Rudolph, J.
  1989   *Lawyers, Courts, and Professionalism: The Agenda for Reform*. Westport, CT: Greenwood.

Gershman, Bennett L.
  2002   "A Moral Standard for the Prosecutor's Exercise of the Charging Decision." In *Criminal Courts for the 21st Century*, edited by Lisa Stolzenberg and Steward J. D. D'Alessio, pp. 57–72. Upper Saddle River, NJ: Prentice Hall.

Gest, Ted
  1993   "Doing Good is Doing Well." *U.S. News & World Report* (March 22): 60–61.

Giannelli. Paul C.
  1994   "When the Evidence Is a Matter of Life and Death." *New York Times* (August 21): E15

Gillers, Stephen
  1996   "The American Legal Profession." In *Fundamentals of American Law*, edited by Alan B. Morrison, pp. 151–176. New York: Oxford University Press.

Gilmore, Grant
  1977   *The Ages of American Law*. New Haven, CT: Yale University Press.

Glaberson, William
  2001a "Juries, Their Powers Under Siege, Find Their Role is Being Eroded." *New York Times* (March 2): 1, 15.
  2001b "A Study's Verdict: Jury Awards Are Not Out of Control." *New York Times* (August 6): 9.
  2000a "Fierce Campaigns Signal a New Era for State Courts." *New York Times* (June 5): 1, 22.
  2000b "A Spirited Campaign for Ohio Court Puts Judges on New Terrain." *New York Times* (July 7): 11.

2000c "States Rein in Truth-Bending in Court Races." *New York Times* (August 23): 1, 16.

2000d "Chief Justices to Meet on Abuses in Judicial Races." *New York Times* (September 8): 12.

2000e "To Bear or Not to Bear: It Depends on How You Read History." *New York Times* (September 24): WK 7.

1999 "State Courts Sweeping Away Laws Curbing Suits for Injury." *New York Times* (July 16): 1, 13.

1990a "Confronting Assembly-Line Justice: Tumult in New York's Courtrooms." *New York Times* (Jan. 16): 12.

1990b "Caught in the Nightmare of New York City's Holding Pens." *New York Times* (March 23): B10.

Glater, Jonathan D.
2001a "Women Are Close to Being Majority of Law Students." *New York Times* (March 26): 1, 16.

2001b "Law Firms Are Slow in Promoting Minority Lawyers to Partner Role." *New York Times* (August 7): 1, C2.

Glendon, Mary Ann
1994 *A Nation Under Lawyers*. Cambridge, MA: Harvard University Press.

Glenn, H. Patrick
2000 *Legal Traditions of the World*. New York: Oxford University Press.

Glick, Henry R.
1983 *Courts, Politics, and Justice*. New York: McGraw-Hill.

1982 "The Politics of State-Court Reform." In *The Politics of Judicial Reform*, edited by Philip L. Dubois, pp.17–33. Lexington, MA: D.C. Heath.

Gluckman, Max
1955 *The Judicial Process among the Bartose of Northern Rhodesia*. Manchester, England: Manchester University Press.

Goff, Lisa
1989 "Firms See Hot Commodity in Prosecutors." *Crain's Chicago Business* (Feb. 20): 3, 29.

Goldkamp, John S., Doruis Weiland, and Cherly Irons-Guynn
2001 *Developing an Evaluation Plan for Community Courts: Assessing the Hartford Community Court Model*. Washington, D.C.: Bureau of Justice Assistance.

Goldman, Sheldon, and Thomas P. Jahnige
1985 The *Federal Courts as a Political System*. New York: McGraw-Hill.

Goldman, Sheldon, and Austin Sarat, eds.
1989 *American Court Systems: Readings in Judicial Process and Behavior*. New York: Longman.

Goldstein, Abraham S.
1996 "Converging Criminal Justice Systems: Guilty Pleas and the Public Interest." *SMU Law Review* 49 (March/April): 567–577.

Gollner, Philipp M.
1994 "Consulting by Peering into Minds of Jurors." *New York Times* (January 7): B11.

Goodman, James
1994 *Stories of Scottsboro*. New York: Pantheon.

Goodrich, Chris
1991 *Anarchy and Elegance: Confessions of a Journalist at Yale Law School*. Boston: Little, Brown.

Goozner, Merrill
1992 "Courts Add to Pain of Pollution Victims." *Chicago Tribune* (February 13): 23, 26.

Gordon, John Steele
1991 "Reforming the Law." *American Heritage* (September): 18–20.

Gorr, Michael
2000 "The Morality of Plea Bargaining." *Social Theory and Practice* 26 (Spring): Internet.

Gould, Carole
1986 "When to Turn to a No-Frills Law Firm." *New York Times* (Nov. 9): F15.

Gourevitch, Philip
2001 "The Crime Lover." *New Yorker* (February 19 and 26): 160–173.

Granfield, Robert
1986 "Legal Education as Corporate Ideology." *Sociological Forum* I: 514–523.

Granfield, Robert and Thomas Koenig
1992 "Learning Collective Eminence: Harvard Law School and the Production of Elite Lawyers." *Sociological Quarterly* 33: 503–520.

Gray, Jerry
  1993   "Trenton Court Upholds Senate's 'Courtesy' Veto." *New York Times* (December 24): 10.

Greenhouse, Linda
  2001a   "The High Court's Target: Congress." *New York Times* (February 25): WK 3.
  2001b   "Punitive Damages Must Get a Searching Review on Appeal, Justices Rule." *New York Times* (May 15): 18.
  2001c   "Justices Try to Determine the Meaning of Disability." *New York Times* November 8): 16.
  2000   "The High Court Rules; the Law of the Land Changes." *New York Times* (July 2): WK 1, 5.
  1999   "States Are Given New Legal Shelf by Supreme Court." *New York Times* (June 24): 1, 22.
  1996a   "Taking States Seriously." *New York Times* (April 14): E3.
  1996b   "How Congress Curtailed the Courts' Jurisdiction." *New York Times* (October 27): E5.
  1994   "High Court Opens Its Fall Session by Refusing Cases. *New York Times* (October 4): 1, 10.
  1993a   "Life and Times." *New York Times Magazine* (March 7): 84.
  1993b   "Has the Supreme Court Become Irrelevant? Or Will History Again Demand to Be Written There?" *New York Times* (September 10): B10.
  1991a   "Justices Back Shareholders' Suits." *New York Times* (May 21): C7.
  1991b   "A Longtime Precedent for Disregarding Precedent." *New York Times* (July 21): E4.
  1991c   "Conservatively Speaking, It's an Activist Supreme Court." *New York Times* (May 26): E1, E3.
  1990   "As Curtain Is Lifted, Rehnquist Is Off Cue." *New York Times* (March 16): 8.
  1989   "High Court's Reticence Raises Questions of Rules." *New York Times* (Nov. 22): 11.

Grossman, Joel B.
  1965   *Lawyers and Judges: The ABA and the Politics of Judicial Selection*. New York: Wiley.

Guidorizzi, Douglas D.
  1998   "Should We Really 'Ban' Plea Bargaining? The Core Concerns of Plea Bargaining Critics." *Emory Law Journal* 47 (Spring): 754–783.

Guinier, Lani
  1997   *Becoming Gentlmen: Women, Law School, and Institutional Change*. Boston: Beacon Press.

Grunson, Lindsey
  1986   "Tiny Delaware's Corporate Clout." *New York Times* (June 1): F6.
  1983   "Second Opinions on Medical Examiners." *New York Times* (May 15): E6.

Grutman, Roy and Bill Thomas
  1990   *Lawyers and Thieves*. New York: Simon and Schuster.

Gulati, Mitu and C.M.A. McCauliff
  1998   "On Not Making Law." *Law and Contemporary Problems* 15 (Summer): Internet.

Gutman, Amy, ed.
  1998   *A Matter of Interpretation. Federal Courts and the Law: Antonin Scalia*. Princeton, NJ: Princeton University Press.

Haar, Charles M.
  1986   "Need Services? Try Common Law." *New York Times* (May 14): 25.

Haar, Charles M., ed.
  1965   *The Golden Age of American Law*. New York: George Braziller.

Haar, Charles M., and Daniel W. Fessler
  1986   *Fairness and Justice: Law in the Service of Equality*. New York: Touchstone.

Haley, John Owen
  1991   *Authority Without Power: Law and the Japanese Paradox*. New York: Oxford University Press.

Hall, Kermit L.
  1989   *The Magic Mirror: Law in American History*. New York: Oxford University Press.

Hall, Kermit, William M. Wiecek, and Paul Finkelman, eds.
  1991   *American Legal History: Cases and Materials*. New York: Oxford University Press.

Hamilton, Alexander, John Jay, and James Madison
  1937   *The Federalist Papers*. New York: New Modern Library. (Originally published in 1788.)

Hamilton, Walter H.
  1999   "The Path of Due Process of Law." In *The Lanahan Readings in Civil Rights and Civil Liberties*, edited by David M. O'Brien, pp. 3–19. Baltimore: Lanahan Publishers.

Handlin, Oscar, and Lillian Handlin
1982 *A Restless People: Americans in Rebellion, 1770–1787*. Garden City, NY: Doubleday.

Hanna, Janan and Eric Ferkenhoff
2001 "Hillard Orders Probe After Cocaine Evidence Disappears." *Chicago Tribune* (April 21): 1, 18.

Hans, Valerie P., and Neil Vidmar
1986 *Judging the Jury*. New York: Plenum.

Harlow, Caroline Wolf
2000 *Defense Counsel in Criminal Cases*. Washington, DC: Office of Justice Programs.

Harmon, Amy
1998 "The Law Where There is no Land." *New York Times* (March 16): C1, 9.

Harper, Robert Francis
1904 *The Code of Hammurabi*. Chicago: University of Chicago Press.

Harrell, Mary Ann, and Burnett Anderson
1982 *Equal Justice Under Law: The Supreme Court in American Life*. Washington, DC: The Supreme Court Historical Society.

Harrington, Christine B.
1985 *Shadow Justice: The Ideology and Institutionalization of Alternatives to Court*. Westport, CT: Greenwood.

Hart, H.L.A.
1961 *The Concept of Law*. Oxford, England: Clarendon Press.

Hartnett, Edward A.
1999 "A Matter of Judgment: Not a Matter of Opinion." *New York University Law Review* 74 (April): 123–160.

Hastie, Reid, Steven D. Penrod, and Nancy Pennington
1983 *Inside the Jury*. Cambridge, MA: Harvard University Press.

Hay, Bruce L.
1994 "Civil Discovery: Its Effects and Optimal Scope." *Journal of Legal Studies* 23 (January): 481–515.

Hazard, Geoffrey C., Jr. and Michele Taruffo
1993 *American Civil Procedure: An Introduction*. New Haven, CT: Yale University Press.

Heilbroner, David
1990 *Rough Justice: Days and Nights of a Young D.A.* New York: Dell.

Heinz, John P., and Edward O. Laumann
1982 *Chicago Lawyers: The Social Structure of the Bar*. Chicago: Russell Sage Foundation and the American Bar Association.

Henderson, Thomas A., Cornelius M. Kerwin, Randall Guynes, Carl Baar, Neal Miller, Hildy Saizow, and Robert Grieser
1984 *The Significance of Judicial Structure: The Effect of Unification on Trial Court Operations*. Washington, DC: U.S. Government Printing Office.

Henley, Patricia
1996 "Improving the Jury System: Peremptory Challenges." *Public Law Research Institute Reports* (Spring): Internet.

Henriques, Diana B.
1995 "Top Business Court Under Fire." *New York Times* (May 23): C1, C6.

Henry, James F.
1985 "Alternative Dispute Resolution: Meeting the Legal Needs of the 1980s." *Ohio State Journal on Dispute Resolution* 1 (Fall): 113–120.

Herget, James E.
1990 *American Jurisprudence: 1870–1970*. Houston, TX: Rice University Press.

Hensler, Deborah R., Bonnie Dombey-Moore, Beth Giddens, Jennifer Gross, Erik K. Moller, and Nicholas M. Pace
1999 *Class Action Dilemmas: Pursuing Public Goals for Private Gain*. Executive Summary. Santa Monica: RAND.

Hepburn, John R., C. Wayne Johnston, and Scott Rogers
1994 *Do Drugs, Do Time: An Evaluation of the Maricopa County Demand Reduction Program*. Washington, DC: National Institute of Justice.

Herget, James E.
1990 *American Jurisprudence: 1870–1970*. Houston, TX: Rice University Press.

Heumann, Milton
1978 *Plea Bargaining*. Chicago: University of Chicago Press.

Heymann, Philip B., and William H. Kenety
1985 *The Murder Trial of Wilbur Jackson*. 2d ed. St. Paul, MN: West.

Hinds, Michael deCourcy
1994 "Compiling Data, and Giving Odds, on Jury Awards." *New York Times* (January 21): B12.

Hines, Crystal Nix
2001a "Competition Sprouts One-Stop Law Firms," *New York Times* (May 31): C1, 7.
2001b "Without a Lawyer." *New York Times* (July 31): C1.

Hittinger, Russell
1998 "Introduction" to Heinrich A. Rommen, *The Natural Law: A Study in Legal and Social History and Philosophy*. Indianapolis: Liberty Fund.

Hobson, Wayne K.
1986 *The American Legal Profession and the Organizational Society: 1890–1930*. New York: Garland Publishing.

Hoebel, E. Adamson
1974 *The Law of Primitive Man*. New York: Athenuem.

Hoffer, Peter Charles
1992 *Law and People in Colonial America*. Baltimore: John's Hopkins University Press.
1990 *The Law's Conscience: Equitable Constitutionalism in America*. Chapel Hill: University of North Carolina.

Hoffman, Jan
1998a "Police Tactics Chipping Away at Suspects' Rights." *New York Times* (March 26): 1, 21.
1998b "Police Refine Methods So Potent, Even the Innocent Have Confessed." *New York Times* (March 30): 1, 17.

Hoffman, Paul
1982 *Lions of the Eighties: The Inside Story of the Powerhouse Law Firms*. Garden City, NY: Doubleday.

Hogue, Arthur R.
1966 *Origins of the Common Law*. Bloomington: Indiana University Press.

Holland, Kenneth M.
1982 "The Twilight of Adversariness: Trends in Civil Justice." In *The Analysis of Judicial Reform*, edited by Philip L. Dubois, pp. 17–29. Lexington, MA: D.C. Heath.

Holmes, Steven A.
1996 "Pact Overhauls Accreditation of Law Schools." *New York Times* (June 28): 1, 9.

Honderich, Ted
1993 *How Free Are You? The Determinism Problem*. New York: Oxford University Press.

Horowitz, Donald L.
1977 *The Courts and Social Policy*. Washington, DC: Brookings Institution.

Horowitz, Morton J.
1977 *The Transformation of American Law, 1780–1860*. Cambridge, MA: Harvard University Press.

Howard, J. Woodford, Jr.
1981 *Courts of Appeal: A Study of the Second, Fifth, and District of Columbia Circuits*. Princeton, NJ: Princeton University Press.

Huff, C. Ronald, Arye Rattner, and Edward Sagarin
1996 *Convicted But Innocent: Wrongful Conviction and Public Policy*. Thousand Oaks, CA: Sage.

Hughes, Graham
1996 "Common Law Systems." In *Fundamentals of American Law*, edited by Alan B. Morrison, pp. 9–25. New York: Oxford University Press.

Hunt, Morton
1982 "Putting Juries on the Couch." *New York Times Magazine* (Nov. 28): 70–72, 78, 82, 86, 88.

Hurst, Hunter
1999 "Family Courts in the United States." *Family Court Bulletin* 1 (Fall): 1–5.

Hurst, James W.
1956 *Law and the Conditions of Freedom in the Nineteenth-Century United States*. Madison: University of Wisconsin Press.

1950   *The Growth of American Law: The Law Makers*. Boston: Little, Brown.

Hutchinson, Allan C., ed.
1989   *Critical Legal Studies*. Totowa, NJ: Rowman and Littlefield.
1988   *Dwelling on the Threshold: Critical Essays on Modern Legal Thought*. Toronto, Canada: Carswell.

Hyman, Harold M., and William M. Wiecek
1982   *Equal Justice Under Law: Constitutional Development 1835–1875*. New York: Harper and Row.

Illinois Criminal Justice Authority
1999   "Drug Court Provides Treatment Alternative to Incarceration." *On Good Authority* 2 (April): 1–4.

Israel, Jerold H., and Wayne LaFave
1980   *Criminal Procedure: Constitutional Limitations*. St. Paul, MN: West.

Jacob, Herbert, and James Eisenstein
1977   *Felony Justice*. Boston: Little, Brown.

Jacobs, Nancy F., and Ellen F. Chayet
1986   "Court Dynamics and Disposition Time: The Realities of Case Delay." Paper presented at the annual meeting of the American Society of Criminology, Oct. 30, in Atlanta, GA.

Jaffa, Harry V.
1988   "Judge Bork's Mistake." *National Review* (March 4): 38–40.

Janofsky, Michael
1999   "Baltimore's Push on Crime Creates a Backlog of Cases." *New York Times* (January 7): 14.

Jennings, Dianne
1989   "King of Torts." *Chicago Tribune* (July 25): Sec. 5: 1–2.

Johnson, Charles A., and Bradley C. Canon
1984   *Judicial Policies: Implementation and Impact*. Washington, DC: Congressional Quarterly.

Johnson, Earl, Jr.
1977   *Outside the Courts: A Survey of Diversion Alternatives in Civil Cases*. Denver, CO: National Center for the State Courts.

1974   *Justice and Reform: The Formative Years of the OEO Legal Services Program*. New York: Russell Sage.

Johnson, Kirk
1993   "Public Judges as Private Contractors: A Legal Frontier." *New York Times* (December 10): B9.
1986   "Lawyer Hires an Ex-Juror for Retrial." *New York Times* (Jan. 31): 15.

Johnson, Sally
1991   "Depositions by Witnesses Are Restricted in Vermont." *New York Times* (July 12): B7.

Johnston, David
1997   "Report Finds F.B.I. Lab Slipping from Pinnacle of Crime Fighting." *New York Times* (January 29): 1, 12.
1989   "A.B.A. to Resume Rating of Judicial Nominees." *New York Times* (June 1): 7.

Joint Committee on New York Drug Law Evaluation
1977   *The Nation's Toughest Drug Law: Evaluation of the New York City Experience*. New York: Association for the Bar of the City of New York.

Jones, David M.
1997   "Judicial Federalism and Prosecutorial Vindictiveness: State Responses to Bordenkircher and Goodwin." *Journal of Criminal Justice* 20 (1): 73–90.

"Judge Voids Suit on Harvard Hiring"
1991   *New York Times* (February 26): 12.

Kaczorowski, Robert J.
1987   "To Begin the Nation Anew: Congress, Citizenship, and Civil Rights after the Civil War." *American Historical Review* 92 (Feb.): 45–68.

Kagan, Robert A.
1994   "Do Lawyers Cause Adversarial Legalism? A Preliminary Inquiry." *Law and Social Inquiry* 19 (Winter): 1–62.

Kahlenberg, Richard D.
1992   *Broken Contract: A Memoir of Harvard Law School*. New York: Hill and Wang.

Kahn-Freund, Otto, Claudine Levy, and Bernard Rudden
1991   *A Source-Book on French Law. Public Law: Constitutional and Administrative Law. Private*

Law: Structure, Contract, 3rd ed. New York: Oxford University Press.

Kairys, David
1982 "Legal Reasoning." In *The Politics of Law: A Progressive Critique*, edited by David Kairys, pp. 11–17. New York: Pantheon.

Kalman, Laura
1986 *Legal Realism at Yale: 1927–1960*. Chapel Hill: University of North Carolina.

Kamisar, Yale, Wayne R. LaFave, and Jerold H. Israel
1986 *Basic Criminal Procedure*. St. Paul, MN: West.

Kant, Immanuel
1949 *Critique of Practical Reason*. Translated by Lewis White Beck. Chicago: University of Chicago Press.

Karp, David R.
2001 "Harm and Repair Observing Restorative Justice in Vermont." *Justice Quarterly* 18 (December): 727–757.

Kassberg, Maria
1989 "Alternative Dispute Resolution to the Rescue." *Update on Law-Related Education* 13 (Winter): 3–4, 64.

Katz, Stanley M.
1971 "The Politics of Law in Colonial America: Controversies over Chancery Courts and Equity Law in the Eighteenth Century." In *Law in American History*, edited by Donald Fleming and Bernard Bailyn, pp. 257–284. Cambridge, MA: Harvard University Press.

Kaufman, Irving R.
1986 "What Did the Founding Fathers Intend?" *New York Times Magazine* (Feb. 23): 42, 59–60, 67–69.

Kaufman, Leslie and Anne Underwood
1997 "Sign or Hit the Street." *Newsweek* (June 30): 48–49.

Kay, Fiona and John Hagan
1998 "Raising the Bar: The Gender Stratification of Law-Firm Capital." *American Sociological Review* 63 (October): 728–743.

Keeva, Steven
1993 "Unequal Partners." *ABA Journal* (February): 50–54.

Kelly, J. M.
1993 *A Short History of Western Legal Theory*. New York: Oxford University Press.

Kelman, Mark
1987 *A Guide to Critical Legal Studies*. Cambridge, MA: Harvard University Press.

Kendall, Peter
1991 "Indebted New Lawyers Shunning Public Service." *Chicago Tribune* (January 29): Sec. 3: 1, 2.

Kennedy, Duncan
1982 "Legal Education as Training for Hierarchy." In *The Politics of Law: A Progressive Critique*, edited by David Kairys, pp. 40–61. New York: Pantheon.

Kennedy, Leslie W.
1990 *On the Borders of Crime: Conflict Management and Criminology*. New York: Longman.

Kens, Paul
1990 *Judicial Power and Reform Politics: The Anatomy of Lochner v. New York*. Lawrence, KS: University of Kansas Press.

Kessler, Mark
1993 "Legal Discourse and Political Intolerance: The Ideology of Clear and Present Danger." *Law and Society Review* 27 (3): 559–597.

Kiernan, Louise
1997 "Trial: At Juvenile Court, an Ongoing Struggle to Mend Broken Lives." *Chicago Tribune Magazine* (January 19): 11–18.

King, Anthony
1997 "Running Scared." *Atlantic Monthly* (January): 41–61.

King, Nancy Jean
1999 "The American Criminal Jury." *Law and Contemporary Problems* 41 (Spring): Internet.

Kirby, Michael P.
1977 *The Effectiveness of the Point Scale*. Washington, DC: Pretrial Services Resource Center.

Kirschenbaum, Aaron

1991 *Equity in Jewish Law. Halakic Perspectives in Law: Formalism and Flexibility in Jewish Civil Law*. Hoboken, NJ: Ktav Publishing House.

Klein, Eric C.
1998 "Dennis the Menace or Billy the Kid: An Analysis of the Role of Transfer to Criminal Court in Juvenile Justice." *American Criminal Law Review* 35 (Winter): 371–401.

Kolata, Gina
1993 "When Court Decisions Vanish from the Record." *New York Times* (June 18): B12.

Kolbert, Elizabeth
1990 "In Civil Liberties Cases, New York's Court Leans on the State Constitution." *New York Times* (Jan. 8): 12.

Korobkin, Russell B. and Thomas S. Ulen
2000 "Law and Behavioral Science: Removing the Rationality Assumption from Law and Economics." *California Law Review* 88 (July): Internet.

Koski, John C.
1994 "Mandatory Disclosure: The New Rule That's Meant to Simplify Litigation Could Do Just the Opposite." *ABA Journal* (February): 85–87.

Kreindel, Burton, Robert H. Adams, Robert V.D. Campbell, Susan P. Hobart, and John P. Moreschi
1977 *Court Information Systems*. Washington, DC: U.S. Government Printing Office.

Kreinler, Lee S.
1989 "Monetary Awards Can Soothe the Pain." *New York Times* (Oct. 8): Sec. 3: 2.

Kress, Jack M.
1976 "Progress and Prosecution." *Annals* 423 (Jan.): 99–116.

Kritzer, Herbert M.
1996 "Courts, Justice, and Politics in England." In *Courts, Law and Politics in Comparative Perspective*, edited by Herbert Jacob et al., pp. 81–176. New Haven CT: Yale University Press.
1991 *Let's Make a Deal: Understanding the Negotiation Process in Ordinary Litigation*. Madison: University of Wisconsin Press.
1990 *The Justice Broker: Lawyers and Ordinary Litigation*. New York: Oxford University Press.

Kronman, Anthony J.
1993 *The Lost Lawyer: Failing Ideals of the Legal Profession*. Cambridge, MA: Harvard University Press.

Kumble, Steven J. and Kevin J. Lahart
1990 *Conduct Unbecoming: The Rise and Ruin of Finley, Kumble*. New York: Carroll & Graff.

Kunkle, Wolfgang
1972 *An Introduction to Roman Legal and Constitutional History*. England: Oxford University Press.

Kurki, Leena
1999 *Incorporating Restorative Justice and Community Justice into American Sentencing and Corrections*. Washington, DC: National Institute of Justice.

Kynge, James
2001 "China's Amateur Judges in the Dock." *Financial Times* (July 14–15): 4.

Labaton, Stephen
1992 "Solution to Wasteful Lawsuits Becomes a Problem." *New York Times* (June 14): E2.
1988a "Federal Court Rules Challenged after 50 Years." *New York Times* (Oct. 14): 23.
1988b "U.S. Law Firms Expand to Reach Global Clientele." *New York Times* (May 12): 1, 43.

Lacasse, Chantale and A. Abigail Payne
1999 "Federal Sentencing Guidelines and Mandatory Minimum Sentences: Do Defendants Bargain in the Shadow of the Judge?" *Journal of Law and Economics* 42 (April): 245–268.

Ladinsky, Jack
1963 "Careers of Lawyers, Law Practice, and Legal Institutions." *American Sociological Review* 28: 47–54.

Landon, Donald D.
1990 *Country Lawyers: The Impact of Context on Professional Practice*. New York: Praeger.

Landsman, Stephen
1999 "The Civil Jury In America." *Law and Contemporary Problems* 285 (Spring): Internet.
1993 "The History and Objectives of the Civil Jury System." In *Verdict: Assessing the Civil Jury System*, edited by Robert E. Litan, pp. 22–60. Washington, DC: Brookings Institution.

Lane, Eric
1999 "How to Read a Statute in New York: A Response to Judge Kaye and Some More." *Hofstra Law Review* 28 (Fall): 86–125.

Langdell, Christopher C.
1871 *A Selection of Cases on the Law of Contracts.* Boston: Little, Brown.

LaPiana, William P.
1994 *Logic and Experience: The Origin of Modern American Legal Education.* New York: Oxford University Press.

Lawrence, Susan E.
1990 *The Poor in Court: The Legal Services Program and Supreme Court Decision Making.* Princeton, NJ: Princeton University Press.

Law School Admission Council (LSAC)
1996 *The Official Guide to U.S. Law Schools.* New York: Bantam.
1995 *Thinking About Law School: A Minority Guide.* Newtown, PA: LSAC.

Lee, Eric
2000 *Community Courts: An Evolving Model.* Washington, DC: Office of Justice Programs.

Leeson, Susan M. and Bryan M. Johnston
1988 *Ending It: Dispute Resolution in America.* Cincinnati, OH: Anderson.

Lempert, Richard, and Joseph Sanders
1986 *An Invitation to Law and Social Science.* New York: Longman.

Levi, Edward H.
1955 *An Introduction to Legal Reasoning.* Chicago: University of Chicago Press.

Levin, Martin A.
1977 *Urban Politics and the Criminal Courts.* Chicago: University of Chicago Press.

Levrant, Sharon, Francis T. Cullen, Betsy Fulton, and John Wozniak
1999 "Reconsidering Restorative Justice: The Corruption of Benevolence Revisited?" *Crime and Delinquency* 45 (January): 3–23.

Levy, Leonard W.
1988 *Original Intent and the Framers' Constitution.* New York: Macmillan.

Lewin, Tamar
1986a "Leaving the Law for Wall Street: The Faster Track." *New York Times Magazine* (Aug. 10): 14–19, 42, 48, 53.
1986b "A Legal Curb Raises Hackles: It Punishes the Frivolous." *New York Times* (Oct. 2): 25, 31.
1983 "A Gentlemanly Profession Enters a Tough New Era." *New York Times* (Jan. 16): Sec. 3: 1, 10–12.

Lewis, Neil A.
2001 "White House Ends Bar Association's Role in Screening Federal Judges." *New York Times* (March 23): 13.
2000 "Edward H. Levi, Attorney General Credited with Restoring Order after Watergate, Dies at 88." *New York Times* (March 8): C25.
1996 "Clinton Vetoes Liability Limits in Product Suits." *New York Times* (May 3): 1, 8.
1990 "Non-Lawyers to Be Partners in Firms in Nation's Capital." *New York Times* (March 2): B10.
1989a "Legal Panel, 6–5, Keeps Disputed Chief." *New York Times* (Dec.16): 11.
1989b "Legal Skills and Legislation: Washington Growth Industry." *New York Times* (Dec. 29): 1, 26.

Lewis, Peter W., and Kenneth D. Peoples
1978 *The Supreme Court and the Criminal Process: Cases and Comments.* Philadelphia, PA: W.B. Saunders.

Lieberman, Jethro K.
1989 "What Courts Do and Do Not Do Effectively." In *American Court Systems: Readings in Judicial Process and Behavior*, edited by Sheldon Goldman and Austin Sarat, pp. 18–32. New York: Longman.
1981 *The Litigious Society.* New York: Basic Books.

Linowitz, Sol with Martin Mayer
1996 *The Profession Betrayed: Lawyering at the End of the Twentieth Century.* Baltimore: Johns Hopkins University Press.

Lisagor, Nancy, and Frank Lipsius
1988 *A Law Unto Itself: The Untold Story of the Law Firm Sullivan and Cromwell.* New York: William Morrow.

Litan, Robert E., ed.
1993 *Verdict: Assessing the Civil Jury System.* Washington, DC: Brookings Institution.

Litras, Marika F. X., Sidra Lea Gifford, and Carol J. DeFrances
2000 *Tort Trials and Verdicts in Large Counties, 1996.* Washington, DC: Office of Justice Programs.

Llewellyn, Karl N.
1989 *The Case Law System in America.* Edited and translated by Paul Gewirtz. Chicago, IL: University of Chicago Press.
1960 *The Common Law Tradition: Deciding Appeals.* Boston: Little, Brown.
1951 *The Bramble Bush.* Dobbs Ferry, NY: Oceana Press.

Lloyd-Bostock, Sally and Cheryl Thomas
1999 "Decline of the 'Little Parliament': Juries and Jury Reform in England and Wales." *Law and Contemporary Problems* 7 (Spring): Internet.

Locke, John
1952 *The Second Treatise of Government.* Indianapolis, IN: Bobbs-Merrill. (Originally published circa 1688.)

Lofgren, Charles A.
1987 *The Plessy Case: A Legal-Historical Interpretation.* New York: Oxford University Press.

Loh, Wallace D.
1984 *Social Research in the Judicial Process: Cases, Readings, and Text.* New York: Russell Sage.

Lomasky, Loren E.
1989 "The Selling of Jury Deliberations: Commentaries on the Issue." *Criminal Justice Ethics* 8 (Winter/Spring): 33–34.

London, Robb
1991 "New Technology Sends Law Firms Recruiting Scientists to Be Partners." *New York Times* (March 22): B8.

Lorch, Robert S.
1980 *Democratic Process and Administrative Law,* revised edition. Detroit, MI: Wayne State University Press.

Lou, Herbert H.
1972 *Juvenile Courts in the United States.* New York: Arno Press. (Reprint of a 1927 edition.)

Lynch, David
1994 "The Impropriety of Plea Agreements: A Tale of Two Counties." *Law and Social Inquiry* 19: 115–133.

Lynk, William J.
1994 "The Courts and the Plaintiff Bar: Awarding the Attorney's Fee in Class-Action Lawsuits." *Journal of Legal Studies* 23 (January): 185–209.

Lyon, Jeff
1991 "Chicago Law." *Chicago Tribune Magazine* (June 9): 14–21.

Maag, Gordon E.
2001 "Forum Non Conveniens in Illinois: A Historical Review, Critical Analysis, and Proposal for Change." *Southern Illinois University Law Journal* 25: 461–527.

MacDonald, H. Malcolm
1961 "Government Under Law." In *The Rule of Law,* edited by Arthur L. Harding, pp. 3–21. Dallas, TX: Southern Methodist University Press.

MacFarquhar, Larissa
2001 "The Bench Burner." *New Yorker* (December 10): 78–89.

MacNeil, Ian R.
1992 *American Arbitration Law: Reformation, Nationalization, Internationalization.* New York: Oxford University Press.

Madison, James
1987 *Notes of Debates in the Federal Convention of 1787.* New York: Norton.

Maestro, Marcello
1973 *Cesare Beccaria and the Origins of Penal Reform.* Philadelphia Temple University Press.

Mahoney, Barry
1988 *Changing Times in Trial Courts.* Denver, CO: National Center for State Courts.

Maine, Henry S.
1861 *Ancient Law: Its Connection with the Early History of Society, and Its Relation to Modern Ideas.* New York: Cockcroft and Company.

Malcolm, Andrew H.
1989 "More Americans Are Killing Each Other." *New York Times* (Dec. 31): 14.

Maloney, Dennis M. and Mark S. Umbreit
1995   "Managing Change: Toward a Balanced and Restorative Justice Model." *Perspectives* 19 (Spring): 43–46.

Mann, Dale
1976   *Intervening with Convicted Serious Juvenile Offenders.* Washington, DC: U.S. Government Printing Office.

Mansnerus, Laura
2001   "Shortage of Lawyers for Poor Nearly Stops the Wheels of Justice." *New York Times* (January 17): 21.

Manza, Jeff
1990   "Critical Legal Studies." *Berkeley Journal of Sociology: A Critical Review* 35: 137–150.

Margolick, David
1994a   "At the Bar." *New York Times* (February 4): B9.
1994b   "The A.B.A.'s Party of the First Part Can Play as Many Parts as Anyone." *New York Times* (Feb. 6): E7.
1991a   "Target: Drexel. Weapon: Tom Barr." *New York Times* (April 7): F1, 6.
1991b   "Address by Quayle on Justice Proposals Irks Bar Association." *New York Times* (August 14): 1, 9.
1989a   "Annual Race for Clerks Becomes a Mad Dash, with Judicial Decorum Left in the Dust." *New York Times* (March 17): 24.
1989b   "Glimpse at Secret System of Punishing Judges." *New York Times* (July 14): 1, 21.
1988a   "For Trial Lawyers in Big Firms, Arguing a Case Can Be a Remote Possibility." *New York Times* (Sept. 9): 19.
1988b   "Turning Economic Theory into Legal Practice and Spectacular Profit." *New York Times* (June 17): 22.
1988c   "Increasingly, Legal Firms Find Themselves in the Dock as the Litigation Explosion Boomerangs." *New York Times* (Nov. 18): 25.
1985   "The Legal Aid Society on the Defensive." *New York Times* (Aug. 4): E4.
1983   "The Trouble with America's Law Schools. *New York Times* (May 22): 20–25; 30–37.

Marks, Jonathan B., Earl Johnson, Jr., and Peter L. Szanton
1985   *Dispute Resolution in America: Processes in Evolution.* Washington, DC: National Institute for Dispute Resolution.

Marshall, Tony F.
1998   *Restorative Justice: An Overview.* London, England: Restorative Justice Consortium.
1988   "Out of Court: More or Less Justice?" In *Informal Justice?*, edited by Roger Matthews, pp. 25–50. Beverly Hills, CA: Sage.

Marvell, Thomas B.
1978   *Appellate Courts and Lawyers: Information Gathering in the Adversary System.* Westport, CT: Greenwood.

Mather, Lynn M.
1988   "The Outsider in the Courtroom: An Alternative Role for Defense." In *Criminal Justice: Law and Politics*, edited by George F. Cole, pp. 253–270. Pacific Grove, CA: Brooks/Cole.

Matthews, Roger, ed.
1988   *Informal Justice?* Beverly Hills, CA: Sage.

Mayer, Martin
1969   *The Lawyers.* New York: Dell.

Maynard, Douglas W.
1988   "Narratives and Narrative Structure in Plea Bargaining." *Law and Society Review* 22 (3): 449–481.

McCarthy, Belinda R., and Charles A. Lindquist
1985   "Certainty of Punishment and Sentence Mitigation in Plea Behavior." *Justice Quarterly* 2 (Sept.): 363–383.

McClosky, Robert G.
1994   *The American Supreme Court*, 2d ed. Chicago: University of Chicago. Revised by Sanford Levinson.

McCormick, John P.
1999   "Three ways of thinking 'critically' about the law." *American Political Science Review* 93 (June): 413–424.

McCoy, Candace
1993   *Politics and Plea Bargaining: Victim's Rights in California.* Philadelphia: University of Pennsylvania Press.

McCoy, Candace, and Robert Tillman
n.d.   *Controlling Plea Bargaining in California.* Sacramento: California Bureau of Criminal Statistics.

McDonald, William F.

1985 *Plea Bargaining: Critical Issues and Common Practices.* Washington, DC: U.S. Government Printing Office.

1983 "In Defense of Inequality: The Legal Profession and Criminal Defense." In *The Defense Counsel,* edited by William F. McDonald, pp. 13–38. Beverly Hills, CA: Sage.

McDonald, William F., Henry H. Rossman, and James A. Cramer

1982 *Police–Prosecutor Relations in the United States: Executive Summary.* Washington, DC: U.S. Government Printing Office.

McDowell, Gary L.

1990 "The Politics of Advice and Consent." In *Judicial Selection: Merit, Ideology, and Politics,* edited by Henry J. Abraham, Eugene W. Hickok, Jr., and William Bradford Reynolds, pp.xiii–xix. Washington, DC: National Legal Center for the Public Interest.

1988 *Curbing the Courts: The Constitution and Limits of Judicial Power.* Baton Rouge: Louisiana State University.

1982 *Equity and the Constitution: The Supreme Court, Equitable Relief, and Public Policy.* Chicago: University of Chicago Press.

McGee, Jim and Brian Duffy

1996 *Main Justice: The Men and Women Who Enforce the Nation's Criminal Laws and Guard Its Liberties.* New York: Touchstone.

McGillis, Daniel

1998 *Resolving Community Conflict: The Dispute Settlement Center of Durham, North Carolina.* Washington, DC: National Institute of Justice.

McGillis, Daniel, and Joan Mullen

1977 *Neighborhood Justice Centers: An Analysis of Potential Models.* Washington, DC: U.S. Government Printing Office.

McGuire, Kevin T.

1993 *The Supreme Court Bar: Legal Elites in the Washington Community.* Charlottesville, VA: University Press of Virginia.

McIntyre, Lisa J.

1987 *The Public Defender: The Practice of Law in the Shadows of Repute.* Chicago: University of Chicago Press.

McKean, Dayton

1963 *The Integrated Bar.* Boston: Houghton Mifflin.

McKenna, Marian C.

1986 *Tapping Reeve and the Litchfield Law School.* New York: Oceana.

McLaughlin, Charles H.

1984 "Common Law." *The Guide to American Law.* St. Paul, MN: West.

McMillian, Theodore

1999 "Early Modern Juvenile Justice in St. Louis." *Federal Probation* 63 (December): 4–7.

McNamee, Kathleen

1998 "Another Chapter in the History of Scholia." *The Classical Quarterly* 48 (Jan.–June): 269–289.

Meese, Edwin

1986 "Interpreting the Constitution." *USA Today* (September): 36–39.

Meier, Barry

2000 "Bringing Lawsuits to Do What Congress Won't." *New York Times* (March 26): WK 3.

1997a "Class-Action Consciousness." *New York Times* (February 18): C1, 11.

1997b "In Fine Print, Customers Lose Ability to Sue." *New York Times* (March 10): 1, C7.

1996 "Lawsuits to End All Lawsuits." *New York Times* (January 10): C1, 5.

1995 "Math of a Class-Action Lawsuit: 'Winning' $2.19 Costs $91.33." *New York Times* (November 21): 1, C4.

Melville, Herman

1961 *Billy Budd.* New York: New American Library. Originally published in 1924.

Menand, Louis

2001 "Civil Actions: Brown v. Board of Education and the Limits of Law." *New Yorker* (February 12): 91–94.

1986 "What Is 'Critical Legal Studies'? Radicalism of Yuppies." *New Republic* (March 17): 20–23.

Mennel, Robert M.

1973 *Thorns and Thistles: Juvenile Delinquents in the United States, 1825–1940.* Hanover, NH: University Press of New England.

Mercuro, Nicholas and Steven G. Medema
1997   *Economics and the Law: From Posner to Post-Modernism.* Princeton, NJ: Princeton University Press.

Merryman, John H.
1985   *The Civil Law Tradition: An Introduction to the Legal Systems of Western Europe and Latin America,* 2d ed. Stanford, CA: Stanford University Press.

Michalowski, Raymond J.
1985   *Order, Law and Crime: An Introduction to Criminology.* New York: Random House.

Middlekauff, William Bradford
1994   "What Practitioners Say about Broad Criminal Discovery Practice. More Just—Or Just More Dangerous?" *Criminal Justice* 9 (Spring): 14–19, 54–58.

Milford, Maureen
2001   "New Home for Delaware Chancery Court." *New York Times* (February 4): 38.

Miller, Jerome
1992   *Last One Over the Wall: The Massachusetts Experiment in Closing Reform Schools* Columbus, OH: Ohio State University Press.

Miller, Perry, ed.
1962   *The Legal Mind in America: From Independence to the Civil War.* Garden City, NY: Anchor.

Mills, Miriam K., ed.
1991   *Alternative Dispute Resolution in the Public Sector.* Chicago: Nelson-Hall.

Montesquieu, Charles de
1949   *The Spirit of the Laws.* Trans. by Thomas Nugent. New York: Hafner Publishing Co.

Moore, Christopher W.
1986   *The Mediation Process: Practical Strategies for Resolving Conflicts.* San Francisco, CA: Jossey–Bass.

Morgan, Edmund
1956   *The Birth of the Republic: 1763–1789.* Chicago: University of Chicago Press.

Morris, Richard B.
1964   *Studies in the History of American Law.* New York: Octagon Books.

Morrison, Alan B.
1996   "Litigation." In *Fundamentals of American Law,* edited by Alan B. Morrison, pp. 61–81. New York: Oxford University Press.

Müller, Ingo
1991   *Hitler's Justice: The Courts of the Third Reich.* Cambridge, MA: Harvard University Press.

Murphy, Walter F., and C. Herman Pritchett
1986   *Courts, Judges, and Politics.* New York: Random House.

Nagel, Robert F.
1989   "The Selling of Jury Deliberations: Commentaries on the Issue." *Criminal Justice Ethics* 8 (Winter/Spring): 31–33.

Nardulli, Peter F.
1978   "Plea Bargaining: An Organizational Perspective." *Journal of Criminal Justice* 6 (Fall): 217–231.

Nasheri, Hedieh
1998   *Betrayal of Due Process: A Comparative Assessment of Plea Bargaining in the United States and Canada.* Lanham, MD: University Press of America.

National Council of Juvenile and Family Court Judges
1989   *Court-Approved Alternative Dispute Resolution: A Better Way to Resolve Minor Delinquency, Status Offense and Abuse/Neglect Cases.* Reno, NV: National College of Juvenile and Family Law.
1988   *Glossary of Selected Legal Terms for Juvenile Justice Personnel.* Reno, NV: National College of Juvenile and Family Law

Navarro, Mireya
1997   "Doubts about F.B.I. Lab Raise Hopes for Convict." *New York Times* (April 22): 8.
1995   "Entangled by Law, Boy Stays in Hospital That Failed Him." *New York Times* (March 10): 1, 13.

Neely, Richard
  1985 *Judicial Jeopardy: When Business Collides with the Courts.* Reading, MA: Addison–Wesley.
  1981 *How the Courts Govern America.* New Haven, CT: Yale University Press.

Neubauer, David W.
  1974 *Criminal Justice in Middle America.* Morristown, NJ: General Learning Press.

Newman, Katherine S.
  1983 *Law and Economic Organization: A Comparative Study of Preindustrial Societies.* Cambridge: Cambridge University Press.

Newmyer, R. Kent
  1987 "Harvard Law School, New England Legal Culture, and the Antebellum Origins of American Jurisprudence." *Journal of American History* 74 (Dec.): 814–835.

Noonan, John T., Jr.
  1976 *Persons and Masks of the Law.* New York: Farrar, Straus and Giroux.

Novak, William J.
  1996 *The People's Welfare: Law and Regulation in Nineteenth Century America.* Chapel Hill NC: University of North Carolina Press.

Novick, Sheldon M.
  1989 *Honorable Justice: The Life of Oliver Wendell Holmes.* Boston: Little, Brown.

Orlando, Leoluca
  2001 *Fighting the Mafia and Renewing Sicilian Culture.* San Francisco: Encounter Books.

Orth, John V.
  1987 *The Judicial Power of the United States: The Eleventh Amendment in American History.* New York: Oxford University Press.

Packer, Herbert L.
  1968 *The Limits of the Criminal Sanction.* Stanford, CA: Stanford University Press.

Palermo, George B., Maxine Aldridge White, Lew A. Wasserman, William Hanrahan
  1998 "Plea Bargaining: Injustice for All?" *International Journal of Offender Therapy and Comparative Criminology* 42 (2): 11–19.

Pallasch, Abdon M.
  1998 "Napping Juries Giving Courts a Wakeup Call." *Chicago Tribune* (April 16): 1, 17.

Palmer, John W.
  1974 "Pre-Arrest Diversion: Victim Confrontation." *Federal Probation* 38 (September): 12–18.

Parsa, T. Z.
  1999 "The Druge Report." *New York* (June 21): 24–31.

Parsons, Christi
  2000 "Prosecutors, Defenders Are Called Ill-Equipped." *Chicago Tribune* (May 19): Sec. 2: 7.
  1997 "Constitution Shmonstitution" *Chicago Tribune* (June 8): Sec. 2: 1, 7.

Passell, Peter
  1994 "Contingency Fees in Injury Cases Under Attack by Legal Scholars." *New York Times* (Feb. 11): 1, B12.

Patterson, James T.
  2001 *Brown v. Board of Education: A Civil Rights Milestone and Its Troubled Legacy.* New York: Oxford University Press.

Paul, Jeremy
  2001 "CLS 2001." *Cardozo Law Review.* 22: 701–720.

Pear, Robert
  1999 "Group Asking U.S. for New Vigilance in Patient Safety." *New York Times* (November 30): 1, 18.

Pérez-Peña, Richard
  2002 "Passing a Health Measure Without a Second Thought." *New York Times* (January 17): 27.
  1994a "Private Colleges are Criticized for Their Brand of Justice." *New York Times* (June 1): B8.
  1994b "When Lawyers Go After Their Peers: The Boom in Malpractice Cases." *New York Times* (August 5): B12.

Perry, H.W.
  1991 *Deciding to Decide: Agenda Setting in the United States Supreme Court.* Cambridge, MA: Harvard University Press.

Pertschuk, Michael, and Wendy Schaetzel
  1989 *The People Rising: The Campaign Against the Bork Nomination.* New York: Thunder's Mouth.

Peterson, Joseph L.
  1987   *Use of Forensic Evidence by the Police and Courts*. Washington, DC: National Institute of Justice.

Peterson, Melody
  1999   "Her Partners Can Call Her Ms. Chairman." *New York Times* (October 9): B1, 4.

Pettibone, John M., Robert G. Swisher, Kurt H. Weiland, Christine E. Wolf, and Joseph L. White
  1981   *Major Issues in Juvenile Justice Information and Training; Services to Children in Juvenile Courts: The Judicial–Executive Controversy*. Washington, DC: U.S. Government Printing Office.

Pierce, Richard J., Jr., Sidney A. Shapiro, Paul R. Verkuil
  1999   *Administrative Law and Process*, 3rd edition. New York: Foundation Press.

Pileggi, Nicholas
  1982   "The Last Liberals." *New York* (Sept. 13): 28, 30–35.

Plapinger, Elizabeth and Donna Steinstra
  1996   *ADR and Settlement in the Federal District Courts: A Sourcebook for Judges and Lawyers*. Washington, DC: Federal Judicial Center.

Platt, Anthony M.
  1974   *The Child Savers: The Invention of Delinquency*. Chicago: University of Chicago Press.

Plunknett, Theodore F. T.
  1956   *A Concise History of the Common Law*, 5th ed. Boston: Little, Brown.

Pohlman, H. L., ed.
  1993   *Political Thought and the American Judiciary*. Amherst, MA: University of Massachusetts Press.

Polin, Raymond
  1986   "The Supreme Court's Dilemma and Defense." *USA Today* (Sept.): 43–45.

Posner, Richard A.
  2001   *Breaking the Deadlock: The 2000 Election, the Constitution, and the Courts*. Princeton, NJ: Princeton University Press.
  1995   *Overcoming Law*. Cambridge, MA: Harvard University Press.

  1990   *The Problems of Jurisprudence*. Cambridge, MA: Harvard University Press.
  1987   "The Decline of Law as an Autonomous Discipline: 1962–1987." *Harvard Law Review* 100 (February): 761–780.
  1985   *The Federal Courts: Crisis and Reform*. Cambridge, MA: Harvard University Press.

Possley, Maurice
  1999   "Kids Get Right to Murder-Trial Jury." *Chicago Tribune* (April 13): Sec. 2: 1, 4.

Post, Robert C.
  1995   *Constitutional Domains: Democracy, Community, Management*. Cambridge, MA: Harvard University Press.

Pound, Roscoe
  1975   *An Introduction to the Philosophy of Law*. New Haven, CT: Yale University Press.
  1953   *The Lawyer from Antiquity to Modern Times*. St. Paul, MN: West.

Powell, Michael J.
  1988   *From Patrician to Professional Elite: The Transformation of the New York City Bar*. New York: Russell Sage Foundation.

Precker, Michael
  1996   "Is It Justice or a Legal Loophole?: Nolo Contendere Skates Line Between Guilt, Innocence, Experts Say." *Dallas Morning News* (July 22): 1c.

Prelaw Handbook 1982–83
  1983   Association of American Law Schools.

President's Commission on Organized Crime
  1986   *The Impact: Organized Crime Today*. Washington, DC: U.S. Government Printing Office.

Price, Marty
  1997   "Can Mediation Produce Justice?" *ADR Report* 1 (October 29): Internet.

Provine, Doris Marie
  1996   "Courts in the Political Process in France." In *Courts, Law and Politics in Comparative Perspective*, edited by Herbert Jacob et al., pp. 177–248. New Haven CT: Yale University Press.

Puritz, Patricia and Wendy Wan Long Shang
 1998 *Innovative Approaches to Juvenile Defense.* Washington, DC: Office of Justice Programs.

"Q & A."
 1991 *Chicago Tribune* Magazine (June 16): 6.

Quillen, William T. and Michael Hanrahan
 1993 "A Short History of the Delaware Court of Chancery" pp.1–29. Widener University School of Law.

Quinn, Jane B.
 1986 "Cutting Back Verdicts." *Newsweek* (July 7): 44.

Rabkin, Jeremy
 1989 *Judicial Compulsions: How Public Law Distorts Public Policy.* New York: Basic Books.

Rakove, Jack N.
 1996 *Original Meanings: Politics and Ideas in the Making of the Constitution.* New York: Knopf.

Raven, Robert D.
 1988 Letter to the Editor: "In Legal Aid Chicken Coop, the Fox Is King." *New York Times* (Dec. 9): 30.

Ray, Larry, Prudence B. Kestner, Lawrence Freedman, and Anne E. Clare, eds.
 1983 *Alternative Dispute Resolution: Mediation and the Law: Will Reason Prevail?* Chicago: American Bar Association.

Re, Edward D.
 1975a *Stare Decisis.* Washington, DC: Federal Judicial Center.
 1975b *Appellate Opinion Writing.* Washington, DC: Federal Judicial Center.

Rehnquist, William H.
 1999 *All the Laws But One: Civil Liberties in Wartime.* New York: Knopf.
 1996 "Remarks of the Chief Justice at the Washington College of Law Centennial Celebration Plenary Academic Panel: The Future of the Federal Courts." American University, April 9.
 1987 *The Supreme Court: How It Was, How It Is.* New York: William Morrow.

Reich, Cary
 1986 "The Litigator." *New York Times Magazine* (June 1): 18–24, 48, 50, 70, 74–76, 84.

Rembar, Charles
 1980 *The Law of the Land: The Evolution of Our Legal System.* New York: Simon and Schuster.

Reuters
 1996 "Malpractice Awards Tied to Disability." *New York Times* (December 26): 11.

Richert, E. Susanne
 1987 *Equal Justice Under Law.* Washington, DC: Judicial Conference of the United States Committee on the Bicentennial of the Constitution.

Ritchey, Joan Grace
 2001 "Limits on Justice: The United States' Failure to Recognize a Right to Counsel in Civil Litigation." *Washington University Law Quarterly* 79: 317–341.

Roberts, Sam
 1985 "For One Zealous Judge, Hard Bargaining Pushes Cases Through the Courts." *New York Times* (April 29): 13.

Roehl, Janice, and Larry Ray
 1986 "Toward the Multi-Door Courthouse— Dispute Resolution Intake and Referral." *NIJ Reports/SNI* 198 (July): 2–7.

Rohde, David
 1999 "A Glut of Minor Cases Swamps City's Courts." *New York Times* (February 2): 19.

Rommen, Heinrich A.
 1998 *The Natural Law: A Study in Legal and Social History and Philosophy.* Indianapolis, IN: Liberty Fund. Originally published in 1936.

Rothfeld, Charles
 1989 "Law Firms Moving Rapidly into New Businesses." *New York Times* (June 9): 27.

Rottman, David B.
 2000 "Does Effective Therapeutic Jurisprudence Require Specialized Courts (and Do Specialized Courts Imply Specialist Judges)?" *Court Review* 37 (Spring): 22–27.

Rottman, David and Pamela Casey
 1999 "Therapeutic Jurisprudence and the Emerging of Problem-Solving Courts." *NIJ Journal* (July): 12–19.

Rottman, David B. and William E. Hewitt
1996 *Trial Court Structure and Performance: A Contemporary Reappraisal.* Arlington, VA: National Center for State Courts.

Rottman, David B., Carol R. Flango, Melissa T. Cantrell, Randall Hansen, and Neil LaFountain
2000 *State Court Organization 1998.* Washington, DC: National Institute of Justice.

Rousseau, Jean Jacques
1954 *The Social Contract.* Chicago: Regnery. (Originally published in 1762.)

Rubin, Emily
1998 "Ineffective Assistance of Counsel, and Guilty Pleas: Toward a Paradigm of Informed Consent." *Virginia Law Journal* 80: 1699–1722.

Rubinstein, Michael L., Stevens H. Clarke, and Teresa J. White
1980 *Alaska Bans Plea Bargaining.* Washington, DC: U.S. Government Printing Office.

Saari, David J.
1985 *American Court Management: Theories and Practice.* Westport, CT: Quorum Books.

Sabatino, Jack M.
n.d. "ADR as 'Litigation Lite': Procedural and Evidentiary Norms Embedded Within Alternative Dispute Resolution." Internet.

Sack, Kevin
1990 "Thousands of Medical Errors, But Few Lawsuits, Study Shows." *New York Times* (Jan. 29): 15.

Sagatun, Inger, Loretta McCollum, and Michael Edwards
1985 "The Effect of Transfers from Juvenile to Criminal Court: A Loglinear Analysis." *Journal of Crime and Justice* 8: 65–92.

Salomone, Rosemary C.
1986 *Equal Education Under Law: Legal Rights and Federal Policy in the Post-Brown Era.* New York: St. Martin's Press.

Salpukas, Agis
1997 "CSX and Others Ordered to Pay Billions in '87 Rail Chemical Fire." *New York Times* (September 9): C1.

Samuelson, Robert J.
1992 "I Am a Big Lawyer Basher." *Newsweek* (April 27): 62.

Sanborn, Joseph B., Jr.
1986 "A Historical Sketch of Plea Bargaining." *Justice Quarterly* 3 (June): 111–138.

Sanders, Joseph
1996 "Courts and Law in Japan." In *Courts, Law and Politics in Comparative Perspective*, edited by Herbert Jacob et al., pp. 315–388. New Haven CT: Yale University Press.

Savage, David G.
1991 "Supreme Court's Rulings Rankle Business Lawyers." *Los Angeles Times* (March 10): D1.

Scalia, Antonin
1996 "Speech before The Catholic University of America," October 18.

Schlossman, Steven L.
1977 *Love and the American Delinquent: The Theory and Practice of "Progressive" Juvenile Justice, 1825–1920.* Chicago: University of Chicago Press.

Schma, William
2000 "Judging for the New Millennium." *Court Review* 37 (Spring): 4–6.

Schmetzer, Uli
1991 "China Judges Hail Imprisonments." *Chicago Tribune* (April 4): 5.

Schubert, Frank A.
2000 *Introduction to Law and the Legal System,* 7th ed. Boston: Houghton Mifflin.

Schulhofer. Stephen J.
1994 "A Wake Up Call from the Plea Bargain Trenches." *Law and Social Inquiry* 19: 135–144.
1992 "Plea Bargaining as Disaster." *Yale Law Journal* 101: 1979–2009.
1986 "The Future of the Adversary System." *Justice Quarterly* 3 (March): 83–93.

Schur, Edwin M.
1973 *Radical Non-Intervention: Rethinking the Delinquency Problem.* Englewood Cliffs, NJ: Prentice-Hall.

1968   *Law and Society: A Sociological View*. New York: Random House.

Schuster, Richard L.
1979   "Prosecutor–Police Relations: An Overview and Case Study from an Organizational Perspective." Paper presented at the Annual Meeting of the American Society of Criminology, Philadelphia, Nov.

Schwartz, Bernard
1996   "Administrative Law." In *Fundamentals of American Law*, edited by Alan M. Morrison, pp. 129–150. New York: Oxford University Press.
1993   *A History of the Supreme Court*. New York: Oxford University Press.
1988   *The Unpublished Opinions of the Burger Court*. New York: Oxford University Press.
1974   *The Law in America: A History*. New York: McGraw-Hill.

Schwartz, Richard D., and James C. Miller
1964   "Legal Evolution and Societal Complexity." *American Journal of Sociology* 70 (Sept.): 159–169.

Scott, Robert E. and William J. Stuntz
1992   "Plea Bargaining as Contract." *Yale Law Journal* 101: 1909–1968.

Seelye, Katherine Q.
1997   "Conservatives in House are Preparing an Impeachment List of Federal Judges." *New York Times* (March 14): 13.

Seligman, Joel
1978   *The High Citadel: The Influence of Harvard Law School*. Boston: Houghton Mifflin.

Sengupta, Somini
2000   "Youth Court of True Peers Judges Firmly." *New York Times* (June 4): 1, 29.

Seymour, Christopher
1996   *Yakuza Diary*. New York: Atlantic Monthly Press.

Shaibani, Sahand
1999   "Psychodynamics of the Judicial Process." *Stanford Journal of Legal Studies* 1 (December): 1–10.

Shaman, Jeffrey M.
1992   "Interpreting the Constitution: The Supreme Court's Proper and Historic Function." In *Judicial Politics: Readings from Judicature*, edited by E. E. Slotnick, pp. 37–55. Chicago: Nelson-Hall.

Shamir, Ronen
1995   *Managing Legal Uncertainty: Elite Lawyers in the New Deal*. Durham, NC: Duke University Press.

Shapiro, Martin
1988   *Who Guards the Guardians? Judicial Control of Administration*. Athens: University of Georgia Press.
1981   *Courts: A Comparative and Political Analysis*. Chicago: University of Chicago Press.

Shea, Dennis
1997   "Impeaching Abusive Judges." *Policy Review* 83 (May–June) 62–63.

Shepherd, George B.
2000   "Cartels and Controls in Legal Training." *Antitrust Bulletin* 45 (Summer): Infotrac.

Sherrid, Pamela
2001   "Lawyers on Trial." *U.S. News and World Report* (December 17): 34–40.

Sherry, Suzanna
1998   "Independent Judges and Independent Justice." *Law and Contemporary Problems* 15 (Summer): 15–20.

Shuster, Beth
2001   "The Science of Getting Inmates from Jail to Court." *Los Angeles Times* (August 3): Internet.

Sigler, Jay A.
1986   *An Introduction to the Legal System*. Homewood IL: Dorsey.

Sigmund, Paul E.
1971   *Natural Law in Political Thought*. Cambridge, MA: Winthrop.

Simon, James F.
1989   *The Antagonists: Hugo Black, Felix Frankfurter and Civil Liberties in America*. New York: Simon and Schuster.

Sinclair, Andrew
  1962   *The Era of Excess: A Social History of the Prohibition Movement*. Boston: Little, Brown.

Sinclair, Jim
  1994   "APPA's Public Hearings Explore Probation and Parole's Response to Victims of Crime: Speakers Call for a New Approach to Victim Issues." *Perspectives* (Special Issue): 15–17.

Sinha, Surya Prakash
  1990   *What Is Law? The Differing Theories of Jurisprudence*. New York: Paragon House.

Slade, Margot
  1993   "Billable Hour, a Centerpiece of American Law, is Fading." *New York Times* (October 22): 1, B9.

Slotnick, Elliot E.
  1992a *Judicial Politics: Readings from Judicature*. Chicago: American Judicature Society.
  1992b "The Place of Judicial Review in the American Tradition: The Emergence of an Eclectic Power." In *Judicial Politics: Readings from Judicature*, edited by E. E. Slotnick, pp. 3–17. Chicago: Nelson-Hall.

Smigel, Erwin O.
  1964   *The Wall Street Lawyer: Professional Organization Man*. Glencoe, IL: Free Press.

Smith, Christopher E.
  1997   *Courts, Politics, and the Judicial Process*, 2d ed. Chicago: Nelson-Hall.
  1993a *Courts, Politics, and the Judicial Process*. Chicago: Nelson-Hall.
  1993b *Courts and Public Policy*. Chicago: Nelson-Hall.

Smith, Reginald H.
  1919   *Justice and the Poor*. New York: Carnegie Foundation.

Smith, Rogers M.
  1985   *Liberalism and American Constitutional Law*. Cambridge, MA: Harvard University Press.

Smith, Steven K. and Carol J. DeFrances
  1996   *Indigent Defense*. Washington, DC: Bureau of Justice Statistics.

Smothers, Ronald
  1994   "Court-Appointed Defense Offers the Poor a Lawyer, But the Cost May Be High." *New York Times* (February 14): A9.

Solomon, Harvey E.
  1987   "The Training of Court Managers." In *Court Administration: Issues and Responses*, edited by Charles R. Swanson and Susette M. Talarico, pp. 15–20. Athens, GA: University of Georgia.

Sosin, J. M.
  1989   *The Aristocracy of the Long Robe: The Origins of Judicial Review in America*. Westport, CT: Greenwood.

Spaeth, Harold J.
  1979   *Supreme Court Policy Making: Explanation and Prediction*. San Francisco, CA: Freeman.

Spangenberg, Robert L., Marea L. Beeman, David J. Carroll, David Freedman, Evelyn Pan, David J. Newhouse, and Dorothy Chan
  2000   *Contracting for Indigent Defense Services: A Special Report*. Washington, DC: Office of Justice Programs.

Spangler, Eve
  1986   *Lawyers for Hire: Salaried Professionals at Work*. New Haven, CT: Yale University Press.

Spencer, Herbert
  1961   *The Study of Sociology*. Ann Arbor: University of Michigan Press. Originally published in 1871.

Stanny, Claudia J. and Thomas C. Johnson
  2000   "Effects of Stress Induced by a Simulated Shooting on Recall by Police and Citizen Witnesses." *American Journal of Psychology* 113 (Fall): 359–386.

"State Courts Providing Broader Constitutional Protections in Criminal Cases Than U.S. Supreme Court."
  1993   *NCJA Justice Bulletin* 13 (No. 7): 1, 6, 9–12.

State Felony Courts and Felony Laws
  1878   Washington, DC: U.S. Government Printing Office.

Steinhauer, Jennifer and Ford Fessenden
  2001   "Doctors Punished by New York are Still Prized by Hospitals." *New York Times* (March 27): 24.

Stevens, Ed
1999 *Due Process and Higher Education: A Systemic Approach to Fair Decision Making.* Washington, DC: Washington University, Graduate School of Education and Human Development.

Stevens, Robert
1983 *Law School: Legal Education in America from the 1850s to the 1980s.* Chapel Hill: University of North Carolina Press.
1971 "Two Cheers for 1870: The American Law School." In *Law in American History*, edited by Donald Fleming and Bernard Bailyn, pp. 403–548. Boston: Little, Brown.

Stevenson, Carol S., Carol S. Larson, Lucy S. Carter, Deanna S. Gomby, Donna L. Terman, and Richard E. Behrman
1996 "The Juvenile Court: Analysis and Recommendations." *The Future of Children* 6 (Winter): 4–28.

Stewart, James B.
1987 *The Prosecutors: Inside the Offices of the Government's Most Powerful Lawyers.* New York: Simon and Schuster.
1984 *The Partners: Inside America's Most Powerful Law Firms.* New York: Warner.

Stienstra, Donna and Thomas E. Willging
1995 *Alternatives to Litigation: Do They Have a Place in the Federal District Courts?* Washington, DC: Federal Judicial Center, Internet.

Stolle, Dennis F., David B. Wexler, Bruce J. Winick, and Edward A. Dauer
1997 "Integrating Preventive Law and Therapeutic Jurisprudence: A Law and Psychology Based Approach to Lawyering." *California Western Law Review* 34: 15–51.

Stoner, James R.
1992 *Common Law and Liberal Theory: Coke, Hobbes, and the Origins of American Constitutionalism.* Lawrence, KS: University of Kansas Press.

Story, Joseph
1962 "Discourse Pronounced upon the Inauguration of the Author." In *The Legal Mind in America: From Independence to the Civil War*, edited by Perry Miller, pp. 176–190. Garden City, NY: Anchor.

Stott, E. Keith, Jr.
1987 "The Judicial Executive: Toward Greater Congruence in an Emerging Profession." In *Court Administration: Issues and Responses*, edited by Charles R. Swanson and Susette M. Talarico, pp. 21–36. Athens: University of Georgia.

Stout, Ronald
1986 "Planning for Unified Court Budgeting." *Judicature* 69 (Dec.–Jan.): 205–213.

Stover, Robert V.
1989 *Making It and Breaking It: The Fate of Public Interest Commitment During Law School.* Urbana: University of Illinois Press.

Strauss, Peter L.
1990 "Too Often, the Buck Stops in the Appeals Court." Letter to the *New York Times* (April 14): 14.
1989 *An Introduction to Administrative Justice in the United States.* Durham, NC: Carolina Academic Press.

Stryker, Robin
1989 "Limits on the Technocratization of the Law: The Elimination of the National Labor Relations Board's Division of Economic Research." *American Sociological Review* 54 (June): 341–358.

"Study: Obstetrics Suits Make Doctors Wary"
1989 *Chicago Tribune* (Oct. 12): 5.

Stumpf, Harry P.
1988 *American Judicial Politics.* San Diego: Harcourt Brace Jovanovich.

Stumpf, Harry P. and John H. Culver
1992 *The Politics of State Courts.* New York: Longman.

Subin, Harry I.
1990 "Why the Bar Exam Is Absolutely Crucial." Letter to the *New York Times* (August 3): 10.

Sudnow, David
1965 "Normal Crimes: Sociological Features of the Penal Code." *Social Problems* 12 (Winter): 255–264.

Sumner, William Graham
1992 *On Liberty, Society, and Politics: The Essential Essays of William Graham Sumner*, edited by Robert C. Bannister. Indianapolis: Liberty Fund.

Sunstein, Cass R.
2000a "Dred Scott v. Sandford and Its Legacy." In *Great Cases in Constitutional Law*, edited by Robert P. George, pp. 64–89. Princeton, NJ: Princeton University Press.
2000b "Cognition and Cost Benefit Analysis." *Law and Economics Working Paper No. 85*, University of Chicago Law School.
1996 *Legal Reasoning and Political Conflict*. New York: Oxford University Press.

Sutherland, Arthur E.
1967 *The Law at Harvard: A History of Ideas and Men, 1819–1967*. Cambridge, MA: Harvard University Press.

Sutton, John R.
1988 *Stubborn Children: Controlling Delinquency in the United States, 1649–1981*. Berkeley: University of California Press.

Sviridoff, Michele, David Rottman, and Richard Curtis
1997 *Dispensing Justice Locally*. New York: Center for Court Innovation.

Tabarrok, Alexander and Eric Helland
1999 "Court Politics: The Political Economy of Tort Awards." *Journal of Law and Economics* 42 (April): 157–188.

Talbac, William L.
1987 "Crossfire at the Bar." *New York Times Magazine/Business World* (May 3): 30–31, 47, 50, 55.

Taragin, Mark I., Laura R. Willett, Adam P. Wilczek, Richard Trout, and Jeffrey L. Carson
1993 "The Influence of Standard Care and Severity of Injury on the Resolution of Medical Malpractice Claims." *Annals of Internal Medicine* 117 (November 1): 780–784.

Tarr, G. Alan
1999 *Judicial Process and Judicial Policymaking*. Belmont, CA: Wadsworth.

Task Force on Administration of Justice
1967 *Task Force Report: The Courts*. Washington, DC: U.S. Government Printing Office.

Taylor, Ian, Paul Walton, and Jock Young
1973 *The New Criminology*. New York: Harper and Row.

Taylor, Stuart, Jr.
2000 "Bush v. Gore May be Just the Beginning." *Newsweek* (January 1): 50.
1988 "The 'Judicial Activists' are Always on the Other Side." *New York Times* (July 3): E5.
1986a "Vigor in the Court, Laughter in the Court." *New York Times* (Oct. 14): 12.
1986b "Tasting the Salty Air of Politics and Criticism." *New York Times* (July 18): 8.
1986c "An Inside Look at Supreme Court and Its Cases." *New York Times* (June 24): 10.

Tegland, Karl
1984 *Mediation in the Western District of Washington*. Washington, DC: Federal Judicial Center.

Texas Criminal Justice Council
1974 *Model Rules for Law Enforcement Officers: A Manual on Police Discretion*. Gaithersburg, MD: International Association of Chiefs of Police.

Tiersma, Peter M.
1999 "Jury Instructions in the New Millennium." *Court Review* 36 (Summer): 28–36.

Tigar, Michael E. and Madeleine R. Levy
1977 *Law and the Rise of Capitalism*. New York: Monthly Review Press.

Toch, Hans
1982 "The Role of the Expert on Prison Conditions: The Battle of Footnotes in *Rhodes* v. *Chapman*." Criminal Law Bulletin 18: 38–49.

Todd, A.L.
1968 *Justice on Trial: The Case of Louis D. Brandeis*. Chicago: University of Chicago Press.

Torbet, Patricia, Patrick Griffen, Hunter Hurst, Jr., Lynn Ryan MacKenzie
2000 *Juveniles Facing Criminal Sanctions: Three States that Changed the Rules*. Washington, DC: Office of Juvenile Justice and Delinquency Prevention.

Torbet, Patricia, Richard Gable, Hunter Hurst IV, Imogene Montgomery, Linda Szymanski, Douglas Thomas
1996   *State Responses to Serious and Violent Juvenile Crime.* Washington, DC: Office of Juvenile Justice and Delinquency Prevention.

Treaster, Joseph B.
1994   "Hard Time for Hard Youths: A Battle Yields Few Winners." *New York Times* (December 28): 1, 8.

Tribe, Laurence H.
1985   *God Save This Honorable Court: How the Choice of Supreme Court Justices Shapes Our History.* New York: Random House.

Tribe, Laurence and Michael C. Dorf
1991   *On Reading the Constitution.* Cambridge, MA: Harvard University Press.

Tsai, Betsy
2000   "The Trend Toward Specialized Domestic Violence Courts: Improvement on an Effective Innovation." *Fordham University Law Review* 68: 1285–1327.

Turkel, Gerald
1996   *Law and Society: Critical Approaches.* Needham Heights, MA: Allyn and Bacon.

Turow, Scott
1977   *One L: An Inside Account of Life in the First Year at Harvard Law School.* New York: Penguin.

Tushnet, Mark
2000   "*Marbury* v. *Madison* and the Theory of Judicial Supremacy." In *Greatest Cases in Constitutional Law*, edited by Robert P. George, pp. 17–54. Princeton, NJ: Princeton University Press.

Tybor, Joseph R., and Mark Eissman
1986   "Study Confirms Crime Lab's Lag Let Drug Cases Fail." *Chicago Tribune* (March 3): 11.
1985   "Judges Penalize the Guilty for Exercising the Right to Trial." *Chicago Tribune* (October 13): 1, 6.

Uchitelle, Louis
1992   "The Art of a Russian Deal: Ad-Libbing Contract Law." *New York Times* (January 17): 1, 6.

Uhlman, Thomas M., and N. Darlene Walker
1980   "He Takes Some of My Time, I Take Some of His: An Analysis of Judicial Sentencing Patterns in Jury Cases." *Law and Society Review* 14 (Winter): 323–341.

Umbreit, Mark S.
2001   *The Handbook of Victim Offender Mediation.* San Francisco: Jossey-Bass.
1994   *Victim Meets Offender: The Impact of Restorative Justice and Mediation.* Monsey, NY: Willow Tree Press.

Umbreit, Mark S. and Mark Carey
1995   "Restorative Justice: Implications for Organizational Change." *Federal Probation* 59 (March): 47–54.

Unger, Roberto M.
1986   *The Critical Legal Studies Movement.* Cambridge, MA: Harvard University Press.
1976   *Law in Modern Society: Toward a Criticism of Social Theory.* New York: Free Press.

Uphoff, Rodney J.
2002   "The Criminal Defense Lawyer: Zealous Advocate, Double Agent, or Beleaguered Dealer?" In *Criminal Courts for the 21st Century*, edited by Lisa Stolzenberg and Stewart J. D'Alessio, pp. 84–117. Upper Saddle River, NJ: Prentice Hall.

Utz, Pamela
1979   "Two Models of Prosecutorial Professionalism." In *The Prosecutor*, edited by William F. McDonald, pp. 99–124. Beverly Hills, CA: Sage.

Uviller, H. Richard
1996   *Virtual Justice: The Flawed Prosecution of Crime in America.* New Haven, CT: Yale University Press.

Van Alstyne, W. Scott, Jr., Joseph R. Julin, and Larry D. Barnett
1990   *The Goals and Missions of Law Schools.* New York: Peter Lang.

Van Caenegem, R. C.
1994   *An Historical Introduction to Private Law.* Cambridge, England: Cambridge University Press.

Vandall, Frank J.
1989 *Strict Liability: Legal and Economic Analysis.* New York: Quorum Books.

Van Hoy, Jerry
1997 *Franchise Law Firms and the Transformation of Personal Legal Services.* Westport, CT: Quorum Books.

Vera Institute of Justice
1977 *Felony Arrests: Their Prosecution and Disposition in New York City's Courts.* New York: Vera Institute of Justice.

Vermeule, Adrian
2000 "Interpretive Choice." *New York University Law Review* 75: 74–149.

Volcansek, Mary L., with Elisabetta de Franciscis and Jacquiline Lucienne Lafon
1996 *Judicial Misconduct: A Cross-National Comparison.* Gainesville, FL: University of Florida Press.

Wachtler, Sol
1990 "Grand Juries: Wasteful and Pointless." *New York Times* (Jan. 6): 15.

Wagner, Diane
1986 "The New Elite Plaintiff's Bar." *ABA Journal* (Feb. 1): 44–49.

Walker, Samuel
1980 *Popular Justice: A History of American Criminal Justice.* New York: Oxford University Press.

Wall, Joseph F.
1981 "Lochner v. New York: A Study in the Modernization of Constitutional Law." In *American Industrialization, Economic Expansion, and the Law*, edited by Joseph R. Frese and Jacob Judd, pp. 113–141. Tarrytown, NY: Sleepy Hollow Press.

Walsh, Mary Williams
2001 "Ruling Likely to Bring Changes to Many Jobs." *New York Times* (March 22): C6.

Waltz, Jon R.
1997 *Introduction to Criminal Evidence*, 4 ed. Chicago: Nelson–Hall.

Ware, Stephen J.
1999 "Arbitration and Assimilation." *Washington University Law Review* 77: 1053–1063.

Warren, Charles
1966 "The Supreme Court in United States History." In *The Historian's History of the United States*, edited by Andrew S. Berk and James P. Shenton, pp. 941–953. New York: Capricon Books.

Warren, Donald
1996 *Radio Priest: Charles Coughlin, the Father of Hate Radio.* New York: The Free Press.

Wasby, Stephen L.
1993 *The Supreme Court in the Federal Judicial System*, 4th ed. Chicago: Nelson-Hall.

Wasserstrom, Richard A.
1961 *The Judicial Decision: Toward a Theory of Legal Justification.* Stanford, CA: Stanford University Press.

Weber, Max
1967 *On Law in Economy and Society*, edited by Max Rheinstein. New York: Simon and Schuster. (Translated from the 1925 German edition.)
1958 *The Protestant Ethic and the Spirit of Capitalism.* New York: Scribners. (Originally published in German in 1905.)

Weisberg, Richard H.
1997 *Vichy Law and the Holocaust in France.* New York: New York University Press.

Weisheit, Ralph H., and Diane M. Alexander
1988 "Juvenile Justice and the Demise of Parens Patriae." *Federal Probation* 52 (Dec.): 56–63.

Weller, Steven, and John C. Ruhnka
1978 "Small Claims Courts: Operations and Prospects." *State Court Journal* (Winter). Reprinted by National Center for State Courts.

Westin, Alan F.
1990 *The Anatomy of a Constitutional Law Case: Youngstown Sheet and Tube* Co. v. *Sawyer, the Steel Seizure Decision.* New York: Columbia University Press.

Wexler, David B.
1999 "The Development of Therapeutic Jurisprudence: From Theory to Practice." *Revista Jurídica* 68: 691–705.

Wheeler, Russell R.
1992 *Origins of the Elements of Federal Court Governance*. Washington, DC: Federal Judicial Center.

Wheeler, Russell R., and A. Leo Levin
1979 *Judicial Discipline and Removal in the United States*. Washington, DC: Federal Judicial Center.

White, G. Edward
2000 *The Constitution and the New Deal*. Cambridge, MA: Harvard University Press.
1980 *Tort Law in America: An Intellectual History*. New York: Oxford University Press. (Paperback edition 1985.)
1976 *The American Judicial Tradition*. New York: Oxford University Press.

Whitehead, Jason E.
1999 "From Criticism to Critique: Preserving the Radical Potential of Critical Legal Studies Through a Reexamination of Frankfurt School Critical Theory." *Florida State University Law Review* 27: 701–742.

Whitman, Mark, ed.
1993 *Removing a Badge of Slavery: The Record of Brown* v. *Board of Education*. New York: Markus Wiener Publishing.

Wice, Paul B.
1985 *Chaos in the Courthouse: The Inner Workings of the Urban Municipal Courts*. New York: Praeger.
1983 "Private Criminal Defense: Reassessing an Endangered Species." In *The Defense Counsel*, edited by William F. McDonald, pp. 39–64. Beverly Hills, CA: Sage.
1978 *Criminal Lawyers: An Endangered Species*. Beverly Hills, CA: Sage.

Wiecek, William M.
1988 *Liberty Under Law: The Supreme Court in American Life*. Baltimore, MD: Johns Hopkins University Press.

Wiehl, Lis
1989a "New Law Erects Barriers to the Federal Docket." *New York Times* (May 12): 22.
1989b "After 200 Years, the Silent Juror Learns to Talk." *New York Times* (July 7): 20.

Wilkerson, Isabel
1990 "As Indiana Debates Its Malpractice Law, So Does the Country." *New York Times* (August 20): 11.

Williams, T. Harry
1969 *Huey Long*. New York: Bantam.

Wilson, James Q.
1989 *Bureaucracy*. New York: Basic Books.

Wilson, James Q. and George Kelling
1982 "Broken Windows: The Police and Neighborhood Safety." *Atlantic Monthly* (March): 29–38.

Wines, Michael
1989 "Thornburgh Abandons Choice for Top Justice Post." *New York Times* (July 7): 1, 9.

Winfree, L. Thomas, and Lawrence Kielich
1979 "The Prosecuting Attorney and the Labeling Process: An Analysis of the Application of Official Sanction." In *Legality, Morality, and Criminal Justice*, edited by Nicholas Kittrie and Jackwell Susman, pp. 161–179. New York: Praeger.

Winick, Bruce J.
1997 "The Jurisprudence of Therapeutic Jurisprudence." *Psychology, Public Policy, and Law* 1: 184–206.

Winter, Greg
2000 "Legal Firms Cutting Back on Free Services for Poor." *New York Times* (August 17): 1, C5.

Wishman, Seymour
1986 *Anatomy of a Jury: The System on Trial*. New York: Times Books.

Wold, John T., and John H. Culver
1989 "The Defeat of the California Justices." In *American Court Systems: Readings in Judicial Process and Behavior*, edited by Sheldon Goldman and Austin Sarat, pp. 323–329. New York: Longman.

Wolfe, Christopher
 1986 *The Rise of Modern Judicial Review: From Constitutional Interpretation to Judge-Made Law*. New York: Basic Books.

Woodiwiss, Anthony
 1990 *Rights v. Conspiracy: A Sociological Essay on the History of Labour Law in the United States*. New York: Berg Publishers.

Wright, Martin
 1991 *Justice for Victims and Offenders: A Restorative Response to Crime*. Philadelphia: Open University.

Yarbrough, Tinsley E.
 1995 *Judical Enigma: The First Justice Harlan*. New York: Oxford University Press.

Yeazell, Stephen C.
 1987 *From Medieval Group Litigation to the Modern Class Action*. New Haven, CT: Yale University Press.

Yiannopoulos, A. N
 1974 "Jurisprudence and Doctrine as Sources of Law in Louisiana and France." In *The Role of Judicial Decisions and Doctrine in Civil Law and in Mixed Jurisdictions*, edited by Joseph Dainow, pp. 69–90. Baton Rouge: Louisiana State University Press.

Young, Malcolm C.
 2000 *Providing Effective Representation for Youth Prosecuted as Adults*. Washington, DC: Office of Justice Programs.

Zane, John Maxcy
 1998 *The Story of Law*, 2nd ed. Indianapolis: Liberty Fund. Originally published 1927.

Zawitz, Marianne W.
 1988 *Report to the Nation on Crime and Justice*, 2d ed. Washington, DC: U.S. Government Printing Office.

Zehr, Howard
 1990 *Changing Lenses: A New Focus for Crime and Justice*. Scottdale, PA: Herald Press.

Zeisel, Hans
 1982 *The Limits of Law Enforcement*. Chicago: University of Chicago Press.

Zobel, Hiller B.
 1991 "Naming a Justice Has Always Been Political as Usual." *American Heritage* (October): 94–101.

Zweigert, Konrad, and Hein Kötz
 1987 *Introduction to Comparative Law, Vol. I: The Framework*. Oxford, England: Oxford University Press.

CASE INDEX

In an appellate court citation, the first name is that of the party making the appeal; the second name is the party against whom the appeal is directed. The first number(s) is the volume of the court reports in which the decision may be found, followed by the name of the reporter system, with the second number(s) designating the first page of the decision. The year of the decision is always in parentheses.

For example, in the famous school desegregation case, *Brown* v. *Board of Education*, 347 U.S. 483 (1954), Brown refers to the appellant, the party who lost in a lower court and is appealing the decision; Board of Education refers to the school board of Topeka, Kansas, the respondent who won at the lower court level; 347 is the volume number of *United States Supreme Court Reports* (U.S.), and 483 is the page on which the case, which was decided in 1954, begins. There are also three private reporter systems for Supreme Court cases: *Supreme Court Reporter* (abbreviated S.Ct.), *Supreme Court Reports, Lawyer's Edition* (abbreviated L.Ed.), and *United States Law Week* (abbreviated LW). There are also some discontinued systems: Cranch, Wharton, Pet. (Peters), Wall. (Wallace's), Dall. (Dallas'), Wheat. (Wheaton's). A Supreme Court case may also be cited by its original Court number (No.) until the reporter systems provide a citation. Each case submitted to the Supreme Court—whether or not it is granted certiorari—is assigned a docket number. The first two digits indicate the calendar year in which the matter was brought to the Court, while the next set of digits represent the case's sequential position among cases presented that year. In states that do not provide an appellate process for juvenile court cases, they are cited as *In re* (in the matter of); thus *In re Gault* instead of *Gault* v. *Arizona*. Citations of state appellate cases follow the same format except the abbreviated name of the state, for example, Mass., will appear with the year in parentheses; if the date is preceded by a number such as 2d Cir., (Second Circuit), it is a U.S. Court of Appeals case. In some cases, there is only one federal district in a state so the reporter system, such as F.Supp (Federal Supplement) would reveal the type of case, state or federal. (For a useful summary guide to legal citations, see Bouchoux 2001.)

AUTHOR INDEX

∫UBJECT /NDEX